# Nuts & Bolts

The ACORN Fundamentals of Organizing

by **Wade Rathke**
Chief Organizer and Founder of
Assocation of Organizations for Reform Now (ACORN)

Copyright @2018 by Wade Rathke

All rights reserved. No part of this publication may be reproduced, distributed, or transmitted in any form or by any means, including photocopying, recording, or other electronic or mechanical methods, without the prior written permission of the publisher, except in the case of brief quotations embodied in critical reviews and certain other noncommercial uses permitted by copyright law.

For permission requests, write to the publisher below

Social Policy Press   2221 St. Claude Avenue, New Orleans, LA 70117 (physical)
                       PO Box 3924, New Orleans, LA 70177 (mailing)
                       Tel: (504) 302-1238
                       www.socialpolicypress.org

Ordering information
Quantity sales
Special discounts are available on quantity purchases by corporations, associations and others. For details, contact the Publisher at the Social Policy address above.

Individual sales
Social Policy Press publications are available through bookstores. They can also be ordered directly from Social Policy Press at the above numbers and through socialpolicy.org.

Orders for college textbook/course adoption use
Contact Social Policy Press (504) 302-1238

Orders for U.S. and other trade bookstores and wholesalers
Please contact Social Policy Press or visit our website's

Social Policy Press is a registered trademark of
Labor Neighbor Research and Training Center, Inc.

Printed in the United States of America.

Rathke, Wade
Nuts and Bolts: The ACORN Fundamentals of Organizing
ISBN 978-0-9970943-1-2

1. Community, labor, and political organizing
2. Media and service delivery
3. Building mass organizations

First edition
Layout and design: Jim Lowe, designSphere, Vancouver, Canada
Copyediting: Beth Butler, New Orleans
Index: Marie Hurt, New Orleans

Social Policy PressPaperback $35

Dedication

To all of the great leaders, members, and organizers
that have worked in these same vineyards
to empower people and force their voices to be heard,
and especially to all members of the ACORN family,
its peoples' army, and our allied forces
with whom I've been honored to serve.
And, to my family, Beth, Chaco, and Dine'
who have always helped me
stay my course with love and support.

Table of Contents

Dedication	....	i
Prologue	....	v
Preface	....	ix
Chapter I:	All About the Base – Who Do You Organize and Why?	1
Chapter II:	Structure Counts: Form Determines Function	4
Chapter III:	Money Matters	39
Chapter IV:	Dues and Don'ts: Lessons and Learning from Unions	56
Chapter V:	Organizers, Staff and the Allied Trades	80
Chapter VI:	Learning to Swim	102
Chapter VII:	Managing Organizers and Staff	115
Chapter VIII:	Maintaining Organizers: Training, Dialogues and Meetings	152
Chapter IX:	Care and Maintenance of Leaders	224
Chapter X:	Governance, Leadership Development, and Structure	239
Chapter XI:	Conventions	267
Chapter XII:	Where Do Issues Go? Campaigns!	308
Chapter XIII:	Strategy and Tactics	316
Chapter XIV:	Architecture and Engineering of Actions	338
Chapter XV:	Big Actions	352
Chapter XVI:	Organizing Math	368
Chapter XVII:	Constituency, Institution, Network, Alliances, Advocacy	388
Chapter XVIII:	Politics – Proving the Base, Initiatives, and Alternative Parties	400
Chapter XIX:	Communications and Media	438
Chapter XX:	Why Work and Workers	451
Chapter XXI:	Services	493
Chapter XXII:	What in the World	513
Chapter XXIII:	Odds and Ends	543
Epilogue:	Going Forward..	551
Acknowledgments	....	552
Exhibits	....	553
Photographs and Illustrations	....	555
Index	....	559
About the Author	....	566

Prologue

Where do you start, when organizing stands on so many shoulders? How do you finish when the work continues interminably? There are no simple answers to those questions for an organizer. Sometimes though, the work is clearest, when reduced to basics. Not where we have been or where we are going, both of which are fool's gold of hopes, dreams, and the weird angles of perspective, but simply popping open the hood and pulling the wires away so that the nuts and bolts that build and bind the whole engine together are finally revealed.

When I began as an organizer out of anger against the war, conviction over welfare rights, and a vision of political change and empowerment for low and moderate income families in the community, organizing was, thankfully I thought, a radical thing, one step up from the underground. There weren't many of us, but we were everywhere. Just behind the scenes. Just off towards the edge of the stage, yet vital in putting together all of the pieces. We made a difference. We made things happen, even though we were unknown and unsung, a hardworking invisible cadre, fiercely competitive with each other, working outside of the straight lines, yet part of a proud, even revolutionary, tradition that had left barely visible footprints on history for years. Mao instructed us to be like "fish in the sea of the people." I liked that. Pope Francis now calls us "social poets." I love that! This was not work for everyone or perhaps much of anyone, but it was perfect for me.

Then Barack Obama was is elected as President of the United States in 2008. Big country. Big job! Part of the historic election's backstory was his elaborate and conclusive rejection of his undistinguished stint as a community organizer in Chicago.

Nonetheless the genii had been increasingly escaping out of the bottle, and more and more people, politicians, and institutions made their wishes known for certain skills that came with organizing, even if they had little interest in the whole package. In some diluted mix, organizers became "animators." In perhaps the greatest perversion, as a weak chaser to the bitter pill of austerity and a rending of the social safety nets in the country the conservative David Cameron, Prime Minister of the United Kingdom, established a national community organizing program in England. Increasingly, people wanted to put starched shirts and ties on community and other organizing, embrace it in a suffocating bear hug, pimp it out, and squeeze it for everything it was worth using the pulp, while separating out the heart and soul of the work. Everywhere organizing was in danger of becoming little more than transactional, rather than transformative.

Nonetheless, the sudden and surprising prominence of community organizing in the reflection of the Obama election prompted speculation, exaggeration, and conversation about how the experience might impact his leadership in government and the world, and what this might mean for all of us. With this sudden prominence and new light being shown on a small and largely previously unknown subculture of activism and organization, it is not only important for everyone to understand that *listening*, and a concept of change from the bottom are important, but also to recognize that there are lessons for us all from community organizing principles and that some of the lessons might be much different than might be imagined because they flow from a unique view of power and participation that might have something to teach a lot of people. Arguably, Obama may not have embraced these lessons fully while rejecting the path for other directions in "public life" as he has stated, but that does not mean that many others might not find the "nuts and bolts" of community organizing, especially as practiced by ACORN, which was the largest community organization in the United States, when community organizing was increasingly prominent, and continues to practice and innovate both there and around the world.

It is disconcerting and confusing that these recent years have also led to a revival of interest in another famous community organizing evangelist, Saul Alinsky. Right wing activists in the United States sometimes quote one "rule" or another from Alinsky's *Rules for Radicals*, and act as if they have uncovered hidden truths. In modern parlance Alinsky has become something of a "brand" with contentious claims on all sides and in unusual places. Not long ago in Korea and Japan, I was asked serious questions about Alinsky and how his thinking might have influenced building ACORN and ACORN International. It is a great big world, but I have found it smaller and smaller than many might think over the last decades.

Frankly though, none of these developments in recent years really prompted the genesis of this book.

Having founded ACORN in Little Rock, Arkansas in 1970, I began writing this book more than fifteen years ago while Chief Organizer for ACORN at a family fishing camp across Lake Pontchartrain. An easy commute, it was only 35 minutes from our Bywater neighborhood in New Orleans.

ACORN was growing rapidly across the country as we expanded to meet the challenge of "devolution," which was pushing more power and resources from the federal government to the state government, stranding our city-based organizations and thwarting their ability to deliver what we needed to give our members and what they demanded. In the sweltering heat of August, the plan was that I would start writing about ACORN's philosophy and methodology for a couple of weeks while our family stayed and worked from the camp, just going into the office at noon and taking a week of vacation. Or, so it began.

August ends, organizing begins again, and the writing is set aside for a couple of years. We started organizing in Peru, Mexico, and then Argentina. My family took a vacation in Buenos Aires, I picked up the writing again every morning. During the next spring trying to raise money on the road in the Netherlands, Germany, Sweden, Norway, and Denmark for several weeks, I continued to push forward writing in postage stamp rooms in Stockholm and stranded weekends in Copenhagen.

Then in another August in 2005 Hurricane Katrina came to land and the world around us changed completely. It was two months before we could return to the city. ACORN's national headquarters was in New Orleans. Thoroughly damaged, our offices were out of commission. Similarly, though our house didn't flood, it was a new year before we could come home. The family fishing camp was washed away completely with nothing but some pieces of decking, piling stubs, old photos, and a monthly mortgage payment as reminders of our times there. My writing changed as well to a book about Katrina, New Orleans, ACORN, and the struggles and lessons of rebuilding took center stage which became *Battle for the Ninth Ward* which began another period of long starts and stops… *Nuts and Bolts* was for organizers and activists. It could wait.

In the summer of 2008 I left ACORN, but already had a contract to write *Citizen Wealth: Winning the Campaign for Working Families* to try and explain how large scale organizing, ACORN style, had created the promise and proof of "citizen wealth," which is to say, income security. More books continued with *Global Grassroots: Perspectives on International Organizing* that came out in 2011 to help introduce the growing, widespread impact of community organizing around the world, not just in the United States, and to position ACORN International's growth in Canada, Latin America, India, Africa, and even Europe in this emerging movement for citizen and community based change and empowerment.

So, why finish the book now?

Basically, because I am personally once again back organizing at the nuts and bolts level in building ACORN International's federation of city and country-based affiliates around the world and am asked every day how – and why – we did what we did, and what lessons we learned, and, more importantly, what we should do now. ACORN in the United States surrendered under assault at the barricades in late 2010. The mourning never ends, but the learning also continues with the work itself as I had learned from experience with Katrina and that informs resilience and rebuilding as well. What needed to be done differently to have a different result? Could we learn to build better and more securely? Could we ever create something bigger than ACORN had been in the United States?

Once again organizers were asking the hard questions about building something powerful. In Edinburgh, Scotland activists wanted to know how to calculate membership density in the neighborhoods. What a great question. How long had it been since anyone had asked me this important and obvious question? In Quito, organizers wanted to know how we could build a national, mass-based membership organization in Ecuador alongside a growing progressive political formation. What a great puzzle to solve. In Jakarta, Indonesia a presidential election was coming and community organizations of the poor wanted to have impact and be heard. How? Will you help? Civic movements building in Sicily, Italy wanted to build organizations and win elections at the same time. Could it be done? Will you help? In the United States, calls from Austin, Memphis, California's Central Coast, Charlotte, New Orleans, Juneau, and Pittsburgh. …led me to joke that I was becoming the St. Jude of Lost and Hopeless Causes and Campaigns, but I couldn't resist, "Will you help?" or "Could it be done?"

So it was back on the road and the writing began again in Tokyo, Seoul, Victoria, Quito, and even when I was lucky, New Orleans, and finally over a half-dozen long stretches of "workations" off-the-grid on Rock Creek, Montana before the fish would bite as dusk came over the canyon and mottled the stream and on the Jourdan River in Mississippi after canoeing or kayaking to get a glimpse of eagles, ducks, and cranes nestled along the waterway and anywhere and anytime that I could get a moment.

It was time to get back to the nuts and bolts and see whether it could all be put together again.

Fishing Camp. Chaco fishing.

Preface

So, what do you have here and what can you expect to find? Nuts and bolts of course! Here there are tools and even diagrams and exhibits of how the organization worked in practice since 1970, and this is how it continues to function around the world.

In some chapters you will find that you are taken by the hand and walked point by point through the methodology of ACORN organizing. For some those chapters will be easier, perhaps even invaluable, and for others that will be something quickly scanned to return and read more closely later when needed, especially for organizers, or maybe even never for many others. I understand that completely and am comfortable with it. In other chapters you are offered a window into how the house was built from room to room, floor to floor, through a combination of historical narratives. They are joined with the chapter and verse of stories along the winding path that necessarily shaped both the history and methodology of the organizing. In those chapters the would be organizer, activist, member, or random reader will not find themselves shuffling through the toolbox, but rather walking with us side by side and finding how we got there in the real world. When my brother and I were young we read all of the "We Were There" series of books in our local library like "We Were There at Pearl Harbor" or "We Were There with Lewis and Clark" or "We Were There on the Chisholm Trail." You get the idea. These sections of *Nuts and Bolts* are "We Were There with ACORN When…."

At the same time this is not a "do what I say, not what I do" book. You won't find any sugar in your coffee between these pages. This is a book about the ACORN Fundamentals of Organizing, so the focus is not on woulda, shoulda, coulda, but on what ACORN has done (and is doing!) to organize low and moderate income families in community organizations, workers' associations and unions, tenant organizations, and other formations, as well as how we used issues, campaigns, politics, media, and anything else.

So, I hope we are clear. This is not a novel. This is not a manual. This is also not poetry.

I have made my life as an organizer. In reading over this book, there are some sections I worry that I should have made clearer, and I wish I was able to do so. There are stories that sometimes I worry were twice-told in the curious way that I cobbled this book together in spare moments, vacations, weekends, airports, trailers, and wherever over so many years. I am truly sorry for that. I feel the same way when I leave a visit on the doors and feel like that family should have become members and active in the organization, if only I had done a better job explaining this or that or had answered some question some other way. I am not going to rationalize any shortcomings of this book by saying that it is the way it is because I "was trying to keep it real," or some lame excuse like that, because it just plain isn't true. So at the bottom line I may not be the best writer, but I'm not bad, and regardless of my merits or demerits as an author, at the least I am, as characterized by our organizers, as fearless a writer as I hope I have been as an organizer. Either way this is the start of our dialogue about organizing, hopefully not the end of it, and at worst if there is a point left vague or something mangled past understanding or a rough edge dragging, my email is in the Author's Note, so reach out or call me, maybe.

I am not trying to write a best seller here, but I am trying to get the word out to people that want to organize that the ACORN methodology is worth a hard look and has something to say to you. There are lessons that can be learned from not only what we do, but what we tried to do and even failed to do, and how we thought about and puzzled through the pieces to do the work.

For this book to succeed it has to find its way into the hands of men and women who want to make changes in this world. For people trying to build power by doing the hard, tedious work of building a mass-based organization, I am hoping this book is as much a weapon as a tool.

When I was working on the final version of *Nuts and Bolts* and had decided the book should have some exhibits of how ACORN really works, I reached out to a number of ACORN veterans to see if their files were better than mine or if they had some things handy that were no longer accessible. Some did, and some didn't, proving again how much an oral tradition organizing continues to be, or at the least, what sorry record keepers many of us are in a takeoff of the old Dylan song, "we were organizers and we don't look back." Some of what I did receive was fascinating, because either it never crossed my desk, had slipped out the back door of my memory, or I had just tossed it in a pile and kept moving to the next problem, the next action, and the next thing that HAD to be done.

One piece that fascinated me that I must have skimmed and forgotten was a piece in our new ACORN organizer training manual that was entitled "Principles and Foundations."[1] The title of the piece was confusing because it spoke of being eleven of the twenty such cornerstones even though it only included about eight of them. Perhaps there are more to come.

Regardless, this seems a perfect preface to the book, because it works as such an excellent summary of the value structure and ideology of the organizing.

Silver Bullet at Rock Creek, Montana

---

[1] Thanks especially to Kevin Whelan, ACORN's former communications director, for taking the time to send me an entire UBS drive where I found this document and a treasure trove of other materials!

PRINCIPLES and FOUNDATIONS of ACORN

Two Primary Principles:
1. The principle of Commitment and Responsibility
2. The principle of Personal Initiative.

Other Principles:
1. Growth
2. Self-sufficiency and Internal Financing
3. Coordinated Autonomy
   a. organizing against conflict
   b. attention to detail
4. Issues as Vehicles for Building Power
   a. will it build the organization?
   b. is it on the agenda?
5. Actions secure wins
6. Leadership is shared and functional
7. Ownership of the organization
8. Distinct role of the Organizer

Of course the training document immediately talked about ACORN's commitment to organizing a "majority constituency" which is fundamental to our work, recognizing that to build power we needed to assemble a majority constituency from the low and moderate income population to realize our goals and objectives. Power is of course mentioned. Democracy is of course fundamental in ACORN's motto, "The People Shall Rule," but you don't see it on this brief list either. Another principle, obliquely presented, involves winning. Coordinated autonomy was incorrectly handled, although it was right to include "organizing against conflict" as a fundamental principle, but the point of the document was to give a brand new organizer some introduction to an amazing new world they were about to enter that might have been unimaginable even days before. Winning, organizing 10% of the constituency, handling conflict, endless organizing, paying the bills (where was dues mentioned as a foundational principle?!?), consensus, the real-politic that measured whether or not the issues increased membership and built the organization, and more, were all embedded in the document, no matter how many bullet points or whether the numbers added up.

For example, in number 7 concerning the "ownership of the organization," I can easily imagine a trainee trying to memorize the list of items and being glued in amazement at this new world they were now preparing to enter as organizers:

Preface xi

7. OWNERSHIP of the ORGANIZATION

These are the principles ACORN operates by, and every member, leader, and organizer must know these principles and know that we abide by them.

Organize every member on every issue

Decision by consensus

Executive Board accountable to their groups

Maximum participation

From the bottom up

Or, how about this one:
BELONGS to its MEMBERS

ACORN is the members' organization. To make our organization work properly and successfully, we want to have, indeed, must have, access to as much information as possible. Occasionally we may think we don't have enough time to make sure everyone is as fully informed and part of the planning processes as possible. We cannot afford to skip over any of this. The process of getting other leaders and members to see and understand the organization, gets right to the core of what ACORN is trying to do. It's not enough that you understand why dues are important or self-sufficiency as a goal is important, if the members and leaders that you work with don't understand either one. If all the ideas, all the skills, all the understanding about the local group are only in your head and you're not transferring that information and that way of thinking to other leaders and members, then it is not really the members' group and the principles are just so much hot air.

And, that's what we are going to do now with you as well! All of these principles and more will get full attention in the coming pages.

Since *Nuts and Bolts* is about building an organization, it is also only fair to say that the organization of this book in the following chapters will work like this.

If you are going to build an organization it all begins with a set of decisions on who you are organizing, why you are organizing them, and where you are organizing them, in short, as **Chapter I** says, it's **All About the Base**.

Chapter II warns you in excruciating detail that "the beginnings prejudice the ends," (another one of those ACORN foundational principles!) so you need to avoid foolish advice, which seems all too common, and think very carefully about the questions of how to structure the organization, because, like it or not, **Structure Counts and Form Determines Function**, and inadvertent steps might stunt the potential of the organization from the beginning. Changing a mass-based organization is almost impossible midstream, so suffer through this chapter because the organizer it saves, could be you.

And, since you are taking your medicine, it is never too early to learn that it is not the sizzle of the issues or the excitement of the members that sometimes determines the eventual success or failure of the organization, but as **Chapter III** indicates unfortunately **Money Matters** and is often life or death. There is probably no more fundamental ACORN cornerstone than the importance of the dues paid by members to support and sustain the organizations, and since this book is not a two-handed piece of liberalism but about the nuts and bolts of ACORN's organizing methodology **Chapter IV** is all about the **Dues and Don'ts** and a lot of this has been learned from unions, so we get pretty deep into the weeds with labor organizations and the **Lessons and Learning from Unions**. Yes, yes, members paying dues is yet another fundamental ACORN principle!

As you will read repeatedly, I am a huge believer – and tremendous beneficiary – of what I frequently call the "volunteer army." Members, researchers, lawyers, you name them, I've loved them all, but to build a mass-based membership organization there is no way around the fact that we have to have organizers, so next up you will find as we travel this path, **Chapter V: Organizers, Staff and the Allied Trades**. And, if we are going to have organizers, that also means that they have to be trained, and we cover that first in **Chapter VI: Learning to Swim** and then in even more detail in **Chapter VII: Maintaining Organizers: Training, Dialogues and Meetings**. Did I mention that organizers were essential? Yes, I guess I did! Well, I should add that they are "made" not born, and that's another fundamental ACORN principle.

But, as important as organizers are, if you decide to build a membership organization along the lines of ACORN, leaders are even more important. We have to recruit members, involve them deeply, determine who has a base and is therefore is a leader, so **Chapter IX: Care and Maintenance of Leaders** looks at the undercarriage of this process in some detail. If leaders are pulling from the front of the organization and organizers are pushing form the back, as they are in ACORN's world, then that means they have to have the power to participate fully and run the organization, which we cover in **Chapter X: Governance, Leadership Development, and Structure**. And, when the confluence of all of this comes together it is a big, powerful deal in **Chapter XI: Conventions**.

By this time we have traveled almost to the midpoint of the organizing path, and you have been stuffed to the gills with steak and potatoes, but, tell the truth, you're flagging, because you were hoping for more sizzle. You drifted into this because you wanted to see something happen on issues that you really cared about and you didn't want to talk, you wanted action, right? That's where we will go next in **Chapter XII: Where Do Issues Go? Campaigns!** Then we will go deeper and look at **Chapter XII: Strategy and Tactics** and we won't play around, but go all the way to the bottom with **Chapter XIV: Architecture and Engineering of Actions (and Campaigns!)** and then jump as high as we can in **Chapter XV** on **Big Actions**.

Now that I have your attention again, some adrenaline starting to flow, you are starting to breathe deeper, your heart is pounding, and you're ready to go, I hate to bring you down hard, but none of this works without **Chapter XVI: Organizing Math**. Now, I've gone and done it. I could have tried a bait-and-switch and snuck all of this in under something blah-blah like Accountability, which is certainly part of it, or Performance and Production, and given it a bit of an industrial tilt, because using the "m" word and

Preface xiii

speaking about math to most organizers is a little like holding up a cross in a vampire movie. Unfortunately, yes, you may owe some high school teachers an apology, math does turn out to be important even when organizing low and moderate income families into community and labor organizations, and it does lead to accountability, performance, and production, so, now I've said it, stop your whining, read the damn chapter and pay close attention if you want to win and build power, and we'll get past this together.

Once you get your arms around "organizing math" (one of the principles!), we might as well understand how we work with others, because if you did any of the math at all, you can tell that we can never get to the scale where we can do it all by ourselves. **Chapter XVII: Constituency, Institution, Network, Alliances, Advocacy** looks at how to navigate this organizationally and constructively in spite of the fact that one of ACORN's fundamental principles is that you only join others to "borrow power, not to loan it."

If you build it, they will NOT come. The organization will have to go and get them to build power. Actions and campaigns are part of it, but when we talk about power, there is no getting around the importance of politics (yes that is a foundational principle of ACORN nuts and bolts as well) and we go there, where no community organization ever really ventured to travel in **Chapter XVIII: Politics – Proving the Base, Initiatives, and Parties**. Sadly, having the numbers in the majority constituency is not enough to build power or win. **Chapter XIX** our adventures in **Communications and Media**, including this book itself, as you must have figured out by now. In **Chapter XX: Why Work and Workers** we look at ACORN's work in building unions and worker associations. I mentioned we were a constituency organization more than a pure-and-simple community organization, and perhaps one of our boldest moves and one of the one of our most important was also organizing lower income workers first in the United States and now in India, Argentina, North Africa, and coming soon to a job near you, proving perhaps that "fools tread where wise men" avoid, which is NOT one of our principles.

As significantly, we also embraced the full lives of our members and what it took to deliver "citizen wealth," and **Chapter XXI: Services** we make the case that the members demand services, so their demand must be heeded, and providing such services creates both concrete results and wins, as well as loyalty and resources to keep the organization working.

One problem, challenge, whatever you want to call it, I say TOmato, you say toMATo, is that in a democratic membership organization and an organizational culture that believes in growth and scale, it is exceedingly difficult to ever say, "NO!" to people who want to organize. At least it was for me, which we cover in **Chapter XXII: What in the World**, as well as in every day of our working lives.

And, finally, when we come to the end of our journey, rifling our hands through the toolbox of ACORN's nuts and bolts and methodology, we come to the **Epilogue** with some relief for me to finish this book after more than a decade of peripatetic, stops and starts, and some recognition that every day is a new one and marks a beginning more than an end to the never ending process of organizing **Going Forward**.

Chapter I
All About the Base – Who Do You Organize and Why?

Everybody has to start some place.

Some people come looking for an organization. For work? For a job? For a way station between this and that? For their resume? They are just passing through. Part of the transient workforce of social change. They may not know better, but they at least want to do no harm. Sometimes they even provide real skills and excellent contributions.

Everybody has been somewhere and done something before they work for an organization. Often the stories seem happenstance. Sometimes they seem determined and destined.

Sometimes they just finished school. Other times they left school running. Some hated their other jobs. Some had never worked before.

We will look at what brings people to the work, as we look at what makes an organizer, but for now, however you come to be an organizer and join an organization or begin to build an organization, the first questions are always, "Who?" and "Why?" After that will come the nuts and bolts: how does it get built and how will it work?

The first principle of organization is that it is never about you and always about the base. An organization can be many things, a mutual project, a fighting force, an ad hoc group, a political power, but it is always a collective endeavor. Whether working for an organization or founding one, the decision to build an organization is a commitment to serve and represent the people being organized, whether it be a described constituency, a defined membership, or a group of people just like yourself.

People, a constituency, a base. That's what it is all about in building an organization.

If you want to join or form an organization you have to first decide where you stand with people.

If you want to speak *for* them, there are groups that certainly do that: advocacy groups, environmental groups, public interest groups, and countless nonprofits. And that's not counting the lobbying, research, and for-what-it's-worth shops that line K Street, inside the Beltway, and a thousand other streets around the world. You can be a catalyst, an activist, an agitator, and try to make these happen. You can even be an anarchist and wear your unaccountability and righteousness like a loose sweater, and profess to not believe in any organizations and speak truth to power.

If you want to speak *to* them?

There are groups for that as well. That almost defines most modern political parties these days, "muscling" the message into bits-and-piece to make the sale for a candidate or a cause or an organization using a thousand data points, surveys, prospecting, and micro-targeting. Facebook faux organizations spring up for this and that on a daily basis, so the opportunity is huge and the entry level for access is less than ankle high, so if this is who you want to organize or join, all you have to do is find the "group" or throw something out there and see what the response might be. Or, you can canvass, persuade, raise vital resources, see the world from busy streets and front porches, and start assembling something from the issues that appeal and the actions that seem to resonate.

For an organizer the base is all important. That is the "who" that determines eventually the "what" of organization.

If you are going to organize tenants, you will be building a tenant organization, a tenant union, or whatever. If you are going to organize workers, then you will be building a union or a workers' association or maybe even a cooperative. If you are going to organize residents of a community, then you will be building a community organization or a civic association or a block club. If you are trying to organize a base more broad than narrow, you will be building an alliance, a coalition, or perhaps even a federation. If you only want to organize women, or African-Americans, or seniors, or Somalians, or gays, or students, or the disabled, or groups smaller and larger, then that will also define the "what." There are also a lot more "what's," than what I have listed above, but it all starts with the base. If it doesn't start with the base, then there is bound to be trouble ahead.

Some people start organizing because they feel strongly about an issue. They care about housing or the environment or the rights or one group or another or some place in the world. They have strong points of view about what needs to be changed and the platform that must be implemented. They may not care if they lead, but they are clear that they want others to come aboard, work, and maybe even follow. If they can narrow the issue down, they want to organize a campaign to take action to win the changes they want.

This is all well and good. The inspiration to organize comes from a thousand sources, but eventually the stone that will dash their feet will be the base, finding the people who will take up the banner of their cause, and if the question of the base has not been answered, then the form and function will surely fall, saved only by luck and the kindness of friends and strangers. For an organization or campaign that survives and sustains, there are thousands that fall on the hope that "if you build it, they will come." The "they" is the base.

ACORN members assembling for Los Angeles ACORN Convention 2004.

If this all seems painfully obvious, then you are already many leaps ahead of those who did not look closely at this question from the beginning, and are ruing the day. Their numbers are legion. I have spent more time with great, talented, motivated, and wonderful men and women, desperately passionate to make things happen who were dissolving in frustration because they had not defined their base from the beginning of their work, allowing them to inform the organization, participate fully, and give the organization life after the initial inspiration. Facing the question of the base is often what separates organizers from activists and advocates.

So, the first question is "who?" The answer is the base that you have chosen to organize. Whether they want to organize – and organize with you – involves a whole different set of questions. Before you get there, it is worth asking in some depth, the question of "why" you want to organize that base, because that is going to make some of the other questions a bit easier to handle.

It is not enough for the response to the "why," to be simply that you realize that you cannot win by yourself. Yes, it is true that on one can win anything by themselves, but if that is the answer to the question of "why?", then keep it to yourself, and please do not try and build an organization. An organization, by definition, will always be bigger, better, and different than any one individual, even its founder. Similarly, if the "why" is that you are looking for followers or people to listen to your wisdom on the goals, objections, the issues, or the platform, don't try and build an organization. Go look for one where you might fit and see if you can join and close ranks with them or jump to the front of their pack. If they will have you.

For ACORN and our family of our organizations, we were always clear that our "who," our base, our constituency, as we called it, was low-and-moderate income families. We were always clear that the "why" was to build power so that these families could make the changes that they demanded on the issues they determined.

How you answer the "who" and "why," might determine whether or not the nuts and bolts of organizations has any interest or appeal, much less the fine art and principles of organizing, because these were the items we needed to deal with on the order of "first things first," and from here we go next to the "what" and on beyond.

ACORN India members gather in assembly in Delhi.

Chapter I: All About the Base – Who Do You Organize and Why?

Chapter II:
Structure Counts: Form Determines Function

In organizing the beginnings prejudice the ends.

This is not exactly an iron law, because it is not totally impossible to change or redirect an organization from its original purposes, but it is highly unlikely, very improbable, and many organizations have died trying. So, structure counts, and it counts for a lot.

This should be an area where employing skilled organizers really matters and means something, though surprisingly many seem to take structure for granted and to their peril.

Corporate Structure and Tax Status

Take for example the area of tax status and corporate structure. It is hard to think of something more important in some ways, or of a decision made more cavalierly by many organizers and organizations. Many think that they simply *must* build organizations that are tax exempt, and if not they will not be able to raise money, and so forth and so on until wreck and ruin. This is often simply a self-serving recommendation from funders themselves and lawyers neither of whom give the matter little thought past billing hours, protecting their own liabilities, and insuring their own convenience, or for virtually no good reason. More tellingly it totally violates a first principle of organizing that one should not build an organization tailored to external demands, but instead build an organization accountable to its own constituency, membership and interests. At the least concede that there are in fact many options and decisions have to made, and in that sense there is no substitute for good judgment.

In the United States the Internal Revenue Service in order to facilitate the creation and implementation of a tax system dependent on the good will of the rich and maximum inequity for most of the rest of us, has a number of sections of its code that are designed to ostensibly encourage certain general charitable activities for education, health, and other purposes. The most favorable status is a 501(c) 3 ruling, which allows the recipient institution to escape taxation on all donations from institutions and individuals as tax exempt and allows the donor, at least the rich donor, a tax exemption as well. Another common organizational status is a 501(c) 4 ruling, which allows an organization a broad degree of latitude in communication with its "members," however that might be defined. A contribution to such an organization by these members and many, many others is also tax exempt. Similarly a labor union is usually tax exempt under 501 (c)5, although this simply means that unions do not have to pay taxes, rather than giving union members a tax exemption for their dues equivalent to what the rich might receive from the IRS in (c)3 or (c)4 situations – members can only receive deductions for their dues as a business expense if they are filling out a "long form, " and, for my good Americans, you know what I am taking about here, I know, since the long form is for the big whoops and the short

Exhibit 1a: Organizational Flowchart

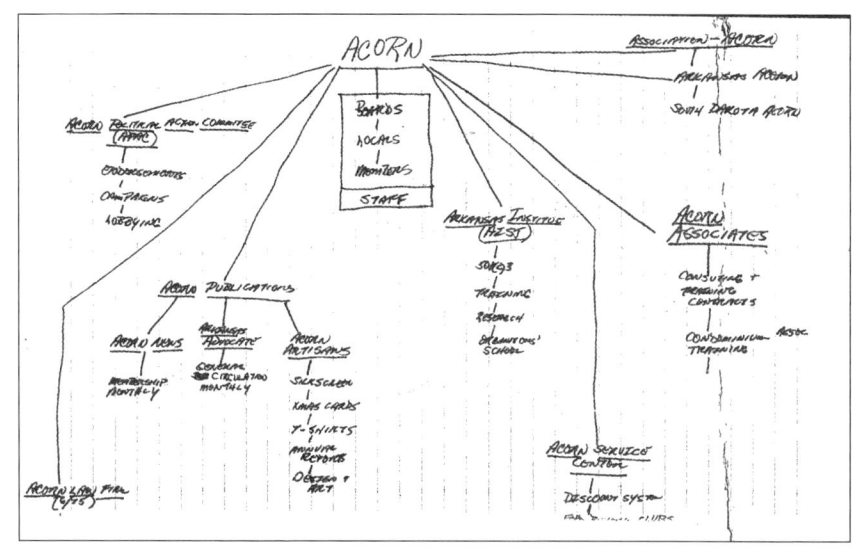

ACORN Organizational Chart c.1975.

form is for the rest of America. There are some other tax rulings which allow a special status for organizations that engage in voter registration on a multi-state basis or to create cooperatives, but if you have these numbers firmly in your mind, you understand the basic things you need to know – or not know, as the case may be – about the IRS that is, but decidedly not about how one might or should structure an organization legally. Ditto for Revenue Canada, registering a charity or trust in the United Kingdom, France, or the arcane laws of scores of countries for nonprofits with or without tax benefits. For way too many people this is the beginning and end of the conversation about structure.

In reality there are really two threshold questions an organization has to answer from the beginning. One is whether or not to be or not to be incorporated formally at all. The other, which is usually the easiest, is whether or not you want the outfit to make money, and if you are really organizing, you will not make money no matter what you might hope, so this is purely a structural question, not a substantive one.

Incorporating or not is actually a very important political question with tactical implications, so it really is worth some thought, rather than a knee-jerk response. Certainly an organization can incorporate and many do, but it is not the only choice, or necessarily the best choice depending on the circumstance. Businesses routinely incorporate because they are interested in shifting and limiting liability from individuals for particular activity to the corporate structure. One has to consider exactly what kind of liability one wants to shield in a corporation? Unions for example at the local level and the national or international level are in fact rarely if ever corporations, and instead operate as "unincorporated associations." In welfare rights we were always unincorporated

Chapter II: Structure Counts: Form Determines Function

associations of groups. ACORN from 1970 – 1978 was not incorporated, and simply operated as an unincorporated association.

One of the good reasons not to be incorporated, and the reason we were not for a long time, has to do with injunctions on associational activity and the attendant liabilities that flow from such activity. In order to enjoin the activity of such an organization one has to name individually all of the organizational participants one wants to enjoin, rather than simply enjoining the organization in a blanket way, which one can do with a corporation, thereby stopping everything and everybody in their tracks. Let's say there was a demonstration in a housing authority office demanding the rights of public housing tenants in Chicago, and CHA simply had its attorneys go into court to seek an injunction to prevent the Chicago Fighting Tenants Union from sitting in at the authority offices. In an unincorporated association the unnamed members could continue the activity, one after the other, following the footsteps of those that went before, theoretically until we either won or ran out of members who were willing to take part in the action. If the Chicago Fighting Tenants Union were incorporated though the injunction would have immediate success, because it would bind all of the members of the Fighting Tenants Union, since the corporation would be liable for the activity of its members, and any CHA lawyer could stroll into court and get daily fines and other prohibitions making the organization responsible for all manner of madness and mayhem. In the United States injunctions have long been a favored weapon in stopping the organization of unions, protests, and demonstrations.

These are real threats. The NAACP as a corporation[2] in the famous buying boycott in Mississippi in the 1970's[3] was held liable for more than a million dollars for lost revenue for businesses in early court decisions that held it responsible for the impact on the businesses whose behavior they were successfully trying to modify. On the other hand when institutions moved to enjoin ACORN in early campaigns in Arkansas they were forced to get it all right down to the last detail in order to stop any activity – and in a leadership run, democratic organization this can be especially difficult to do, since so many can come forward to replace those falling or taken from the front. Tactically, this lack of a standard – or expected – corporate structure tended to allow the organization more leverage in its earliest days, when it needed it the most, because the organization was highly fluid and mobile, and therefore more difficult to fix firmly, and stop dead in its tracks.

None of this means that you get free ride from injunctions, especially in America, where property and corporations have more than rights than real people can ever hope to win. Unions may be unincorporated but judges do not hesitate to award injunctions and process and levy huge fines. The annual teachers' strike season every fall used to bring the customary news clips of teacher leaders being led to jail for not complying with an

---

[2]   NAACP affiliates are organized as subsidiary branches of the central corporation, a New York-based membership corporation, much as ACORN was structured as an Arkansas-based corporation eventually.

[3]   The U.S. Supreme Court overturned in NAACP v. Claiborne Hardware fortunately. A local branch along with field secretary Charles Evers initiated a boycott in Port Gibson, Mississippi in Claiborne County that ran from 1966-1972.

injunction. Certainly Richard Trumka[4] made his name when he and the Mine Workers accumulated some $64 million dollars in fines in the Pittston Coal strike from local judges in Virginia. Organizations, even unincorporated associations, cannot escape the courts, but if the organization – and the organizers – knows it is going to be in a fight, it better be at the right strength and weight to take the heat it has coming.

More simply there just is not that much hurry in some cases to set the structure of the organization in stone – either literally or legally. Sometimes new organizations would be well served to run for a while, even years, as an unincorporated association, even a project of another sponsoring organization, until the full range of the goals and objectives and institutional nature of the organization emerges and consolidates.

Many more mistakes are made through structural certainty than structural flexibility.

The other question: to be, or not to be, non-profit, really is a bit easier, but the implications are profound. Being for-profit simply means that you will be taxed at the corporate rate for surplus income, which might be described as "profits." Being for-profit also means that the organization could have shareholders, and that these profits could be distributed to such shareholders. The default choice really is to establish the organization as a non-profit, although there are a few advantages for a membership organization to be for-profit or some kind of hybrid. Though these may be time-dated fads, there are emerging social benefit structures and even in some states L3C's or Low Profit Limited Liability Corporations.[5] Given the wide ranging expansion of powers both financial and political that the Chief Justice John Roberts US Supreme Court is currently giving to for-profit corporate entities, this situation warrants constant attention.

Here is a point frequently missed though: being non-profit does not mean that the organization *cannot* make money – in fact there are some *huge* non-profit organizations, cooperatives are one example, that make beaucoup money, but the difference is that they *cannot* distribute profits to shareholders. That's just about it. If a non-profit corporation makes money, then such a corporation is also required to pay taxes; that is unless it is tax-exempt under an appropriate application and ruling by the IRS. Without such a ruling, and therefore submission to the full brunt of the IRS regulations for such a privilege, a non-profit corporation would simply pay taxes on excess resources that were not allocated against other current and expected expenses. What are the chances of that? And, if you somehow miraculously were to make money, why not pay taxes?

In fact this is the status that ACORN finally chose in 1978 when incorporated in Arkansas as a non-profit corporation under the laws of that state. ACORN has never been tax exempt. Non-profit and tax-exempt are two states of being in totally different worlds, and it is a severe and potentially fatal mistake to confuse these two realities. As the organization was consolidating in multiple states after eight years of activity, and, perhaps more importantly, starting to acquire this, that, and the other, including property for the first time, owning our own buildings in Little Rock and Dallas, then like burghers everywhere, we had both assets and people to protect, so it finally made sense

---

[4] Richard Trumka is President of the AFL-CIO in the USA at this writing.

[5] ACORN Global Enterprises (AGE), a Louisiana-based corporation which owns Fair Grinds Coffeehouse and other businesses is an L3C, and may have been the first with this status in the state of Louisiana from what we understand.

to incorporate, and we did so. We were operating in a wider world and there might be some crazy stuff happening between Little Rock and Sioux Falls and Des Moines and Fort Worth and Houston and St. Louis and Memphis and New Orleans, so following the examples of many before us, we hunkered down behind the corporate walls we needed to protect everything in such a different internal and external environment.

There are entirely different decisions though that must be made in choosing to structure the organization as either non-profit or tax-exempt. Much, in fact almost all, of what any and all non-profits do fits the definition of tax-exempt purposes, and is educational, charitable, and so forth. All of that is right and good. On the other hand choosing to seek privileges from the IRS as a tax-exempt organization also embraces huge restrictions, not the least of which have to do with direct politics and what is referred to as "grassroots lobbying." A tax exempt organization makes an overt decision to eschew any form of direct or partisan political activity as an absolute pre-condition for maintaining an exempt status. Various amendments of the tax code have also created increasingly rigid prohibitions on the form and function of what an exempt organization can also do in terms of direct advocacy with public and governmental bodies. No one who has served on the board of an exempt organization with a heartbeat of any kind has avoided hearing the percentages and kinds of allowable activity and the penalties for breaching the walls of permissible behaviors.[6] Even decades after the promulgation of such regulations the real practice and rules continue to be shrouded in the kind of foggy ambiguity that earns specialized lawyers' fees that range hundreds of dollars per hour. Given the make-believe "scandal"[7] involving the politicization of the IRS exempt section and the proposed rules to codify and restrict any activity, especially by c4's that has been temporarily stalled by a record number of letters and comments on the rule setting, it is fair to state that everything is currently "up for grabs" in the US. In plainer English, that also essentially means "when they want you, all they have to do, is come and get you."

This seems a tough and unacceptable trade. In effect one is exchanging the freedom of the organization and its membership to choose any available and effective tactic or strategy, no matter how aggressive the advocacy or direct and overt the politics, for a floating crap game run by the government where the odds are still going to be in their favor and the enforcement at their discretion or whim in their own good time. On either ground it seems amazingly worthless, yet, paradoxically, organizations routinely seem to choose such options for few good reasons.

The "good" reason inevitably cited has to do with the presumed necessity of offering a tax benefit to the donor or the requirement of exempt status from some significant foundation or institutional giver. Let's take a closer look at these necessities.

---

[6] Sadly, this is not even simply a phenomena of the US Tax Code. When working to direct the Community Labor Training Centre from Vancouver, I was constantly confounded by the same fears and paranoia of non-profits in Canada over the 10% limitation on such activity that are faced by organizations there. My best understanding to date (2016) is that the IRS has never made any percentage of political activity a settled matter, rather than lawyers" speculation.

[7] The Tea Party and its supporters in 2013 claimed that their applications for tax exempt status were being given extraordinary scrutiny by the IRS, though there was little evidence that they were being denied. Investigations found that groups on the left, particularly ex-state affiliates of ACORN were also being given additional scrutiny for their applications, many of which were denied, including Action United, formerly Pennsylvania ACORN.

As we discussed earlier, tax benefits for membership dues *per se* often do not exist, for example in the case of union dues where the only deductible status lies in its role as a "business expense" which are of marginal utility to the contributor. For the average working family a contribution of $50, $100, $200, or even more is not likely to be motivated specifically by a desire for favorable tax treatment. Instead the contribution is going to be driven by passion, politics, impulse, or whatever else may have motivated the individual reaching for the purse, pocketbook, or wallet to write a check or shell out the money. Having done this for more than 45 years and counting, I can assure you that the number of questions raised by low and moderate-income families, as they get ready to pay ACORN membership dues about the tax consequences of such a decision are microscopically small. Direct door-to-door canvassers in middle and upper middle-income neighborhoods report being asked the question from time to time, but the answer was usually irrelevant to the decision to contribute. These are not huge sums after all; so neither is their tax consequence likely to be that significant to the donor. Whether dues or another contribution is made for the "cause," the community, or the general support and solidarity of it all, this is not the reason to choose to apply for a tax exemption for an organization committed to the struggle for social change. In short one does not need an exemption to appeal to the "biscuit cookers"[8] that provide the primary constituency support for your organizing.

Rather it is the "stud ducks"[9] that will be looking for the edge and the tax benefit in exchange for their contribution. They are not motivated by natural support or solidarity, but by the separate calculus of association and advantage that moves the rich, whether old or new. Perhaps this is compelling and argues that despite all of the steel walls and high ceilings created to shield your activity that it is worth it in compensation for the resources needed to fuel the fight. Truth is though that even when the activist, social change driven outfit has a bright, shiny tax exempt certificate hanging on the wall, nearly every early potential supporter would much, much prefer to still give the money to some middle ground broker for their own security at least until the organization has reached its prime. At that point the mass-based organization can probably – usually – channel the money through its own associated tax exempt organizations.

There are a lot of reasons for this, some of which are good ones, it would appear. The contributor is typically risk adverse. Even if not anonymous, many sizable contributors would just as soon forego the hassle of identification, investigation, and public inspection that goes hand and glove with contributions to publicly active and therefore controversial organizations. Once the contribution is made the last thing any contributor wants to find is that they are caught up in the muck and morass of the consequences of the contribution.

---

[8]   The populist sounding head of the ARKLA gas company, Witt Stephens, in appealing for rate increases before the Arkansas Public Service Commission would often sway the day with his appeals on the part of the biscuit cookers that ARKLA was dedicated to serving, harkening back to an era in which uneven fire could ruin many a batch of the best biscuits that the even temperature of gas could cook undisturbed.

[9]   I owe this expression to Max Allison, a legendary political organizer in Arkansas whose "fine hand" was seen in all Wilbur Mills campaigns from beginning to end, who across countless cups of coffee at the Woolworth's on Main Street in the early 70's was more than willing to tutor a young organizer in how politics and power really worked in the state and the "stud ducks" and "fuzzy balls" that called the shots and how to counter them.

And, as much as they want deniability, they also want some distance from the contribution. They do not want to be attached, preferring instead to have hoped that their contribution alone spoke to what needed to be said and done. It was a learning experience for me to hear – or overhear is probably more accurate – the complaints and the whining from people who had made contributions to bail funds or whatever in the civil rights days, who years later were struggling to disassociate themselves from their "friends" in that struggle who were now caught up in the daily struggle to live with the attendant strains and stresses of that period which often scarred them not only psychically, but also fiscally for the future. There would not be so many middlemen in this process if it were not more than a convenience, but an absolute necessity for the rich to have them.

There are so many 501(c)3 organizations out there, that it is not that hard to get the occasional church or community center or whatever to accept and transmit the contribution thereby acting as a "fiscal agent" for your organization. A fiscal agent takes responsibility in the eyes of the Service, as the IRS never seems to tire of describing itself, of assuring that in fact the monies spent by the organization were in pursuit of a tax-exempt purpose, whether or not the organization itself was tax exempt. A church or other institutional supporter will not necessarily see this as a trivial decision and may be as challenged in accepting the risk of acting in your behalf as any of the intrepid rich were originally. Nonetheless one can almost always get this done either for love or money. Love meaning for support of your cause, and money meaning your willingness to pay for the service to compensate them for whatever love did not quite take care of completely.

When the contributions of this size and scale go from the occasional to the commonplace, one inevitably confronts the question of tax exemption once again, because one needs a *real* fiscal agent or at the least a real plan for how to handle all of this. Once again there are other ways to go rather than adapting the operating organization into a tax-exempt institution.

The most significant alternative available in the United States is to become a sponsored project of one of the various incubating institutions that exist for this purpose, the most exceptional and largest of which has been the Tides Center in San Francisco. There are others that provide a similar service in specific cities or as one of a number of services, but Tides is a good example of the best and biggest of the lot. There are even community organizations themselves, like Virginia Organizing, directed by Joe Szakos, that provide this service and receive a significant percentage of financial support for their own organizing by doing so.[10]

The Tides Center is a partner organization to the Tides Foundation also located along with the entire family of organizations at the Thoreau Center on the Presidio in San Francisco. Tides was founded in 1978 somewhat uniquely for this purpose by Drummond Pike[11] as a vast improvement on similar work done by the now defunct Youth Project[12],

---

[10] Personal conversation.

[11] By way of full disclosure, I was proud to be – along with the attorney drawing the papers – the other initial incorporator and board member of the Tides Foundation and Tides Center in one capacity or another for over 30 years.

[12] Where – once again by way of full disclosure – I had also served a stint on the board in the early-mid 70's, but from which I was long, long gone years before its unfortunate demise.

where he had formerly worked as West Coast Director. Often Tides confuses organizers given its dual status as an unendowed foundation, where its role is not insignificant, but not as revolutionary as its success and strength in operating as the structural architecture, and therefore fiscal agent, for more than 300 different organizations both permanent and ad hoc. Here in the delivery of "excellent core services" Tides has developed a back shop capacity which has historically provided top service to the constituent organizational projects, while also providing unparalleled security to the source contributor, whether foundation, church, or private individual. Furthermore, it provides this kind of fiscal competency – which is often the bane of struggling organizations and their organizers – at a reasonable cost, based on the size of the project and the source of the funds, from soup to nuts, benefits to payroll to audits. Tides has grown big at this, handling some tens of millions in gross income and expenditures for its combined projects, and is able to achieve efficiencies through scale, centrality, and computerization that are not often available for smaller organizations, time sensitive campaigns, or temporary projects. At the least it represents a viable alternative for many organizations compared to making the unnecessary compromises on program and politics that separate c3 status would entail, and in many cases has meant the difference between life and death for organizations in legal and financial protections that would have been difficult to provide independently. The number of organizations that have crashed on the simple shoals provided by the fiscal temptations of spending payroll tax withholding when they get caught in a cash flow crunch are inestimable, and incidentally, corporate status does not protect anything or anyone from liabilities and penalties imposed by the IRS to restore such withholding dollars, since the Service holds individual board members personally liable for restoration and repayment of such funds.[13] The Tides Center offers a viable model for organizational activity that has not been sufficiently explored, but extends resources and protections importantly, and should be more broadly used, though now the minimum financial threshold to be part of the Center makes it less accessible as an incubator.[14] Tides/Canada is also offering similar services with offices in Vancouver and Toronto, which have also been an exciting development in recent years.[15]

There is an irony that is impossible to completely avoid or escape, since in most ways we still are talking about providing a service to donors, and surprisingly these donors are frequently churches and foundations. The core of the paradox is that the organization itself is paying for this service to the funders, rather than having the funders absorb the cost, especially since the cost is in many ways an unnecessary transfer of expense to the project or organization. There is no legal or accounting reason that mandates that a foundation has to give a grant solely to a tax exempt organization, only that it has to give grants

---

[13] ACORN affiliated the Citizens Action League in California in the early 80's after its second episode of spending its withholding in order to prevent the IRS from being in a position to seize the homes of some of the lower income elected board members.

[14] I was surprised in 2016, when I made an inquiry for an organization in Alaska that Tides Center seems to require considerably over $100,000 in confirmed funding before a project will be selected to sponsor.

[15] I was the Chair of the Tides Center board when it became a separate partner organization of the Tides Foundation (where I was also on the board and a former Chair) some years ago by way of full disclosure.

for tax exempt purposes. In order words the same burden that is taken on by the "fiscal agent." A foundation could – and should – simply take on this responsibility itself, which is a matter of requiring reporting and some semblance of oversight to be able to vouchsafe that the actual expenditures in the field are in line with the tax exempt purposes indicated in the original proposal or other timely reporting. The Tides Centers of the world or the integrated c3 organizations working with many activist outfits are really fiscal agents *for* the foundations, more than they are for the projects and organizations themselves. Where there is often even a sharper edge to the irony is when some funders, including the rich themselves, complain about the fees and related costs from the fiscal agents, even while requiring these expenditures themselves because of their unwillingness to undertake the necessary review and oversight internally. The funders are getting a service and in essence *allowing* a shrinkage charge from their grant, rather than either shouldering their burden or increasing the grant sufficiently to allow the recipient to receive the full benefit of the award. Bizarre! But, because of the common unwillingness by many to point out the stark nakedness of the emperor, the beat just keeps on rolling here.

Churches are also spectacular examples of the same thing, and some of them at least understand and act correctly on this issue. Because some national religious denominations give grants of assistance from the contributions of many small givers themselves often in their collection plates, they are exempt because they are in fact religious institutions, they have no requirements to give to tax exempt organizations whatsoever. The requirements of a public charity – that contributions in the main are coming from the public – are therefore easily met. The organization therefore should be able to directly receive the contribution regardless of its own tax status. The main exception here has been the Catholic Campaign for Human Development, at its zenith an almost $10 million per year funding source for community organizing, and therefore the single most significant source of funding in the United States for community organizing. CCHD has required – for no really good reason – tax exemptions or fiscal agents because of its own concerns for its own tax exemption given the level of lobbying and political activity the Catholic Church engages around abortion and other social issues. Essentially, the Catholic Church and its ruling Bishops were willing to risk their own exemption for their own political advocacy, but created a stringent policy for CCHD disavowing any political relationships, no matter how indirect, in order not to risk its tax exemption through the work of its grantees. It is an interesting contradiction that in this situation where no exemption should be necessary or required, we are essentially having to make "hard" money – usable for anything – go "soft" – avowedly apolitical – so that the Church can make its own soft money, go hard. CCHD has also been the only funder of this nature to ever rescind a grant to an ACORN affiliate because of a mention on our website that some ACORN in New York was involved in the creation and activity of the Working Families Party in that state.[16] Goes to show that you just never can tell. Also goes to show once again that since this is all about the funder, and not the real use of the funds, and about reporting requirements and

---

[16] During most of its history, CCHD has been the single largest funder of community organizations in the United States and needs to be categorically praised for its history in this regard. CCHD has also routinely blocked grants to community-based organizations that were even remotely involved, even in coalitions, with other groups that may have advocated a woman's right-to-choose.

accountabilities that protect the funder, it should be a simple part of the package that the funder should pay the piper, and not the grantee. But, I guess that's just me!

Money like water can be "hard" or "soft," and the best money is hard as rock. Soft money can only be spent on charitable and other tax-exempt purposes, while hard money can be spent without qualms or second thoughts to build the organization any way that it needs to be done. The right is absolutely correct: money is fungible. As such any time one can get a hard contribution straight into the organization without any dilution, then it frees other money, like dues money or similarly unrestricted contributions as well to move to the highest level that the water can flow, and where the need is greatest. One hears of these distinctions around political money as well, and the parallels are pretty close to exactly the same. With political contributions hard money can be used by a candidate or a campaign anywhere that it needs to be spent, while soft money can only be spent on voter education or voter registration and so forth. It really should not be so much to ask the rich to pay a piece of their taxes in order to harden the money and let us do what needs to be done!

All of these devices allow the organization to structure "projects" that segregate its educational or other tax exempt work from the rest of the organization either through segregated fiscal sponsors, like Tides, or even through integrated sponsors, like the creation of independent, but related, c3 organizations created by the organization itself. The organization may in fact want to create 501(c)3 organizations and sponsor them through the application procedure, and in many ways as the scale of the organization and the diversity of its activity grows, this makes very good sense. Nonetheless, this does not encourage, much less mandate the organization itself to become a c3 thereby crippling opportunities for flexibility and the future.

The other reason that I would encourage some serious rethinking of these structural issues is that 501(c)3 status is getting harder to achieve, not easier, especially as the federal administration has become increasingly conservative. Over recent years it has become virtually impossible to obtain status for any activity *once* it has begun operations – my advice: forget about it. Unless you can apply for exempt status for an empty shell without any prior activity you may be waiting for years, if not an eternity.[17] This is not to say that with aggressive appeals and some intercession from Congressional offices that one cannot jimmy lose some of these knee-jerk rejections from the Service, but it is going to keep getting harder for the foreseeable future. In the IRS in 2014 in the more progressive "age of Obama" announced a streamlined procedure for applying for tax exempt status in the wake of its other political problems in this area. Little optimism has been expressed by organizers that this initiative has changed the basic problems to the degree that they have embraced this openness as real, and no figures are available yet on whether general

---

[17] At least this was our experience for many years for ourselves and infrequent others. Tides Center during my time there found that some of our projects incubate out to their own c3 status, and we speculated that that may have had as much to do with a regional IRS anomaly given the number of West Coast projects in the Tides stable and that it may still be catching up to the conservative drift on these issues in other IRS regions in the country. Atlanta, Austin, and Memphis where we do much of our work are in the "forget about it" categories at this point.

applications have risen. Hope springs eternal, but until realized, caution is the watchword still.

One step will follow the other as well. What is harder today to obtain is eventually going to be more difficult to retain. During the Clinton Administration the number of IRS personnel in enforcement and overview of tax exempt organizations declined, which meant a welcome decrease in politically inspired audits which had been increasing in the first Bush administration. In the defunding of the left strategies that Karl Rove and his ilk were continually and aggressively managing from the White House in the early years of the 21st century one can expect that there will be surges of such audits in the years to come depending on who is in the White House, Westminster, Ottawa or elsewhere. It is simply foolish to believe that we can successfully operate for long periods of times close to the line between exempt and non-exempt status and successfully surf past the high waves of political change that are coming with increasing regularity towards the beach. We do not just need firewalls; we are going to need great walls worthy of the ones built by Hadrian or Emperor Qin Shi Huang and later the Ming Dynasty.

Protecting an integrated c3 is not an easy matter in the world of activist organizations committed to social change. Though we may not have incorporated ACORN until 1978, we moved to incorporate the Institute for Social Justice[18] in late 1970 under the laws of the state of Arkansas, and secure a 501(c)3 for the Institute as early as 1972. When ACORN members in great numbers were elected in a *de facto* takeover of the Pulaski County Quorum Court in 1974, it was only a matter of months before the IRS did a thorough investigation and review of the tax status and exemption of the Institute, even though it had never been publicly identified in any way as connected to ACORN or any activity other than training and research. Compared to some of the conservatives in Washington these days, Nixon was a liberal, so it is foolhardy to believe that many organizations are not going to be fighting with both hands and feet to hold onto tax exemptions in the near future.

Let me mention one other corporate structural decision as we move past these detailed matters, and that has to do with the advantages of creating stock based non-profits, which is a possibility in the United States at least. This would seem at first a contradiction in terms, since we have already defined a non-profit as something that cannot distribute profits to stockholders, and for many it would seem strange to conceive of a non-profit that could be *owned* or have stockholders of any kind. In fact there are quite a number of states that allow this option, and in our experience it is quite a good one. Arkansas along with about twenty other states had such an option. For example all of our building corporations were stock based non-profits so that the participating non-profit organizations each held a share of stock and participated on the board of the corporation that collectively owned the property, almost making it a "corporate cooperative" of sorts.

Many of these corporations would not exist other than to do two critical things: (1) absorb liabilities separately that can arise from property ownership, and (2) shield

---

[18] Originally called the Arkansas Institute for Social Justice, the Institute was incorporated and handled by the late Jay Lipner, a VISTA Attorney, and Steve Herman, a Reginald Heber Smith attorney, in the early 70's. In the 21st Century we also incorporated the ACORN Institute in order to further segregate our c3's that accepted government contracts with our c3's that did not to limit the range of exposure and requirements of various audits.

real property assets from other kinds of politically inspired and dangerous litigation that aggressive and activist organizations, like unions and ACORN attract like honey. Having them stock based actually helps strengthen and resolve control and corporate accountability issues in a constructive way. Other stock based non-profits particularly where there is a membership-derived benefit are healthy alternatives to common practice rather than simply creating a self-perpetuating board, which at some future time could take on a life of its own. When you are building a membership based organization, like an ACORN, then a stock based non-profit is irrelevant to you, since the members "own" the organization itself and hold the power. Where you are building non-profits in other ways, then I would not hesitate to advise that you look at a stock based structure to create some accountability when everything goes south, as it inevitably always seems that it will, sooner or later.[19]

Does all of this really matter to organizers or are these just matters for lawyers and other obsessive types? Let me share a painful story of unintended consequences where organizers, leaving matters to lawyers, paid heavy dues. As the story came to me in a visit to ACORN's office in Hawaii, Arthur Rutledge was a seminal organizer in Hawaii who built both HERE Local 5 on the islands into a powerhouse, particularly in the Waikiki tourist mecca in Honolulu, and also had a charter to organize in other jurisdictions with the Teamsters, building their organization as well in the heroic days for labor in the islands. In the normal way of the world the two locals needed a headquarters and meeting hall and bought one off the Waikiki Strip along the beach on the island of Oahu. The corporate structure to create Unity House, as they called the joint building corporation, was created by Tom Gill, the attorney for Local 5. Gill having watched the red-baiting and hard handed attack on Harry Bridges and the ILWU, which was the premier union on the islands in these days, correctly advised that one needed a separate building corporation in order to shield the assets against fairly predictable McCarthyism attacks that might be coming the way of any big union on the islands. Because of the particular nature of the partnership Rutledge and Gill constructed a membership base for Unity House though, which created a different animal all together. Unity House was not a union, nor was it simply a building corporation, but it was an actual voting membership body composed of members of both HERE and IBT who could elect a board to govern its affairs.

There is certain logic to all of this of course. In the unique way that land is the delimiting resource on the islands, the building over the decades thanks to the natural course of inflation, the Japanese bubble economy, and to some shrewd timing by the senior Rutledge sold at the top of the market for the astronomical sum of $55,000,000! Given the vicissitudes of time, Arthur was replaced as the manager of HERE Local 5 by his son, Tony, and in the close work that is not uncommon in the islands, his political opponent trying to clean-up and bring the local union back to some power, is Eric Gill, one of the sons of Tom Gill, the former attorney for the local. Eric became the President of HERE Local 5. One is surprised though to meet him at his leased space off the path

---

[19] This comment seems prophetic when examining the dissolution of ACORN in 2010 and some of its reorganization and realignments after 2008, when I resigned. Many of the stock-based nonprofits survived like the building corporations in Arkansas and Pennsylvania, as well as similarly structure nonprofits like the Affiliated Media Foundation Movement (AM/FM).

downtown near the auto repair shops, which is fine, but seems cramped compared to what one might have expected to find. Owing to the complexity of this structural architecture, when I met him, Eric Gill was running the local union and though Tony Rutledge lost election at the union, Tony did not lose the election to continue to run Unity House, which though it no longer has a building, nor does it house the local union, is still sitting on the remainder of the multi-million dollar big real estate score! And, just to put a finer point on this situation, Unity House would then have no real purpose other than its own existence and some minimal services to its "members." Meanwhile, HERE Local 5 could have been sitting on a war chest with millions and millions of dollars, if one had looked at the long term structural consequences as they evolved through the years to these fine days. Who knows how and whether this all worked out, since it is not the kind of thing that hits the papers, but my point remains the same: structure matters![20]

Organic, Natural, and Flexible

A mass organization's structure is not a Robert's Rules of Order thing. Structure has to be organic, natural, and flexible.

What do I mean by that?

The structure is "organic" in the sense that it must be deeply rooted in the constituency or membership and therefore resonate culturally, sufficient to allow the reinforcement or the creation of a community within the organization. Artificiality in the structure is poison, even if the death might be slow in coming. There was an organization in Virginia years ago whose structure was based on the British Parliament, which seemed quite impressive to the organizer. In the US it had little chance, though in the UK, it might have been seemed more organic, although now that ACORN International has a strong affiliates in England and Scotland, I am pretty sure no one there would have thought so there either.

The structure is "natural" in the sense that the organization needs to operate with an order and harmony that needs to be straightforward, transparent, and above all, simple, rather than complex and legalistic.

The structure is "flexible" in the sense that it creates a big tent allowing diversity of constituency, multiplicity of actions, events, and campaigns, and elasticity of strategy and tactics over time. Such a structure makes action easy, not hard, and facilitates change when necessary.

The smartest thing I did in designing the structure of ACORN was to realize that I was not smart enough to accurately and exhaustively predict the future of all that the organization might want to do and be, and having realized that, devised a structure that would be simple and flexible in order to allow the future to fit freely, but firmly within the organizational architecture. As we have already discussed, this also led to he abhorrence

---

[20] Although I've spent a lot of time, perhaps too much time, on this question here with a USA lens, having experienced the process in Mexico, Honduras, India, Peru, England, Canada, Italy, the Czech Republic and elsewhere, if this is a problem an organizer confronts, contact me, and perhaps we can discuss and assist in resolution.

of artificial ceilings and constructs either legally or financially that would make the organization unnatural or foreign to its own membership.[21]

I have made my life and living organizing working families – low and moderate income people – not doctors, lawyers, or big whoops, but plain spoken and down to earth families. A lot of the best and worse results of public school education will assemble in these meetings, and it will be spiced heavily with the kind of life experience and shoulders to the wheel that took mothers out of school to have and raise children and fathers out of school to make a living on the street the best way they could with books and the learning that came from them taking the hindmost. A community or workplace meeting is not a prototype of a seminar attended by PhD's, legal eagles. or a society book club. Therefore for the process to work the structure of the organization has to put everyone on hard, solid, and very even ground. One cannot make the mistake of inadvertently empowering the one eager beaver who believes he or she knows the best and only way to make a motion, run a meeting, or take some minutes, because to adopt as part of the process some bit of such an esoteric world that only a select few can understand and follow is to cede the leadership of the organization and the fundamentals of its operation to the select few who have been admitted to that holy order.

Natural and organic works, but it may not be easily confused with democracy in a classic sense. Experience teaches what our politics and commitments abhor: the roots of democracy do not naturally run deep through our constituency. There is a tendency to defer to strength, not the nicety of democratic procedure. Which is not to say that people do not believe in democracy or that organizations should not operate democratically, quite the opposite! It is to say that democracy is a struggle and takes a huge investment in time and energy – it is not in fact natural for people. Therefore it takes a lot of hard work! The old saying that there are some things that are not pretty to watch in practice – making sausage and democracy – can be easily and often demonstrated in countless worksite and neighborhood meetings any day of the week.

We have found that the discomfort with voting in general and the mechanics of voting in particular strengthen a commitment to a group process that operates with a high level of consensus though. People in the same organization and community for the most part are conflict adverse, so part of their commitment is a flight from controversy to a common denominator, no matter how low, while the other, and perhaps the lesser part, is a genuine commitment to everyone owning and being comfortable with a decision and course of action.

Similarly in the main few want to be identified as leaders, and it is often that those that do are more aberrant than most, but we will address this at greater length later. The point here is that people flow naturally to the collegial and the collective – they are willing to share work, take parts of the agenda, sit together at the front, carry huge burdens equally for long distances, but frequently they are most uncomfortable standing alone or taller than their neighbors or co-workers. We have produced a dysfunctional civil and public society, which has systematically stunted the growth of the vast majority of our

---

[21] Obviously this was also a lesson I took from my experience as an organizer with the National Welfare Rights Organization as well, and its inability, and then disinterest, in broadening its base.

citizens, and the internal life of mass organizations has to provide prescriptive antidotes to ameliorate, if not cure, this terrible disease. Organizers cannot assume that just because the goals and objectives of the organization are antithetical to mass society and its maladies, that members will not bring every bit of the mass society baggage into the internal life of the organization. The structure has to provide soft landings, gentle slopes, and ample padding to allow people to find the proper space to successfully run their own organizations.

All of this is a work-in-progress. It is a mistake for the organizer to believe that there is an end to the learning curve or that there is an expectation that she will have all of the answers backwards and forwards from the first day on the job. Fortunately our constituency is also very forgiving on these details and quick to join something they see as a joint project. The mutuality of purpose and struggle is a vast open limit credit card for the organizer, unless abused in some critical way, and then one can follow the curve as people vote with their feet and pull themselves out of the organization.

In short with structure, keep it simple! From ACORN's experience I would also add, keep it equitable. I refer to this principle as *coordinated autonomy*, which was a fancy, if not fanciful, way of having the discussion with other organizers, but in truth worked for the groups because it seemed fair, and, therefore, natural.

The coordinated autonomy in structure was based on all groups having an equal say within their area of operations with all other groups that worked in the same area, but allowed them the main say – the autonomy – within their own area as long as they were consistent with the rest of the principles of the organization. An ACORN local group in north Philly or Scarborough in Toronto or the East End of Little Rock or the 9th Ward of New Orleans or in the flats of Oakland, would be able within the democratic process of the members of their own community organization to handle their own affairs: elect officers, raise funds, determine issues, plan and design campaigns, execute tactics and strategies, and, in short, do whatever was necessary within the boundaries of their geography to operate effectively. But, once the local group was dealing with an issue that moved past the boundaries of their neighborhood and involved either other communities where there were other affiliated ACORN local community organizations, or focused on targets and forces larger than the neighborhood to deliver the relief, provide the solution, or realize the victory, then coordinated autonomy in practice meant that the local organization needed to appeal to the other ACORN organizations structurally at the citywide level in order to get not only their concurrence, but also their necessary support. To win would require the highest level of consensus available at that structural level, so it required a dialectical process of different groups pushing and pulling with each other to set the priorities for common and mutual action sufficiently to get their issue prioritized at the citywide level. Once again all local groups are structurally represented equally on the ACORN citywide board, so the opportunity to win – or lose – in achieving this level of coordination is also equivalent.

The same structural imperatives operate at the state, national, and international level within ACORN. All the groups need to combine to set a priority and come to a consensus when the issue involves a statewide action or a statewide legislative priority. Similarly, the national board is made of an equal number of representatives of each state affiliate (two delegates per state) meeting several times per year. No individual state could presume to suddenly begin a national campaign without the concurrence – and enthusiasm – of all other state affiliations, though certainly many campaigns began in different cities and states and found themselves rising to a level where everyone has to come into the fight to have a chance of winning. Globally, same, same.

At all levels one finds some tension at vulnerable spots in the structure when pressed by aggressive interests. Politics is certainly one of the prime tests of ACORN's structural tensile strength. Politicians want any endorsement they can get and often are willing to calf off from the herd, rather than take a chance at losing the full endorsement. ACORN nationally went through this structural experience on the feasibility of opposing or supporting intervention by the United States in Iraq in 2003 during the first George Bush presidency. Various city and state organizations were of course solicited particularly in the early "hot spots" of anti-war sentiment in places like New York and Chicago to take positions, sign ads, and join local coalitions, as if, structurally, something like a position on the war could have been anything other than a national organization decision. The national board ended up going through a lengthy six-month process to arrive at a position, which was virtually moot by the time it was taken, but nonetheless preserved the structural and leadership integrity of the organization because it was organic, natural, and transparent, therefore represented a deep consensus when a position was finally taken.

As an organizer, one has to continually ask in these circumstances – Does it matter. How much? And, what is the price of the fight?

I part ways with many, because I believe in fact it does matter – intensely – and that one has to be willing to allow, if not encourage, quite a bit of conflict over these kinds of issues, and if you do not, you will not be able to hold the organization together against the constant hurricane winds of internal and external conflict that will inevitably blow it apart. We protected the political structure of the organization at critical historic intervals in order to establish a tradition, protocol, and shared experience that leadership was willing to protect and advance.

The first crisis came – and this is to be expected – early in the political history of the organization in Arkansas right after 1972 when we first began making endorsements in local political races. To the surprise of all of the leadership an article ran in the local papers indicating that the chair of an ACORN local group in Levy, then a largely white, working class neighborhood of North Little Rock, had personally endorsed a candidate running for mayor of that fair city. If this behavior had been allowed, the impact would have been devastating and likely irreparable. Accountability would have been impossible to maintain for any leader or member to the structure of the organization, since any could go and do likewise. There would have been no commitment to the integrity of the shared endorsement process.

Additionally, the intractable issues of race lie beneath some of these problems. Many of the other local ACORN organizations in North Little Rock, which under the structure would have had an equal say in the decision to make an endorsement in the mayor's race, were largely black for example the Dixie neighborhood, Shorter College Gardens, and Eastgate Terrace. The price of such conflict inevitably though, is that there are winners and losers. If one does not fight for the structure, then the organization operates at the whim of charismatic leaders or motivated outsiders with their own agendas. Dominant leadership styles constantly test the boundaries and operate in some ways uncomfortably within any structural confines. Needless to say, it was a bitter meeting, but important for all the participants in bringing other white and black leaders of these embryonic and immature ACORN chapters into a shared experience of conflict to decide to "protect" their organization against the "embarrassment" of a politician having been able to so easily turn a local chapter leader's head. The conflict and the experience itself welded the process back in place so firmly that such an incident became part of the foundational ideology of the organization at least in Arkansas. The leader obviously resigned in a huff and a puff, and there was a protracted struggle to keep the local group in Levy alive through the conflict of contending sets of leaders, but once it was all said and done it was something that no one – even within ACORN – really remembers – an isolated episode lost even to the archives and history of the organization – but in my view these are the foundation stones on which the rest of the weight of the structure was borne into the future.

The equivalent crisis, nationally, came as ACORN was branching past Arkansas to include other states and was initiated by delegates from the ACORN organizations in Reno, Nevada around 1978. At that point there were less than a dozen state affiliates of ACORN – we had only begun to expand outside of Arkansas in early 1975 first to South Dakota, then to Texas, Louisiana, Tennessee, Missouri and so forth, and to Reno of all places. The leader in Reno was another strong white, working class guy – a mechanic in one of the casino's from the Sparks chapter of ACORN. He insisted on bringing forward a resolution to put the ACORN national board on record against President Jimmy Carter's Panama Treaty. What in the world did we have to do with Panama one might, rightfully, ask, but nothing is quite that simple. The question here was not the integrity of the process, since after some early pushes and shoves there was a commitment to make the fight – for or against – at the national board meeting, rather the problem, as was once again the case, as we saw more recently in the national board's debate over the Iraq war, was how one conceives of the legitimate role of the national organization. How does one weigh credibility? How does one assess the impact of leadership positions on the membership? And, importantly, on all sides of the question – how would ACORN operate as a truly *national* organization?

The undercurrent issue here was less race, than it was ideology in a classic sense, even if it was simply a lower key *Readers' Digest* sort of conservative semi-republicanism. The organization was non-partisan, so the decision would turn on whether or not one spent whatever credibility and legitimacy the organization had built nationally solely on our own specific, generic constituency issues or whether or not we believed we had a separate voice that could be extended to matters outside our normal and natural practice. Such structural issues cut both ways. These issues are almost always fought at the lowest common denominator. For example as one of our Portland leaders argued in 2003 on whether or not the vision of the organization is *minimalist* and ACORN exists as a collection of *civic* and neighborhood improvement organizations around the country, or whether the vision is more expansive and one believes the organization should play on a larger stage. Allies for each position can come to the debate and at the issues from all directions, though the impact of polarizing ideological decisions can cast large shadows on both sides of the street.

On both the Panama Canal and Iraq the issue turned in some ways off to the side of the main question as it did right on the issue itself, but that is neither here or there. On a very, very close vote the ACORN national board ended up after extensive debate deciding to take no position whatsoever on the question of the Panama Canal Treaty. Twenty-five years later on an equally close vote an entirely different set of leaders constituting the ACORN national board barely decided by only the slimmest of margins that it was inappropriate for ACORN to take a position about the war, even though the board individually almost to a man and woman personally opposed the war in Iraq. If I had more time and thought that the reader had more patience, I would argue that these are case studies in the evolution of the organization's own internal, structural legitimacy, but it's enough to say that these issues are critical, and literally the life and death of organizations can rest on such questions and how they are handled.

And, in organizations of low and moderate income families there are no simple, intellectual debates. The losing leader from Nevada resigned in defeat, conflict, and turmoil – tried to get the head organizer fired, and instituted years of trouble trying to reconcile a separate space for his position and dominance in that area in opposition to the national organization. In fact ACORN was not able to support a viable office in Reno for 20 years. In another example the national ACORN executive board, dominated by African-American and Latino women, debated the organization's position on choice for women on birth control, and though almost all of them personally disagreed with abortion, as leaders they believed the organization needed to politically support a pro-choice position, because as many of them argued in the meeting held on a cold New Orleans January in the back of my office on Elysian Fields Avenue, "it was best for the organization." An organization's culture is forged in steel – and conflict.

Severability and Conflict

One critical element of structure in fact has to have severability. One might say that it is the other side of the coin from flexibility. Severability allows the organization to mix and match pieces, insert and extract projects or campaigns or initiatives, and any number of other constructive things, but it also allows one to jettison mistakes, cauterize problem areas, and continue to drive the organization forward on the main line. Perhaps as much as organizational structure has to accommodate growth and change, in order to survive, the structure has to accommodate conflict and reverses as well.

Conflict is the gorilla in the room that no one likes to acknowledge or discuss, but in many ways the real test for both an organizer and an organization is the ability to weather the storms of internal and external conflict, and believe that there is a safe harbor on the other side, and finally secure the port. Conflict is inevitable – a fact of organizational life and a force of nature in working with people. Yet, conflict is very disorienting to many organizers and most other civilians.

The confusion is easily understood. In building and working for mass organizations or any organization trying to create social change, only the most naïve would not expect some level of external conflict, even if the level of intensity might surprise. Men and women signing up for the work with any level of awareness then correctly expect that the institutions, governments, and corporations that are the targets of their activity, or the resistance to their force, or simply have the power to resolve the issues in their campaigns, will invariably push back and in most cases have more resources to give back even, better than they get. Organizers and organizations are buffeted by their belief in the cause, the solidarity of their work with their comrades and colleagues, and the good will and appreciation of the constituency they serve and organize. This is the nature of the fight after all. In the immortal words of Fredrick Douglass "power concedes nothing without struggle," so this is flatly the ground on which we stand, the nature of the terrain on which we work. Like it, or leave it.

One of the simplest structural protections for ACORN lies in the definition of exactly who is eligible to be a member and what constitutes membership. In a community organization of low and moderate-income families the eligibility is not based on income, but geography – if you live in the neighborhood, then you are eligible to me a member, and therefore if you move out of the neighborhood, you may be a member of the overall organization, but your status in the local group, as the central organizational unit, is altered.

This alone can regulate, or at least define, the field of battle engaged by some external forces. In late 1970 in one of our first drives in Pine Bluff, Arkansas we did a drive in Watson Chapel, a largely white, working class area right outside of the city, and the organizing committee meeting was broken up by the Ku Klux Klan. The tactical objective of the KKK members was to outnumber the committee itself, join the organization, and thereby, take over the group. Being able to define the limits of membership as only the

Early Little Rock Board Meeting Walter Nunn and Wade 1973-74.

neighborhood boundaries saved the group in this instance from being taken over. Usually these external threats are more about preventing the group from organizing, than they are designed to permanently take control of a local ACORN community organization. In the Barelas neighborhood of Albuquerque in 1981 a local civic organization packed the first meeting of the local ACORN chapter as it was forming and tried to vote against forming the group. At the end the fact that they did not join, meant that they lost their voice and were not there in subsequent meetings. Smarter was the state representative in south Philly in 1977 who showed up with over 40 neighborhood folks to a first meeting of that chapter, had them all sign up and join ACORN, and they promptly created a voting bloc in the meeting of 100 or more people such that they were able to win all of the local group officer elections, and effectively disband the group at the birthing. One does not see much of that kind of "close work" in organizing, because it requires a well-organized and disciplined base – perhaps that neighborhood was organized after all! One would expect this kind of external interference with the organizing process in "machine" cities, but at the street level outside of the election cycle, many of them simply cannot compete with a door-to-door, close-to-the-ground organizing model – we never had problems of this kind in Chicago for example under either Daley regime. More frequently one will simply have the isolated discordant voices who come to argue for either special interests or the status quo, and that kind of problem is just part of the mix: sparks that start the engine of the organization.

This is essentially turf conflict, which can be pretty tough, though it is interesting to observe how different organizers see turf conflict compared to the expectation of outsiders. ACORN finds the occasional politician or civic association that wants to fight block-by-block, but frankly, most organizations simply do not have that deep a base, nor has the base been well tended, and it is not that difficult to get under them on a door-to-door based methodology along the lines employed by ACORN. In all these years we have never had any turf problems with church based organizations of which the IAF is the best example. We have frequent examples in fact, and I can personally remember them as early as the late 1970's in Houston, as one example, where an ACORN local group meeting in one neighborhood would be held in the same church as the IAF meeting, and we would be breaking up, as they were walking in to start. In New Orleans Blessed Seelos Catholic Church (formerly St. Vincent de Paul) in 1999 had a sign made after they rehabbed their meeting room with pictures of the organizational insignia that used their hall with ACORN's logo right next to the name of a church based group in the city. No big deal. The organizations work with different constituencies, different models, and only the politicians getting jammed by both or the funders who want to become partisans and advocates believe there is any problem whatsoever. These are simply different planets going around the sun.[22]

Where a donation, instead of dues, equates to membership, one can automatically tell that if that is the only membership engagement, then membership will have a proportionately diminished power and voice in the organization. Certainly that is almost uniformly true of organizations that solicit through direct mail or various forms

---

[22] Perhaps I'm gilding the lily, since ACT at that time an affiliate of a national church-based network tried to prevent ACORN in New Orleans from meeting in any other Catholic parish.

of "canvass," as door-to-door solicitation is termed. There really are not that many opportunities for members to move program or exercise democratic practice in these kinds of organizations, if any, but neither do they pretend differently for the most part. They are "representative" organizations, rather than "participatory" organizations. In such organizations all of the conflict is internal within the staff or external with the institutional targets of their activity, since the membership, are usually passive supporters at best, and are essentially watching the main show through a small side window. They can vote with their feet and shift allegiances based on the public and private perception of the effectiveness of the organization and the contribution or controversy it creates, but the methodology is efficient and can maintain itself almost mechanically, independent of membership voice and affection. Attention should be paid, respect should be given, but they are not mass-based community organizations along the lines of our interest or often even little "d" democratic community organizations.

Such organizations can handle conflict only within the context of clearly defined enemies and the structural framing of their issues and identity. The barometer of so-called membership is often easier to read based on the popular perception that people *need* representation more in different times than others. The Bush election in 2000 and its lack of concern for environmental and other issue areas could be monitored through the increased membership recruitment rates in some of the national environmental organizations, not because there was proof that they were more effective, but because the public believed that they were more essential in times of strain, and felt that they needed the representation more, than previously. At the same time a hard wind can blow some of these same organizations and their members away as well, because in a classic sense there are "weak ties" between the members and the organization.

For unions and community organizations like ACORN, it is often hard for our opponents to understand why we cannot be beaten easily. Frequently we are the subjects of bad press, editorial harangue, political reaction and abuse, and constant accusation and conflict. There are just plain a lot of people who do not like unions, period, and do not like organizations like ACORN, exclamation point.

Tight structural protections and clear membership involvement and participation in campaign planning, strategy, and tactics builds a base level investment and ownership that makes it possible to withstand significant and continual public and private attacks, and in fact to condition the membership to expect such attacks as part of the standard operating procedure in the milieu of social change. The impact of such attacks are not irrelevant, because the ability to change the perception of the field of battle, condition the moral rightness and rectitude of the campaign or issue, or polarize and alienate the non-combatants within the organizations' own constituency can all spell defeat for the organization, if it is not able to anticipate and offset these attacks. But with good planning and preparation of leaders and members, aggressiveness in the field, and persistence in the endeavor, we cannot only take a number of good hits without falling, but we can eventually win in a way that others cannot imagine being able to sustain. And, severability is essential so that it is not possible to move leaders in another direction or prevent interference with the heart of the organizations financial base. Then eventually, even though the target may not concede the issue at hand, neither can they ignore the fight and not engage fully.

ACORN concluded a protracted three-year struggle with Household Finance (later HSBC after their purchase of Household Finance) in 2003 against predatory lending, which demonstrated many of these themes at a larger level. Household believed that it could simply have spokespeople attack our credibility; spin the story through the *Wall Street Journal* and the *American Banker*, and it would all go away someday. When that did not work, while attacking us directly and indicating that they would never negotiate with ACORN, they tried a parallel cooptation strategy by making financial contributions to middle ground organizations who would then say that they had worked with Household, that Household was reforming their practices, and even – when the money was right – that Household was not involved in predatory practices. As a multi-billion dollar outfit they had a lot of resources, both politically and financially, to continue the fight almost indefinitely, even as they were losing – and given the amount of profits they were realizing from these practices, frankly it paid for them to continue the strategy. Long and short of it, once we won in addition to the $400+ million in settlements we helped the state attorneys general give to victims of predatory lending from Household, we also negotiated an additional package of another $100 million or so in reparations and rehabilitation for victims of such practices, and when it came to the ACORN share, the only thing that I ever insisted to our negotiators, leaders, staff, and lawyers, was that the number of dollars to ACORN had to be at a steep multiple over what they had been willing to pay other organizations to sell us out. And, it was: $2 M per year over 3 years for ACORN to do direct outreach to inform our members and others of the settlement.

Nonetheless, membership definition is essential. The Knights of Labor in the late 1800's were the first of the major non-craft unions and had a very broad definition of their potential membership base, but it notably excluded and made ineligible bankers of course, and, very smartly, lawyers. The Knights were on to something. Lawyers *as members* are the bane of any grassroots organization, since obviously it is anathema for them to want the structure to work organically, naturally, and flexibly, since the nature of their business is artificially rule bound, rigid, and unnatural. ACORN had targets of actions and campaigns attempt to send in dues and join the organization in order to try to subvert the efforts against them. Billy Rector, a legendary real estate magnate and political manipulator in Little Rock, who was the target of many ACORN campaigns to prevent blockbusting in the early and mid-1970's constantly tried to figure out ways to pay his dues so that he could come to meetings – I left Little Rock in 1978 with an uncashed check from him still in my drawer. One cannot be a liberal. If they want to make a contribution, so be it, but if they want to be a member, at the least they must move into the neighborhood.

What shocks and confuses many organizers, particularly the first time they confront reality, is that in fact their orientation to serve and organize the constituency is not a safe travel pass allowing them to escape internal conflict with the members themselves. The structural divisions between staff and leaders/members, which exist in ACORN, and some other organizations, are a structural firewall that attempts to keep the two sets of problems separate, so that one does not eliminate the other, but unless the structure is secure and rigorously protected, no simple artifice can keep conflict from leaping the walls and burning everything to a crisp.

Aversion to conflict is frequently fatal not always to the organizer, but almost always to the basic democratic fiber of the organization. Strong leaders always trump weak structures, unless one forces the issue. Time after time in city after city, we have dealt with leadership and staff conflict, and almost invariably the problem will lie in the short circuit of structural accountability. The little litany of horrors is common. Sometimes it was simply a failure to hold regular group elections in order to hang on to a board seat. More frequently the group might have ceased to be active, yet the "leader" continued to sit regularly on the board and "represent" the interests of the members who were no longer meeting and frequently were no longer members. Sometimes contrary to all advice and the clarity of the bylaws, a leader who might have come in as part of an issue campaign or an ad hoc effort to report to the board during the campaign, through habit continued to attend and through excessive good manners was never asked to leave. Whatever it might have been, unless one respects the simple provisions of democratic operations that move people in and out, up and down within the organization, a deeper natural order takes hold and can strangle and suffocate the organization itself, and that is a Darwinian law of survival, which will drown the process of the organization itself against whatever will dominates.

Yet, ironically, even strong leaders believe in the process and structure of the organization, because it grants the very act of their leadership some legitimacy. Some scholars looking at social movements tend to argue that it is only the charisma of individual leaders that can hold together a social movement in its growing and non-institutional phase, and perhaps there is truth in that, but we have found that the folkways of our simple structure and its traditions have served that function adequately if in fact members and staff will act with accountability within these requirements.

The Problem with Democracy?

I am often troubled by the tension involving democratic operations in popular organizations. I can admit and understand that it is not naturally the way people seem to operate; yet the obstacles put in its way and, frankly, the minimal commitment to the process itself leaves our efforts in a quandary. At the same time I understand that social movements are in a hurry and social change cannot wait. Nonetheless, I am sobered perhaps by too many years inside the autocracy of labor institutions, where democracy, as practiced, is at best simply a legal requirement that binds the leaders to the members more in the letter than the spirit of the law. My cynicism has succeeded increasingly in making me an idealist in this area, increasingly unable to shave off the edges of the means, while trying to still clearly recognize and understand the ends.

The worst example of this was a some years ago in a ridiculous skit, probably long forgotten, written by someone for a meeting in Colorado of the National Organizers Association as part of a send-up on the "sacred cows" of organizing – an attempt to belittle and denigrate organizing principles, particularly of constituency based organizations' that got "in the way" of some activists. Incredibly the notion of having "democracy" in membership organizations was one of the "sacred cows" both the "actors" and the "audience" seemed to believe was worth scrapping. For what, it was unclear? And, that's often the problem as well.

It is not the soft hands and new agers of the Estes Park crowd, but the hard men of the movement, especially in labor unions, but not infrequently in other organizations where someone else "knows best," who are driving this discussion further and further away from the main path of organizing work. Part of it derives from the inexperience, and therefore distrust, that many of these hard men have with elections, because they are not coming to power in the traditional way. They have not built local unions or other organizations from scratch or in many cases moved from the political cauldron at the local level where they ran to replace or displace someone else before them. These new hard men were "staff officers" in the peoples' army, so to speak. They rose because of their proximity to power, rather than through their own exercise of political skills and their survival in the yes-and-no of democratic and regular elections. Having perhaps been once in a local somewhere down the line, they wanted, it seems, to be as far from that experience as possible, and while disdaining those who came before them as baseless labor politicians, they instead have substituted themselves as the new men – and women – of labor, moving forward from the bureaucracy, rather than the shop floor or the local union base. Power was too often a matter of anointment, rather than ascendancy. They moved from staff slots to trustees, and as trustees of large locals, they might be blessed with running the new local over the dead body of those before them. The national or international union was the only real "local" union they understood or saw as their base. In many of these mature unions this has become the path to power. Such a path would not put much faith or trust in the members making the right decisions, or even how to bring it to the members. Like media age politicians of every stripe, they poll the members to find out what they think of the union and their program, and trim the sails according to which wind is blowing hardest.

The layers of rationalizations pile on from there. Ends and means in constant collision. Colonialism, imperialism, paternalism, what? Amartya Sen, the Nobel Prize winning economist, argued an interesting theme in a book called <u>Development as Freedom</u>,[23] which speaks to these issues in some ways, though at a different level, but some of his points on macroeconomics resonant down to our smaller world. Sen's argument is quite simply that democracy is almost a precondition for successful economic development. The hard men in these areas that argue that a Chinese model or this model or that model is better at achieving prosperity in underdeveloped areas, partially because it is autocratic and allows a level of controlled state planning that can force achievement of these benchmarks, and that one has to be willing to forego popular participation, democracy, free speech and any number of other freedoms that the we might assume essential in order, so they rationalize, to achieve orderly economic progress.[24] Sen argues compellingly, that democratic systems not only outstrip others, but that democratic systems – even with their faults and failings – are the systems that do not allow famines

---

[23] Amartya Sen, *Development as Freedom* (Knopf, 1999).

[24] William Easterly, *The Tyranny of Experts: Economists, Dictators, and the Forgotten Rights of the Poor* (Basic Books, 2014)

Chapter II: **Structure Counts: Form Determines Function**

for example, where other systems are unable or unwilling to respond sufficiently to such popular catastrophes. This is convincing. Saving tens of millions of lives has a value greater than the relative difference of a couple of hundred dollars per year in annual income.

These arguments against democracy, whether at the large scale of governments or the small scale of unions and community organizations, are often buffeted by public opinion polls holding that there is popular support for virtually any kind of government that will deliver more economic security. Had the concept of false consciousness not already achieved currency, this would be a classic case for its conception. Such polling has to rank somewhere between a deathbed confession and whatever might be heard from people at the point of a gun. A drowning man does not care who is throwing the rope, but that hardly should have weight as an endorsement of anything but the rope itself. Unions do similar polling where members in these difficult economic times are also enthusiastic about almost anything that will move the economics forward in their lives, and therefore willing to sacrifice many other things that have been – and might have continued to be – bedrock principles and foundations of the union itself, including the very existence and democracy of their local union.

Getting things done regardless of the price that includes diminishing people and their capacity, is the supreme rationalization and may have a certain cache with activists and advocates disinterested in the hard, close work of building a popular base that allows the base to *participate and determine* organizational direction. Taking directions from the schoolyard or the library shelf or the caucus of the like-minded and righteous is virtually always easier and quicker than the painstaking, arduous, and, sometimes, risky process of popular and democratic participation.

The question that cannot be answered in this methodology of expediency is how it might ever be possible to truly make change and exercise power differently if democracy is diluted and members are denied the experience and transformation involved in direct participation, debate, and decision. Denied a voice in the discussion, their participation becomes passive at best, cutting the heart out of the action that organizations promise and promote to create change.

Mergers

The 21st century "line" around union structure is that no one would have fabricated the structure of unions today in the way that made sense in the late years of the 19th century and the early days of the 20th century, yet within national and international unions and within larger federations, we are still working under the shadow of some of these structural expectations and requirements, and they have consequently stifled our groups, prevented innovation, and left us ill prepared to deal with the ruthlessness of the modern employer. Some of that may even be true. Few may realize that Samuel Gompers fashioned the structure and financing of the Cigarmakers Union – before he became head of the original American Federation of Labor – in such a way that all funds were "pooled" rather than kept in any one local in order to advance organizing more expeditiously and deal with all protection and servicing matters on equitable and centralized basis. Seems like he had a good grip on structure more than 100 years ago, though he seems not have paid it much mind at the AFL. And, it is inarguable that employers are almost omnipotent now and the law is justly ridiculed, but hardly worse than employers then, including the Standard Oil of John D. Rockefeller, way, way before the foundation, the Ludlow Massacre, steel combines, Pinkertons, and god knows what else. Of course there was no law whatsoever, so it is not like unions at their birthing were playing patty cake with bosses that were soft and fluffy.

The real point the *mergeristas* try to make is that they have to be, at the least different and at the most, more, in order to face the future, because the essential "business model" of many local and 'national" unions has inalterably changed. Certainly, it goes without saying that when the jurisdiction of a union has been made obsolete by commerce or technology, then it's time to throw in the towel and either combine or die. For many local unions these are contradictions when viewed in structural terms, because they can survive quite a long time in an uneasy, queasy compromise with their employers on the local level because of either spatial strength, employer indifference, or the luxury of the "union shop," where it still exists. Mergers of these unions are really more questions of capacity and resources than they are issues of structure, and hearing the death rattles of organized labor from the inside, these questions often rightly trump concerns of local effectiveness, leadership development, and membership democracy. The ends and means get terribly twisted in the life or death struggle that propels many of these mergers in the labor world. To paraphrase what a friend and comrade, later executive vice-president of the Service Employees, used to say, "if we get 3 out of 5 of these right," speaking of mergers and reorganizations, "then we're ahead, and, if not, we'll have to do it all over again."

No matter what the argument, in the world of labor "necessity has been the mother of invention" propelling most combinations. Why are there not more mergers in the world of community organizations? Why in fact does there continue to be such a proliferation of non-profits regardless of sustainability and such a dearth of combinations for any reason whatsoever?

Burnaby chapter of ACORN Canada preparing to vote.

Chapter II: Structure Counts: Form Determines Function

Among the default reasons that cannot be on the list, you would have to include ego, since that would be a "push." I could never argue that there are any fewer egos in labor, than there are in community organizing. I could also never argue that "job security" or basic employment was any more an issue in community organization rather than in labor formations, since if anything the opposite prevails. A labor soldier never wants to go "back on the tools," while many community practitioners simply flop to working somewhere else for something else and someone else.

Perhaps I am also looking backwards rather than forwards. In recent years there have been mergers of sorts that have created the organizing support organization, the Center for Popular Democracy, that included a remnant of the old ACORN national support system, that had been recast as the Center for the Common Good or some such, Make the Road by Walking, a dynamic New York City based organization, and others. Many of the community based components consist of "rebranded" former ACORN state affiliates. There has also been a merger between the Seattle-based Alliance for a Just Society, formally the Northwest Federation of Community Organizations, US Action, formerly Citizen Action in the 1970s and 1980s, and National Peoples' Alliance (NPA), which had grown from Shel Trapp and Gail Cincotta's old NTIC, the National Tenant Information Center. This amalgamation would also include other organizations like Virginia Organizing, founded by Joe Szakos. One long-time organizer told me the impetus for this later amalgamation was the inability to raise external resources without a larger footprint, and, indirectly to effectively compete as an alternative to the Center for Popular Democracy.

I've been a part of negotiating various mergers or affiliations of other community organizations with ACORN, as well as a host of partnerships, so I know how difficult it can be to achieve, develop, and nurture these relationships and create synergies from differing experiences and structures despite the best of good will and intentions. In the late 1970's ACORN affiliated the Carolina Action network in North and South Carolina and Georgia, whose staff was directed by Jay Hessey at that time. In the same period we were unsuccessful in affecting an affiliation with the Citizens' Action League (CAL) in California under the staff direction of Josie Mooney and Tom Newberry, but later during a pronounced financial crises, we merged the organization in order to protect the elected, citizen leadership from the liability of having to take personal financial responsibilities with the Internal Revenue Service for a payroll tax payment problem. CAL merged with ACORN because the government in fact held the gun and pointed it at their heads! These amalgamations were never easy to achieve even though they were founded on vision and commonality not external money, but under any circumstance mergers are challenging.

Partnerships, associations, affiliations, alliances, and whatever else we might call them have value, but many contain such weak links and easy exits with constant decisions points that although strengthening relationships between organizations and networks, often seem to take more work than the value that they produce in real or measurable terms. Within the internal life of such arrangements, participants often feel that they are struggling to define the relationship and create opportunities to achieve real synergy, much less power, which is the point after all. For years ACORN for example had "affiliation" relationships in the 1990's with Montana Peoples' Action (MPA) and the South

Carolina based, CAFÉ – Carolina for Fair Employment. Under these arrangements they had one representative at the board governance level of national ACORN (rather than the standard two for a full affiliate), participated in trainings at the staff and leadership level, and nominally in joint campaigns when the issue and spirit moved them. Interestingly after much work the relationships simply drifted apart. There was never any ill will, simply ennui and boredom. There were staff changes. When there was no one pushing the relationship steadily, like old couples, we just drifted apart, until neither seemed to notice anymore, and not long afterwards both organizations disappeared as well.

In the 2000[ths,] we had "partnerships" at different levels with the Gamaliel Network in Chicago led on the staff side by Gregory Galluzzo and with PICO founded by John Bauman and now directed by Scott Reed from California. Both of these community organizations are church-based and largely church funded. After meeting for years there was recognition that the church-based methodology was so different than the community based, membership model used by ACORN that there was no real competition practically speaking. We worked together on specific things and did so without difficulty. At the same time these relationships also take constant attention and care or months go by and nothing has happened and one can forget that there was a relationship at all, much less a partnership.

As much as anything these partnerships are "non-aggression" pacts or "no raid" agreements similar to what is sometimes practiced in the labor movement. They create a way of speaking well about each other and importantly define boundaries for work, which when respected, can have positive benefits. We had a partnership with Gamaliel in opening our offices in San Diego, which was largely positive, and our relationship with PICO was useful in dealing with difficult pressures in the Camden, New Jersey organizing area as well as assuring best practices and coordination in the wake of Hurricane Katrina in New Orleans.

I actually suspect that many of the real barriers lie in two very simple circumstances. First, there is no real constituency or membership existing behind many non-profits **demanding** continuity of services, support, and action from their own organizations, and, secondly, many of the organizations are so dependent on external support from sources outside of their own constituency, that survival issues are more often determined externally where a funding source can either turn the spigot off, and watch the organization wither and die, or has a greater investment in the continued autonomy of the particular enterprise than in any great mission, which might force realignment or merger. The lists of funders are countless who encourage organizations to "work together," but it would be past most acceptable boundaries for funders to "force" mergers between organizations and enterprises at least publicly.[25] The net result is a rate of demise of organizations probably equal, if not greater, than found in any set of small business ventures anywhere.

---

[25] My information may be time dated now that I haven't trafficked in the funding world for some years. See Brian Johns and Ellen Ryan, "*Leadership Development is Not a Deliverable*" in Social Policy, V.43#4.

Workarounds and Adaptations

There are a lot of old houses that look one way from the street as you drive by, but once you park and walk up close or perhaps knock on the door and go inside and visit, you realize that they started as one thing and then became another. A bathroom was added where one used to walk back to the yard. A room was added here or there. An attic was built out. A carport was covered and became a den. Families grew and changed, parents moved in, children brought spouses and more children under the roof. This was the family house, and everyone made do and made it work, either with good grace or until they moved on to something else and maybe better. Many organizations are the same way, especially with the passing of time and achievement of any permanence and success. Sometimes the structures accommodate purposes unimagined by the founders. Other times the structures seem inadequate or even at cross purposes to the smooth functioning of the organization. I strongly believe that the best organizational structures have to be built from the beginning to allow growth and change, and that form must follow function, yet I also know that just as in that old house, people come first and you make allowances for them every day, or at least as long as you can.

ACORN internally was a good example of both the best and the worst of this. Success is not only built on structure and the effectiveness and discipline of our organizing model, membership, and leadership, but also the ability to both attract, and then hold, a brilliantly accomplished and committed community of talented organizers. This has been no one person band, but an orchestra of accomplished players, and we can count many warriors and generals in this number who are the veterans of ten, twenty, thirty, and more years of these wars and importantly made their decisions and lives to build the whole, rather than run off alone. All of their names are clearly marked on this organization; I simply got here first and stayed the longest, as I often said. In order to keep them from their youth to their dotage, I managed them with equal doses of collective ambition, inspiration, commitment, and huge degrees of autonomy in their operations, which allowed them to run their operations with great authority, while part of a centralized whole. Big pieces of the operation and many of ACORN's largest city operations were part of this kind of "coordinated autonomy."

A simple minded "command and control" structure could not effectively conceive of a situation like we saw in mid-2006, where simultaneously we were dominating the news and agenda of cities like New York, with the Atlantic Yards project, Chicago with the fight to raise the minimum wage for retail workers, New Orleans was moving tens of pieces around the Katrina recovery including being selected as one of the district and neighborhood planners to everyone's surprise, Houston where we continually were in the middle of every fight, Illinois where we signed the first contract through SEIU Local 880 for more than 30,000 home health care workers, to Denver, Phoenix, Columbus, and St. Louis where we mounting huge statewide efforts to put minimum wage efforts on the ballot. The scale of this kind of accomplishment is due to the efficiency of the organization and part of this accomplishment comes from the clarity of the overall structure as well as its flexibility and adaptations that are not easily drawn on an organizational chart, but work because of individual arrangements with great operations and organizers to allowing

Mary Gonzalez and Greg Galluzzo at Organziers Forum Board Meeting with Barbara Bowen.

the best work to get done, regardless. In geology, there is a recognition of the rock strata holding, essentially, that if it happened, therefore it must have worked somehow, even if it might take decades and centuries to figure out the "how" and "why" of it. In that sense the ACORN structure worked for a very long time.

Ironically, ACORN underwent an extensive and expensive management review of our field operations structure at the same time many of these potentially individually cataclysmic efforts were happening. The consultants in looking at the ACORN field structure were correctly evaluating two things. First, would the structure allow us to build from 250,000 members to ten times that number in order to reach 2,500,000 members in five years, and, secondly, would the structure work the way it was, if I was not part of it? These were fair and important questions. To achieve critical changes for poor and working people, it was necessary to be as large as we needed to be and to organize and service a mass membership as large as we can possibly accommodate. We also realized that though I was hopeful I could spend fifty years or more with the organization, I could not continue to be the driver of the field operation, and there needed to be a responsible plan for the organization that was independent of any individual (including me!) and of every individual (including everyone else as well!). Looking through that lens, we were forced to agree that in fact, the consultants were right, and our structure was too much like the old house with additions and "make do's," which worked under the same roof, but had limits, and in fact could not work at the level of growth we were striving to reach.

We had a "legacy" problem in the consultants' terms which forced too many "workarounds." When forced to confront this situation frankly, I had to admit that this was a "problem" of my making, and one I was going to have to somehow help fix. Essentially, we had some supremely talented and deeply experienced organizers running operations that went back to the "heroic" original organization building period of ACORN in Arkansas and had done thirty or more years with me, and were willing to work with me and even for me, but had no time or tolerance for trying to adapt to some new fangled structure that might have developed in the last five or ten years. What did it have to do with them anyway? They could organize and they could run their operations,

John Bauman PICO.

and if they needed any help, they could just call me, and if the organization needed them to do anything more or different, then I would ask them, and that was enough said about it! And, that worked for both of us, but once forced to look at this from another side, clearly it could only work for us individually, and was inadequate and destructive for where we needed and wanted to go now.

An organizational chart would have had a line off to the side, broken and jagged, outside of field operations that only linked these offices and individuals – the legacy organizers – just to me. Everyone else had to work around this. Worse perhaps, this became an inadvertent model for others. If a legacy organizer did not have to get their statistics in on time, then why should a regional organizer with ten years, have to do it? Inadvertently, such behavior was being modeled. There became "wannabe" legacy organizers, even though we did not recognize the terms at the time, which would drive energy and attention away from the mission of field operations. Fortunately, this was ACORN and the strength of the community then was such that once we all looked into the mirror this way, we were forced to get on about it, and fix the problem so we could get where we all wanted to be, and this was better for both the legacy organizers and the hundreds of organizers that have come behind them and for whom they have been the best models and trainers.[26]

---

[26] This may seem dandy to you, gentle reader, and like a big fat lie to you, professional organizer, so let me admit that, yes, this was hard and wrenching for all of us, and that there were certainly rough edges still dragging, but at the end of the day, organizers are organizers, not freelance activists, and they understand intuitively and completely the compelling logic of what makes organizations work, and then did what is necessary in fact to make them work, even when it means that they had to make some changes themselves, thank you! On the other hand perhaps lingering resentments and unresolved issues from this experience made it more difficult for my successors at ACORN to hold the organization together, if they had wanted to do so, when ACORN in the United States came under fierce attack in 2008 and 2009. Historians, when and if they are interested, will have to sort this out, and in the meantime the rest of us will keep organizing and hope to continue to learn as we go.

The Internet Assault on Structure

Increasingly, organizers hear about "new" structural inventions, many of them flowing from the experience with the internet, especially the notions of "network" organizations and "hub" organizational formations. Still sitting in too small a chair at the back of the old school, I may not be the absolute best commentator on the claims and potential outcomes that might flow from such new forms.

A network organization, as best I can tell, follows ad hoc lines structurally and focuses primarily on exploiting linkages between various organizations, campaigns, interests, and individuals in order to move forward. The attraction, especially for the "un-based" activist or organizer is the appeal of a shortcut. If, computer style, one could "network" multiple organizations together, then, wham-bang, on a much quicker timeline and at a fraction of the development cost, one could have an "organization" up and running on some cause or concern. As a campaign structure, the network operation has significant appeal. Other organizations can opt in or opt out, as can anyone or anything else. The disadvantage is the same as the advantage, since the entry level is low to get in; the exit is also as easily achieved. Easy come, easy go. Once again for an effort with limited objectives and a short anticipated shelf life, who cares, as long as no one pretends it is something other than what it is meant to be. A computer network is valuable in allowing you to use fewer printers and to back up the work centrally that is produced separately. Few networks achieve the power that might be potential in a real mutuality of purpose and work, and this is likely to be the problem in such organizations as well.

In theory and in practice when one looks at Al-Qaeda and similar outfits, the real power of "network" organizations is their ability to achieve some level of operational effectiveness based on autonomy and independence of operations compared to either hierarchical, centralized, or bottom-up, mass-based organizations. In such organizations one unit of the whole can be dismembered or ineffectual, while the rest operate within their own context to engage the targets or move their own constituencies into distinct operations. The links between units are both strong and very weak. They are weak in terms of operating structure and any methodology along the lines of "command and control," but they are stronger in their ability to function separately independent of the victory or failure of other units based on shared adherence to common principles or common enemies or other forms of adhesiveness. Such organizations do seem somewhat unique contemporarily, though it is unclear exactly how this would be applied to non-profit or social change structures. Let's just leave the jury out. There is something clearly there, but how replicable it might be is hard to determine at least at the present time.

Similarly, "hub" organizations are becoming a conceptual framework heard about more often and, in my way of thinking, creating great confusion. The hub follows the function of a router in the computer world, which is a way to hook things together and allow them separate functionality. SEIU's Andy Stern's original concept of an organization to oppose Walmart on many fronts was to create a "hub" following this model. There would then be "spokes" (like a wheel) engaging the company on various levels. I was going to take responsibility for the "worker" spoke and the "community" spoke, and later acquired a piece of the "international" spoke when we began working in India to oppose the expansion of foreign direct investment (FDI) in retail, which would allow Walmart and other big box retailers into that country. The hub was to be a smaller structure which operated largely to coordinate between the spokes. Each spoke would be able to operate independently and perhaps even autonomously with its own responsibility for funding, staffing, and so forth. I argued in such a hub/spoke operation applied to a campaign structure that we would need to agree to "terms of engagement" that we all had in common, particularly on whether or not any spoke could settle with the company without consideration and concessions to the entire campaign. In other words an "environmental" spoke could not simply decide that Walmart was now more "green" and settle separately, allowing for example the "worker" or "community" spoke to hang out in the drift by themselves. In real terms in the Walmart campaign the hub/spoke system may have been either ahead of its time or so poorly understood by the participants that there developed a mismanaged anarchy of self-appointed "spokes" who wanted to attach themselves to the campaign and when not fully integrated then had issues with the campaign itself.

Once again in theory this all should work. What impacts one "spoke" should not impact the other "spokes," therefore the campaign structure could be both independent and interdependent. In real terms, partly drawing on what I saw in the Walmart campaign startup, this decentralized structure obviously does not allow you to pick which spokes succeed and which ones might fail because of their interdependence. Many people wanted to build spokes, but did not have the independent capacity to resource the effort or the commitment and initiative to be able to sweat out the work to make it happen. Smaller "spokes" withered quickly and with hard feelings when resources were not forthcoming. There was a political connection and mission commitment, but not the powerful motivation of an ideological or political conviction and a replicable, simple model. Such a formation might have promise with simpler moving parts and a less daunting target than Walmart. It is also may be that such a structure was so foreign to the standard operating procedures for big unions, like SEIU, that what we articulated, we did not yet know how to practice. Either way, more tests of this structure will have to determine whether or not it holds interest for organizers in the future.

A Final Word on the Wild World of Structure out There

Almost everything I have said goes in spades for work around the world. Every country has its own systems of law and order, most of which are designed to make operations of all kinds of formations, including non-profits, very, very difficult. At one level this encourages a "wink and nod" kind of system where people try and go around the formal procedures in every way possible by working with partners or other "agents" allowing the organization to avoid having to go through all of the formal procedures of registration and legality. As ACORN has begun to expand and work in other countries on the globe as ACORN International, we have found the learning experience very difficult and wildly expensive, so I will give some quick examples:

- In Canada there is a somewhat similar registration system as we find in the United States, except that it is more important how you define your purposes under the charter of the organization. The differences between tax exempt and

Exhibit 1b & 1c: Organizational Flowchart

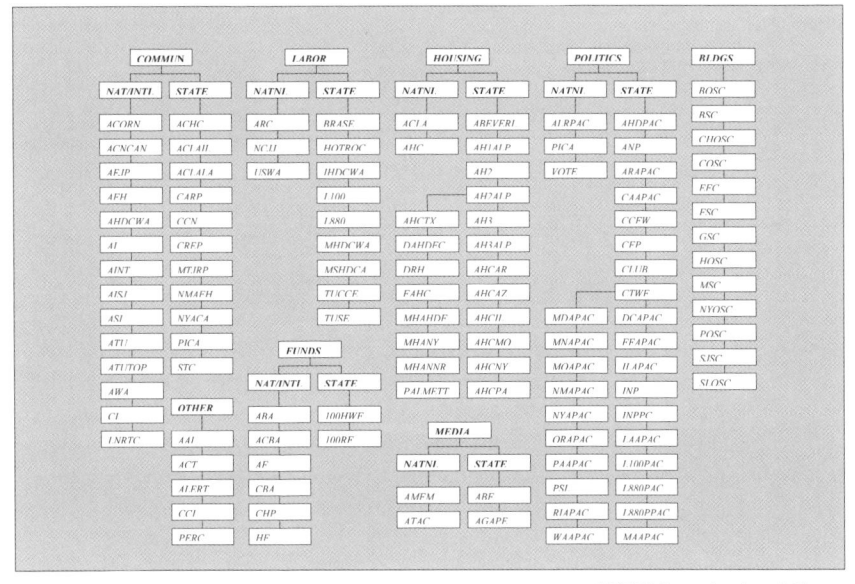

ACORN Organizational Chart.

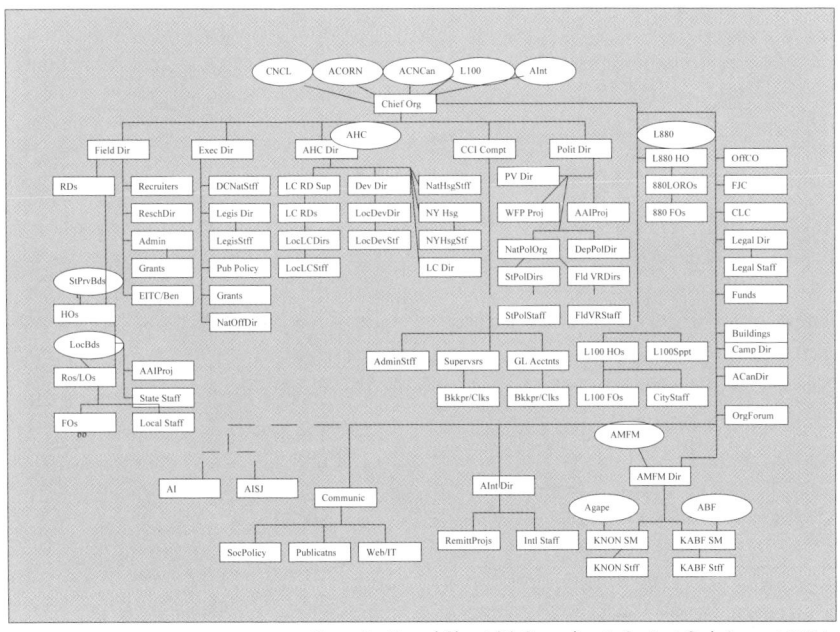

Organizational Chart (2) Consultants Project Oak August 2004.

Chapter II: Structure Counts: Form Determines Function 37

taxable organizations are also substantial and even though the registration and procedures follow closely those of the US, the particularities are enough to keep battalions of lawyers fully employed.

- In India contrary to common belief, it is possible to register, but an organization can only do so in order to operate with funds raised and then being spent in the India. A step cousin to the post-colonial vestiges that bar foreign direct investment (FDI)[27] also makes it difficult for organizations that are non-native to India to easily operate without fear of expulsion. The AFL-CIO for example ran its Solidarity Center operation for this part of Asia from Sri Lanka for exactly that reason. Community organizations that are part of a long standing network in India at one time received twenty-years of advance funding from German sources in order to prevent the money from being expropriated.

- Mexico is particularly difficult in our experience, partially because the lawyers are easily confused with the criminal element and being forced to settle differences with local arbitrators is risky. Registration requirements are also wildly different between states and the Federal District. Contracts have to be exacting and supervised meticulously. We bought this lesson several times and found each lesson very expensive until we got it right.

- Peru allows there to be a penalty for employees without a "contract" prior to legal registration which plants a land mine every time an organizer is hired, because any dismissal can lead to bonus severance payments in the absence of a contract. Nonetheless, it is not a quick process and requires extraordinary attention.

- In Honduras it has taken ACORN years to figure the whole system. More than six years in fact, so you figure!

- In places like Italy, Kenya, Czech Republic, and the United Kingdom, it's more a matter of money than any other particular barriers.

These are quick examples and by the time you read this all of these countries might have made the process of legal operations easier or they might have once again increased the barriers to legal operations. Part of the siren call of the "informal" economy in one country after another, particularly in the developing world, is the huge difficulty of being formal.

I left the soapbox on the last section. I will try and stop whining on this afterword.

---

[27] This is the core of a large campaign that ACORN directed nationally in India to make any modification of FDI in retail such that it forces the large, big box operations like Walmart, Carrefour, Metro, Tesco, and others to be good corporate citizens in India or not be allowed to enter the country. More on that elsewhere in Nuts and Bolts.

Chapter III:
Money Matters

Many years ago in a rare occurrence I was invited for several weeks to participate in a unique program at the University of Wisconsin at Madison where I was to be an "activist-in-residence." The obligations were minor, the hosts no doubt assuming if you were willing to freeze in the stark Wisconsin fall, then you had already paid some amount of dues. When we bundled up two small children for the adventure and the opportunity with a mix of vacation and work time there was a chance to think through a couple of things and make notes.

One of the small requirements was that I participate in a graduate seminar with students and professors studying social movements. I was intrigued and impressed. The whole notion of social movements as a topic of serious scholarship was fascinating. I made a few notes on the kinds of political and issue undercurrents that shaped ACORN, assuming these would be the themes of the seminar. After making a couple of preliminary remarks along these lines that sketched out the history of ACORN, its roots, and branches, I asked for questions. I later described the session to my old friend UW Professor Joel Rodgers, saying that I was a little confused, because by the end of the session I felt that I had just defended our budget to a group of auditors, rather than our program to a bunch of students.

Virtually all of the questions were about the raising and spending of money. The students – and professors – seemingly could have cared less if we had ever moved people on the street or won any of the myriad campaigns we had waged. Joel explained to me, much in the tones one uses with the smallest child, that the current direction of social movement theory at that time concluded that one could not easily isolate why, when the circumstances seems to be similar, in some situations social movements rose and in others they did not, so increasingly theorists and their students were focusing on the anomalies that drove such activity, and a main variable in either jumpstarting movements or stopping them at birthing seemed to be resources – or the lack of resources.

No question: money matters. For that reason we are going to spend an inordinate amount of time on the subject, though we come to the subject somewhat backwards. As an organizer, I had always looked at money as the backend of the work, rather than the front end.

My perspective on money had always been much like the slogan helping drive settlement in the US West: rain follows the plow![28] If one had a vision – a plan – and if it were solid and you were committed to making it happen – I mean really committed – then money would always follow. As a guiding principle, this philosophy had worked for me, and in almost a mystical way, I still believe it is largely true in the main. You have

---

[28] Obviously the slogan was a great example of 19th century marketing. And a lie!

to believe some things, and this just happens to be something that I believe. Naively, irrationally, and without doubt.

As an organizing principle, such a philosophy is just as false as its historical antecedents. No matter how many pioneer families were convinced to travel thousands of miles through great hardship to settle the western United States, breaking sod does not in fact bring rain to the aridity of the desert that is at the heart of the west. On the other hand through pluck and luck, there are also some pioneers that crossed through the mirage and made the transition as settlers. As we have said elsewhere, sometimes it's not being right, but being persistent that matters, and at the end of the day, as I have already admitted, I had to believe in something, and one simply cannot organize for social change and believe that the existence or absence of money gets to decide whether you work or not, or whether you win or lose, even if in fact that is often the case.

So, let's look at the problem of money.

Rain follows the plow – Go west!

External and/or Internal Money

As a matter of category, I defined money as either external or internal. Follow closely, because some of this is tricky, since the driver turns out to be as important as the destination.

External money is clearly money that comes from *outside* of the organization, most typically from churches, foundations, or wealthy individuals. This is the swampy quagmire of philanthropy.

Internal money is money that flows directly from work done *inside* the organization. Best examples would include membership dues for community organizations like ACORN and of course labor unions, but internal money also includes a host of other sources that are directly generated by an organization's constituency: bake sales, raffles, block parties, pancake breakfasts and potlucks, Las Vegas nights, bingos, and hundreds of other events.

How does one categorize other activities like tagging (standing at street corners or in the street) asking for contributions for the organization or a campaign, and giving those that donate a "tag" – a slip of paper – that thanks them and explains the campaign) or street canvassing (going door to door with either trained canvassers or others to solicit contributions and support for the issue or organization) or a number of other things from annual community and corporate solicitations from banquets to annual walks and other events? Some of these activities can net little more than silver and single bills depending on scale, while others can bring in hundreds of thousands, if not millions, of dollars. Since many of these dollars are not coming from the organizational base itself, are they appropriately seen as internal or external sources of money?

This is actually a problem that is more fundamental than the simple semantics would seem to indicate, particularly when one looks at the raw realities of organizational survival. Roughly, within the ACORN world we define external money as money that is really *outside of the control of the organization,* while internal money is money that is driven directly by organizational decision and therefore is money *within the control of the organization.*

As a simple rule, we believe that external money is a crapshoot, transcending rhyme or reason. In managing our field offices in this area we have even found a statistical pattern, similar to the laws of pure chance, that indicates that an office will be successful for 1 out of every 5 proposals submitted, independent of the so-called "merits" of the proposal, theme of the request, or funding source.[29] Funders were constantly haranguing our development staff to get them to harness and coordinate the number of applications for funding received from various ACORN operations and offices, but at a fundamental level the decision making of funders is equally rational (or irrational), and increasingly we have found that the only offices (even in the external bare cupboards of America in the fiscal badlands of a Louisiana or an Arkansas or an Iowa or South Dakota) that are uniformly

---

[29]   This ratio is not scientific, but subjective. Could be better, and often is worse.

unsuccessful in raising external money are those that do not apply, and do not apply enough! But, we'll look at this more deeply a little later.[30]

In internal money we think of internal *systems* when we sort through the elements of a street canvass by staff and volunteers or an annual corporate fundraiser or awards banquet. Because the heart of ACORN's funding, along much the same lines as labor unions are membership dues so we build the budget on the belief that dues should provide at least half of the money necessary to support the full operation of the local office. Generally, we believe each office needs at least two other internal systems in order to be sufficiently self-sustaining to make it.

These systems work better or worse in building the actual organization based on how they fit organically within the basic methodology of the organizing model. Within ACORN the basic methodology is constructed around door knocking – home visits by teams of members and organizers to communicate, recruit, mobilize, and develop the membership and general organizational constituency. Not surprisingly it is logical then that the more that we can privilege the basic "street" work and add on pieces to the fundamental structure that both build the organization and increase organizational resources, then the stronger we build the organization. I cannot begin to tell you how hard this is!

It worked only where the constituency is the *a priori* for the whole program. Keep in mind my continual obsession with the importance of clarifying the base. It worked for example when there was interest in assuring that all the low and moderate income families in our communities were registered to vote, so that the "add-on" of the home visit also determines whether everyone eligible is actually registered, and where we could trigger a premium paid for each new registrant from Project Vote, one of our family of organizations, or others. It also worked when in partnership with a union we can add-on identifying a worker from our membership who might be interested in being involved in an upcoming organizing drive or union representation election or legislative battle (home daycare workers in Chicago or Walmart "associates" or clients with disabilities in California). Here we not only provided more benefits to our own members by allowing them to access other fights where they had an interest, but also increased support for the basic daily work of the organization without having to create new and parallel systems. It worked when we could move entitlements, like Earned Income Tax Credits (EITC) benefits to our members through our standard program and link the work to additional support wedded to specific interests in EITC full participation that ACORN shared with many others from local cities, counties and states to outside funders. It worked when the local business puts an ad on the ACORN neighborhood flyer that is going to be distributed anyway before the upcoming meeting, so means a little more money for the sweat and effort involved in what had to be done anyway. All of these efforts privileged our base.

---

[30] I have not found this true internationally. My experience has been that pretty much no number of proposals predict success because pretty much for all of the sound and fury no one cares about what's happening much past their nose, at least when it has to do with lower income and working families.

Rather than adding value, some internal funding systems taxed the basic program differently, and therefore created a set of real tensions. A "street" or phone canvass often meant assembling an entire parallel staff of professionals and others whose real *raison d'etre* is simply raising money, which is vital of course and builds the capacity of the organization, rather than building the program of the organization. The work takes place in different neighborhoods with a different income constituency only linking, as best one can, an issue or campaign sufficiently broad to bridge the organization with financial supporters. This is not to say that tactically organizations have not found a real use for the tens of thousands of petitions signed in a canvass or the calls generated in support of program objectives from time to time. There is political value that adds to the financial weight, but the money is everything here. The same could be said for lower tech tagging operations running on weekends at busy intersections as well as for high end work with corporate executives pledging contributions for community support or the inside game that puts together big award banquet functions that are such an important and common fundraiser in large cities on the East Coast, Midwest, and West Coast. At many levels one can argue – successfully – that these events build power along with support, but the tensions are real and unavoidable.

The core tension is fundamental to the very existence of the organization and its survival. Whenever the vast majority of the money derives from the sources and systems external to the organizational base, then such money implicitly is at the throat of the future of the enterprise. The diminishing production of external and contract street canvassing systems in the 1980's, led to the collapse and curtailment of many organizations who had based their entire financial structure on the net delivered by such operations. Massachusetts Fair Share and the Citizens Action League in California were two outstanding examples for slightly different reasons, and the entire Citizen Action [now U.S. Action] network of organizations felt the reverberations. The same can also be said for many corporate schemes. At the most extreme the entire scam of "consensus" organizing, which expressly counterpoints ACORN and others, is based on snake oil sales to community and financial institutions with little input or activity from the purported constituency, if any. Faith based community organizations link their support to institutions of faith, particularly the Catholic church, so the tragic Catholic crisis around sexual abuse by priests and, along with other establish religions, its loss of membership is threatening them not only financially, as contributions diminish to support community organizing, but the credibility of the institution and its leadership – much of which is also synonymous with the leadership in the faith based organizations – also suffers. When someone or something else is paying for the song, there is never a guarantee that they will not decide to be the piper.

We take the fundamental organizing principle here from Mao's dictum that an organization and its organizers should essentially be like "fish in the sea of the people." Say what you will about Mao, and rightly you may, but let's not argue about whether or not the fellow knew something about building social movements and organizations. As an organizer building ACORN more than 45 years ago, this simple statement propelled my conviction that for the organization to grow and build power, it had to drive it's life support from the people – from the constituency that fought for change and that won

Canvass Team in Arizona on Min Wage.

the benefits, when there were benefits won, and stood to exercise the power when it was created.

My time as an organizer with the National Welfare Rights Organization brought these simple lessons home hard. When I was first building the WRO chapters in Springfield, Massachusetts, at the first meetings we were collecting the nominal dues that defined membership – literally a dollar a year. (I later learned that many state organizations of NWRO bothered neither to collect the dues, nor to send the money into the headquarters in Washington, D.C, but I was very young, and what did I know.) In the early months of organizing we were winning easily – and big – on what we called "minimum standards" campaigns, where much of the hardest ground had already been broken elsewhere in Massachusetts. For example if AFDC mothers had won furniture vouchers and checks for household supplies in Boston or Worcester or Haverhill or Hyannis, in retrospect it was largely a matter of engineering for me to organize and win similar victories with recipients in Springfield.[31]

And, win we did! The novel feature of these victories, due to my own naiveté, was the fact that I was organizing multiple groups simultaneously in different neighborhoods to sequence them into the campaign, and we were demanding – and winning – check pickup days where after we had demanded and won certain payments, we would add that we were coming back – hell or high water – to pick up the checks and vouchers or whatever in exactly two weeks, and they had best have it ready for us. So, you can imagine what developed, a rising tide of people with demands being met and unmet. The original demand might have been made in a sit-in demonstration of 150 ladies from two communities, but by the time they came back two weeks later to pick up their checks – and lo and behold, the checks were actually there and waiting for them so that their elected leaders could stand on tables and pass them out, one after another – the crowd

---

[31] My thanks to Bill Pastreich and his great organizing work – along with many others – before me at NWRO.

would have swelled with the original folks there to get the checks and a lot more people there to turn in the forms to get their checks, and on and on the momentum built.

But, part of what struck me later, as I struggled to organize ACORN, was that we were passing out checks, sometimes for thousands of dollars for household supplies – these were checks so they were just "free" money really – and vouchers for furniture also worth hundreds, if not thousands, and all of this for members paying $1 in dues per year. What dues would they have been willing to pay to fight and win? $12 per year? $25? What? Who knew, and it's a longer discussion, but I at least knew that I did not want to be a fish downing in the sea of the people, but one swimming in that sea, and that meant figuring out what people would pay to support their own organization.

It is often simple truths that define a lifetime. I can recall later trying to work out the question in 1974 of whether to continue to be ACORN's Chief Organizer or move on. The dominant ideology at the time (thanks to Saul Alinsky's dicta) held that after three years an organizer needed to move on. I was in Honolulu where my dad had proposed we take a week to spend away the last of what had been their savings for me to finish college, which was clearly never going to happen. One day while there I read that Kalihi was the "ghetto" of Honolulu, so I spend the day walking through and thinking about what it would be like to organize there in the low rise housing projects filled with yards that seemed, so uncharacteristically to me, bursting with flowers and greenery. Walking through this unique community and standing for a while and watching the old men playing and betting on dominos in other languages under a banyan tree, I came to a realization that has comforted me throughout my lifetime as an organizer, and that was the simple truth that one way or another, I could always find the money to do this work. I had a trade that could travel, and I could always find work.

From that minute forward organizing fixed in my mind as a trade – a set of skills that could never be taken away, just like any other trade. Having built an organization that relied on dues and internal fundraising, I could literally go anywhere and build an organization because the money would always be there, wrapped in the hands and lives

Wade in Springfield WRO Action 1969.

Chapter III: Money Matters

of the people joining the organization and moving its agenda and its actions. No matter what I was making then, I could never really starve, because I could always depend on the members, and for that matter go right into the street or door to door for support for the work, and I knew what very few others really either knew or believed. I knew the support would be there. If I just asked.

I had learned the hard part about asking very early. Originally, I founded ACORN as an affiliate of the National Welfare Rights Organization. Early in 1970 this had come to pass in the kind of complex, indirect, and wandering negotiation that George Wiley practiced so famously. Which is to say that walking one freezing night down a Boston street after George had given a speech at Harvard with Tom Glynn, Michael Kerr, and others, George was ambling ahead talking to my wife. Later that evening she told me that he kept asking her about her family and didn't she miss them far away in the south and wasn't she ready to leave the bitter cold and get closer to home. Huh? The next day when I asked George what in the world he was up to it turned out that he had been pushing his foundation friends about an NWRO "southern strategy" to go after Congressman Wilbur Mills, the powerful chairman of the House Ways and Means Committee from Arkansas, Senator Russell B. Long, who headed a similar committee in the Senate from Louisiana, and others. He had raised a little money, but had no horses. So George was stuck, and I had this idea for ACORN as a more broadly based organization of low and moderate income families, not just welfare recipients, that I wanted to try, so if he backed my play, I would back his, and so a deal was struck.

But, within a matter of months after I began, the deal unraveled, as the welfare recipient leadership of NWRO became uncomfortable with ACORN's direction once they saw the other issues, the different leaders, and the local groups, so we all came to a collision at the crossroads. I was summoned to a meeting in the middle of the night – literally – in a beaten down hotel off Peachtree in Atlanta and interrogated by Johnnie Tillmon, Beulah Sanders, and the other top leaders of NWRO. It became clear that they wanted a craft "union" of welfare recipients, rather than a broader AFL-CIO of diverse constituencies and community organizations. George couldn't, or wouldn't, protect this embryonic organizing experiment. Within weeks in a special meeting at the UAW Hall on Rebsamen Park Road in Little Rock, members and leaders of ten of the ACORN affiliates in the spring of 1971 voted to disaffiliate from NWRO, while one group decided to stay with welfare rights. ACORN went on its own on that momentous Saturday, but that also meant that I had no salary, and ACORN had no money in the bank. Uh-oh!

Creating a dues system became a matter of necessity, and necessity is the mother of invention. Most of my staff then were VISTA volunteers[32] that I had cadged from their agencies to work virtually full-time organizing with ACORN, so I didn't have to make their payroll, thankfully. We weren't paying rent because we were moving from office to office – using the Arkansas Council of Human Relations some days and Pulaski County Legal Aid some nights – phones here, typewriters there, mimeograph paper from somebody somewhere in the trunk along with a box of stencils, so we could fire it up wherever we could get access to a machine, talking secretaries here and there into taking

---

[32] Donna Parciak, Sue Hannah Marcus, Melva Harmon, and Carolyn Carr. Carolyn worked for me until the day I left ACORN – god bless her!

Gary Delgado laughing at Fair Grinds Dialogue (Pat Bryant and Beth Butler in background).

messages for us with the rare permission and usual ignorance of their bosses. Besides myself, I had one organizer – the first I had hired for ACORN – Gary Delgado[33], and we had to be paid. In the early months sometimes we would make $28 in a week, sometimes $35, and so forth – living off the land, fish in the sea of the people. Unitarians paying $100 for a presentation. Catholics passing the hat after meeting our leaders. On the trail. In the hunt.

We survived thanks to constant hustle. We were able to finally get an office – a storefront on Woodrow Street behind Central High School – and our own phone, hire an office manager, and another organizer[34] thanks to a deal we made to help to do voter registration as an add-on to an action we were doing to demand books from Title I. We billed the action in the neighborhoods when the buses showed up as a "1-2 Punch" – hitting the school board and then the voter registrar. A woman named Pat House, a veteran of the school desegregation fights in Little Rock and a masterful voter registration organizer, was the angel there, and I have never felt like I was walking in higher clouds or lower valleys than when I walked out of her office with a paper bag, and counted the money in the street and knew we were going to finally make it. I finally knew why political operations call it street money! The next time we made it around the corner was our first, legitimate grant thanks to the intercession of Rev. Wellford Hobbie, the pastor of the giant, rich Second Presbyterian Church in the fancy Pleasant Valley neighborhood in western Little Rock, who had come to appreciate the work thanks to a support group called the Citizens Against Poverty, which I had paid his son to help organize. He was able to get

---

[33] Gary Delgado went on to get a PhD from the University of Santa Cruz and write a book about ACORN called *Organizing the Movement: The Roots and Growth of ACORN (1986)*, as well as founding the Center for Third World Organizing, and then the Applied Research Center in Oakland, CA.

[34] We took both – Cheryl McCleary from Fort Smith and Bobbie Cox from Gould from one of our "landlords," Elijah Coleman at the Arkansas Council of Human Relations who said memorably that we were getting to be like relatives, and if we stayed longer, he was going to have to build another room.

the Southern Presbyterian Church in Atlanta to grant us $9000 in general support.[35] The check showed up made out to Wade Rathke, and we all stood there in the office looking at it and deciding whether or not to pay the bills and call it a day or finally open an account for ACORN, and go forward to live this tough dream, or as I joked at the time, cash it and head for Mexico. Like I say, you have to ask, and then you have to live with the consequences that come with the answers.

Dues came naturally though because this was all "hit and miss." Twelve dollars per year per family, if you paid by the month, $10 if you paid by the year, became the foundation of the organization. More than thirty years later it is unsurprising to see my Social Security records for those early years in the 70's when I was making $1600 a year or $2000 or $2500, and somehow making it, but we all were, one way or another. One of the many nice things about a dues system is that there is a pure and perfect democratic accountability to the system: the members vote with their feet! When they are paying dues, the organization is healthy and well. If they stop paying dues, the organization is dead as a doornail. Thousands and thousands of individual decisions every year – to join or not join, to renew or not renew, to go to a bank draft or stick with cash – that multiply and accumulate to determine the daily work and long term future of the organization. This is no rich person's whim or charity or some program officer's initiative on a three-year plan, but a symbiotic relationship that translates the real work into life support.

Flowing from such a philosophy, increasingly, we try to use external money in a series of ways to prevent co-dependency, and actually build the organization. Clearly, external money is cheap capital, since it does not have to be repaid in most cases, at least directly, especially when we are talking about grants. In that sense external money is well used in our view as venture capital or spending on "luxury" items,[36] rather than being part of the core budget. Much of the growth and expansion of ACORN was made possible thanks to our ability to convince specific funders to make the investment solely in ACORN's expansion,[37] and expansion is by definition appropriate for venture capital.

At the back end of these many decades my comrade reader might note that paragraph and the footnote with eyebrows raised and nose twitching at an early warning of gross groveling, thinking simply, "that must have been easy, how hard could it be for some foundation executive or program officer to decide to give money to ACORN to let it grow." The truth is, very, very hard, because that's not really the way funders, particularly foundations, really work. Foundations, both big and small, have developed their own subculture and bureaucracy that construct a series of rewards and prerequisites, very few of which are based on success of the kind that one might measure in social movements or mass-based organizations. This world is peer-based, rather than outcome based, and

---

[35] The first "big" grant that put the icing on the cake came later than year from Grace Oliverez and a program she ran called *Food for All* and away we went.

[36] Meaning the new Xerox or Gestefax machine or phone system or predictive dialer or whatever we might have "wanted," but also knew we could somehow live without.

[37] In the 70's that meant David Hunter and the Stern Fund, Drummond Pike and the Shalan Fund, and the Veatch Program, in the late 90's that meant the Schuman Foundation, then in the 21st century it meant Beth Rosales and Luz Vega-Marquis at the Marguerite Casey Foundation. This was money I raised, and I love these people and their institutions for what they allowed ACORN to become in the United States.

where outcome based, is more often done so in column inches, rather than social change. A Berlin wall is constructed between grantor and grantee with few escapees or survivors in order to hermetically seal off the wardens from the inmates. To the degree these folks are betting, they are doing so "on the come," not on institutional construction and long term delivery and results.

ACORN had not been the darling new thing for foundations since the mid-1970's[38] so a grant simply to allow a now established organization to grow on its own terms would often be seen as prosaic, even if the program proposed was unique and innovative. Too much of philanthropy is about issues and interests, projects and initiatives, new themes papered over in tired visions lost in the jargon-speak of countless single spaced memos marked "confidential" or "for discussion only." It is no wonder after a generation of exciting and creative organizing that there are so few permanent institutions that have been created from such a dysfunctional, self-serving, in-bred, and isolated culture.

Is that sour grapes? Hardly. I was good at raising money. Still might be, if I were willing. I just hated every minute of it. One advantage I have had of both founding organizations and running them, is that there finally can come a point where you don't have to do what you hate to do. Furthermore, it was a task of diminishing returns given my alienating cynicism. My eclectic fundraising practice and philosophy tended to polarize sharply, so there were people in foundations that loved me, and an equal and growing number who felt just as strongly the opposite way. A thousand well-meaning foundations explained to me that when all was said and done, foundations invested in the individual, not the proposal or the organization. I understood that and exploited it I'm sure, but I just for the life of me could not come to either believe in that or take comfort from it.

The examples were legion. The legendary foundation innovator of the last third of the 20th century, David Hunter, who trained a generation of thoughtful and progressive foundation officers, when director of the Stern Fund came and visited Arkansas to take a closer look at ACORN. Subsequently, he called me and invited me to attend a board meeting of the Stern Fund in New Orleans at what was then the family property, the Royal Sonesta Hotel in the French Quarter. I declined. I argued to him that the family was paying him as executive director of the fund, and was more likely to listen to him if he was making a recommendation and arguing our case to the board, than they were to me coming in out of nowhere – if he couldn't get the job done for me, I didn't think I could get it done by myself, so I would take a chance on his winning the day. This seemed simple logic to me, and I was surprised to learn later that no other prospective grantee ever turned down an invitation to attend a meeting with the Stern board. I was also pleased when the Stern Fund ceased doing business to find that ACORN was the largest total grant recipient in the history of the foundation.

---

[38] Thanks to Ruth Abrams, then running the Norman Foundation, who took me by the hand and forced other foundations to pay attention by doing whatever it took, including inviting a good number to dinner at her home with her family – an invitation impossible to refuse because of her charm and grace. No surprise that Ruth did not find foundation work agreeable, though she was a gifted fundraiser, and created the Lower East Side Museum, as a monument to a certain time and people of New York City, which will long survive her and serve as her testament as well.

I was probably a case study in what not to do with foundations – I raised money largely without proposals or any paper, solely on the visit and a follow-up letter; I refused to go to New York more than a couple of days in the spring each year to talk to foundations there and another couple of days in San Francisco to work the other side; but I was a relentless advocate for ACORN, making both friends and enemies, many of which endure to this day, but it's no way to live or work, and neither was my practice a model that I would recommend. Fundamentally, the work needs to be able to speak for itself, but increasingly it became clear for us to move the dollars we needed this was a fight, no matter how important, that I was not likely to win.[39]

Nor is anyone, barring the occasional exceptions to the rule, likely to succeed on a long term basis, which is why we continued to believe that when such external money is not venture capital, it should fund the "luxury" or non-vital operations of the organization. Our core operations were in the cities and states and the backup support that was essential for the survival of that program. In the first dozen years of organizational life all of the operations' funds were held essentially in one financial pot and a principle of rough equity prevailed: all bills for all operations were paid centrally, all salaries were on the same scale, everyone was paid or no one was paid, and so forth. In the early to mid-1980's we couldn't financially sustain a totally centralized expenditure equity, because we could no longer develop the internal "subsidy funds" to support the financially weak cities and states at parity with the financially strong cities and states. We realized that there were market inequities in external wealth and resources between a New York or a Chicago and an Iowa or Arkansas or Texas, but one has to be able to fund internal socialism, and the inability of the canvass and other dues supplements to generate sufficient revenues finally forced us to allow all operations to "go to market" and find their "own water level."

There may be no other decision that I hated making more in my time at ACORN because it conflicted so severely with the organizing principles of the organization, but faced with severe financial crises including scores of staff owed months and months of back wages, we had to let each individual operation float on its own weight or the whole enterprise would sink. We were forced to retrench and close marginal operations that could not survive in thin local markets where outside resources were rare and we had not developed institutional partnerships at that point in our development. In some cases it took us 15 – 20 years to rebuild a number of offices in the wake of those decisions so many years ago, and in others (Reno, Sioux Falls, Rapid City, Davenport, Grand Rapids, and Lansing) we never worked our way back.

"Luxury" in our definition might translate into core operations in any other organization. It would include our Washington legislative staff, at one time part of our publications and political operation, our research teams, most of our legal staff, and other functions, including communications would seem heretical in the 21st century. The core operations are those that directly organize and service the membership. Within an internally financed organization these are also the elements that generate income to sustain their operations. Any part of the overall operation that pours money out of the bucket without replacing that cash flow is non-essential. Every piece has to contribute to

---

[39] We created a position of "executive director" for this purpose, so that foundations would feel like they were dealing with someone real.

the whole or it can endanger the entire organism and become cancerous both financially and psychologically to the morale and *espirit de corps* of the organization. Clearly this can become controversial and conflictual as well, because all of these support functions are important. Very important. Just not essential. Simply put at the end of the day, my view was that we owe the membership an organization – we do not owe anyone a job.

The bedrock financial principle that has always driven ACORN in this area is *self-sufficiency*. From the earliest years of our work this has been an operating obsession. The organizing math that propelled planning was both hypnotic and addictive. One can calculate down to the member the number necessary to pay dues to sustain an organizer to support and organize a certain set of communities and generate the additional income which would also provide the office backup for that organizer from telephone to office rent to reams of paper for flyers to whatever. Forty years ago one of the first memos I wrote on these self-sufficiency formulas focused on an annual dues income collecting $4000 per year sustaining a wage rate of $2500 per organizer and backup for the rest. Approximately 400 member families paying 1970's dues rates averaging $10 per year would provide the float for the entire system in that formula. Seems miniscule in retrospect, but it is really not that much different fast forwarding to these times. With dues rates per family at $10 per month $120 per year and an average payment of $100 per year, the same complement of 400 families per organizer could provide $40000 per year to support an average wage per organizer at $25000 and backup for the rest, as I said.

Whatever the dues and whatever the wage, the model was self-sufficiency, and more than that it was about power, and in that sense the students and professors at the University of Wisconsin had it right. Remembering the old memos and the visions that continue to propel the organization, if we could succeed with a formula of $4000 in dues per organizer, then we could expand exponentially – there were no longer limits imposed externally on the organization, its leaders, and its vision – because money would no longer be the delimiting resource controlling growth and expansion. We dreamed then around a small table with a dozen staff in Little Rock of the "100 Plus Plan" – the financial model which would allow us to build an organizing staff of first one-hundred organizers and then an infinite number up to the unknown point of whatever might be our capacity to hire and supervise them. This is heady stuff at any age. It is also very hard to achieve, and requires (as we will discuss elsewhere) tremendous discipline to realize in no small part because it imposes inflexible ceilings on individual incomes, which runs counter to pretty much every dominant cultural trend of the last number of decades!

The problem of sustainability in social movements of every stripe and variety is unavoidable. External support from foundations and other funders may create an illusion of viability over a short run, but building to win and building permanent organizations requires sounder economics. Nothing outside of the organization itself can ever guarantee such support. At best such organizations are caught under the circus big top as permanent juggling acts – keeping some foundation pot of money up in the air as other sources dry up and fall towards the ground – really nothing more than a perpetual motion machine of cash that unfortunately is not perpetual. This can work for many years, but it can never work forever, therefore the end result is not additional popular capacity within social movements or long term institutional change.

Unfortunately what this has often created is a lowering of ambitions and acute scarcities of capacity. There are thousands of civic associations and neighborhood groups around the country that are self-supported in one way or another through small dues or annual fairs or one creative volunteer project after another. Though self-sustaining these groups have limited range and even more limited ambition. To be wholly supported by volunteer effort also often requires a community with an income range that can afford the luxury of such an energetic capacity not otherwise chained to income acquisition in the formal or informal economy. Historically this has not been the case in the low and moderate income communities where ACORN organizes anywhere in the world. One might speculate that it could be to our advantage that changing demographics in the next several decades that will leave more seniors still healthy and vital though pushed out of the formal job market could be one of the huge resources to propel our growth in the future, but that's another subject, and it has not been the history or much of the contemporary experience, and in the wake of the Great Recession and higher retirement ages they may have to stop by and do their shift at McDonald's first, before they join our "volunteer army." We may or may not be "bowling alone" these days, but for sure we are all working together – and the more bodies we are throwing into the economic engine, the less time there is at home and on weekends to support families, much less communities and the myriad activities that would create real organizational capacity on the local level through volunteerism.

A related problem exists in union organization and support and defines the current conflicts pressing for an "organizing model" unionism versus a servicing model unionism. A local union with decent and well-trained stewards and a "live and let live" relationship with employers on a normal dues system and in peaceful times can self-tax to create sufficient support and services to exist in a relatively calm equilibrium at the local level. As part of the per capita based taxing or dues system, sufficient revenue will be generated in such times to support other federated labor bodies for mutual support and assistance as well as some level of regional, national, or international union support to assist the local on everything it might need: collective bargaining, grievance handling, legal resources, political help, and so forth.

In both cases the world falls apart when there is either local struggle or conflict, or, importantly when it is necessary to grow and expand. One passes the line from extra and part-time to the need for full-time. Full-time capacity means organizers, who at the least have to be paid, and, eventually, to be successful it means also good training and supervision. If the dues or internal systems are only generating survival or maintenance income, there is no additional capacity to meet anything but the rarest emergency, and that's not what faces low and moderate income communities that are involved in these days in constant combat to survive. For unions the extra income that was devoted to better servicing and support of the local unions and their members and some limited organizing *has been insufficient to face the onslaught of company pressure and economic and social changes that have decimated the labor movement over the last 50 years.* The unions attempting to survive now, similar to ACORN on the community level, are the ones that are changing to organize by going through the structural – and political – upheavals to reallocate and increase resources to organize to achieve market and sectoral density sufficient to build power.

Small is not beautiful when one examines the capacity of social movements and our institutions. The local neighborhood group and the local or branch union are essential building blocks of organizational life, but there is no simple stasis that allows an equilibrium of stability when either one of these basic units is integrated into institutions that are trying to create real change which means building real power. So the financial model at the base level has to generate enough income to sustain local activities – subsidized, if you will, by millions of hours of volunteer labor by members – and to support full-time, and, increasingly, professional staffs, the financial model has to create the capacity to both expand the organizations by organizing new members in communities or workplaces and to create additional infrastructure and support to counter the opposition in on going struggles.

Doing all of this with dues is not without issues – a lot of them!

The simplest problem is one of the most difficult, and that revolves around dues levels. How really does an organization make the decision about how much or how little the dues rate for members should be? And, how does one keep it equitable – which is a very difficult and challenging issue also worth addressing.

One could figure out what dues income the organization needs and then do the long division and calculate the number of members one would need to carry the weight and at what annual rate. Seems easy enough, though it's really not, because an organization has to constantly calculate what the market, meaning members, can bear.

But, even if it were that easy, we cannot avoid stumbling on simple decisions that carry their own fundamental logic. Presumably, if one charges less dues for example, one will recruit more members, and conversely, charging more dues is bound to cause some drop off of lower income adherents who cannot afford to pay the higher dues.

This is a classic organizing conundrum because as a fundamental principle in a democratic system we believe in people power – majority will – and the fact that the more people we have, the more power we can demonstrate, both politically and morally, as we translate our cause into action within the public forum. In the old axiom organizers for generations have argued the simple facts, universally accepted and understood, that because we aren't rich, we cannot buy votes and politicians, so we don't have economic power in that sense, so we can only build power in numbers – so that we have enough votes to move the polls, so that we have enough feet to block the streets, and so we have enough hands to stop the factory wheels from turning. These five fingers alone can do many things, but when they are bound to each other in a fist, then they can make things happen. And, so on and so on, etcetera, etcetera.

In practice these roads cross and collide differently than in theory and that has to do with simple engineering – the methodology of the organizing model.

A simple example is with members like those that some organizations claim based on a simple designation regardless of the level of the contribution who are more accurately classified as supporters or even contributors more than members in a more participatory sense. If an organization is recruiting its members through a street canvass or phone canvass or even direct mail, its basic engineering cost is the same regardless of the donation made by the individual, as long as it at least recovers its basic recruitment investment. If a canvasser is walking the block in an upper middle income neighborhood, she's hitting every door on the block and it's random selection who opens and turns on the light for her, but once the door is open and the rap is presented, any contribution could equal membership by this measure, and the only variables are the skill of the canvasser in realizing the maximum gain from the householder and the generosity and self-interest of the householder in deciding to give a donation and the level to award. These are faux members because frequently these are simple transactions involving impulse decisions without commitment or participation. In direct mail the attachment is even more ephemeral. Marketing the message to the recipient and a decision to give based on support of the issue is hardly the stuff of long term struggle, as important as the dollars are. Nevertheless in this kind of juggling, like the other forms of juggling we have discussed, many organizations can thrive and survive for long periods with good engineering that continues to mine the methodology and create sustainability out of duplicate transactions across the probability of millions of opportunities for similar decisions with reasonably predictable results. Who knows how we might try to describe "friends" and "followers" or "likes" on social networks, but they are not "members," even though some social network organizations count them as such. There are damned few that would take a bullet for you.

There are probably university statisticians, who could tell all of us more about the odds here, but we are addressing the basic engineering, not how long the structure will stand. The question of dues levels is not a purely theoretical guess that equates lower dues with more members and higher dues with less members, if the primary methodology is such that basic levels of competency in organizing will predictably yield a reliable level of support that is inelastic compared to the income constituency.

Ok, what do I really mean here? Well, at the most basic level, you can only run so fast. Let's say the organizing methodology is such that a team of organizers and community residents are home visiting every house, block by block, in a neighborhood to organize their community. No matter how the spirit is willing, there are only so many hours in the day; there are only so many hours that the team is available; and, there are only so many hours that the work will be productive and one will find a sufficient number of people at home to justify the results and yield. Let's say that happy figure turns out to be four working hours when this team will be on the doors, which is the number ACORN settled on. They can only run so fast from door to door, and they can only talk as quickly as they can be understood as they visit with the neighbors so that there will in fact be a predictable number of doors that they can hit and visits that the team can complete.

If that is the basic methodology then, whether or not one was charging $1 per year as we did in NWRO or $12 per year as we did in the early days of ACORN or $120 as we did in 2008 or $15/month as ACORN Canada does in 2015, one can only get to so many people in a day so the number is no longer theoretical and inflexible. So, sure out of an infinite number of people many, many more might "join" – if they gave it any thought at all – at $1 per year, but the maximum number of members would still only be the number one could reach through a specific method. Once one has a grip on the numbers available, one really has to determine what is the threshold level at which the number of dollars charged in dues starts to actually decrease the number of families that will make the decision to join purely for economic reasons – where is the limit of economic elasticity in the decision. An organizer for such an organization knows – hopefully – what it takes to run the railroad, so a constant dialectic in the street determines the market value of participation in the organization as expressed through payment levels of dues. There are obviously variables that make this more art, than science, because the factors of organizational performance and production are critical; consistency and effectiveness of communication between the organization and its members are essential; and in some cases general community standing, visibility, and representational positioning can be vital, all of which can create the climate for a potential participant to decide the importance of becoming and maintaining membership in an organization.

A related membership dues issue revolves around whether or not for exactly these reasons it is sometimes advantageous to tier a dues system with a distinction between entry-level dues and permanent dues. One can argue that there are advantages to making the entry-level lower and therefore more accessible to the potential member, so that once enrolled the member increases their understanding and appreciation for the work and results of the organization, and therefore is more inclined to renew at a higher level, once they have come to value their membership more highly. In building a mass-based organization these issues still involve problems because inevitably the question of dues levels does impact total membership capacity, no matter what the decision.

The simple truth is that after a generation of community organizing where ACORN has pioneered a membership dues system, no matter the merits, principles, and philosophy, most community organizations still do not go there, and often when they do, it is not in a systematic fashion, although this also argues why there is not more community organizing today, and why what we have is not more effective.

Regardless, at the "nuts and bolts" level the point is inarguable whatever decision is made, whatever the source of funds: money matters. Nonetheless, we really see the issues more clearly, and in some ways more complexly in unions, and if you can bear it, let's go there, and if not, skip a chapter and hope for the best and pray the wheels don't come off.

Chapter IV: **Dues and Don'ts: Lessons and Learning from Unions**

Unions are about dues in all shapes and sizes. Making a list of various unions would reveal an almost infinite variety of dues systems – and manners of collection. There are also dues, fees, fines, and assessments – all different, though all about money, indeed mainly about money, though sometimes about protection or defense or benefits as well. Construction trades have bench dues and working dues. Some trades along with others have hybrid systems that will combine a fixed per capita dues level along with a certain percentage of income. Straight percentage dues systems would seem the easiest to understand and administer, though sometimes they are coupled with a joining fee, a cap, or a minimum, and they may be calculated on either gross monthly income, gross monthly income with overtime, or net monthly income. Probably the majority of local unions – and their national or "international" parent organizations – use fixed per capita systems determining a set amount that will be due to the parent organization – with the rest staying with the local union.

Fixed dues systems can be arbitrarily determined – though based on the requirements of federal labor law in the United States at least one should remember that arbitrarily also means democratically, since all members have to be allowed to vote on dues levels and increases, before they can be enacted – or fixed to a level equal to one or two hours of pay particularly in industrial unions. Dues can also differ within individual local unions with different levels and rates for different kinds of worker classifications or sectors. Finally, let's remember the additional overlay of law that differs within the United States from state to state involving so-called "right-to-work laws," union shops, closed shops, maintenance of membership, and agency fees. Oh, and the means of collection are important as well: hand collected, payroll check off, and so forth. Are you still running with me, brothers and sisters? If so, you are now way ahead of the members!

Ok, I've sketched out the forest, so let's see if we can identify some the trees and hack a path through this wilderness.

First, some definitions:

- **Per capita:** From the Latin and a couple of thousand years ago the way taxes built the empire, can you believe it – means by the head, the amount paid for each individual member.

- **Dues:** The regular engine that runs the train, and also the defining characteristic of all union membership – you pay dues, then you are a member, you do not pay dues, then you are not a member. Never confuse these terms!

- **Fees:** Fewer of these in the modern labor movement, but there are still joining fees, particularly in the trades, and this is the price of admission – or exclusion – from some unions. Typically, most public sector unions these days have minimal to non-existent joining fees – my union, Local 100, states a $5.00 joining fee, but the board waves it as new units come in, and we never collect it. In the trades though the joining fee can be hundreds of dollars at the entry gate to control membership access.

- **Fines:** A ridiculous practice that is also increasingly archaic and usually divisive. Fines can run from the simple quarters and dollars paid into the kitty for being late for a meeting or other reasonably good-natured infractions like cursing to significant amounts administered literally by union trial boards for criminal felonies like scabbing – crossing the line and going to work in a strike – to working non-union in general to a host of other problems, large and small.

- **Assessments:** The sun is not large enough to shine over this earth. If there is something needed by the local – or larger – union, where dues is not sufficient to cover the cost, then the members will be asked to dig deeper and vote to assess themselves an additional amount. Assessments are commonly used to finance the purchase or construction of local union halls. Fans of HBO's "The Wire" in the USA heard the longshoreman checkers local union president give a report to his executive board on the political leverage they were gaining from contributions in Annapolis derived from membership assessments to try to create more work on the docks.

- **Bench Dues:** Dues paid by a member who is "sitting on the bench," which is to say not working.

- **Working Dues:** An additional amount, frequently a percentage, added to the standard dues for when the tradesman is, working.

- **Cap:** The maximum dues that can be paid in a single month.

- **Minimum:** The minimum dues that can be paid. Both of these are usually absolute dollar amounts, rather than percentages. The careful listener and the wary worker will hear the dues expressed as say, "1.5% of gross monthly with a minimum of $15 and a cap of $50," and be able to figure the dues accordingly.

- **Gross Monthly, Net Monthly, and Gross Monthly with Overtime:** You understand the English and the math is simple. The definition lies in the politics of the local union.

- **"Right-to-Work:"** This is the dues reality imposed state by state by legislators once they were allowed under Taft-Hartley in the US or national policy in the United Kingdom to dilute the federal policy encouraging union dues payment for representation. So, R-t-W has nothing to do with actually getting any work. In the states with R-t-W laws, a local union cannot negotiate with the employer any method which requires all workers in the bargaining unit to pay either dues or some sum for union services and representations. The vast majority of the R-t-W states are in the South and Mountain West, but its spreading. Like a disease. Internationally, such a voluntary "open shop" dues program is the norm not the exception. I dare say that the open shop is vastly more prevalent across the globe than any other dues system.

- **Union Shop:** In the other states one has the right to try and negotiate an arrangement with the employer that makes the workplace a "union shop." This is a matter of bargaining, so please do not automatically assume that this is universal or easily achieved in many, many workplaces! Where an agreement is made, a union shop gives every worker in the bargaining unit a fixed period of time – 30, 60, or whatever number of days – to decide to join the union or pay a representation fee, or to start finding a new place to work.

- **Closed Shop:** For all intents and purposes the "closed shop" has been illegal in the United States for more than 50 years at this writing, though it has taken over a legendary, rhetorical life among union bashers that has no time limit. Essentially, the closed shop meant that one had to be a union member *first* in order to get a job later. There are some gray areas around the docks and trades where this might still be a matter of interpretation, but generally speaking, it's simply not kosher over the last generation.

- **Agency Fee:** The increasingly complex calculation that determines exactly how much the worker, who elects not be become a union member, pays for representational services of the union. Remember under the National Labor Relations Act the unions are bound by a "duty of fair representation" to equally represent all workers in a bargaining unit under their union contract, whether this worker is a member or not. Essentially in half of America the political authorities allow a fee to be fixed to prevent "free riders," as they are known, and in the other half of America the members subsidize the non-members to fulfill the identical obligations. No one said this was about fairness – these are just the facts, ma'am. Sadly the US Supreme Court just decided that there was even such a thing as a "partial public employee," and they now do not have to pay servicing fees. Soon the Supreme Court may made agency fees for public employees a relic of the past and illegal for the future.

- **Maintenance of Membership:** A middle ground negotiation – where legal – that essentially means that once a worker decides in the course of a contract period to become a union member, the membership must be maintained without any withdrawal or cessation for the period of the collective bargaining agreement or whatever term is bargained.

- **Hand Collected:** A system of dues collection – still widely used in the trades – and on the doors – where a member has to go to the hall or pays her dues through a union steward or representative at the workplace. One gets their "book stamped" or a new button indicating payment for that month, or a card punched or whatever might be the system. This is close work – and possible where there is a union shop requiring a worker as a matter of the contract to pay or not have a future in that shop – but very, very difficult in R-t-W states. Sadly this was the history, and may become the future after a fashion.

- **Check-off:** Upon receiving a signed authorization from the employee, the dues is checked off from the payroll wages of the worker – the amount is subtracted from the total wages and paid to the union. In more refined parlance this is referred to as a payroll dues deduction system. This system is also under attack by politicians as well as by the contingent nature of the economy leading some unions and even large ones in the United Kingdom to eschew payroll deduction systems in factor of direct debit, bank draft, and other arrangements between the member and the union.

Now, we have reached a patch of clear ground, and can look at the real issues, which is still about money, as you will recall, and how much it matters in building capacity for social change. First, one has to be amazed not at the architecture of the labor movement these days, but really the sedimentary geology of the movement, which is nowhere more evident than in examining issues around dues collection. Dues systems seem to have rarely changed. New layers were simply added on to the old structures to produce systems that were known as much by their differences as their similarities. History trumps philosophy at every turn.

A labor movement founded in secrecy in the 19th century shrouded in the hostility and opposition of much stronger and more ruthless employers had little choice but to develop simple systems that could be maintained through concerted and collective will. Printers, typesetters, trades of all descriptions assembled in a preindustrial brotherhood to attempt to fix fair wage rates for their labor and combine to create a voice at the workplace where they had none previously. Their voice may have been marginally legal then, but the attempt to combine to set labor rates was seen as a restraint of trade by employers and their friends at the U. S. Supreme Court.[40] It is sobering to think that some workers and their unions successfully hand collected dues for more than a hundred years and maintained the core and spirit of unionism in their hearts and hands decade after decade. Union halls and meeting places had to be built by hand or purchased with hard earned dollars because these were illegal assemblies that could find no roof to safely shield them in many cities and counties.

So of course dues were at fixed levels and dollar amounts, because they were paid right from the pockets and not from the employer's check. No other member could know correctly what the income of their brother member might be, so for the union the equity was in the equal share of dues payments to support and own the enterprise. The history defined the archeology.

As an organizer it seems to me the great "reforms" in dues systems, and others may disagree, were three fold.

The first was the system that propelled Sam Gompers to his success as an organizer and leader of the cigar workers union and therefore later to the head of the American Federation of Labor, I have discussed earlier, but will underscore again. Local unions

---

[40] *Loewe v. Lawlor, 208 U.S. 274 (1908)*, also referred to as the Danbury Hatters' Case.

were by definition "local" – they covered a single, local geographical area or they covered a particular local work site – and they represented largely the craft – the work trade – in that space. Gompers' innovation was not so much in the way dues were collected *as the way they were uniquely aggregated.* All dues from all locals in the New York City area were held centrally, despite the varying size of the individual locals, because Gompers was able to convince all of the locals that if they did not pool their dues they would not be able to organize the entire jurisdiction, leaving them with only pockets of varying levels of strength depending on the effectiveness and clout of each individual local. Consequently, rather than the level of power for cigar workers falling to the lowest watermark set by the weakest or smallest local, the level rose to an equal level allowing the cigar workers to consolidate and organize their entire jurisdiction. All for one, and one for all.

The dominant historical trend of aggregated dues for local unions in Gompers time in the late 19th century continued in a largely unbroken line to the 21st century. In the main the local union pays the fixed per capita rate to the national or international union and keeps the rest. The rest may be a little or may be a lot, but whatever it may be it is all retained at the local level and spent accordingly. Not surprisingly, the decision made by Gompers' cigar workers is the rarest of decisions – to agree to pool everything for the greater good and to understand that the individual member – and of course the individual local – benefited most – when *everyone was organized.* Unions are at the base political institutions vesting members – appropriately – with huge democratic rights both by

Samuel Gompers.

history, political practice, and, now, law.[41] Members accordingly, since they are paying the dues, as a natural impulse would want to see their dues spent as close to home as possible in hopes of realizing the benefits in direct services, representation, bargaining, or whatever. Which is not to say that they are unwilling to make different choices when they are given the opportunity to evaluate them, it just says that they are often not given the right options in order to make the right choices, so it is hard to expect different decisions.

The next real effort to do it right and differently then came with the creation of the Congress of Industrial Organizations, the C.I.O. Several of the major industrial unions, particularly the United Auto Workers and the United Steel Workers Union implemented two major reforms around dues. First, dues were tied more closely to the individual worker, than to a fixed rate. The system was based on dues equally the number of hours worked. The system was based on the amount of dues worked by the member equaling a certain number of hours. A different kind of equity therefore made its appearance. Each member would pay an equal amount based on the ability to pay, rather than a regressively fixed amount. In current terms, a member who earned only slightly more than minimum wage, say $7.00 per hour at a 2 hour rate would pay $14.00 in dues to the union, while a better paid member making $20.00 per hour at a 2 hour rate would pay $40.00 in dues per month to the union. Part and parcel to this system working was the second innovation – a centralized dues collection mechanism.

The CIO was creating new national unions virtually from scratch, marking a watershed change in the construction of the labor movement. Most, though not all, other unions in the AFL's history had traditionally been constructed from the locals up. Many national unions historically had been built by local unions, having proven their ability to survive in a Chicago, or a New York, or San Francisco, or Atlanta, and recognizing a greater strength or advantage in consolidating the standards of the craft or jurisdiction past the local area or head-to-head with non-local employers, were also nationalizing, came together to form a national union. National unions that were built by strong local unions or coalitions of existing unions inevitably would construct a dues system that recognized the primacy of the locals and thereby build largely weak national structures to coordinate specific functions with limited staff. In such organizations it was natural to determine a per capita that the locals would pay at some small amount that would be sent over to the national union to maintain these functions in Indianapolis or Washington or Chicago or wherever the headquarters of the national union might be in those days. The power of the locals was both the strength of these unions in spatial and economic markets, and also the practical and political regulator and paymaster that could either veto or vouch for expansion or growth of the overall union. The creation story is vital in the lives of labor organizations in understanding much about their operations and challenges to this date and in the future – just as it is in all mass organizations. I cannot make this point too strongly!

The CIO had the advantage of starting organizations from scratch so, just as decisions about equity were vital in the apportionment of dues per member, the opportunity also existed to turn the tables on the relationship of power, so that it flowed down from the national to the local, rather than up the other way. The CIO was now the parent of

---

[41] This is not to say that they are democratic institutions just that they are political institutions, which is an important distinction.

the organization, where in many, many other unions the locals had borne the national union as their child. CIO unions like the UAW and USW created a dues collection system whereby they collected all of the dues centrally and nationally and essentially rebated either a per capita or a percentage *back* to the local, rather than the other way. Consequently, one would have a strong, well-financed national union with relatively weaker local bodies without much in the way of financial resources. The local union's job would be basic representation under the contract, and in many industrial settings, once again auto and steel being prime examples, union stewards were paid by the employer – often full-time – thereby also (a third huge reform!) transferring a huge and expensive responsibility over to the employer and off of the members backs and the dues system. The local union's share of the dues coming back was virtually for beer money at that point since the administration of the contract was covered in parts by the boss and the national union. Renting or buying the hall, the occasional clerical, the Christmas party, and odds and ends were under the control of the volunteer and elected officers, and they had the minimal dues to move the program. The leavening in this basic alteration came from the history of the organization and the development of strike funds. Industrial unions retained significant amounts of the dues (or through special earmarked assessments) in order to administer the collective strike funds to allow members in disparate locations to take on clearly national and multi-national industries. The UAW has a strike fund alone today that virtually equals the assets of the rest of the labor movement combined, though I might add that's another problem worth discussing as well at some point.

 The third major area of change in the last one-hundred years of the dues system is the growth of percentage dues systems in many unions, particularly in the service sector, which established even more clearly the principles of equity in dues payment. In a pure percentage dues system one creates virtually perfect equity in the burdens shared by individual members, since whatever the percentage applied, it will impact each individual member exactly the same. If the percentage is 1% of gross income, a lower waged worker making only $15000 per year knows that the $150 per year he pays hurts as little – or as much – as the higher income worker making $45000 per year who is paying $450 in dues per year, despite the fact that one member is paying three times the amount per year that the other member is paying. Because the system is identical and equitable, both members own and invest equally in the union, and at least in theory, even if not in practice, have an equal say and are of equal importance.

 Dues are a form of self-imposed taxation though, so just like other forms of taxation, some are more progressive and some are more regressive. An income tax is a progressive tax – in theory – whereby we all are at least supposed to pay the same rate of our gross income to the government to equally support the common functions as citizens. A sales or property tax is regressive because it hurts the family or individual more with less income because it is a fixed amount and does not take anything into account about overall income or wealth and the ability to pay. These are important public issues, and usually unions in fact are on the right side arguing as a cornerstone of labor's platform that taxation should be progressive.

Often inside the house of labor the taxation system gets bundled by political compromises into very regressive systems because of the fixed level of many per capita taxes paid to national and international unions. Here's how it works.

The first steps backward are at the ceiling and floor of the system. The imposition of a floor, let's say $15.00 per month on the system, takes the same lower waged member we discussed earlier and hikes their dues from $150 per year to $180 per year – a 20% increase! A ceiling on the high side at even $50 per month or $600 per year would mean that a better paid member making more than $60000 would in effect get a dues reduction not only affecting the purity – and equity – of the percentage system, but a discount against their higher wages and a better ability to pay dues to the union. An $80000 a year worker in our example of a 1% dues rate should pay $800 per year, but with a ceiling would have $200 lopped off the top getting a 25% discount. Arguably, the union would be even stronger if it had the higher resources represented by the equitable payment of the higher paid worker – in fact arguably the higher paid worker has gotten *more* benefit from the union than has the lower paid worker – at least at this historical moment – and should be delighted to pay more. Math works this way, not the world, but we'll get to that later.

But, before getting there we have to face up to a much more crippling problem at the next level of taxation, which is imposed by the national or international union on the local body. International union per capita taxes are invariably calculated as a fixed dollar amount, rather than as a percentage amount. The same is true for the AFL-CIO and its sub-components in state federations and local labor councils.

Using as an example the relatively low international per capita imposed by the Service Employees International Union with which I am intimately familiar, for sake of this discussion – to keep the math easy – let's call the per capita paid to them, $7.00 per month per member or $84 per year, and then let's see how it all works. Our lower waged worker at $15000 with a 1% dues system was paying $150.00, so suddenly we can see the problem when the International per capita takes more than half of the gross dues at $84 per year. Add on payments to the state, central body, and this, that, and the other, adding up to at least another $1, and the local union's share of the dues drops down to only $50.00 per year of the gross dues. The higher waged $45000 per year worker is paying the same percentage in our model at $450, but leaving the local union with almost $300 per year on the gross dues – so the bite is not the half of the total dues for the less well paid member, but no more than a third of the obligation for the higher waged member.[42]

At the simplest level the archaic fixed per capita level system, which dominates the financial relationship between union locals and their parent bodies creates huge structural anomalies. Though the revenue may be falsely balanced for the national or international union, since all members are ostensibly paying the "same" tax, it creates significant dysfunctions between locals, essentially allowing the larger locals to retain more income

---

[42] In 2000 SEIU broke new ground among all AFL-CIO unions when delegates to the Pittsburgh Convention approved creating an organizing war chest through a New Strength Unity Fund which would add a $1 per month per member to special funds for organizing until reaching $5 per month for this purpose in 2005. As critical as this was for the whole union it capsizes our financial model, since a union made of lower waged workers goes under water financially unless exempted from the payments, while the a local union with the higher waged workers moves to the point where it is retaining only 53% of the members' dues.

Chapter IV: Dues and Don'ts: Lessons and Learning from Unions

at the direct expense of the smaller and poor locals by directly impoverishing them. The political exigencies are such that the structural inequity becomes virtually impossible to reform within institutional labor, since the political oligarchies are constructed around the size of the locals with very, very few unions utilizing direct membership election procedures (as opposed to delegate assemblies in conventions) and no large locals – and few leaders who depend on their votes and support – having a self-interest to reform the equities of the system.

Does this have consequences? Oh, mercy yes, and they are myriad!

First, local unions are enriched or impoverished right at the crossroads determining which came first, the chicken or the egg. One could speculate whether wages in labor markets are higher because unions are stronger or lower because unions are weak as a causal factor, or one can stand with macro-economists and realize that a series of historical factors have led to spatial market variations so that wage rates are *structurally* lower in the South, rural areas in general, and so forth. Either way, a local union trying to maintain its density or share of the labor market within its sector, craft, or jurisdiction, in a wage market that is generally or significantly larger is going to have less total dollars in dues to spend to either organize or maintain its membership on a percentage dues system, than a union that has exactly the same membership in a market with generally higher average wages. If a local union has nothing but plumbers or janitors or any other job classification where wages are adjusted to the local market, then unions in such markets on a percentage dues system will always have less absolute dollars. Given the cost of organizing and servicing members it is unclear whether or not these costs shrink in the market or are inflexible. And, either way a flat rate fixed per capita system will unfairly tax the local union facing structural economic market challenges in its work of either new organizing or delivering good wages and benefits to its members. The union in such markets will be at an unfair competitive disadvantage with another local union in the same national or international union simply on the random economics of the market – virtually an accident of a union leader's birth or at least workplace.

Secondly, the economics of unions are powerful drivers pointing down one clear highway: **it pays to organize high wage workers, and it does not pay to organize low wage workers.** Once again we have a little of the chicken and the egg going here – there is no question for example that industrial workers have become well paid and benefited thanks to the labor movement, and in unionized sectors even non-union workers are reasonably well waged as part of competitive labor market pressure for the same skills as well as union avoidance schemes. Higher wage sectors – transportation, maritime, rail, skilled construction, utility workers, communications – consequently continue to enjoy extremely high levels of relative union density – it pays for the unions to maintain their membership in these areas – even as the total levels of employment in these and industrial sectors plummet.

The economy has been growing most rapidly in the service sector though, and that sector has historically been extremely low waged, and continues to be so: retail, tourism and hospitality, food service, most health care, security work, janitorial, laundry, and so on. Public workers are an exception in many areas since the levels of organization are high and relative wage rates are higher than the rest of the service sector, so not surprisingly the public sector continues to attract a lot of organizing interest and resources everywhere in the country. At least until recently.[43] The wages in many of these industries are structured around the minimum wage, which at this writing for full-time work would be less than $15080.[44] Running successful local unions of minimum wage workers within the structural economics of institutional labor as it exists now in the United States is a virtual contradiction in terms. The system of taxation produces an unsustainable financial model. A local union can survive with either financial subsidies or financial exemptions, but is still sentenced – along with its members – to a permanent structural weakness unless it can blend its membership with higher waged workers to essentially subsidize the lower waged part of its base, usually by organizing in another jurisdiction. Add on a flat rate fixed per capita by the parent organization, and such local unions are permanently crippled institutions if they represent nothing but low waged workers, even though lower waged workers are where there are increasingly massive numbers of the unorganized.

Thirdly, do not forget the other structural problem of wage differentials is not just the hourly rate but the number of hours worked. A nursing home worker with a fixed week of 35 hours, which is the industry standard, is going to need to make more per hour, not less in order to have the same buying power as other minimally waged workers. Same for a janitorial worker in the cleaning industry in downtown buildings who is lucky to get 20 hours per week at night, or school support workers in the public sector, or hospitality workers whose hours come and go with the occupancy rate in the hotel or the season or the conventions setting up and pulling out. The burgeoning growth of the home health care industries and the workers employed there constitutes a public health breakthrough and a structural savings in the industry, but also leaves hundreds of thousands of workers scrambling between enough clients to make 40 hours of work. Earlier the signs may have been clearly pointing a local union to higher waged workers rather than lower waged workers, but there are big warning signs and flashing lights if the local union got on the wrong road and organized not only lower waged workers but contingent workers and workers with less than full-time hours. A sustainable organizing model for local union created for skilled workers one-hundred years ago cannot even conceive of these problems, yet the American labor movement is still being run this way.

Finally, what masks – and drives – this problem inside unions, yet has led to the patchwork quilt of increasingly weak local and national unions, is the difference in state laws on dues creating right-to-work states and markets and union shop states and markets. The existence of union-shop agreements in almost half of the states allows unions to avoid the problems of dues inequities and other economic anachronisms, which would normally cripple all local unions, because such agreements allow for inflexible collection systems in a captive market. Simply put, every worker has to pay – at least something, and that something is a hardy percentage of the total dues rate even for an agency fee payer – under a union shop agreement in order to stay employed as a condition of the overall collective bargaining contract. Based on union constitutions and bylaws, legitimized by

---

[43] Conservative political forces in the USA have increasingly targeted public sector workers in recent years at the state level and in court.

[44] $7.25 per hour in 2014 times 2080 or 40 hours times 52 weeks.

federal labor laws, of course only union members can vote on any matter from the cast of characters that make up their leadership to approving a contract or going out on strike to whether or not to increase and how to apportion dues to the tax itself. In union-shop states one can create anomalous dues systems and support gross inequities, because everyone or virtually everyone has to pay, assuring a base income to the local union and therefore sufficient resources as well to pass on up the line to the parent organization or other affiliated bodies, reducing any economically rational incentive to move to more equity or eliminate regressive flat and fixed rate per capita systems. Furthermore, union shop states at least give the promise of economically paying back the investment of new organizing – which as we have seen and will continue to see – is expensive and risky. If the union succeeds against bad odds to organize a new employer and against yet more terrible odds wins a first contract at least with a union shop provision the workers in the bargaining unit will all pay dues or fees, then the books get balanced and away we go. In right-to-work land – remember all of the South and most of the Mountain West and increasingly in the great Midwest here and there in between the coasts – the wages are worse, the workers are poorer, and the chance of a union recovering organizing costs are much, much slimmer. Additionally, in R-t-W states local unions will have to make continual investments in "internal" organizing in order to enroll new bargaining unit workers as union dues paying members, which is not a cost borne by unions in non-r-t-w states. And, remember, the pie is also still smaller since in these situations since the dues are going to likely be proportionately lower and the local union doing the work or ending up with the members, proportionately weaker as well.

If you did not understand why conservatives around the world, led by the rightwing in the United States are now attacking agency fee and union shop systems in order to implement right-to-work regimes, you surely get it now!

Not to put too fine a point on it, but it must be obvious by now that one of the reasons that the millions and millions of workers in the South and elsewhere are unorganized is simply that based on the existing dominant labor organizing models it does not pay unions to organize them, and even if organized the financial structure inherent in today's unions ends up crippling most of the unions built in these areas. In the "small business" model that is at the archaic heart of institutional labor, everything militates against real work that would turn the tables on such a financial model. Not that this is the way it has to be, but simply because it is the way it is. An old organizing comrade of mine in Boston used to refer to this problem by saying that running a local union "was a nice small business for an Irish guy," but Irish or whatever, where his quip came close to the truth was that the model only works for a small outfit – it is not scalable on these numbers, or worse, it is only scalable, but one cannot aggregate the resources to get large enough to achieve economies of scale in unorganized areas.

A final paradox that flows from these arguments is that the lowest income locals are in effect subsidizing the highest income union locals and of course their national unions, when clearly, if anything, it should be the other way around. That is ironic particularly because one of the functions of the labor superstructure's allocation of per capita dues should be redistribution to where needs for organizing and program support are highest, which one might think would include the South, lower waged workers, and other challenging areas for labor. It is a different discussion whether a local would ever fully realize the full value of per capita on normal rates of exchange, or even should, because many functions of national or international union are collective and critical. Nonetheless the dysfunctional economics that prevail create such a skewed imbalance of payments that often inadvertently the local unions are being financially bled to death without full recognition of the pain and suffering being administered. A local union of 5000 members paying per capita to a parent organization of ten dollars per month would be sending out $600000 per year. Even in the best of unions in the best of years, there are going to be few times when the local union "breaks even" with money or staff or support coming back at the full value of the resources they exported.

I thought of this problem some years ago when hiking with a friend, Emmet Aluli, on Maloka'I, while making the contacts to open an ACORN office in Honolulu. We stopped by a huge indentation that native Hawaiians had dug in the mountain that fit the dimensions of the hull of a ship in the late 1800's. Hawaiians were early examples of the current crises in third world debt and owed the great powers hundreds of thousands of dollars in loans that could not be paid back. The banking countries demanded the payments be made in sandalwood, so hundreds scoured the mountains for sandalwood, lugging it back into the hull hole until it was full, indicating another shipload was fulfilled. There is almost no sandalwood left in Hawaii anymore, and the same may become the case for union members in the South and elsewhere unless the impacts of these imbalances of payments are soon corrected.

Ship indentation in Hawaii for measuring sandalwood.

Chapter IV: Dues and Don'ts: Lessons and Learning from Unions

The result is that the growth and prospects of unions – and therefore workers – in these markets are in fact *structurally stunted* by such policies, creating inflexible barriers to their potential. Looking at a series of local unions across a national union the pattern become fairly clear. Parent organization per capita payments run on average about 30% of the total income of a local union[45]. Affiliate per capita payments perhaps add another 2-3% to the tax paid by the local union on its members. The average local union then would be paying roughly one-third of its total dues income to the organizations at all levels where it has an affiliation. But, since these are flat and fixed amounts, obviously the richer the local union, which is to say the higher the membership dues paid by workers in such a local union, then the lower the percentage of external per capita payments the local pays to affiliate bodies, and the more of their members' dues it is able to retain. The obverse is also true. The local union with a more progressive percentage dues system representing lower waged workers, particularly in right-to-work environments will pay a disproportionate amount of their members' dues to affiliate bodies – frequently between 45-55% of their total dues. Where the local union is in fact not just representing lower waged workers, but also battling the requirements of right-to-work laws, the half or less of its remaining income has to provide the resources for internal recruitment, maintenance of the legal representative functions of the union, basic operations and legal requirements of day to day union administration, *and* external, or new, organizing to recruit unorganized workers. One might say that based on this economic model, it is a surprise that any new workers are ever organized, but in fact the hemorrhaging of membership in the labor movement indicates that in fact they are not, and the archaic and structural inequities that are now ingrained within the system guarantee that it will stay that way barring the occasional exception or extraordinary event.

One could equalize resources through several structural reforms. One could turn the clock back over a hundred years and borrow from Gompers playbook and equalize and redistribute resources based on the analysis that the entire jurisdiction simply must be organized. It is the rare national union leader who can effect such a redistribution. The Service Employees International Union's initiative to create a separate dues pot through the New Strength Unity Program is one of the rare examples of a modern redistribution formula, though it was not meant to equalize resources, it was certainly meant to create the resources to create innovative and breakthrough organizing opportunities. The more common political maneuver has been to shore up the existing membership base which the Teamsters locals did to Ron Carey to virtually strangle the international union under his leadership or when the Steelworkers politically redistributed all of their organizing resources to regions rather than run a national program. They all no doubt had their

---

[45] Given the history, it is not surprising that many national and international unions have at best an imperfect understanding of the local union dues systems within their own union, since the locals were father to the child, no matter who is seen as parent now. When the national union only collects the per capita payments it has no way of knowing anything other than their part of the elephant. Therefore it is difficult to determine whether or not the figures on local union comparisons that I discuss here are relatively common, as I assume, or distinct. These figures derive from the volunteer submissions of close to 100 of the total locals of the Service Employees International Union (although close to 70% of the total membership of the whole union), which were provided to me as a member of an International Resource Committee that was debating the very topics being discussed here some years ago.

reasons, and this is ancient history to many, but the point remains inarguable: there have to be dues resources to organize new members and existing bureaucracies and the political life of institutional unions continue to claim priority.[46]

It would seem easier to simply convert the parent organization's per capita payments either to a percentage or to levy an equitable flat percentage on the gross dues income of all local unions. Such a step would be "revenue neutral" in order to maintain the same budget for the national or international union taking away that potential political problem. Essentially the change would be more mathematical than structural – a non-ideological conversion of a flat rate to a percentage rate. In the earlier example where the average parent union per capita payments were coming in around 30%, one would simply convert all national union per capita payments for all local unions to 30% of the total dues income.

In theory one would wonder, who could disagree? The salutary impact at the "bottom" of the system would be enormous though, since local unions organizing and representing lower waged workers, southern workers, and workers in right-to-work states would all be paying 30% (or less!), just like all other locals, but based on this simple statistical change would be gaining almost 40% more income. Additionally, the efficiency of such a modernized system would create economies at all structural levels of the union. The task and expense at the national or international union level would be streamlined. Elaborate field audits of all local unions to determine whether or not the locals are paying on a "fair and accurate count" of their members would be reduced to a mathematical exercise against the gross dues receipts and deposits. The extensive clerical staffs at the local and upper reaches of the dues chain would also be rendered obsolete – the constant figuring of per capita would not be formulaic, and instead could be redeployed more effectively and strategically at list and data management befitting a more modern organization.

Practically the only resistance to such a much needed modernization and a more equitable financial and economic model for unions would have to be found by looking to which unions were benefiting most from the current inequitable systems, and that would obviously be any local union that was paying less than the average percentage of their income prior to the recalculation. Problem is, as we indicated earlier, that tends to be the richer – and therefore often larger – local unions, so in this way unions mirror the larger community where regressive tax practices are buttressed by the similar fixed formulas benefiting the rich by assessing less of their actual income through fixed cap systems like property taxes or sales taxes which disproportionately burden the poorer families and working families. Not surprisingly such an atrophied movement will find that this financial structure assures that the rich get richer and the poor unions stay poor, if they survive at all as marginal worker organizations.

Besides the political dysfunction which supports such a system internally within the house of labor, there are huge external costs as well which critically weaken the power of labor, because they impact on similar "engineering" problems that we reviewed earlier

---

[46] For SEIU most of these maneuvers seem not to have worked out, and rather than solve the problem of organizing the unorganized in places like the United States southern states, all indications as of 2015 are a withdrawal from the South except Florida. The most recent sign was abandoning its share of city workers local in Houston, subsidy cutbacks in Louisiana, and a general retreat.

Chapter IV: Dues and Don'ts: Lessons and Learning from Unions

in community organization dues systems. Fundamental axioms of organization would hold that in building power at the workplace or in the community one wants more members, rather than less members. In bargaining and representing workers or citizens, one also wants to be able to define the organization's representative ability by looking at the percentage density of membership to the whole constituency or jurisdiction of workers. Unless there are huge reasons otherwise, as a general rule anything that limits the potential membership of the organization is a structural inefficiency that competes with the overall goals and objectives of the organization. Artificially inflated dues structures do just that or it would seem so for labor unions, because they introduce an economic inflexibility that depresses the total membership numbers in the union.

Take my own local union, Local 100 when we were still affiliated with SEIU[47] we faced the labor equivalent of triple jeopardy: lower waged workers, the South, and right-to-work. Add the fact that we organized many part-time and contingent workers in high turnover sectors (nursing homes, janitorial, and so forth) and public workers without clearly defined and accessible collective bargaining rights in states with ultra-conservative politics, and we have a trifecta of obstacles to surmount, just to make it through the day, much less grow and aggregate power. Finally, especially in the public sector without clear bargaining definitions, there are a lot of competing organizations seeking to represent all or pieces of the workforce with different packages and inducements. Dues levels in all of these areas become vital questions for workers, since whether to pay dues at all in a right-to-work environment starts with a threshold choice about joining period. Additionally, in many, many situations workers can come in and out of membership repeatedly by joining and paying dues one month and then dropping their membership the next month.[48] As Justice Sotomayer noted recently in her opinion in *Harris v. Quinn*, there is an economic disincentive to pay dues to a union – period – if you don't have to pay something.

As an independent union coming into SEIU in 1984 our dues system was simple and clear – 1% with no minimums and a cap at $25.00. When we affiliated for the first number of years our international per capita were rebated back to the local, so in effect we were paying no international per caps. Finally in the late 90's we gradually worked our way into the position where we paid full per caps. In the mid-80's organizing janitorial workers made sense even at 1%, and we could build power in the buildings, which made a difference sometimes enrolling 90% of the unit and more into the union. It became quickly evident as we began paying international per capita that we were in fact, *losing money every time we recruited a member at 1%* with no minimums. This was part-time work and the union premium was no more than $1-$2 over the minimum wage, so a member would only be paying $4 - $6 in dues to Local 100 per month. Organizing janitorial workers did not make economic sense for the local union, if we were going to have to subsidize every member that joined with some other member's dues. It would only be financially within the local's self-interest if we controlled the entire market and could leverage wages high enough to allow us to recover sufficient dues. Were that possible, it

---

[47]   Local 100 was affiliated with SEIU from 1984 until 2009 when the local returned to the United Labor Unions.

[48]   In the Baton Rouge school system several years ago we were amazed to watch the pattern for one member who came in and out of the union five times in one year!

would take more resources than the local could amass, so over the years we adapted the local dues system in order to survive with various percentage increases over 20 years so that now members pay 1.75% and a minimum of $15 per month and a maximum of $50 per month. Local 100 still retains janitorial contracts and on this, much more regressive dues system, instead of membership levels over 80% in these units, we are lucky to maintain levels of 30%, which also reduces the power we have at the bargaining table with the employers obviously. As an independent union since 2010, we no longer have to pay per capita, and can invest in ourselves to the level of our membership strength.

The same situation occurs among nursing home workers. We organized a good number of nursing homes in a spurt of organizing in the mid-1980s especially around Shreveport where we gained a significant density in the total beds in the market. Given the wage rates over time the same financial reality depressed the membership and therefore the organizing program. Virtually all members were minimum dues members and a single arbitration case could decimate the whole enterprise by sucking up any space between the members' dues payments into the local union and the payments of per caps out of the local union. It made little economic sense to send organizers to organize more nursing homes under such an economic model and unless workers self-organized and almost knocked down our door to come into the union, it was crazy to expand our work in this area, because it was such a terrible financial proposition. Similarly it was also financially absurd to expend significant organizing resources to keep membership levels high, because the dues did not offset the labor costs, so truly one had to have the perfect union model to build power – good union stewards and in-house capacity. Constant structural turnover in the janitorial and nursing home and home care and many other sectors makes stable, good leadership a largely transitory phenomena as well. As my comrade and brother, Keith Kelleher, would sometimes say to me, calling from Chicago, "some days it's not fun 'playing' union anymore."

Where we face competition in the public sector, workers are frequently recruited on the basis of price, just as in other competitive enterprises. The AFT in trying to build a market presence among school support workers will frequently charge nominal to no dues

Warren, Arkansas local 100 Labor Day Picnic Setup.

Chapter IV: Dues and Don'ts: Lessons and Learning from Unions

until it charters a chapter at a certain membership threshold (say 200 members), and then gradually move dues up to their normal levels. Such a strategy is very smart marketing, and draws its inspiration right from Madison Avenue. One increases price at the point that one has built brand loyalty. Sometimes that works as a business plan and sometimes it does not, but at least it is a plan. Assessing dues rates without any notion of the market and its likely, if not predictable, response is the most common organizing strategy for unions. Assuming pricing is irrelevant is one of the most quaint and archaic aspects of the labor movement.

Of course there are always situations where it could be worse. Currently (2015) ACORN International's street vendors union based in the south India cities of Chennai, Hyderabad, and Bengaluru has 35,000 members. Since most unions in India are partnered directly with political parties some of our sister unions trying to also organize street vendors charge no dues whatsoever, believing that the base itself is sufficient for them, for the day that votes are counted in an election. The dues rate is set by the level of competition.

Unions try to artificially limit competition within the AFL-CIO by imposing conditions on the market. Under Article XX one AFL-CIO union cannot "raid" the members of another AFL-CIO union. Out in the hard scrabble organizing vineyards, this is almost impossible to really enforce and is honored in the breach by one and all. Nonetheless, independent unions – and there are a host of them, particularly in the public sector – compete without any such restrictions and therefore can do so solely on price. Because they are independent, and often local, they do not have the burden of paying per capita to other bodies, therefore not only can they offer equivalent representation at a lower price, they can even make that financial model work better, because they can retain more of the income. In Texas there are literally a dozen organizations that represent school workers throughout the state on this basis, and sometimes in the larger districts like Houston or San Antonio or Dallas there may be that many and more in a giant district like the Houston Independent School District alone.

Local 100, healthcare rally.

One wonders in a dues and membership based organization why the organization does not do everything possible to maximize membership and whether or not that program would also maximize dues? This is a threshold problem for a membership-based system, where there is a level of choice, particularly in right-to-work areas. If minimum dues for a local union were $20 for each member, the question would be whether or not one might be able to enroll four members for each one if the minimum dues were $5 per month instead of $20 per month? The equally important second question would be whether or not one could *retain* the member longer with a lower dues rate, rather than a higher one? In these situations – different to some degree than in community organizing – there is less of an engineering problem. On a worksite or within a group of workers, one is going to end up talking to everyone over some time frame, so everyone will have the opportunity to make a decision about joining – or quitting. The engineering problem in community organizing that created a structural ceiling, as we discussed earlier, is the access to the potential member, which often would be determined by the physical number of doors that could be hit during a time period and the number of residents that would be home. Eventually one would reach maximum saturation, but it would be over a longer time period, so there was no simple math that allowed one to calculate the differences in membership that were cost sensitive as clearly.

There are no firm or scientific tests with sufficient variables to allow one to unequivocally answer this question with finality, so one is forced to deal with a certain amount of inescapable bias and assumption. Logically, most of us would reason that a penny on a dollar is not going to be missed as much as 2 or 3 pennies on a dollar. When dues starts to hit 2% of every gross dollar, there are huge economic pressures that are attendant. In bargaining and representation situations that are wage driven, particularly when bargaining is dominated by concession demands or low inflation levels, it is simply not that easy to get increases in the contract that are significantly over 2% per year, especially in the current periods of low inflation. Any member – and certainly their union representative – can start to figure out, particularly on first contracts where this pressure is most acute (and the rate of failure also the highest partly for this reason), that the size of the increase has to dwarf the level of the dues burden. Politically 2%, and certainly 3%, just feels like it represents something of a sound barrier for leadership and an increase in membership accountability. Once the union is asking to take that much of the gross pay of a member, the results have to warrant the payment more strenuously.

Surprisingly, unions do not keep good statistics of the number of members lost by locals in right-to-work situations based on dues increases even though this is obviously critical. The information therefore is anecdotal, and therefore suspect for all of the usual reasons. There was no question though in the 1990's that state employee unions in places like Georgia lost thousands of members when dues minimums were increased. Unions of nursing home workers in south Florida experienced similar problems converting dues systems from an organizing program to a more mature servicing model. Moving minimums and percentages up within Local 100 cost us more than 1000 members,

ACORN Street Vendors Union convenes in marketplace in Bengaluru, India.

moving us from the mid-6000 range to closer to 5000 on the transition.[49] Part of the reason that national unions do not track such figures is because they monitor those things that are *revenue neutral, like their own per capita income from the locals, and not the numbers that move under the total dollars.* Overall per capita increases for national unions are simply good news, even if they mask devastating losses of members in the colonial backwaters of the national unions in the south and right-to-work geographies.

On a business model, one can say, one still has the same approximate level of income even after the loss of roughly 20% of the local's membership, and with fewer members theoretically the servicing costs would also be reduced, so financially perhaps no real harm was done. Problem is, as we know, unions operate on a connected economic and political model, so the loss of members is noticed both in the larger community around market share or union density and by the individual employers, especially in right-to-work environments, who reason that the union with less members is therefore weaker. It is harder to maintain the same economic threat represented by the price of the workers' exit through strikes or whatever on a particular employer, when the employer is able to clearly calculate reduced strength in the union through diminished membership numbers.

On a national basis the annual obsession – and depression – that accompanies the release of union density figures by the DOL and the Bureau of National Affairs is the barometer for the health – or sickness – of the labor movement. Temperature rising is indicated when at least absolute numbers go up, even when the percentage of unionization falls. When both fall, the storm clouds are coming and on us!

National unions do know something about it though in their own internal reckoning of the number of members who are dues payers versus agency fee payers. Between 15 and 20% of total membership come from fee payers. In some unions this figure moves closer

---

[49] Certainly one could argue that there were other salient factors in such precipitous declines (resources, staffing, opposition, circumstance), but the coincidences seem overwhelming when a triggering event is so easy to determine.

to a quarter of the total membership.[50] Some local unions make the financial decision that it is not worth the money to enroll the members and cheaper to simply assign the fees and run the locals on the other side of the statistics with only 20-25% actual members and the vast majority fee payers. In essence these are "discount" members. Unions still in most cases pay per capita to affiliate and parent bodies – including the AFL-CIO – so the total membership figures everywhere also reflect non-member fee payers – with the numbers consolidating members and non-members. Inevitably though the final affect is to reduce the strength and power of the union, because the relationship between the union and its members has been altered, usually permanently.

Assumptions, presumptions, and bias – and of course talking to workers – indicates that with a minimum dues level, seen as non-consequential, and a percentage system, seen as equitable without being exorbitant in the market, like our earlier example of a $5 minimum and a 1% gross dues amount per month, one might eliminate most of the workers who decide not to join because of the influence of financial factors, so that instead the union could concentrate on educating and agitating workers who have some antipathy to the union to move across the line and come on in. A lower dues rate also influences the requirements for organizer cost and skill as well as the comfort levels of members and stewards acting as the central recruitment arm for new members in the workplaces. The higher the dues level the more likely the interchange is not about information, but about persuasion. The greater the level of persuasion, the higher the level of skill necessary, therefore the increased likelihood of investment in skilled labor, meaning organizers – and better organizers at that – than in volunteer labor, meaning members, stewards, and local leaders.

Does it matter? You bet. Local 100 had roughly 1000 members in the Houston Independent School District. There are a dozen other organizations with check-off among support workers. There are more than 10000 workers in the available pool. Competing on the level of the highest dues rate means that even though we are growing annually, it required three (3) full-time organizers constantly working with this unit to maintain the existing membership and recruit new members. With the same expenditure of resources and a dues system that was more accessible, it is not far fetched to believe that we could have three or four times the number of members. In a right-to-work non-collective bargaining environment the level of power an organization has with the employer with 1000 members is substantial, but with 2000, 3000, 4000 or more, because of what it states clearly about the significance of the organization and its relationship with the workforce, the level of management attention and concession on issues and interests dramatically changes. Furthermore, the local income changes. The main barrier to lower income workers is eliminated, when the barrier is the minimum dues amount. A percent stays a percent in any system. More members at the ratio of twice to four times existing

---

[50] I may be simply projecting figures that I knew well when I was on the International Executive Board of SEIU, but conversations with many other organizers in many other unions leads me to believe that these general figures are reasonably accurate, if not conservative. With the more aggressive imposition of right-to-work in the Midwestern states in the years between 2010 and 2015, and the ruinous impact of the *Harris v. Quinn* decision, the numbers may have fallen along with the general membership of unions like SEIU, NEA, AFSCME, and others with significant numbers of public sector members.

Chapter IV: Dues and Don'ts: Lessons and Learning from Unions

membership even with lowered rates still ends up producing more income to the local, if other factors were equalized, like national and affiliated per capita. Along it does not convert into more income for the national or other affiliated bodies.

Union density is a tremendous issue and an important achievement in the world in which we operate politically and economically. Somehow, perhaps inadvertently, we have allowed our internal politics and economics trump our external political and economic agenda. We desperately need to create a majoritarian movement. There are certainly ideological and religious reasons why some workers will never (or rarely) join local unions and so be it, but within some level of pricing – coupled of course with actual organizing and really winning – virtually every worker would join existing unions where they work.

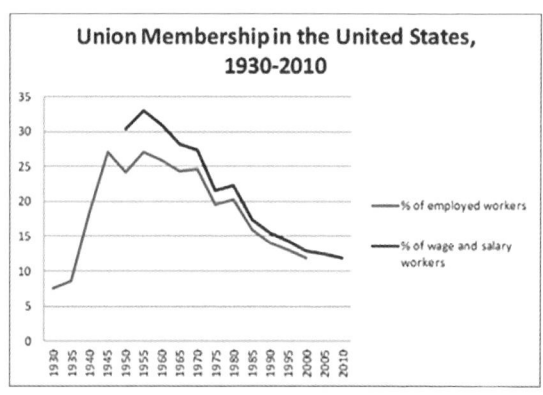

Union Density 1. Union membership in US 1930-2010.

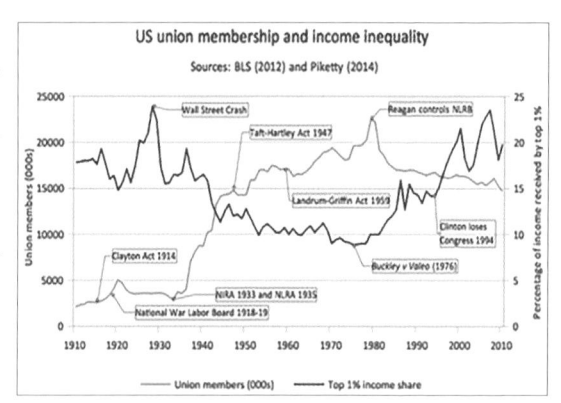

Union Density 2. United States union membership and inequality, top 1% income share, 1910 to 2010.

Unionization migrates from necessity to luxury item for the decision makers who value the cost of organizing more than the millions of workers and the bargaining agreements in right-to-work environments. For example all federal workers covered by collective bargaining – regardless of the state where they are employed – are working under "open shop" agreements, where membership numbers typically top out at 30% of the size of the unit. This is a condition of the Federal Labor Relations Act, flowing from the original order. Many state public employees are also in open shop situations, and of course in the private sector the examples are legion, particularly in the south where job growth is leading the nation. The employers know the strength of their unions because they are administering the dues remittance and distribution system to the union: total transparency – no secrets there. The public also knows the size, and therefore putative strength of labor as an available calculation in the open forum of information. Converting these numbers into political power means moving members, not non-members, even though they are co-workers in the same soup. Somehow our economics have moved us to

76 Nuts & Bolts – *The ACORN Fundamentals of Organizing*

the place where we are polarizing the shop floor, so to speak, between who is in the union and who is not in the union, based on their membership decision, rather than polarizing the greater community of workers based on who is covered by a union and who is not, or the greater political community and the public on the issue of who is with the union and who is against working families. Something is very wrong with that. We have become trapped in a strategic box through a combination of tradition and bad habits without even realizing we are so shuttered in the box that we cannot see the light clearly enough to out again.

The labor movement needs to recalibrate the economics of building a majority. We need to lower the financial barriers to the level that we can first capture 90% or better of the workers in the bargaining units we already have under contracts and the places where we already have a union. Our organizing and economic models have to finally align themselves, rather than allowing the local union – small business system defeat all other efforts for unions to expand and grow. Removing as much as practicable the economic barriers to membership would recreate the community of workers solidarity in the workplace, and therefore allow unions to once again operate and speak for *all* workers, rather than just members.

Would this be financial suicide? Hardly, and here are my arguments. Though let me add as well that the labor movement in the United States (and some other countries) seems destined for suicide anyway, so why not die fighting, which is to say organizing, with our boots on?

Where unions do not labor under right-to-work laws, they do not need to take the risks at all, as one of my sisters from San Jose, California once said to me, "we're running unions in heaven, what is it like in the rest of the world?" They do not need to find out. On the other hand even in heaven unions would be wise to look at the concept of *organizing dues* which lowered the barriers to increased union growth by not arbitrarily equating the dues of new and embryonic units with mature bargaining units. So in those states at the worst case, it is a wash – and that's where the largest bulk of the union resource originates anyway.

Secondly, people will voluntarily pay more than their mandatory assessment for various reasons: good will, ideological conviction, and particular engagement with specific programs.[51] Most vividly, unions see this in the area of federal political contributions, which are voluntary as a matter of law. Routinely, no less than 25-30% of members will agree to political or COPE donations simply because they are asked and believe politics is connected to their economic security increasingly – and correctly – as an article of faith. Allowing the dues threshold to be lowered does not automatically mean that the total dues collected would decrease, if a union can effectively package and communicate its programs, members would as likely be open handed in support of paying additional sums for necessary and popular programs, just as they do for political work, if not more so, and, importantly, there would be a larger pool of participants in making these additional, though voluntary, payments, because the size of the total membership pool would dramatically expand as well. A salutary indirect benefit of restructuring union economics

---

[51] This is not to be confused with mandatory assessments already discussed.

Local 100 Houston Cafeteria workers.

would also be the increase of effective democratic participation within unions that would now provide economic rewards in terms of increased dues revenue to union leadership that are able and willing to bring programs to their membership, debate the merits, win support, and enlist their participation in securing maximum feasible financial investment in the collective enterprise. A measure of specific and real financial accountability on both the front and back end of the program is achieved, which is overwhelmingly not the case today.

There are numerous – and well publicized – examples, though of course they are anecdotal given how little work is done in really understanding mass organizations. Offering another example from the Service Employees, local leaders in unions where membership votes were required on the increases mandated by convention for the New Strength Unity Program. It was found in case after case that the members responded overwhelmingly. Many leaders reported that they could have gotten even greater financial commitments from members given the enthusiasm for the program and the fact that members were being allowed to participate in the decision. Local unions involved in difficult, and extensively reported, battles with employers in meatpacking in Austin, Minnesota and food processing in Decatur, Illinois self-assessed themselves huge amounts to build funds to maintain contracts and engage in survival efforts that ran to $50 per month per member and even more in struggles in the later part of the 20th century.

Strategically, a local union could attempt to merely realign dues programs to achieve revenue neutrality in these right-to-work conditions. Lowering minimums or eliminating them, lowering percentages to 1%, and other similar programs would allow one to calculate at various levels of density in the workplace what economic impact could be predicted. Then packaging programs to access voluntary membership support for politics, organizing, bargaining, health and safety or whatever, at varying levels of participation would allow one to look at overall budgeting.

I would then argue that asking existing members *if* they supported the alteration of the dues program would very likely agree to maintain their existing dues levels *in order* to lower the dues rates to achieve higher density in their workplaces, which would in fact mean that the local union did not experience any decrease in income, but implemented this program to increase income. Think I am wrong? Maybe, but some organization would have to do me the favor of trying it, and *proving* me wrong. I'll bet on the members and on workers and win or lose the bet that way. I think my money is safe.

I do not want to gild the lily by repeating the argument yet again about how much more powerful any mass organization would be, if it were larger, rather than smaller. This seems so simple that its reiteration borders on an insult, despite the fact that we are missing this forest for the trees on a routine basis. Employers and politicians – and our own members – care primarily about how big, and therefore, how strong, we are and that's based on our ability to move larger numbers both positively to promote our interests and negatively to protect our interests. None of them – including really our members[52] – care about our internal economics and whether or not we are balancing our books! The real point is that in order to build mass organizations, particularly mass-membership organizations, we have to focus on the real objective – building a mass membership, not money maximization!

This chapter may have focused on unions, but it serves as a case study for identical issues confronting other mass-based organizations and community organizations. The same challenges and decisions face all organizations.

Money matters but in too many cases the money is driving the program around membership, rather than the base understanding of power and politics which is essential. Everything is built on these blocks whether it is power in the community or at the ballot box or at the workplace. If we are building irrational obstacles to the relationships between members and their unions based on inflexible economics, then it is past time for a change. We need to get about it.

---

[52] Certainly this is not true in all cases, and this is not an argument for financial mischief or unaccountability – we have laws for that anyway – but it is an argument that mass membership organizations need to be just that and need to be willing to build a social movement, not a social club.

Chapter V: **Organizers, Staff, and the Allied Trades**

The members are everything. They drive the truck and determine the direction, but a mass based organization has to have staff – organizers – working as the mechanics, building the engine, holding the map, getting the gas, and a million other tasks. I am certain this is true, but for many this is something of an uncomfortable reality – an elephant not discussed, but standing in the middle of the room.

The existence of organizers is also a lightning rod for much of what attracts the controversy from opposing forces. Everyone from mayors and council people, farmers and factory bosses, and many in between redden in the face and stammer in their speech on the issue of organizers. These are "outside agitators," "troublemakers," and clearly people who do "not have the best interest of the community at heart." Add in some of the history of the last several generations and of course that's additional seasoning in the gumbo, since organizers – by definition, I assume – are communists, and not just commies, but "red to the core," or they are too often "uppity," as in uppity women or uppity blacks, or speaking of the issue of race – too often we had organizers who might have been white while working in black neighborhoods or vice versa, and of course too often they were young, so all this makes for a highly combustible, devil's brew. Maybe? Everything matters. Many of these questions are for outsiders. The real question for insiders is whether or not they can do the job and the job gets done.

Then throw in a bit of spice from the mass culture, *Norma Rae* or *Matwan*, maybe think about Merly Streep in *Silkwood* or Jack Nicholson in *F.I.S.T.*, a picture of Huey Newton and the gang in black jackets and guns, a poster of Malcolm speaking, King dying, and the occasional fresh faced youngster with a tattered copy of *Rules for Radicals* or *Reveille for Radicals* by Alinsky, and it's not too difficult to whip up a little local, downscale version of mass hysteria in town or a workplace over the mere idea of organizers. It's Hollywood, and it is hell. It's a magnet for the passionate and the misbegotten, just as it is repulsive to the status quo and the powers that be.

Part of what we have is a process of evolutionary bureaucratization of mass organization, and since we are locked in a particular warp of time in the maturation of such organizations, there are many rough edges dragging and edges that will require a lot of hard sanding before they smooth out. For me it is always helpful to look at the history of other organizations to try and plot the points on the road we are currently traveling. Much of this history involves the internal transition from movement roots to organizational branches.

A warning: no matter the history, wherever there is an organization of any kind, one will find **someone** performing the role of "organizer," whether they are self-identified as such, paid or volunteer, or seen that way by others, inside or outside of the organization, so put the rose colored glasses aside and the myth making machine on idle – we're taking a trip, but it won't be Hollywood when we get there. In the populist movement of the Farmers' Alliance the organizers moving through Texas, Arkansas, Oklahoma, and neighborhood states were called "travelers." Arthur C. Townley built the Non-Partisan League in the Dakotas on what he referred to as "five dollars and a Ford," referring to the membership dues and the vehicle that revolutionized the way Townley and his organizers were able to spread the organization county to county in the Great Plains. In the Bible they were called "disciples" and more recently they have been bundled up somewhere between preachers and missionaries.

In these foundational periods the organizers were largely "members," taking on part or full-time duties to build the organization because of their conviction, skill, or simple availability to undertake the tasks at hand. If they were paid, it was damned little, if anything at all, expenses and a farmhouse meal with the family. They were in fact those "fish in the sea of the people" that we were talking about earlier.

The same was true in the labor movement. Workers were organizing other workers in a cooperative enterprise of mutual help and assistance. As the labor movement gained structure and consolidated as local unions, dues income and democratic process combined to begin to create "staff" from these small volunteer collectives. As local union leaders and stewards were elected, the dues income began to allow enough that some compensation could finally be paid, particularly in the late days of the 19th century and the early years of the 20th century, so that officers could gradually lay down their tools to do union business on a part-time basis, and as the organization grew the level of administrative, bargaining, representational work, and, even organizing, led to some officers of larger local unions working full-time for the union during their terms of office.

Part of this, particularly in the trades, became critical because the job of these union officers was in fact organizing employers, if you will, to hire their members and give them sufficient work to make their daily living. These "business managers" or "business agents" were primarily devoted to the task of securing work and their continuing in the position rose and fell with their ability to keep their members employed in their crafts. These were not really organizers in ways that we would understand today, because "organizing" flowed from the employers – if there was enough work, everyone was happy; if there was more work than the members could handle, then the shortage created demand, which led to wage increases; if there was more work than the members could handle, then recruitment of new members into the apprenticeship program or enlisting non-union members into the union was finally important to prevent the work from finding a non-union market. As this kind of "paid staff" position moved over to fixed workplaces on construction sites and shop floors, these "walking delegates," or "labor skates," or "pie-cards," depending on the eye of the beholder, became a source of tension between the real need for people to enforce the contracts and protect the work competing with the natural pressure of working members enforcing accountability on brother members who were a half-step removed from the manual labor of the job and whose cleaner hands came from the dues paid from their labor.

In the 1920's labor bureaucratization began to also consolidate at the level of the national union as more locals combined to attempt to keep up with the growth and structural patterns in industry. Union officers whether Terrence Powderly of the Knights of Labor, Big Bill Haywood of the Western Federation of Miners, or a Samuel Gompers

Chapter V: Organizers, Staff, and the Allied Trades

of the Cigarmakers or the local officers becoming national leaders in new unions in the trades or other affiliates of the American Federation of Labor were expected to do the work and in turn expected to be paid for the work they did to administer and build the union. Perhaps a larger union paid a couple of officers and added a secretary or more, but gradually in steps both small and large, the growth of the union and its dues base created the expectation for increased services, just as the newly minted union staff created the demand for exactly those services, and more. In other social movements there might be "speakers" or "lecturers," who made their money here and there, who were the "activists" of those days and organizers in our terms. It is easy to understand how it starts, but no one can be quite sure where it will end.

Nonetheless the issues involving pay and volunteerism are critical, and perhaps as essential, because theses issue define the conflict between simply being paid, and being "professional." These are all matters fraught with weighty ideological and cultural baggage that have huge practical consequence and therefore cast shadows from the past far into the future.

In community organizations, especially a mass-based, membership organization like ACORN, the bright line test between staff and leaders is drawn around pay, as well as responsibilities. The constitution and bylaws of the organization clearly states that one cannot be a leader or member of the organization and also be paid. Some unions operate on similar lines in barring union staff from being dues paying members of the organization, even though in most unions key leaders are in fact paid. In such cases these organizations are more clearly demarcating the political life of the organization, just as ACORN does, by establishing two separate organizational tracks and therefore rigidly segregating the staff structure from the membership's democratic process and leadership selection procedures. Other unions, perhaps most of them, blur these lines deliberately

Big Bill Haywood.

in order to not only allow, but encourage, staff to dominate the political life of the membership. This is equally true for ideologically left organizations like 1199 both from its days as an independent union and now to its life as part of either AFSCME or SEIU, as it can be for ideologically right organizations.

The primary cultural tradition in classic trade unions not surprisingly creates a weighted advantage for staff having come "off the tools" of the trade to work for the union. Privileging such experience puts the premium of course on the "representative" function of union staff, rather than the organizing function, since the expectation and presumption is that the shared identity and understanding of the work will allow the union employee to better represent the interests and needs of the members, having been part of the collective experience and struggle. Certainly, there are many experienced and skilled tradesmen and women who also turn out to be talented and gifted organizers, but there is certainly nothing inherent in any craft that would allow one to predict that that would be the case, and often it is, spectacularly in fact, not the case. Part of this is about class of course, and if one cannot appropriately find class-consciousness in a union, then where in the world can you find it![53] And, class without question is critical. The homogenization of unions which deteriorates their ability to truly act as pillars of working class culture and the foundation of class institutions is an ongoing, contemporary tragedy, bankrupting our potential, our future, and our critical content. A caricature is not the same as a symbol.

This is not a narrow tradition limited to the building trades, but extends more broadly even to more general worker unions like the Teamsters, where even as the drivers portion of their membership plummets, the cache of having been behind the wheel, especially of an over-the-road vehicle is enormous.[54] In an industrial model union like the Mineworkers, one may have been a skilled lawyer, like Richard Trumka, but one has no political life in the union without some time underground in the mines. Even some of the dominant Congress of Industrial Organizations (CIO) industrial unions, like the UAW and the Steel Workers, both of which could have created different traditions, and perhaps should have, since their key organizing staff were certainly in many cases not auto workers or steelworkers, evolved cultural and political traditions which created virtual requirements that staff, particularly staff with any kind of future, had to come out of the shops.

Part of the impetus for this kind of CIO reverse class elitism came as a direct countervailing measure to John Lewis' reputation for a willingness – and need – to use any organizers he could find to build the CIO, when it had to be built.[55] Communists,

---

[53] A sad note in a university based study in the 1990's about "bargaining success" for unions, or in other words the likelihood of successfully winning a contract and continuing to do so, found through an exhaustively comprehensive survey that the likelihood of success was significantly increased by the degree that the employer representative was able to "identify" with the union representative at the bargaining table. Which is to say that the more "middle-class" or "professional" identified the union representative was, the more likely that he or she is able to in fact secure a contract for the workers from the employer, as opposed to the more clearly identified son or daughter of the working class. This brings the concept of class collaboration to a very fine point indeed.

[54] Unless one enjoys some offsetting compensation, like the last name of Hoffa, or something.

[55] Confirmed pretty clearly in Saul Alinsky's semi-approved biography of Lewis, *John Lewis: An Unauthorized Biography (1949)*.

socialists, and leftists of all stripes as well as motivated college students and others came with commitments, discipline, and a willingness to go anywhere and do anything to build the labor movement. Lewis was starting a war, so he needed troops that could move into battle. Organizers had a value, which they had not had earlier, and would not again have for quite a long time. Nonetheless, when the cultural traditions of the unions matured in the freezer of the cold war climate, unions retreated back to the more reliable class-and-trades basis as a priority for paid staff coming out of the shops, and did so more rigidly than some of the craft unions in some cases, rather than simply double tracking the political and staff sides of the organizations, so they could more effectively continue to cross fertilize the organizational development. This is largely true to this day within auto and steel unions – which is not to say that one cannot get a job there without an auto or steel background, just that there's a limited future in it. With less jobs available that will become less true. John Sweeney first with the Service Employees, and later with the AFL-CIO, was as willing, as Lewis was, to recruit anyone because he was first trying to build a base, and willing to do whatever it took with whomever would take him there to do so. Then later with the AFL-CIO he was facing a crisis and needed any help he could get in trying to mobilize an army to organize enough workers to salvage what was left of institutional labor.

Not that this is not done self-consciously. Sweeney's Service Employees in the mid-1980's had considerably less than a score of headquarters and international union staff that had ever worked in local unions (much less came from local union membership) out of just less than 200 staff at the time, and since this included the union's officers, it was a sensitive matter in the internal culture of the organization, regardless of the expediency that produced such a staffing pattern. Within a union dominated by lower waged workers, women workers, immigrant workers, and therefore not statistically likely to be in the new middle class that is often synonymous with the old working class, the internal political culture can easily devolve to the ridiculously, if not racist, lowest common denominator of the symbolic by simply trying to "color code" or ethnically brand the leadership appointments of staff to be anointed as leaders of the locals, rather than expecting to see the rise and development of genuine indigenous leadership. This would be an area where class-consciousness could be a welcome relief. A more bizarre identity crisis was the effort some years ago by a former Secretary-Treasurer of the Hotel Employees Restaurant Employees, Vincent Sirabella, widely reported in the *New York Times* and elsewhere to recruit from the Ivy League to build their union, partially to "re-brand" the union since it represented Yale workers and wanted to be seen as something other than the low waged, women and immigrant workers' union that it was.[56]

Service worker unions like the United Food & Commercial Workers (UFCW), Service Employees, HERE, AFSCME, AFGE, and of course the teachers unions have difficult class and craft identities, which foment these kinds of internal culture wars. Within such unions, one can have a mixed bag of public and private sector employees ranging from the

---

[56] This was also good public relations since it put some distance from the constant mob related rumors that haunted the President of that union, Ed Hanley, for years until his retirement and death, and led to the federal supervision of the union for almost as many years as the Teamsters.

lowest paid janitors or or dishwashers or nurses' aides to doctors, registered nurses, and social workers, teachers with a collection of degrees, licenses, and certifications. Class is shifting sand in such unions, though it can produce wild schizophrenia internally. Face it, anyone anywhere who has worked for a living can move through numerous service sector jobs without being class bound. From 13 to 20, I personally worked as a groundskeeper, busboy, oil field roustabout in Oklahoma and in the Gulf of Mexico, office clerk, janitorial floor-waxer, bookstore clerk, shift working coffee company shipping clerk and lift-truck driver, laundry truck driver, and microfilm print dryer, but that did not mean that I was not a full-time student the vast majority of that time. It just meant that we weren't rich or raised that way, and had to work to make it all come together.

Service worker unions could accommodate wide ranges of experience and in some cases utilize the skills of people. It's not surprising that a John Sweeney never worked the tools, but was always local union staff and moved up the union bureaucracy career ladder, nor is it surprising that some of the brightest and most forward looking labor leaders in the 20th century were HERE's John Wilhelm, a Yale graduate, SEIU's Andy Stern, a University of Pennsylvania graduate, and Bruce Raynor from UNITE-HERE and Cornell were also products of the internal union bureaucracies that nurtured them and allowed them to rise to power. But, what will this all mean to the future of these institutions as class based organizations of working people and has it already produced internal cultural tensions that cannot be resolved? All the results are not yet in, but the legacy issues of the Ivy Leaguers of labor have been mixed.

For the most part in the labor movement organizers did the grunt work for one hundred years, and generally that's true across the board. Organizers are not on a career ladder moving up, they are in a skilled trade honing their craft year by year. At least if they can hang on, that is. Since organizers sometimes came willy-nilly from here and there as opposed to the normal tracks that determined the internal life of the local, only the few who could make the viral leap over to the leadership track could move forward, unless in fact they were not "organizers" per se, but simply had the title of organizers as one of the appointed jobs they grabbed as they moved off the tools and trade within their jurisdiction. It is only in the current desperate straits of foundering institutional labor that one sees organizers coming out of the cold to actually run and lead unions at both the local and national/international level, because organizing in some places has gradually started to become a first priority to survival.[57]

Certainly not everywhere, and this is one of the great ironies of the early 21st century American labor movement. A lot more people are still counting the chairs on the deck of the *Titanic* than are getting the ropes and the lifeboats into the water. The much vaunted programs of both the AFL-CIO Organizing Institute and the touted success of the AFL-CIO's Union Summer programs are good examples of this paradox.

The Organizing Institute was created under AFL-CIO President Lane Kirkland and was one of the few heartbeats of life in his reign. The model, especially in its heyday,

---

[57] Once again Andy Stern (SEIU), John Wilhelm (HERE), Bruce Raynor (UNITE), and Larry Cohen (CWA) were all former organizing directors running or near the top of their respective unions. Even the UAW elected Bob King as Vice President for Organizing and then President in a major reform. There's movement here, though for Stern, Wilhelm, and Raynor there was a residue of mess as well, so who knows....

evolved into a straight forward system. The OI recruited from the general population, rather than just the rank-and-file, and the real recruitment was heavily weighted to *certain* college campuses, which OI recruiters crawled over like ants. The recruit who made first muster would go to a so-called "3-day" where a combination of OI staff and cooperating union staff would put a bunch of recruits together in different cities and run them through the basics, mostly light lifting, but providing a close opportunity to evaluate the crop and determine which prospects were eligible to proceed to door number two. The "three-days" though would have a mix of participants who were either "sponsored," which means that a local or international union had recruited them already and would pick them up going to the next round, but wanted them either to have the 3-day experience or was looking for the OI staff to give them a second look and evaluation. The unsponsored were "free agents" on tryout essentially. A participating union helping out would be doing so in order to have the first crack at picking up a promising free agent and then drafting her into their organizing program, or if the OI's own staff evaluated a free agent highly they would try to place her with a cooperating team – I mean union – for the next round. Football aficionados will recognize this dilemma quickly, but for the rest of the world, it was most people's high school movie on slow rewind, where the free agent is waiting at home for months for a phone call to join a campaign, which may never come. Recruits selected into the second round were placed in a 10-14 day campaign. This evolved over the life of the OI, but essentially this was a closer look in actual organizing field conditions in some union's real campaign. Survivors went to the third and final OI round – the apprenticeship. Once again sponsored recruits had the "pass go" card and other promising free agents hit the bench and hoped to be picked up. The apprenticeship involved actually organizing under the supervision of a host union with the presumptive guarantee at the end of that rainbow that one would then go to work as an organizer with the original sponsoring organization. Remember as well that all of this is highly Darwinian with folks falling off the curb and into the streets along the way regularly throughout the process.[58]

Why didn't this program have the effect of dramatically increasing the number of organizers in the labor movement?

First, there were not that many cooperating unions for all the sound and fury accompanying this program for exactly the reasons we have discussed extensively all ready. Publicly this may have seemed a popular program, but internally within the AFL-CIO, it's a whole other story. The "organizing unions" were the sponsoring institutions – SEIU, UNITE, HERE, AFSCME and LIUNA were at the core – and occasionally other unions tried their hand with the program like UAW or USW or whomever. The low roar of criticism for the Organizing Institute came from the vast majority of unions who were not utilizing the program at all, but were obviously participating in its financing as part of the federation's dues base. In essence these unions were arguing that they were subsidizing the internal organizer recruitment program for a handful of their co-unionists.

---

[58] A similar union program evolved early in the 21st century with similar results in the United Kingdom according to *Union Voices: Tactics and Tension in UK* by Jane Holgate, Edmund Heery, and Hilary Simms (2013).

Secondly, this is the equivalent of an "Ivy League" education for a few organizers, because it was a very, very expensive program. Once an organizer-trainee hit the field on the 2nd and 3rd rounds of the training, the sponsoring union was committed to paying a lot of freight, which included the trainee's salary, while putting rent-a-car wheels under them and a hotel roof over them for every day they were in the program. For a long time the OI required the 10-day campaigns involve a complement of ten or more organizers in that part of the program. The math is easy to do, and before you sober up, you find that you have spent $25-30,000 for an operation that threw "green as grass" folks at a campaign in a matter of less than two weeks, and that does not count a dime put into the cost of supervision, since the host union was absorbing that cost on the cuff, and the OI and sometimes an International was also putting supervisors in to help do the training and run the crew, which is also costing real money even if it shows up on some other budget line somewhere else. In the vicious cycle where one needs organizers to drive campaigns, and one then needs campaigns to train and develop organizers, the decisions to spend these resources were not trivial, which tended to drive the training not necessarily to the "best" campaigns, but to the campaigns that were best resourced and could carry this weight. This was not necessarily good training, but more another question of practical engineering, where one needed the input of a certain number of live bodies moving on the grid to get a piece of work done.

Similarly, Union Summer had been a public relations celebration for the AFL-CIO and its gradual demise was backstory to the press release of its existence. Union Summer

AFL-CIO Organizing Institute Trainees in Action.

Chapter V: Organizers, Staff, and the Allied Trades

was roughly a three-week sleepover camp for largely college kids and the random rank-and-file worker's kid or union official's child that slipped through the cracks into the program. If working for a union is the major leagues for union organizers, the OI was the minor leagues while working one's way into the big show, then Union Summer was strictly sandlot. This is not to say that no one has made it from Union Summer through the process and into an organizing position, but it is to say that that was still not common. Union Summer was also very expensive for everyone involved. The *summeristas* would get a stipend of $200 per week paid by the AFL-CIO, and the AFL-CIO would provide a site coordinator, while the local or international union or central body would have to provide the local housing and transportation, and integrate them into real work.

In my brief college career I had the opportunity to study closely with Robert Gaudino, a political science professor at Williams College, who had studied the impact of the early years of the Peace Corps program in several countries during the 1960's. He concluded that the program had little or no positive impact on the host countries – in the main the Peace Corps Volunteers did not have the skills or wherewithal to accomplish the goals and objectives to affect the countries in the ways hoped – but he found that the program was a great *experience* for the young people who had served in the Peace Corps.[59] This insight has traveled with me many miles, and I would posit that it probably is echoed again for Union Summer participants. Union Summer in short was not really organizer training, development, or identification program, but was "union summer camp" – an opportunity for a certain number, declining rapidly to the vanishing point now, of young people to have a good experience with a union that might add up to something sometime in the future.

For those of us who believe we need more, rather than fewer, organizers none of that was bad. We have to wade out in the stream and sluice a lot of rock to find gold. As vital as organizers are and as critical a resource, there just are not that many of them. Best guesses at the broadest numbers are just that, guesses. It would be surprising to find more than 1000 constituency based community organizers, and the number is likely far lower, since ACORN by that count would have 20-25% of the total and its diminished role in the USA would invariably lower the count. All of institutional labor might not have but another 1000 organizers. Marshall Ganz, who served as Caesar Chavez's chief organizer in the heroic era of the United Farm Workers Union, later in life ended up as an academic, looked deeply at this issue. One of the things he tried to research exhaustively was the level of staff capacity of unions just in California, though given the size of the labor movement that would be a big "just." He found that with the hundreds of millions of dollars' worth of dues collected that there were about 2500 staff working for California unions at every level, but that the total number of actual union organizers in the whole state was hardly one-hundred. Ganz looked in the mid-1980s. There may or may not be more now. SEIU because of the great expansion of its program could count about 200-225

---

[59] Robert Gaudino, *The Uncomfortable Learning: Some Americans in India* (1974)

Wade at Year End / Year Beginning to back. Dewey Armstrong Standing. John Beam looking and Others.

by the early years of the 21st century, but this could easily have been 20-25% of the total capacity of institutional labor.[60]

Obviously this does not count everyone in the allied trades. Unions have large staffs of representatives, researchers, communications and publications people, educators, health & safety people, lawyers, accountants, bookkeepers, secretaries, and clericals. Community organizations, like ACORN, have a lot of these same kinds of folks along with housing developers and housing loan counselors, web designers, and political campaigners (unions have these, too!). Both have a lot of other specialists on staff and on contract as consultants from experts and actuaries for pension funds to software designers and direct mail houses and expensive pollsters and telephone call centers, social media folks, and god knows what else. That listing does not pretend to accurately count the capacity of all of the progressive forces. I have certainly not mentioned street canvassers, and even as that program has declined in the last 10-15 years, there still are way more than 1000 canvassers plying their trade door-to-door in the course of a year.[61]

Nor am I counting the innumerable "activists." Not because I disparage them, though many organizers do, but virtually by definition this is a hard category to fix with a number, since it is self-defined and may mean on one level a very good member putting in significant hours of personal time building organizations or working on campaigns, or someone working part-time in some capacity so that they can finance their own activism, or whatever, including "lost-timers" who are compensated by large unions for

---

[60] In These Times in a story by David Moberg dated August 19, 2016 claimed there were 75 members of SEIU's Union of Union Representatives – the union's staff union for organizers.

[61] I better say here that I'm talking about full-time equivalents (FTE's), because many more thousands of actual warm-blooded folks will pass in and out of these jobs and be sent a W-2 statement by January 31st of the following year. Educated guess, seat of the pants, I would multiply everything by four to try and estimate the flowing river of people in and out of the work every year. In ACORN's case in the first decade of the 21st century we frequently filed 15-20000 W-2s *annually* throughout that period.

Chapter V: Organizers, Staff, and the Allied Trades

time they are losing from their job hours. Frequently, these are "campaigners" more than they are organizers in the way we are defining the terms, but certainly they are part of the progressive capacity and part of the larger catchment pool from which many organizers eventually migrate. Part of the reason that I am easy on the issue of activists is that I value the *political impulse* that drives many to become organizers, though many institutions are uncomfortable on these grounds, we certainly found them valuable in ACORN as well as in the unions we have built.

How do we sort all of this out? Not well unfortunately, and a lot of rough edges will be dragging.

Part of the problem is that I believe that *we need many, many thousands more organizers* than we have now, both in community organizations and in unions. The constituency targeted for organizing in the community and the workplace is enormous in the tens and tens of millions, and it needs to all happen yesterday. Communities are in cities and towns everywhere obviously, and so are the workplaces that demand organization. One needs an army of organizers to win this war!

This may seem obvious to me, and even to most people, but not everyone thinks this, and the reasons are complex. Part of the problem lies with the dilemma of "professionalism," and the wages that some would argue should follow closely behind such a classification. I have earlier spoken of organizing using the terminology of a trade and a craft. Some think of themselves as professionals and talk of being professional organizers and part of a self-certified group of professional organizers. Some of this is bound up in its own ideology, while some of it may just mask self-interest. The issues are important though, because it has a lot do with what either makes the work accessible or builds barriers to entry.

Historically the most vocal proponents of professionalism in community organizing have been adherents of the methodology and practice of the Industrial Areas Foundation (IAF), created by the legendary Saul Alinsky before his death. The IAF was designed, harmlessly enough to train and develop organizers. After Alinsky's death in the early 1970's, the IAF became the central source from which disciples of his tradition operated and were dispatched. The IAF is not an organization *per se*, but an institute or center, which administers contracts between itself and organizations in various cities. The nature of the contracts may vary, but they involve a certain commitment to send local leaders to training, a level of consultation, and a supply of organizers.[62] The IAF has gone through a number of permutations over the years since Alinsky's time, evolving from a methodology of building "an organization of organizations" of the powerless, low income, and minorities to Alinsky's own conversion to organizing the middle class before his death, and now under his disciples to focus on building institutionally based organizations concentrating on the church, particularly the Catholic church and doing so by building

---

[62] This story is impossible not to tell. For more than 30 years and counting I have been asked to describe the differences between the IAF and ACORN, but the best explanation I have ever heard was in 1976 in Houston, Texas, when a local ACORN leader named Ed Foote, was asked in a radio interview to explain the difference between ACORN and the IAF, both of which were getting started in Houston around that time. Ed thought about it and answered that he wasn't really sure, since he didn't know that much about the IAF, but he thought the main difference was "…that they seem to organize 'industrial areas,' and ACORN just organizes neighborhoods." Says it all.

"relationships" through "one-on-one" meetings with the organizer.

It is somewhat ironic that the IAF has become the bastion of a kind of professionalism for organizers, given Alinsky's own predilection for publicly evangelizing, anywhere and everywhere in the late 60's and early 70's that anyone could, and in fact, everyone should organize and become organizers. Exactly right, I would say, and I can personally remember going back to Williams when I was organizing for welfare rights in Springfield at that time, and standing in the back of the hall, when he spoke there. I can remember even better when Saul would come meet with the Massachusetts Welfare Rights staff whenever he happened to be speaking or visiting in Boston, when I worked there as head organizer. Saul was a tireless promoter of organizing and organizers as critical agents for social change and crisscrossed the country from campus to campus from venue to venue with an extremely entertaining presentation that issued the clarion call to organize. Personally, I believe that that public advocacy and the myth making embodied in his books, were his most effective contribution, and they certainly overshadow any "peoples' organization," as he used to call them, that he actually assisted in organizing.

Saul Alinsky.

Privately, Alinsky was anything but welcoming to the many hearing his call. He felt a real threat, partly I imagine because community organizing was in its infancy and trying to still get its sea legs under it, from movements and movement organizers, because they represented a counterpoint in style and speed when compared to the painstaking, institution and organization-based work that went into building a first "congress" to create an organization. God help you in those days, if you were also a young woman who caught the fire and wanted to organize. Saul was a product of his time and not able to see past it. He was routinely dismissive, and with charm and wit would tell them to come back when they were 40 after they had finished raising children. Nuns were the only women who they could tolerate, because they were unlikely to run away and get married or need to take breaks to have children. Unfortunately, too often this ended up being his legacy outside the IAF, and not his missionary work among so many that – luckily – helped drive more organizers into the work.

On another level it is precisely this contradiction that plays out around the professionalism polarity. Regardless of what might seem the obvious logic in my earlier argument that we need more organizers in every shape and size to undertake the work at hand, the IAF tried to develop a model that attempted to assert hegemony over organizing based on elite premises, and a central cornerstone was professionalism. They were like a craft union trying to limit the amount of work just enough to keep their members fully employed and well-compensated while developing a scarcity which kept the wage floor

Chapter V: Organizers, Staff, and the Allied Trades

sturdy. They were anti-ideological, but to a degree that created their own ideology. They were both apolitical and anti-political, because they feared the cauldron and confusion of movements that vied for community leadership with alternate agendas and interests in power, particularly in minority communities among African Americans in the 1960's where the Alinskyites were also organizing in Buffalo, Chicago, Rochester, Kansas City, and elsewhere in older industrialized cities. An Alinsky organizer was, supposedly, a pure technician, nothing more than a skilled social engineer, neither soft-hearted like social workers trapped in the settlement house organizing methodology of an earlier time nor soft-headed like the organizers building sweeping movements and mobilizations for change. The organizations were indeed about power, but somehow not about politics, perhaps an Achilles heel in this model, but one that flowed directly from Alinsky's own understanding that the Daley machine in the Chicago where he began his work, would not be easy competition if these neophyte, peoples' organizations tried to contend for political power in an electoral framework. Such an organizer, supposedly, just built the car, and then dutifully watched, moved, and got out of the way three years later, as the organizations leaders drove the car straight, left, or, not infrequently, right, down the road. This was the ideology of such professionalism.

Other organizations, particularly community organizations, were not "real" organizations building "real" leaders or "real" power or of course "permanent" organizations (whatever that might turn out to be), and certainly "real" organizers – men only – did not staff them. How could they? There were too many of them, and they were not paid enough, so by definition they were not professional organizers, and that's what was needed, or so it seemed, in the essential marketing message for the IAF.

Given the way they tended to recruit there was certain logic here. Alinsky and his cohorts liked flipping men who were dissatisfied with existing careers as salesmen, journalists, priests and preachers, lawyers and businessmen, social workers and academicians into a switcheroo to organizing. One had to purge the old ways, the old life, and the old career in a form of "ego-dump" in Alinsky training, which stripped them bare to be reprogrammed and rebuilt. These were not kids just coming out of college who might move with the wind from this job to another, but stable, angry, unsatisfied sorts who had an analysis about what they had been doing and why it did not work, and had open ears to a call for change and felt the swift kick in the backsides.

But, there's "change" and then there's change, and this was a generation that still needed to believe that even if they ere switching at least they were switching careers to something that might be different, but would still be long-term, stable, and structural when all was said and done. They were also men who not infrequently had families, houses, and other responsibilities, and they were being asked to hit the road and commit to being uprooted on a regular and on-going basis. If they had been political at all, they could have been communists or fellow travelers, but since they were not, they had to be compensated; therefore they had to see themselves, and be seen, as professionals. Fortunately for them at that particular time most of what looked at them across the table in the halls of the establishment, the church, foundations, newspapers, and businesses also looked – and thought – much as they did, though they used different tactics, they were cultural twins. So the combination had a certain cache and resonated for a time. And without an argument senior IAF organizers were bastions of the middle and upper middle class, and as professionals paid well, even if it did limit their ability to grow and expand, and organizations rose and fell like leaves in the seasons of their work.

No reason to believe that that time is now, because it is not, and time has not been kind to the IAF as a methodology. Some of their organizations and organizers are outstanding. Seemingly the IAF has also had to come back to solid ground though in order to keep up and survive. They are still woefully insular and inbred, but they increasingly recruit younger and more diversely experienced organizers in order to try to inject life in the methodology. The rap may be the same, but the reality has turned increasingly away. The IAF seems to not believe in mass organization now any more than they did in the past. Holding on to their structural model still means that even the largest IAF organization will only have a couple of organizers – COPS in San Antonio, one of the oldest and most esteemed, continues to run on no more than three organizers with one fairly senior, one a journeyman of sorts, and one an apprentice.

To build mass organizations we have to open access to members and leaders to believe that they have an equal opportunity to become organizers and staff of the organization. In fact ACORN's experience and belief is that unless we can build a steady and secure flow from our constituency, membership, and leadership into the ranks of the organizing staff, we cannot institutionalize the program over time.

Why would we not want that?

Perhaps there is something inherent about having a good job that produces something like a genetic instinct to try to keep others from taking it away? There are a number of successful and time honored strategies: manufacturing "requirements" that we may not have had to meet ourselves, fabricating rationalizations direct from the factory to create an impenetrable mythology around the job, deliberately mystifying the process of work, elongating the hours to separate the martyrs from the mavens, or just in general making the job of organizer impossible to do and even more unlikely to want. Is this deliberate or inadvertent? All of these are used by different organizations without thinking, or at least without thinking hard.

Part of the conundrum has to do with whether or not there is in fact a "bright shining light" division between organizers and other staff and members and leaders, similar to what exists in ACORN. One wisely would not want to politicize the membership around issues relating to job seeking, which would seriously obviate the mission of the organization. Even in ACORN there are mixed messages, but these distorted signals usually revolved around money, hours, and travel – all of which are part of the chemistry of the job.

Recruiting Organizers

Having run an organizing staff since 1968 and counting, frequently I have been asked, "Wade, what do you look for in an organizer?" I always answered that I look for three things: a sense of humor, ability to listen, and whether or not they owned a car. The first makes it easier for me to live with them, as well as everyone else in the world, the second makes it possible for them to become organizers, and the third, outside of a couple of big cities in the country and around the world, makes it possible for them get out and about to do the work. Does that mean that those are the three essentials I maintain in order to hire someone? No, the only absolute essential to get the job – at least in the United States – was having access to transportation, the rest you need to keep the job.

I usually let just about anyone try the job, who is willing to do the work, as I describe it, for the pay we are offering. Fundamentally, I have more faith in our organizing model and organizational culture than I do in anyone walking through the door looking for the job. We routinely wind people up and put them in the neighborhood working the street with existing organizers and members to see how they perform and make hiring judgments based on this field-testing.

Some of these definitions are circular in organizing. A leader is someone who has followers. An organizer is someone who moves people. A good organizer is someone who moves lots of people a long way.

Within a secure methodology, like ACORN's practice, one can maintain many diverse organizing styles within a framework that only judges performance. This is more novel than one might think.

Many people have elaborate stereotypes about what makes an organizer. The first time I walked into the west coast office of the Youth Project in the 1970's, the office manager who had spoken to me on the phone a score of times, looked at me hard and with obvious surprise. Finally, she said, "I didn't expect you to look like this?" I made some kind of joke about being good looking, and still very seriously, she said, "I thought you would be short and swarthy." Thankfully, she didn't also then add that I was required to be Jewish and from New York as well, but clearly a redheaded guy born in Wyoming with a y'all still stuck in his mouth after years in New Orleans was miles away from the picture in her mind. I can remember equally well going to a meeting at the Catholic diocese office in Springfield, Massachusetts when I was working for welfare rights, and having the woman who opened the door, measure me from head to toe, and then ask me to come around back to the service door to make my "delivery," if I had any hopes of gaining entry and an appointment. I guess I should add the obvious, that it helps to have a thick skin to make it as an organizer!

How about other personal attributes like passion and commitment? Certainly, these are both nice things to find in an organizer, but neither is very reliable or at all predictive of how an organizer will last over time. Passion comes and goes after all, and time alone and routine familiarity are hard water pounding on soft rock, breaking it down at will. Passion may bring someone to the door of organizing, but it will not keep them there. Daily work inures you to all manner of horror and the most terrible things can become almost trivial with constant exposure. People adapt or in more modern terminology are resilient. Part of the nature of human survival is the ability to develop a coat of indifference as we become part of the scene so that symbols become people, and circumstances become routine.

The same can be said about commitment. Commitment must be proven, not promised. When a young organizer looks me in the eye, and tells me that she will be an organizer forever and with the job until the end of time, I know that I am simply listening to an exercise in self-delusion. They cannot know what they will find in the work and whether or not they will be comfortably at home with their future. Frequently the organizers who will proclaim their permanence the loudest and longest will be the first to drift off course. They are looking for a cause to define themselves, rather than a career of work that can be their small mark upon the world.

Yet, you might easily say to me, Wade, then why does ACORN require new organizers to make minimum commitments when they come to work for the organization if you have so little confidence in what they are promising? Good question, but it is not hard to answer either. When hiring an organizer we are acting as representatives of the membership and it is our duty to translate to new recruits their responsibilities to fulfill their obligations because there are hundreds and thousands of people who depend on them and their jobs are vital to the entire project at hand. Depending on the job we required one or two years, sometimes more as the responsibilities, and therefore the dependence of the membership on their performance, increased. It is important that people take that seriously, and we enforce it with every ounce of suasion we can bring to the task.

Managing 100 offices or more around the country, and working with Head Organizers in 18 other countries, there was not an anteroom where replacements are sitting and waiting to be called into action. The replacements are out beyond the parameter waiting to be found, nurtured, and trained to step into the jobs, and that takes time and notice. I once had a young man working with me as an assistant, who came in and wanted to give me two weeks' notice, because he thought that was "standard" in the world of work. I suggested he either give me the time needed for an orderly transition of his tasks to a replacement or he just not pretend he was doing me or the organization any favors, and simply leave forthwith, since if he was going to screw us, then he might as well get on with it. No one does anyone a favor by simply foisting one's responsibilities off on someone else, so why should those of us on the mop-up detail be expected to thank someone after we have something suddenly dumped in our laps?

Glib and fast talkers are also unlikely candidates for organizing and often this separates the independent activist and advocate from the career organizer. One has to hone skills in trying to assert themselves into situations, grab the moment, seize the headline, and move the faceless crowed, or simply stand still and speak truth to power in one setting or another. The organizer though has to listen and listen hard for the issues that enrage others and help them move to the unusual and uncomfortable to make the transition from follower to leader. An organizer has to move people from the back to the front, and the best arguments for doing so are the ones that people themselves articulate, rather than being the lines of rhetoric spun from another's lips.

Organizers, often operating with miles of rope in singular situations on far flung frontiers, have to be able to work in cooperative and interdependent situations, rather than being freelance operators. This is also not easy for some people. Some of the skills seem to conflict with each other. The toughness and self-assurance that lets an organizer move into a difficult situation with no support, no contacts, and essentially no net, and begin to build something from scratch in a community or workplace tends to produce fiercely self-confident people (if it does not destroy them, I should add), which is not necessarily the classic definition of someone who plays well with others. But, somehow this person with these attributes must be able to fit into an organizational structure which requires discipline, accountability, and invariably a high degree of understanding of rules, procedures, and traditions. None of this is easy, so we will spend more time on how to manage organizers once we figure out how to recruit and train them.

In the terms I hear around the work today, an organizer needs to be "relational." Please do not mistake that word for rational, since, frankly, that is still not a requirement in this particular field of work! By relational it means that they need to be able to work and get along with people. I hope this means that they need to be able to move people. But, let's say it means that, as well as being someone who has a sense of humor and some other evidence of good character.

At the bottom line an organizer simply must *like* people! It is sometimes amazing to me how many people one sees around this work that in fact seem not to genuinely like people at all. Organizing is a bad career choice for misanthropes, or at least misanthropes who don't like people.

Liking people trumps other values like politics. Outsiders always assume that there must be a political litmus test that determines whether or not one can be an organizer. That is absolutely false, as it turns out. I have had organizers work with me for thirty years who hardly have a political bone in their bodies, and I have had organizers work with me forever who could handle finely constructed debates in any political discussion in the world. Neither mattered or was determinant in whether these organizers could last a lifetime or make a contribution in this work, it only mattered that they possessed a fundamental value that resonated with people and that people were also drawn to them. As we frequently say at ACORN, "it's all about the members," and this is part of what this means.

So, people skills made a lot of difference for an organizer. A smile means something to people and is a lot more appreciated than a scowl. The fire of anger may sear your soul, but if it is worn on your face, frankly, people find that very off-putting. There are many mothers out there that are inadvertently helping their children become organizers, because they are imparting basic social skills and, though this may surprise you, manners, God forbid! All of these things communicate respect and dignity to people we are working with and trying to organize. I am not saying that it is impossible to be an organizer, even a good organizer, if you lack some of these things, because I have to admit, I know a number of long time organizers who totally lack any of these attributes and somehow still move people. They just have different problems in holding and keeping people, especially staff working with them.

Even charm helps. Charm communicates good will and what seems like deep interest in another person and their well-being. It also surprises. People have expectations of what an organizer is and to the degree the most common caricatures seem to involve sharp teeth and long tails; it helps to lower the guardrail at the border boundaries with some charm. I was raised to it, and do not apologize for it. As an organizer part of the job involves using all of your tools. If you have fewer tools, it doesn't mean you can't build anything, but the work is hard enough not to use everything you have.

Flirting on the other hand is greatly overrated and frankly dangerous, both for men and women organizers. In one case it can be threatening and competitive in ways that an organizer does not want to encourage, and in the other it can be misconstrued and put an organizer in situations that can be personally threatening, especially for women organizers in strange and hostile areas and environments, and can also move the wrong people into the organization and keep some of the right people from joining. Sex is everywhere around people, so it should not be a surprise that sexual politics are important to understand from soup to nuts, if one is going to effectively do this work. Flirting, off color jokes, use of innuendo, are all tricks, not tools, and they may have worked once as a shortcut for someone somewhere, but then they just erode the values of the enterprise and the confidence that people must have in the organizer, because they change the vantage point of judgment in a way that a serious organizer cannot allow.

Age turns out to not matter as much in hiring organizers, though it is important and cannot be overlooked, and does require various forms of compensation, when either relatively younger or relatively older. Organizers in their very early twenties are fresh and energetic, but have to be prepared to handle reservations from older members of the constituency who are, correctly, more skeptical of the advice and assistance of the young. Organizers hired and trained in their forties or fifties usually do not have that problem, but may be harder to train.[63] They also often have to offset the fact that they are at an age that might prefer the clutter and comfort of the office to the clamor of the streets. We have found success across all generational divides, but the obstacle to hiring older candidates for the work is more often the level of the wages, rather than the constraints of the work. On a seniority based scale, such as ACORN uses, starting from scratch is one thing at twenty-five and another thing at forty-five. Regardless, please do not misunderstand: organizers, great organizers, can be found at all ages, just listen carefully and make a training and supervision plan that recognizes the challenges in retention and performance at various levels. My old comrade and friend, Bill Pastriech, used to tell me when I started that we generally would be able to hire and retain people five years older or five years younger than we were. I am not sure where he got that figure, though I assume it was his own experience, and I used to think it was true, but the longer I do the work the more I realize from my own experience that there are always young people who can – and should – be hired, no matter their age, and there are older people who can – and should – be hired, no matter their age, and both can be retained and supervised regardless of the supervisor's age.

Experience is also greatly overrated in hiring most organizers. Most of the "organizing" experience people have too often consists of the wrong lessons drawn from unfortunate work experiences with people who have created deeply set bad habits, and therefore contributes little to the necessary openness you need to have in learning how to organize, especially in a system that is grounded in the clarity of an organizing model along the ACORN lines. In almost every case it is easier to train organizers who have no organizing experience, because they are more open to learning based on what they hear, see, and find in the work itself. Fighting through prejudices and preset conclusions and life experiences is difficult, and too often such experience becomes the default position that people revert too when faced with something challenging or unknown. Certainly, this is natural, but that does not make the task for the trainer or supervisor any easier. Sad to say,

---

[63] Two good examples of many were Christina Ford and Lynette Johnson from the New Orleans ACORN staff who led the organizer performance charts for years in the late 1990s.

nevertheless true, but an open mind, is the easiest to work with in molding an effective organizer.

Life experience in general on the other hand is invaluable. Given the choice, I would also prefer to hire as a new recruit someone who has had at least some previous experience working almost anywhere for almost anybody. First, they know what it is like already to be unhappy and miserable in a job, so they do not come in all dewy-eyed with expectations that are naïve and impossible to meet. They know that you have to actually show up, that people get fired in the real world, and that there is a difference between a good boss and a bad one, and good working environment and one that is stifling and oppressive. Organizing does very well against normal work benchmarks. There is more independence and freedom than in most jobs, and having had a job; people know this, rather than somehow believing that the job is supposed to be all about freedom and independence. Small benefits derive from bad work that saves time for good work – as another example, understanding that vacations and benefits are fixed and matter, rather than are discretionary and negotiable. I have hired great organizers by walking into offices and seeing people doing clerical work or something else that is unfulfilling but who are locked to the treadmill, like social work or teaching or whatever, and essentially using their obvious unhappiness and the clear underutilization of their talents as motivation for them to quit and become organizers. Such people can weather many storms that come with organizing, because they have some grip on life and, as importantly, work, so they know to hold on to good work when they find it, and many of them have now make a lifetime of it. Certainly my own work experience, as I mentioned earlier, taught me exactly these lessons, so perhaps I have been successful in recruiting such people because I can feel their pain and can argue more convincingly for the salve.

All of which explains why ACORN does so much of our recruiting **not** from the ranks of the recent college graduates, though we were – and are – blessed with many of these candidates as well, but from the ranks of our own constituency, where we could retrain people with the good fundamentals, personal skills, and particular interests to the life and work of organizers. Within our framework this is also more accommodating for several reasons. First, it gave us the diversity that reflects our constituency and a sense that what they are being asked to do, can be done, since in many cases they can see it in the face of the organizers themselves. This was particularly helpful in organizing immigrant communities where language is an issue. Secondly, it helped our sustainability model toggling between the maximum dues and viability of our wage scale. An effective rate of ten or fifteen dollars or twenty dollars an hour may not look like great money to some college graduates (though many these days jump at it as well!), but to someone who might have been underemployed in the service sector or doing manual labor or sales or a thousand different jobs at minimum wages or pay that runs half of ours, the wages were good, the benefits were great, and the future was unparalleled, and manifested clearly in the regular, annual increases of the wage scale.

Recruiting in this way is not without its own set of obstacles and barriers. Often people do not have the writing skills and confidence that organizers are sometimes expected to have in doing sophisticated research or formulating proposals or helping leaders and members with communication projects like writing press releases, speeches, and postings for the websites and news reports. In fact sometimes organizers who are giftedly bilingual verbally may have difficulties in writing in either language. We learned all of these lessons, like most lessons in organizing, the hard way. We do organize in the real world still, and a monolingual Spanish speaking organizer with the right supervisor can make huge organizing contributions in organizing Spanish speaking neighborhoods in California barrios and Texas _colonias_ and elsewhere, but they cannot direct a staff and build power as easily without having the ability to operate as effectively in English since that is the _lingua franca_ of politics and business. What this means practically speaking is the need for better supervision and support for such organizers to succeed. It did not mean that we should not recruit such organizers and train them to be great organizers.

The biggest problem in recruiting, especially for organizations who believe that they only need one or two organizers in their operations and are not building mass organizations is in fact keeping people from not hiring people who are identical to themselves. The hubris of cloning seems inadvertent, but remains irresistible to many managers. Almost unselfconsciously they develop a prototype for a successful organizer that seems most like the characteristics and background that they themselves bring to the work. If they write well, they believe that writing well is an _a priori_ for the job itself, rather than an added value that they have contributed. If they are college graduates, then they believe it might not be essential, but inevitably prefer to hire college graduates. All of this is natural. People are always drawn to people with whom they are most comfortable, and that is often people just like themselves. This just happens to not be good for organizing or building organizations, so we need to place some barriers in the way.

So, how were organizers recruited, especially by an organization like ACORN that needed hundreds, if not thousands of organizers to staff its large membership and more than one-hundred offices? The short answer is any way we could think of, anywhere we think they might be, and however we could afford!

For decades ACORN ran newspaper ads galore. In some cities it goes without saying that this was horribly expensive. We ran public service announcements constantly on our own radio stations in Dallas and Little Rock and on any other stations that would have them. We did email bulletins and mailings to college professors, friends and family of existing staff, and in magazines and user groups that potential organizers might stumble upon. We used craigslist, no matter how objectionable some of their practices are, and we have done well, thanks be to Craig! The most visited section of the ACORN website was almost always the recruitment section. We put small "ads' on the back of monthly meeting flyers for our own local neighborhood groups. We posted notices with tear-off slips at the bottom in laundry mats in our neighborhoods, on college campuses, and in popular haunts of all types from grocery stores to record shops to bars and restaurants. I have stopped people cold on the street, and of course run the rap on scores of secretaries, UPS delivery drivers, and bored salespeople, as I have already admitted. Members below the top leadership ranks are frequently queried about their interests in embarking on a new career – and many have done so! And, none of this is ever really enough, and the recruitment process can never be allowed to stop.

When we look at existing organizers, can we find a pattern? This is hard to answer, since we go everywhere and people come from everywhere it seems. The woman running our office in Lima, Peru was a nurse. The woman who ran our office in Buenos Aires was a teacher. I know ex-med students, lawyers who couldn't stand the law, ex-truck drivers, former factory workers, college graduates who never worked anywhere else, college dropouts who worked everywhere else, speech therapists, occupational therapists, unhappy bellmen and alienated waitresses, ex-journalists, discharged soldiers, and so on and so forth. Of course we also have lots of organizers who we have found from what I call the "allied trades," who were researchers or activists in college or with other non-profits or unions, former canvassers who went door-to-door for one cause after another, ex-politicos who couldn't see where one campaign began and another ended, ex-VISTAs, ex-Peace Corp, ex-Teacher Corps, ex-Jesuit volunteers, current Quakers, ex-Catholic Workers, and lost Catholics, ex-whatever, former union or community organizers from some other situation, and of course members who made the jump from dues payers to dues collectors, so to speak. So, the answer to the question about a pattern is "not really," and that is actually good news, because it means we might find a potential organizer around every corner and under every rock, if we keep turning them over and looking.

ACORN's system, as I've already hinted pretty broadly, is that we bring in lots of people, because we trust that we will find the "keepers" in the net. We increasingly ran what we called "organizer academies," meaning a concentrated recruitment and hiring campaign, which then had lots of men and women begin the work together in a full-fledged "try-out" and training exercise to see how many we could determine that had the attitude, character, and, potentially, the aptitude to make it worth our time and money to put them into training as an organizer. We would hire literally everyone who shows promise in such an ACORN Academy. Even if an office only has the finances and placement opportunities for two or three organizers, if we were able to flush out more than that number, we would try to send them for training elsewhere in the country in order to see how many and who might make it, so that we can fill the needs of staffing in that office and potentially others. It still comes down to "many are called, and few are chosen," but to choose enough to grow at the rate we found necessary in those days and times, we have to keep calling lots of people into the ranks.

Before I leave the issue of recruitment and what makes a good organizer, I suppose I cannot avoid dealing with the issue of whether or not the nature of organizing attracts a lot of misfits, people who might not make it in the regular world, though they seem to thrive in the subculture of organizing. This is an uncomfortable question, and I am not sure that I am the best qualified to answer it well. I am honest about the fact that a primary motivation for my ability to become and remain an organizer for all of these years is anger – a deep, raging, and howling thing, which is always lurking not far beneath the surface in dealing with me even on the best of days. As much as it is motivating to me, and as lucky as I personally feel to have found organizing because it gave me a wide and deep channel to fill with all of the anger I have and to translate it into political expression, to fight inequity, class barriers, racism, and find voice for what a high school counselor told me was my "unfortunate" Manichean sense of justice and injustice. Nonetheless it is wrong to believe that this is in fact simply a haven for the maladjusted. ACORN's open door and acceptance of staff from various backgrounds gives a wide tolerance for such people finding a place in organizing.

Hard work in community organizing is an expectation in building something as large and strong as ACORN in a world of adversity. These values contributed to a certain stage in our development, and no doubt attracted others with similar inclinations – all good people in most every way, but hard edged, tough, and driven. We depended on each other in a narrow circle of trust and loyalty, and joined together to build something together, anyone else be damned, and the devil take the hindmost. I used to say, perhaps too many times, that people had to get "used" to me, because "I came with this shop." I just wanted to be a good soldier in a real peoples' army that meant something on a long march that was going somewhere. I was surprised – and disappointed – to find that the march was this long and that I ended up this far in front.

Perhaps that's not completely true.

The other primary motivation for me, and many others, besides anger is an intense competitive spirit. We want to win. In campaigns I wanted to be part of something that beat the target and won. It is amazing to me in talking to organizers sometimes how many of them were able to sustain commitments to the work over the years without being part of winning campaigns, elections, or whatever defines victory over the opposition in their area of the work. There's never been a question in our organizing about the positive value of competition in performance from charts on the wall showing the number of new members, dues, and turnout to monthly reports and everything else. There is only a fine line between that kind of clarity and the fun and spirited back-and-forth between organizing offices and hard core, flat out competition.

I believed it was us against them and that we had to win the fight, and that it was a fight. I would not pretend that is how everyone sees the world. I also always felt that we were part of long tradition and a history of struggle written in sweat and blood, and that part of what was glorious about our work and lives was the honor to be part of bending the trajectory towards justice for millions. I wanted ACORN and the many organizations I helped build to really matter and to mean something forever. So maybe I'm not being disingenuous to say that I saw myself and others as soldiers on the long march, and admitting at the same time that we wanted to be toward the front of the line, and not just eating dust at the back of the column.

Organizing though is work on the fringe, behind the scenes, and outside of the smooth lanes for easy travel. For the most part organizers are not going to be elected to office, appointed to boards and commissions, quoted in the press, presented loving cups or gold watches, or, god knows, given any of the few awards that might exist for making a difference in our world. Perhaps with the pure scale and scope of ACORN (and others) we changed that somewhat, but it is hard to imagine that people doing this work of fighting for and winning social change are going to someday wake up and find themselves comfortably mainstream, even if some of them can pretend – or presume – in some circumstances to be middle class.

Organizing is not just for misfits, any more than it is work that fits just anyone. The work flows from a wonderful tradition of struggle and that has been its hallmark in my career as well. It is hard for me to imagine it being any different.

Chapter VI: **Learning to Swim**

The fundamental training model for ACORN organizers has always been an elaborate "apprenticeship" training experience where the organizer is walked through the fundamental steps involved in building a local community based organization following the ACORN Model[64] with a trainer, who is always a more experienced organizer or journeyman. The experienced organizer acts as the guide not only to the model but to questions that inevitably arise through the new – and often foreign – experience of organizing. Within the ACORN system the trainer, not the trainee, is therefore *responsible* for the conduct and success of the organizing drive[65] for the simple reason that the members and the community obviously have the right to always expect that ACORN will faithfully assist them in organizing their neighborhood within the range of their hopes and expectations. Trainees may fail in short, but an organizing drive cannot be allowed to fail.

This does not mean that "all groups are created equally." The core of the model is not the organizer, but the organizing committee. The critical concern for the trainer has to be that no shortcuts are taken which would weaken the building of the organizing committee composed of community residents. We both believe, and it is our experience, that if we create a solid organizing committee that can shoulder the drive, then systematically following the outlined steps in the model will at the end of the "organizing drive" produce a strong organization, even if it turns out to be the case that the trainee does not succeed in completing the drive or becoming an organizer.

All of this is easier said than done. The average community "drive" includes an area that is ideally between 1500 and 2500 families. Membership, recruited during the drive, is tabulated regularly and is in fact an excellent barometer of support of the organization in the community. The omnipresent danger is that a trainee, unless supervised closely, will simply plunge into the community and begin door knocking with a weak or non-existent organizing committee, escape detection at the onset of the drive, and be able to mask the full range of performance by simply beginning to "chart" some number of members enrolled in the organization. Unless there is careful supervision and training the full range of this problem will not be revealed until the first meeting of the new organization when the attendance will be weaker than expected and the leadership will be either non-existent or ill-prepared. The ACORN Organizing Model that I wrote in 1973, teaches well the various components of direct community organizing.

Knowing the risks on the back end forces the training process and supervision to be more exacting on the front end, obviously, and that is exactly what we constantly endeavor

---

[64] Written in 1973 (*www.chieforganizer.org/writing*) and obviously dated and in many ways a quasi-historical document, the model is an outline of steps necessary to systematically follow to create a local group.

[65] This is obviously more difficult in ACORN's international work, since the "trainer" may be on Skype thousands of miles away, but the same practice and principal prevails, even the implementation is vastly more difficult and sometimes uneven.

to maintain. Nonetheless, some operations are stronger than others for a host of reasons indigenous to the community, the issues, and even resistance, and some organizers are more exacting, disciplined, and talented trainers than others lacking the same level of patience or interest in training, so the constant challenge is also making sure that trainees are matched to the best training situations. This turns out to be difficult for us, because most staff are locally hired, and therefore are not part of an organization wide system of training as much as they are integrated into the best (which may be quite good, though the point being made here is simply that it is not going to be uniform) that can be offered in the local office, partially because they are likely to be employed exclusively in the office where they were hired. Internationally, it also means a lot of work via Skype and, when we are lucky, being able to parachute in an experienced organizer for a time to help bring everyone up to their potential, but it also means that in many areas language is a mountain to climb.

This is not our ideal training model. We believe strongly that an organizer needs to be trained outside of the city where they have the most experience for a number of reasons.

- It allows them to totally concentrate on the training without distraction.

- The trainee is less likely to fall into a "leader" pattern or be threatening to local leaders they are developing, because they are not from the same communities.

- It allows the trainee to get more experience in organizing styles in addition to the experience where they will end up being assigned after training.

- It allows a first expression of commitment to the organization and to the depth of the job.

Having said that, what is involved in training?

We get people into the field lickety-split. In some offices this is not the first day, but in most offices a trainee will see the streets before the end of the first day at the least with one of the other organizers as a navigator or observer. Usually, the first couple of hours are spent on paperwork – got to keep the government informed and happy – and reading background material about ACORN in general and its work in that city or around the world, so that the organizer-to-be has a growing grasp of what is happening. There is time to ask questions. This is a relaxed day allowing people to get their feet on the ground. As a first day on the job, they are already nervous enough! Certainly, when we are training someone who has already been an organizer elsewhere or even a leader in our own organization, the background is easier for them, though they very likely have never seen or read a copy of the ACORN Model, and may not know it exists. In an ACORN Academy setting there are some advantages because there is a slightly reduced level of pressure given that there are more people starting from scratch at the same time. Of course this also makes it both easier and harder for the trainer. Easier, because with more than one trainee, you can feel like all of your eggs are not in just one basket, and someone is bound to make it to the end of the process, but harder as well, because new people can bond with each other, both positively and negatively, and reinforce both good habits and bad ones equally, unless the trainer is especially attentive to this problem.

As an aside, let me mention that this is actually the same problem expressed in another way, when organizing groups of people: the yield might be higher, but so are the attendant risks. When approaching a group of neighbors gathered together on someone's porch or stoop or whatever or when approaching a group of workers at a check-cashing side, break area, or in the "open field," the odds are actually not good that an organizer will get everyone, even though one-on-one, the odds might be excellent at organizing all of these contacts or the vast majority. In a gaggle of people the one sour expression or negative response from one person will tend to lead everyone to at the least defer decision on the organization. Most organizers, especially the less seasoned, will go "all or nothing" in such situations. You know when an organizer has increased their skills, when they can approach such situations and end up with some people on board or signed up, perhaps even a good majority, while isolating the few negative voices as simply negative voices. Most new organizers are flatly advised to avoid such "group" situations, if possible, until their skills are a lot better, because the odds of failure are so high. For the same reason you know that anyone who has ever told you that places like bars are good for making organizing contacts is also either a hard drinker or a good liar. Bars are nothing but groups of people in difficult situations without even the good grace of their "normal" selves and when someone is calved out of the herd in the bar, the chances are best that this is not going to be a person who moves others and may just be someone who is a serious partier. Save your money, and do not bother wasting your time at bars unless it is to drink yourself or for your own pleasure, but never claim that this is where you can do some good organizing.

The same is true in training. While writing this section years ago in our office in Buenos Aires, I was listening in my woefully inadequate Spanish to a conversation in the next room where there was a "training" discussion about the language that is on the ACORN Argentina membership card. On the back of all ACORN membership cards there is a commitment the member signs that they will vote in all elections. A trainee is challenging whether or not this should be on the card, based on the lack of value she personally feels that her vote has. The trainer figures out quickly that in fact the trainee does not vote and believes that no one should vote. Now, we may at the end of the day be able to make a very good organizer out of this woman, but in the beginning all another trainee would know is that – suddenly – the language on the membership card itself was an object of disagreement and contention. Other trainees are not likely to understand what in the world all of this was about, and are going to be uncertain whether or not they should have engaged in the discussion or stayed as far away as possible. When the trainees are talking separately at some later point (and they *always* do!), if the trainee was not handled both firmly, and gently, there may be way too much talk about a lot of extraneous issues, like whether or not the language was accurate, whether it was necessary, whether the trainee was handled too softly or too harshly, justly or unfairly, whether the trainer was sensitive or brusque in the handling this, and a whole lot of other malarkey about something that perhaps 99 of 100 members do not even read when they decide to join the organization and on a question that is absurd on its face since in Argentina (as in 25 or more other countries around the world) voting is mandatory! The point here is simply that part of the dynamics of training (and staff management as we will examine later) rests on how well the senior organizer or trainer can switch between dealing with the individual versus dealing with the group. Little things, as always, can make a huge difference, and in this case the differences may mean the loss of potential talent to the movement for social change in this country (in this case, Argentina!). That is a serious weight for the training process to shoulder.

There are some other near "universal" truths about training that show up from the very first day.

One is that there is no way to ever satisfy a new organizer's **demand** for training. Every new organizer wants more, more, and then more and more training, preferably before ever hitting the field for the first time. Trainees always want more to read, have more explained, more practice, more role plays, more time, more questions, and then yet even more. This is natural. They are entering a wild new world in the workplace or community, and it is important that they be allowed to succeed. It is also very tempting for organizers who are acting as trainers to also want to give the trainees more to read, watch, or do, partially, if not solely, because this is not their full-time job and they are also trying to cadge time for the "rest" of their work, and also would prefer to have something that fills the trainees' time which is not lunch, gossip, make work projects, database entry, social network stalling and cruising, and, perhaps best of all, that will help cover something that the trainer is also worried about forgetting.

The demand and desire for good information in this area is like filling a bottomless pit. Enough will never quite be enough. More recently, we are also surprised, especially since we are producing a steady stream of information these days, how little of it is actually used. This speaks to our own continual need for a better protocol for training or guidebooks which helps us as we increase the scale of our training.

Written materials only meet part of the demand especially as we train more and more organizers who are less comfortable in certain languages or are less comfortable with written materials in any language. As our society has become more visual and immediate, our ability to produce the same level of professional grade training and organizing materials has not grown as rapidly as needed to meet the impatient user of such information. So, we soldier on and now create more materials on video and spent more time and money doing it. With help the materials are even improving gradually, but the yawning maw continues to seem gaping.

There is just no substitute for putting people on the streets and letting experience be the primary teacher, changing the trainee from the student, and the trainer into the interpreter, guide, and mentor. No matter how much people read and watch, it all takes on a different, and more real, meaning once they begin to engage the organizing process directly.

So, we quickly, and frequently on the first day, come back from lunch to do "role plays" that prepare people for the field. Role plays are funny things. There is no way to not see them as somewhat hokey. This is definitely something that many people have spent a lifetime avoiding as well. Frequently, people are reticent to dive right into role plays for all of these reasons. They are what they are: an artificial mimicking of real experience. They are also **incredibly** helpful to people learning the work, and when people take the role play seriously, the experiential practice can be as effective a training tool for organizers

ACORN Scotland Doorknocking Crew Gathers.

as a flight console might be for a future pilot – an accessible way to become skilled in the language and exchange of the work.

All of that is also easier said than done. Some people are too easy when acting as members and some are too hard, though at the end of the day, it does not particularly matter. The key for the trainee is getting their "raps" in – giving them more and more repetitions in the language of the "doors," so that their level of comfortability, and therefore effectiveness, increases. We have found that before people can concentrate fully on listening, which is the superior skill, they have to be able to move their concentration outside of their self, and as long as they are not comfortable with the structure and environment of the visit, then they will not be truly listening. Instead they will be fretting over the words and the structure of the rap.

I am not referring to a set speech, but something more along the lines of an outline of critical points that have to be communicated in the exchange, whether on the doors or in the workplace. Things along the lines of the following:

- Who is organizing?
- What is our organization?
- What is the organizing about?
- What are their issues?
- What do they feel about all of this?
- When is the next opportunity for them to participate?
- What do they need to do now in order to get involved and join?
- What other questions or ideas do they have for the organization?

In the community context the "who" is the organizing committee and "people in the neighborhood." The same is true in the workplace in many ways, where the "who" is also the organizing committee of co-workers and others in the workplace. The organization is ACORN, or the union, or the workers association, or the campaign, or whatever the operating organizational vehicle might be.

When I was on the streets, I used to describe the organization briefly at this point (Like I said, I'm Wade Rathke, an organizer with ACORN, the membership organization of low and moderate income families working with neighborhood residents in communities in your city and 100 others around the country [or the world] around issues that are democratically decided and therefore most important to you….), and then I would say, "You've heard of ACORN right?" Often I would be out with a new team of organizers and members in a brand new city somewhere in the world. Usually, these were situations in the earlier days where ACORN had never been within miles of these neighborhoods, or involved in any local campaigns, or mentioned in the newspapers or on television. In almost every case, we would both look each other in the eye at this point on both sides of the door, and they would then say, quickly, "Yeah, I've heard of it." Had they heard of it? Possibly, but probably not, but once they responded this way, what they were **really** telling me is that they **wanted** to have heard about it, and that was precisely the message I was listening to hear.

Once I heard it, I would ask if I could come in for a minute so we could visit briefly about what was going on, and I would go through more pieces of the rap while sitting in their front room or kitchen or wherever. Getting in the door is very important in organizing and strengthens the whole visit immeasurably, as does making the visit as part of a team with someone from the neighborhood (or workplace!).

Without further burdening this subject one can easily determine that the point of the outlined rap structure is an exchange that establishes that there is a basic dialectic providing give-and-take between the resident or worker in the visit with the organizing team, and, equally importantly, there is a level of essential bottom-line information that has to be communicated as well (who, what, when, and how about the organization, the organizing drive, the next meeting of the organizing committee for identified leaders and the general meeting of the group for everyone being recruited, as well as asking them to actually join the organization by becoming a member and paying dues). A trainee has to become comfortable enough with the structure of the rap that they do not get flustered at the door trying to remember what they have to communicate and then not being able to hear clearly the other critical part of the visit, which is what folks **want** you to hear about their neighborhood (or workplace), its issues, and concerns and what they believe needs to be done to make it better. Greater comfortability equals better listening.

One of the key problems that role playing helps to address directly is what I have always called "testing" that happens in first conversations with neighbors and workers. My view is that it does not just happen some of the time, but virtually all of the time. In the same way that people *want* to believe that things could be better and that something could make a difference, they also *don't* believe it is really possible so they find that it is important in many cases to be skeptical, shrewd, negative, or whatever and push back just enough to make sure they are not seen as a sucker or a mark. From my personal experience I can tell almost anyone that there must be a thousand ways for people to tell an organizer, "what's the use, why bother, or why do you think any of this could make a difference?" In fact there are three, right there! Depending on the person talking and what else you are hearing, if the organizer does not have an effective response to "testing," you are dead on the doors. The response also has to be well measured and calibrated. Too flip or smart-alecky, and you are out of there. Too serious, might seem fragile and hurt. You have to come back, but you have to comeback in like manner to the test given, which also requires listening once again. Where there is a real sensitivity to testing, role playing allows "no fault" practice with a lot of tests and responses, and upgrades the organizers skills immeasurably through a dry run.

Some testing by people is hard and harsh, personal and direct, so none of this should be confused with a game. When you are on the streets and are asked with a harsh, sneer, "What is a white boy like you doing down here?" "Changing the world" may be your core response, if so, it's real and it will likely be well received. No matter how good your sense of humor, a joke is unlikely to work in this context, because the questioner, perhaps more than anything else, is asking you whether or not you respect him and his community, so flippant will not get the job done. To organize you have to learn to be comfortable, very comfortable, with this question asked repeatedly time after time. In fact you are only lucky when it is actually asked, rather than when you read it in someone's face or eyes, and have to answer it even before it is vocalized in some roundabout way. This kind of testing is epidemic in all manner of circumstances, and perhaps that is why organizing is such good training for life in our world.

Organizers have to learn to meet testing appropriately and head on and go forward. Good lessons for everyone really, and role playing armors people and thickens their skin before they go out the door and hear that "all unions are sell-outs," "we tried that and it never worked," and of course "our neighborhood (or work, or city, or country, or people) is different," and nothing can be done here. If as an organizer you agree, then get stepping. If you don't, then there's a test being given, and you need to take it, pass, and get on with it.

The first day and sometimes the first several days in the field are teamed up with an experienced organizer, which is precisely where the "apprenticeship" part of the training program is so important. The first afternoon in many cases the trainee will only observe, listen, smile, and acclimate to the settings of the work and the interchanges. The most important part of this training is the debriefing after each door where the exchange is dissected and analyzed thoroughly so that the lessons are pulled from each part of the conversations about what was happening, and of course what was working and what was failing. Critical in this part of the debriefing is the assessment of the contact based on the visit.

A lot of the "assessments" in community organizing, including what we are doing in ACORN, have become softer over the years for both good and bad reasons depending on the organizer's perspective. For years the dominant assessments were yes, no, or maybe around meeting attendance and membership. There has been an evolution since I have been less in touch with the field organizing now, where there is little assessment past whether someone enrolled as a member of not, and these newly signed up members are the core group being recruited to the first meeting. Part of this is obviously due to the fact that the ACORN organizing staff and doorknocking teams have improved immeasurably over the years in signing up members on first visits on the doors, and without a doubt signing up indicates a commitment from the member that has real meat and meaning, especially compared to either their promise of future attendance or the estimation and assessment of their credibility by the organizing team. Membership is an unsurpassed barometer of community strength, as is the signing of membership or authorization cards in a labor context, but the old union adage is still true: "cards cannot walk and talk." In other words assessments are still bread and butter in organizing.

In the community a "yes" was an assessment of whether or not you were *likely* to attend the first meeting, become active, and join the organization. A "maybe" meant the obvious, that all things in a perfect world were possible, but it was less likely this person would be in that number. And, once again, let me remind, these are assessments, which is different than what the person might have said. Sometimes the individual promises to the sky that they will do a million things. And, I fully believe that they are not lying. I fully believe (and perhaps this is what has sustained me as an organizer so long) that when they tell you that they want to be a member, be active, and do these million things, that when they say it, they *want* it to be true.

The same thing is true organizing workers. The assessments are different and are more varied and harsher, partly because the dues litmus test is not normally present, and even the signing of membership cards, authorization cards, or various promises and pledges, which all tend to "toughen up" the verbal commitments and assessments, are substantially less than guarantees. We tend to use a four-part or five-part assessment which allows more judgment and forces more returns and contact with the worker, partially because as organizers we believe that people can be "moved" from one category to another, and we recognize that the employer is also an active campaigner in many cases and pushing back, so we have to constantly check and revise assessments so that tactics and strategy on an organizing campaign can be determined, especially if there is an election. Here the assessments additionally note whether someone is leaning yes or leaning no. Sometimes this same battle back and forth is true in communities either because of political machines, established civic organizations (if they exist), or institutional and other organizational interests, but frankly it is much rarer to find any real organization in

Bristol ACORN Easton chapter door knocking role playing.

communities where ACORN organizes, meaning not that there are not organizations, but few have a discernible base, particularly at the street or grassroots level.

Part of the fundamental job of an organizer is to help people become active in the organization, just as they want to do, by making it harder and harder for them to say "no" to the organization, and lowering the barriers more and more to make their participation possible, if not inevitable. It is still true in organizing that you are door knocking both to bring some people into the organization and to keep some people out of the organization (which I will explain more when we talk more about leaders), but people respond differently and need different inducements to mass participation. One visit may just not be enough for many people to decide to make a deep and defining organizational commitment. The best example I give of this is always the perhaps apocryphal story of Fred Ross, Sr. and his pursuit of Cesar Chavez as a leader for the Community Service Organizations (CSO) in California, *where legendarily he visited his house four times* before he was able to successfully engage him in a visit and convince him to host a house meeting, and the rest, as they say, is history, and the moral is that many people are worth the pursuit, perhaps not for four visits, but certainly not everything can be accomplished for everyone in one.

In training organizers I always suggest that the best barometer on this question might frequently be to look at themselves and what it would take for them to get involved in an organization where they lived, as well as all the reasons – honestly – that might lead them to join an effort or walk the other way. I would not be a quick joiner, so perhaps I feel like I understand people that might not jump in my lap the first time they talk to me. There are lots of groups, and it is a good exercise to think about why we say "yes," and why we say "no" as individuals to various solicitations. These are life lessons that we can apply to our own work and translate from our own experience. The point here is that we have to train organizers around *the values of persistence and pursuit*. The more the organization is able to steadily pursue a potential member to become active and join, while avoiding accepting with some style and panache an individual "rejection" and letting it stand for a final verdict on the organization and their participation, then the higher the probability in most cases that we will be able to activate that resident or worker at some time or another or some issue or another.

The natural reason why less and less of this may be done in community organizing, and even in labor work, is that the scale of the task before mass organizations is so huge and the ocean seems so infinitely populated with fish that it is reasonable to simply keep throwing out the net and knowing that the catch is there, rather than spending the same amount of time pursing individual fish, unless they are of huge and dramatic importance. In many ways this is a bright shining test for the type of organizer we are developing. A standard issue neighborhood organizer whose turf will only be defined by the rigid boundaries of one neighborhood is more likely to understand the value of constant pursuit in steadily increasing the percentage of organization (and membership) in a particular area, than is an organizer working for a mass organization that is looking at constituencies of an entirely different scale. My bias is that both organizers need to be similarly trained so that they can appreciate the tasks and skills necessary in the work for training purposes if nothing else. Even a mass organizer, like those working for ACORN, need to be able to impart these lessons to workers and members themselves so that they can finish the job in their own areas, even while the organizer moves other programs and projects in order to develop scale. Such an organizer, if well trained, can be more valuable in assisting the resident leadership in deepening the penetration of the organization to the maximum extent possible.

In short the assessments need to mean something for them to have value, just as recording the issues raised on the doors needs to get into the database so that other organizers and leaders dealing with these members can start the next conversation from the end of the last conversation, not from the beginning all over again. People need to feel that in fact there will be a reaction and response from the organization and its leadership, not simply a call, flyer, letter, or email announcing a meeting. People, these days as much (more?!?) than ever, want to feel and believe that they are being heard. The organizer needs to be trained in these early visits on the doors that they are the steward upholding the essential good faith of this unspoken contract with their prospects and members.

It takes a lot of watching to start to understand all of the weight, both obvious and hidden, that is freighted in all of these visits with prospective members. We do not leave time for much of that watching though, because we firmly believe that there is no real advantage in standing by the water with one toe in and thinking about whether the waves will be warm or cold, when the only certainty is that they will be wet. Usually by the second day, the trainer will be alternating raps with the trainee between doors, taking one, then allowing the trainee to take one, and so forth, and then doing a quick evaluation on pros and cons and assessments between visits in the car on work visits or walking between the doors in the community. Canvass programs have something that they used to call a "trunk talk," which would be exactly this kind of debriefing by a supervisor at the end of the night in order to put the work in perspective. In training this is more of an ongoing, running conversation between steps, as it were, for people to be ready for the next piece of wood under the skin of their knuckles.

There is no way of avoiding the fact that some element of sinking and swimming comes into all of this. The trainer and the trainer's supervisor spend a lot of time with the trainee at the end of the evening helping them come to an understanding of their experience and how it plays out with their expectations of the work, and drilling into them the fact that it takes patience to succeed. Inadvertently, some level of quantity control, rather than quality control, comes into play here when the accountability of statistical measure intercedes. There is a lot of interest in performance standards. It begins to matter a lot once the trainee goes solo, whether or not they are producing, as well as performing. Were members enrolled? Were "count-on-me's" signed? Were authorization cards collected? How many "yesses" on the doors? How many 1's and 2's on the assessments?

An experienced organizer quickly begins to come to an analysis of the trainee which can be hard to shake. For example if the trainee reported 20 visits and said that they spoke with 15 people and that 13 of them said "yes" that they would be at the meeting, but no one joined, there would be concern, because the results would be outside of the normal range of experience and credibility for organizers. 13 of 15 people are never "yesses." And, this is particularly true if of all of these "yesses," not a single one is a solid enough yes, to have forced the trainee to let them join the organization. Once again, this is not to say this is not possible, because I guess anything is possible, but, wow, is this street one to mark down on some permanent record as being something unique and different in the history of organizing or what? The same thing can be said if someone said that they had 40 visits in one night or had 20 visits and only 1 person was a yes and no one joined. In the first case the organizer knows that the trainee was just "burning turf," which in organizing means that they were running through the doors without doing real visits, but simply marking turf or canvassing, rather than organizing – since these techniques are much, much different. In the second case the organizer would probably suspect and then ask as many questions as necessary to determine whether the trainee in fact "blew off" the doors, meaning they either froze in the neighborhood and hung out at a café or *mercado* until time to come into the office or they are telling less than the truth and just didn't work that day at all. Attentive trainers will telephone the one "yes" and see if it was real. Most will simply leave the trainee with enough questions so there is a realization that something is not adding up. All of this is about work patterns, normative experience, and predictable outcomes. Anything can happen once to the best potential organizer, and a good trainer knows to throw out the bad day in order to get the trainee to where they need to be. When the same thing happens more than once or repeatedly, then the pattern becomes undeniable, and may lead to the conclusion that organizing may not be this recruit's personal destiny.

Training someone to success is the objective, but experience teaches hard lessons, and one of the most fundamental is that nothing about organizing comes without hard work. Results obtained too quickly or easily are as much a warning sign of trouble as no results being achieved at all. Where someone is doing the work and not succeeding, the odds are that one can still with perspiration, if nothing else, get them to a level of competence as an organizer. When someone is taking short cuts or cannot face the weight of the work, they are not going to make it, so the quicker one gets to the heart of this problem, the better. Finding that the work is hard is also frequently a surprise for many trainees coming not from the membership or general constituency, but from the outside. Perhaps they had always been successful in school or were activists back home or at college. There is culture shock for many finding that those experiences and even successes do not translate well. There are natural talents that some people have, but all of organizing takes work whether in shaping the talent into analysis and skills or working from the blank slate of commitment and concern.

My old high school Latin teacher, Dr. Romeo, used to repeat daily to all of us: *repetitio est mater studiorum* – repetition is the mother of study. Nowhere is that more true than when a fledgling organizer in training hits the doors day by day by day honing their skills. One of the nice things about the ACORN training drive model is that it puts a new organizer in the field virtually daily for up to six weeks or more organizing their first group. The trainee working with the more senior organizer can gauge their own progress on the doors, week after week. The size and character of the weekly organizing committee meetings should also demonstrate the same progress. The leadership visits and preparation for the first, big meeting and first actions are telling and reward hard work well done.

Training is an ongoing process. So is supervision.

ACORN also does two other major training programs with organizers, largely to evaluate their performance and standardize the work, which is more and more an issue as we increased the size and scale of our staff. Every organizer after completing between six months and one year with the organization went to a week of special training run by the national organization. A year later they would go to advanced training for several days to do another "time and temperature" check on their skills as well as work with their individual development plan. Subsequently, on an annual basis there were regular weekend training "dialogues" where each organizer who was eligible could participate on a variety of different topics, as well as the workshops and planning sessions at mid-year and year end/ year begin meetings.

Central to all of this of course is that organizing is a way of thinking, both distinct and unique from other ways that people view the world and think about it. Consequently, there is no end to the dialectic of learning, watching, and listening that develops a good organizer. It takes years of development and experience to produce a competent organizer who can land on their feet in myriad situations, while protecting and servicing the organization and its membership.

Outsiders used to ask me how long it took to train a good organizer. This is not a fill in the blank question from multiple choices. It is a cinch that the person asking would not have any idea whether we were selling sheets or shingles. Within five years you have to deal with most of the problems, but it could be more or less, depending on the speed, pace, and scale of the operation where you are organizing. In a big, bruising operation with lots of actions and campaigns, you will learn a lot more quickly, assuming you survive the pacing and the racing. In a smaller operation you may learn a few things more deeply, but some things not at all.

Nonetheless in even less time than this, you will start thinking like an organizer, and that change will be permanent. Take something simple, like reading the newspaper or watching the news. Before becoming an organizer, you can read stories about this or that at face value thinking perhaps that you are getting something in the vicinity of the facts. After becoming an organizer, you know better, and start looking for the "fine hand" behind each piece, what is at the table, what is hidden underneath, what is said versus what is meant, who and what is benefiting, and whose ox is getting gored. The basic suspension of disbelief that goes with everything is converted quickly to an understanding of how the world and its actions are really put together, piece by piece. At one level thinking like an organizer is exhilarating, and at another exhausting, but at either pole, once you have learned the language and the process, there is no going back.

Sometimes I wonder about people who learned just enough and for whatever reason, either professional or personal, did not make it or stay in the work, and how they live the rest of their lives with an understanding of what they see and what needs to be done, and the fact that they can clearly view the inside of events and movements, as if they were a low-grade superman with x-ray vision of a type, but then are no longer able to act on that knowledge, having left the work, and therefore lost their voice. It makes me sad for them in a way, but it's still a gift to learn another language and intellectual discipline, and that's what the training of an organizer produces.

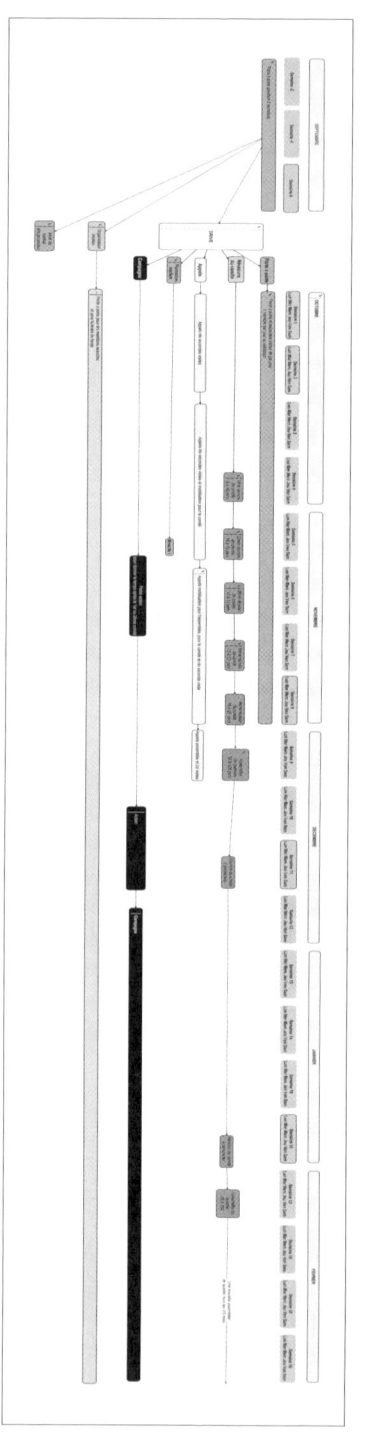

Organizing Drive Chart
(adapted by Alliance Citoyenne ACORN)

Chapter VII:
Managing Organizers and Staff

Let's say we figure out how to find and recruit organizers and then we manage to do a reasonable job at training them, how in the world does anyone manage this unruly bunch of free-wheeling, wild eyed, independent, hard-edged folks in any one room or anywhere around the world, much less in any one organization? Very, very carefully! Ba-boom!

Let me quickly point out that I tend to believe that there are many types of organizing staffs. Many of the faith based organizing networks have a fair number of former clergy and religious within their value based foundation. I assume that a staff with a lot of people motivated religiously, rather than say politically, would be different to manage, but from what I've observed that's more the veneer than the core.. Union staffs are sometimes a little different than community organizing staffs, but only by degree.

Coming out of the sixties, organizing staffs were much more male and macho. These tendencies are more repressed now, thankfully. I remember feeling like a solid citizen when I would hear stories of staff meetings in other operations that would go all night long, where there would be drinking, where people would stand up on tables and tear phone books, where organizers were sent out in the middle of the night to steal change from vending machines and newspaper boxes – truly weird and bizarre stuff! Relatively speaking, our operations were way tamer than any of these tales, especially if the tales were true? Which is not to say that there are not stories that people could tell, but whatever? One of our organizers in Bristol, England is also a cage fighter in his "free" time, so maybe it's just that these days there are more "hobbies" that can channel some of that wild and woolly stuff, rather than set off the bells and whistles at work?

There are some basic principles of staff management that we used. Three of the central tenets that we value from the very beginning of the organization are: consensus, commitment, and final responsibility. These three things, perhaps more than any other, define how I manage an organizing staff.

The membership operates as a democracy, the staff does not. The staff makes decisions based on consensus. There are no votes in our staff meetings. At the same time neither is there endless discussion, and individuals who essentially "withhold consensus" and stubbornly dig in to block achieving consensus, are also neither able to prevail or allowed to prevail.[66] The arbiter resolving such questions is the staff member that has "final responsibility," meaning that they are both accountable to superiors or the board for their performance or at the end of the day are "tasked" to have to make the decisions and do the job, therefore their view has more weight than others, and their say is the last say on a question. This runs all the way up the Chief Organizer and all the way down to the

---

[66] Recently I learned a technique meeting with our French staff during an impasse of consensus where they drew an invisible line on the floor, and everyone had to choose which side of the "river" they were on, and the moderator would ask each in turn what – if anything – it would take to get them to the other side of the river.

office director or head organizer of an individual project. There is never a place where, despite the belief and practice of consensus, the organization will not act because there was no way to define consensus, especially if the organizers are not easily able to achieve consensus. This is the nuts and bolts of ACORN consensus, not the finger wagging of an Occupy meeting. It neither looks nor feels the same, and there is always action or a decision at the conclusion of the meeting.

Final responsibility and commitment dovetail in a similar way. When we recruit staff, as I said earlier, we require a commitment. Once an organizer is on staff, a commitment is demonstrated and over time that turns into seniority. In an argument over tactics, it is obviously more likely that an organizer with final responsibility will prevail in the discussion – everything being equal – than the organizer who is just offering their two cents in the discussion, as helpful as that might be. On strategy the same is true on the long term consequences. It is only natural that the person who will do the hard time and the mop up over the years within the framework of the decision's consequences, should have the heavier value ascribed to their point of view, because by virtue of their commitment and proven work, they will carry the heavier burden as well into the future.

To me this seems obvious, but to many this is a wake-up call about organizing and our special world order of reality. I have been in absurd situations in which organizers who have already told us their leaving date will try to argue long and hard individually and in staff meetings before their departure on some course of action, thinking that their point of few should prevail and never understanding the irony that it is only a commitment to excessive liberality that allows them to speak at all once one of their foot is out of the door. Certainly since they will neither endure nor shape the consequences of whatever decision

George Wiley.

is made or course of action is chosen, given their diminished commitment, their view should have no weight in any determination.

As commitments turn into seniority, it should be no surprise that a basic value of staff management, as I managed the system, is that the longer you have worked with the organization, demonstrating time and again your value and contribution, the more that your voice should be heard and heeded in the councils of serious staff consideration. This seems natural, though perhaps uncomfortable, for the younger or less senior hands around the table, though their role is to help in the calculation of accountability. So, we place more weight on the opinion and point of view of organizers having more seniority, than we do on those with less time in the job. The ACORN pay scale is similarly structured to measure rewards to time served, but more on that later.

Some of these lessons I learned in reaction to the wild days working in the welfare rights movement under Dr. George Wiley. George was well loved and respected for his open hearted sincerity and demonstrated commitment, skill, and passion in service to the National Welfare Rights Organization (NWRO), but he was not an organizer, nor did he pretend to be. Furthermore, his academic and scientific background, led him to be more interested in an "open mic" approach to the world and to staff and strategy meetings. He seemed to have an equal interest in every opinion from any quarter, be it the highest performing organizer, the guy who might have wandered in from the print shop and pitched his opinion on the pile, or the visiting academic, friend, or social worker who might have been at the meeting by happenstance. Everybody and every point of view were in the gumbo. He was a "let a thousand flowers bloom" kind of guy when he managed the meetings, and in truth though he was the weight in the room, he frequently

Bill Pastriech at Local 100 Training.

did not manage the meetings at all, but would hover around them, half in and half out of the process, and therefore neither accountable nor responsible for the process at all. All of this would make Tim Sampson or Hulbert James, the sort of staff director and the sort of field director, have fits trying to ride these bronco busting national staff meetings when they would happen ever so rarely, and it would drive the organizers literally crazy! I will never forget the arguments when I was 20 and 21 years old working for NWRO in Massachusetts between Bill Pastreich, then in Connecticut, Rhoda Linton, and Andrea Kydd both working in Brooklyn over just these kinds of issues. Pastreich was perpetually befuddled that certain organizers, who were not producing, could both make and win arguments on strategy and tactics, where he could not, and he felt he was producing, which usually was true, though Bill rarely actually thought about how to "organize" *in the meeting* enough to have his views prevail, retreating usually to some outrageous expression of pique or exaggerated position, which would almost always drive Rhoda and Andrea even crazier. I loved every minute, as scary as it all was, since yelling and harrumphing of all sorts could break out at any moment, and it was all a great lesson in work and life for me, and of course the antithesis of boring!

The lessons in staff management I took away from those somewhat searing (scarring?) experiences were first, only to let the staff in the room for staff meetings. Staff meetings were serious business and not pickup games for passersby. They were mandatory unless properly excused and they were closed to everyone not on the staff. It was an honor and responsibility to attend. They needed to be held regularly, and people on payroll should have a right to know what to expect in terms of agenda and participation.

This question of voice is central in managing a staff, especially an organizing staff, and I think it is part of what rendered welfare rights and so many other movements of that era challenging internal experiences. To not properly credit voice proportionate to contribution, responsibility, and commitment was essentially also to devalue all the very lives of the people who were working for the organization invariably at low pay and sometimes at significant personal price and occasionally peril. Allowing the creation of a false equity in voice may have seemed to some a correct commitment to "participatory democracy" or some other waving flag marching by in the rhetoric of the moment, but in reality it inadvertently, but directly, called into question the very work people were doing by privileging others equal to those doing the time and carrying the weight. There is really no positive outcome that comes from anarchy in managing a staff and one cannot be a steward of the memberships' interest without being willing to discriminate among opinions and be forceful in presenting operating premises and principles at work. Part of what holds organizers in the work for literally lifetimes is the fundamental recognition that apart from the organization itself they would have no voice in the affairs of the world and their stake in changing so much of it, therefore leaving the organization means losing the voice that they have spent a lifetime learning to use effectively.

Additionally, contributions simply need to be weighted appropriately. This did not mean that all voices were not heard, that discordant views were not allowed time and accorded proper discussion and struggle, but that there still has to be a shared hierarchy of accepted principles that rule the way the staff operate, and especially the way it handles disagreements so that the final product is consensual, unified, and able to be presented to the membership with one voice. In the early days of ACORN in working these principles out in the crucible of fumbling new experiences, this was not easy. The boundaries were less clear and the order less assured. Meetings on key questions or campaigns could literally go forever, whether standard or special. Every Wednesday night at 8pm was staff meeting night in Little Rock in the early days. Maybe the meeting would be over in a couple of hours on a normal week, but just as easily something could come loose, and it might be midnight, or 2 AM, or god knows what time cows come home in Arkansas, we would do whatever it took to come to a consensual conclusion. My hand was there, but it was less heavy in building the system. Being young, it was also easy to lose control of these things as well and get *way out there*. We needed every one of these organizers to build this operation, so they **all** had to own the whole, by damn, whether they wanted to or not

Similarly, keeping staff business within the staff itself is a critical value to maintain in staff management. One cannot allow internal voice in staff affairs to be robust and even unruly at times and also worry that it might be repeated outside the staff itself, particularly to the membership, where it could affect not only the credibility and working relationships of an individual organizer, but also the entire staff and its viability and advice to the leadership and counsel to the membership. We have always been clear that repeating staff business to the leadership was past the pale, and in fact was grounds for termination. Not only was it grounds, but we terminated staff for just this kind of thing. Loose lips cannot be tolerated or the internal process then takes on the color of a public forum, and voice and debate are permanently destroyed as effective tools for policy making within staff councils.

Needless to say, if an organizer can be terminated this way, without a doubt if a staff member runs their mouth not just within the organization's membership or leadership but actually *outside* of the organization to allies, friends, or strangers, you are a long gone, pecan, cher! Primary loyalty to the organization, including its program, policies, and procedures has to have a clear value without dilution or equivocation.

I am unabashedly serious about this, and I am so even realizing that this is hopelessly passé in these modern days. I believe in loyalty, and, frankly, both expect it and categorically practice it. ACORN is a better organization because of this, and I mourn the deterioration of loyalty and its value elsewhere, including in the institutional labor movement, as a sad thing, even if effectively rationalized for scores of reasons. It is about people first and finally for me, and it only works with people, if you are able to work with them in the utmost trust and care, which translates back into loyalty.

How hard is this really? It devalues brazen, ruthless ambition, and that is good. It means that one accords the benefit of doubt and good will to proven people in an organization over time, and how bad is that really? It means that one counts and reckons where stands will be made and, dare we say, bullets taken. I think that one of the reasons some very great men and women worked (put up?) with me, through thick and thin, good and bad, has a lot to do with loyalty. They know that at the bottom line, I would do anything for them and that represents a categorical commitment that transcends minor, and even major, differences against the weight of years and decades. Loyalty is a non-refundable currency that acts as amazing cement within an organization. People who do not have it, have trouble understanding it. People who have it, know that it is a gift and an obligation.

The criticism of both seniority and loyalty is whether or not these are shelters for staff that allow non-performers to find a sinecure of sorts and whether or not more talented performance goes underappreciated and rewarded, while disproportionate weight, and even wages, are expended on those whose contributions may, arguably, be more in the past, than in the present. Of course I am comfortable offering a rendition of the critique, because I believe it is unwarranted in the case of staffs that I manage, but past such an obviously self-serving assertion, the very "dog eat dog" nature of survival within the marginally sustainable enterprises of progressive movements tends to mitigate strongly

Little Rock Staff Meeting 1976. Dewey Armstrong, John Beam, Kaye Jaeger.

against anyone being provided a sinecure or carrying the water for others performing less ably.

The problem arises more in offering an extra chance. If one has an organizer with twenty years' experience running an office in a certain city, and the job is being done, but perhaps not within the full potential or promise that is possible there, of course one lingers much longer before making hard decisions and sudden changes in staffing because of the body of the contribution, the seniority, and the loyalty to the organizer that is systemic within our staff management system. How long is the right length, and how long is too long, when measured against such stewardship?

The members are almost never the problem. They are usually dealing with their immediate expectations rather than measuring organizational performance against other offices or market potential, so the issue is more on whether or not, I am doing the job they demand of me, than whether or not they might be satisfied with the individual organizer. We are paid money to make these hard calls and decisions, and as part of the exchange for our own job security, we have to answer for them regularly, and sometimes no matter the years, the past, or the loyalty, change has to come, that may not make the individual organizer happy.

I believe it is still better this way, and, frankly, more palpable when even the person on the wrong end of this trade has to face the call, knows the system has been transparent, has included deeply shared values, and has worked in their favor, even if they are not happy at the outcome. They are then more likely to accept with some good grace the decision, and in some cases we have found they do so mutually, recognizing that there are other ways that a new and better contribution can be made that exploits more ably the strengths they still have to offer at that time. Furthermore, even the young, brash, and hot to trot, need to realize that the system bends to the arc of their progress as well, even if it only does so over time, and therefore there will be a reward for their service in the same way.

All of this informs the way we look at wage scales as well, since the guiding principle is equity and that has translated into seniority for most of the life of the organization. Nothing can be as corrosive for an organizing community as a belief that the pay is unjust or that others doing the same work are paid differently, independent of performance or anything extenuating. No matter what any might say about the pay levels within our operations, there is clarity and an equitable standard of fairness. You start at the same gate on wages as everyone else and know with a certainty that as low as our wages might be that they represent a commitment by the organization to being able to pay an organizer at least that amount with a level of certainty and timeliness. You know within our system that there was a wage increase for every year that you successfully completed. You knew that the increases are actually "frontloaded," meaning that more junior organizers go up more quickly in the beginning – which speaks to the high consensus within the community about both recruiting and retention – and more senior organizers have smaller adjustments at the top of the scale. You also knew that you will never lose ground because even in years when there is not an overall scale adjustment, there would still be a cost of living adjustment (COLA) figured to the recognized and accepted governmental index. All of these things are tried and tested within the system and are baseline components of our wage scale for decades. They signal equity and they assure that, if you serve continually and consistently, you will steadily see your wages rise in recognition to your service. Fair enough!

We are always clear that our people are invaluable and that all of them are underpaid and none of them are paid based on any market calculation or comparability of their worth. We spend a lot of time with organizers making sure that they hear, whether they agree or not, that they must not allow money to become the standard by which they

Exhibit 2

United States Council Compensation

SENIORITY	BASIC SCALE 1/1/2008	INCR /YR	BI-WEEKLY	WEEKLY
40	$71,553	$1,231	$2,752.02	$1,376.01
39	$70,321	$1,231	$2,704.67	$1,352.33
38	$69,090	$1,231	$2,657.32	$1,328.66
37	$67,859	$1,231	$2,609.97	$1,304.98
36	$66,628	$1,741	$2,562.61	$1,281.31
35	$64,887	$1,119	$2,495.65	$1,247.82
34	$63,768	$1,119	$2,452.60	$1,226.30
33	$62,648	$1,119	$2,409.55	$1,204.78
32	$61,529	$1,119	$2,366.51	$1,183.25
31	$60,410	$1,629	$2,323.46	$1,161.73
30	$58,781	$1,007	$2,260.80	$1,130.40
29	$57,773	$1,007	$2,222.06	$1,111.03
28	$56,766	$1,007	$2,183.31	$1,091.66
27	$55,759	$1,007	$2,144.57	$1,072.29
26	$54,752	$1,517	$2,105.83	$1,052.92
25	$53,234	$895	$2,047.47	$1,023.74
24	$52,339	$895	$2,013.04	$1,006.52
23	$51,444	$895	$1,978.60	$989.30
22	$50,548	$895	$1,944.16	$972.08
21	$49,653	$1,405	$1,909.72	$954.86
20	$48,247	$839	$1,855.67	$927.84
19	$47,408	$839	$1,823.39	$911.69
18	$46,569	$839	$1,791.10	$895.55
17	$45,729	$839	$1,758.82	$879.41
16	$44,890	$1,349	$1,726.53	$863.27
15	$43,540	$839	$1,674.63	$837.31
14	$42,701	$839	$1,642.34	$821.17
13	$41,862	$839	$1,610.06	$805.03
12	$41,022	$839	$1,577.77	$788.89
11	$40,183	$1,349	$1,545.49	$772.74
10	$38,833	$839	$1,493.59	$746.79
9	$37,994	$839	$1,461.30	$730.65
8	$37,154	$839	$1,429.02	$714.51
7	$36,315	$839	$1,396.73	$698.37
6	$35,476	$2,424	$1,364.45	$682.22
5	$33,052	$1,119	$1,271.21	$635.61
4	$31,932	$1,119	$1,228.17	$614.08
3	$30,813	$2,694	$1,185.12	$592.56
2	$28,119	$1,619	$1,081.51	$540.75
STARTING	$26,500		$1,019.23	$509.62

allow themselves to judged or a measure of their worth as individuals or professionals. We have found that arguments around political principles in this area have no meaning. Most do not care if they might have come to us with a bourgeois backgrounds or middle class aspirations, so simply to point out the obvious is not a good learning experience or teachable moment.

We do much better conceding from the beginning that their value to us is inestimable and incalculable, and instead talk to them about the organizational sustainability model under which we operate and the membership that finally determine the wage scales and how they are paid and how they think about money. These points are both true and irrefutable. An organization committed to a sustainability model that rests on dues and produces internally based income, even though supplemented sometimes significantly by external sources, cannot base salary scales for a significantly sized staff on whatever might have come through the door yesterday or might be expected tomorrow. There has to be a bottom line logic to budget, income, and expenses that all ties together.

The membership that approves salaries is also low and moderate income. The members fight endlessly for better wages, increases in minimum wages, and realization of living wages. There clearly cannot be a double standard, where the members have to reach deeply for their dues, while the staff is living high on the hog. Needless to say, there is no danger of this happening in an ACORN operation! If salaries were disproportionately high, members and leaders would be steadily arguing that they should be on staff. The salaries have to seem fair to the members in their experience and from their observation of the work itself and its difficulty. In Local 100 ULU for example the constitution and bylaws holds the pay to 90% of the average of what our members make in order to define this message even more starkly.

Organizers also understand easily that we have to have more organizers rather than fewer to do the work. Not all organizing communities resolve this question the way that we do, but within our fundamentals, there is no belief that the organization only needs "one ranger for one riot."[67] Instead there is a recognition that if we are to organize a critical mass of the constituency, it will always mean that we will need more organizers and not less. When there is only so much money, there are important programmatic judgments that have to be made about whether it is more important to hire more or pay more. As a matter of operating principle, we always elect the former over the later.

Over the years our wage scale grew from abysmal up to merely low. We pay about two to two a half times the minimum wage in the USA and other countries, so the salaries are less minimal, but also a long way from grand. We get fewer questions from outsiders and relatives about whether "care" packages are needed or whether or not their people are in danger of starvation. On the other hand, we also find some head scratching about whether or not this is a cult or calling. Whatever? It works!

I am not proselytizing. Our scale is certainly not perfect and our resources are thinner than others, mission is different, and values are as I have stated, and certainly not universally shared. Under any circumstances though, *every* organizing project has to have a scale, and if it does not arise through an internal process, as our does, it will

---

[67] The old Texas Rangers motto.

Chapter VII: Managing Organizers and Staff

be forced from some direction eventually. A scale is a system, and without a system the organization cannot grow. Within the ACORN family of organizations at our high point we had 1200-1500 regular employees and during special projects the number of people on staff ballooned up past 5000 workers and over 10,000 annually including part-time staff. Needless to say, an individually based payroll negotiation can never work once any kind of real size is achieved.

Over the years there have been adaptations and amendments that have given the scale a slightly more human touch and allowed some flexibility to the increased requirements brought by the growth and range of the organization. The crack in the door was always around "need." The twin pillars of the salary scale were "equity," which was obvious, and "need," which could be very personal. The concept of need allowed just enough discretion to be able, particularly on very little money, to handle the occasional car loan, college loan payment, or day care problem not shared equally by all on staff, but vital to allow equity, particularly at the lower salary levels, to work for the vast majority of people. The system had to be one where everyone had an equal chance of surviving and living reasonably, even if not living well. The concept of need gives room for the rest of the scale to work.

Another adaptation that is fair, but always has the ability to be contentious, especially as the organization ages, has to do with how one "credits" organizing seniority outside of our family of organizations. If someone had organized for another community organization or union, should they get any credit on the salary scale thereby advancing them up some number of levels above the starting pay? Reasonably, there is a case that should be made that sometimes that experience is valuable to our organization, therefore some level of credit should be applied, but how does one handle vacation time earned then, or how does one not create a "false equity" that might in the rush to hire, dilute time served within our community by saying it had the same value as time served elsewhere. We ended up developing a board approved measure which allowed some seniority credit but barred 100% credit. Nonetheless, there are traditionalists, usually some of our best senior people, who still cannot reconcile full seniority credits as part of affiliations almost thirty years ago, so they certainly were not applauding such credits later for various comparable experiences elsewhere.

Where "need" became a more difficult principle to manage is when the organizations' developed different needs that we had not anticipated fully over the decades for particular skills and people where we could not "set the market" as we could in organizing. Our first lawyers, bless their hearts, came on at scale, but as the climate and markets changed, to stabilize them we had to make some movement towards a separate, though related scale to handle positions that were more market impacted. This was also true for some finance positions. The overwhelming size of the financial operation eventually meant that a professionally trained and experienced controller was needed and that CPAs had to be hired, so an organizers' scale was the rock on which all of this was built, but there were differentials.

These kinds of issues though are slippery slopes for wage scales. There were already "fundraising" exceptions, but to the degree that virtually all staff has financial responsibilities, the debate, if ever joined, would be difficult to mediate easily. Political organizers in some ways broke the back on the scale, because they were simply organizers in most peoples' minds who were used to getting paid higher and working in shorter spurts therefore demanding more money, rather than people who necessarily had different or superior skills. Gradually, the board also became displeased looking at the wild ranges that they could not reconcile with how they valued particular staff, and found these situations harder and harder to resolve from their perspectives as well.

As size increased there also became issues with whether or not seniority based scale properly recognized the difference in the jobs of similar people in different offices with larger staffs and budgets. Responsibility pay[68] at various levels was finally introduced to address this issue, and to some degree it did, but to the degree there was a gradual hybridization of the scale, one always had to make sure that it remained as defensible and above challenge as we needed to allow for maximum effective operations.

Cost of living was a good example of a staff management system that totally did not work, though we tried it for years. Adjusting the wage scales based on local living standards would seem on its face to have merit; particularly since we were working in cities as diverse as New York and Little Rock, San Jose and Miami, and everywhere in between. We would use the Bureau of Labor Statistics figures issued during January by city tabulating the changes in cost of living for the previous year. Everything would be measured to Little Rock at benchmark zero since that was the original ACORN city, and the rest of the increases would be lumped in groups first with the top being $3000 extra per year for the allowance, and before we abandoned the policy it added $5000 extra per year added onto the wages in the most expensive cities.

As an administrator, I have to say this was a largely thankless and dysfunctional system. No one *ever* believed their city was getting a fair break, and particularly those in cities that putatively might have believed that they were "high cost" cities, always thought that there was a conspiracy afoot somewhere. Lord help us the years that San Jose was seen as the most expensive city, rather than New York – those arguments could be endless. The Little Rock's would chafe because they were required to own (and therefore buy!) a car, pay insurance, and gas with minor reimbursements, while in the New York's or Boston's or other "high cost" cities, the transportation was subsidized completely through the organizational purchase of bus and metro passes. Moving staff from a "high" COLA adjusted city to a "low" one was also difficult and painful, and sometimes impossible, because it mean a reduction of pay for the organizer being transferred, and even though reason might have told them that it was a better deal, seeing their check go down started the kvetching. Who had cheaper housing versus where there was cheaper food and so on and so on: *ad nauseum, ad infinitum.* For the organization this policy was an absolute bust, because it was not only expensive, but precious dollars bought controversy, rather than happiness. Finally, it was easier, though it was hugely expensive, to buy our way out of the regional cost of living adjustment programs, and simply leapfrog the entire pay scale high enough over what everyone was making to run from this problem. Once we were a couple of years away from these regional adjustments, it was possible to smile a little about the mess, but that is still the only way to describe what happens when one tries to run a

---

[68] Responsibility pay meant that if you directed an operation or a city or state, you might be paid slightly more for doing so.

national organization on a program that can easily be sabotaged by a local and provincial bias that trumps the good of the whole. Been there, done that, never going back!

In a perfect salary system there would simply be one system, and that's it and no questions asked. People neither think, nor work that way, so the real situation is that one finally makes a determination based on where the highest level of consensus and support lies, and then you hang on for dear life. As great a job as it is running an organization, if you lose control of the salary structure, you will spend all your time in a constantly losing and unsatisfactory battle trying to manage the individual salary demands of staff. I didn't sign up for that, and can't imagine that anyone would.

I am reminded of this constantly as we continue to build an international operation and work in other countries. Some staff people may suffer episodic myopia. They can look at policies where there are more than a 1000 people employed, and in a twist of parallax vision of some kind, because they are one of a couple of people working in the same organization, but in a different country, they can believe with sometimes righteous indignation that, "thank you, sir" but everything should work differently for me! The issues, or more accurately, the "interests," usually start with wanting to be paid in United States currency, rather than the currency of their own countries. The next hope often expressed would be that the scale would not be adjusted to their local circumstances and currency, but that the whole US scale would simply be imported wholesale into their country. There is no logic to any of this. The missing link is sustainability obviously. There is no way to collect dues from members in the soles, pesos, or rupees from member families calibrated to the equivalency of the membership dues rates for members in the US, and then somehow turn around and pay the organizers based on US rates, when we have collected local dues in local currency. This is so clear as to really be inarguable.

The reason, besides naked self-interest, that it was ever even arguable is the disease of NGO-ism that runs deeply around the globe. Whether in Canada or Mexico, Kenya or India, there are people who know that other people who work for large non-governmental

ACORN Board and Staff Meeting in Santa Domingo 2008.

Exhibit 3

ACORN INTERNATIONAL COMPENSATION SCHEDULE 2012

	United States 1/1/2012 US$	Mexico 1/1/2012 US$	Mexico 1/1/2012 Pesos	Canada 1/1/2012 US$	Canada 1/1/2012 CND$	Peru 1/1/2012 US$	Peru 1/1/2012 S/.	Honduras 1/1/2012 US$	Honduras 1/1/2012 HNL	Argentina 1/1/2012 US$	Argentina 1/1/2012 ARS	India 1/1/2012 US$	India 1/1/2012 Rs	Kenya 1/1/2012 US$	Kenya 1/1/2012 Shillings
35	$69,812	$32,252	$415,419	$68,218	$68,337	$8,972	S/. 78,396	$11,130	L. 212,073	$20,507	$89,153	$4,807	INR 236,935	$11,333	KES 939,067
34	$68,607	$31,678	$408,020	$67,040	$67,158	$8,812	S/. 77,000	$10,931	L. 208,296	$20,142	$87,565	$4,721	INR 232,716	$11,131	KES 922,343
33	$67,403	$31,104	$400,629	$65,864	$65,979	$8,653	S/. 75,605	$10,733	L. 204,523	$19,777	$85,979	$4,636	INR 228,500	$10,930	KES 905,635
32	$66,199	$30,530	$393,237	$64,688	$64,801	$8,493	S/. 74,210	$10,535	L. 200,749	$19,412	$84,393	$4,550	INR 224,284	$10,728	KES 888,926
31	$64,995	$29,956	$385,846	$63,511	$63,622	$8,333	S/. 72,815	$10,337	L. 196,976	$19,047	$82,807	$4,465	INR 220,068	$10,526	KES 872,217
30	$63,242	$29,121	$375,079	$61,798	$61,906	$8,101	S/. 70,783	$10,049	L. 191,479	$18,515	$80,496	$4,340	INR 213,927	$10,233	KES 847,878
29	$62,158	$28,604	$368,429	$60,739	$60,845	$7,957	S/. 69,528	$9,871	L. 188,084	$18,187	$79,069	$4,263	INR 210,134	$10,051	KES 832,845
28	$61,074	$28,087	$361,771	$59,680	$59,784	$7,813	S/. 68,272	$9,692	L. 184,686	$17,859	$77,640	$4,186	INR 206,337	$9,870	KES 817,796
27	$59,991	$27,571	$355,121	$58,621	$58,724	$7,670	S/. 67,017	$9,514	L. 181,291	$17,530	$76,213	$4,109	INR 202,544	$9,688	KES 802,763
26	$58,907	$27,054	$348,464	$57,562	$57,662	$7,526	S/. 65,760	$9,336	L. 177,892	$17,202	$74,784	$4,032	INR 198,747	$9,507	KES 787,714
25	$57,275	$26,276	$338,445	$55,967	$56,065	$7,310	S/. 63,870	$9,067	L. 172,778	$16,707	$72,634	$3,916	INR 193,033	$9,233	KES 765,065
24	$56,311	$25,817	$332,529	$55,026	$55,122	$7,182	S/. 62,753	$8,909	L. 169,757	$16,415	$71,364	$3,848	INR 189,659	$9,072	KES 751,692
23	$55,348	$25,358	$326,613	$54,084	$54,179	$7,054	S/. 61,637	$8,750	L. 166,737	$16,123	$70,095	$3,779	INR 186,285	$8,910	KES 738,319
22	$54,384	$24,898	$320,697	$53,143	$53,235	$6,926	S/. 60,520	$8,592	L. 163,717	$15,831	$68,825	$3,711	INR 182,911	$8,749	KES 724,946
21	$53,421	$24,439	$314,781	$52,201	$52,292	$6,799	S/. 59,404	$8,433	L. 160,697	$15,539	$67,555	$3,642	INR 179,536	$8,588	KES 711,573
20	$51,910	$23,719	$305,503	$50,724	$50,813	$6,598	S/. 57,653	$8,185	L. 155,961	$15,081	$65,564	$3,535	INR 174,245	$8,335	KES 690,600
19	$51,007	$23,288	$299,958	$49,842	$49,929	$6,478	S/. 56,607	$8,036	L. 153,130	$14,807	$64,374	$3,471	INR 171,082	$8,183	KES 678,065
18	$50,103	$22,858	$294,413	$48,959	$49,045	$6,359	S/. 55,560	$7,888	L. 150,299	$14,533	$63,184	$3,407	INR 167,919	$8,032	KES 665,529

Chapter VII: Managing Organizers and Staff

Exhibit 3

ACORN INTERNATIONAL COMPENSATION SCHEDULE 2012

	United States 1/1/2012 US$	Mexico 1/1/2012 US$	Mexico 1/1/2012 Pesos	Canada 1/1/2012 US$	Canada 1/1/2012 CND$	Peru 1/1/2012 US$	Peru 1/1/2012 S/.	Honduras 1/1/2012 US$	Honduras 1/1/2012 HNL	Argentina 1/1/2012 US$	Argentina 1/1/2012 ARS	India 1/1/2012 US$	India 1/1/2012 Rs	Kenya 1/1/2012 US$	Kenya 1/1/2012 Shillings
17	$49,200	$22,427	$288,867	$48,077	$48,161	$6,239	S/.54,514	$7,739	L.147,468	$14,260	$61,994	$3,342	INR 164,756	$7,881	KES 652,994
16	$48,297	$21,997	$283,322	$47,194	$47,277	$6,119	S/.53,467	$7,591	L.144,637	$13,986	$60,804	$3,278	INR 161,594	$7,729	KES 640,459
15	$46,845	$21,305	$274,408	$45,776	$45,856	$5,927	S/.51,785	$7,352	L.140,086	$13,546	$58,891	$3,175	INR 156,509	$7,486	KES 620,308
14	$45,942	$20,874	$268,863	$44,893	$44,971	$5,807	S/.50,738	$7,203	L.137,255	$13,272	$57,701	$3,111	INR 153,346	$7,335	KES 607,772
13	$45,039	$20,444	$263,317	$44,010	$44,087	$5,687	S/.49,692	$7,055	L.134,425	$12,998	$56,511	$3,047	INR 150,184	$7,184	KES 595,237
12	$44,136	$20,013	$257,772	$43,128	$43,203	$5,567	S/.48,645	$6,906	L.131,594	$12,725	$55,321	$2,983	INR 147,021	$7,032	KES 582,702
11	$43,232	$19,582	$252,227	$42,245	$42,319	$5,448	S/.47,599	$6,757	L.128,763	$12,451	$54,131	$2,918	INR 143,858	$6,881	KES 570,166
10	$41,781	$18,890	$243,312	$40,827	$40,898	$5,255	S/.45,917	$6,519	L.124,212	$12,011	$52,217	$2,815	INR 138,774	$6,638	KES 550,016
9	$40,877	$18,460	$237,767	$39,944	$40,014	$5,135	S/.44,870	$6,370	L.121,381	$11,737	$51,027	$2,751	INR 135,611	$6,487	KES 537,480
8	$39,974	$18,029	$232,222	$39,062	$39,130	$5,015	S/.43,824	$6,221	L.118,550	$11,463	$49,837	$2,687	INR 132,448	$6,335	KES 524,945
7	$39,071	$17,599	$226,677	$38,179	$38,246	$4,896	S/.42,777	$6,073	L.115,719	$11,190	$48,647	$2,623	INR 129,286	$6,184	KES 512,410
6	$38,168	$17,168	$221,131	$37,296	$37,362	$4,776	S/.41,731	$5,924	L.112,888	$10,916	$47,457	$2,559	INR 126,123	$6,033	KES 499,874
5	$35,560	$15,925	$205,122	$34,748	$34,809	$4,430	S/.38,710	$5,495	L.104,716	$10,126	$44,021	$2,373	INR 116,992	$5,596	KES 463,685
4	$34,355	$15,351	$197,724	$33,571	$33,630	$4,270	S/.37,313	$5,297	L.100,939	$9,760	$42,434	$2,288	INR 112,772	$5,394	KES 446,961
3	$33,152	$14,777	$190,332	$32,395	$32,451	$4,111	S/.35,919	$5,099	L.97,165	$9,396	$40,847	$2,202	INR 108,557	$5,192	KES 430,252
2	$30,253	$13,652	$175,839	$29,562	$29,614	$3,798	S/.33,184	$4,711	L.89,767	$8,680	$37,737	$2,035	INR 100,290	$4,797	KES 397,490
STARTING	$28,511	$13,078	$168,448	$27,860	$27,909	$3,638	S/.31,789	$4,513	L.85,993	$8,315	$36,151	$1,949	INR 96,075	$4,595	KES 380,781
Dues	$10	$5	$67	$11	$11	$0.47	S/.4	$1	L.27	$1	$4	$1	INR 33	$1	KES 117

Note: Over the five years in fact between 2009 and 2014, ACORN International resized with a twist, similar to that of ACORN US in 1984. We abandoned a set salary scale, even while keeping the salary formula, and instead in developing countries provided a fixed subsidy

128 Nuts & Bolts – The ACORN Fundamentals of Organizing

agencies (NGOs), commonly funded by donor governments or some other weirdness (like the AFL-CIO's Solidarity Centers that are all funded by the US government so their staff is living in high clover on most local currencies!). Or, they might have run into someone on a plane or at a club or wherever that works for a multi-national corporation, and is on assignment, and being paid to live differently for the short stint in the host country. NGO-itis is corrosive and parasitical. There is no pretense to integrating an operation indigenously or achieving any sustainability, it is all about another way into the high air and the upper class of the local country and the ex-pat, globally transient community. Visiting Nairobi is a tonic for this kind of toxicity. The name of the city might better be NGObi! The donor community is a major income source for the city and a visitor drives mile by mile in some sectors past one gated, signed, NGO headquarters, compound, or office after another.

There were early NGO lessons for ACORN International. With a membership based organization the preference on hiring should be indigenous anyway, so at one level this is less a problem, except that one still has to translate the organizing model and methodology into the local community and country somehow, and then comes the rub. We were fortunate in Canada that the harsh immigration policies between the US and Canada, forced Judy Duncan, a Canadian working on a visa and being trained in Seattle, to have to go back home, and we were smart enough to follow her there with the organization. The same situation led to our initial breakthrough in Latin America and, especially, Argentina, with Ercilia Sahores, who for a while ran all of Latin American operations from Buenos Aires, but who trained with ACORN in Florida for six months and then returned home to work to build ACORN. But, we have almost as many failures and near misses where US trained organizers, recent immigrants from other countries, would not go back to organize in their home countries, unless they were paid some kind of premium based on a US wage scale. Without that problem there would have been ACORN organizations in Honduras and Guatemala many years earlier, but organizers balked at the last minute about being paid in local currency. In India it has been an experience having local staff come to grips with a wage scale based on rupees and the poverty of the population, rather than their hopes of what working for an organization with US roots might mean. We are not outsourcing, but laying permanent and deep roots in local communities and countries, and that is a hard message to accept until an organizer senses that it is common and it works, so we had to relive some of the early struggles around wage scales that ACORN in the US had grown past over the its four decades.

As I indicated earlier our basic scale is internationalized by roughly taking the base line from the United States, where the scale begins at roughly two and a half times (2 ½) the minimum wage, determining the minimum wage in the country, multiplying, and doing the same adjustments to the dues. The real problem that worried me is that I was still not sure that we could be financially sustainable in our other countries. For example Mexico, compared to other Latin American countries where we are organizing, is a relatively high waged country, if we paid on our formula. Dues though, are low. The mismatch between our costs and our dues are horrendous still, and it is unclear to me how we make this work without something breaking on one end or the other.

Over the five years in fact between 2009 and 2014, ACORN International resized with a twist, similar to that of ACORN US in 1984. We abandoned a set salary scale, even while keeping the salary formula, and instead in developing countries provided a fixed subsidy, allowing the difference in salary and expenses to be set by the level of success in dues receipts and internal financing. We became convinced that the venality and power of the NGO model of operations between richer countries and poorer countries was such that unless we changed the system we would never be able to have a chance at building permanent, locally sustainable operations. Furthermore in more recent years when ACORN International has had the opportunity of also organizing in higher income countries (United Kingdom, Italy, the Czech Republic, and France), we provide no external financial support thereby forcing the self-sufficiency process to be immediate from the beginning and permanent for the future. Having now grown to more than 17 countries at this writing and 200,000 members, I am convinced, as painful and difficult as the process and as uneven as the results in some of the initial countries, this was a right-sizing, not simply a re-sizing.

The truth is that people – for the most part – come to our work for two reasons, either because this is what they believe in or because they need a job. The ones that need a job, but don't believe, are never going to be happy, nor is happiness waiting for the ones who are more committed to a certain life-style rather than to our work. Neither of those potential recruits, no matter how individually valuable they might seem, are going to make it over time. The people who need a job are solid prospects because they are rooted in our world and constituency, and many once involved in organizing in fact come to believe in the work, and therefore are invaluable. The ones who need a job and never believe in the work and culture, are going to be gone if they ever get a better offer, so we cannot expect otherwise. For everyone, fairness, a decent work environment, and basic support and encouragement can win a lifetime of work. The ones who come to us because they believe it the mission of the organization, our politics, our culture, the community they find here, and other "values" based reasons are also going to be able to stick, as long as the wages are fair and equitable and they are not abused or alienated in some way. These two sectors are both large, so we have to focus on what needs to be done to recruit and develop them permanently from either orientation.

We manage one of these groups around ambition and realization and the other around competency, continuity, and standards. Yes, all of these are important regardless of the initial orientation of the individual, but we are looking here at emphasis, not exclusivity, and there is no substitute for good judgment and discernment in all of these areas.

Ambition is a great and fierce motivator, particularly for staff drawn to the "cause" of the organization. These are people who have been trained and raised, sometimes from birth, to believe that they should be at the top of any heap, and they will fiercely want to succeed, if there's any way possible for them to do so, in the organization. These are race horses that one has to teach to run and somehow keep them in the lanes so that they can make it to the end of the race.

Ambition is often the hand maiden of competition, and putting these two explosive pieces together so that the thrust propels the organization can be a tricky procedure either allowing fast progress or blowing up everything in its path. In a smaller organization with a narrow set of aspirations, these kinds of motivations are probably inappropriate. In organizations with the broad mission and aspiration of unions or community organizations like ACORN, I believe that you might as well recognize the existence of these potentially creative, yet centrifugal forces, and try to manage them to the benefit of the enterprise.

Our record is good at handling these kinds of explosive combinations for the most part. We have had limited experience over almost five decades with the common problem in business (and in some non-profits) where individuals have begun competitive organizations.

Running local unions within a larger international there is a constant encouragement for disloyalty and subterfuge in the increasing corporatization of large unions and there are political alliances which shift and can therefore strand organizers and leaders as the tides move in and out within such institutions. For the most part this has not been a terrible problem for us, but we have seen and experienced the phenomena, and found little to recommend or respect in the way this works out. The move to make local unions mere shells, rather than operating entities of large unions is the wider trend here, though I am not sure that it will be the final paradigm.

The plus side of managing along these lines built a core and deep reserve of very talented, top flight people who could manage virtually anything anywhere, and we were – and are – fortunate that they have yoked their futures to these organizations and our mission. Managing along these lines, one might reasonably ask, how I survived for all of these years? Good question! And, the answer is not measurably different than how anyone survives at the top of any large, aggressive combination.

First, it is always critical on the bottom line to correctly understand and maintain your base. I often joked, unsmilingly, that I am still a local group organizer, and the very large local group that I have had to grow and maintain constantly is the staff itself. To be a boss and manage people one has to always remember that you have to maintain significant consensual support among the people you supervise in order to be their boss. A fundamental error many supervisors make is not understanding that their ability to drive staff is based on the *support* of the staff, not simply their own brilliance, grueling work habits, personal charisma, or any number of other very temporary and tenuous things. All of these other assets are important and may help give you the respect and edge you need to operate, but to manage a staff you have to be able to drive the staff and without the clear or unspoken "consent of the governed" a revolution is as likely as a successful program. This is especially true in a non-profit, and absolutely true in a more poorly paid group of outfits like our own, because we do not have the corporate alternative of simply buying silence and support and throwing money at the problems. In such a culture an imperial or autocratic style might work for a limited amount of time, especially if you were also the rainmaker and were driving in the income that was greasing all of the wheels. New supervisors often make the first mistake of believing that they can actually tell someone what to do and get them to do it. Sure you can tell people anything, but they will do what they want to do until you can make them realize that anything other than what you are proposing is impossible, everything being equal.

Secondly, regardless of the first proposition, you also can never forget who your boss is, and though you need the support of the people you manage to succeed and get the work done, you do not work for them, and they cannot fire you, though they can try and sometimes succeed if you forget this rule. You have to communicate frankly and fully with your employers and make sure that on both easy decisions and hard calls that you have their support. In my case my bosses have always been boards of either elected leaders or others, so it is a matter of making sure they understand my job, can fairly evaluate my performance, and know clearly the boundaries between what they have to do and what they are paying me to do. If one makes a mistake with the first rule, doing well on this second rule can save you temporarily, and perhaps that will allow you enough time to fix the first problem and survive.

Thirdly, never make the mistake of believing that friendship is possible in a professional context on either side of this equation. You can neither show preference nor can you hope to be shown quarter based on friendship. This is different than loyalty or many other sustaining values that are work and performance tested. If it is personal, it will not help you and could hurt you, so be careful. Being a boss is not a thankless job, and if you believe in your work, the accomplishments of the organization will be your reward, but it is a hard job. Neither is this to say that you will not make deep, permanent, lifetime friends in the work especially among your organizing comrades – you will and I did – but staff management cannot be based on these issues and in fact it is important to steer a straight path around any perception of bias or preference.

Fourthly, flowing from the last rule, keep relationships clear and the structure uncluttered and transparent, so relationships have boundaries and therefore authority and responsibility are fully understood.

Fifthly, always avoid having to give orders and ultimatums or anything that puts authority to a test, at least until, and unless, you know that your authority will prevail and be unassailable. Suasion is a more powerful administrative tool than stark power. The threat is always more dangerous than the delivery, and the more you get involved in situations where relationships are polarized, the more likely conflict will ensue, and no one ever wins all the time, so beware of being caught in this open ground.

Sixthly, always deal with individuals in private rather than in public whenever possible in order to allow embarrassment to be avoided and authority to be exercised without being complicated by an individual's fear of losing face or honor.

Seventh, regardless of the sixth rule, always remember that the group is more important than the individual, and in a "public" or group setting you cannot necessarily protect people from themselves, because then it is your job to maintain the organization, not the individual, the culture and mission, and not the personal and its prerogatives. Protecting the individual may confuse the larger staff about what is permissible, appropriate, and even legitimate, and the individual has to fall before the collective interests.

Eighth, don't manage based on trust. If you are going to be a the boss in a large organization, you have to be about the job, and as much as you like people and enjoy the work environment and community created, trust is a different and dangerous thing. Always better to ask, than it is to assume. Always be prepared for the worst, so that you can be pleased with the best. Create the collectivity around shared principles and commitments, which are then depersonalized, rather than allowing something like "trust" to be an operating value. Make the work speak for itself, rather than allow the person to speak through different values. Trust is fundamental, but you can never ask someone to do something, saying "trust me."

Ninth, always remember that you are expendable, no matter who you are, how long you have worked, or how well you have performed. To hold onto a job at the top you have to set the standard for value produced, and there is never a relaxation on such production. You can be thanked even while you are being fired or pushed out. If you want to stay on the job, learn to live without thanks and continue to be willing to push the envelope.

Tenth, learn to manage conflict and survive controversy calmly. You have to be able to take a punch without falling. Most punches are meant to hurt you, not kill you, so if you can take them and keep standing in the ring, you will heal, sometimes stronger, and fight again more favorably.

Eleventh, give people wide authority to do their jobs, so that your relationship to them is not defined in a boss/worker framework. Let people develop constructive relationships that mirror your own with their teams and responsibilities. This builds the organization, encourages loyalty, and creates innovation and learning.

Finally, if you are going to survive as the boss of a large organization, I think you have to always look at the next day as the time for your most important contribution. No matter what power you may exercise, the focus needs to be on the challenge and your ability to provide the leadership and skills to get where everyone agrees we need to be. The security in your vision and conviction in the necessity of your participation makes you part of the permanent furniture of the organization.

Managing people, and this is increasingly the majority of the staff, who come looking for a job, rather than a cause, is more straight forward because their long term tenure is based more on the ability of the organization to create a high and consistent level of competence in their performance and a work atmosphere which is both stable and secure. We tend to devise a training program that is one size for all. Whether this is the best way to produce the results for our people, or simply the most convenient and affordable for the organization is a question that needs constant attention and more debate, but in the management of people our watchwords are order and clarity.

Where the mission-oriented staff sometimes wishes they could shape the rules to suit themselves, the task-oriented staff wants more than anything else for the rules to be clearly expressed and uniformly applied. Their frame of reference is other work, not other movements, so that they want to know exactly how the rules shape the work, so that they can perform within expectation. Managers who are not specific about work tasks pay penalties in confusion and performance.

Miscommunications are frequent in bridging these two contending staff orientations.

Traditionally and historically, we simply defined the hours of work as essentially "until the job was done." This could translate into some days that were endless and potentially some days that were abbreviated. It might mean two or three weeks of constant work followed by some days off, rather than some more regular schedule. In managing a task-oriented staff though, it became more important to define the hours of work as 11 AM to 9PM with specific breaks or 10 AM to 8:30 PM or whatever and how many hours they were expected for work on Saturdays and the fact that Sunday was an "official" day off. The larger the organization's staff and the more diffuse the commitments, the more we also had to pay attention to things like defining the regular workweek and overtime as well.

In the United States, ACORN had prevailed in numerous situations on the issue of whether or not an organizer's work, as a job classification, was exempted in terms of overtime definitions of the Fair Labor Standards Act. We held that the work was discretionary and required independent judgment. The increases in the salary scale pushed wages over the level defined in 1978 as eligible to avoid overtime payments for hours in excess of forty per week. The revision by the Labor Department in 2015 under the Obama Administration that propose to boost the exemption over $50,000 per year, though arguably long overdue, worries some organizers sympathetic to movements and the growing pains of mass organizations, but the DOL rules specifically exempt smaller organizations and nonprofits, so practically this should not create a problem, though the "optics" might be challenging publicly.[69]

Another issue had to do with "quotas." Managers in ACORN had an expectation that a certain number of members would – in the normal course of the work in the neighborhood – be recruited, if an organizer was working with the community effectively. Managers did not care particularly whether these members were enrolled at neighborhood meetings, by membership recruitment committees, or by the organizer on home visits, as long as the numbers balanced out at the end of the month. Task-oriented staff quickly concluded, whether this point was made by management or not, that there must be a "quota" that allowed them to prove competence and to indicate that they were doing the job well enough to be retained and move forward. If the average in the office were such that two or three members per day would come in under the responsibility of an average organizer then, especially in absence of any other clear standard, the task-oriented organizer would make sure they were producing that average, because they saw it as their daily quota.

Quickly, there evolved a lack of connection in the work. Managers bridled at the notion that the exalted culture of struggle and aspiration which was organizing was being reduced almost to the level of sales expectations with a daily and monthly production quota by some new organizers. Furthermore, too many of the task oriented organizers due to the absence of other clearly expressed objectives, would begin to see the job as solely about the one or two things that could be crystallized into specific, quantifiable numbers and production quotas. The art of the job was being subsumed into the simple, though important, craft of the work.

Both the managers and the organizers were coming from valid experiences, but the inability to construct a common language about organizing was too elevated and ambiguous on one side and too narrow and routine on the other. Managing a large staff with an expanding organization means recruiting more and more people who are attracted to the organization because it is good and steady work, rather than a grand adventure, and this has to be seen as a normal thing, even if it is not the best thing for the

---

[69]   With the election of Donald Trump as President and the court order blocking implementation of this newly proposed rule, it is unclear if anything will happen along these lines.

organization's purity of purpose. The challenge for managers, and the entire organization, is being able to articulate the significant components and tasks involved in the work, so that the architecture of the organization gets built without losing the soul and spirit of the mission. Regardless of the initial motivations at the point of recruitment, there is a confluence at the end of the process, as the mission-oriented organizer has to come to grips with the importance of real performance and discipline, and the task-oriented organizer has to assimilate and learn to support the goals and aspirations of the work past the simple translation of specific objectives.

With an expanding organization more and more people are recruited to handle certain specific tasks and roles, sometimes even on a part-time basis. Phone callers, canvassers, registration workers, petition gatherers, are all good examples of people recruited to handle jobs, sometimes on an on-going basis, and sometimes for specific campaigns or programs with a start and end date. Some of these are shift workers coming on for 4 or 6 hours to do a specific task and are paid on an hourly basis. All of these jobs have been done by organizers, but in the evolution of job classifications within a mass organization, especially since we passed the point where it was reasonable to expect any one person to simply work forever and do all of the jobs, then specialization inevitably, and appropriately, begins. More recently we have spent time trying to breakdown the tasks of organizing in various checklists in order to make the infrastructure of the work more accessible and stress-free for the organizer, allowing more creativity elsewhere in the work.[70]

Such specialization and development of specific sectors within the craft of organizing also challenges managers to learn more appropriately how to manage specialists in organizing. Add to this the fact that there are also in many ACORN offices additional people doing research, housing counseling, tax and benefit preparation, labor organizing, and specialized outreach in each of these areas and one can quickly overwhelm the

Phone bank training in Vancouver.

---

[70] We have been fascinated and found Atul Gawande's *The Checklist Manifesto: How to Get Things Right* published in 2009 very helpful in this regard. ACORN Canada has led the way in this area.

managers, who usually had earned their jobs based on their talent solely as a field organizer. Communication also increasingly became another new specialist category that required more management skills especially as the tactical advantages and low-cost recruitment potential of internet-based work and campaigning developed and social media became more important. The ways in which people are aggregated through web-work is vastly different than the ways that we assemble people in the neighborhoods and workplaces. Like fax machines, autodialers, high speed copiers, cell phones, and so many other things that have made a substantial difference in organizing in recent years, we have not been as aggressive in learning the lessons and moving them down to the local level of our campaigns as we are going to need to be, and it is not hard to imagine any large program needing capacity at all levels to use this technology. Since this is not just a tool, but potentially a new addition to the craft that means another specialist category is evolving as internet campaigners or "organizers" may become increasingly necessary and regular organizers have to acquire some of these abilities as well. We finally added such a department to ACORN in the 21st century, and it made a huge difference, and seeing its effectiveness during the post-Katrina work in New Orleans, we added communication people in more and more of our larger offices.

This demands a different kind of training for managers and a more subtle and nuanced exercise of their skills as managers. We were only in the early stages of appreciating this problem, and our response undoubtedly needed improvement as we continually were forced to make adaptations in our model and field operations systems. In the ACORN methodology organizers are at the back and leaders and members are in the front. This culture has posed problems for communications departments believing that staying on message was vastly more important than the messenger, where we had always believed the messenger spoke as loudly as the message about the importance of an issue, campaign, and the organization itself.

Part of the evolution of our systems organically combined organizing and our constant concerns with sustainability while trying to integrate all parts of our operation more effectively with our staff and members' experience. It has to seem natural to see money as intrinsically woven into the organizing process *and* the motivation for all organizing staff of all descriptions, regardless of orientation or motivation. Money cannot be an afterthought or the medicine that one takes in order to do progressive or political work. The process has to be natural and seamless. I think this is a challenge for all progressive movements, and if we hope to win at the end of this long march, we have to be able to resolve this threshold issue in every part of our work, or our capacity will always be inadequate and our potential always stunted.

One of the long term issues faced by all levels of management of organizing operations will always be planning and preparing for both the unexpected and its attendant crises, and the future and its unpredictability. A good friend of the organization once asked a fair question: where would the intellectual capital that drives organizing come from in the coming generations of organizers? In some ways the answer to this question lies in the process of organizational experience itself. The process of responding to constant assaults and crises that confront our constituency is a continually disciplined and aggressively dialectic process that allows only the best ideas and projects to survive. The members will always be voting with their feet and constantly demanding *something must be done,* and the very insatiability of their demand and their constant and implicit threat of exit from the organizations, will maintain permanent accountability. This kind of process has been proven over and over in the history organizing. I see no reason why it would not continue.

The problems of managing risk and innovation are constant and always current. There is always a disincentive to create change and innovation, perhaps appropriately when a certain set of methods and strategies have produced reliable success. There are no guarantees in organizational life obviously and unions prove that the problem of managing these two elements particularly in political institutions is very difficult, if not fatal. We have to be able to assure membership that we are rewarding and encouraging innovation constantly, and as current managers there has to be sufficient protection for the next levels of management in advancing new programs with support and encouragement. Within organizing programs this is not a pretty process, but an evolutionary one, and we have to create the best protections that we can devise, and then write the "insurance" policies on them, so that there are not inordinate obstacles to innovation.

Handling risk may be more difficult for managers. They are stewards of the operations' legacy and future, and no one wants to be part of management whenever production and performance start to trend downward. Organizing can bend to the reckless and ruthless, so there has to be an internal balance wheel protecting against adventurism or escapism. Having the experience of taking over Massachusetts Welfare Rights Organization early in my career, I can still remember the pressure at 21 years old, trying to both make the transition as head organizer in a new and unfamiliar set of circumstances, and at a point when the organization's founder was seeking new challenges. But even in crisis and on the verge of professional failure, there was personal relief and peace that could be found in the few calm moments, when I felt that I had done the best possibly I could do, even though I might not have been able to fix something that was broken. The risks are real, so we have to create management protections and encouragements that allow failure without putting the organization in jeopardy. In early organizational life I believe that institutionalization is a protection against this level of risk, and in a large organization the very size of the organization itself and its complexity can militate against most kinds of fatal misjudgments or miscalculations.[71] It is the slow death that is most frightening for large scale organizations, when death can come from a thousand cuts. You hope that when the entire organization is harder to steer, it is also harder to crash. You hope that in times of trouble there are a lot of drivers with many miles of time on the road, who can make sure the organization can always go the distance. Sometimes the hope is real, and sometimes you can end up disappointed.

Managing crises is more difficult of course, and therefore always worrisome. Some crises are almost predictable for managers of change-based operations, and I can think of four quickly: (1) funding, (2) attack, (3) separation and internal conflict, (4) external

---

[71] Ironically when ACORN in the United States was attacked in 2009 after I had left, the rightwing used the very complexity of the organization and myriad corporations as one of the "talking points" to stir opposition to the organization, using the organization's own defense, as an attack.

takeover, and we even had the experience with another that shaped our future in the wake of Hurricane Katrina, (5) disaster. All of these are different, and I believe in managing staff and organizations we have to prepare differently for each, but extensively for all of them.

Money problems are constant and debilitating, even though predictable. Money is a little like the problem of "water on the rock" in that it can seem merely aggravating, until it overwhelms, inducing defeatism and panic, and then crumbling the hardest rock into sand. In non-profits there is "always more month than money," it seems. There are twin problems with resources. One is just being short. The other is betting wrong. Even though internally driven resources ranged between one-third and two-thirds of our total income in ACORN, experience with the radio stations and labor unions that are part of our family of organizations has also taught us that organizations totally supported by members (or listeners in radio world) are not immune from financial constraints either. In either case the problem of money is rarely one of survival, but rather more commonly one of managing capacity or managing the implementation of the plan. This may not be much comfort, but as long as you keep moving, keep working and pushing, you can usually make it. I am a huge believer in resilience. If you don't quit and keep fighting, you can make your own breaks and even the odds, eventually.

The hardest problem ACORN managers faced was when they had to lay off staff because offices were unable to financially sustain themselves. As we have seen, the process of recruiting and training staff is burdensome and expensive, so, not surprisingly, it is always wrenching whenever managers have to layoff personnel because of financial shortfalls. The entire notion of a "layoff" seems foreign to the language of normal non-profit communications. It is hard for managers to believe that they are ever going to have to tell staff that they do not have a way to pay them, so they need to hit the road.

Many of the crises around money are also based on our infinite capacity as people to live in denial of reality, which confronts our managerial responsibility with what we want, versus what we know. Information is obviously important here, and it needs to be accurate and timely. This is easier to say than do. We once incurred a huge bill from lawyers in Tijuana, Mexico that was more than we were spending on the organizing operation itself. We were simply being ripped off, but because our financial reporting system on our international operations was not really responsive yet in the early days of these offices and was so minor compared to the overall scope of the organization, no one realized fully what was happening, including me, and god knows I should have been all over it, until we had almost inadvertently capsized the entire operation in Mexico.

Someone could say, well this is only possible in a larger organization, a smaller one would know immediately. I am not as sanguine about that being the case. We find that supervisors in the field are almost always infected with the common organizers' syndrome – undaunted and irrepressible optimism; we *always* think things are going to get better, and we *always* think we can save the day, and we are *always* surprised somehow when we find this not to be the case, no matter how frequently it occurs. In a national operation there are loans, gifts, and grants, so a manager can believe that an office does not have structural problems, but simply problems based on the timing and sequencing of cash flow. Sometimes that is even true. Just not as often as we would hope it is true.

Managing cash flow in itself is a barely legal art form for most organizing operations. For one very difficult year we had a policy in such circumstances that I called "float, stretch, and burn," which succinctly summed up the way that creditors might be dealt with in times of financial emergency in any particular office. Outside of the Walmarts of the world or other totally computerized, real-time monstrosities, which we can only dream about, it is relatively easy in a national or international organization to incur bills locally in the normal course of business without there being any full appreciation of the scope of the local indebtedness. Such a high-flying way of managing cash flow can complicate management systems all along the chain. In short if everything **seems** to be all right and working, as a manager you can never assume that in **fact** that is the case, except at your peril. Rent payments may have been deferred. Bills may have been left unopened in a drawer. Shuffling money back and forth between other unrelated operations in the same office where perhaps a copier is paid by one and simply seen as a bill to another, allows one to seem to be floating along atop the waves until the water rises and splashes into the boat, and that usually happens on big items that cannot be shuffled, like payroll – and payroll taxes of course.

Payroll though is inescapable, because no matter the level of denial or even delays, after a week or two, the whole world will come crashing down, the code of silence will be broken, and stuff will be flying. This is a perplexing problem on all fronts. If a manager hires too few people, then the program will perform under capacity, and the loss of any one organizer for any reason can be crippling to maintenance and expansion of the local operation. If a manager hires too many people, and slips past available income, then the whole operation could be jeopardized as well. One would think in a large operation it would be possible to simply "adjust" staffing and move people from an overstaffed situation to an understaffed one, when resources existed in the alternative location. Unfortunately as scare and valuable a commodity as organizers are, there is no "internal market" that we were ever able to create that works on anything other than the most temporary basis, partly because organizers are simply not as mobile as one would wish. They are tied to local communities by children, relationships, leases, and a hundred other issues. At the end of the day the lesson about managing financial crises we have "bought" over and over, though god knows if we ever really owned it, is that as bad as money problems are, they can be weathered over time since they are rarely "life and death" and that no matter how bad the money problem is, it is better – and cheaper – to deal with the problems early, rather than late.

The other side of the money "crises" is the inability to realize plans and support the necessary work. The problem of just "not having enough" especially in fully self-sufficient operations creates crises because of the inability to access capital for expansion or any ventures that allow growth and victory. These are the days when managers can identify most closely with small business people, land rich/cash poor farmers, and other operating, but marginal businesses. There is probably no more gratuitous piece of advice in the world than to hear some outsider, no matter how well intentioned, telling an operation in this situation that they need to "invest in the future," "pay now to save later," "don't be pound wise, and penny foolish," and "why don't you pay more?" Individual organizing operations can be very marginal even when aggregated into something as large as some unions or an ACORN, and it is often their economics which drives decision making.

I find this problem actually more painful than the ebbs and flows of cash and the crises that arise there, because an office director unable to finance being able to participate fully in the present, or even possibly in the future, is managing an operation involved in a slow death and a decline of the spirit. It is at this point that staff managers, even good ones with earlier potential, either are able to move through the crises, or are on a gradual countdown to either taking themselves out of the work or making it more and more about themselves, rather than the institution. One minute you might be the ship sailing, and the next minute you are the rat jumping.

An organization's migration from being mission-driven and cause-oriented to being another small business with a limited payroll is a sad, sad thing, when it is limited by rigid financial ceilings, independent of either an expansive or limited vision. Local unions stop worrying about organizing the unorganized, and simply try to do the best job for their members, which is important, but in the end simply marking time to the finish. Community groups continue to be active, but increasingly are only holding on to turf where they were rooted and gradually become more and more conservative – growth and change produce expansive politics, holding on is just holding on. Both of these financial crises can *potentially* be avoided, so we have to train managers to recoil at these options and avoid them like the plague!

Being attacked is a different thing entirely. Planning and preparation are critical and invaluable, but a manager needs to realize that essentially the organization is the target of a campaign being run *against* them, when normally we are sitting on the other side and running the campaign against someone else as the target. The trick here for an organizing director is being able to turn a switch inside your head in order to think in reverse. Frankly, we know how hard every campaign is to win and how close we have come to losing time and time again. [See Chapter on Campaigns]

My advice from the bunker is not the stuff that will please your communication director or your special foundation paid public relations adviser, but it all starts with pulling out the mattresses and hunkering down. As a first principle, what many outside of our world do not fully understand is that there are people who in fact want to totally destroy our organizations and drive us from the world, obliterate any sign or footprint that we ever existed.

A couple of quick examples just to make sure we are on the same page:

- Ku Klux Klan breaks up an ACORN organizing committee meeting near Pine Bluff in 1971.

- Arkansas State Senator Boyce Alford declares on the floor of the state legislature that ACORN is all communist and must be stopped in mid-1970's. His position is seconded by Pulaski legislator, pharmacist, and Mayor of Little Rock, George Wimberly.

- Pulaski County District Attorney declares that he is going to subpoena ACORN's membership lists to stop the organization's growth and determine where ACORN gets its money.

- The <u>Arkansas Democrat</u> led an effort to force ACORN to open its finances to the public[72] and to open our board meetings to the public. Board refused to do so despite a barrage of editorials, news reports, and editorial cartoons, and the necessity of barring a reporter physically from the meeting in the mid-1970s. We did not relent.

- In 1978 Congressional hearings are held around the expenditure of VISTA monies by ACORN and whether or not the monies were used inappropriately. Sam Brown, head of ACTION, and Margery Tabankin, head of VISTA, distance themselves. We agree to simply end the grant.

- ACORN does an action disrupting speech by Speaker of the House Newt Gingrich at a luncheon being held by National Association of Counties around cutbacks in the budget. Gingrich makes sure that an AmeriCorps grant being held by ACORN Housing Corporation is terminated based on allegation that one of the AmeriCorps volunteers may have been present or nearby. Director of AmeriCorps, Harris Wofford, distances himself from the matter. We pay no restitution.

- Grand jury investigation of Local 100 goes on for 4 years under President George Bush (the 1st) on the grounds that because of its relationship with ACORN, "it may be involved in social change with membership dues money." Never targeted, never called, and records were returned after four years without comment, but only after we had spent more than $100,000 in preparation and attorney's fees.

- For years the Employment Policies Institute[73] in Washington, D.C., and the Manhattan Institute in New York, have attacked ACORN as a leader in the "evil empire" of progressive forces. At the ACORN Convention in Columbus, Ohio, the "evil" EPI, as we called it, issues a report trying to slam ACORN and drives a billboard truck around the convention and its activities to attempt to disrupt the convention.

- In 2006 Senator Grassley announces that he is going to call hearings to investigate ACORN and how to remove its tax-exempt status.[74]

- In 2006 former lefty, David Horowitz, publishes a book claiming that ACORN is one of the organizations leading a silent takeover of the country from the left.[75]

---

[72]   Not required, we were not a tax-exempt 501c3. See chapter on Structure.
[73]   As distinguished from the outstanding Economic Policy Institute.
[74]   ACORN was not tax-exempt and had no special tax status. See chapter on Structure.
[75]   Silent? Takeover? Huh?

Chapter VII: Managing Organizers and Staff

I do not mean to belabor this point, but simply to pull some quick examples to mind. We have a lot of experience that it is not a friendly world out there. We were not paranoid, but neither were we naïve. We did not believe there was some conspiracy trying to get rid of us, although there might have been. We believe in fact there is an articulated program, which we have experienced steadily over decades which was dedicated to that proposition. It is not a pretty world out there, and we try to prepare managers for that reality, and the fact that they are going to have to be ever mindful of external attack on the organization.

I do want to add that other than the incident with the *Arkansas Democrat* a million years ago, it is not even worth talking about bad press in the same breath as an actual "attack" on the organization. Press of all descriptions and orientations just goes with the work. Expecting credit is pointless, even when deserved, and as organizers we simply have to hope that we will get as many good breaks as bad ones from the press along the way. It is always hard to tell which is more painful, attack or indifference and deceit. For example, there was a post-Katrina article in the <u>New Yorker</u> in which in order for the author to avoid mentioning ACORN or crediting any of our work, he used sources directly obtained from us, but of course credited differently, and even referred to interns working with the organization, looking at maps of the Lower 9th Ward, where they were working for us, whom he met in our building, who were employed by ACORN doing ACORN work, but he named the praline shop behind our office rather than write "ACORN" in the article.

Internal crises are more personal, and less professional, than any of the other crises that managers are called on to handle. The bonds formed in this work under stress and toil are very strong and enduring, so when there is any rupture, it is especially painful to all parties because these are friends, comrades, and *companeros* of long standing.

Managing conflict is different at all levels. Leadership is a separate problem because it has more to do with governance in many ways than it does management, strictly speaking, so that will be covered elsewhere. Conflict among or between staff is more clearly, and solely, the director or manager's job, so we will examine that fully. The problems of

ACORN "nut" ad.

organizational disaffiliation or abandonment are sundering, and external takeovers are certainly important and worth examination as well.

At the simplest level ACORN has a procedure for handling internal staff problems which works reasonably well. When there is an issue between organizers or co-workers, there must first be an attempt to directly resolve the issue between the staff themselves before bringing other staff or supervisors into the matter. If resolved, the problem dies there. If not, then it goes to the first level supervisor, who has a shot at resolving the matter at that time. Essentially, it moves up the line within an operation along the chain of staff supervision. If the matter involves a state level staff person and there is no resolution, but the issue is felt important, then the head organizer or state director would bring the matter to the state board (composed of elected leaders) and the board would act and that would be that. There is no justification in this system for jumping out of line and going to a higher supervisor first or involving leadership. Within our management system in fact it was the upper level supervisor's job to "push down" the problem within the structure or "back up" the structure so that it stops with them.

Going over the line and involving leadership in an internal staff matter was in fact grounds for discipline and termination within our family of organizations. Doing so was both contrary to the express language of the constitution and bylaws, and in general creates mayhem and distrust of all staff regardless of the instant concern.

The other is a somewhat related situation and could be grounds for termination and that is a disagreement between staff in public. This could be the case particularly in an "open" or public meeting of a local group, or even worse, in a public action or event. The reason for having final responsibility is to have a "chain of command" in such situations. If one organizer has final responsibility and another organizer on the scene has a difference of opinion, of course they are required to bring it to the organizer who is carrying the weight on the staff side of the event or meeting, and therefore they also have to be disciplined enough to accept the field decision, if they disagree. Their only recourse would be either gentle suasion or finding another, higher supervisor to make the appeal. If the members were allowed to sense that they were being given conflicting options or a contradictory decision or some kind of "pick and choose" among alternatives presented by staff, then the whole structure of decision making would collapse and anarchy would be at the door. If the second organizer makes the misjudgment of arguing their case in front of the membership, and the disagreement, publicly and loudly, about whatever it might be, regardless of the merits, the lesson might only be fully understood at a great distance from the work, or at least our work, which can be virtually guaranteed to be immediate and forthcoming within our internal procedures. In the organizing army there can be field promotions, but there certainly also can be field dismissals! These things are important. Albeit, terminations were very rare occurrences.

Every community must have rules for its protection and advancement, and there must be penalties when these rules are abridged and there must be sanctions when the mores of the community are breached. An organizing community operates just this way. The bar is low to come in, but high to leave. Trying to split the community by disaffiliating an entity within the whole, would obviously be met with disagreement and contempt. Though ACORN is one organization, so this is not legally or structurally possible [see chapter on structure], and the family of organizations pulling all of our non-profit entities into one overall operation is federated and linked tightly through interlocking board and staff ties, but nonetheless composed of many distinct organizations with their own boards and corporate lives. The notion of dissolution or separation is outside of the values of the organization, therefore it is *exactly* the kind of crisis that would be unexpected and leave management unprepared. I witnessed this problem from a board seat in another organization, where first the director of one entity tried to pull the entity out of the "family," and was fired for it, and then in a larger crisis, the director of one of the fundamental units of the operation also seemed to be proposing separation of some sort. This was a full, institutional survival crisis, and as the chair of the "committee of a whole" created by the entire board to weld the pieces back together, I had more insight into the grueling impact of such a problem than I would have ever wanted to witness first hand in any of our membership organizations.

Speaking not simply as a founder, but as one of the construction workers over all of these years, my first reaction was foolish – that it could never happen here! But, upon reflection I believe that the seeds of this kind of potential problem are planted around every large organization. Why? Well, simply put, it is always more tempting to steal something that is already running, than to have to build and grow it from scratch. Our job as managers is to keep that from being easy; no matter how tantalizing to the characterless or the hyper-ambitious or even to the good soldier that feels this might be an entitlement because of dissatisfaction with a current or presumed future regime. A related problem has to do with internal "takeovers" or coups that would try to wrest control of operating entities outside of the consensus of staff or vote of the membership.

In private business in the United States one would lock the doors using "poison pills," creating super-voting powers for some over others, manipulating the variety and powers of stock and so on. In non-profits there are stock-based corporations as well [see chapter on Structure] and this is particularly useful in maintaining the property assets from capture since they are all stand-alone corporations. There are other safeguards and guarantees. The first is to create interlocking boards or even simply good boards of people where there is a high commitment of shared loyalty and vision for the future and to the entire community of organizations and its culture. Another is viable, renewal, and long-term, evergreen contracts that provide linkages to common and shared services that cannot be voided unless there is bad faith or inept performance. Formal agreements on loans and cash transfers requiring full payments, repayments, renewal interest without forgiveness, and so forth all clarify the financial benefits to continued community membership and support. At the end of the day a manager still has to have the majority support of staff and members behind the community, but it is a good manager's responsibility to push temptation way past arm length. Ambition and greed, no matter how well rationalized, are part of the human condition, so we have to make sure that collective rather than individual values are always locked down and able to prevail.

External takeover is not as easy, though not impossible particularly in heavily regulated areas like unions, radio stations, and tax exempt operations. With unions once we made the agreement to affiliate to the Service Employees International Union in 1984, we ceded the ultimate fate for our own autonomy and the future to whims of the larger organization.

There was an exchange of resources duly approved by membership action, but still twenty years on, the bottom line is that a vote outside of the immediate community determines the future, or even if there is one, at that. We have been given jurisdiction, and we have lost jurisdiction over both workers and geography at different times.

What we learned hardly predicts success for others. One lesson seems to be that within larger institutions, there is almost always a way to make a better deal (not necessarily to be confused with a good deal), by making a deal when push comes to shove, rather than forcing them to do what they have threatened. Another seems to be that without an independent and deep base both within and outside of the local union, you have no way to survive when they move on you. A large organization needs to be able to compute the price and the pain of trouble you represent as well as what your "good will" might mean with a more equitable settlement. The problem is that most of their experience is simply "buying out" the individual, rather than coming to an agreement that allows the local to continue to function, and grow. They can also be ruthless about what they want, when they want it, and how it is going to happen, so it is important to be able to judge very, very accurately when the discussion is over and something has to happen definitively. A local union can never be confused that somehow it is the tail that can wag the dog. There is neither equity nor is there power sharing and our notions of operating by consensus and so forth are at best quaint. Make your first deal your best, because after that every deal will be harder and harder. Unions are autocratic, political organizations walled up to face adversity and conflict and often drawing no lines between combatants on the outside and friendly fire casualties on the inside.

Radio stations are usually tax exempt in non-commercial broadcasting. All frequencies are regulated by the Federal Communications Commission (FCC) in the United States. A station can bully – or be bullied – off of its frequency by complaints at licensing time that are included in your "public" file, constant nitpicking about problems with volunteers and programs, and pure financial inducements common between bigger players (like mammoth churches or state universities) and smaller operators, like KNON or KABF, our affiliated stations. The most important concern here when confronted by an avaricious suitor is to properly value the asset. These stations are core communication tools, but of course they are not actually community organizations. I can only hope that future managers will value these assets as importantly as I have. The external threats to these institutions have lessened in recent years.

This is not true for ACORN or any of our family of organizations, but having read extensively the bylaws of many organizations, it is not uncommon to find that a takeover could be very easily accomplished by simply signing up members. In 1980 we scared the wits out of the Michigan Democratic Party, which at the time was one of the few membership based parties in the country, by producing a huge number of members to what had usually been a "country club" caucus during our campaign to force low and moderate income political participation. Low threshold membership requirements also exist in a lot of United Ways and other social service nonprofits. I am not sure anyone would *really* want to take them over, because then you might have to run them, but as a protest or a tactic in a larger campaign, certainly opportunities exist. Most nonprofit takeovers are 5th column affairs run by big donors or foundations, who attempt to leverage their resources to win a higher level of control in the organization. We have found this common in both the US and Canada. Managers have to be prepared, quite simply, to say no.

Challenges to the legal status of the entity through Internal Revenue Service investigations of the tax status of 501c3 exemptions or Department of Labor investigations of Landrum-Griffin filings and accuracy of LMDA (Labor Management Disclosure Act) reports are also aggressive external threats. No matter the temptation and cost, this is the second best reason to pay for good external audits which provide huge protection when there is a level playing field and a fair process of appeal. It is also one of the reasons that we maintained an internal legal department and large network of attorneys on specialized issues including organizational protection throughout the country and the world. This is serious business, and people take it seriously.

In the United States we can become lulled into ignoring the external threats that are common for our type of work around the world. We assume that our right to do this work without severe restraints will continue to be possible, even though we watch restrictions around voter registration and participation multiply through repressive legislative activity. Challenges are being made to organizational work directly from the White House and Congress, yet we continue to work in normal fashion without fear of constraints. We can't be naïve or a Pollyannaish in the way we protect institutions in America in the light of the history of repression for social movements at different times in the United States over the

Organizers Forum meets in Moscow with persecuted nonprofit of Soldiers Widows and Mothers.

last 100 years, especially in times of external threat and war, as experienced by the leaders of the Industrial Workers of the World, civil rights movements, the Non-Partisan League, and others which were obliterated.

With the Organizers' Forum we have visited Russia and talked to nonprofits whose ability to work has been curtailed or stopped completely. We met with organizers and organizations in Egypt after the revolution and then heard with horror of their arrests, sentencing, and banning from the work. In India the ascension to power of the BJP party and Prime Minister Modi has also meant severe harassment and often delisting of nonprofits. We have visited Cameroon, and Poland, where the work often proceeded underground and in fear. Even working in other countries, especially now in Peru, Brazil, and Argentina and meeting organizers from countries like South Africa and Indonesia only recently freed from the yoke of dictatorships, military repression, and oppressive governments of one stripe or another, I have been heartened by the survival and the stories of many organizers working in such harsh conditions, but I am also sobered at thinking how inadequately we are prepared for anything but the products of indifference and liberal American institutions in our own country. As I said earlier, I am not paranoid, but that does not mean I do not respect history, world experience, and just plain, good old Boy Scout preparation.

Additionally, there are natural disasters! We thought that we had done some preparation for such crises. We had a small office in Oakland during the earthquake in 1989, though the impact on us was minor. Our television station antenna was located right on the San Andreas Fault line though! We had members scattered all over New York on 9/11. We had done some planning memoranda on how to react to uprisings in center cities in the wake of the Miami riots in Liberty City in 1980, and we had certainly reflected on the Los Angeles outbreak in 1992. In those cases we had seen the challenge more at the level of how to activate and keep our membership moving on our issues and to use whatever opportunities that might be presented to address membership issues and concerns. Unquestionably all of that helped prepare management in different ways for such a cataclysmic event as the devastation of Hurricane Katrina, but we found that we were in no way prepared at the level required!

As a community based organization with 9000 members in neighborhoods across New Orleans, we saw low to moderate income areas at the heartland of the ACORN base decimated by the flooding. None of our planning had ever focused on what to do when not only the telephones, mail, internet, and other communication channels for our membership were down, but when in fact their houses were gone or, worse, they were lost all around the country like small boats riding the giant waves of the storm. I have detailed at length elsewhere[76] some of the small things that we take for granted as organizers that turn out to be pivotal. We assume at the worst that, when all else fails, we can go door to door in the neighborhood and find our people or that we can show up at the shift change at work with our unions and find our members somehow. We never realized that there might be, quite literally, ghost towns in the middle of the city and that the workplaces would also immediately and totally disappear.

The lessons are numerous. Get cell phone numbers for **all** members on the database, because text messages work to contact people even when cell towers and land lines are down. Somehow get more access to email addresses for members via children if not

---

[76] For Katrina related articles I have written on this, particularly Squires/Hartmann book, see *www.chieforganizer.org* under "writing." Also of course, my book, *The Battle for the Ninth Ward: ACORN, The Rebuilding of New Orleans, and the Lessons of Disaster*.

No Bulldozing.

directly. Make a note to get backup generators for offices in the storm zones.[77] Take hard drives with you when you evacuate, so you are up and running quickly.[78] Invest in sufficient redundancy to allow operational processes to be seamless. Unfortunately, there is never enough that can be done. New Orleans was our national headquarters, so the staff and members were wildly supportive, but patience is as easily forgotten as today's headlines. We were reminded of that when an organizer in San Diego complained about her payroll check being a couple of days late, and said to Helene O'Brien, ACORN's national field director at the time, "Well, don't they know better than to put the office in New Orleans!" Sitting alone at the edge of the San Andreas Fault, she of course was in a perfect position to give us such a well-received lecture.

There were two additional, unforgettable lessons we learned about our management and organizational operations in the wake of Katrina. First, we learned that in a crisis that trumps the imagination, our top managers and on down the chain of our staff had the ability to put every problem aside and come together immediately to put their shoulders to the wheel. We had volunteers throughout our management structure offer to come to Baton Rouge or Houston were we relocated and to "hit the mattresses" for weeks to tide the organization over through the crises. Our top management division directors were a seamless operating team in moving to respond. Mike Shea, director of ACORN Housing, in a matter of hours calling through our banking partners was able to raise more than $1

---

[77] We bought generators for all of our Florida coastal offices and in Louisiana. Our two coffeehouses in New Orleans have generators and having one smoothed the transition in our Mid-City location after a small storm swept through shutting down power for almost a week. We powered up the generator and were about the only place for miles with coffee. After the storm, customers literally applauded when I walked into the dining area for the first time when it was over.

[78] We did that!

million dollars, which allowed the organization to immediately respond to our members and our own need to rebuild and occupy our offices.

And, that was the second unforgettable lesson – when in trouble, call on your friends! Heck, even call on your enemies! In many cases they will respond in ways that both surprise and shock you with their pure generosity. It confirms one of the first principles of organizing: **ask!** In some ways the response of our banking and financial allies[79] made sense in retrospect, because they knew it was *in their interest* for ACORN to survive and be at peak capacity in New Orleans. In fact those friends on the more charitable side responded, but less quickly than the commercial side, because their donations were based on the generosity of the heart, rather than the gross self-interest at the heart of the bankers, which served us better.[80] We had never been supported heavily on the internet, but Kevin Whelan's[81] quick action in getting the ACORN Hurricane Relief and Recovery Fund on our website within 24 hours of the storm meant that we raised $400,000 from individuals who reached out for us and were very generous. Many of these were our friends, former organizers, and allies as well as the general public who simply wanted a way to help. We also found our friends in New York in the wake of their own experience in the post-9/11 world, were hugely helpful in extending help on the professional, planning, and architectural sides, and continue to be our partners now in rebuilding the city.[82] The same can be said for volunteers who have come, and even some who continue to return, in the thousands to work on ACORN projects in New Orleans! There also turn out to be people who are willing to uproot their own lives for months (maybe years!) to respond to others in crisis. Scott Hagy drove in from Wyoming with a U-Haul and a service truck full of tools to begin the rebuilding for the office and staff with his bare hands and wits. There are people who for whatever reason have come to understand life in the wake of disaster.

For our part we learned as an organization that we need to be prepared in the future to respond to our membership in situations like Katrina or whatever might come our way. An honest assessment internally of whether or not we would have been so effectively able to respond and act, *if* the same or similar natural disaster had happened somewhere other than our national headquarters or equivalent major operation, led us inescapably to the conclusion that we would **not** have been as able to act or as motivated. The membership needs would have been the same though, so we determined that we needed to be prepared to respond at the membership level in the future when called upon in a way that we would

---

[79] Capitol One, Citigroup, Chase, Ameriquest, and others jumped to our aid.
[80] I must add that the most generous were Herb and Marian Sandler, who combined both the instincts and interests of bankers from their decades of leadership with World Savings in Oakland and an openhanded generosity with ACORN in that moment of need.
[81] Our entire communications department was a huge asset in responding to crisis, which was a nice lesson as well!
[82] Ken Reardon, Cornell, Ron Shiffman, Pratt Center, and David Cronrath, LSU were the heroes here! Yes, LSU is in Baton Rouge, but friends find friends!

not have been able to do before Katrina. Like they say about the levees in New Orleans, we were not ready then, but we would be before something similar happens again![83]

Nonetheless, organizations are perhaps more likely to die of a thousand cuts than sudden and unexpected crises, which brings us back full circle perhaps to the additional challenges and lessons we have learned about managing organizing staffs over the decades. After a couple of more quick notes, it is time to finally say goodbye to this question and move on to some other organizing problems.

- **Organizers Need to be Mobile:** Focusing on local recruitment creates a unique staff development problem for organizers – immobility. Organizers need to be able to learn from different situations and settings, from different supervisors, neighborhood conditions, leadership styles, issue alternatives, and campaign situations. If they are hired, trained, and then worked in the same location throughout their career, the problem of provincialism stunting their growth and creating artificial ceilings for their development is a real one. For all of the strengths of a local organizer's ability to go deep, getting the organizer's full potential forces us to go wide as well to develop the vision needed to sustain the work and grow it.

- **Organizing has to be fun:** An outside consultant reviewing our staff meetings was surprised at the fact that, no matter the subject matter or the weight of the discussion, people had fun! There were constantly jokes in the room. People kept laughing. I think this is essential in maintaining the esprit d'corps of an organizing staff.

- **Organizing Staffs Cannot be Bored!** If bored, they are dangerous! For both leaders and organizers in the old days (anything earlier than yesterday!) we used to joke (with seriousness!) that if there were rumors or reports of conflict and disagreement it usually meant that there must have been a "downtime" where there were no big organizing drives or campaigns happening. Organizers too often are "money" players[84] and when they are not running hard in the game, their energy is aggressive, restless, and looking for action. And, they will find it either constructively or not! So, management needs to not just keep a staff busy, because boredom will follow and that does not work. Keep them challenged. We do that at some level in staff meetings by mixing in regular topics with "speculative" issues forcing the staff to come up with something different – plan to meet a natural disaster, new campaign, money raising project, or just a discussion about organizing issues at the margin and cutting edges of the work.

- **An Organizer Has to Have an Individual Development Plan:** I could just say, "See above!" If an organizer, or for that matter any staff person, does not have

---

[83] For more on all of this see, Wade Rathke, *The Battle for the Ninth Ward: ACORN, New Orleans, and the Lessons of Disaster, Social Policy,* 2011.

[84] For my non-USA friends this is a common "Americanism" meaning someone who wants to take the shot to win the game, catch the ball down field to go for the score, be at bat with a chance to bring in the winning run, or be wherever it counts to win.

an individual development plan that gives them a sense of where they are going, how to get there, and why it's worth it, the manager is simply throwing caution to the wind and hoping that fate, karma, or good luck will somehow make it all work, none of which is my experience. This is not a job for "human resources" though a larger organization probably needs such a department to keep supervisors on their toes and prevent "work drift" on priorities to overwhelm the individual needs that individual staff members are going to have and always want to have recognized. Making a good plan is obviously not easy, but no plan is a handshake and a wave goodbye, either sooner or later. A supervisor incidentally gets huge credit for their organizers for even trying to make a plan, regardless of the quality of the plan!

- **Nothing Works without Teamwork and Discipline Even if that is What Your Mother and Coach in High School Also Told You!** Any good organizing staff has superb team and group discipline. I know there are theories about free spirits and people out there "doing their own thing" and somehow it all working, but I not only do not believe it, but I know that it is not true for an organizing staff. People are dependent on each other, and members are often dependent on the staff for their very livelihoods and jobs, their homes, and community well-being. None of that speaks to anything other than incredibly hard work and endless personal self-discipline. If you do not have it or cannot work with others well, then you need to be a free-lance activist or advocate, and decidedly not an organizer or part of a mass-based organization. This work is an honor to be a part of a seamless, historic and honorable trade dating back centuries and marked by great sacrifice and great victories, but none of that ever happened alone or without huge mass support and amazing disciple and teamwork. The strength of the community of organizers is at the heart of what makes all organizing happen.

At the end of the day an organizer learns fairly quickly in building mass organizations that they cannot do all of the work single handedly. From that terrible moment forward when they realize they have to hire others, they become interdependent on a staff, as well as their members. Many organizers atavistically talk about their "best days" or most "fun" being back when they were by themselves and on the streets organizing in the beginning when they only had to worry about themselves and their work. Maybe? But only in their dreams and the nostalgic stories they tell each other with a beer in hand long after the work is done.

Once an organizer embraces building power and the fact that the organization has to be large, that means building a staff, and from that point on the work keeps getting harder and harder, even at the same time as it becomes more and more important. Having a staff may be a problem for many, but you cannot do the work without others, and we need a lot of them.

Chapter VIII: *Maintaining Organizers: Training, Dialogues, and Meetings*

There are two crucial elements in building and maintaining successful organizers: skills and vision. Without a hard reality, field-tested set of practical skills, techniques, and basic methodological framework, an organizer cannot survive in the work on a day-to-day basis, much less year over year. Even with a skill set though, an organizer can also not survive without a vision of the organization and what they are trying to help build, and particularly the fact that the organization, or the organizing project, is bigger than themselves, and in fact better, grander, and more important than any of us individually. In focusing on these dual concerns we devised a number of programs that became part of the ACORN routine and practice, so let's look at them more closely to see how the tools worked.

In understanding the entire system, perhaps it's important to understand general staff policies which were always entitled "Certain Staff Policies" in the USA, indicating that the policies never pretended to be complete, but at least pulled together the key elements.

Exhibit 4. Looks at the initial staff policies for ACORN Canada in 2004 which were adapted from the US policies.

Exhibit 4: ACORN Canada Staff Policies

SUMMARY OF CERTAIN STAFF POLICIES
September 2004

All policies governing compensation, benefits, and conditions of employment are established by the elected leadership. The following is a summary of major staff policies:

I. Compensation

    A. Compensation will be either semi-monthly or weekly as determined by the individual office. Semi-monthly pay periods end on the 15th and the last day of each month. Weekly pay periods end on Saturdays. Paychecks will be issued seven days after the end of the pay period. No payroll shall be requested or disbursed until the employee has turned in approved and signed timesheet(s). ACORN Canada will withhold all required and permitted withholdings and deductions from all compensation.

    B. Payment will be by check.

    C. The compensation scale and policy are detailed in a separate attachment.

    D. Hours to be compensated. Hours of work are established by management and may vary according to specific operating circumstances.

    E. Employees who work more than 5 consecutive hours are entitled a meal break of 30 minutes to be scheduled at the discretion of a supervisor. Meal breaks, and any other authorized breaks, are not included in the hours for which staff is compensated.

F. Staff is not compensated for time on administrative suspension or while on voluntary leave.

G. Hours and Calculations. The regular workweek for staff in British Columbia and Ontario is 45 hours and compensation (including any overtime which might be owed) is calculated with this schedule in mind. By way of example, starting salary is $19,635 for 40 hours at straight time, with five additional hours at time and half bringing the compensation for the regular workweek to $23,307. Overtime is not permitted unless authorized in advance by management. Employees must receive prior approval from management to work specified overtime hours in order to receive corresponding overtime pay.

II. Benefits

A. Statutory Holidays.

B.C. statutory holidays are New Year's Day, Good Friday, Victoria Day, Canada Day, British Columbia Day, Labour Day, Thanksgiving Day, Remembrance Day and Christmas Day.

Ontario public holidays are New Year's Day, Good Friday, Victoria Day, Canada Day, Labour Day, Thanksgiving Day, Christmas Day and Boxing Day.

B. Insurance.

ACORN Canada will make available to employees insured benefit plans as described in separate materials and ACORN Canada will pay the premiums for such benefits, with the exception of family health coverage. An employee's eligibility and entitlement to benefits will be determined by the terms and conditions of the insurance plans or programs established or purchased by ACORN Canada. ACORN Canada may amend, add, eliminate, or modify, in whole or in part, any benefits or the level of any benefits, from time to time with or without notice.

C. Sick Leave.

All staff with at least six months of seniority is eligible for five days of sick leave available annually. This is not cumulative across calendar years or available upon termination. Staff supervisors must receive notification by 10 AM for any sick leave to be approved and may require subsequent documentation. For major medical leaves, the organization allows one week of paid leave per year of seniority as approved by Staff supervisors: this major-medical leave therefore accumulates at a rate of one week for each year of service and is depleted as it is used by the individual. Sick leave is not a holiday and if taken as a holiday is grounds for discipline up to and including termination. Employees may use any sick leave to which they are entitled not only for themselves, but to care for a sick child, spouse, parent, or domestic partner. Employees shall not be entitled to be paid out unused "major medical leave" upon termination.

D. Vacation.
Vacations must normally be scheduled each year before the February 1st and must be approved by the staff supervisor in all cases six weeks or 45 days prior to the scheduled vacation time. Although every effort is made to accommodate individual vacation requests, we reserve the right to determine and/or change the dates of scheduled vacations to meet changing operational needs. At termination, employees are paid the equivalent of any earned but unused vacation pay that they have accrued up to that point. Vacation benefits are provided in accordance with an employee's length of service as follows:
    In B.C., employees are entitled to two weeks' vacation after 12 consecutive months of employment. After five consecutive years of employment, employees are entitled to three weeks' vacation.
    In Ontario, employees are entitled to two weeks after each year of employment.

E. Parental Leave.
Employees will only be entitled to leave in accordance with the applicable ESA.
    In B.C., a pregnant employee is entitled to up to 17 consecutive weeks of unpaid pregnancy leave. A birth mother who has taken pregnancy leave is entitled to 35 consecutive weeks of unpaid parental leave. A birth mother must begin her parental leave immediately after her pregnancy leave ends, unless she and the employer agree otherwise. A birth father or an adopting parent is entitled to up to 37 consecutive weeks of unpaid parental leave. An initial period of parental leave may be extended up to five consecutive weeks if the child requires an additional period of parental care.
    In Ontario, a birth mother is entitled to both "pregnancy" and "parental" leaves. Birth mothers are entitled to 17 weeks of unpaid pregnancy leave. Those who take pregnancy leave are entitled to up to 35 weeks of parental leave. Birth mothers who do not take pregnancy leave, and all other new parents, are entitled to up to 37 weeks of parental leave.

F. Discretionary Leave.
Discretionary leave is a paid merit leave and not an automatic prerogative throughout the year. No more than five days are available each year, with the approval of the appropriate head organizer, staff director, or division head, and discretionary-leave days may not be consecutive.

G. Family Leave.
The organization has no separate funeral-leave policy, and in general such situations would be treated as uncompensated leaves of absence. In certain circumstances, however, supervisory staff may consider requests under the terms of the discretionary-leave policy.
    In B.C., employees are entitled to up to three days of unpaid leave on the death of a member of the employee's immediate family. These days do not have to be consecutive, or start on the date of death. In addition, an employee is entitled to up to five days of unpaid leave in each employment year to meet responsibilities related to the care, health or education of any member of the employee's immediate family.

In Ontario, employees are entitled to an unpaid leave of absence of up to 8 weeks to provide care or support to an individual if a qualified health practitioner issues a certificate stating that the individual has a serious medical condition with a significant risk of death occurring within a 26-week period. In addition, employees who work for employers that regularly employ at least 50 employees are entitled, in certain circumstances, to unpaid emergency leave of up to 10 days each year.

H. Negotiated Seniority.
If an individual's rate of compensation includes a credit for years of service with non-COUNCIL organizations -- as approved by the Chief Organizer – that credit only applies to the compensation and not to any other organizational benefits.

I. Retirement Benefits.
All full-time staff with at least a thousand hours of service registered in a given year is eligible to participate in the COUNCIL Beneficial Association. This is a multi-employer defined-contribution retirement plan established by a group of organizations whose employees support and work with low-and-moderate-income people. For more specific details, please refer to the Summary Plan Description provided to you for the COUNCIL Beneficial Association. In general, however, the organizations' discretionary contributions to the plan on behalf of employees' vest 100% after five years of service have been completed, and any contributions to the plan by individual participants vest 100% immediately.

J. Workers Compensation.
Staff is covered by applicable Workers Compensation legislation when engaged in the performance of their duties. Accidents occurring, or injuries sustained, in the performance of duties, however minor they may seem at the time, must be reported to the Supervisor immediately.

III. Required Meetings

A. Year/End Year/Begin Meeting. At the end of each year, generally in mid-December, required to attend. There is a women's meeting from 6 PM to 10 PM the evening before the YE/YB meeting. The YE/YB lasts a full day and evening on Saturday and a half day and evening on Friday. Generally, it is held on weekends to minimize the field days lost. The YE/YB is part of the regular annual work hours on which the compensation scales are computed. Those who miss the meeting are subject to discipline up to and including termination.

B. Annual Staff and Board Retreat. Certain COUNCIL organizations regularly schedule meetings each fall for leadership and staff for the purposes of workshops, discussions, evaluations, and planning. The retreat is held over a weekend period, and attendance is mandatory. Those who miss the meeting are subject to discipline up to and including termination.

C. Convention and Conferences. Every other year, in even-numbered years, members of COUNCIL organizations hold a national convention, in which all staff from all the COUNCIL organizations participates with duties that depend upon the size of the delegation sent. Staff services the members at the conventions, and hours are geared to ensure that members are comfortable, informed about the organizing plans, and on time for all events. The Convention is part of the regular work hours on which the compensation scale is computed. Those who do not attend are subject to discipline up to and including termination.

D. There may be other meetings from time to time that are scheduled and where staff participation is mandatory, and such meetings will be announced with sufficient advance time for scheduling.

IV. Reimbursements

A. Travel. Work-related intra-province travel is reimbursed at a per-kilometer rate established by the leadership. Transportation from home to office or office to home is not covered. Approved inter-province travel is reimbursed from actual gas and oil receipts submitted, together with a travel voucher setting forth the purpose of the travel.

B. Long-Distance Telephone Calls. Personal long-distance telephone calls are not permitted.

C. Other Expenses. Other authorized expenses are reimbursable upon submission of the actual receipts with express advance approval from their specific authorized supervisor.

V. Drugs

Employees must not possess, use, sell or distribute illicit drugs while at work or on the property of the organization. In addition, employees must not be impaired by or under the influence of illicit drugs while at work or on the property of ACORN Canada.

If, after conducting an investigation, we determine that an employee is impaired by drugs while at work or has otherwise violated this policy, we will take appropriate action. Appropriate action includes the removal of the employee from duty until the employee can work safely and may include the mandatory referral of the employee to a substance abuse professional or physician approved by ACORN Canada for evaluation, treatment and aftercare and discipline up to and including dismissal.

VI. Employees, Supervisors, Employment, and Policy

A. Grievances . Employees who have complaints about various organizational matters should discuss them with their immediate supervisor, including matters involving harassment and/or discrimination.

B. Supervisors . Employees should learn the name of the supervisor of their immediate supervisor, in the event that they need to raise issues concerning their immediate supervisor which they have not been able to resolve or cannot resolve with their immediate supervisor (e.g., harassment, discrimination, or inability to communicate) All employees should contact their immediate supervisor concerning promotion opportunities, performance evaluations, harassment reporting procedures, and so forth

C. Termination. We may terminate your employment without further obligation or liability of any kind, including without limitation, any notice or severance, by giving you only the minimum notice or pay in lieu required by the applicable employment standards legislation. Notwithstanding this, if just cause exists, we may immediately terminate you without further obligation or liability, including without limitation, any obligation to provide notice or severance pay.

D. Grounds for Termination. The following is a non-exhaustive list of examples of conduct which may amount to just cause to immediately terminate an employee's employment without notice or severance pay: insubordination; organizational disloyalty, e.g.; organizing against the constituency and/or membership; appropriation of organization records and/or membership lists; disparaging the organization or its members; assaulting another person; falsification of any records, whether personnel, membership, or client, including personnel information, reports, time sheets, invoices, and expenses; theft; violation of organizational policies; dishonesty about job-related matters to staff, leaders, or members; misuse of organizational resources; deception in securing employment; gross misconduct; possession of alcohol or illegal substances while working; conviction for a felony or imprisonment; failure to perform to organizational standards; failure to carry out supervisory instructions; neglect of duty; unauthorized absence; tardiness; abuse of leave.

E. Resignation and Termination Procedures. Written notice of resignation should be provided as far in advance as possible, but not less than thirty days in advance for exempt personnel and not less than two weeks in advance for non-exempt personnel. At resignation or termination, final time sheets should be submitted; office keys and other organizational property should be returned; and the organization should be reimbursed for any financial obligations owing from the employee. Final paychecks will be paid within 72 hours. If an employee has given more than 72 hours' notice, however, final paycheck will be paid on the last day of employment.

F. Personal Information. We will collect, use and disclose personal information only where reasonably necessary for security, employment and business purposes. Employees hereby consent to ACORN Canada collecting, using and disclosing personal information about them only where reasonably necessary for security, employment and business purposes in accordance with applicable legislation and any privacy policy of ACORN Canada that may be in effect from time to time.

G. Jury Duty. An employee who is required to attend Court as a juror is considered to be on unpaid leave for the period of the jury duty.

H. The Media. No contact with the media regarding the organization, its operations, its policies, or any other COUNCIL organizations is to be initiated without specific prior approval from the appropriate supervisor. If an employee is approached by any representative of the media concerning a particular organization, the representative should be referred to the Staff Director for assistance or to a designated organizational officer.

I. Inquiries. In general, all inquiries about the organization, its operations, its policies, or any other COUNCIL organizations are to be referred to the Staff Director in writing. If the request is in person or by telephone, the name, address, and telephone number of the requesting individual should be secured.

J. Discrimination. We are committed to providing a working environment that is free from any form of harassment or discrimination prohibited under applicable provincial human rights legislation. It is the employee's responsibility to let us know if he or she feels that harassment has taken place, even if it is not directed towards the employee. Any incident of harassment should be immediately brought to the attention of the employee's supervisor, who will thoroughly investigate the matter. After reviewing all evidence, a determination will be made concerning whether reasonable grounds exist to conclude that harassment occurred. Any employee making a report of harassment may do so without fear of reprisal. Disciplinary action up to and including termination will be taken against any employee who is found to have engaged in harassment. Individuals whose accusations are found to be malicious or vexatious in nature will be subject to disciplinary action up to and including termination.

K. Sexual Harassment. Sexual harassment is against specific organizational policy, and an employee or supervisor who is found after appropriate investigation to have engaged in such activity will be subject to disciplinary action up to and including termination. The organization's policy statement concerning sexual harassment appears in Section VIII of this summary.

L. Lists and Work Products . Membership, contributor, and/or client lists and all employee work products are the exclusive property of the Organization and are only made available to particular employees at the discretion of the staff supervisor for the specific organizational purposes. Any distribution of such lists or materials and any other use of these lists or materials shall constitute grounds for discipline up to and including termination.

M. Activities Which Hinder Organizing. Activities, dress, or conduct which, interfere with the organizing process, with the conduct of business in COUNCIL offices, or with organizational activities and functions are specifically prohibited and are subject to discipline up to and including termination. This would include making statements publicly or to the membership which disparage the organization, its goals, and or its activities; wearing clothing,' pins, or buttons at organizational functions or in the course of organizational work which promote other causes or organizations; and engaging in activities which disrupt organizational business or functions.

N. Solicitation. No solicitation is permitted during working hours on working time.

O. Personnel Files. Personnel files are confidential and are maintained by the Payroll Department.

P. **Staff Policies.** Any staff member may propose policies which s/he feels would benefit the overall effectiveness of the organization. Such proposals must be directed specifically to the, appropriate staff supervisor, and final approval is the responsibility of the senior supervisor and the highest body of the elected leadership.

VII. SEXUAL HARASSMENT POLICY STATEMENT

Sexual harassment is prohibited in the workplace by any person and in any form. All allegations of sexual harassment brought to our attention will be promptly investigated. Appropriate action will be taken whenever an allegation is determined to be valid.

Definition of Sexual Harassment

Sexual harassment includes, but is not limited to:

Unwelcome sexual advances, requests for sexual favors, and other verbal or physical conduct of a sexual nature constitute sexual harassment when one or more of the following apply:
• submission to such conduct is made an explicit or implicit term or condition of employee's employment;
• submission to or rejection of such conduct by an employee is used as a basis for employment decisions affecting the employee; or
• such conduct unreasonably interferes with an employee's work performance or creates an intimidating, hostile or offensive working environment.

"Verbal or physical conduct" includes, but is not limited to: sexually related comments; sexually suggestive pictures, notes or signs; unseemly gestures or sounds; touching; use of demeaning or inappropriate terms or names; crude or offensive language; or discussing sexual activity to or around others. Such conduct need not be limited to conduct at the work place or during working hours.

Responsibility of Supervisors

All supervisors have a responsibility to be sensitive to and deal with sexual harassment as with any other form of employee misconduct. This responsibility includes monitoring the work activities for indications of sexual harassment, and contacting a higher-level supervisor, or the Chief Organizer or Executive Director, if it is reasonably believed that sexual harassment may have occurred. Any such report will be investigated regardless of whether a complaint has been made by the affected employee.

Remedies

Any employee determined to have committed sexual harassment will be subject to disciplinary action up to and including termination.

There will be no retaliation against any employee who makes a good faith complaint of sexual harassment, regardless of whether it is ultimately determined that, such sexual harassment has in fact occurred. Nor will there be any retaliation against any employee who provides information in the course of an investigation into alleged sexual harassment.

Complaint Procedure

If you believe that you are or have been the subject of sexual harassment, it is important that you report the conduct in question immediately. The report should be made to your supervisor, or to the Chief Organizer, or to the Executive Director. You may be requested to provide a written complaint detailing the allegations. We will conduct a prompt and complete investigation. Every effort will be made to restrict discussion of the complaint to a need-to-know basis. Where necessary, we will take reasonable protective measures while the investigation is being conducted.

Upon completion of the investigation, if it is determined that the complaint is valid, we will take appropriate action, including discipline up to and including termination of the responsible employee or employees. We cannot emphasize strongly enough the importance of following this reporting procedure. We cannot achieve our goal of preventing sexual harassment in the workplace unless affected employees report it as soon as it happens. Do not assume that "everyone knows" about sexual harassment if it is happening to you. Report it, so that we may investigate and take appropriate action.

Employee Certification

I hereby certify that I have read the Summary of Certain Staff Policies, revised September 2004, that I have asked any questions I have about these Policies, and that I understand and agree to abide by these Policies.

Name _____

Date _____

Signature _____

First meeting of Easton chapter of ACORN Bristol.

In the USA "certain staff policies" there were always snickers at Policy #4, entitled in the earlier years of the organization, "That's Why They Call it Dope," which laid out the political perilous position of organizers involved in social change if they were ever involved in using illegal substances and the consequences in the public perception if any were arrested for using dope, therefore requiring potentially immediate termination. As you can see many of the Canadian policies were cut-and-pasted from the original US-version right down to some programs that did not include Canada (benefit associations) to the Chief Organizer as the final arbiter (me, rather than Judy Duncan, head organizer of ACORN Canada as it should have read), but, they got the job done and the message delivered.

Training

Initial training, as I have discussed in the earlier chapter, is all about the organizing drive and learning the mechanics of the drive within the structure of the ACORN Organizing Model, first written in 1973.[85] This is an evergreen document. Recently in Bristol, England the launch of the first organizing committee meetings in Easton was accompanied by an appeal on the ACORN Bristol website *asking for one-hundred people to pledge that they would join ACORN through the website* to support the progress of the organizing drive. In the classic way of all organizers, we immediately added this feature to the organizing drive in Leith in Edinburgh and now in Reading, Newcastle, and London we are doing the same. If it works, it becomes part of the checklists for new drives that accompanies the work and keeps it fresh and evolving in our ongoing process.

A good summary of the ACORN Organizing Drive Model, produced as a training document by ACORN Canada is in Exhibit 5: Overview of the Organizing Model.

---

[85]   Available currently at *www.chieforganizer.org/writing* in English, Spanish, Italian, French, Polish, and Korean.

Chapter VIII: Maintaining Organizers: Training, Dialogues, and Meetings

Exhibit 5: Overview of the Organizing Model

OVERVIEW OF THE ORGANIZING DRIVE

PURPOSE OF THE ORGANIZING DRIVE

The main purpose of an organizing drive is to build a functioning, strong, and democratic ACORN chapter in a neighborhood. What that means in concrete terms is that:

- The group represents a significant portion of the neighborhood (at least 5% of the households are full members of ACORN, with 10% closer to ideal).
- The group has the capacity to turn out large numbers of residents for events and meetings. Usually the founding meeting should have at least 100 people attending, with the first kickoff action on a campaign turning out 50 people.
- The group has an understanding of how politics in their neighborhood works, with an idea of how many registered voters there are, and how many votes it takes to win local elections.
- The group has chosen an issue that affects the entire neighborhood and has kicked off a campaign on the issue.
- The group has elected a board through a democratic process, and has an additional 20-30 block captains responsible for informing their area of ACORN events, as well as mobilizing around elections.
- The group is involved in and knows about other local, state, and national ACORN events and campaigns.

This means a few things. To get to 5% of a neighborhood of 2,000 households, 100 member families must join. Breaking it down, that means that over the 8-9 weeks of the organizing drive, the organizer and the organizing committee made of members from the community must sign up around 11-12 members per week. In order to turn out 100 people to a big meeting, 1,000 names and phone numbers must be collected. If strong leaders are going to be elected to the ACORN board, then a process of leadership identification and development must occur through the process of Organizing Committee Meetings.

Exhibit 5: Overview of the Organizing Model

PREPARATION FOR THE NEIGHBORHOOD DRIVE
- Identify possible neighborhood boundaries, usually by looking at major streets, and while trying to include around 2,000 households.
- Get the voter list for that area (if possible) from the political department, including an analysis of frequent voters (often good potential ACORN members and leaders).
- Begin identifying potential contacts/allies to contact for support in the organizing drive.

TIMELINE AND PROCESS
An organizing drive takes 2 months minimum to take from start to finish. Generally, the first month is spent building a core organizing committee and narrowing down the initial campaign focus. The second month centers around building for the founding meeting (Big Meeting) and campaign kickoff action.

First and second week:
- Sign up 20 full members.
- Identify potential big meeting locations
- Second visit and solidify relationships with the initial organizing committee
- Organize a quick hit
- Make a list of community institutions, including banks, churches, schools, social service agencies, day care centers, legal services offices, doctors, etc and begin setting up meetings with people within those institutions

Third week:
- First Organizing Committee (OC)—members only
- Confirm Big Meeting location and date
- Print and mail/distribute Organizing Committee letter to the community
- Doorknocking and petitioning with OC members to sign up new members
- Sign up at least 10 new members

Chapter VIII: Maintaining Organizers: Training, Dialogues, and Meetings

Exhibit 5: Overview of the Organizing Model

Fourth week:
- Second OC Meeting
- Doorknocking and petitioning with OC to sign up new members
- Sign up 10 new members

Fifth week:
- Third OC Meeting
- Invite target to first action for the campaign, make initial action plan
- Begin turnout for founding meeting and action, making initial phone calls and getting commitments to turn others out.

Sixth week:
- 4th OC Meeting
- Final turnout for founding meeting and action, including daily phone banking, flyering at gathering places, church announcements, putting up posters and yard signs, etc.

Seventh week:
- Rehearsal meeting before the big meeting
- Confirmation phone calls starting at least two days before the meeting
- Founding Meeting!
- Big Campaign Action!

Eighth and ninth week:
- Sign up all non-members who came to Founding Meeting and Campaign Action
- Identify and finalize block/precinct captains, flyer captains, and phone captains
- Further planning with OC on neighborhood campaign (see Campaign Planning Worksheet)
- Work with Chair, Co-Chair, Secretary, Treasurer, and APAC Representative on identifying their responsibilities for the neighborhood and city-wide.

Exhibit 5: Overview of the Organizing Model

ROLE OF THE ORGANIZING COMMITTEE
The Organizing Committee forms the leadership for the drive. For our neighborhood groups to develop leaders, membership, power, and self-sufficiency, the OC must take responsibility. Over the course of the drive, the OC does the following things:
- establishes legitimacy by voting to organize their community through ACORN
- develops leaders and ownership of the group
- prioritizes issues
- makes decisions about the first campaign
- makes a plan to involve the whole neighborhood
- builds a team that will maintain the chapter and build power in the community, whether a full-time ACORN staffer is assigned to the area or not.

OC Meetings are very different from the founding meeting. Everyone in the neighborhood is invited to the Founding Meeting, but only members who are potential leaders and hard workers are invited to the OCs. OCs are held informally, in people's homes, not in a public meeting space. The atmosphere is less formal, the agenda is more flexible, and discussion are more open-ended than at the Big Meeting.

ACTIVITIES TO BUILD THE DRIVE
Doorknocking
Primary Purpose: Sign up new members

Secondary Purposes: Develop leaders by having them come out with you; developing good contact information for the big meeting; and updating voter files for election purposes.

Notes: Use the voter registration file for doorknocking wherever possible. It should be in a format that allows the organizer to use it as a doorknocking sheet. When doorknocking, the organizer can ask for the name listed on the sheet, and make corrections as needed (this information becomes very useful as the group becomes involved in election campaigns). Many houses will not be listed if no one is registered voter, in which case they can be flagged for future voter registration efforts. Whenever possible, a member should doorknock with the organizer, introducing the organizer to people they know, and helping make the case for people to join.

Chapter VIII: Maintaining Organizers: Training, Dialogues, and Meetings

Exhibit 5: Overview of the Organizing Model

Petitioning

Primary Purpose: Gather names and contact information for Big Meeting turnout.

Secondary Purposes: Develop a petition that can be used for leverage on the campaign.

Notes: This is an easy project for members to do with a little training. After spending an hour with a member at first, members can go on to do it on a regular basis. It also builds a relationship with grocery stores and other businesses that will allow us to set up future petitions.

Quick Hits

Primary purpose: Sets the tone and builds momentum early in the drive by quickly moving membership into action.

Secondary purposes: Develops leaders, get a small win early on, builds excitement about ACORN being in the area, and strengthens legitimacy

Notes: Quick hits are very good early on in the drive. Be careful, though, because after a certain point in the drive, they can sap energy away from the OC and Founding Meeting process.

Meetings with other institutions in the community (churches, service agencies, etc)

Primary Purpose: Building relationships that will be useful later on for the local group

Secondary Purposes: Organizing against conflict by defusing concern about ACORN's presence in the community, answering questions, and getting referrals and other community contacts to build the group, using these connections later on to help get the word out about the Founding Meeting

Notes: Other community groups and established leaders often don't relate well with ACORN if they aren't approached carefully. They often have a significant stake in the status quo, and ACORN will probably upset that status quo. We do not want to cause avoidable conflict within the community, so it is usually good to meet with these groups and leaders early on, to help them understand that we're here to work with them, not against them. During those initial meetings, approach them as an organizer by asking questions about the things they think need changing in the area, and working to bring them around to a vision of

Exhibit 5: Overview of the Organizing Model

power in numbers. Get contacts of community residents from them that they think would be interested in joining ACORN, and open the door to future relationships in neighborhood campaigns. Explain ACORN's organizing process as well, so that they understand that community residents will be making the decisions about issues.

Mailing the OC Letter

Primary Purpose: Builds the buzz about the first meeting.

Secondary Purposes: Builds legitimacy for the Organizing Committee, and paves the way for future doorknocking.

Notes: The OC letter should go out to every household in the neighborhood if possible. It should explain briefly some of the issues identified in the OC Meeting, have a brief description of ACORN, and tell the Founding Meeting date, time, and location. Have members write it using a sample for reference, and they can help stuff envelopes and mail it out.

Yard Signs Announcing the Founding Meeting

Primary Purpose: Turnout for the founding meeting

Secondary Purpose: Owning our turf.

Notes: Along with giving every member a sticker to put in their window or on their car, this helps us own ACORN turf in a very visible way.

See sample agendas and notes for more information about OC meetings, and the bottom line for what should happen at each one.

Organizing committee meeting in Edinburgh, Scotland.

For organizers to succeed, training has to break the overwhelming enormity of the tasks into smaller bits, easier to remember and through constant repetition part of the daily grist for the mill. Exhibit 6 for example is a checklist used by ACORN Canada for what we call "quick hits," or *rapides accions* as our Latin American staff refers to them in all of their reports, which are small actions that help move the campaigns along or as that fulfills that purpose as well:

Exhibit 6: Organizing letter

ACORN

March 2, 1972

Dear Neighbors:

For years we have been talking about the problems in Garden Homes. Now we feel it is time for us to get together and do something about them. Our community needs a neighborhood park for our children, better drainage, and an end to the heavy traffic coming through our neighborhood.

We have decided to form a Garden Homes Community Organization, with the help of ACORN, and with everyone in the neighborhood working together we can solve our problems. ACORN is a statewide organization of over 3,000 families who work together to solve their own community problems. ACORN is not supported by any government agency. It is run entirely by its members who pay membership dues to meet their expenses.

On March 16 at 7:30 p.m. at the Welch Street Baptist Church Education Building on Roosevelt and Welch, we will have our first meeting. At this meeting we will:

1. Elect officers
2. Discuss our organization and what it can do
3. Plan how we can get a neighborhood park
4. Discuss some good new news on the drainage
5. Explain ACORN

Before the meeting, one of us will visit you to talk more about our community organization and to find out what you would like to see done. If you would like to help, please call one of us.

Mrs. Shirley Burks
1700 E. 21st

Mr. & Mrs. Jack Deese
1816 Security

Mr. Morris H. Rhoads
1724 E. 20th

Mr. & Mrs. William N. Quick
1718 E. 16th

Mr. & Mrs. Edward W. Short
2008 Security

ARKANSAS COMMUNITY ORGANIZATION FOR REFORM NOW
523 W. 15th Street   Little Rock, Arkansas 72202   376-7151

Exhibit 7: Quick Hits Checklist

QUICK HITS

WHY DO THEM?
- Gets a quick win on an issue people care about
- Makes clear right away what it means to be an ACORN member
- Helps build momentum during an organizing drive
- Attracts new members and builds ownership/develops new leadership by getting people to take responsibility for the action
- Shows that organizing and taking action gets results
- At least two during org drive

WHAT ISSUES ARE GOOD FOR QUICK HITS?
- Ones that only take one action to solve (don't cost much to fix, so some lower level official can agree to it on the spot)—getting a stop/slow children sign, cleaning a vacant lot, boarding an abandoned building, getting a school crossing guard, cutting trees off of power lines, fixing streetlights, cleaning trash and alleys, removing abandoned cars, and you name it. [versus issues that require bigger actions and a campaign—getting a stop light, changing city policy on vacant lot cleaning and maintenance, tearing down an abandoned building, getting more money for school safety, getting new streetlights
- Affect a small area—block or two
- Ones that a lower level official can commit to solve on the spot.

HOW TO ORGANIZE ONE?
- Look everyday on the doors for quick hit issues
- After you identify a problem that people on the block feel strongly about, ask someone who is fired up about it, if they can make a call to get somebody out to fix it, and if they can get their neighbors to join in. Must be a member.
- Set a date, time and location for the quick hit. (time when people can come out—late afternoon—pre meeting 6:00, official at 6:30, weekend)
- Work with this person to identify an appropriate target and rehearse the phone call by role playing it with them so that they'll feel comfortable making it, and also so that they won't do the action over the phone (It's VERY IMPORTANT that you work with them on this, since targets often try to work things out over the telephone to avoid coming out to the neighborhood)
- Get a commitment from your leader on how many people from the block they will turn out. Discuss their personal network and how many of these people they can produce, and offer to get them a petition that they can take door-to-door on the block for phone numbers and commitments to turn out.

Chapter VIII: Maintaining Organizers: Training, Dialogues, and Meetings

Exhibit 7: Quick Hits Checklist

- Check in a couple of days before the meeting to see how turnout is going.
- Have a member get fliers out about the quick hit. Be sure to make issue, time and place clear.
- Doorknock in the immediate area with a member on the day of event.

QUICK HIT TIMELINE

Day 5—**id the issue** Identify a local issue we can win quickly. Doorknock the area to get members and talk up this issue.

Day 4—**recruit members and call targets** Recruit a member to call the target and set the quick hit up. Prep them for the call.

Day 3—**turn-out** Get from members to lead the action, distribute fliers and make phone calls, and doorknock on day of action. Give fliers out. Role play phone calls. Follow up on results.

Day 2—**prepping & press calls** Work with at least two of these people on the agenda for the quick hit and get commitments on what roles they will play.

Day 1—**action day** press calls in morning. 90 minutes before meet with member for doorknocking "An official will be out at 5:30 to hear from us about clreaning up the lot down the street. Do you want to get it cleaned? [urgency] Great, can you join us? We're meeting at…" half hour before make last reminder calls. Pre-meeting—What is ACORN and membership, agenda, What-ifs/excuses/demands/bottom line, stick around for evaluation afterwards.

Etc—check on yeses daily
Prep—preferably a couple of people take roles
Make sure someone is coming, and get a commitment on who it will be. Need to be forceful—folks will be v. upset if no one meets with them about this…

Tour problem, member testimony about it, demands with a card to sign, commitment to go downtown on specific day if no-show
Follow-up with everyone who was there and sign up non-members
Get out win fliers—do them w/member who did the work

Perhaps even more valuable in Exhibit 8 is a detailed look at the interplay between the training organizer and the trainee organizers on how to handle membership recruitment through doorknocking or home visits. This detailed description comes from a transcription of a training film produced by ACORN and used in the early 21st century. If put before a dozen ACORN organizers it might yield a book length critique of its own, chock full of suggestions, modifications, stories, and lessons, but as a guide this is a handy and accessible tool in the way it presents issues and alternatives.

Exhibit 8: Membership Recruitment and Building Your Rap: Video Transcript

MEMBERSHIP RECRUITMENT—BUILDING YOUR RAP

[Opening Scene: Long follow-shot—organizer walking through the neighborhood and up to a door, knocking, then being invited inside]

(Voice over: footage of an organizer walking up to a door and knocking; music "Can't You Hear Me Knockin"
If organizing people to raise hell about injustice is your idea of a good time, this job might be for you. At ACORN, we think it's a problem that politicians and business leaders think they know what's good for low and moderate income people without ever talking to them and asking. As an organizer, your job is to find out what folks care about and motivate them to get organized and do something about it.
Organizers challenge people to take action rather put up with injustice. Most people in the neighborhoods where we organize want to fight back but aren't sure how. That's where you, as the organizer, come in. Talk is okay, but action's better".

[Scene #2--footage of an action]

(voice over)

"ACORN's prescription for justice is clear: Your children are stuck in lousy schools—get organized
Budget cutbacks for the poor and huge tax breaks for the rich —get organized
No affordable housing or health insurance—get organized
Trash in overgrown vacant lots, abandoned buildings on the block landlord not making repairs, too many speeders and too much crime—get organized
Ready to fight for your fair share—GET ORGANIZED!
The first step to getting organized is joining as a member. Here's how we recruit new members in the community":

Chapter VIII: Maintaining Organizers: Training, Dialogues, and Meetings

Exhibit 8: Membership Recruitment and Building Your Rap: Video Transcript

```
[S2-Part two: shot of organizer being invited
inside and walking through front door]

[Scene #3: Group of organizers doing role play]-
group sits in a circle for role play.
Part one: Trainer explaining the role-play process
Unscripted brief explanation of how and why we do
role plays. Gets two volunteers.

One-shot of Organizer (A) doing New Orleans rap

Trainer
"So what did you think? What did you like about
it?

Shot of group briefly discussing the overall rap
[we need two cameras, don't we?—one for speaker
and one for group?]

Trainer
Unscripted—asks what people thought of the
introduction (the part before getting in the door)

Group briefly discusses the introduction

Trainer
Unscripted—asks group if they would have let him/
her in to talk more

Group responds

Trainer
Unscripted
1. Brief description of introduction sample
points:
   •   importance of making a good impression right
away—you just have a few seconds to connect
   •   we want to know what their issues are—purpose
is to get them involved, not push a particular
issue
   •   key thing is to get them involved quickly by a
question that focuses on the issues
   •   we want to get in to talk further, and asking
about the issues at the door gives them a reason
to let us in
```

Exhibit 8: Membership Recruitment and Building Your Rap: Video Transcript

2. Use issues to help get you in. If folks don't come up with an issue when you ask what their concerns are, you can say that plenty of folks are talking about the problem with speeders, or with the trash in the alleys, then ask if that concerns them.

3. It's not just what you say but how you say it that matters. Ask group what they think that means.

Group answers question

Trainer responds to those answers and then lists on butcher paper the following points about how to make it easier to get invited in:
- Good eye contact.
- Good body language.
- Smile and be friendly
- Keep it short and simple
- Ask a question about issues
- Ask to come in and talk

Then review each item

Sample points:
Good eye contact—crucial. Keeps you focused. Helps your confidence.
Gets their trust. Keeps you talking with them instead of at them.
Good body language—no slouching, fidgeting or looking down at the ground. Carry yourself like you believe in yourself and what you're doing.

Smile and be friendly—act like someone you'd want to talk to yourself

Short and simple—concise and clear. Speak slowly. Don't make a speech, drown them in details, or preach at them.

Ask a question about issues— We want to hear what they have to say. Get them engaged right away.

Chapter VIII: Maintaining Organizers: Training, Dialogues, and Meetings   *173*

Exhibit 8: Membership Recruitment and Building Your Rap: Video Transcript

Ask to come in and talk — tell them it will just take a couple of minutes. Can't get in without asking.

Then say we'll move on to the second part of the rap. First part is
Introduction, where you make a connection, Second part is the conversation, where we you find out what issues they care about and help them see that organizing can help them build the power to solve them.
[writes down Introduction and Conversation

Then asks what group thought of how _____ did with the conversation inside the house

Brief discussion by group about the conversation part of the rap

Trainer responds to their critique, offers own critique, and then adds:
Writes on paper
- No preaching

"It's not about giving them some fancy presentation or slick rap, and we're not out there to convert anybody. This needs to be a conversation, so talk with them,
not at them."
- Keep asking questions

ACORN Scotland Doorknocking Team.

Exhibit 8: Membership Recruitment and Building Your Rap: Video Transcript

```
And listen closely to their answers. Then use
these to create agreement between the two of you
and to build positive momentum.
•  Think on your feet
No two conversations are just alike, and you've
got to think on your feet and make adjustments,
not just go through the same spiel with everybody.
You're an organizer, not a salesman.
•  80% listening
Which means that only 20% of the time you're
doing the talking. So if you're there 15 minutes,
they're talking for 12 and you're talking for
3. Got that?

[Then writes on paper]
Investigation
Polarization
Solution
"It helps to break the Conversation down into
these three sections.
What do you think we mean by investigation."

Group responds

Trainer
Unscripted description of interview
Sample points about the investigation:
•   We want to draw them out on the issues—how
long this has been a problem, what anyone has
tried to do about them
•   Start by finding out something about them—how
long they've lived here, what changes they've seen
•   Don't just sit there and let them go on. Keep
yourself involved by clarifying and emphasizing
what you're hearing.
•   Look around. If they've got young children,
ask about issues parents care about—how are the
schools, is there somewhere for children to play
•   Build on their answers. To get them to join,
you need to build positive momentum in the
conversation.

Trainer asks what polarization means.

Answers from group
```

Chapter VIII: Maintaining Organizers: Training, Dialogues, and Meetings

Exhibit 8: Membership Recruitment and Building Your Rap: Video Transcript

```
Trainer
Unscripted description of polarization
Sample points:
•   Get them fired up!
•   Find out if anyone's tried to fix the problem,
and if so, why do they think it didn't work
•   Ask if they think a wealthy neighborhood would
have to put up with this? Or if the mayor would
stand for it in his neighborhood?
•   Ask why they think politicians don't care
about this neighborhood's problems.
•   Then ask what they think it would take to fix
the problems.

Then ask group what they think it would take to fix
the problem.

Group responds

Trainer
Responds to the group
Says this brings us to the Solution section
Gives advice about how to get people to see
organizing as the way to solve their problems
Sample points:
•   If they say they don't know what it would
take, ask them if they think taking 30 people down
to city hall, or getting folks together and the tv
stations to come out, would make a difference?
•   Tell them that's what ACORN does—strength in
numbers, everyone working together

Trainer then says "let me show you how" and gets
a volunteer (someone experienced) up for a brief
role play

Role Play
Unscripted
Sample:

Trainer: So, what do you think it would take to
get the trash in these alleys cleaned up?

Trainee: I'm not sure.
```

Exhibit 8: Membership Recruitment and Building Your Rap: Video Transcript

Tner: Do you think if everybody stuck together it would help?

Tnee: Yeah, if you can get people around here to do that. We had that meeting before about the trash and nothing else ever happened.

Tner: Do you think it would work out better this time if 30 people went down to city hall and demanded that they clean up the trash, and told them you were coming back in two weeks if they didn't clean it up? You think they'd listen to that?

Tnee: Maybe.
Tner: Are you willing to work with your neighbors to get the trash clean up?

Tnee: Yes.

Tner: Great! A lot of people are already involved, and they've been joining as ACORN members. We got the trash cleaned out of the alleys over in the Ninth Ward recently when everybody got organized. And we're the group that just beat back that electric rate increase that you saw on the news. We get results when good people like you join the fight. Can we count on you?
Tnee: Sure.

Tner: Then let's get you started by signing up as a member. Here's a membership card. Let me tell you how the membership works.

Trainer
Asks what people think about the role play

Group responds

Trainer responds and adds advice
Sample points
- Build momentum here by making the connection between organizing and solving the problem
- People talk themselves into joining through the questions we ask.

Chapter VIII: Maintaining Organizers: Training, Dialogues, and Meetings

Exhibit 8: Membership Recruitment and Building Your Rap: Video Transcript

That works better than us trying to talk them into it.
- When they say, "Yeah, this problem sucks. Complaining about it isn't going to solve it. Us poor folks need to stick together and fight," you've got them.
- Once you've got them, ask them to join.
- Timing is important. What if you knocked on their door and immediately said, "Hi, I'm Steve with ACORN. I need for you to join ACORN today by signing this bank draft authorization for $10-30 per month. I'll wait here while you get your checkbook." That wouldn't work, right? You build up to it.

Says we're now up to the third part of the rap [writes down Close—Commitment under Introduction—Connection and Interview—Conversation]

Asks group to tell him some of the do's and don'ts of asking people to join

Group discussion

Trainer
Asks how _____ did on the membership ask

Group responds

Trainer comments on discussion and adds tips on closing the deal:
[writes them down]

Sample points:
- Be direct. Get to the point, don't beat around the bush. Don't spend a lot of time justifying why we ask them to join. Organizing speaks for itself
- Sound confident. You get back what you put out. If you're hesitant, they'll be hesitant. You're unsure, they're unsure. You're confident, they're confident. You have to believe in yourself and in what you're doing to organize people.
- Make it easy for them. Make it sound like you're asking for a little bit, not a lot. And

Exhibit 8: Membership Recruitment and Building Your Rap: Video Transcript

stress what's in it for them, not what's in it for us.

Here's what I mean—I'll give you two versions of the "ask." [we could get someone else up for this if we want—they just need to be prepped]
Here's the "make it easy" version.

So I've got the membership card in her hands after we've had a good conversation and she's down for getting involved. Now I say something like:

Sample:
ACORN works like your church, or like a union. The more members we have, the stronger we are, and when a whole lot of people pitch in a little bit every month, that makes us a strong, independent group.
Folks pay between 10 and 30 dollars a month in dues—less than what one soda costs every day—to build the group and pay for our office. The way your neighbors are joining is through an automatic monthly payment from their bank account. It's safer and easier that way—you don't have to remember every month and we don't have to carry cash around the neighborhood. It just takes a voided check to get your membership started. If you want to get that, then I can start filling out this card.

Now here's the "make it hard" version—where I make it sound like I'm asking for their first-born child.

Sample:
Uh, we ask people to join as members. Folks pay 10 to 30 dollars per month through a bank draft. We need that money to run our office. Do you think you could possibly do that? It would really help us out.

I know that one sounds exaggerated, but I've heard people sound like that out there. Guess what? They didn't sign anybody up!

Chapter VIII: Maintaining Organizers: Training, Dialogues, and Meetings

Exhibit 8: Membership Recruitment and Building Your Rap: Video Transcript

The other way you make it easy for them is to give them options that don't let them off the hook so fast.
"I don't have a checking account..." That's no problem, we can do it through your savings account.
"No savings account either."—We can take a credit card, too. We want to sign you up today so you can get to working with your neighbors now.
"I don't have a credit card."—We can give you a receipt for cash.
We're going to get results with good people like you involved.
"I don't have much around."—We ask that you do at least $30 for the first three months.
"I don't think I have that much."—Why don't you check. We have three levels of membership, and can sign you up today as an associate member if you can't do 30. That will get you started.
[goes off and returns]
"I can do $10."—Great, we'll put you down as an associate member, and you can move that up to a full membership soon.

Trainer
If she'd come back and said she only had $5, I would have signed her up as a provisional member. Remember, you're negotiating. This is a positive person with issues and a willingness to work together with others. No way I'm walking out of there without some level of membership commitment from her. The key is to keep coming back at them in a positive way.

Trainer
Asks if people get the difference
Adds more tips for making it easy [writing down]
Sample points:
• Don't let them off the hook—an organizer's job is to challenge people to take action
• Give them options—negotiate: no checking account, no problem, we can do it with your savings account, etc.
If they hesitate, ask again if they're willing

180   Nuts & Bolts – The ACORN Fundamentals of Organizing

Exhibit 8: Membership Recruitment and Building Your Rap: Video Transcript

to work with their neighbors to get the problem solved. When they say yes, you say, "That's what we're doing—getting organized. Plenty of people are already involved, and we're out here today looking for more good people like you.

How about we get two folks up here to show us how you negotiate with folks about joining. a and b. b, you be the person who's got questions and hesitating, and you lead it off.

A. "Do I have to join with my bank account?"
B. "That's how we ask everyone to do it. That way we can spend more time organizing to get the streetlights fixed and less catching up with everybody once a month."

A. "What's the money used for?"
B. "Our general budget is mostly paid for with dues— office rent, phones, fliers, and the organizing staff working full-time in the neighborhood to get action on these problems. We're not funded by the city or corporations because we fight them when we have to. Our members own and control ACORN—nobody's telling us what we can and can't do—and your dues make that possible."
A. "How much is it again per month."
B. "The minimum is just $10, but we ask you to do as much as you can so that we can get more done here in the neighborhood.
A. "You know, I go to community meetings over at the Baptist church, and they don't make you pay dues."
B. Sure, that's the group that the city pays for. ACORN members don't want to depend on the city because they know we can hit them harder for streetlights and trash clean up when we're raising our own budget."

A. "Yeah, that group doesn't get much done. How long has ACORN been around?"
B. "Forty-five years, all over the nation. We have almost 500,000 members. We're just starting out in this neighborhood, so we can work to get vacant

Chapter VIII: Maintaining Organizers: Training, Dialogues, and Meetings

Exhibit 8: Membership Recruitment and Building Your Rap: Video Transcript

lots cleaned up here just like we just did over in Homewood. You might have heard about that on the news. And we work on big issues, too—improving schools, getting more jobs and raising wages, getting better health care coverage for children and families.

If it's an issue poorer people are facing, we're probably working on it right now."
A. "You know, I'm short in my bank account right now. Maybe it's better that you come back."
B. "It's no problem if you're short today. The payment does not come out until the fifth of each month, so you've got plenty of time. We ask you to join when we stop by."
A. (laughing) "You've got an answer for everything, don't you?"
B. (laughing) "Hey, joining ACORN is a great investment. That's why
I'm out here.
A. "Well, all right. Hang on for a minute and I'll find my checkbook."

Trainer
Like b, you get pretty relaxed doing this after a while, but everybody's nervous to start. You'll get plenty of training your first few days about how to respond to just about anything people come up with. We spend a lot of time practicing answers to typical questions—and we've got an answer for just about any question. Not that having an answer gets everyone to join, but we're always in there pitching, sounding positive, and not taking "no" for an answer without challenge folks to get involved.

The key is finding people who care about getting problems solved, and then helping them make a connection between organizing, joining, and solving that problem through ACORN. Folks might raise some smoke about coming across with the membership dues, but don't just give up. Work with them. You're negotiating about getting them involved, not haggling with them over $10 a month. Tell them the dues are only $10-30 per month, not

Exhibit 8: Membership Recruitment and Building Your Rap: Video Transcript

10 a month "if you can afford that much." And always make you first ask for a bankdraft. Always. You can bargain down if you need to, but you can never bargain up. And always personalize your ask, no matter what you're asking for—dues, to chair a meeting, to lead an action. Don't say to someone, "We're asking people to join." Say to them, "We're asking you and everyone else to join." Confident and direct—that's how to ask.

No two conversations are the same, but when you use the structure of the rap to move the conversation in a positive direction, you'll stay more focused, you'll feel surer of what to say next, and you'll get more people to join. The structure keeps us on track

[add some practical advice here at the end]

Remember the levels of membership and join up every interested person at the highest level you can
Ask and be quiet
Don't mention meetings before asking to join
Get a voided check or deposit slip to verify the account number
Always get referrals and use them
Set a second visit when they join
Get e-mail address
Use positive language—we're working, not trying; demanding, not asking. A lot of your neighbors are concerned just like you and are getting involved, and we've gotten great results whenever folks get organized; not, have you ever heard of us before? Always make us sound big and exciting, which we are, not small and weak. People want to invest in a winner!

This is also a good snapshot of a training "exercise" with a group of trainees, all of whom likely had some experience, but are together in a situation as part of formal training or a training session embedded in some form of staff meeting or gathering.

One of the more interesting training experiences for many ACORN organizers came at the next level if they had more than six months experience and gathered for either the mid-level training or the advanced training. The initial staff-wide trainings were organized while Madeline Talbott was Field Director and were held largely in religious retreat areas in the Chicago area and later the meetings were held in various locations, though mostly in the middle to late summer in California around Los Angeles or the Bay Area, particularly at Point Reyes. Most of the later mid-level trainings were run by Pat McCoy, ACORN's Training Director, and Helene O'Brien, when she was ACORN's Field Director. I would handle the advanced training track which was usually only one-and-a-half days compared to up to three days for the other training.

The general training would include features like the Melian Debate, the classic exercise from Thucydides where the Melians are debating whether to surrender to the Athenians and the dire consequences of various bargaining strategies based on practical or principled grounds. Other readings would include Warren C. Haggstrom's "Money for the Poor," the Montgomery Bus Boycott piece from *Bearing the Cross* by David Garrow, the ACORN Model, and a summary of ACORN Principles. These training periods were also invaluable in the cultural cross-fertilization of ACORN values and experiences between various organizers in the same cohort of sorts, but hired in offices throughout North America, so that they could get to know each other. For management the sessions were also invaluable in allowing us access to all of several groups of organizers to discuss future assignments, the need to make deeper and longer commitments, consider transfers, and, invaluably, and try to ascertain that there continued to be a consistent and uniform training experience not only in these short bursts but also in their home offices where they were being recruited and receiving their organizing drive training.

We even had a separate head organizer to new head organizer training component to ease the transition into the job of directing staff and servicing members in new offices for the first time.

Exhibit 9: Agenda for Lead Organizer Training (Canada)

ACORN Canada Lead Organizer Training
Day 2 – Niagara Falls, Ontario

Campaigns

- Building blocks from Street Corner to Parliament and Corporate Hdqs
- Power Resource Theory vs. Pluralism for the Poor
- Allies, Base, Pressure, Press, and Understanding the Target
- Demands and Negotiations
- Privileging the Base to Agreements
- Institutionalizing Relationships

Fundraising and Sustainability

- Driving Capacity through Resources from Dues to Don'ts
- Diversification in Funding
- Simplicity to Scale
- Mixing and Matching Resources to Sustainability

Politics and Power

- Districts to Ridings: Role of Members
- Relationships to Party and Power
- Inside and Outside
- Thoughts about the Role of Lower Income Families in Canadian Future?
- Seizing our Ground and Staking our Claim

Melian Debate from Organizers Training at Colby Ranch in Los Angeles County.

Exhibit 10: Agenda for New Head Organizer Training (New Mexico 2008)

ACORN Field Operations
New Head Organizer Training

Mid-Year Management
Albuquerque, New Mexico
Thursday May 22, 2008
9am to 5pm

AGENDA

I   Introductions/ Overview

II Goals for Today

III Money: Raising It, Tracking It, Reporting It

IV Unions and Coalitions: Understanding and Evaluating Them, Approaching Them, Partnering With Them, Costs and Prices

V   Managing the Head Organizer Life: Time Management, Stress Management

VI Other Stuff?

The advanced training would be available to those organizers and other staff that had completed the mid-level training and had another year of experience. The advanced training agenda was more focused on readings and exercises that allowed people to learn more about "thinking" like an organizer and other levels of planning. The format also allowed time for more free flowing conversations that allowed organizers with 18 to 24 months experience to take advantage of the ability to get access to me and other senior organizers and to ask any questions about organizational history, policy, perspectives, or plans that they might have on their minds.

Dialogues

The advanced training was somewhat similar to the "dialogues" in that they were optional attendance offerings available annually to all staff that had completed both the mid-level and the advanced training components. All senior organizers and staff were also welcome to participate on a voluntary basis in whatever dialogues interested them. These dialogues were also organized around themes (politics, campaigns, civil rights, etc.) and based on required readings distributed in advance of the sessions along with discussion questions. The venues were diverse and since the meetings were usually held in the later winter not surprisingly they were held in locations like San Diego, St. Petersburg, and Charleston, South Carolina over a weekend period.

The structure of the dialogues, which I directed, was built around required readings within an overall topic. Various participants would summarize the readings and their reactions, and then specific questions would be designed to provoke wide ranging discussion that hopefully would reflect on ACORN's work, challenges, or future directions. Readings included such classics as Taylor Branch's treatments of leaders in the civil rights movement from his trilogy or Charles Payne's, *I've Got the Light of Freedom: The Organizing Tradition and the Mississippi Freedom Struggle,* probably the best book written on the organizer's role in civil rights organizing. We also examined less well known but invaluable pieces on issues like "how cities worked," using readings from *A Prayer for The City: The True Story of a Mayor and Five Heroes in a Race Against Time* by Buzz Bissinger, a former *Philadelphia Inquirer* reporter that ironically featured the machinations of David Cohen among others, who more recently has become one of our chief opponents in winning digital access in his newer, and more lucrative, role as Executive Vice-President of Comcast. We discussed book chapters on Cesar Chavez, John Lewis, and various critiques of strategy and organizing in the labor movement. This was also true not only for the winter dialogues but also for the fall advanced training dialogues.

Exhibit 11: Sample Agendas and Readings from Dialogues

DIALOGUE #5: POLITICS
Highlander Center
February 9 - 11, 1996

Friday, 2/9 -- 7-9 PM

    General Discussion on Weekend Objectives
    Piece that People Liked Best
    Organizing Ourselves to Understand Politics
    Organizing Ourselves to Understand Ideology

Saturday, 2/10 -- 9-12 Noon -- Using the Base Electorally...

    Readings: Reuther, Quinn, Chicanos, Fink - Knights of Labor, Greenstone

Saturday, 2/11 -- 1 - 3 PM   Takeovers and Movements

    Readings: Diamond - Right Wing, Quorum Court, MFD, Populists

Saturday, 2/11 -- 3 PM- 5PM   Building Local Parties and Politics

    Readings: Green - SW Socialists, Lowndes County, La Raza- Crystal City, United Labor Party of San Francisco

Saturday, 2/11 -- 7- 9 PM   Independent Parties

    Readings: American Exceptionality (marks), and others (*Finks*)

Sunday, 2/12 -- 9 - 11:30 AM   Where Do We Go From Here

    Applying the discussion to a discussion of the New Party, ACORN and union electoral politics, and future political strategies

----

Four Groups of 3-4

Sometimes the dialogues were convened across various operations within the ACORN family to try to cross fertilize the programs. A good example was a dialogue convened to discuss training programs and training models in St. Petersburg.

Exhibit 12: Dialogue on Training, St. Petersburg, February 2006

AGENDA
Organizing Dialogue on Training and Training Models
St. Petersburg, February 18-19, 2006

1. Introduction and background
2. What are we doing now?
3. What training programs and models do others use?
4. Needs for materials and techniques for contemporary demands
5. Training locations and training dislocations
6. Training programs for leaders
   a. Leadership School
   b. Local training programs
   c. Other offerings and venues
7. Training in special programs and interests
   a. Labor
   b. Politics
   c. Communication
8. Training in other forums
   a. Dialogues themselves
   b. Utilization of mid-year and year end meetings
9. Priorities for Training
   a. Campaigns
   b. Staff/management
   c. Budget/finance
   d. Communications
   e. Diversity
   f. Other
10. Training Past the Lowest Common Denominator
    a. Supervisors?
    b. Annual senior training?
    c. Cross-training and replacements
    d. Mentoring and shadowing
11. Succession
12. Cultural Transitions and Training
13. Other Thoughts and Themes

Chapter VIII: Maintaining Organizers: Training, Dialogues, and Meetings

Meetings, Meetings, and More Meetings

And then there were meetings. Lots of meetings. From the very beginning and forever more.

In the beginning in Arkansas we had a staff meeting every Wednesday at 8PM. For years in the 1980s when I was acting as Regional Director in the West, there were a series of phone calls every Sunday night to each of the head organizers in Texas, Colorado, New Mexico, Arizona, and so forth, week in, week out. Staff meetings were part of the routine, just like charts on the wall for all offices with multiple organizers.

As the organization grew, there were also statewide meetings on a regular basis, head organizer and regional director meetings of the field operations, division directors or management council meetings, and of course staff wide management meetings like the Mid-Year Meeting, usually held in the West in Colorado or New Mexico in the summer, and the annual, all hands' mandatory meeting of all staff, the Year End/ Year Begin Meetings, held initially on the weekend after the beginning of the year, but eventually moved to mid-December at the staffs' request, and always held in New Orleans or the New Orleans area, except in one instance in the immediate aftermath of Katrina when no hotel was able to accommodate us and we met in Houston.

ACORN Canada head organizers. Judy Duncan, John Anderson, Scott Nunn, and Jill O'Reilly with Wade.

Exhibit 13: Head Organizers' Agenda – ACORN Canada – Gatineau, Quebec March 2015

Head Organizers' Agenda ACORN Canada Gatineau, Quebec March 2015

WEDNESDAY night –

BC, NS, judy

THURSDAY:

Broadbent 9am – 3pm (judy)

11.30 – 3.30pm –Location Ottawa Office
- 11am pick up at Hotel
- 11.30 – 12.30 (jill) tour of Ottawa ACORN office [all BC Staff + NS]
- 12.30 – 3.30 (Scott) door knocking in Vanier (all BC staff + NS]

5pm – 6pm – HO meeting (Judy) location – Hotel (john Pizza)

6pm – 9pm: – Reports – (Judy) all staff
- National
- National Communications
- BC
- Toronto
- Ottawa
- NS
- International

9pm – Solidarity

FRIDAY:

9am – 10.3am0
- Gaelen, Andrew, David, Adele, peggy (Wade)- main room 2
- Rory, Mandi – Drive Reflections (John) –Break out room 1
- Cory, Clarissa Vincent, Heather, Tyler (Marcos) – Power - Main room 1
- Scott, Shay – Building allies (Jill) [role plays building allies, planning Allie Fundraising Events] – break out room 2. (union, university partnerships, interns, students,

10.30 – 11.30am
- Data, communications, email training - (peggy/john/marcos) – [eblast, how to use excel and do custom sort, gmail – search, labels, more] – clarissa – cory – tyler – rory – mandi – david – gael – Andrew – shay (Main Room)
- **Excel – everyone needs to know how to delete columns, rows, custom sort, cell boarders**

Chapter VIII: Maintaining Organizers: Training, Dialogues, and Meetings

Exhibit 13: Head Organizers' Agenda – ACORN Canada – Gatineau, Quebec March 2015

- French Rap training – French (Adele); Main Room 2
- Tax site Jill / Scott / wade – deep thoughts Break our Room 1

LUNCH – on your own

12.30:

- Campaign planning I (Judy) – Vincent, Clarissa, heather, Cory, Tyler (Main Room 2)

1pm – 3pm

- Campaign Planning II – (do 3 month calendar)
- Andrew (HH) Andrew ~[City Wide Housing - get city to ensure that fines are knows throughout city, get city to better inform tenants of enforcement process, incorporate tenant rights forums into building base] Gaelen (stop the above GL rent icreases ex), David (IZ), Adele(min wage), Mandi (disability), Rory (inclusionary zoning, but an "expanded tenants rights") (Judy) (Main Room 1)
- Grants – Scott, Shay, Peggy (John) - Break Out Room 1
- Building Power – Jill, Marcos – (Wade) – Break Out Room 2

3pm – 3.30: campaign planning report backs (Judy) all staff main room

3.30pm – 4.30pm

- Group 1: (Andrew) rap training – Shay, Mandie, Clarissa, Vincent, Heather, Tyler (Main Room)
- Group 2: (Jill/Judy) – Donor / FR Events
- trivia night reflections (pros and cons)

4.30 – 5.00: goal setting by office

DINNER -- (Peggy Coordinating)

6.30 – 7.30: Convention – all staff –(Judy)

- - Convention Agenda
- -Convention Action Brain Storm

7.30 – 8.15: National Campaign Discussion

- Wages Rising (Judy)
- Digital Access (John)

8.15 – 8.45: -Smart saver

9pm – Solidarity

Exhibit 13: Head Organizers' Agenda – ACORN Canada – Gatineau, Quebec March 2015

Saturday

10am – 3pm

HO meetings:

10am – 12: more convention

- Firm up real numbers
- Labour delegates? SEIU
- Workshops (get out the vote, DD, Housing, workers centre Montreal, Wages Rising, predatory lending)
- French door knock + petition anglaphone problem ??
- Action ideas – DD? conservative target?
- Speakers – CLC ?, labour council Montreal?,
- Child care staff
- Translation captains (jill)
- Food

- AGM –
- International meeting

LUNCH – quick (peggy)

12.30 – 1.30pm

- national platform and campaign updates
- National Platform - Beyond Harper: the People's Charter (send to 3 major parties)
- Leader process with meetings and fed politicians ??
- National campaign updates
  - DD
  - Wages Rising–
  - Remittance bill
  - Predatory lending

1.30 – 2.00pm

- Checklists

2.00 – 2.30: new report

2.30 – 3.00: smart saver

3.00 – 3.30: staying on top gov, press etc

3.30 – 4.00: operating budgets

Chapter VIII: Maintaining Organizers: Training, Dialogues, and Meetings

Exhibit 14: Division Directors' Meeting Agenda

ACORN Division Directors Meeting
Atlanta
July 14, 2003

1. Review of the Meeting
2. Review of Goals and Objectives Planning
3. Review of Progress on Directors' Objectives
4. Review of Priority Operational Challenges
    a. Relationships with Other Organizations and Networks
        i. PICO Summit: 10/30 Oakland
        ii. Gamaliel Report
        iii. NEA Discussions
    b. Financial Sharing Arrangements and Distributions
        i. AHC [also include Household Settlement update]
        ii. Political
        iii. Other
    c. Joint Staffing Arrangements and Protocols
        i. Discussion of Communications Director Position
        ii. Discussion of Legislative Director Position
        iii. Other
    d. Budgeting Needs and Developments
        i. Cash Flow issues and expectations
        ii. Other financially related issues
5. Big Themes for Planning and Coordination
    a. New Brooklyns – Metro Strategy
    b. Office Categorization Discussions
    c. Predatory Lending – Wells?
    d. ACORN Ventures?
    e. Self-Help Expansion and Relationship?
    f. ACORN Financial Justice Center
        i. Casey Proposal Development
        ii. EITC – Report and Issues Raised
    g. Political initiatives: status of capacity and fund development; Chicago?
    h. Los Angeles Convention
6. Discussion on Projects Managed by Chief Organizer
    a. Majority Unionism
    b. International Operations
    c. Community Labor Center -- Vancouver
7. Discussion of Other Items, Opportunities, and Business
    a. YE/YB
    b. Next Meeting
8. Other Business – Time Available

Division Directors' meetings were held two times per year, usually around the times of the mid-year meeting and year end meetings.

Management Council meetings included the division directors, but also head organizers and any operations director for an operation that spent more than $500,000 per year (labor, radio, CCI, New York, California, Louisiana, and other states, as they grew). The Management Council met shortly before the two Association Board meetings usually in the fall in New York City and during the spring in Chicago for many years and then later in Denver frequently as the organization grew stronger in the west.

Exhibit 15: Management Council Meeting

Management Meeting Agenda

Brooklyn and Manhattan
March 22-23, 2001

Special Notes:
- The meeting on Friday evening will convene between 7pm and 9pm at the Brooklyn office to get a jump on the business. It is assumed that we will cover some of the internal items at that time, particularly reviewing CCI progress and operations.
- The meeting on Saturday will be held at the CWA offices on 80 Pine Street in the Wall Street area in their conference room.

Agenda

    Work with Other Organizations
        Discussions with Gamaliel on San Diego
        Discussions with DART on joint projects
        Progress on the Organizer Forum
        Discussions with SEIU and IAF
        CCC

    Technology Developments
        Review of Wolff Memo and Policy Implications – Past and Present
        Web Sites for States and Offices
        Computer Repayments and Updates on network
        Database Discussion
        Payment Programs

    Campaigns
        Predatory Lending
        Living Wage
        CRA Ongoing
        Education Housing
        Other national: taxes, immigration, etc.

Exhibit 15: Management Council Meeting

WPolitics
    New Party
    WFP
    CT – WFP?
    NAACP Drive
    APAC developments
Field Operations
    Offices: Inventory and Expansion
    Ft. Lauderdale – January 2001
    Tucson – in development
    San Francisco – in development
    Staff transitions
    Troubled list
    Cluster Expansion Program: General and Emphasis on TX, FL, AZ, and CA
        Staff and Recruiting
        Experience with Academies
        Experience with Diversification
        Question of Capacity
        Experiment on Campaigns
        IWW – Update and Status
Development
    Housing
- Status of Bank Partnerships moving forward
- Status of New Construction Project in AZ
- Complying with HUD Predatory Lending grant …community outreach and education…

    Education – progress and plight of our schools…
    Media…
    Training: Future of INA?
National
    Education Conference Question?
    Legislative Conference Report
    Federal Perspectives
    External Fundraising
Internal
    CCI – Review and Update
    Audits – Review and Update
    Payroll Taxes – Review and Update
    CCI Reorganization – Review and Update
    Reconciliations and Confirmations – Review and Update
    Personnel
    Shared Costs and Payment Plans
    Wage Scale – Problems Absorbing the Increases in Offices
    Life with Budgets….

Here's another one from six years later in Denver in the fall of 2006.

Exhibit 16: Management Council Meeting, Denver, September 2007

Management Council Agenda
Denver – September 14, 2007

Morning Session   9 AM – 12:00 Noon
Lunch   Provided
Afternoon Session   1:00 PM – 4:00 PM

Foreclosure and Sub-primes Campaign
- Leverage
- Bargaining
- Program
- Policy
- Objectives

Using a Service Platform as an Organizing Platform
- H&R Block Partnership on Tax and Benefit Access
- Branches from the Tree
- Membership Acquisition
- Membership Activation

Regime Change:
Discussion on Policies and Programs that Build Organization and Opportunity
- Examples from the Past
- Next "CRA"
- Public Lists?
- Maximum Eligible Participation
- Imbedding ACORN
- Change in Labor Law

Internal Affairs
- Upcoming Board Meeting
- Purchase of New National Headquarters
- Compensation Discussion
- Year End Meeting

Information Items
- Direction on Education: Green Dot+ACORN+AFT Partnership?
- Mass Membership Meeting Report
- ACORN International, Mega-slums, and Tele-centers
- Follow-up on Political and Registration Protections for 2008 Cycle
- Staff Announcements and Updates

Chapter VIII: Maintaining Organizers: Training, Dialogues, and Meetings

The Management Council was the key staff "governance" sounding board and consensus shaping body. People pushed to qualify and were unhappy to end up out, if once in. People wanted a seat at the table. As the organization grew, more seats had to be added as more operations qualified, sometimes this was welcomed by other members of the Management Council and sometimes it provoked discussions about whether or not standards should be raised to keep the body smaller and more elite. There were merits to all of the arguments. For my part the more people around the table, the deeper the organizational consensus, for others, perhaps correctly as well, the more voices, the more diluted their own counsel at these meetings.

But of course the really big staff meetings were the all staff Year End/Year Begin (YE/YB) meetings. The tradition of the YE/YB began at least as far back as 1975. The meetings originally were in the first weekend of the New Year but weather concerns and whether or not the scheduling was crimping staff vacation plans moved the meeting after many years towards mid-December.

The stated purpose of the meeting was to evaluate the plans made in the previous year and the results of that work measured against the goals and objectives articulated then, as well as the revised and new plans for the coming year. These reports were lengthy, filling up entire volumes of ring binders from every operation, city, and state. The Mid-Year Meeting (MYM) was designed for the obvious, to check in on what progress had been made, adapt to changing circumstances, and appropriately modify and revise plans to more be more successful in the last six months of the year.

ACORN International head organizers meeting Paris 2016.

Exhibit 17: Mid-Year Agenda, New Mexico, May 2004

MID-YEAR MANAGEMENT MEETING
Abiquiu, New Mexico
May 28 – May 30, 2004

Friday, May 28, 2004

9:00 AM - 9:00 PM   ACORN Housing – New Arts Building
3:30 PM - 9:00 PM   Political Operations – Social Center
3:30 PM - 9:00 PM   Field Operations / Head Organizers
                             – Upper Pavilion

Saturday, May 29, 2004

9:00 AM   Welcome, Introductions, and Agenda
                      – Upper Pavilion

9:30 AM - 10:30 AM
                Major Reports and Highlights – Updates across Operations
    * Field   * Politics   * International   * Internal
    * Finance   * Housing   * Media   * Labor
 * National

10:30 AM - 12:00 N   Emerging Strategies I: Partnerships

12:00 PM - 2:00 PM   Lunch and Break

1:00 PM   Local 100 State Directors Meeting

2:00 PM - 3:30 PM   Special Guest: Gail Stoltz, ACORN Political
                            Consultant Washington, DC
                            Analysis of the 2004 Election
                            Effort and Building Power When it's Over

3:30 PM - 4:30 PM   Emerging Strategies II: Corporate Campaigns
                            – Case Studies

4:30 PM - 5:30 PM   Emerging Strategies III: Corporate Campaigns
                            – Core Elements

5:30 PM - 7:00 PM   Dinner and Break

6:00 PM   Home Day Care Association Caucus

7:00 PM - 9:00 PM   Framing and Communications

Exhibit 17: Mid-Year Agenda, New Mexico, May 2004

Sunday, May 30, 2004

9:00 AM - 12:00 N   Management Themes

9:00 AM - 10:30 AM   Review of Goals & Objectives
(By Division & Operation)
A Review of Objectives Established in YE/YB Reports and an Assessment of Priorities over the Remaining 7 months of 2004 Prepared for MYM 04

10:30 AM - 12:00 PM   Impact of DOL Overtime Rulings
Budgetary Issues
Staff Policies and Revisions
2004 Convention Update and Planning

12:00 PM - 12:30 PM   Summary and Conclusions
Announcements, Other Business, Good & Welfare
Evaluations and Summary

2:00 PM - 9:00 PM   Management Training
[Lead/Head Organizer Training] – New Arts Bldg

Monday, May 31, 2004

9:00 AM – 9:00 PM   Management Training II

Ghost Ranch Mealtimes

Breakfast   730 – 800
Lunch   1200 – 1230
Dinner   530 – 615

Here's another one in Exhibit 18 from the next year in Glorieta, New Mexico in 2005.

200   Nuts & Bolts – *The ACORN Fundamentals of Organizing*

Exhibit 18: Mid-Year Meeting, Glorieta, New Mexico, June 2005

MID-YEAR MANAGEMENT MEETING
Glorieta, New Mexico
June 3 – June 5, 2005

Friday, June 3, 2005

3:00 PM - 9:00 PM ACORN Housing
3:30 PM -9:00 PM Field Operations / Head Organizers

Saturday, June 5, 2005

9:00 AM Welcome, Introductions, and Agenda

9:15 AM - 10:00 AM Major Reports and Highlights
– Updates across Operations
* Field   *Politics   *International
*Finance   *Housing*Training
* Communications   *Labor   *National

10:00 AM - 1:00 PM Emerging Strategies I: Branding
Chuck Pettis, Branding Solutions,
Seattle, Washington

1:00 PM - 2:30 PM Lunch and Break

2:30 PM - 3:30 PM Emerging Strategies II: Mass Membership Strategies

3:30 PM - 4:30 PM Emerging Strategies III: Service Programs
– Tax and Benefits
Brief Remarks: Rawlin Tate, IRS Representative

4:30 PM – 5:30 PM Emerging Strategies IV: New Campaigns
** Hospital Charity Care Ordinances
** Credit, Pay Day Lending, & Predatory
Next Steps
** Political and Field Integration – Minimum Wage

5:30 PM - 7:00 PM Dinner and Break

7:00 PM - 9:00 PM Emerging Strategies IV: New Formations

** ACORN Community/Labor Organizing Center

** Working Parents' Association

** WARN and the Walmart Organizing Project

** Evangelicals, Mega-Churches and ACORN

Exhibit 18: Mid-Year Meeting, Glorieta, New Mexico, June 2005

Sunday, June 6, 2005

9:00AM - 12:00PM   Management Themes

9:00 AM - 10:30AM Review of Goals & Objectives
(By Division & Operation)
A Review of Objectives Established in YE/YB Reports and an Assessment of Priorities over the Remaining 7 months of 2005 Prepared for MYM 05

10:30AM - 12:00PM   Liberty Tax – Lessons Learned
Managing Relationships
Budgetary Issues
Salary Adjustments Process
2006 Convention Update and Planning

12:00 PM - 12:30 PM   Summary and Conclusions

Announcements, Other Business, Good & Welfare

Evaluations and Summary

Glorieta Mealtimes

Breakfast 6:30am-8:30am

Lunch 11:30am-1:30pm

Dinner 4:30pm-6:30pm

Estes Park mid-year meeting in 1990s.

Year End / Year Begin Meetings

These were the big whoppers. In the early years of the 21st century the meetings were so large with over a thousand participants from the staff that they would rate a notice that we were meeting in the *New Orleans Times-Picayune* under convention news for the normally sparse weeks before Christmas. Talking to Pat McCoy, then an ACORN training director, and now Executive Director of Action NC, the successor of North Carolina ACORN, recently about what he missed in the wake of the dissolution of ACORN United States, he mentioned, the "conventions," and the Year End meetings, and I knew exactly what he was talking about. It was truly a gathering of the ACORN tribes.

Year End meetings dated back to the expansion of ACORN in 1975, as opportunities to bring back the organizing staff to recharge and refocus, plan, and make plans and do the myriad other meetings, personal and professional, that fuel the work of people who make organizing their lives. Meetings evolved from office meeting rooms to small conference rooms in cheap motels in central Little Rock or Aldersgate, the Methodist campgrounds in Pulaski County for the mid-year meetings, to the New Orleans area after 1978 when the headquarters moved. For many of the early years in the late 1970s' and early 1980s few of the old-time organizers would miss an opportunity to tell colorful stories of meetings in the fog and cold at Fontainbleau State Park in their cabins on the north shore of Lake Pontchartrain. Not only would we pack everyone into hard benches and picnic tables in one long, narrow room squeezing in up to 100 people by the early 1990s, but we would also communally cook breakfast and lunch together adding yet more chaos and charm to the event. By that time adding some children to the mix just made it even more wonderful. It was bunk bed heaven!

Once the money was paid for transportation, the task became to put as many meaningful meetings and trainings into the space of a couple of days as possible. By the end of my 38 years as Chief Organizer, some of the senior organizers were complaining of "YE/YB exhaustion" after what could easily turn into 5 to 7 days' worth of straight non-stop meetings.

The meetings evolved over the years. In the 1980s and 1990s when the staff was somewhat smaller, these meetings functioned as a key forum for major internal and external policy initiatives. In Fountainbleau we would debate the pros and cons of private health insurers handling our group plan versus what evolved as first a staff and organizationally funded health discretionary benefit called the ACORN Fund, and later a qualified labor-management multi-employer plan that covered all eligible staff or establish a pension benefit or undertake initiatives in labor or media or politics. By the 21st century the meetings were invaluable but they were also expensive, costing several hundred thousand dollars to put together in transportation and housing, most of which was a shared cost by each state and individual operation, but for the ACORN Family a major investment.

Chapter VIII: Maintaining Organizers: Training, Dialogues, and Meetings

Exhibit 19: YE/YB Agenda 2006 New Orleans

YEAR END – YEAR BEGIN 2006
December 14-17, 2006
Sheraton Hotel – Canal Street
New Orleans, Louisiana

PRE-MEETING, December 12-13, 2006

ACORN Housing Staff House Gutting and Cleaning (optional)
Contact: supportrebuildingnola@acorn.org

ACORN and Other Staff House Gutting and Cleaning (optional)

Tours of New Orleans Neighborhoods and the 9th Ward (optional)
Contact: laacornlower9@yahoo.com

THURSDAY, December 14, 2006

8:30 AM - 9:00 PM	ACORN Housing Counselors Meeting
9:00 AM - 12:00 PM	Big State Head Organizers Meeting
9:00 AM - 12:00 PM	LEAP II - Lead Heads Meeting
1:00 PM - 9:00 PM	Field Operations Meeting and Training
1:00 PM - 8:00 PM	Political Operations Small Group Meeting
9:30 PM - until	Women's Caucus

FRIDAY, December 15, 2006

8:30 AM - 11:30 AM	ACORN Housing Counselor Meeting
8:30 AM - 11:30 AM	Political Operations Meeting
9:00 AM - 11:30 AM	A-CLOC Meeting
8:30 AM - 11:30 AM	Head Organizers Meeting

Exhibit 19: YE/YB Agenda 2006 New Orleans

12:00 PM - 2:00 PM **Plenary**
Introduction and Welcome
Discussion of Agenda &
Goals for the Meeting

Chief Organizer Report
Field Director Report
Political Director Report

2:00 PM - 2:45 PM **Organizing on the Web!**
Justin Ruben, Organizing Director, Move On - Austin

2:45 PM - 3:15 PM Housing Director Report
Executive Director Report

3:15 PM - 4:00 PM **Re-thinking Education for Low Income Families**|
Mike Feinberg, Co-Founder, KIPP Schools, Superintendent - Houston

4:00 PM - 6:00 PM **Operational Meetings**
Financial Operations   Housing Operations
Field Operations   National Operations
Political Operations Labor Operations
Communications Operations
International Operations (w/ Field)

6:00 PM - 7:30 PM **Dinner Break**

7:30 PM - 8:30 PM **Preparing for Power: The Next Cycle?**
John Podesta, Center for American Progress

8:30 PM - 10:00 PM   **Campaign Workshops**

- Money Mart / Payday Lending: Jordan Ash (Financial Justice Center), Matthew Henderson (New Mexico, Southwest Region), Katrina McKeown (Vancouver)

- Pressing Ahead to Combat Neighborhood Violence: John Eller (San Francisco), Robin Hood (Chicago), Liz Kropp (Cleveland), and Ben Winthrop (Tampa)

- Healthcare Expansion & Environmental Health Campaigns: Jose Manuel Escobedo (El Paso), Derrick Jessup (Baltimore), Beth Butler (Louisiana), and David Sharples (San Mateo)

- Targeting Developers in the Housing Market: Anthony Panarese (Oakland), Harold Miller (New York), Peter Kuhns (Los Angeles)

- Tenant Organizing – Lupita Gonzalez (Los Angeles), Ryan Spangler (Madison), and Julie Roberts (Paterson), Sergio Aguirre (NY)

Chapter VIII: Maintaining Organizers: Training, Dialogues, and Meetings

Exhibit 19: YE/YB Agenda 2006 New Orleans

- Getting 150,000 Votes on Your Own Ballot Line: The WFP Story! Emma Wolfe (Organizing Director – NY/WFP), Theo Moore (NYC Organizer, NY/WFP), Louisa Pacheco (Upstate NY, NY/WFP)
- Research for campaigns – Liz Wolff (Research Dept), Val Coffin (Fair Housing Dept), Marc Seiden (Campaign Dept), Gina Vickery (New Orleans – Katrina Projects), and Greg Mellowe (WARN Research Director – Orlando)
- Wal-Mart – Rick Smith (WARN – Florida), Wendy Torrez (WARN-Merced), and Madeline Talbott (Illinois)
- From Living Wage to Paid Sick Days – a Working Families Agenda: Jen Kern (Living Wage Resource Ctr), Mimi Ramos (Massachusetts), Neil Sealy (Arkansas), Orell Fitzsimmons (Local 100 – Houston)
- Working with Unions –Leslie Mendoza Kamstra (CLOC), Brandon Nesson (Minnesota), America Canas (NY Childcare Organizing Project), and Myra Glassman (Local 880)
- Taking on the Utility Companies – Eric Weathersby (Northern Indiana), Allison Brim (Dallas/Ft.Worth), Deidre Murch (Lansing)
- Building Organizational Power Through Ballot Initiatives – Katy Gall (Ohio), Ben Hanna (Colorado), Andrew Ginsberg (Kansas City, MO)
- Building the Working Families Party - Clare Crawford (WFP Field Director 07) Dan Cantor (Director, NY WFP)
- Immigrant Organizing Plans for 2007 – Brenda Muniz (Legislative Director), Damaris Rostran (New Jersey), Alain Cisneros (Houston), Teresa Castro (New Orleans)
- Building the Base and Moving Campaigns through VITA and Benefit Centers: Jayne Junkin (Houston), Laura Godines (San Francisco), Urell Spain (Philadelphia), Marie Flores (Dallas)
- Organizing Against Voter Suppression Efforts – Mike Slater (Project Vote – National), Ali Kronley (Philadelphia)
- Campaign Finance 101 – the Rules of the Game – Jeff Robinson (Deputy Political Director / Electoral – DC), Steve Bachmann (General Counsel – IN), Hollis Shepherd (CCI Legal – New Orleans), Brian Mellor (Legal – Political, Boston), Jessica Kudji (CCI)
- Brave New World: Campaigning On-line -- Kevin Whelan (Communications), Nathan Henderson-James (Oakland Political), Tunde Obaze (KNON)
- AHC – Converting Production to Leadership in the Housing Industry – Richard Hayes (DC, Moderator), Bruce Dorpalen (Philadelphia), and others TBA

Exhibit 19: YE/YB Agenda 2006 New Orleans

10:00 PM Queer Caucus
Organizers of Color Caucus I

10:00 PM -Until **Solidarity**

Saturday, December 16, 2006

8:00 AM - 9:00 AM Dawn Patrol: Special Session with Nathan and Denis on Using the Database More Effectively

9:00 AM - 9:20 AM Media – Communications Report
CCI Report

9:20 AM - 10:00 AM Shelter from the Storm: Explanation and Response to Attack
Steve Bachmann, General Counsel &
Kevin Whelan, Comm Director

10:00 AM - 12:00 PM **Services and Skills Workshops**

- Performance Based Management – Beth Butler (Middle South Region) and Matthew Luskin (SEIU 880)

- Basics in Using your Local Website: What to Do and How to Do it! - Mark Madere (Webmaster), Nathan Waldrip-Fruin (Communications), Laura Goodhue (Florida)

- Design Upgrades: Help to Create Better Fliers and Materials! – Ricco Robichaux (Communications Dept - Designer), Jewel Bush (Communications – Writer/Editor)

- Getting Good Press: Charles Jackson (Communications Dept) Sonya Murphy (Jackson)

- Innovative Electoral Campaign Tactics: Dear Neighbor and Friends & Neighbor Programs – Emma Wolfe (Organizing Director – NY WFP), Bill Lipton (Deputy Director – NY WFP)

- Building and Maintaining Large Electoral Canvass Programs – Johanna Sharrard (Pol Ops – CO/MO), Debaniesha Wright (Pol Ops – OH), Beth Berendsen (Pol Ops – OH), Jake Olsen (Pol Ops – MO)

- AHC Managers (ONLY): Increasing Local Capacity and Time Management – Jean Withers (Seattle) (Moderator), Rosalind Carroll (Philly), Alex Dicotighano (Las Vegas), and Ernie Boyd (Seattle)

- AHC: Creating Successful Post-Purchase Classes – Tara Benigno (Moderator - Brooklyn), Reagan Brewer (Chicago), Fantaye Akbar (Dallas), Alexa Milton (St. Paul) Munai Newash (Chicago)

- AHC: Housing Counseling 101: Making the Most Out of Our Lending Agreements – Doris La Torre (Moderator - Bridgeport), Christy Leffall (Oakland), Raquel Ravelo (Brooklyn)

Exhibit 19: YE/YB Agenda 2006 New Orleans

- Fundraising from Issue Campaigns – Steve Bradberry (New Orleans), Maryellen Hayden (Pittsburgh), Dave Lagstein (Detroit)
- Working with Navision – Denis Petrov (CCI), Mary Ann LeBlanc (CCI), and Irvine Figueroa (CCI)
- How to Build Power in your City and State – Jon Kest (New York), Ginny Goldman (Texas), Derecka Mehrens (California)
- Event Based Fundraising – Dave Chaos (KNON), Sara Albee (New Orleans Rebuilding Program)
- Moving Members to be Volunteer Organizers – Chris Entrikin (Pol Ops – Los Angeles), David Perkins (Albuquerque), Carrie Guzman (Michigan), Amanda Thorson (AZ), Tai Smith (Cleveland), Becky Wagner (Rhode Island); Amy Teitleman (Cincinnati), Marie Hurt (New Orleans)
- Alternative Membership Strategies / house meetings – Alain Cisneros (Houston), Barbara Clark (Cleveland)
- How to Pass State Legislation: Brian Kettenring (SE RD/ Miami), Amy Schur (Campaign Director), Ronald Coleman (New Orleans)
- AHC: Get Ready for 2007: Organizing Successful Fundraising Events – Jose Luis Trevino (Moderator – San Jose), Munai Newash (Chicago), Sherry Randall (Dallas), Pam Beard (San Diego), Lydia Lopez (Fresno), Susan Wayman (New Orleans)
- AHC: 2006 Production Cinderellas: How to Blow Away Everyone's Expectations! Angie Oliver (Moderator - Boston), Jorge Guerrero (Dallas), Alex Dicogtinano (Las Vegas), Theresa Naylor (Springfield), Carmen Blatt (Kansas City), Michelle Celestin (Ft. Lauderdale)
- Housing Development: How 2006 Experience Informs 2007 Plans – Mary Shalloo (Development Director, Chicago), Ismene Speliotis (MHANY, NY), Marie Lee (New Orleans), Marilyn Perez (Phoenix), Tony Fuller (Chicago)
- Mind Meld: Researchers Coordination Meeting (Invitation Only) – Liz Wolff, Research Director
- Dues and Don'ts Without Bargaining – Barbara Watson (Wal-Mart Workers Association - Orlando), Rosa Hines (Local 100 – NO), Maria Castilleja (Working Families Association – Houston)

Exhibit 19: YE/YB Agenda 2006 New Orleans

12:00 PM - 1:30 PM   Lunch Break

       Special Meeting: ACORN and Allied Tech Staff Discussion – Place TBA

       Special Caucus: Footprint Meeting to Discuss Citigroup and ACORN Partnership with Eric Eve

1:30 PM - 2:00 PM   You Should Have Been There When Dramatic Re-creations of the "Best of 2006!"

2:00 PM - 2:30 PM   Labor Report – 880
                                    Labor Report – 100
                                    ACORN Community Labor Organizing Center (A-CLOC)
                                    ACORN International Report

2:30 PM - 3:30 PM   New Initiatives

- Corporate and Volunteer Contributions – Mitch Klein (Office of Chief Organizer) and Darryl Durham (NO Clean-out Program)
- Katrina Update – Wade Rathke and Steve Bradberry

3:30 PM - 5:30 PM   **Organizing Workshops**

- Organizing and Operating VITA and Benefit Sites-- Jeff Karlson (New Orleans), Maryellen Hayden (Pittsburgh), Urell Spain (Philly), Tanya Hicks (Cincinnati)
- Moving Volunteers – Sara Albee (New Orleans Gutting), Karen Elben (ACORN Tax and Benefit Centers – New Orleans)
- Working with Clergy – Leiland Woods (Dayton), Bertha Lewis (New York)
- Working in Coalitions – Dave Lagstein (Michigan), Katy Gall (Ohio), Anthony Panarese (Oakland)
- Building Organization from Provisional Members – Brennan Griffin (CO Office / NO), Ali Kronley (PA), James Wardlaw (Toronto), Jeff Partridge (Rhode Island)
- How to Fundraise Canvass – John Anderson (Ottawa), Kris Harsh (OH), Ryan Spangler (Madison)
- Intakes and Membership – Tiffany Jones (WARN), Mimi Ramos
- Creating Big Turnouts: Aimee Olin (Providence), Derrick Jessup (Baltimore), Christina Spach (Atlanta)

Exhibit 19: YE/YB Agenda 2006 New Orleans

- Organizing in Middle-Income Communities: Antoinette Krause (SE PA), Amanda Thorson (Mesa), Brandon Nessen (Minneapolis)
- Associate Membership Canvass – Greg Basta (New York), Neil Herman (SE PA), Brittany Petit (RI)
- Organizing Informal Workers – Brynne Seibert (880-Chi), Julie Roberts (Paterson),
- Organizing Partnerships with Labor -- Derecka Mehrens (California), Ross Fitzgerald (A-CLOC), Rosa Hines (SEIU 100 – New Orleans)
- Getting the message: Working with leaders to build ACORN's Brand -- Kevin Whelan (Communications Director), Toni McElroy (Houston),
- Developing International and National Campaign Strategies: Amy Schur (Campaign Director) and Judy Duncan (Canada), and Dine' Butler (Argentina)
- Writing Grants -- Janet Reasoner (Wyoming), Camellia Phillips (New York), Carolyn Carr (DC)

6:30 PM - 9:00 PM Dinner and Banquet

6:30 PM Seating and Social

7:00 PM Dinner Served

7:45 PM Program

Awards: ACORN President Maude Hurd
Local 100 SEIU President Mildred Edmond
Local 880 SEIU President Helen Miller
AHC President Alton Bennett

Special Guest Speaker: Eric Eve, Senior Vice-President, Citigroup on the Value of Partnerships

Sunday, December 17th

9:00 AM - 3:00 PM Political Operations Meeting

ORGANIZE EVERYTHING THAT MOVES!

BEST WISHES FOR A GREAT 2007!

The YE/YB 2006-7 agenda is a good snapshot at how these meetings worked. They were in New Orleans, so we let the "play" happen for people wherever they could find it, and believe me, they found it everywhere. Otherwise the meetings were packed, there was wide participation in leading workshops on any number of topics, and operations with multiple staff assigned folks and woke folks up to get people moving, packed up and out, very much like a bi-annual ACORN Convention. Once the size of the meeting moved to a convention-type facility like the Sheraton or Hilton downtown, it also meant that people were chockablock in twos, threes, and fours in a room with as many rollaway beds as they could pack in and still be able to visit, party, and just get to know each other from the hallways to the lobby to the elevators and escalators packed in the mornings.

These meetings were invaluable to the staff and in building the entire culture and direction of ACORN. Running the meeting was both exhausting and exhilarating!

I've already established it was a marathon of meetings, as the agenda more than indicates, but besides that, it was meetings within meetings. Staff on the bubble who needed encouragement and a conversation to renew their commitment and enthusiasm, vacancies that needed to be filled with the acquiescence of both supervisors and the organizers themselves, people who needed to change jobs, locations, and projects. Organizers who were doing a great job who needed to hear from the Chief that it was recognized. Organizers who were unhappy that needed a conversation to push them further in or further out.

And, it all had to run on time while a staff more young than old was almost giddy at being in the meeting and getting to be a part of the largest and most powerful membership organization of low and moderate income people in the country, and saw a friend from training, grabbed a cup of coffee with an organizer who might lobby for

At ACORN YEYB 2006 John Podesta Answers Questions from Tanya Harris, New Orleans ACORN organizer.

Chapter VIII: Maintaining Organizers: Training, Dialogues, and Meetings them to be transferred closer to home, or someone who seemed to have the secret sauce to filling a hole in the skills that was still one of their weaknesses, or anything else in the world. Herding the back of the room, so that the front of the room, and the business of the agenda was still the priority was a lift. It took a lot of us putting our shoulders to the wheel, and there's no question, sometimes I was begging, and sometimes I was barking, but anyway it happened it was still an amazing organizational experience that tempered commitments with fire and steel for the future and for living and working past the boundaries of our dreams.

As the organization got larger the YE/YB meetings were also opportunities for us to run a three-ring circus worth of related business. Our allies loved the opportunity to see the "show" and address the troops. Key staff from MoveOn, TruCorps, Gamaliel Foundation, US PIRG, and many others made appearances at different times. Certainly good examples are in the agendas including John Podesta, former chief of staff to President Clinton and special adviser to President Obama, among other things, Cecilia Munoz, later the top immigration aide to Obama, Cecile Richards, head of Planned Parenthood, Henry Cisnernos, former Mayor of San Antonio and Secretary of HUD under Clinton, Mayor Bill White of Houston, New Orleans Councilman-at-Large Oliver Thomas, and a host of other politicos. People who wanted the chance to move us, one way or another, like the co-director of the KIPP charter school network or people we were trying to move as well, like Eric Eve, our partnership manager at Citibank, who once helped give the awards at the final banquet that usually ended the YE/YB in the later years.

The formal meetings were also accompanied by various caucus groups that also began meeting during the open periods of the meeting involving women, the oldest group, and later the Caucus of Color, and finally the LGBT. Reports were given to the full body, but the agreement upon the creation of a caucus was that they not impede on the agenda.

Some features of the meeting changed over time. When the meetings were smaller for several decades of the 20th century at the end of the meeting in an effort to ensure maximum participation and some sense of consensus and effective voice, I would moderate a closing where everyone there would have opportunity to speak, hopefully briefly, and give their evaluation of the meeting, a tradition that was deeply cultural for ACORN. Whatever they said, stood as stated, without debate, modification or argument. Often times the comments were very constructive, frequently deeply personal, including comments on quality of the food, bunks, and general housing, and often totally inspiring with expressions of renewed commitments, excitement for the coming year, and pleasure with the meeting. And, sometimes not. As the organization grew this final summary could take hours and often was redundant and harder to hold everyone's attention. I would call on each person in order and take notes, as best I was able, on all of the comments, so people had the feeling their comments were taken seriously by the body and by the Chief Organizer. Once the meetings passed a couple of hundred in attendance, there was no way to continue this tradition. The compromise for several years was to call on random people as well as those that wanted to speak, but this defeated the proposition of both consensus and participation, since it did not afford opportunity for the silent or new voices and tended to privilege those with an agenda. Finally in the 21st century I just

Madeline Talbott, Peter Wood, Fran Streich, Jeff Elmer at Year End/Year Begin Meeting in 1990s.

dropped this final evaluation, offered anyone the opportunity to send me their comments or suggestions, and let the meeting end on its own weight.

Other pieces that evolved were more fun for the staff and communicated extremely well. These features involved "re-creations" of significant events or actions in cities or nationally that organizers wanted to share with everyone. Along with another feature called, "I wish you were there when….," which featured a surprising, embarrassing, inspiring, or exciting event, often in an action complete with role playing, sometimes costumes, and spoken parts. These two meeting additions were fun and often hilarious. Both provided highlights and were great for *espirit de corps*.

Every YE/YB included a session based on small group discussions in addition to the workshops and plenaries. The toughest part of the small groups for years was the painful process of the staff "counting off" the numbers to determine who was in which numbered group. Disastrous! But, unthinkingly I continued to do this for years no matter how poorly it worked until we got large enough that we had to register the staff coming into the YE/YB, give them their packets, and report books and so forth. From that point on we pre-assigned numbers to everyone, thankfully!

Changing tradition came slowly, like using microphones and not allowing smoking in the meeting, but over 38 years, eventually we got there. Exhibit 20 is another agenda for YE/YB 2001 as well as Exhibit 21 which is the small group topic for that particular meeting, both of which reflect their proximity to 9/11. Perhaps more representative of a YE/YB small groups session is Exhibit 22 from YE/YB 2003, which forced people to dig deeper with each other and look at a major initiative of the organization.

Chapter VIII: Maintaining Organizers: Training, Dialogues, and Meetings

Exhibit 20: Year End – Year Begin 2001 New Orleans

YEAR END – YEAR BEGIN 2001
December 13-16, 2000
Hyatt Hotel
New Orleans, Louisiana

THURSDAY, December 13, 2001

9:00 AM–10:00 PM	Organizer's Forum Board Meeting - Fairmont
9:00 AM–9:00 PM	AHC Loan Counselors Review and Training
7:30 PM–9:30 PM	Political Operations & Party-Building Meeting

FRIDAY, December 14, 2001

9:00 AM–1:30 PM	Organizer's Forum Board Meeting - Fairmont
9:00 AM–12:00 PM	AHC Loan Counseling Meeting – Hyatt
9:00 AM–6:00 PM	Party & Political Operations Meeting
12:00 PM–5:30 PM	AHC Loan Counselors Computer Training - UNO
5:00 PM–8:00 PM	Head Organizers' Meeting
2:00 PM–5:00 PM	Management Council
8:00 PM–10:00 PM	Women's Caucus

Nota Bene: All meetings at the Hyatt unless otherwise indicated. All reports are due at Hyatt on arrival.

Hyatt Regency Hotel – 500 Poydras Plaza, New Orleans (504) 561-1234

Exhibit 20: Year End – Year Begin 2001 New Orleans

SATURDAY, December 15, 2001
PLENARY

9:00 AM–10:00 AM   Introduction
        Welcome
        Discussion of Agenda & Goals for the Meeting
        Operations Highlights (2001 Big Hits!)

10:00 AM–11:00 AM   **Campaign Developments:**
        Measuring Progress 2001
        Lending, Education, Living Wages, Politics!

Lisa Clauson (Education – Edison Campaign), Lisa Donner (ACORN Financial Justice Center – Household Campaign), and Jen Kern (ACORN Living Wage Center), and Joanne Wright (ACORN Deputy Political Director)

11:00 AM–11:45 AM   **New Perspectives: Faith Based Work**
        John Calkins (DART – Miami)

11:30 AM–11:45 AM   **Report from Washington:**
        Charlene Sinclair,
        National Campaign for Jobs & Income

11:45 AM–12:00 PM   **Convention 2002 – Chicago**
        Carolyn Carr (DC-National)

12:00 PM–1:00 PM   **Lunch**

1:00 PM–2:00 PM   **Skills and Campaigns Workshops**

1. Fighting for Schools and School Support
   Marianna Davenport (NY), Jeff Ordower (Philly),
   Bertha Lewis (New York), Ken Stretcher (100-Dallas)

2. Meeting the Housing Credit Needs of ACORN Communities
   Bruce Dorpalen (AHCLC), Doris LaToree (CT/AHC),
   Ismene Spiliotis (NY)

3. Nuts and Bolts of Political and Electoral Work
   Beth Butler (Louisiana), Sasha Baltins (San Antonio),
   Alliea Groupp (Detroit), Dan Cantor (NY WFParty)

4. Metropolitan Organizing, Growth, and Sprawl
   Brian Kettenring (Sacramento), Madeline Talbott (Illinois),
   Will Ward (DC)

Exhibit 20: Year End – Year Begin 2001 New Orleans

    5 Living Wages: Where are We Going
Rosa Hines (100-NO), Leslie Haber (100-AR),
Keith Kelleher (880-IL/MO), Jen Kern (National)

    6 Housing Campaigns
Mike Shea (AHC), Marilyn Perez (AZ AHC), Becky Gomers (MN), Kate Atkins (Jersey City), Oriana Saportas (Los Angeles)

    7 National Action Days: II – Bigger and Better– Clean-up and Traffic
Christal Padilla (San Diego), Cledell Kemp (Dallas),
Derecka Mehrens (San Jose), Adam Lang (Chicago)

    8 Childcare Organizing
John Jackson (LA), Maggie Laszlo (880-Chi),
Moricka Johnson (100-NO), Kenneth Stretcher (100-Dallas)

    9 Moving Tenant Campaigns
Heather Appel (Long Island/NY), Peter Kuhns (LA), John Eller (SF), Peter Santiago (Bronx)

  10 Welfare Re-authorization Fight
Neil Sealy (AR), Eric Thompson (Miami), Marie Hurt (New Orleans), Charlene Sinclair, National Campaign on Jobs & Income (DC)

  11 Building Local Campaigns from Scratch
Mitch Klein (Baltimore), Clare Crawford (San Diego), Dave Langstein (Providence), Liz Wolff (Research – Field), Pat McCoy (Field)

  12 Local and State Predatory Lending Campaigns
Matthew Henderson (Albuquerque), Amy Schur (CA),
Doug Bloch (Oakland)

2:00 PM–3:30 PM	**Notes from the Underground: Perspectives on Media** Jen Angel and Jason Kucsma, Co-Editors, clamor Magazine Bowling Green, OH
3:30 PM–5:30 PM	**Operational Meetings** Internal Operations Housing Operations Media Ops Field Operations National Operations Political Operations Labor Operations
5:30 PM–7:00 PM	Dinner
5:30 PM–7:00 PM	Gay/Lesbian Caucus
6:00 PM–7:00 PM	Caucus of Color
7:00 PM–7:30 PM	Dramatic Re-creations of the "Best of 2001!"

Exhibit 20: Year End – Year Begin 2001 New Orleans

7:30 PM–8:45 PM **Politics in a Parallel Universe**
What are we Learning – and Does it Matter?
Zach Polett (Political Director), Jon Kest (New York),
Bertha Lewis (NY WFP), & Jim Fleischmann (New Party)

8:45 PM–10:00 PM **Small Groups: Organizing after 9/11:
Impact of War and Recession**

10:00 PM–Until **Caucus of Color Deuce**

10:00 PM–Until **Solidarity**

SUNDAY, December 16, 2001

8:00 AM–9:00 AM **Implementation and Program**

1 Organizing Academies: Recruitment and Stability
Carolyn Siegel (Denver/ Field), Andrew Ginsberg (Portland), Melanie Marcus (Bost), Myra Glassman (880-IL)

2 Moving the Message: Spin City and How to Message
David Swanson (DC), Jeff Karlson (NOLa), Kimberly Olson (Dallas), Mildred Brown (National)

3 Organizing Immigrants in Changing Times
Ginny Goldman (Chicago), Teresa Castro (Phoenix), Julie Roberts (Paterson NJ)

4 Raising Money from our Organizing
Matthew Henderson (Albuquerque), Josh Miles (Boston), Glenda Kizzee (Houston), Chris Leonard (Boston)

5 Raising Money from Foundations: How-to-Guide
Steve Kest (National), Camillia Phillips (National), Nathan Henderson-James (CA-Oakland), Ron Niemark (100-LA)

6 Predatory Options in the Street and Courtroom
Elizabeth Andrades (Ft. Lauderdale), Jordan Ash (AHC-Midwest), Rose Alanis (AHC), Jose Gonez (AHC)

7 New Systems: How to Work 'Em!
Barbara Faherty (CCI), Steve Bachmann (Legal), Maisha Jamerson (100), Marsha Henley (880)

8 Bringing Politics Home: State and National
Chris Saffert (Leg Dir), Beth Pease (AR-100), Jerry Jones (Project Vote), Cindy Boland (880-IL)

Exhibit 20: Year End – Year Begin 2001 New Orleans

   9 Organizing with New Technologies – Practical Lessons
Karen Bahow (100-SA), Greg Heller (New York), Richard Schwartz (100-NO), Val Coffin (National)

 10 Building and Working with Coalitions
Mitch Klein (Baltimore), Clare Crawford (San Diego), Ken McCoy (St. Louis), Lisa Clauson (Campaigns), Steve Bradberry (NO)

 11 Expansion Program and the Challenges of Building New Program and Staff
Kevin Whelan (Field), Henrietta Hill-Murray (Jacksonville), Pat McCoy (Field), Doug Bloch (Oakland)

 12 Managing Staff through a Drive
Becky Gomers (Twins), Jenny Lawson (Seattle), Jon Kest (New York), Orell Fitzsimmons (100-TX)

 13 Leadership Development
Amy Schur (California), Kate Atkins (New Jersey), Madeline Talbott (Illinois), Bertha Lewis (New York)

 14 How to Canvass
Alliea Groupp (Detroit), Ali Kronley (Philly), Marc Seiden (Philly)

PLENARY

9:00 AM–10:00 AM **Techno Wonders at the Edge of the New Frontier of Organizing**
Peter Compagno (CCI), Mark Madere (CCI), Eric Stenstrom (Chicago), and Greg Heller (New York)

10:00 AM–10:30 AM	Operations Reports
10:30 AM–11:00 AM	Report from Small Groups
11:00 AM–11:30 AM	You Should Have Been There When….
11:30 AM–12:00 PM	2001 ALLSTARS
12:00 PM–12:30 PM	Summary of Other Business
12:30 PM–1:00 PM	Evaluations

ORGANIZE EVERYTHING THAT MOVES! BEST WISHES FOR A GREAT 2002!

Exhibit 21: Small Groups Topic 2001

Small Groups Topic
This topic "writes itself."
The twin tragedies of war and recession impact on our work, clearly. But, how?
Recession and the downturn in the market say something about both internal and external resources. How does this affect our work? How does this affect campaigns? What does this instruct about the construction of budgets for all operations?
The notions of war, terrorism, security, and various rights for citizens – and non-citizens – are all up for grabs today. Many of these issues – if not all – impact all facets of our work. How? What should be our response? Are there different issues, we should engage or the same issues in different ways? How will this impact our access in communities, workplaces, and public spaces?
These are our times now. What should be done?

Small group meeting at ACORN International organizers meeting in Paris 2014.

Here's another example of a small group feedback discussion at a Year End/Year Begin meeting. This one in 2003.

Exhibit 22: Small Groups Topic YE/YB 2003

YE/YB SMALL GROUPS 2003
Privileging the Base

What are we talking about here: privileging the base? Is this just another way of saying that we need to build the base? Is this a weird expression about income transfer to the members? Is this some other conversation we have had in the past with a peculiar name?

The base of all of our operations is low and moderate-income families. We organize and service that base in a variety of ways. We organize them systematically into neighborhood, community organizations so that they can make decisions about community issues, resolve long-standing grievances, take action, and operate in the public sphere to build power. We organize this same constituency into associations and unions as workers, so that they can act on concerns not in the neighborhood, but at the workplace or as workers in much the same process. We create vehicles for them to communicate with each other and at large through our radio stations, websites, newspapers, and journals. We create bridges and services that both fulfill our members and other constituent families' aspirations and distribute the results of victorious campaigns that have permanently changed lending institutions to these families so that they can find decent and affordable housing – some of which we directly provide – or can become home owners with access to reasonable mortgages. In a few cases we bridge the educational grievances and aspirations with our own schools. In a few other places we can surround our members with the sound of our radio stations. We want to be the home page for our members as they increasingly become on-line.

As the institutions and formations we construct become larger and larger with roots and branches entwined anywhere and everywhere around the family of other organizations and the often dauntless requirements and burdens of each part, the whole can become harder and harder to see clearly. The list becomes longer. The architecture becomes more intricate. The pieces squeeze tighter in the puzzle. We can all easily become lost in the details of the

Exhibit 22: Small Groups Topic YE/YB 2003

engineering and lose sight of the vision that unites and propels us all. We have had these conversations before about integration and synergy. Looking at the organization in a holistic manner is critical, and we really cannot do enough of that.

Nonetheless that is not this conversation.

This dialogue is about the methodology of all of our operations. When we speak of privileging the base, we are talking about adding value to daily work. We are talking about understanding what others call "our core competencies." Stripping off the extra layers of all we do in order to look closely at what we do well – the very uniqueness at the heart of all of our operations.

Drilling to the core, we want to then determine if we can add value to work with our constituency – privilege the base – by deepening that work. Mixing metaphors, we would be adding tributaries to the main stream; we would look at the natural branches that could be grafted to the trunk; we would super-size the basic portions of our work – are you following me yet?

What are examples of privileging our base – looking at our methodology more holistically? This after all is the point of these small group exercises!

When AHC counsels homebuyers how can we make sure that same user of our services is also being registered to vote? What is the cost of this slight extra addition to the program?

When ACORN organizers and members are door knocking in the community how can we also test eligibility for EITC at the same time? And, check voter registration? And, determine interest in AHC's loan counseling service?

When Project Vote is doing "site" registration, how can we also identify families interested in getting involved in organizational campaigns? With their email addresses?

When our local unions are communicating with their members at the worksites or at meetings, how can they let the members know about loan counseling services, voter registration, or community activities?

Chapter VIII: Maintaining Organizers: Training, Dialogues, and Meetings

Exhibit 22: Small Groups Topic YE/YB 2003

You get the idea, right? These are core competencies. In the ACORN field program that may be (should be!) door knocking – the fact that every day and night, six days a week, more than 200 organizers are visiting 5000 households and having thousands of conversations a day about the organization. In the AHC loan-counseling program we are watching tens of thousands of interested homebuyers walk through our doors to our meetings or individual counseling sessions. There are somewhere near 80000 people listening to our radio stations daily.

Too often when we think of how to move an additional program – register voters, move people to the polls, raise more money, whatever – or when we look at fundamental institutional issues like governance, financial sustainability, staff recruitment and training, communication, or the like, we look at parallel architectures: grant writers, canvassers, special crews, separate operations, discrete functions, additional competencies, new skills. In privileging our base we need to instead confront how to maximize what we are already doing well, focus more crisply and deeply on these demonstrable proficiencies, and determine how to make slight alterations that add value and benefits to existing work, rather than embracing greater risks and redundancy in the hopes of recreating something additional that we are not doing now or not doing well now.

We would be doing something differently than we have done or are doing now. We would be experimenting with new forms and styles, which would mean that success is not guaranteed and risk are embraced in tinkering with proven methodology and firmly rooted institutional ideologies. But, we also would potentially be making our own work more sustainable, deepening our base, creating value to existing work, extending resources and capacity, and more.

So, this small group exercise focusing on privileging our base, asks the small groups to do the following:

Analyze and list core competencies.

Inventory strengths and resources.

Exhibit 22: Small Groups Topic YE/YB 2003

> Inventory strengths and resources.
>
> Identify best practices where they exist throughout operations.
>
> Detail interlocks that are not being sufficiently integrated, and determine why or why not.
>
> Assemble options and alternative practices in methodology that would result from privileging our base.
>
> List areas that need further work and discussion in the future.
>
> The results of all of the small groups will be collected, digested, and assembled to create one report on this work product and its recommendations, which will be posted on conference and distributed to all staff as part of the planning for the coming year and future directions for the organizations and operations.
>
> Thanks!
>
> Wr/12/09/03

Eventually reports changed so that they featured the "big hits" forcing people to read the full written reports for more detail, which people sometimes did in the months after the meeting was over. Once we started binding all the reports that were in early, this also helped. For decades there were tables set out with copies of all of the reports from the newest office to mine, as well as reams of financial materials all laid out so that there was often a scrum at the start of the meeting, even though the reports were required to be put out the night before.

Like I said, traditions were hard to change, and many were important to protect.

Chapter IX:
Care and Maintenance of Leaders

In the simplest definition a leader is someone who has followers. In the technical definition within democratic, mass based organizations, a leader is also politically adept enough to get enough votes to be elected, and sometimes to continue to be elected.

All of this seems very simple and straightforward. Nothing though in my experience in working with leaders in our organizations is in fact simple and   .

This is not a criticism, but an observation from experience. Working with leaders in ACORN and our unions and everywhere else that I have plied this trade has been without doubt the most rewarding part of the job. At the same time working with leaders in some situations can be terribly difficult, and missteps can lead to disaster.

Leaders within the low and moderate income community are very, very special, and though they may fall in certain types and categories, as perhaps we all do, they are often unique, adaptations to hard scrabble conditions and bring the same levels of brilliant contributions and just plain orneriness that is both a thrilling, roller coaster surprise every minute mixed in sometimes equal measure with a combination of stress and mayhem. Finding a perfect leader or the pure balance of all skills and requirements in one person is the unobtainable holy grail of the work.

There are some things we know about leaders though that are worth keeping in mind.

- **To Get Someone to Do Something, We Have to Ask!** This point keeps showing up on all of my lists. People will do amazing things, but they have to be asked. Very few can guess what the organization needs or wants. Many though will try and succeed in some unexpected areas, if they are asked, and when they are allowed, which is a necessity in a membership-based organization.

- **Leaders Want Information** No one wants to be embarrassed in front of big timers or their fellow members. They are used to people disregarding their point of view, turning a deaf ear, or refusing to listen, but they do not want to be subjected to anything like humiliation, *especially* if it could have been avoided. Good staff work is the antidote to this problem, time and time again.

- **Leaders Are Not Normal, They Do Think Differently** It is a mistake to think otherwise. This point deserves special attention.

- **Leaders Want Preparation** Spending the time, both formally and informally, having the conversations about meetings, actions, politics, and other events is rewarded many fold.

- **Written is Good, but Oral May Be Better** Some of our most brilliant leaders are not necessarily most comfortable with written information, so there are no shortcuts brochures, memos, or emails to sitting across the kitchen table and spending countless hours talking it through.

- **Leaders Do Not Expect You to Know All the Answers** Do yourself a favor and do not pretend that in fact you *do* know all the answers. Ask *them* about the question at hand.

- **Leaders Appreciate the Fact that You Are Listening** This is true for everyone all of the time. The sad truth an organizer learns early and often is that no one really cares all that much what you have to say, they care about what **they** have to say, and it makes a difference if you are listening – really listening – and paying attention to what they have to say.

- **Input Has to Mean Power** If you want to build a successful organization, make sure that leadership input is translated into the program, giving the leader's voice real power. This is actually fairly easy to do, because it will make the program better!

- **Oh, Don't be Naïve!** These are just people, not dolls on a pedestal, so they have the same weaknesses that all of us have, just combined with some compelling strengths that make them worth the risk for many others to follow and for us to service. An organizer can never make the mistake of thinking that they are ever anything other than just regular old "pants on one leg at a time" folks or the organizer will not be able to do their job in the organization because of blinders and rose colored glasses getting in the way. Worse the price of naiveté is disappointment and unfulfilled expectations. It is our job as organizers to create expectations, not to believe in them. We feed the beast, so we have to be careful not to worship it!

The amount of anger pent up in many excellent leaders is palpable (once again, remember that this is also true for some of our best organizers, yes, me included!). The anger alone can sometimes make leaders unpredictable and dangerously exciting in many public actions and other settings.

Here are some examples that come quickly to mind:

- **Gloria Wilson** Gloria was one of the first members I ever signed up in Arkansas with ACORN. She was hardly older than I was, and had plenty of spark to her. We finally won negotiations with Governor Winthrop Rockefeller in late 1970. We were demanding a program be established that would grant furniture allowances to welfare families. In the middle of the discussion in his office in the state capitol, Gloria was making a point about how much the program was needed and started talking about the fact that welfare mothers were normal people but the stress of coping with divorce, young children, and then no money was terrible. With a flourish she then pulled the wig off of her head, and said, "Governor, look what all of this has done to me!" She was not bald, but here was an attractive, young woman not yet 24 years old, though I did not realize it at the time, who hardly had any hair – she had just worried it off! The impact was dramatic, sudden and changed the whole tenor of the meeting, and from that minute on, this brave and impulsive action – which no one could have known or suggested – meant in my mind that there was no way we could lose.

- **Mother McKeever** Was a leader of the old Parents for Justice in the Grove Hall area of Roxbury, Massachusetts, which had been a precursor of the Massachusetts Welfare Rights Organization. In the middle of a convention being held at Boston College and during an election of officers for MWRO, she and many of the old warriors realized that their candidate was losing and would not be re-elected, because of what they called, "these new women from Springfield." She was seated in the thick of the audience and she yelled, "Knife!" and kept yelling and headed for the door, because she was trying to clear the room. It took every organizer I could muster to stand in the exits and herd the majority of the people back into the room, but of course, the out state people could not leave, while the Boston people could find their way home somehow, so as brilliant a tactic as "Mother" had, it did not achieve its desired result, though I stand in awe to this day of her insight.

- **Vera Smith and Barbara Rivera** Vera was originally from Tuscaloosa, Alabama and I never knew how she really got to Springfield, Massachusetts. In October of 1969 though she was the elected president of the Hill Area WRO and one of the four or five groups in Springfield WRO that was sitting in the welfare office not far from her own neighborhood demanding that "Boston," as we referred to the state headquarters, relent and provide the funding for winter coats for mothers on welfare. Vera and Barbara Rivera, the president of the North End WRO, were leading the remaining members out of the building believing that they were on their way to police paddy wagons after the negotiations seemed to have broken down and police had begun pulling people out of the old supermarket serving as the welfare office. Barbara was in the lead and while rocks and bottles were flying managed to get all of the 200 women remaining formed into a picket line after they realized that the police had simply tricked them into leaving the building. Vera was at the tail end and looked behind her to see if everybody was out of the building and saw the police manhandling a white woman who was a member from the South End WRO. Vera physically ran through the locked glass door and grabbed the woman and got her out of the welfare office to the amazement of the police who stood there dumbfounded and ducking from the barrage of projectiles flying through the air. What wild and crazy courage is all of that? Simply what you can find in real leaders!

I deliberately picked those examples just from the late 1960's and 1970 to make the point of how fortunate I was to learn some of these great lessons so early in my journey in this work, but there are as many examples I could give both at the front lines and behind the scenes in the closed rooms, and I probably will. The first point I want to make is that leaders are the **real** thing. They are not blow up dolls or puppets on a string that one can bounce from this to that. They are people capable of amazing things, and sometimes the key job we will have as organizers is to **get out of their way and let them lead!**

Gloria Wilson, top row middle, between Wade Rathke and Maxine Nelson, Steve McDonald and Mildred Brown in front, at 20th Anniversary 1990.

We used to have a saying in my early days in this work that, "you need crazy leaders to win, but good leaders to survive." We *all* knew exactly what that meant, too, as contradictory and confusing as it seems to read on paper.

We all understood that in the beginnings of an organization when everything is most fragile and it seems like a gentle wind can blow all of the work away, and as an organizer you know deep down to the hard pit in your stomach that you have to win the first campaigns and establish credibility for the organization, or there may not be second chances and second campaigns. You know you simply **cannot** fail! Because you know that, you are sometimes willing to take all kinds of chances with leaders who can bring just the right level of suspense and surprise to every part of the work, particularly the actions and negotiations, that their pure unpredictability will be an extra intimidation and advantage in dealing with the target, even though you also have to know as deeply that you are playing with fire and may not be able to contain some of these leaders inside that same fragile and embryonic organizational structure later. So, you make a deal with the "organizing devil" and integrate some wild pieces into the puzzle, hoping you can ride the wave all the way into the beach. You also know, as an organizer, that these leaders will not make it long term in the life of the organization as it stabilizes and institutionalizes. You need "good leaders," which is to say more stable, sober, and steady personalities to make it for the long haul to grow and maintain the organization. Sometimes people in fact develop and change, but usually you thank your stars you did not get burned, that you won, and that you grew, so you keep on running.

Inexperienced organizers frequently make the mistake of settling for "angry" people because, and it is a prejudice unfortunately, they believe this represents leadership or charisma, when it may in fact just represent anger. Shouters and screamers are pretty frequently just shouters and screamers, and not leaders at all. When pushed, a green organizer often answers by saying the "leader" had emerged because s/he was not "afraid to speak out" and that people felt that was needed. One needs to "test" this conclusion pretty rigorously, because it also is equally possible that no one could have prevented this individual from speaking out and as likely the group itself had no easy way to control

Chapter IX: Care and Maintenance of Leaders

the person. Sometimes of course it may develop that such people are in fact leaders, but it is very rare (at least in my experience), and in fact more likely that they will push other people *out* of the group, rather than bringing people into the organization. They often shout away any potential membership base they have other than a small group of sycophants in the usual "amen" corner that you will find around such people. To further complicate this leadership type, the anger will eventually be turned against the organization and particularly other leaders and the organizers quickly as well.

Rage is something more normally present, but suppressed at least to a manageable degree in better leaders, and it is certainly common. Organizers have to be able to work with difficult and angry people, if for no other reason that many of our best leadership types have this attribute just beneath the surface. In many ways people ***should*** be angry. They are reacting to discrimination frequently; they are undervalued at work because besides some form of discrimination; their families are in pain and peril; they also did not have the same educational advantages, though they might be whip smart; and, not uncommonly they are the products of life stories that would shock and appall, all of which can, and likely should, produce a devil's brew of roaring rage.

As common as it is for novice organizers to sometimes settle for screamers, especially in organizations where there is a steady diet of direct action and protest, it is also common for them to slip the other way with compliant, accepting, stable, and nice people, who are often the greatest members in the world, but also are just plain not leaders. Novices can confuse the person with plenty of time to sit and visit with them, who is always glad to talk on the phone or stand on the stoop, with someone who others would follow. Sadly, it is not the case. A pleasure cruiser in a safe harbor is different than a warship.

The additional complication also common among talented leaders finds them compensating, feeding, and even fueling their rage at the hand they are playing in the world, sometimes with alcohol or drugs. We have of course never done a survey of our members or queried them about items this personal, but from observation, it feels like a higher percentage of talented leaders are battling demons along these lines than you find in the general membership population. This is a cross borne inordinately in the ranks of the low income and working class, and because leaders are clever they are often more adept at covering these problems than others, so organizers simply need to be savvy and shrewd as well in picking up the signs.

Just as an aside, this is also one of the big reasons that I joined the church ladies in not allowing booze or beer around any ACORN or union meeting. First, why offend anyone for any reason when you are trying to attract everyone for every reason. Secondly, why put pressure on your members and leaders to try to handle something that they cannot handle that is nearly death of them? To me this all seems so obvious, but it may just be experience. Many other organizing cultures, particularly on the labor side, are much less prudish about imbibing than I am, so there are certainly other views, but I come down with a comment in this area that George McGovern made as he prepared for his presidential race, that "those who would be most radical, must appear most conservative." I think that is solid and useful advice!

I hate to make too much of this, but often leaders, real leaders, come into our lives and work in order to find an area where they and their unique contributions can be accepted

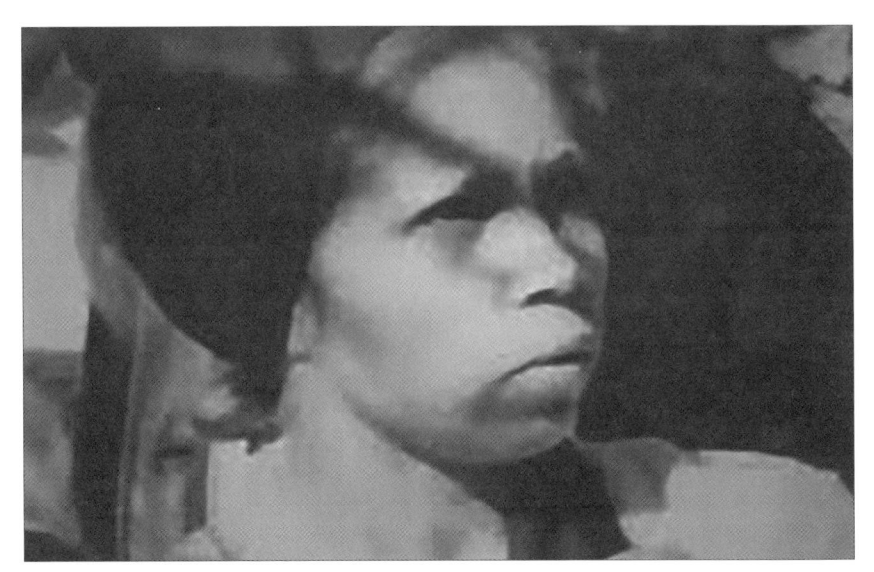

Carmen Rivera, Springfield Welfare Rights leader speaking in 1969.

at face value regardless of the rest of their lives. There are often situations over the years that our organizations provide opportunities to avoid and forget and therefore create an opportunity to move forward with a new slate.

An organizer will often be surprised though, and here are a couple of stories to help keep this in mind:

- Local 100 had an excellent, young African-American leader in Baton Rouge named Larry Roddy who was our Chief Steward in the school district and an officer of the union. It was very important for him to be identified in situations by a title, even if not his. He was loud and vocal in a hail fellow well-met way that is attractive in a labor setting and he was also active in his community. He was a superb off-the-cuff speaker who could jump up in school board meetings and committees with a good feel for the business and the great quote for the media. When prepped by staff, he was often excellent. He also had a propensity for pushing with a little arrogance and would over claim and over promise both attracting and repelling followers. On the union board he would frequently raise issues about money before the meeting, but in the meeting would always stand down once he saw the figures and was with other leaders. It took years for the organizer, who dealt with him every day, to finally say to me on the phone, and, once he had discovered it, it was obvious to me as well, that as clever and effective as the Chief Steward was, he was also completely illiterate. Everything he was able to achieve was based on an excellent "ear" and "memory," which would allow him to literally look at the pages and mask the fact that he could read none of it!

Local 100 officers at Lake Charles Retreat
Rebecca Hart, Vickie Cisneros, Larry Roddy, Linda Lathers.

- Charlie Anderson, my auto mechanic for many years had been the rock on an organizing drive at a car dealership in New Orleans East that we had narrowly lost. I knew him well. We did literally scores of house visits together. He ran a "favor" bank among many of the other workers because of his seniority and his willingness to help out his co-workers either on the job or at his garage at home when they had something else they were trying to piece together. He was older and knew the ropes, but he also was simply one of the most straightforward guys you could imagine. Unusual to me, when he was pulled into a management run "one on one" at a shop floor dinner being held to fight the union a couple of days before the election, he, unlike so many others, told me all about it, almost immediately. When they told him he was going to lose, he told them, he knew that, but that he had been there the whole way and was going to stick it out, and he said they understood. We did lose the vote. Not among the mechanics that Charlie led, but because of the expansion of the unit by the company that was designed to overcome the number of workers who would vote for the union. I was still surprised to read a couple of months later that Charlie was thrown off a jury in Jefferson Parish when the opposing counsel moved that he be disqualified because he was a felon and barred by Louisiana law from jury service. I did not know that though I knew him well. I asked him about it, and he said, as honestly as always, that he thought he could get away with it. Clearly, during the election, the boss had known this fact, and I had not. It might have mattered.

- One of the ACORN state operations elected a treasurer for the board. The leader had been outstanding at the local group, campaign, and state board level and was an inspiration for others because of his sound judgment and hard work. He reached out for me though with a question since we had met at several meetings and visited in the past. He was unclear if he should accept the position as treasurer of his state board because he had had to resign a position in his union decades earlier because money came up missing on his watch and in his pocket. I assured him that there was no problem since he would not have signing authority on any checking account. As long as there was full disclosure, why shouldn't there be forgiveness for a good leader?

So, even good leaders can have imperfections that can be used against the organization, but it is not necessarily a given that their history may be weaponized. Our society is hard on our people. Success is defined in such stark economic terms, and this trend has been accelerating as we all recognize, so that virtually by definition these days, our members and leaders are losers. They do not wear the mantle easily or necessarily with a smile, but society's judgment is harsh and hard to shake. The "good" leaders are often people who for one reason or another have simply come to find a peace with their situation and their lives. Here are some examples:

- Steve McDonald was the first national president of ACORN and his contribution is inestimable, but he was also a man of depth and contradictions. He was African-American, but also went to a mainline Episcopal Church in Little Rock where he was one of the few non-whites. He had been a career military man until he was diagnosed with multiple sclerosis and essentially came home to die after a long absence. He deteriorated steadily during our time together. He first walked into the organization as a member of ACORN's Vietnam Veterans Organizing Committee (VVOC) and left ACORN in a wheel chair. He believed that ACORN was his opportunity to participate actively since he felt he was not able to carry his share of the load during the civil rights struggle, because he had been overseas. He brought calm and courage to the business and a sense of gravitas that a 20's year old kid like me could not have mustered. He was unflappable but also had a temper and an anger at the world and fate that had put him in the situation he was in now. His clearest accomplishment was convincing the leaders from Arkansas to not dominate the national organization as it was building and forcing acceptance of the one state / two delegates system, rather than weighting the delegates by membership which would have stunted, if not stopped, the ability to build a national organization by rendering everyone outside of Arkansas second-class. His unique sense of fairness and his even handedness made his position unassailable and gave us all the opportunity to grow thanks to that contribution.

- Bill Whipple was a character. He was from Nebraska, and though he told me the story a million times, I was never really clear how he ended up in Arkansas, but one got the feeling he was chased. He was a carpet cleaner. Drove a panel truck that touted the steam cleaning process. I had George Wiley meet him in 1973, and George, a PhD chemist and former professor from the University of Syracuse before heading NWRO, immensely enjoyed talking to him about the chemicals and the cleaning process. He would work many nights, and still be

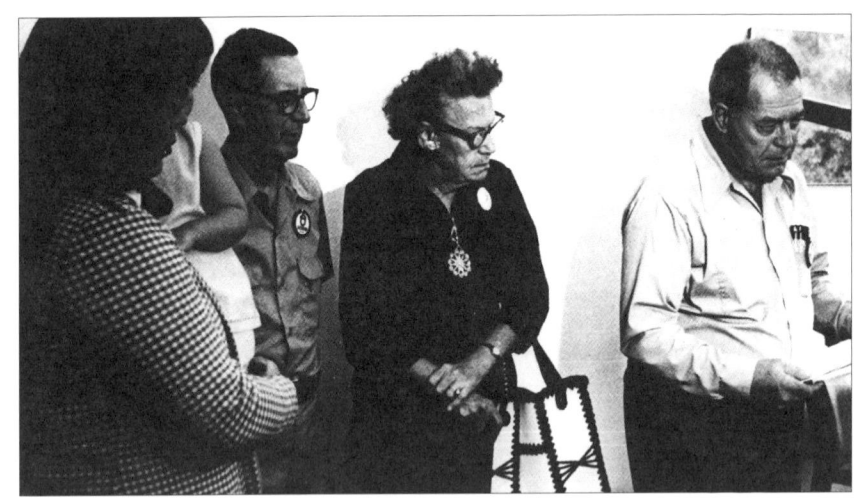

Elena Hanggi, Bill and Mrs. Whipple, and Willard Johnson.

ready and able to show up at neighborhood meetings or actions. He fancied himself a homespun philosopher. Two of my favorites Whipple-isms, which I have often repeated, were his definitions for the words "expert" and "rationale." An expert in Bill's words is nothing but a "pressurized drip." A rationale on the other hand is a "lie in the skin of a reason." Bill was also white, which helped sustain the multi-racial cast of the organization which was essential in building a majority and building power. When some of the other white leaders reared back in huge conflict around the expansion of the organization, Bill's respect for his fellow leaders, like McDonald, Larry Rogers, and others, helped stay the course. Importantly, Bill also had enough ego and drive to run for the Pulaski County Quorum Court when it shrank to single districts and was elected from his large, mixed area. His value to building the organization was reflected in naming a leadership development internship the Whipple-Bell Leadership Award.[86]

- Maude Hurd is tougher than anyone ever wants to believe. She was the national president of ACORN for more than a dozen years. She was from a small, rural community in Georgia and with nothing more than pure pluck and less than $100 in her pocketbook, left at 18 having decided for reasons hard to describe that she was going to the big city and that the city was going to be Boston, which she had never visited before. She showed up on a bus, and got a job quickly, and somehow made it with sheer grit and determination. She married there and had children, eventually buying a house in Dorchester. Maude is normally more quiet, than loud. A charming individual and powerful listener,

---

[86] Geraldine Bell of New Orleans was another one of the great early leaders and a mainstay of the powerful New Orleans organization and a member of the national board for years in the 70's and 80's until her untimely death.

she holds respect by her constancy, rather than a dramatic speech. She is steady and solid. She takes a week of her vacation every year to run the ACORN Leadership School and forges deep bonds with upcoming leaders which let her lead by example. But, importantly, no matter how often other up and coming leaders underestimate her, she is deceptively ambitious and holds on to her responsibilities with a firm hand and constant patience. She knows who to trust and then trusts completely within normal limits. Where she doesn't trust, she is open, but watchful. Winning power is something, but holding on is a lesson in shrewdness, and Maude provided that lesson regularly.

The point is that even good leaders, just like good organizers, have individual strengths and specific weaknesses. To serve them well, requires a clear analysis of both sides of this ledger. To see their role in the organization in the most constructive terms requires open and frank assessments with dialogue that forges the range as well as the limits.

Before looking at some of these issues, let me address the question of term limits, since as we discussed Maude Hurd's contribution, clearly she was at the top of the ACORN leadership structure for quite some time. We do not believe in term limits, because we believe in elections and democracy. It is the duty of the incumbent to protect a base and of the challenger to build a base. These are not campaigns that involve expenditures of funds so financially it is a level playing field. The organization grows increasingly larger and more complex, so has no institutional interest in frequent leadership turnover for its own sake, especially since that would only empower the staff even more deeply, since their jobs would be protected while leadership's would be constantly under challenge. The National Education Association (NEA) in the United States is a good example of what happens in these situations. The executive director at the national and state level essentially controls the organization by controlling the bureaucracy and budget, while the leadership constantly turns over every several years with a maximum of two terms served. At the national level the terms in ACORN are only for two years which forces

Maude Hurd with Judy Duncan and Wade Rathke Boston 2012.

Chapter IX: Care and Maintenance of Leaders

regular elections. There were many years when Maude had only token or no opposition. In the later years there was a leadership division around policy and somewhat around personality which more acutely challenged national officers, including Maude, to engage in robust campaigns. This was all healthy and forces internal debate in a way that a mechanical switch of officers would not. We believe in democracy both inside and outside of the organization.

Part of the care and feeding of leaders involves remembering that they are not organizational fixtures but real people made of a hank of hair, a piece of bone, and a little honeycomb. This seems painfully obvious of course, but in public and political life, there is always a knee jerk temptation to dehumanize the individual and transform them into simply a position. A sophisticated leader over years, like a Maude Hurd, will eventually, in order to survive, learn how to depersonalize herself and the position, but this is a challenge for people unaccustomed to public life in both the leadership and the staff. In one of the early ACORN Leadership Schools we added a section (which became a permanent and popular part of the program) which allowed people to talk about how to balance their personal life with their leadership responsibilities. Leaders jumped on this topic like dogs on a bone! They were desperate to be able to share the problems that they could not easily discuss at home: why their boyfriends or wives were jealous of the other members or the staff; why they felt guilty being away from home at meetings and actions; why they felt inadequate to the jobs they were elected to hold because of their education or grammar or whatever; how to handle suddenly being recognized by strangers when they were on television and used to their own anonymity; and a score of other issues. They also had to have a forum to talk about how to handle simply "standing out" and being controversial, which is not normal at least for the normal among us, and not just being on the outside, but being scorned because they were in the opposition. Some of these challenges for leaders are different for women than for men, but all of them are challenges that cannot be ignored, so people like letting down the guard and talking seriously about strategies for personal survival, so it is important for the organization to make space for this.

Importantly, this is also why it is essential to make a space for leaders to interact with each other on a personal level. Such experience builds bonds that protect people and under gird the subculture of the organization and its own set of mores and principles. At trainings, meetings, conventions, workshops, public actions, and planning meetings, leaders and members find the space regardless, so good organizers learn quickly that what cannot be controlled, should be managed appropriately and constructively, especially since it is going to happen anyway. Church based organizations do this under the cover of religion and prayer that automatically connects to a tradition which is constructive and protective. More political and oppositional organizations like ACORN and unions need to realize that people are searching for social networks through their activity in the organization, so should assist in supporting one that works for the individual as well as the organization.

Nonetheless, the organizer should never be confused or naïve in thinking that all of this is about pursuit of lofty goals and Utopian visions. People, even potential leaders, join the organization for scores of reasons. It is probably as common that they joined out of boredom, an excuse to get out of the house and leave the kids with someone (anyone!) else, hoping for a job, and god knows what else might have come to mind more frequently than the notion that they were joining in the fight for social justice. Members talk about why they joined and like working with a group to feel empowered and get something done, but frequently, it was nothing more than curiosity and a promise made to someone who showed up from ACORN at their doorstep. We should never be confused that this is a spontaneous, mass movement for social change, when it is as likely something much more prosaic that brings people in the organization's door and makes it even more our job to lock the door behindthem and keep them active and involved.

Information and Input

I've said this before, and I'll say it again. The simplest advice that I have always given in training organizers to work with leaders and members is to think back to any experience they ever had as a member of an organization or even officer of something, whether in school, scouts, social, political, or whatever. I ask them to first look at their own experience and whether it was good or bad. I ask them to look at why they joined and then to examine why they quit, if indeed they left or dropped out of the situation. Then I ask them whether or not they felt they were on the "inside" of the organization? Did they feel they were part of the inner circle or simply a member on the fringe or one of the soldiers making up the troops along the march? Did having baseline information about what was happening and what was going to happen matter to them as a member or leader of this group make a difference? Did they feel they had any input on the decisions and directions of the group? How did they rate the care in which they were managed? Was the situation chaotic and disorganized or efficient and responsive? You get the message: I ask organizers to dig deep in their own experience and then empathize with the feeling of a leader or member to more clearly evaluate the potential factors giving rise to real inclusion and investment in ACORN versus alienation, detachment, and dropping out as a member or leader. The trick of successfully working with leaders (and members!) is to make sure that you create a systemic experience for them that would have been sufficient to maintain your own membership (and leadership!) in the organization as well. This operates as a sort of "do unto others, as you would have them do unto you" rule, and. when kept in mind, it works.

The problem of retention and activism of leaders and members is complicated by two things in organizing: systems and scale. Organizations need a very good system of constant information and contact in order to maintain information needs required by members as the *a priori* to their full involvement and participation. Over reliance on events, like monthly meetings, is a common error because attendance is never going to be greater than a percentage of the total membership, and unless the organizer has a more comprehensive plan, the meeting experience is still largely passive for most members and active primarily for the leaders. Even a highly engaging meeting and agenda will still leave many members with question marks that need to be answered, which once again leads to the question of systems. Scale also comes to play as the size of the organization and its project increases, along with hopefully the size of its membership. There are going to be mounting demands placed on the communication and activation systems to maintain increasing participation and constantly combat drop-off and disaffection.

Some passive systems, performing admirably and at low-cost efficiency, certainly include email bulletins, website notices, and autodial telephone messages. The expense of mail and the innumerable surveys that indicate that newsletters are simply not read (and therefore not worth the money) have made these instruments more sporadic and somewhat traditional and sentimental communications choices, rather than effective in laying the necessary information base for serious participation. All of this helps, but there is still no substitute, particularly for leaders, for personal contact. ACORN schedules its organizers for hours of phone calls on a daily basis to the general membership call list and on a regular basis to leaders even more frequently on a set pattern of subjects and needs. Additionally, we schedule organizers for 2nd visits and leadership visits before and after regular periods in the field. Regular planning committee meetings and events that integrate the agenda with staff support and build bridges to the rest of the members, and most importantly create a critical role for leaders in actually doing the communicating, informing, and, actually leading, is the critical final ingredient in making it all come together well. There are always good ideas, so the job is making them *pro forma* and part of the regular daily and weekly work plan for the staff and expectation for any elected leader.

Internal Conflict

Understand this, if you understand nothing about organizers: they love the members and worship the leaders! This is something that outsiders can't comprehend, but it is at the bedrock of all organizing. None of this is to say there aren't top-of-the-lungs arguments and disagreements, but these are squabbles in a very close, tight knit family.

If there is anything that destabilizes newer organizers though, it's internal conflict between staff and leadership. We can all talk about how conflict and its eventual resolution can deepen bonds, but first you have to live through it, and it's a challenge when the leaders you serve, find fault despite best intentions of well-meaning organizers. Telling organizers that it's natural or having them intellectually understand the chasms that exist between race, class, gender, and any number of other misunderstandings, may find them nodding in agreement but don't necessarily convince them that this is something they should embrace as a regular part of their future. Conflict is inevitable, but resolution is critical, if everyone is going to survive.

No one likes conflict. Internal discipline and accountability within an organization's leadership corps is hard on everyone. When leaders have to hold each other's feet to the fire, they are uncomfortable doing so, they drag their feet, they make excuses, rationalize bad behavior, and organizers too often are caught having to push for action, risking being caught in the middle themselves or going through the same process of denial the leaders are struggling through. Most often the difference is that the organizers' know there is trouble coming, and their job is to head it off – to organize against conflict – while for the leaders hope springs eternal, and with luck the members hardly notice a ripple on the waters.

When leaders are in conflict with other leaders there is no safe haven. If there was one story I told more than any other in my years with ACORN, it was one from my early months as head organizer of Massachusetts Welfare Rights Organization in 1970. There had been a convention and an election of officers. It had been a donnybrook, and it ended when a slate of new leaders was elected after many had cleared the hall in Boston College where we were meeting. The new president was a solid, though uncharismatic, woman from Grove Hall in Roxbury named Mamie Wilson along with a slate of others from Springfield and around the state replacing the old leaders who dated themselves from the early, brutal fights with the welfare department in Boston. The old leaders did not want to leave their positions and saw the elections as illegitimate. The staff was caught in the middle. I was twenty-one, young, green, and by-the-book Manichean. This was the members' organization. The staff had to be neutral and stay out of it. In a late night meeting of the senior staff at my apartment on Rutland Square in the South End we went back and forth. At one point it seemed clear, and Bill Pastreich, who had come over by then, also seemed to conclude along with most others that the situation was hopeless, the organization was too divided to survive, and there was nothing that could be done to save it. Somehow we came back from that precipice, but the plan I developed was to simply close the office at 17 Brookline Street in Cambridge until the conflict settled down, and there was a way forward. And, that's what we did.

An image I will take to my grave was standing at my bay windows overlooking the street and the green space in the middle of the square, or what we call a "neutral ground" in New Orleans, and seeing the former treasurer, the famous, tough but erratic, Ruth Barkley, walking up and down both sides of the street, waving her gun, and, yelling, "Rackley, Rackley, I'm looking for you, Rackley," until she became bored and left for home in the Cathedral projects that were also in the South End. Later I found that one of the volunteers and a sometime organizer had stumbled into the whole former leadership team when they tromped into Anna's Brookline Lunch, just a few doors up the street from our office, where he happened to be at the time. They seized him and let loose all of their anger about the situation, until satiated, and then moved on.

I got it then and understood a lesson I would never forget about leadership conflict: face it and take it. I could have locked the door, but I should have set up a folding chair and sat out front on Brookline Street until the old leaders came around. I should have taken the charge, let them have their pound of flesh, and quietly explained what I was doing and why. They would have respected that, but having taken my path out of the way, I had just driven them to a frustrating boiling point.

I didn't necessarily learn to be calm and cool in all situations, because I could be quick, loud, and curt from time to time, but I learned to weather the storm, hang in there, and make sure we all came to a quiet harbor sooner or later, so the organization could move forward. When leaders had to work it out with other leaders, I learned to pave the way, rather than to claim a pure path and try to get out of the way.

There may be other and better strategies, but cutting and running is never one, so I am a firm believer in taking the hit and then quickly returning to my work.

Regardless, It's Never About You

Whether community organizations or unions, John Lewis or Saul Alinsky, the most important thing to always remember no matter what anyone whispers in your ear or how you daydream or suffer or scheme, membership organizations are always about the membership. The organizations endure if the members stay, no matter how many leaders come and go. No matter how autocratic or democratic or somewhere in between, if the organization serves the membership, it survives any and all of us as we pass through.

 I learned at twenty-one that I had no right to decide to kill an organization, no matter the problem or challenging the circumstances. I could hurt an organization with a false step or a wrong move, as I did then, but organizations with purpose and value are resilient. They endure and persist as vital institutions no matter how ill-served, if they have worth to their members, as long as they keep working and keep serving that membership.

 Organizers are easily confused and sometimes lose perspective in the swirl of events and tasks of the day. Organizations for low and moderate income families where they live and work are rare. We may believe in revolution, power, and justice. Our members are more often willing to settle for relief, change, and a chance. We might not think that's enough, but it's something, and it's more. It's our job to push and pull, but we should never be confused that a membership-based organization is anything other than all about the members. It's never about us.

 Leaders often get this message more clearly than organizers, which is why we work for them, not the other way around, and why the best of them are invaluable, and why we are always replaceable. Lots of books are written about leaders and a few are written by organizers. There are a host of reasons why it's not the other way around.

Chapter X: **Governance, Leadership Development, and Structure**

Leading and governing are two very different things. One can bring you over the barricades and crash through the door. The other makes sure the barricades are actually built and that the door is actually there. Vital to the entire infrastructure of ACORN from the beginning organizing drive to the highest level of board governance through the ACORN Executive Committee and the Association Board, leadership development was intrinsic to the preparation and culture of membership governance.

Organizing Drive

If the heart blood of an ACORN organizing drive is the process of hitting the doors and putting flesh to the wood to contact everyone possible in the community, the head of the drive is the organizing committee meetings where leadership is developed, nurtured, and manifested through the sweat equity of the work and decisions directing the drive. In our classic model, these four organizing committee meetings much of what shapes the values of ACORN leadership governance are established.

From the first organizing committee meeting people have to take initiative and make decisions. Someone who has never invited strangers into their home has to be willing to put aside fears of burglary and the unknown, and, trustingly, welcome neighbors into the living room or kitchen by taking the lead. People who frequently have never met each other before, who were deliberately recruited from all corners and segments of the community, have to first discover that they have common cause in the issues that they identify as important in their community, sufficiently to agree to vote formally to take the steps among themselves, five, ten, or twenty in a community of thousands of households, to actually form an organization. They also have to commit to the process of the drive, from filling their name in on the calendar when they are willing to hit the doors with the organizer or in teams with other members of the committee, to their participation in the full process of the drive from the coming organizing committees every other week or so, to the big meeting. The organizing committee process joins these new community activists to each other in a collective decision making and governance process for the organization until there are formally elected officers at the first large meeting. And, of course they also have to lead by formally joining the organization as dues paying members.

From these first organizing committee meetings shaping all ACORN leadership there are deep values transmitted that are constantly reinforced throughout the organizing and leadership development process. The values include the following:

- The ACORN leadership process is collective, not individual.

- Consensus comes first, and votes formalize the consensus already developed.

Exhibit 23: Agenda for First Organizing Committee Meeting – ACORN Los Angeles

ACORN

Sample Agenda / *Agenda Borrador*
Organizing Committee Meeting #1 / *Comite Organizativo Reunion #1*

Facilitator/Facilitador: Translator/Traductor:

1. Welcome & Introductions / Bienvenida & Introducciones   (5 min.)
2. What is ACORN? / Que es ACORN?   (5 min.
3. Discussion of Community Concerns   (15 min.
   Discusion de las Preocupaciones de la Comunidad
4. Vote to Organize / Voto para Organizar   (5 min.)
5. Building Our Numbers / Aumentando Nuestros Numeros   (15 min.)
   a. POWER IN NUMBERS / LA UNION HACE LA FUERZA
   b. planning meetings, big meeting, action
      reuniones de planeacion, reunion grande, accion
   c. doorknocking / ir a tocar puertas
   d. house meetings / reuniones de casa
   e. commitments / compromisos
6. ACORN Membership / Membresía de ACORN   (5 min.)
7. Next Planning Meeting / Proxima Reunion de Planeacion   (5 min.)

Who will offer their house for the next meeting?
Quien ofrece su casa para la siguiente reunion?

- ACORN leaders make decisions but these decisions are premised on taking action and making commitments, whether to join, door knock, or come to meetings.

- ACORN leaders accept responsibility for their collective process. The issues found to have consensus in the discussion at the first organizing committee meeting will be in the letter to everyone in the community giving people the reasons that the organization is being built, and all members of the organizing committee will sign that letter.

- The community members will provide the leadership and be the face and voice of the organization. The organizer may have helped find the early members but her signature will not be on the committee's letter and her role will have been defined from the first OC meeting as transitional, helping the committee in the organizing process until the group is established.

- The process continues in the other three main organizing committee meetings directing the drive.

Exhibit 24: Organizing Committee Agenda #2 – ACORN Los Angeles

ACORN

Twenty Eighth Street Chapter
Organizing Committee Meeting #2 / Comite Organizativo Reunion #2
Thursday, January 29, 2004/ jueves, 29 de enero, 2004

1. **Welcome & Introductions** / Bienvenida & Introducciones
   Clementina Caro (5 min.)
2. **What is ACORN?** / Que es ACORN?
   Julia Botello (5 min.)
3. **Discussion of Community Concerns**
   / Discusion de las Preocupaciones de la Comunidad
   Cruz Quevedo (15 min.)
   • long-term vs. short-term issues
   / separando los temas mas grandes de los mas inmediatas
4. **Building Our Group** / Construyendo Nuestro Grupo
   a. review of the process / repaso del proceso
   b. first big meeting: where and when?
   / primera reunion grande: donde y cuando?
   c. what is our goal for attendance? / cual es nuestra meta para asistencia?
5. **Building Our Numbers** / Aumentando Nuestros Numeros
   Marta Perez (15 min.)
   a. doorknocking / ir a tocar puertas
   b. house meetings / reuniones de casa
   c. phone lists / listas de telefono
   d. petitioning at school / consiguiendo firmas en la escuela
   e. Who will be a Block Captain? / Quien sera Capitan de Cuadra?
   f. other commitments / otros compromisos
6. **ACORN Membership** / Membresía de ACORN   Marta Perez (5 min.)
7. **Next Planning Meeting** / Proxima Reunion de Planeacion   (5 min.)
   Who will offer their house for the next meeting?
   / Quien ofrece su casa para la siguiente reunion?

There are no delays in the process as you can see from the action OC agenda from 28th Street in Los Angeles, as opposed to the template. By the second organizing committee meeting there are local leaders taking parts of the agenda for the meeting, so that they can become comfortable running meetings and demonstrate ownership of the of the organizing process, already transferring the authority for the drive from the organizer to the committee.

Chapter X: Governance, Leadership Development, and Structure

ACORN Scotland organizing committee working a street stall.

By the third organizing committee meeting the process introduces the concept and practice of representation for the emerging leadership. In Exhibit 24 from the Organizing Committee # 3 for Los Angeles ACORN, block captains are being recruited as the process is deepening in investigation and planning around the research for the first issue and broadening the outreach to other institutions and gatekeepers including schools and churches now that the organizing committee members have logged hundreds of doors and tens of hours hitting them so that they have built the experiential confidence to engage confidently with long established institutional and community leaders, who may or may not have a base, but are important to neutralize or support the emerging organization.

There are no delays in the process as you can see from the action OC agenda from 28th Street in Los Angeles, as opposed to the template. By the second organizing committee meeting there are local leaders taking parts of the agenda for the meeting, so that they can become comfortable running meetings and demonstrate ownership of the of the organizing process, already transferring the authority for the drive from the organizer to the committee.

By the third organizing committee meeting the process introduces the concept and practice of representation for the emerging leadership. In Exhibit 25 from the Organizing Committee # 3 for Los Angeles ACORN, block captains are being recruited as the process is deepening in investigation and planning around the research for the first issue and broadening the outreach to other institutions and gatekeepers including schools and churches now that the organizing committee members have logged hundreds of doors and tens of hours hitting them so that they have built the experiential confidence to engage confidently with long established institutional and community leaders, who may or may not have a base, but are important to neutralize or support the emerging organization.

Exhibit 25: Agenda for Organizing Committee #3 – ACORN Los Angeles

ACORN
Sample Agenda / *Agenda Borrador*
Organizing Committee Meeting #3 / *Comite Organizativo Reunion #3*

Facilitator/Facilitador:　　　　　Translator/Traductor:

1. **Welcome & Introductions /** *Bienvenida & Introducciones*　　(5 min.)
2. **What is ACORN? /** *Que es ACORN?*　　(5 min.)
3. **Discussion of Community Concerns**
    / *Discusion de las Preocupaciones de la Comunidad*　　(15 min.)
    a. review of last week's list / repaso de la lista de la semana pasada
    b. report – what else do we know about each issue?
    reporte – que mas sabemos de cada tema?
4. <u>**Big Meeting /** *Reunion Grande*</u>
    a. finalize - where and when? / finalizar: donde y cuando?
    b. review of our goal for attendance / repaso de nuestra meta para asistencia
5. <u>**Reaching Our Attendance Goal /** *Logrando Nuestra Meta*</u>　　(15 min.)
    a. Who will be a Block Captain? / Quien sera Capitan de Cuadra?
    phone lists / listas de telefono
    c. flyers / volantes
    d. Where else can we get the word out?
    / En que otro lado podemos publicar el evento?
    schools / escuelas - Who can take a petition & flyers?
    churches / iglesias Quien puede llevar una petición y volantes?
6. **ACORN Membership /** *Membresía de ACORN*　　(5 min.)
7. **Next Planning Meeting /** *Proxima Reunion de Planeacion*　　(5 min.)

Who will offer their house for the next meeting?

Quien ofrece su casa para la siguiente reunion?

Chapter X: Governance, Leadership Development, and Structure

Usually in the 3rd meeting the financial reality of the organization also becomes crystal clear with a discussion of the budget for the local organizing drive. The budget breaks down the expenses in terms of shares of the cost of the organizer, the office, the support in phones, supplies, mileage, and other items from pens to posters that have fueled the organizing drive all compared to the income represented by the number of members recruited to that point in the organizing drive and the amount of dues gained in that manner as well as any other local group fundraisers discussed for the future. Invariably, the cost of the drive, even with relatively low paid staff, is higher than the income produced or even projected by the time of the first big meeting.

The results of this first fundamental financial discussion are foundational principles for ACORN producing almost invariably the following conclusions and consensus:

- We run our own community organization but we cannot survive without working in cooperation with the other community organizations in ACORN to share costs which we alone could not sustain.

- All resources available have to be dedicated to self-sufficiency of the organization and our ability to increase our capacity.

- There are no surplus revenues for local bank accounts, sick funds, donations to local churches, festivals, or politicians.

- The numbers are not huge, but neither are they trivial. It is possible to plan for enough members and events to be self-sustaining between dues and local fundraisers, but only as part of a larger, collective enterprise.

- We cannot afford to have a local organizer spend 100% of their time with our local organization, so we have to be able to step up to the responsibilities of directing and maintaining our own local organization.

From this third OC meeting, these conclusions are fundamental to the understanding of the entire ACORN organizing and leadership culture. Millions of dollars are just a jumble of numbers, but the tens, hundreds, and thousands that made up the cost of an organizing drive are as standard as the money under the mattress or the numbers scribbled along the side of a checkbook balance.

Exhibit 26: Agenda for OC #4: ACORN Los Angeles

ACORN

Comite Organizativo Reunion #4/ *Organizing Committee Meeting #4*
Facilitadora/*Facilitator:*

1. Bienvenidos e introducciones / Welcome and Introductions (5 min)

2. Por que organizarse? Que es ACORN? / Why organize? What is ACORN?
   (5 min)

3. Reunion Grande / Big Meeting (20 min)
   a. finalize place & time / finalizar lugar & hora
   b. asistencia – Cual es nuestra meta final?
      turnout – What is our final goal?
   c. asistencia – Cuales son nuestras metas individuales?
      turnout – What are our individual goals?
      (contact forms) (formas de contacto)

   d. reporte – Quien ha hablado con iglesias, escuelas? Proximos pasos
      report – Who has spoken with churches, schools? Next steps
   e. banco telefonico – Que dia podemos hacerlo?
      phone banking – Which day can we do it?
   f. volantes & peticiones / flyers & petitions

4. Accion / Action (10 min.)
   a. finalizar tema / finalize theme
   b. finalizar lugar & hora / finalize place & time
   c. finalizar lista de invitados / finalize who we want to invite

5. <u>Nominaciones / Nominations</u> (15 min.)
   a. How leadership works in ACORN / Como funciona el liderazgo en ACORN
   b. Nominaciones / Nominations

6. Membresía / Membership
   (5 min.)

7. Otros Anuncios / Other Announcements
   (5 min.)

Chapter X: Governance, Leadership Development, and Structure

In the 4th meeting the rubber hits the road for the emerging leadership with the discussion of taking roles in running the large meeting, and as importantly, starting to figure out the "who" and "how" of nominations for the temporary leadership that will take the organization to the next step.

The actual first meeting agenda features the organizing committee members in prominent places throughout the agenda, because they are now "at the front table," so to speak, and running the meeting. They will also be at the back table handing out the agendas, getting everyone to fill out the attendance list fully, and, importantly, encouraging people to enroll as members. They will also be "working the room" and welcoming people as they enter the meeting and making sure "who is in the room," whether they were house visited, who and how they were recruited to attend, and whether or not there are other agendas that the rest of the committee and the organizers need to know.

For example in the first meeting in East Brixton, London for the first new ACORN local group in London, a fellow came in late, never took off his jacket or sat down for the 45 minutes he was in attendance, and after making some scattered, curious comments questioning the right of people to organize the group, which the members turned back quickly, tried to get the agenda reordered so that he could leave early, and, finally, revealed his real agenda when he passed out leaflets for a citywide housing action as a member of something called the local Radical Housing Network. A tree that fell in the forest that no one heard, but in the debriefing after the meeting, he was a random player that could have been picked up at the gate before the meeting and neutralized or escorted out then. A minor event certainly, but a critical part of both leadership and organizer development that emphasizes in the heart of the organizing methodological practice why success for leaders in running meetings may be in the smallest details and in preventing conflict before it is allowed to develop by rooting it out and confronting it early.

Not surprisingly, when elections of the temporary officers occur the visibility of the organizing committee members, both at the first big meeting and throughout the organizing drive will invariably mean that a high percentage of the first crew of officers will be those that have won their positions not through some special charisma or outburst of anger or speechifying, but through a form of "sweat equity" in driving the organization of the group through their own work and visibility. This kind of "sweat equity" leadership has always been a hallmark of ACORN.

The organizing committee meetings during the drive evolve into planning meetings prior to regular meetings and actions that involve not only the newly elected leaders but also the key members that might have most keenly advocated for a particular action or tactic or are most impacted by the issue or the topics or guests at the meeting. Preparation more than any innate skill or talent is often the defining character of ACORN community leaders, especially as they make the transition from silence having been either never in the room or at the back of the room to leaders responsible for the success and growth of the organization.

Other leadership and structural levels of governance within the organization usually followed along these same lines. Citywide boards within ACORN in the United States were composed of one representative from each affiliated local group, usually the elected chair though sometimes local groups elected a special representative to attend and report back. In Canada, France, and the United Kingdom the citywide structures usually have two representatives for each local group, the chair and one other officer or members. The point being that every local group is represented equally, regardless of size of its membership in the equanimity of the decisions. The same thing is true at the state or provincial level where each citywide formation has several seats at the next level of body and then at the highest level nationally, two seats as well. Officers at the city and state/provincial level are all presiding officers elected by the other board members as officers of the board. Nationally, the overall chair or president of the national ACORN organization usually comes from the general membership, though often they are currently board officers and local group chairs. Other than that election, to move forward at each step requires an elected base at the local level, continuing to privilege accountability and experience within the grassroots ACORN membership. The bylaws of ACORN organizations invariably required that such a level of accountability existed, and when leaders failed to be re-elected or resigned their positions at the local group level, they also forfeited any position at the higher levels, city, state, national, or international as well. Being true to the membership base was an ideological foundation at the nuts and bolts of all ACORN formations.

Similarly, there was a fixed rule that leadership was an unpaid position, and any leader joining the staff was required to automatically resign from their leadership position in the organization at every level. When asked by outsiders if we regularly hired and trained leaders as organizers, we always answered in the affirmative, but answered as quickly that good leaders were rarer than good organizers, so that we were very careful in doing so. And, the training process to produce and develop good leaders was as arduous, and perhaps more so, than what was required to develop good organizers. ACORN was always clear about the priorities within our inner hierarchy.

First meeting of ACORN Scotland neighborhood chapter.

Chapter X: Governance, Leadership Development, and Structure

Exhibit 27: Agenda for a Citywide Board Meeting

Ottawa ACORN Board Meeting
Saturday, June 11, 2016
1230pm-2pm, 404 McArthur Ave

1. Agenda for Change- 2 Year Power Plan- Leading to Municipal Election
2. Funding
   a. Fundraising Needed, Grants Delayed, Increased Staffing
   b. Fundraiser- Art in the Park- 11am-3pm- Minto Park, Saturday July 9
3. Staffing Document
4. Elected Leaders Document- Chapter Meetings in Vanier (290 Dupuis July 13 6pm), Mechanicsville (booking now), more chapter meetings post forum
5. Campaigns
   a) Ottawa Healthy Homes Platform
      i) Report from Councillor's meetings and allies
      ii) Focus on landlord licensing
      iii) Tenant Summit- Saturday July 16 12pm-4pm, city hall (Champlain Room), where to do action?
      iv) Herongate AGI- 5% July 15 Hearing- action to throw it out
   b) Predatory Lending
      i) Municipal -licensing
      ii) Federal - postal banking submission June 30- national office
   c) ODSP/OW
      i) Demands from leadership June 10- to be approved
      ii) Actions last Friday of each month 12pm June 24, July 29, Aug 26- addresses
      iii) Focus of the petition
   d) Make it Fair - OFL - Forum June 14, Tuesday at 630pm at 120 MetCalfe- Ontario labour code review
   e) Healthy Transit
      i) Low income transit pass vote- June 15, city hall 930am
      ii) Audit in Vanier- Saturday, July 9 10am-3pm- 290 Dupuis St
6. Campaigns Gatineau
   a) Forum June 14 at 120 rue Charlevoix -Safety, nature of police interventions
   b) New drive in Hull Right
7. Ontario ACORN Board Meeting June 24-25 – Reps Gisele Bouvier, Ria Rinne, Amber Slegtenhorst
   a) Fundraising needed
8. Tax site- 3 days in June, 2 days in July/August, Wed-Thurs OESP registrations
9. Conflict of Interest Statement- Review

In the early years of ACORN in Arkansas I experimented with rotating chairs, going from one local group chair to another on each successive meeting to run and direct the meeting. The leadership within the first year concluded that this level of equitable participation was interesting and it was not that it could not work, but it did not work as well as having someone elected to chair each meeting and take responsibility for working out the agenda with me as the chief organizer. It was also felt that it tended to more clearly differentiate the roles of the leaders and make the different roles between the leadership and staff clearer and routinized within the organizational culture. Very quickly it evolved that annually the boards would elect officers to run their agendas, and that became the policy in 1978 when the bylaws were finally written.

Decisions in the beginning were largely made by consensus in the leadership deliberations, so all decisions on regular business were unanimous and most decisions on all other items were as well, since striving for consensus guaranteed all leaders from all local groups would have their say. Actual votes, when needed, tended to require supermajorities since the unity of the organization was valued more highly than the decision on any particular item of business no matter how controversial. Under ACORN's operating principle of "coordinated autonomy," the rights of the local branches or groups were seen not as paramount but as foundational to the strength of the decision or action that would be taken, so there was little value in coming to marginally achieved decisions. Not infrequently, controversial decisions were pushed back to the local group level for input in order to instruct their delegates' positions and votes for the eventual decision with the understandings that consensus could not be blocked and a decision would have to be made.

Political decisions always required some form of vote, even when unanimous so that the group could be recorded, and eventual endorsements, were they to occur always required supermajorities depending on the board rules of either two-thirds or three-quarters. These disciplines were hard won. Candidates would attempt to join and pay dues to the organization at the local group or citywide level to gain an advantage in the endorsement process.

Grenoble Citywide Board Meetings Outside in Summer 2016.

Exhibit 28: Statewide Board Agenda

PA State Board Meeting Agenda

Section I: Open Meeting (12-12:15) Saturday July 26th, 2008
I. Opening Welcome
II. Introductions

Section II: Internal Business (12:15-1:50)

I. Elections – 45 minutes
    A. Review job responsibilities of open positions & membership eligibility
    (provided in advance) – 5 Min
    B. Review Structure committee process for running elections
    (provided in advance) – 5 Min
    C. Nominations for All Positions – 10 Min
    D. Nominated members have time to speak to their qualifications – 25 Min
    E. Secret Ballot Vote – 5 min

II. Finance – 30 min - Melvin Starchia
    Please note: expect people to review local budgets in advance of the meeting & be prepared.
    A. Review recommendations from Finance Committee
    B. Specific Highlights from the Statewide account finance report
    C. Sign up to be on a statewide finance committee

III. National Transition Report– 20 minutes

Break (1:50-2:10)
Agenda still needs to be set for this piece

Section III: External Business (2:10-4:30)

I. Campaigns – 1 hr & 30 min
Please note: We are going to start this part of the meeting assuming that people have read the reports, so please read the reports!

    A. Very quick highlights, Legislative Victories this session – 5 minutes
        1. Education Budget Passed: Largest increase ever & New Formula!
        2. Sheriff Sales stopped in Phila & Pittsburgh – Joe Glenn?

    B. Discussion of Recommendations from the committee: 1 hr, 20 Minutes
    For each campaign listed, we would like to discuss the following three items:
        -The general recommendation from committee
        -What activities do we want to accomplish between now and next State Board Meeting?
        - What can each person commit to do to make it happen?

Exhibit 28: Statewide Board Agenda

> 1. Foreclosure Campaign – 30 minutes
> 2. Education Campaign – 20 minutes
> 3. Health Care Campaign – 20 minutes
> 4. Utilities Campaign – 5 Minutes
> 5. EITC/ Wage Campaign – 5 Minutes
>
> C. Are there any important issues that we are currently not addressing that we need to research/ look into in the next three months?
>
> II. Political – 45 minutes
>
> A. Voter Registration Report – Christina & John & (need pbg person)– 10 Minutes
> 1. Goals & Registered to date
> 2. Reports from Boards of Elections/ our message if attacked
>
> B. ACORN Votes (Our National PAC) Recommendations – Donald – 20 Minutes
> 1. Helping Obama: Increasing the voter turnout in our neighborhoods for Obama
> 2. Hurting McCain: Beating up on McCain around our issues (Foreclosure) whenever he is in the state.
> 3. Key Congressional Races: Altmire, Murphy, Sestak
>
> C. PA APAC Recommendations – John – 15 minutes
> 1. Attorney General's Race
> 2. Key Races in places we are near
>
> **Section IV: Wrap up (4:30-5)**
>
> General Evaluation of Meeting, Thoughts for planning next meeting

Other than politics, the most critical decisions at larger, state and national board levels, were in picking and managing the campaigns on issues, which also meant clearing targets, tactics, and acceptable terms in negotiations. Campaigns are organic, living things where actions and reactions create their own fluid dynamics, that cannot be perfectly predicted, so these debates were often either very general or extremely specific. Certain leaders would advocate meeting after meeting for their local group's *primary* issue, sometimes effectively and sometimes not. A new campaign direction had to meet a lot of tests before adoption as an issue or interest searched for support and a critical mass of leadership interest and engagement. Often an ingredient for adoption was whether or not the issue was best resolved at the state or provincial level.

In the early days in Arkansas linking the various city organizations together was sometimes achieved using various tax or regulatory issues, though not exclusively. At one point, led by one of our most conservative and rural groups in Lawrence County in the northeastern part of the state, called TRAG, the Tri-Rivers Action Group, we ended up campaigning around the state against the repeal of the intangibles tax. This was essentially a tax on investments, stock transactions, and similar "intangible" properties, that they, joined by the entire statewide leadership, felt was necessary in order to get upper income groups to pay to offset the regressive property taxes. I can remember a jalopy panel truck we bought to put up posters and barnstorm town to town statewide until it threw an engine rod and stranded us in southern Arkansas between Dumas and McGehee. Every time I drive down Highway 65 towards Louisiana on my route, I see the garage on the side of the road that finally pronounced that van past resuscitation weeks before the highly financed opposition crushed us on that campaign.

More successfully we barely lost a statewide initiative repealing the sales tax on food and medicine in Arkansas and later in Missouri, but won the consolation prizes when the Governors, after our close defeats, quickly moved legislation repealing the taxes on medicine. We were also able to win statewide approvals of generic drugs in Arkansas in a similar way. Campaigns against utility companies, often having statewide or regional footprints, were also tailor made for building a statewide consensus at the board level and engaging the membership deeply in the same way. Where these were regulatory efforts that found their way to the state Public Service Commission or Public Utilities Commission, sometimes still elected bodies in southern and western states with a deeper populist history and tradition, we had more success.

And of course, part and parcel, within the governance mandate of state ACORN organizations were the oversight of staff and money.

The firewalls built within the organizational bylaws and constitution of ACORN are clear that the board makes policy in this area but did not directly manage the staff. The board sets priorities and parameters within the policy directions, and then exercises its responsibility by holding the chief organizer or head organizer accountable to performance on these goals and objectives. As I have indicated, staff could not pay dues, and members could not be paid, so there were clear distinctions around the responsibilities. Board members could recommend potential hires as organizers, but had no ability to hire and fire anyone other than the head organizer, who reported directly

ACORN Canada Board Meeting in Toronto.

to the state board, and even in that situation could only terminate a head organizer after going through a consultation process with the overall Chief Organizer of ACORN. Even an agreement to remove a head organizer from a specific state would not necessarily mean that the organizer was terminated from ACORN overall, because the Chief Organizer could also replace and transfer the head organizer to another state or assignment if there was an office open and interested or in another job within the organization. To terminate an organizer from all of ACORN would have required going to the national board and having them resolve the issue with the Chief Organizer, if there was a disagreement. In truth the relationships between staff and boards were excellent in the vast majority of cases, though the exceptions define the rule. The support for this intricate system assured that the ACORN organizing staff would be managed on the basis of merit and performance, and was not as a popularity contest. More often the real tensions on a board, both state and national, were winning more organizer capacity, defined in time and resource, rather than figuring out how to remove an organizer.

Money, as anyone might expect, was more frequently grist for the mill. There was never enough of it anywhere, and the priority was always to produce more internal and sustainable sources, which means that even in times of plenty, leadership were always under pressure to do more to help raise money through their local groups. All of which also makes it no surprise that leaders spent more time and energy on campaigns and politics during the meetings than on finances. The one thing that was inescapable and vitally connected to the ACORN ideology was going through the numbers, often group by group, to measure the growth of the organization, the amount of dues paid, the amount paid later in the organization's history through the more systematic and reliable bank draft collection methods, and where this stood compared to other organizations within ACORN. This was a part of the organizational culture for all of the leaders, inculcated from the first door knocking and membership recruitment, in the initial organizing drives, so leaders followed this carefully and often competitively.

The same was true at the national board level when the Association Board, composed of two representatives from each affiliated state organization, met in April and October of each year. When the delegates would meet with the members of the Budget Committee they would get questioned about how well they were following their "numbers" and whether or not they were including their "debt sheet" in their projections, but they were almost unchallenged if they proposed an aggressive organizing and membership recruitment plan to beef up their budgets with more dues income, essentially praying at ACORN's own altar.

Exhibit 29: Association Board Agenda, Fort Worth, Texas, October, 2003

Friday Evening
7:30 -- 9:00 PM   Radio Board Meeting

Saturday Morning
8:30 – 11:00 AM Committee Meetings
9:00 – 11:00 AM AHC Board Meeting
11:00 – 1:00 PM Possible Joint Action with Fort Worth ACORN

1. <u>Welcome and Introductions:</u>
   President Maude Hurd

2. <u>Campaigns</u>
   - Report from the Campaign Committee
   - Living Wage Campaigns and Minimum Wage Initiatives
     - *Special Report on San Francisco and Florida Initiatives*
   - Predatory Lending Campaign
     - *Special Report on Household Settlement – Mike Shea, AHC Director*
     - Update: Wells Fargo Campaign Developments
   - Financial Justice Center
   - Education
   - Health
   - Other Campaigns

3. <u>Politics</u>
   - Report from the Political and Legislative Committee
     - *Special Report: District Representation Initiative in Seattle*
   - Working Family Party - New York, Connecticut, and elsewhere
   - GOTV and Voter Registration
   - Proposal on Office Participation
     - *Special Report: Politics in 2004 – Current Alignments – Zach Polett, Political Director*

4. <u>National Operations</u>
   - Relationships with Other Organizations
     - Discussion of Summit Meetings with PICO and Gamaliel Foundation
   - Labor Relationships: Various Cities
   - Discussions with NEA

5. <u>Housing and Development</u>
   - Phoenix Project and Other New Developments

254   Nuts & Bolts – The ACORN Fundamentals of Organizing

6. Field Operations
   - New Offices: Indianapolis, Springfield (IL), Tucson, Harrisburg (PA), Wilmington
   - Re-opened Offices: Columbus (OH)
   - Priorities
     - State Capitals Initiative: Timeline
     - Expansion Lists and Timelines
   - Staffing: Currently - Goal 200+
   - Field Operations Staffing and Locations
   - Field Operations: Financial Support Staff and Campaign Staff
   - National Education Day Report

7. Leadership Business
   - Regional Representative Appointments
   - Leadership School Report from Oakland
   - Convention Planning – Los Angeles
   - Report from the Nominating Committee
   - Election of Officers

8. International Joint Projects and Concerns
   - Report on Peru Initiative and Lima Representative
   - Report on Other Opportunities
   - Report on ACORN Dominican Council

9. Finances
   - Budgets for 2003
   - National Organization's Budget (Consolidated)
   - Financial Committee Report
   - Financial Analysis and Audits
   - Report on CCI and Controller
   - Discussion of Salary Review

10. Labor
    - 880
    - 100
    - American Family Home Day Care Workers Association Plans and Report
    - Working Families Association – Field Tests

11. Media
    - KABF and KNON

12. Other Business
    - Next Meetings: Executive Committee - January 31, 2004 – New Orleans
    - Association Board: April 24-25, 2004 – Kansas City, Missouri or Indianapolis, Indiana?

The second agenda is from the regular spring meeting. This particular agenda is from the meeting in April of 2008 in Minneapolis.

Exhibit 30: Association Board Agenda: Minneapolis, April 2008

Association Board Agenda
Minneapolis, Minnesota
Hyatt Place at Bloomington
April 18 - 20, 2008

Friday – April 18th

4:30 – 6:30 PM	Organizational Meeting of Bylaws Review Committee (Place TBA)
7:00 – 8:00 PM	Orientation for New Delegates (None Scheduled at this Time)
7:00 – 9:00 PM	AHC Board Meeting [Check for Time Confirmation]

General Information and Saturday and Sunday Schedule – April 19 – 20th

9:00 -- 11:00 AM	Committee Meetings @ Hyatt Place
11:00 -- 1:00 AM	Action TBA with Minnesota ACORN
1: 00 PM	Meeting Begins

1. Welcome and Introductions: President Maude Hurd
    Notifications on Guests
    Special Guests Speakers During the Meeting
    Congressman Keith Ellison
    Secretary of State Mark Ritchie
    Attorney General Lori Swanson

Association Board April 2008.

Exhibit 30: Association Board Agenda: Minneapolis, April 2008

2. Campaigns
   Summary Report from the Campaign Committee
   Special Report on Foreclosures Campaign
   - Foreclosures Campaign
     - Negotiations and Agreements Report
       - Countrywide Agreement
       - GMAC Negotiations: Report
         - Introduction of Speaker from GMAC: Sharon Belton, former Minneapolis Mayor
       - HSBC Potential Announcement
       - Citi Negotiations Report
       - Ocwen Negotiations Report
       - Other Companies
     - National Policy Statement on Foreclosures and Regulation
   - Financial Justice Center
     - On-going RALs Campaign and Strategy
   - Immigration Update
   - Education
   - Healthcare Campaign Developments
   - Katrina Update

3.. Politics
   - Summary Report of the Politics Committee
     - Report on DC Legislative and Political Conference by Participants
   - Presidential Primary Report – Impact of APAC Action
   - Report from Political Director on Scope of Voter Registration and GOTV Effort for November
   - Impact of 2006 Convictions

4. National Operations
   - Report on Planning and Details on Detroit Convention
   - Relationships with Other Organizations
   - Role of Organizers' Forum

5. Communications
   - E-mail Communications
   - Progress on new National Database
   - *Social Policy*
   - *ACORN United*
   - Radio Stations: KNON and KABF

6. Housing and Development
   - Development Progress
   - Partnerships

Special Report: AHC Wins $7.8M Grant from NeighborWorks for Foreclosure Work!

Exhibit 30: Association Board Agenda: Minneapolis, April 2008

7. Field Operations
   - New Offices and Re-Opened Offices
   - Building a Mass Membership – Report 2007
   - Special Initiatives
     - United Way Support
     - CFC Support
   - Call Center Establishment
8. Leadership Business
   - Report of Committees
   - Leadership Issues Report
9. International Joint Projects and Concerns
   - Report on ACORN International Board Meeting in Mexico City
   - Report on Existing International Affiliates
   - Discussion and Report on Opening New Offices and Projects
     - Mexico City
     - Quito, Ecuador
     - Santo Domingo
     - Nairobi, Kenya
     - Lagos, Nigeria
     - Mumbai & Delhi, India
10. Finances
    - Budgets for 2008
    - National Organization's Budget (Consolidated) – Progress to Date
    - Financial Committee Report
    - Financial Analysis and Audits
    - Costs, Funds, Etc.
    - CCI Report

    Special Report by Treasurer on the Status of Loans to the Association
11. Labor
    - SEIU Local 880
    - SEIU Local 100
    - A-CLOC Report on Contracts
    - Walmart Organizing Campaign: US + India
    - Waste Pickers in Delhi and Buenos Aires
12. Staffing
    - Staff Internal Process
13. Other Business
    - Executive Committee Meeting: TBA Detroit Convention
    - Next Association Board Meeting: October 17-19th in New Orleans

These same categories would be components of many agendas on the national level: reports from the regions along with additional notes of interest provided by the state delegates, reports from the main committees which were campaigns, politics, and budget, each chaired by officers generally, though not the President, as well as reports and discussion from other parts of the family; housing, labor, media and so forth. The location of the national meeting always moved between cities, generally to encourage new cities recently organized or specific campaigns or elections as they might occur. Frequently, there was an action with the local leadership and membership in the city on Saturday mornings from eleven until one in the afternoon when the formal meeting began with the committee meetings beginning at nine in the morning, commonly running from eleven until one in the afternoon. Sometimes there would be a welcoming event on the opening Friday with local members, sort of a cheese and crackers (yes, you guessed it – never beer or booze!) or a cookies and punch affair. Sometimes there might be a potluck or fundraising dinner the members were having in the city that most everyone would attend on Saturday nights. These meetings were about conducting national business of course, but they were also about transmitting ACORN culture and program to new leaders and cities, and of course they were political, as various leaders looked for opportunities to secure or expand their bases.

    As the organization grew larger and more influential it was also common that the meeting might welcome guests to give greetings or talk on issues, as was evident in the Minneapolis agenda in 2008 where the board was addressed by a number of political figures who were friends and allies of ACORN in that community, like Mark Ritchie and Keith Ellison. During the heat of election cycles there might be Presidential candidates that would come and speak about their issues and common interests with ACORN. Certainly, that was the case for Jesse Jackson, Barack Obama, John Edwards, Hillary and Bill Clinton, Bill Richardson, and others. Association board meetings also became opportunities to try to wrest settlements from negotiations with banks or pay day lenders or tax preparers or many others to bring them in to meet with the negotiating committees, national leadership, and potentially be able, if the agreements were close, to speak jointly to the board, take questions, and hear before leaving town that the board had voted in all likelihood to approve the settlement. Not surprisingly many more of our negotiating partners were offered such an opportunity than accepted it, but some did and many more actually came in on the Friday or Saturday for the opportunity to engage in meaningful efforts to resolve issues. At one Association board meeting in Little Rock relative positions on immigration reform were debated before the board by representatives of the AFL-CIO and SEIU, but that was rarer. These meetings were about ACORN's business and usually ACORN was clear on what it was doing and where it going, particularly on campaigns and politics, so spent the time making sure the consensus was high in these areas.

    Voting is elaborately recorded from the first motions to begin the meeting to the final motions to adjourn with each delegate keeping a tally sheet of the votes so that they were be able to align these sheets when they gave their reports back home to the local state boards or their local groups. It is important that the local members knew their board delegates were accountable to them, not only on their votes of course, but also on their attendance so that there was no perception that being on the board and attending these meetings was a junket of sorts or that their delegate might have spent the weekend visiting relatives, dead drunk, or running the street.

Exhibit 31: Voting Sheet

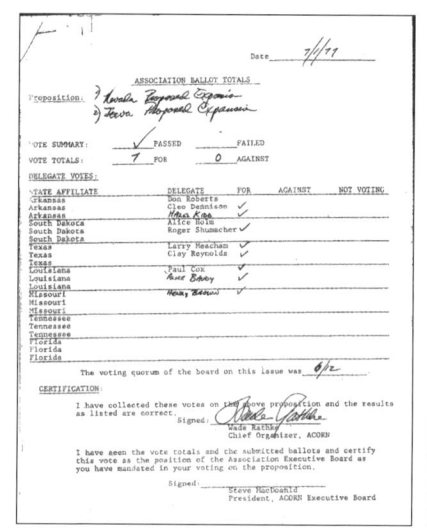

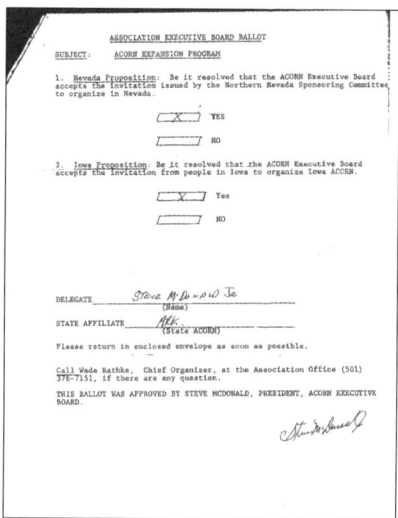

Agendas were finally assembled by the President and other officers, if needed, and by the Chief Organizer at the national level. Key issues often would have been discussed within various staff management grouping so that there could be briefings of delegates by staff as well as regional representatives from the leadership side of the organization before the meeting. Board members always wanted the final agenda in the forms shown in the earlier exhibits. Invariably last minute developments might intrude so usually one to two weeks in advance was the norm for the finalization of the board agenda. Delegates who found that they had come to the meeting unprepared raised heck when they got home because they felt embarrassed or inadequate to the business. On the staff side there was also a report after the meeting of decisions of the board and also usually some information on those delegates that seemed unprepared and whether or not staff had been demonstrably attentive to that responsibility.

More often than not, when the delegates were squirming and monitored most carefully, were during their reports to the committees. A schedule was always part of the delegate packets when members arrived for the meeting that detailed the times that various state delegations would meet respectively with the Politics, Campaign, and Budget Committees. As the organization grew these committees were also broken down in groups of threes and fours to be able to receive all of the written and oral reports and questions from the committee. The budget committee was always staffed and as the organization grew, typically the politics committee was staffed by Zach Polett, the political director, and the campaigns by Mike Shea, who managed ACORN's housing and banking portfolios or Helene O'Brien, the field director, depending on what was happening and who was available. At breakfast, before those meetings the Executive Committee of the officers and appointed regional representatives would meet for an hour with the Chief Organizer, so that they were knowledgeable about the agenda and the internal and external needs of the meeting.

None of these were story telling sessions, though a lot of stories were told of actions especially and these were highlights and affirmations of the ACORN culture and experience. Pending elections and candidates were discussed with special attention given to the status of initiative propositions or party building developments. Campaigns were updated in a specific format. The real crossroads for many delegates was when they met with the Budget Committee and had to defend their budgets, explain deficits, and request subsidies, loans, or other favors from the committee to prepare their final report before the whole board. All of these reports would be pulled together for the committee chairs, and over Saturday night all of the numbers were crunched by the Budget Committee so that the Treasurer usually would give the final report on what was recommended or rejected, along with advice and scolding either welcome or unwelcome to the delegates on Sunday morning. For many newly elected delegates this was a baptism by fire since often they might have risen to prominence in their city or state because of some campaign or action and their leadership of their local groups, and now they were being held accountable for money raised and spent, which might not have been high on their initial list or if the head organizer was also relatively new, might have also not been part of what the local organization was hoping to showcase. It was "family" business so the embarrassment was more of a blush, and never involved humiliation, but the gentle calling out of your state, always had the delegate better prepared for their next Budget Committee and Association Board meeting.

On many key issues there was a board briefing paper prepared by the Chief Organizer for the delegates that outlined the issue, the background to bring everyone up to speed, as well as the discussion points that needed to be resolved, if possible, and either the option for the board to make a decision or the organizational need that a decision be made. An example of such a briefing paper is included below in Exhibit 31A and 31B from the meeting in Cleveland, Ohio in spring 2003. If no decision was necessary at that particular meeting, then the issue could be for discussion and future action. If a decision was essential, then the discussion had to be resolved at some point over the several days. If controversial or divisive, then the matter might be shelved for later, after review, or the next morning, to allow leaders to caucus and try to find compromises that allowed a decision. Most frequently by the time of the final vote the margins were wide, one way or another, in assent or dissent. Sometimes, as discussed elsewhere, critical issues like the addition of associate and provisional membership categories involved three votes in three regular Association Board meetings over 18 months. Barack Obama to be endorsed in 2008 by ACORN while running for President involved three ballots to reach a super majority over one meeting and two board phone calls. Decisions were taken seriously.

The following is a document that lists ACORN's commitment to open new office for expansion.

Exhibit 32A: 2003 Office Development

<u>Association Board Material</u>   <u>Cleveland – 4/03</u>

2003 Office Development List

In implementing our continued program of opening offices that have been closed previously and expanding into new cities within existing states and new states, we have secured financing and we are working on the following program. This list includes state capitals in many cases.

The following indicate the cities and the timeline set by responsible staff:

*	Wilmington (DE)	4/03	New City & State
*	Fresno (CA)	5/03	New City
*	Tucson (AZ)	5/03	New City
*	Detroit (MI)	6/03	Existing City – Field Capacity
*	Atlanta (GA)	7/03	Re-Open City
*	Orlando (FL)	8/03	New City
*	Harrisburg (FL)	9/03	State Capital – New
*	Albany (NY)	9/03	State Capital – New
*	Columbus (OH)	9/03	State Capital – New
*	Springfield (IL)	9/03	State Capital – New
*	Santa Ana (CA)	9/03	New City
*	Anaheim (CA)	9/03	New City
*	Mesa (AZ)	9/03	New City
*	Glendale (AZ)	9/03	New City
*	Honolulu (HI)	9/03	New City & State
*	Jacksonville (FL)	10/03	Re-Open City
*	Riverside (CA)	10/03	New City
*	Memphis (TN)	10/03	Re-Open
*	Cincinnati (OH)	10/03	New City

Exhibit 32A: 2003 Office Development

*	Austin (TX)	10/03	Re-Open – State Capital
*	Kansas City (KS)	11/03	New City & State
*	Waterbury (CT)	11/03	New City
*	Hayward (CA)	11/03	New City
*	Charlotte (NC)	11/03	New City & State
*	Omaha (NE)	11/03	New City & State
*	Las Vegas (NV)	12/03	New City & State

We have already opened the following offices this year:

*	Kansas City (MO)	1/03	Re-Open City
*	Houston (TX)	2/03	Existing City – Field Capacity
*	Buffalo (NY)	3/03	New City
*	Contra Costa (CA)	2/03	New City
*	Hartford (CT)	2/03	New City
*	Tampa (FL)	3/03	Re-Open City

By Categories in 2003:

New States:	Six (6)
New Cities	Twenty-four (24)
Re-Opened City	Six (6)
Upgrading Field Capacity	Two (2)
Total Cities Impacted	Thirty-Two (32)

Action by the Board

　　The Board needs to review the arrangement and authorize the expansion under these terms for this timeline or take such other action as it sees fit.

Chapter X: GOVERNANCE, LEADERSHIP DEVELOPMENT, and Structure

Exhibit 32B: Board Material on Peru Initiative

Association Board Material   *Cleveland – 4/03*

Peru Initiative

In St. Petersburg the Chief Organizer reported on the progress of the partnerships we have been developing with other non-governmental organizations in Peru, particularly in Lima. As part of these commitments, we provided the Commodores Populares and others with the assistance of Lisa Donner, a senior member of our staff, for almost six weeks during the fall of 2002. As part of the agreed exchange the President of the Commodores Populares came to Los Angeles, where thanks to excellent work by the Peter Kuhns, Head Organizer of Los Angeles ACORN, and Lez Trujillo of AHC, she spend a month in training with ACORN.

We have also forged an emerging relationship with the union of water workers in Peru and we are assisting them in increasing capacity and responding to threats of privatization for water services in their country.

The next step seems to be that we need to have someone in residence in Lima as an ACORN representative to assist these two organizations on an on-going basis to improve their ability to deliver for their members and make effective change in Peru. Lisa is in Lima finishing interviews with several candidates in order to select one who would be hired and then sent back to Los Angeles for training and then sent back to Lima to represent us on this basis.

The Frontera Fund of the Tides Foundation funds this project with some small-donated services from ACORN and Local 100 Service Employees International Union.

Action by the Board

The Board needs to discuss the appropriate response on these issues and ask about what questions they might have. After so doing they need to take action on the following:

1. Does the board approve of hiring and stationing an ACORN representative in Lima, Peru during 2003-2004 as the next logical step in our experiment in transferring the lessons from our experience and learning the lessons others have to teach in another country?

2. Any other action that the board finds appropriate on this matter.

There were elements of board meetings, whether local or national, that seemed more like the British question and answer sessions with the Prime Minister in Westminster, particularly about staffing questions. Routinely, there might be contentious discussion about the movement or relocation of staff or, even more pointedly, situations where an office had lost a key organizer and was desperate for the national organization to transfer in a replacement. Almost routinely the semi-annual national meetings and other governance meetings would have some discussion of staff and staff directors where leaders would seek to sort out the issues and find common ground and agreeable action timelines. In a leadership accustomed to winning issues with their fists slamming on doors and their voices raised, these were opportunities to apply pressure and hope that the squeaks got the grease.

Another interesting governance issue between leaders and staff involved matters of compensation. Anywhere and everywhere ACORN deservedly won a reputation for not paying its staff extravagantly. In the early decades of the organization's history perhaps critics were accurate in saying that we underpaid, though from the perspective of a lower income membership the wages were seen as fair and adequate. There was always a pay scale from top to bottom and people were paid within the framework and guidelines of the scale with exceptions made only for equity and need. The scale was also front-loaded for newer staff with raises more modest for more senior staff. Gradually, as the organization grew, wages advanced more reasonably and, aggregated with benefits, the total package was fair, if not expansive, and certainly more than a living wage, even if not a gilded path to the middle class.

Salaries and the wage scales were reviewed every two years generally. In the early decades because of the ACORN obsession with self-sufficiency, any proposals on increases that worked its way up through the staff to finally be presented by the Chief Organizer to the Association Board was based on what was called a "sporting proposition." Usually the proposal involved a two or three-month period where certain goals around increased membership numbers, dues amounts per organizer, and other internal fundraising per organizer were agreed, and, then if met, would trigger at a specific time a mutually agreeable conclusion to the sporting proposition that would create a staff wide increase.

Here is an example from a later period of sporting proposition in Local 100, following the ACORN experience.

Exhibit 33: Sporting Proposition (April 2001)

SPORTING PROPOSITION

BACKGROUND

Besides the annual cost of living and seniority increases for staff, the union would like to raise the entire scale. Our financial condition does not allow this without increases of production that would pay for such increases. We also understand that the current monthly 15 card minimum does not produce a net membership growth across the Local. We also believe that it is important for the Local to develop a more efficient way to reward production.

THE PROPOSAL

All organizers in Local 100 will average 20 members per month over a consecutive three month period – any consecutive period -- and, at that point, salaries will be increased by $100 per month per organizer across the local. A minimum standard of 20 members per month will be maintained. If the average falls below 20 for any consecutive two (2) month period, then the salary level will revert back to the pre-Sporting Proposition scale.

Organizers who hit more than the new minimum of 20 will continue to be eligible to be paid for the bonus at that level as the cards are turned in, provided that the cards continue to check off as they are processed. A % of the total of new sign ups on bank draft would have financial issues with their bank account, so therefore it was made clear that the bankdraft had to be real for the staff to receive credit for it.

Chapter X: Governance, Leadership Development, and Structure   265

Bonus levels:

11-19	+100	(10 per member)
		This bonus would be converted with success of Sport Prop
20-29	+150	(15 per member)
		This would be bonus for higher than average performance
30-39	+170	(17 per member)
40 plus		(10 per member)

Wr/4/06/01

Such a dialectical process was essential. The natural tendency of the leadership, who highly valued the work of the staff, was always to believe that they should be paid more, almost regardless of whether or not there was the money to pay them or any notion of where the money might be found. The rank-and-file organizer was always ready for a raise as well, so the rub was also where the money might be found. Going through the process of a Sporting Proposition put everyone's shoulders to the wheel in trying to work out a satisfactory solution. In reality the concern continued to be that "poorer" offices might not be able to fully afford and actually pay the increases while "richer" and larger offices might have even been able to pay more, but equity throughout the organization was also essential, and a collective leadership and staff process around wage increases shifted the burden for resolution to the whole organization on these issues as well. It might not be a model, but it worked on many levels, and built a governance culture that prepared leaders with usually no experience in paying anyone or making payroll to be good stewards of the organizations in dealing with a staff that they saw as partners and essential to the success of the enterprise.

Mildred Edmond (100) and Kaye Bisnah (AINT) and others touring with San Juan Laranguancho with ACORN Peru Leaders to see Progress.

Chapter XI: **Conventions**

At the pinnacle of ACORN's governance structure and organizational inner life were the biennial conventions held on every even year from 1978 to 2008 which served to provide both the height of the aspirations of the organization as well as a fundamental glue for the leadership, membership, and even the organizing staff. These events meant bringing between one thousand and two thousand members in cars, vans, buses, and planes from across the country to some location for several jam-packed days and then also getting them alive, well, and back home again.

Some civilians might wonder to themselves, "Why do I want to know the nuts and bolts of how to put together conventions?"

The first question in your mind might be how in the world any organization of lower income families could afford to put on national meetings with a price tag in food, transportation, and everything involved costing hundreds of thousands of dollars, it is important to realize that no outside funder would ever be willing to put up the money for such a meeting, so here again we have the classic situation that these meetings were driven by how deeply the members themselves– and their local organizations – were willing and able to go into their pockets to come up with the money and means to make it possible. Doing so meant long timelines, lots of goal setting and planning, and a deep commitment to deliver a meaningful experience worth the individual and organizational investment. If there were a sugar daddy or angel investor that had ever been willing to write a check and underwrite something like an ACORN convention, who knows what the attendance might have been, because the member's own money was the delimiting ceiling on the crowd.

The work on a convention would begin more than a year ahead in the summer meeting of the ACORN Executive Committee when they would start narrowing the list of strategic locations for the convention. There were always invitations from the Association Board delegates to come to their cities or to go to cities that some thought we should collectively visit, like Little Rock where the organization was founded or New Orleans where the national organization was headquartered, though neither were ever chosen. The Executive Committee was more concerned with the key organizational factors, first, where we had the most strategic and political advantages, where there were appropriate targets that we might be able to leverage and move on national campaigns, and how and where the members could finance the trip. The one convention on the West Coast in Los Angeles in 2004 was a hard slough for the organization because it entailed so many delegations that were forced to fly at great expense, but the board felt it was necessary to finally achieve full "western" participation, rather than continuing to force an unequal financial burden on those members every convention.

By the October meeting of the full Association board the decision would be finalized on the location and date for the convention, always held in the summer of the following year. By the Field Operations and Head Organizers' meetings around the same time, each office director would already be reporting their goals for attendance at the meeting in some detail. The estimated cost would be known and the level of deposit required for the members to secure a seat would be established.

Exhibit 34: October 2005 Turnout Chart for 2006 ACORN Convention in Columbus

Office	Number of Members	Convention
Birmingham, AL	106	5
Arkansas ACORN, AR	6935	100
Glendale, AZ	460	7
Mesa, AZ	467	7
Phoenix, AZ	2937	42
Tucson, AZ	495	7
Vancouver, BC	21	5
Bay Point, CA	337	5
Chula Vista, CA	100	5
Fresno, CA	259	5
Los Angeles CC, CA	1268	18
Long Beach, CA	141	5
Los Angeles, CA	6149	88
Oakland, CA	4524	65
Raleigh, NC	106	5
Sacramento CCP, CA	240	5
Sacramento, CA	2075	30
Salinas, CA	9	5
San Bernardino, CA	152	5
San Diego, CA	2597	37
San Francisco, CA	1446	21
San Jose, CA	2600	37
Santa Ana/Orange County, CA	232	5
Stockton, CA	7	5
Aurora, CO	56	5
Colorado Springs, CO	116	5
Denver, CO	838	12

First convention action. Front Line Memphis March 1978.

268   Nuts & Bolts – *The ACORN Fundamentals of Organizing*

Exhibit 34: October 2005 Turnout Chart for 2006 ACORN Convention in Columbus

Office	Number of Members	Convention
Bridgeport, CT	1964	28
Hartford, CT	511	7
Washington, DC	6484	93
Wilmington, DE	389	6
Ft. Lauderdale, FL	960	14
Hialeah, FL	335	5
Jacksonville, FL	58	5
Miami, FL	1034	15
Orlando, FL	1716	25
Palm Beach, FL	396	6
St. Petersburg, FL	355	5
Tampa, FL	464	7
Atlanta, GA	410	6
Honolulu, HI	60	5
Des Moines, IA	7	5
Chicago, IL	3575	51
New Party, IL	23	5
Springfield, IL	13	5
Indianapolis, IN	246	5
Kansas City, KS	102	5
Topeka, KS	12	5
Wichita, KS	13	5
Louisville, KY	649	9
Baton Rouge, LA	1772	25
Lake Charles, LA	466	7
New Orleans, LA	8056	116
AHDCWA, MA	35	5
Boston, MA	12767	183
Brockton, MA	398	6
Springfield, MA	31	5
AHDCWA, MD	59	5
Baltimore County, MD	46	5
Baltimore, MD	3330	48
Prince George, MD	1003	14
Detroit, MI	522	8
Flint, MI	224	5
Lansing, MI	138	5
St. Paul, MN	10642	153
Kansas City, MO	745	11
St. Louis, MO	11204	161
Tijuana	0	5
Charlotte, NC	270	5
Bronx, NY	11156	160
Jersey City, NJ	2961	43
Newark, NJ	1532	22
Orange, NJ	7	5
Paterson, NJ	1536	22
Trenton, NJ	180	5
Albuquerque, NM	2264	33
Las Cruces, NM	0	5
Las Vegas, NV	201	5
AHDCWA, NY	11	5

Chapter XI: Conventions

Exhibit 34: October 2005 Turnout Chart for 2006 ACORN Convention in Columbus

Office	Number of Members	Convention
Buffalo, NY	72	5
Long Island, NY	2018	29
New York, NY	30997	445
Westchester, NY	4	5
Akron, OH	57	5
Cincinnati, OH	1605	23
Cleveland, OH	423	6
Columbus, OH	453	7
Toledo, OH	71	5
Oklahoma City, OK	8	5
Tulsa, OK	6	5
Toronto, ON	563	8
Portland, OR	2600	37
Allentown, PA	378	5
Harrisburg, PA	543	8
Philadelphia, PA	9270	133
Pittsburgh, PA	1078	15
Providence, RI	2081	30
Memphis, TN	135	5
Arlington, TX	36	5
Austin, TX	7	5
AWA, TX	69	5
Dallas, TX	8017	115
El Paso, TX	466	7
Ft. Worth, TX	306	5
Harlingen, TX	35	5
Houston, TX	3654	53
Irving, TX	110	5
Middle South Home Day Care	7	5
San Antonio, TX	1265	18
Waco, TX	106	5
Norfolk, VA	88	5
Burien, WA	2157	31
Madison, WI	5	5
Milwaukee, WI	17	5
	194712	3000

The number of members in the left hand column are those charted as "full" members, meaning they were actual member recorded as paid-in-full dues paying members in the database. Other categories of "associate" or "provisional" members were obviously not "full" members.

The later revisions by field operations separated out the numbers even farther though the bottom line goals and projections based on membership stayed constant, but with the input of the field staff, they shrunk slightly in the face of reality. The numbers though reported by the board members continued with stops and starts to hit the same overall goal.

Exhibit 35: Revised Projections for 2006 ACORN Convention in Columbus

State	Office	Full Members	Calc'd #s	Field #s	Board #s
AL	Birmingham, AL	91	5	10	5
AR	Arkansas ACORN, AR	6809	101	50	100
AZ	Glendale, AZ	322	5	15	7
AZ	Mesa, AZ	335	5	15	7
AZ	Phoenix, AZ	1762	26	30	42
AZ	Tucson, AZ	365	5	10	7
BC	Vancouver, BC	44	5	10	5
CA	Bay Point, CA	225	5	40	5
CA	Chula Vista, CA	63	5	10	5
CA	Fresno, CA	172	5	20	5
CA	Long Beach, CA	80	5	20	5
CA	Los Angeles CC, CA	1268	19	0	18
CA	Los Angeles, CA	6046	90	150	88
CA	Oakland, CA	4433	66	50	65
CA	Sacramento CCP, CA	240	5	0	5
CA	Sacramento, CA	1959	29	15	30
CA	Salinas, CA	9	5	0	5
CA	San Bernardino, CA	138	5	10	5
CA	San Diego, CA	2499	37	40	37
CA	San Francisco, CA	1232	18	45	21
CA	San Jose, CA	2468	37	50	37
CA	Santa Ana/Orange County, CA	143	5	15	5
CA	Stockton, CA	7	5	0	5
CO	Aurora, CO	54	5	0	5
CO	Colorado Springs, CO	73	5	10	5
CO	Denver, CO	754	11	20	12
CT	Bridgeport, CT	1995	30	25	28
CT	Hartford, CT	453	7	30	7
DC	Washington, DC	6532	97	30	93
DE	Wilmington, DE	154	5	20	6
FL	Daytona	0	0	10	0
FL	Ft. Lauderdale, FL	960	14	50	14
FL	Hialeah, FL	243	5	20	5
FL	Jacksonville, FL	58	5	20	5
FL	Miami, FL	719	11	40	15
FL	Orlando, FL	1235	18	60	25
FL	Palm Beach, FL	329	5	10	6
FL	St. Petersburg, FL	243	5	10	5
FL	Tallahassee	0	0	10	0
FL	Tampa, FL	423	6	30	7
GA	Atlanta, GA	347	5	20	6
HI	Honolulu, HI	58	5	5	5
IA	Des Moines, IA	7	5	10	5
IL	Chicago, IL	3246	48	200	51
IL	New Party, IL	23	5	0	5
IL	Springfield, IL	13	5	0	5
IN	Indianapolis, IN	285	5	15	5
KS	Kansas City, KS	101	5	10	5
KS	Topeka, KS	2	5	5	5
KS	Wichita, KS	11	5	15	5
KY	Louisville, KY	671	10	20	9

Exhibit 35: Revised Projections for 2006 ACORN Convention in Columbus

State	Office	Full Members	Calc'd #s	Field #s	Board #s
LA	Baton Rouge, LA	1861	28	0	25
LA	Lake Charles, LA	502	7	50	7
LA	New Orleans, LA	8094	120	0	116
MA	AHDCWA, MA	35	5	0	5
MA	Boston, MA	12471	185	50	183
MA	Brockton, MA	398	6	0	6
MA	Springfield, MA	31	5	5	5
MD	AHDCWA, MD	59	5	0	5
MD	Baltimore County, MD	63	5	10	5
MD	Baltimore, MD	3387	50	50	48
MD	Prince George, MD	937	14	20	14
MI	Detroit, MI	513	8	35	8
MI	Flint, MI	157	5	20	5
MI	Lansing, MI	110	5	20	5
MI	Saginaw	0	0	5	0
MN	St. Paul, MN	10351	154	60	153
MO	Kansas City, MO	694	10	30	11
MO	Springfield	0	0	5	0
MO	St. Louis, MO	11182	166	66	161
MS	Jackson	37	0	6	0
MX	Tijuana	54	5	0	5
NC	Charlotte, NC	232	5	17	5
NC	Raleigh, NC	116	5	7	5
NE	Omaha	0	0	5	0
NJ	Jersey City, NJ	2900	43	0	43
NJ	Newark, NJ	1496	22	50	22
NJ	Orange, NJ	7	5	0	5
NJ	Paterson, NJ	1528	23	30	22
NJ	Trenton, NJ	205	5	10	5
NM	Albuquerque, NM	2249	33	30	33
NM	Las Cruces, NM	0	5	5	5
NV	Las Vegas, NV	168	5	20	5
NY	AHDCWA, NY	11	5	0	5
NY	Bronx, NY	11379	169	0	160
NY	Buffalo, NY	72	5	0	5
NY	Long Island	2000	30	0	29
NY	New York, NY	31068	462	300	445
NY	Westchester, NY	4	5	0	5
OH	Akron, OH	50	5	20	5
OH	Cincinnati, OH	828	12	30	23
OH	Cleveland, OH	395	6	70	6
OH	Columbus, OH	524	8	40	7
OH	Dayton	15	0	15	0
OH	Toledo, OH	59	5	15	5
OK	Oklahoma City, OK	8	5	5	5
OK	Tulsa, OK	6	5	0	5
ON	Toronto, ON	634	9	30	8
OR	Portland, OR	2625	39	20	37
PA	Allentown, PA	378	6	5	5
PA	Erie	0	0	5	0
PA	Harrisburg, PA	560	8	30	8
PA	Philadelphia, PA	9076	135	70	133

Exhibit 35: Revised Projections for 2006 ACORN Convention in Columbus

State	Office	Full Members	Calc'd #s	Field #s	Board #s
PA	Pittsburgh, PA	872	13	40	15
RI	Providence, RI	2147	32	40	30
TN	Memphis, TN	124	5	10	5
TN	Nashville	6	0	0	0
TX	Arlington, TX	37	5	5	5
TX	Austin, TX	7	5	5	5
TX	AWA, TX	31	5	0	5
TX	Dallas, TX	7795	116	25	115
TX	El Paso, TX	332	5	20	7
TX	Ft. Worth, TX	307	5	20	5
TX	Harlingen, TX	13	5	10	5
TX	Houston, TX	3737	56	50	53
TX	Irving, TX	106	5	5	5
TX	Middle South Home Day Care	7	5	0	5
TX	San Antonio, TX	1183	18	35	18
TX	Waco, TX	28	5	5	5
VA	Norfolk, VA	87	5	5	5
VA	Richmond	0	0	5	0
WA	Seattle	2153	32	20	31
WI	Madison, WI	33	5	15	5
WI	Milwaukee, WI	17	5	5	5
		188250	3011	2881	3000

The numbers would ebb and flow as they were counted and revised continuously until members literally climbed onto the bus or boarded the airplanes when a final call would be phoned into the national staff at the convention office along with any revisions that were then required for rooming assignments, meals, childcare, and so forth. Those last calls, once all were on board would finally bring a certain lull in the storm.

Way before those calls came in there are huge numbers of nuts and bolts to tighten down. Every two years, Carolyn Carr, Director of Special Projects, would go into action from her office in Washington, D.C. to put together the pieces. As the conventions became larger, it was not a simple task just finding an affordable venue, and given the size of the conventions, that usually meant university campuses. In 2006 once the Board made the decision to go to Ohio, in order to use the ACORN Convention to support one of our states where we had a minimum wage measure on the ballot, almost immediately that meant securing a location, and fortunately in this instance Ohio State University in Columbus met all of our specifications quite easily. Adequate dorms, many of them air-conditioned, with meeting and workshop spaces in fair proximity to the housing and cafeteria locations, a reasonable dorm and eating package, places to part the buses, varying sized auditoriums, and pretty close to other potential action targets and neighborhoods in Columbus, all of which are vitally important for smooth campaign planning, were accessible there. Additionally, having work space on campus for the pre-convention staff coming in 7 to 10 days before the members to handle the details, and space for all-staff meetings was available as well. We were never looking for tourist destinations, but we knew what we needed in terms of working spaces for convention places.

Three or four months before the summer convention, the planning and discussion was already in earnest. A memo from Steve Kest, ACORN's executive director, to me, the field director, Helene O'Brien, Amy Shur, the campaign director, Mike Shea, the housing director, Zach Polett, the political director, and Lisa Donner, on the legislative and research staff at the end of March (Exhibit 36) is a good example of the details already being shaped and in motion by that point.

Exhibit 36: March Convention Planning Memo

March 29, 2006

To: Wade, Helene, Zach, Mike
Amy, Lisa
Fr: Steve

Re: **Convention planning**

Here are some initial thoughts and questions for further discussion on the Convention. Looking for feedback here, so we can move forward.

Actions/other events
1. Not sure what action targets we'll find, but we can start looking at this. Any corporate HQ or regional offices of any businesses we are remotely interested in?
2. Would we want to march to Sec/State's office (or whatever the appropriate office is) to turn in our MW [Minimum Wage ballot] signatures? Not especially hard-hitting, but could be fun, and could be an excellent press hook.
3. Could we do MW petitioning Sunday afternoon? (Do you have to be an in-state registered voters to circulate petitions? Is there a way to pair people with Ohioans for this?)

Speakers
1. Edwards is pretty-much confirmed; would I think be significant and newsworthy to get others who are on the 08 list to attend, to address issues of concern to our members and constituency. Clinton, Warner, etc.
2. Other national figures: Talking to Bill Clinton's people on whether he can come. Need some thoughts on who we would want to invite, in what categories, for other speakers

Exhibit 36: March Convention Planning Memo

3. OH allies: Makes sense to invite Sherrod Brown and Ted Strickland, our candidates for US Senate and Governor who are running on the MW platform. Possibly the mayor to do a welcome.

Other program ideas

1. Any victories we will be in a position to announce, where we can have the target/CEO come and sign an agreement? Lead paint; Cap One; a payday lender or tax prep company; etc? Or an existing partner with a new or extended agreement?

2. Any partnerships with union allies we want to highlight – SEIU, AFT, others, by inviting their presidents?

3. Is there internal business we want to accomplish? I.e. generate consensus on the 5 million goal, and organize a segment of the agenda around that – including awards for offices with highest membership growth, etc?

4. Minimum wage: we probably need a session that highlights this – perhaps with OH allies; could also invite key allies from our other MW states.

5. Reports on victories: this worked well last Convention; we should probably repeat.

6. Banquet: Assume we want to do this again – but this time with only one speaker! Is there someone we want to honor? Should we try to steer Edwards to this event?

Workshops

1. We probably want to look at Saturday evening on these, as we did last time. If we want to be more ambitious (and if we can't figure out a Sunday action/petition-gathering program) we could do these Sunday as well….

2. Two tracks: issues/campaigns – and internal/organizing?

3. Thinking of inviting allies to issue/campaign workshops as resource people – good way to get folks to the Convention.

As the conventions got larger it seemed we were putting together three-ringed circuses, one part for the members, one part for the public, and one part between the two to engage our allies and targets and use the opportunity of the assembly to leverage and influence both. There were always discussions about how to use the opportunity to move campaigns, first at the level of figuring out the various action-targets for the largest march on the final day, but also any way we could move people effectively on Sunday too. For example at ACORN's convention in New York City in 1992, on the Saturday before the convention began, while meeting at Columbia University, we took advantage of the location to bring together most of our banking partners and adversaries to successfully engage them on housing issues in meetings that paid off on a number of fronts.

We were also able to use the meeting with some of our targets. Ameriquest, the subprime mortgage outfit was a prime example. We launched the beginning of the predatory lending campaign, targeting the company, which was a prime mover of mortgages then with an action in Philadelphia in 2000 at one of their board member's homes on the Saturday and at their offices for the big march and action that following Monday. In later conventions we would announcement settlements with them and others and progress on agreements.

Organizing conventions every other year, trial and error, allowed us to determine the membership enthusiasm through their participation. We found that an open-mic program run by the leadership that allowed all comers to report on their campaigns and work was immensely popular with leaders and members and a better "ice breaker" and informal welcoming to the business of the convention than any other we might have imagined. Run and operated by the leadership, the event also had the advantage of allowing the staff to continue to run around trying to put the heads back on chickens and deal with the myriad logistical details of housing all of the members, last minute transportation problems, and all of the remaining details for the meeting Sunday and Monday.

The workshops were also marvels to behold and an experience for everyone. ACORN had initially stumbled onto this recognition in 1978 in the special convention and Platform Conference in St. Louis at Washington University where the final pieces of the ACORN Platform were written, debated, and approved by the membership. The process had involved a series of meetings on issues beginning at the local group level then moving to the citywide organizations and state organizations where they existed then and finally culminating in St. Louis at the Platform Conference.[87] In the beginning when members were asked what they would see as real solutions around housing or jobs or community development their vision was narrow and obstructed by the difficult experience of fighting for changes against opposition at the local level, but as the process pressed forward and the members realized that the platform was their opportunity to dream, the blossoming made the debate and final decisions one of ACORN's greatest internal accomplishments. The workshops at subsequent conventions continued that trend with good results.

The conventions were about the ACORN members. The staff's job was to spend every second possible figuring out and working to ensure the maximum comfort of and participation of and by each member.

---

[87] Documented in Gary Delgado's book, *Organizing the Movement: The Roots and Growth of ACORN.*

Exhibit 37: Workshop Grid for the Columbus Convention in 2006

Come to the ACORN Workshops

Saturday 3:30-5 and 6:45-8:15

See below for room numbers and which sessions have Spanish translation

Bldg #	WORKSHOP	ROOM	DESCRIPTION	SPANISH TRANSLATION 3:30- 5 pm	SPANISH TRANSLATION 6:45 – 8:15 pm
054	Minimum and Living Wages	Mendenhall Lab ML 100	Learn about ACORN's successful campaigns to raise wages at the city and state level - and even for companies like Wal-Mart - and how you can run them in your own city.		With Spanish translation 6:30
054	Lead Campaigns	Mendenhall Lab ML 131	What should we do to get Sherwin-Williams to pay to clean up the lead paint in our neighborhoods? How can we get landlords to clean up their apartments?	With Spanish translation 3:30	
054	Utilities Campaigns	Mendenhall Lab ML 173	Think your utility bills are too high? Find out what kinds of campaigns ACORN can run to get utilities under control.		With Spanish translation 6:30
054	Predatory Mortgage Lending	Mendenhall Lab ML 174	We have put an end to many predatory mortgage practices, but they've come up with new ways to rip us off. What are the latest loan scams and what we can do to stop them?	With Spanish translation 3:30	
054	Pay Day Lending	Mendenhall Lab ML 175	Find out what can we do about these loan sharks who are stealing billions of dollars from our neighborhoods and from the working families who need it most?		With Spanish translation 6:30
338	Immigration	Independence Hall IH 100	Learn about the status of legalization in Congress and what we can all do on the local level even before Congress acts.	With Spanish translation 3:30	With Spanish translation 6:30
149	Housing	Hopkins Hall HC 262	How are we going to get more housing real people can afford? Find out what other offices are winning.	With Spanish translation 3:30	
065	Tenant's Rights	Smith Lab SM 1005	Tired of your landlord not doing the right thing? Come find out about campaigns in Canada and the US to get renters rights.		With Spanish translation 6:30
065	Education	Smith Lab SM 1009	Come learn about different things you can do to improve the schools in your city.		With Spanish translation 6:30
065	ACORN History	Smith Lab SM 1153	Want to know all about the first 37 years of ACORN? Come find out the history you never knew.		With Spanish translation 6:30

Chapter XI: Conventions

Exhibit 37: Workshop Grid for the Columbus Convention in 2006

Come to the ACORN Workshops

Saturday 3:30-5 and 6:45-8:15

See below for room numbers and which sessions have Spanish translation

# on map	WORKSHOP	ROOM	DESCRIPTION	SPANISH TRANSLATION 3:30- 5 pm	SPANISH TRANSLATION 6:45 – 8:15 pm
149	Third Party Politics	Hopkins Hall HC 162	ACORN is helping the Working Families Party to expand into more states. Come find out where and how.	With Spanish translation 3:30	
054	2006 Elections	Mendenhall Lab ML 115	Hear about voter registration, APAC and election work that we are doing for 2006 so you can do it in your city too.	With Spanish translation 3:30	
054	APAL – Precinct Action Leaders	Mendenhall Lab ML 185	Precinct Action Leaders (PALs)-- Control the votes in your precinct to have power. Learn how to teach others to doorknock, phone-bank, and make good calls to legislators.		With Spanish translation 6:30
054	Building ACORN	Mendenhall Lab ML 191	Want more members at your meetings? Want to have more power in your state? Come find out how.	With Spanish translation 3:30	
339	AHC Credit and Budget Class Demonstration	University Hall UH 0014	ACORN Housing is developing a new Credit and Budgeting Class to help low income households learn how the credit reporting system works, the true cost of credit and establishing and/or improving their credit standing. ACORN Members will provide feedback for final program after demonstration.		With Spanish translation 6:30
017	American Blackout	Knowlton Hall KN 250	See a new film about voting rights & Rep. Cynthia Mckinney (D-GA) and discuss how it can be used as an organizing tool in '06 and '08.		With Spanish translation 6:30
037	Getting Media Coverage	Hagerty Hall HH 180	Find out how to get the media to cover your events and how to get them to get your message right.	With Spanish translation 3:30	

Workshops in the 6:45 – 8:15 timeslot ONLY

150	For Youth to organize	Evans Lab 2004	A workshop for teenagers about what we can do to improve our lives, our schools and our neighborhoods		In Spanish and English

As you can see from Exhibit 37, putting these pieces together, making it all happen, and having it work for the members and the organization and its own ambitions was even more than a three-ring circus. There were multiple tracks and some small lobbing from various organizers and cities to be able to showcase their campaigns or projects on a national level to see if they could create more support and attention for the efforts, and that was a good thing in my view.

As you can see from Exhibit 38 (below), members voted with their feet, and even after a day that would have usually included travel, perhaps tours of the city, moving into the dorms, and a bit of everything else, they was good attendance at the workshops. By counting carefully, we could also measure the interest for the future.

Exhibit 38: Workshop Turnout Numbers Collected on Columbus Convention 2006

WORKSHOP	STAFF	1st session turnout	2nd session turnout
Minimum Wage	Jen	35	75
Lead	Stuart / Amy	15	25
Utilities	Stephanie	35	55
Predatory Lending	Aimee Olin	30	20
Pay Day Lending	Jordan	4	20
Immigration	Ginny, with Victoria & Brenda	40	60
Housing	Julie/Kate	35	50
Tenants' Rights	Judy & Val	15	15
Education	Liz	45	35
ACORN History	Mildred	20	40
Third Party Politics	Clare	7	7
2006 Elections	Brian	50	40
APAL	Kimberly & Ron Sykes	50	50
Doorknocking, House Visits 5 million member presentation	Marc Seiden		
AHC Budget and Credit Class Demonstration	Lez	70	50
Media	Charles Jackson / Kevin		
America Black Out	Jehmu		

Chapter XI: Conventions

The other thing that would be happening simultaneously, and competing with the workshops, showcased both the socializing and entrepreneurial side of the membership. There were no limits to the "block" parties, floor to floor on the convention. In 1978 Mark Splain turned to me after looking up at the laundry the members had hung out on the outside balconies at the dorms of Washington University in the St. Louis suburbs, laughed, and said, "It looks like the members could hunker down and stay here for the rest of the lives!" And, compared to home, many of them would love to have squatted there forever without a doubt.

Exhibit 39: Going to Ground for a Convention

ACORN NATIONAL CONVENTION 2006
Early Staff Arrivals

By Air:
Port Columbus International Airport (CMH)
http://www.port-columbus.com/home.asp

Transportation options to the convention from the airport:
-**Taxi**, The approximate fare to Ohio State University is $18-$24.

- **Shuttle Services**, There are several shuttle companies available upon arrival at the airport or you can schedule their services ahead of time. The costs range from $18-$28 per person, $5 each additional passenger. See the listings on the Airport's website,
  http://www.port-columbus.com/parking/transportation/shuttle.asp

- **COTA bus system**, for schedules and fares visit their website
  http://www.cota.com/COTA/Cotaweb/main.xml

By Car:
Parking will be available in Jesse Owens North Lot. A permit is required and can be picked up at check-in at Royer Student Activities Center.
http://tp.osu.edu/maps/campusparkingmap.pdf

Destination:
The convention will be held on the campus of Ohio State University. Click the link for an interactive map of campus.
http://www.osu.edu/map/

Check-in will be held at:
 Royer Student Activities Center, Room 5
85 Curl Drive

Convention attendees will be housed in:
 Nosker House
136 W Woodruff Ave.

Contacts:
ACORN Convention Office:
Royer Student Activities Center, Living Room
 614-247-4828

My point? Details matter! Getting ready for up to 2000 people is a production. Ten to fourteen days ahead of the convention and the members' arrival, central staff would start relocating to the convention site. Virtually the entire Citizens Consulting, Inc. (CCI) staff would be relocated in stages more than a week in advance. The regular business of the organization had to continue with bills being paid, payroll issued, and everything else, so by the week of the convention there was a "shadow" operation both handling the convention expenses and logistics, making sure buses were paid, invoices received, and a thousand other tasks on the ground, as well as juggling the "normal" business at the same time. Other parts of the CCI crew would drive up in a truck full of old convention's banners as well as the state stanchions with the name of each organization and affiliate for the convention floor. After we acquired two ACORN Mobile Action Vans (panel trucks equipped with sound and computers), we had even more vehicles to get to ground and usefully handle all of the sundry equipment.

Extra staff from the larger offices were frequently detailed to lend a hand with the set up and preparation, whether support staff, new organizers, researchers or whatever. Besides getting the work done, which is always voluminous, it also built camaraderie and solidarity. There were jobs both big and small. Signs had to be made with member-friendly direction signs from dorms to cafeteria to meeting places to auditorium. Posters had to be farmed out as backups to what might not come with the members on the buses for the actions. Packets had to be assembled with the agenda, *ACORN USA's* (our membership newspaper), song and chant sheets, campus maps, food locations, and sundry other items for each member. If there were sights to be seen, materials had to be collated into the packets on that as well. T-shirts, ordered earlier, had to be sorted out, sized, folded, and "sellers" assigned to move the merchandise.

Registration teams had to be assigned and assembled for various dorms and the whole convention. Heading up the registration effort was a Herculean task or perhaps a Sisyphean one, particularly before computers and Excel made some dent. Initially handled by Carolyn Carr and Dale Rathke in various forms, but later transitioned to Joann Wright for several seasons and then Jen Kern, this was a flesh-eating, mind boggling task that would virtually drive whoever picked the straw that convention into bed for a day after everyone was safely in their dorm. The hours were grueling, the work thankless, the migraines immeasurable, and the gratitude for their skill and success endures to this day on my part at least. A bad job, if there ever was one, but a critical one. We found early and often that as easy going and adaptable as the members were and as excited as they were to be at the convention, when they rolled off of those busses, they were beat to a frazzle. We would have crews of volunteers and staff ready to help mule the luggage up the rooms, but if there were problems with the registration, particularly if underage college kids were handling the tasks flippantly, cranky would be a mild way to describe the volcanoes that could erupt over nonworking keys, roommate assignments that did not jell, and other minor matters normally ignored. Members that found a strange man assigned to their room that was outside of their bargain and myriad other problems could turn mean on a moment's notice after a long bus ride to the convention. In short this was one of the key assignments made and the most important, and always handled by heroes!

Exhibit 40 gives some sense even in a pretty well laid out campus like Ohio State the number of locations, varying delegations and logistical challenges that getting everyone into their rooms entailed.

Exhibit 40: Convention Housing Assignments

Dorm	Delegation
South Dorms	
Morrison	Erie
	Philly
	Lehigh Valley/Allentown
	Harrisburg
	Pittsburgh (+)
	MontCo/Philly Burbs
	Alabama
	Arkansas
	Mississippi
	Boston
	DC
	Orlando
	Louisiana (and Canfield)
	St. Pete
	Tampa
	Bus Drivers/Problems
Baker East	Contra Costa
	Orange County
	Columbus
	Midwest
Baker West	Atlanta
	Memphis
	Columbia
	Charlotte
	Raleigh
	Louisville
	Midwest
	Hartford
	Delaware
	ADA Rooms
Canfield	Cleveland
	Canada
	Pittsburgh Overflow
	Louisiana (2 rooms)
Mack	San Jose
	San Francisco
	Los Angeles
	Oakland (plus Stradley)

Dorm	Delegation
South Dorms	
Stradley	Sacramento
	San Bernardino
	Oakland (plus Mack)
	New York
	880 (plus Park)
Park	New Jersey
	Fresno
	San Diego
	Arizona
	Colorado
	880 (plus Stradley)
	New Mexico
	Dayton
Siebert	Cincinnati
	PG County
	Baltimore
	Rhode Island
	Las Vegas
	Oregon
	Washington State
North Dorms	
Scott	San Antonio
Norton	Broward County (with Houck and Taylor)
Drackett	Dallas
	El Paso
	Jacksonville (with Barrett)
	Bus Driver
Houck	Hialeah
	Broward County (with Norton and Taylor)
Barrett	Miami
	North Dade
	Palm Beach
	Jacksonville (with Drackett)
Taylor	Houston
	Broward County (with Norton and Houck)

ACORN Canada leaders running a workshop on recruitment at Ottawa Convention 2017.

Handling the bus drivers and transportation logistics was another hard and critical job. Herding cats hardly describes the anarchy of bus drivers coming from around the country to a central location from different companies with different expectations and contracts. Invariably, the convention crew would insist on getting all of the bus contracts into the national office in New Orleans early. Some offices would have found top-of-the-line companies and others would be in school buses on loan for the short hops. Some offices would have priced the bus right to the dormitory door, not remembering the problem of getting around in the city or off to actions or whatever. This would be an instance were "coordinated autonomy" verged on complete chaos. Fortunately, convention to convention, we got better at this, and it helped that when we found someone who was willing to manage these complicated bus logistics, maps, directions, and drivers, we would dragoon them into the task from year to year, usually from our canvass teams, first Peter Wood and then Fred Brooks who handled the job a number of conventions and then would volunteer to come back and manage the piece even after he had left the staff.

The traditional order in sorting the dorms, buses, seating, or marches followed the order of founding of the state organization with ACORN. Tradition and seniority always trumped something prosaic, like the alphabet.

Exhibit 41: Order of States

Order of Delegates		
45	Arkansas	37
165	Texas	164
50	Louisiana	46
95	Missouri	82
20	Colorado	
120	Pennsylvania	135
75	Michigan	81
55	Arizona	50
31	Connecticut	17
4	South Carolina	2
33	Massachusetts	35
62	New Mexico	60
110	New Jersey	87
60	Minnesota	72
300	New York	
20	District of Columbia	
92	Illinois	137
300	California	300
10	Washington	
80	Maryland 81	
10	Wisconsin	14
200	Florida	190

Order of Delegates		
20	Oregon	
40	Rhode Island	44
190	Ohio	
2	Hawaii	
20	Delaware	19
28	Indiana	17
6	Georgia	5
31	North Carolina	57
18	Kentucky	
20	Nevada	
12	Alabama	
3	Tennessee	4
8	Kansas	10
0	Oklahoma	
12	Mississippi	10
4	South Carolina	
1	Nebraska	1
35	Canada	
	Peru	
	Mexico	1
1	Argentina	1

Exhibit 42. Numbers on the Order of States

Order of Delegations

Arkansas	District of Columbia	Kentucky
Texas	Illinois	Nevada
Louisiana	California	Alabama
Missouri	Washington	Tennessee
Colorado	Maryland	Kansas
Pennsylvania	Wisconsin	Oklahoma
Michigan	Florida	Mississippi
Arizona	Oregon	South Carolina
Connecticut	Rhode Island	Nebraska
South Carolina	Ohio	
Massachusetts	Hawaii	Canada
New Mexico	Delaware	Peru
New Jersey	Indiana	Mexico
Minnesota	Georgia	Argentina
New York	North Carolina	

In the same way the numbers were also monitored closely.

Many are called and then there are all of the ones that make it on the bus. Once at the convention and unpacked and ready to go, the first interactions for the members are informal.

And, entrepreneurial! One of the things that organizers learn, eventually, is that it is a fool's task to try and believe, no matter how well organized, that you can micromanage all of what happens around the convention. We first saw the entrepreneurial impulse in full flower at the 1980 Convention in New York City, the culmination of the 20/80 campaign after years of organizing. Members from right-next-door, so to speak, in Philadelphia jumped off the bus after a quick ride to the city with huge suitcases and big ice coolers as if they were coming prepared to camp out at Fordham University, the Convention's residential site, for months or the rest of their lives.

Andrea Hall, a long time North Philly leader, led the entrepreneurial way, beginning the first night before the cafeteria service opened by serving plate meals by the score. She was not alone in figuring out there were lots of fundraisers that could be used to defray a member's convention costs. Other members operated "blind pigs" or just shared what they had hauled in or bought locally as yard and "dorm" parties seemed to be going everywhere. Sister Hall did learn that there was a line that could not be crossed when during the march down Broadway to Madison Square Garden she delayed one section of the march line hawking water bottles from a rolling cooler, earning her a trip to the back of the line.

Meanwhile the convention staff, exhausted after many 16 and 18-hour days, and the state-based staff fairly well spent after epic bus rides or corralling members successfully to planes and trains, was running on adrenaline and caffeine, but feeling no pain in the excitement. The members might be unpacking, partying, meeting each other informally in the great exchange of making new friends in other states and cities over the shared issues and campaigns that linked all of ACORN, but the staff was assembling for 10 PM meetings to go through the myriad details of getting ready for the main show once the formal convention convened. The meetings were forced marches through forests filled with information that they all needed to have. Every night of the convention involved a rerun of some material interspersed with new information crammed into every minute. More effectively the larger meeting would set the tone and maintain the direction, while smaller meetings would break off to handle preparation for actions, marches, handling speakers, and whatever. Larger delegations and states would also have separate meetings on who was doing the wake-up calls, getting speakers or leaders to early meetings, and knocking on the dorm doors to make sure everyone was up and out. Some of this may sound mundane, but truth to tell, the special moments of walking out of a dorm a dawn and hearing doors slamming, members talking, organizers running down hallways, and then greeting the early risers as the first members hit the cafeteria lines, invariably meeting Carolyn Carr personally supervising her assigned crew of "line" and "tray" handlers, was always a prized and special part of the work for me over many decades.

The ACORN Association Board would also meet briefly several hours before the opening gavel to go through the agenda one last time, get assignments, and clarify their roles in running the meeting, as well as anything else that warranted the leadership's attention. These meetings were always brief. Usually I would meet with the Executive Committee and President at a table in the cafeteria so make sure everything was in good shape. Sometimes we would hear Maude Hurd, ACORN's president for many years run through her opening speech. It was fair to say the work was all over but the shouting.

Bus load up at convention Ottawa 2017.

Exhibit 43. Pre-Convention Board Agenda in 2006 Columbus ACORN Convention

AGENDA
ACORN Association Board Meeting
July 8, 2006

1. Welcome to Convention
   – President Maude Hurd
2. Review of Seating for Leadership and Delegates
3. Review of Agenda and Roles
4. Report from the Treasurer
   - Loans Policy and Procedures
   - Loans Outstanding
   - Other Financial Matters
5. Other Reports
6. Good and Welfare

Crew works to prepare the convention packets before the crowd comes 2004.

Chapter XI: Conventions 287

very delegation entered the hall to find their seating as they marched from the dorms to the auditorium with their own special chant somewhere between shouting and singing, and this was invariably an exciting and beautiful moment as the walls almost literally shook with the members' excitement and the high spirits of what could only be called competitive chanting. Chicago and New York always used their trips wisely and set the standards, but often California challenged, especially with an additional Latin flair, and other states and cities often had their moments as well. Any organizer or leader that passed through these halls always wanted to come back to the next convention bigger and bolder, and undoubtedly with a better opening sound to their steps into the convention. That tradition has been ably kept alive in the ACORN Canada Conventions where even something simple like the loud, repetition of "BC, BC, BC," still brings members to their feet, shouting with smiles across their faces.

The leaders were always moving. The leadership had to be on the stage as the members marched into the convention, but most of them also wanted to be with their states as they hooted and hollered their way into the room. The rough compromise that leaders fabricated had them doing their own version from the stage to support their members. The President would stand at the microphone as the state's marched in, but the stage itself was filled with the elected leadership, standing and swaying with the beat of the crowd.

Exhibit 44: Stage Seating at 2006 Columbus ACORN Convention

Maude Hurd	President	Yvonne Woods	Kentucky
Maria Polanco	New York	Mary Phillips	Tennessee
Maxine Nelson	Arkansas	Yvonne Stafford	North Carolina
Paul Satriano	Minnesota	John Jones	Washington
Toni Foulkes	Illinois	Heidi Johnson	Washington
Fannie Brown	California	Marie Pierre	New York
Tamecka Pierce	Florida	Betty Wilkins	Colorado
Aaron Pridgen	Florida	Jose Jurado	Colorado
Stephanie Canady	Rhode Island	Carmen Arias	Arizona
Laurie Morrow	Michigan	Charlotte Peper	Arizona
Sheila Collings	Michigan	Sonja Jones	Maryland
Johnny Pugh	Arkansas	Marcel Reid	Washington,
Shada Buyobe Hammond	Minnesota	DC	
Carol Culvahouse	Indiana	Louise Davis	Washington,
Barry Hayes	Wisconsin	DC	
Robert Tillman	Missouri	Angela Walker	Delaware
Claudie Harris	Missouri	Stephanie Vaughn	Ohio
Carol Hemingway	Pennsylvania	Mary Keith	Ohio
Gail Williams	Pennsylvania	Pedro Rivas	New Jersey
Ron Sykes	Georgia	Denise Booker	New Jersey
Diana Barnes-Pate	Mississippi	Marva Burnett	Canada

A crew of staff works to fill the hall. Each delegation is greeted in turn as they are ready to come in, invariably with the larger delegations hoping to be among the last to enter so that they could showcase their size and shouts. Organizers "usher" them into their place, and the chants continue at full decibel from that vantage point only pausing briefly to allow a new state to enter the room. The unique super-charged entry of loudly chanting members as they come into the hall to their delegation's seats might then continue in unison, with the entire body chanting for 45 minutes or more. The simply irreplaceable huge actions and meetings set ACORN apart as a group about change and action.

The exact membership count from each delegation was key, because seating was allocated precisely on that basis.

Exhibit 45: Convention Seating Chart – Columbus, Ohio 2006

Columbus Convention Seating Chart

Orchestra Pit

A	(left facing the stage)	B (right facing the stage)
1	AZ	Canada
2	AZ	Canada
3	AZ	Canada/Colorado
4	AZ	Colorado

MAIN FLOOR – MERSHON CENTER

	A	B	C	D	E
1	GUESTS	GUESTS	GUESTS	GUESTS	GUESTS
2	CALI	CALI	KANSAS	GUESTS	GUESTS
3	CALI	CALI	NY	NY	NY
4	CALI	CALI	WASH	NY	NY
5	CALI	CALI	OHIO	NY	NY
6	CALI	CALI	OHIO	NY	NY
7	CALI	CALI	OHIO	NY	NY
8	CALI	CALI	OHIO	NY	NY
9	CALI	CALI	OHIO	NY	NY
10	CALI	CALI	OHIO	NY	NY
11	CALI	CALI	OHIO	NY	NY
12	CALI	CALI	OHIO	NY	NY
13	CALI	CALI	OHIO	NY	NY
14	CALI	CALI	OHIO	NY	NY
15	CALI	CALI	OHIO	NY	NY
16	CALI	CALI	OHIO	NY	NY
17	CALI	CALI	OHIO	NY	NY
18		CALI	OHIO	NY	
19		TENN	OHIO	NY	
20		HAWAII/NEBR	OHIO	NY	
21			OHIO		
22	WISC				GA
23	MISS				KY

BALCONY FLOOR – MERSHON CENTER

	A1	B1	C1	D1	E1
1	LA	FL	FL	FL	NM
2	LA	FL	FL	FL	NM
3	LA	FL	FL	FL	NM
4	LA	FL	FL	FL	NM
5	AL	FL	FL	FL	NM

DOOR   DOOR

	A2	B2	C2	D2	E2
1	MO	FL*	IL/880	DE	NJ
2	MO	FL*	IL/880	DE	NJ
3	MO	MI	IL/880	AR	NJ
4	MO	MI	IL/880	AR	NJ
5	MO	MI	IL/880	AR	NJ
6	NV	MI	IL/880	CT	NJ
7	NV	MI	IL/880	OR	NJ

DOOR   DOOR

	A3	B3	C3	D3	E3
1	PA	TX	MD	CAN	IN
2	PA	TX	MD	CAN	DC
3	PA	TX	MD	CAN	AZ
4	PA	TX	MD	MA	AZ
5	PA	TX	MD	MA	AZ
6	PA	TX	MD	NC	AZ
7	PA	TX	MN	NC	AZ+SC
8	PA	TX	MN	NC	CO
9	PA	TX	MN	STAFF	CO
10	PA	TX	MN	STAFF	STAFF
11	PA	RI	RI	STAFF	STAFF

KEY

*	if FL does not need these rows then Rhode Island should take them.
**	if NJ does not need these rows then Delaware should take them.
***	if MO does not need these rows then Nevada should take them.

When the members walked into the building in the later years of the ACORN Conventions they could see giant video screens with the ACORN symbol and pictures of actions and demonstrations during the year scrolling over them. The agenda was a mixture of campaign reports from the leadership and speeches from allies. To calm the crowd there was always an invocation to begin the proceedings and a welcome by a local dignitary, perhaps the Mayor or in the 2006 convention in Columbus, Sherrod Brown, then a US representative and more recently the Senator from Ohio.

Exhibit 46: Annotated Agenda for ACORN 2006 Convention

Draft 7/7/06b

ACORN NATIONAL CONVENTION 2006
July 8-10, 2006
Columbus OH
Program

SATURDAY

Afternoon	Arrivals and room check-in
2:00	Association Board Meeting
3:30 – 5:00	Workshops I
5:15 – 6:30	Dinner
6:45 – 8:15	Workshops II
8:30 – 10:00	Pre-Convention Plenary: Members Speak Out! *Mershon Auditorium*

SUNDAY

6:30 – 7:45   Breakfast
8:00-8:30: enter Mershon Auditorium

8:00 – 11:30   **Morning Plenary**
Mershon Auditorium
Opening ceremonies (8:00-9:15)
- **March of the States** (8:00-8:30)
- **Gospel Performance: Bishop Giovanni Johnson and the New Shining Light** (8:00-8:30)
- **Roll Call of the States** (8:40-8:50)
- **Opening prayer: Rev. James T. Morris, Pastor, Lane Tabernacle CME Church, and President of the ACORN Clergy Association, St. Louis** (8:50-9:00)
- **Welcome to OH: Rep. Sherrod Brown** (9:00-9:15)
Introduced by Lashon Campbell Smith, OH ACORN

Exhibit 46: Annotated Agenda for ACORN 2006 Convention

- **President's address: Maude Hurd, ACORN National President, MA ACORN (9:15-9:25)**
  Introduced by Toni McElroy, TX ACORN
- **ACORN 2006: Campaign priorities (9:30 – 10:45)**

Responding to Katrina (9:30-9:50)
Gwendolyn Adams, LA ACORN
Vanessa Johnson, LA ACORN
Tyrone Graves, TX ACORN
Takuna Tarhakah, AR ACORN

Fighting for Comprehensive Immigration Reform (9:55-10:15)
Maria Polanco, ACORN National Vice President, NY ACORN
Giselle Quesada, CA ACORN
Stephanie Cannady, RI ACORN
Nina Nunez, TX ACORN

Raising the Minimum Wage (10:20-10:40)
Tamecka Pierce, FL ACORN
Julie Smith, OH ACORN
Rob Tillman and Claudie Harris, MO ACORN
LaMone Noles, CO ACORN
Carmen Arias, AZ ACORN

ACORN Allies (10:45 – 11:15)

Building Alliances: Paul Satriano, ACORN National Treasurer, MN ACORN (10:45-10:50)

- *Chris Redfern, Chair, OH Democratic Party (10:50-10:55) Introduced by Stephanie Vaughn, OH ACORN*
- **John Sweeney, AFL-CIO (11:00-11:15)**
  Introduced by Bridgett Carruth and Jennie Cardona, NY ACORN/UFT/American Federation of Teachers

11:30 – 12:45   Lunch

12:45-1:00   – return to Mershon Auditorium

Exhibit 46: Annotated Agenda for ACORN 2006 Convention

1:00 – 2:30	**Afternoon Plenary**
	 Mershon Auditorium
	 Raising the Minimum Wage in Ohio: (1:15-1:30)
	 • **Mary Keith, Cleveland ACORN**
	 • **Tim Burga, Ohio AFL-CIO**
	   Introduced by Mary Keith, OHACORN
	 • **C.J. Prentiss, Democratic Leader, Ohio Senate**
	   Introduced by Mary Keith, OH ACORN
	 Guest Speaker:
	 • **John Edwards** (1:30-2:10)
	   Introduced by Maude Hurd, ACORN National President
	 • **Canvassing Our Neighborhoods: Sandra Soweto, OH ACORN** (2:10 2:15)

Dismissal:	**Maude Hurd, ACORN National President**
2:30 – 5:30	**Canvassing Our Neighborhoods: The ACORN Campaign to Raise the Minimum Wage** • 2:20-2:30: load and send-off 5 S-W buses • 2:30-3:00: load rest of buses (further n'hoods firsts) • 3:00-3:15: drive to the n'hoods • 3:15-4:30/4:45: canvass (later time – closer n'hoods) • 4:40/4:50: back on buses • 5:00: drop offs at dorms • 6:00 and on: shuttles from dorms to banquet
6:00 – 6:30	**Board buses for Banquet**
7:00 – 9:30	**Banquet** *Columbus Convention Center* **Rev. Al Sharpton** Introduced by Marie Pierre, NY ACORN **Maude Hurd, ACORN National President** • **Report on Sherwin-Williams Actions** • **ACORN National Raffle Drawing** • **ACORN Awards** • **Recognition of Allies and Sponsors**

Exhibit 46: Annotated Agenda for ACORN 2006 Convention

	President Bill Clinton – video Introduced by Johnnie Pugh, AR ACORN
	Roseanne Barr Introduced by Vanessa Johnson Gueringer, LA ACORN
9:30 – 12:00	**Dance**
MONDAY 6:00	**Members drop luggage in dorm lobbies**
6:00 – 7:30	**Breakfast** 7:30-7:45 enter Mershon Auditorium
8:00 – 10:00	**Morning plenary** *Mershon Auditorium*

Welcome to Columbus
Columbus Mayor Michael Coleman (8:00-8:10)
Introduced by Donald Coulter, OH ACORN

The ACORN Precinct Action Leader (APAL) Program
(8:15 – 8:45)
- Maxine Nelson, ACORN National Secretary, Chair, ACORN Political Action Committee, AR ACORN
- Don Robinson, TX ACORN
- Pedro Rivas, NJ ACORN
- Ron Sykes, GA ACORN

Report on Sunday canvass: Toni Foulkes, IL ACORN
(8:50-8:55)

Guest Speakers:
- **Eliseo Medina, SEIU** (9:00-9:15)
  Introduced by Oneal Rayford, Secretary, SEIU Local 880, IL, and Ana Aguilar, CA ACORN
- **Sen Edward M. Kennedy – video (9:15-9:20)**
  Introduced by Allen Booth, MA ACORN
- **Sen. Hillary Clinton (9:30-10:00)**
  Introduced by Pat Boone, NY ACORN

Why we are marching: Julie Smith, OH ACORN
(10:00-10:05)

294 Nuts & Bolts – The ACORN Fundamentals of Organizing

Exhibit 46: Annotated Agenda for ACORN 2006 Convention

	Dismissal: Maude Hurd, ACORN National President 10:05: dismiss 10:10-11:10: load buses; each bus leaves as loaded 11:20: last buses arrive at march start 11:30: march begins 12:00: arrive at statehouse 12:10-1:00: rally 1:00: load buses
11:30 – 1:00	**March and rally: Raise the Minimum Wage!** **Rally Speakers:** **Mary Keith, OH ACORN, Master of ceremonies** • Rep. Stephanie Tubbs-Jones • OH House Minority Leader Joyce Beatty • Tim Burga, Ohio AFL-CIO • Others tba
1:00	**Load buses and head for home**

Looking at the agenda for other conventions over the years indicates the basic format was set for these "mass" meetings, as you can see from Exhibit 44 and the 2002 Chicago Convention early convention agenda draft.

Detroit 2008 Convention from back to leadership on stage.

Chapter XI: Conventions

Exhibit 47. Early Draft of Convention Agenda – ACORN Convention 2002 – Chicago

ACORN NATIONAL CONVENTION
Justice Now, Justice Always
Justicia Ahora, Justicia Siempre

June 29 – July 1, 2002

DRAFT AGENDA

Saturday, June 29

All Day	Members arrive Registration at dorms Tours and Dinner
8:00 – 10:00pm	**Members Speak-Out!**

Sunday, June 30

6:00 – 7:30	Breakfast
8:15 – 8:45	Worship Service
9:00 – 11:30	**Plenary Session**
9:00 – 9:20	Entrances/Roll-call of states and organizations
9:20 – 9:30	Invocation: Bishop John Williams, ACORN leader and Pastor of The New Shining Holiness Deliverance Church, Venice, IL
9:30 – 9:40	Welcome to Chicago: Rep. Jan Schakowsky
9:40 – 9:50	Greetings: Rev. Vitillo, Exec Director of CCHD
9:50 – 10:10	President's Address: Maude Hurd
10:10 – 10:20	Welcome to Chicago: Rep. Danny Davis
10:20 – 10:40	Tribute to Mrs. Somerville
10:40 – 11:00	Guest speaker: Anna Burger, Int'l Sec-Treas, SEIU
11:10 – 11:30	Guest speaker: Jim Hightower
11:30 – 1:00	Lunch
1:00 – 2:30	**Plenary Session**
1:10 – 1:30	Guest speaker: Rich Trumka, Sec-Treas, AFL-CIO
1:30 – 2:30	**ACORN's Campaign Against Predatory Lending** [Reports on the campaign; victim testimony; recognition of allies; prep for action]
2:30 – 4:30	**Taking Action Against Predatory Lending**
2:30 – 3:00	Load buses and roll
3:00 – 3:30	In transit

Exhibit 47. Early Draft of Convention Agenda – ACORN Convention 2002 – Chicago

3:30 – 4:15	March/action/speak out
4:15 – 5:00	Load buses/in transit back to dining halls
5:00 – 6:30	Dinner
7:30 – 9:00	**Workshops**
9:30 – 12:00	Dance/Party

Monday, July 1

6:00 – 7:30	Breakfast
9:00 – 10:15	**Plenary Session**
9:00 – 9:15	Report on Sunday actions/set-up for Fannie Mae
9:15 – 9:35	Guest speaker: Jamie Gorelick, Vice-Chair, Fannie Mae
9:35 – 9:50	Reports from ACORN leaders on immigrant issues
9:50 – 10:05	Guest speaker: Cecilia Munoz, La Raza
10:05 – 10:15	Prep for march
10:15 – 1:00	**March and Rally for Immigrant Rights**
10:15 – 10:30	Load buses and roll
10:30 – 11:00	In transit
11:00 – 11:15	March set-up
11:15 – 1:00	March/rally/action
1:00	**Box lunches and leave for home**

The tone of the Conventions was always and unsurprisingly set by the remarks that would open the convention by ACORN's elected president.

Each convention had a theme or slogan.

List of Conventions and Themes

1.	1978	Memphis	The People Speak
2.	1979	St. Louis	The People Decide
3.	1980	New York	The People Shall Rule
4.	1982	Philadelphia	Draw the Line
5.	1984	Dallas	Out the Door in 84
6.	1986	Washington, D.C.	Building People Power
7.	1988	Atlanta	Our Time Has Come
8.	1990	Chicago	Twenty for the Many
9.	1992	New York	Directions for a New Democracy
10.	1994	Washington, D.C.	Taking it to the Top
11.	1996	St. Louis	Fighting for the a Living Wage
12.	1998	Milwaukee	Welfare, Workfare, Unfair!
13.	2000	Philadelphia	Fighting for our Future
14.	2002	Chicago	Justice Now, Justice Always
15.	2004	Los Angeles	Count on Us
16.	2006	Columbus	Raising Our States
17.	2008	Detroit	Building Dreams Across America

ACORN Canada picked up the tradition and continued to expand it, as the organization grew larger, for its own membership as well as delegations from the USA and other countries affiliated with ACORN International. In Canada the issues were the emphasis rather than a particular overall theme, so focus tended to be on a major, unifying national and international campaign.

18.	2011	Ottawa	Remittance Justice
19.	2013	Toronto	Digital Divide
20.	2015	Montreal	Predatory Lending
21.	2017	Ottawa	Fair Banking-Stop Predatory Lending

A couple of the inaugural speeches during Maude Hurd's dozen years as president are good thumbnails of how she set the theme and got the crowd fired up and ready to go.

Here are her remarks from 2004 in Los Angeles:

PRESIDENT'S ADDRESS!

Good morning, ACORN!!!

Look at you – you are beautiful! And, you are mine!

More than 2000 strong from more than 30 states and 70 cities in the country – ACORN is indeed in the house!

A little more than a week ago, we have just celebrated ACORN's 34th anniversary. It has been 20 years since the ACORN Convention last ventured west when we camped on the banks of the Trinity River in Dallas during the Republican Convention in 1984 and could not stop Ronald Reagan from being re-elected. May he rest in peace, because he sure gave us none! It was hot, and we made it hotter. Some of you were there – you remember!

Now we have come all the way to the Pacific Ocean to celebrate the huge expansion over recent years of ACORN in California, Arizona, and all over the West. We've come a long way from Arkansas, baby!

But, we are all here now, and we are here and everywhere else in the country to serve notice that this time, just like last time, and any other time when things really matter – you can COUNT ON US!!!

Looking back, the world seems to have shifted since our last convention two years ago in Chicago, and ACORN has had to step up on every front to meet these challenges. Our members face a hostile federal government, robber-baron and predatory corporations, broke-ass cities, indifferent states, and an array of forces aligned against low and moderate income families.

Meeting these challenges and facing these threats has meant deep changes in ACORN. We have had to accelerate our growth to unparalleled levels, as we now approach organization in 70 cities in the United States. To meet the problem of devolution, we have had to deepen our base in large states - California, Florida, Ohio, Texas, and others -- to have enough weight to fight in a new class.

Responding to the crises of globalization, we now have offices in Lima, Peru, Vancouver, Canada, soon Toronto, Canada, all of which are coupled with major initiatives in Mexico and the Dominican Republic, where many of our members have deep roots and on-going responsibilities.

We are sharpening and focusing our resources to deal with corporate threats and profiteering practices. Where we are able to negotiate best practices, we are building partnerships. Where we find worse practices, we are digging in for the long struggle until these companies stop or are driven from the field. We have learned the lessons from Household, H&R Block, and others, and intend to put our new schooling into practice! We are creating alliances with others in order to build power deeper and broader in our communities. We are joining with unions in agreements to help drive support to working families. We are undertaking demonstration projects around EITC, remittances, housing developments, and other initiatives to find new ways to support our members. We are also in the fight of our life this election. We're not tired, we're BUSHED! But, the United States of ACORN in 2004 is not Florida in 2000 – we are united and we are clear – you can COUNT ON US!

We said with Project Vote that we would register 900000 new voters this year, but we won't. We have already done 450000, and we will do 1.2 million! AMERICA COUNT ON US!!!

We said we would raise $10,000,000 to bring in new voters, but we won't. We will raise $12,000,000! COUNT ON US!!!

We have committed to the largest Get out the Vote effort in our history and we are trying to raise $10,000,000 to pull our people out. We may not know how our members will vote, but we know they WILL vote – COUNT ON US!!

Once burned, twice learned – COUNT ON US!!

Our past 34 years are now history. Our best years are ahead of us. ACORN is muscling up and digging deeper. It's something we simply have to do. You can COUNT ON US!

ACORN President Maude Hurd speaking at Wells Fargo Action in Los Angeles.

And here she was again in Detroit 2008 in what turned out to be the last ACORN Convention in the United States at least so far.

<u>*Keynote Speech – President Maude Hurd*</u>
June 22, 2008

Hello, ACORN!   (pause)

And, hello, Michigan!   (pause for applause)

Look at all of us now!   (pause!)

Thanks for that welcome from our good friend……..

To (????) on behalf of all of ACORN, (*turn towards the introducer and face him/her*) I will promise you that we will not rest until we do everything possible to stop the march of foreclosures that are destroying homes, families, and communities throughout this state!   (pause)

I just can't help myself!   (pause)

Neither can 2000 of my brother and sister ACORN members! ACORN has come here to Michigan to do everything we can to stop foreclosures in this state. We have hit the streets, yelled at the top of our voices, sent our caravans and loudspeakers blaring, canvassed parking lots, grocery store lines, and, yes, liquor stores, petitioned, leafleted, hollered, and, even sweet talked about the mortgage and credit crises here.

A home should be our castle. That's one of the dreams that ACORN has been building. After decades of campaigns with banks, savings and loans, Wall Street, and even Congress trying to first move money into our communities through the Community Reinvestment Act, we were delighted to see the levels of home ownership rise over the last decade among lower income and working families and among African-American and Latino households. This was a dream come true!

Now though because of unchecked greed, fast dealing, no oversight and government inaction, we have seen almost all of that progress wiped out in front of our eyes in the two years since ACORN's last convention. The dream has become a nightmare!

We're going to keep raising the roof about this crisis and demanding justice, until all of our families are back safe and sound and walking through the front door again.

We have learned something in our 38 years of fighting for homes and communities, and we didn't forget the lesson.

The problem is that for years we have been learning these lessons by ourselves it seems. Foreclosures are a good example of the mess we are now in, but that is just one of many.

For the last 8 years while President Bush has been living the cowboy life in the White House war room, low and moderate income families and our communities in America have been suffering.

We need "regime change" in America! And, we need it now!

Foreclosure prevention is on our list, but that's not all.

How about healthcare? We need something that covers ALL AMERICANS and their families. I live in Massachusetts. The state is trying something there and it's better than nothing, but it's time that America set the standard in family and children's healthcare and took action. American health care protection is not just a city and state problem. It's a national issue. We need a government that understands that lesson. It's time for regime change in America!

How about education? The Bush program has meant that *all children are left behind.* It's time for regime change in America!

What about our cities? Community development used to mean that we saw investment in neighborhood improvement. Now, it seems this is just another developer subsidy. It's time for regime change in America.

There's no end to our list: rising food prices, fuel and gas prices going through the roof, utility bills soaring, immigrants being abused, and recession seems everywhere we look. Why? Who is learning these lessons? How can we get relief? It's time for regime change in America.

Two years ago in Columbus, Ohio, I stood before you and asked what we had learned from Katrina and the failure to rebuild New Orleans. I asked you and anyone in the sound of my voice how many more cities would have to be destroyed before we found a government that would care and act. Now three years after Katrina, we all know that the only hope for New Orleans and all of us is change. It's time for regime change in America now!

Once upon a time, we had a federal government. There once was a place we could go to do this all at once. Remember, it was called congress. Now, it's just us, ACORN and our allies, fighting for justice.

It's time for regime change!

We're trying to teach a lesson to our elected representatives. We're not sure if they are going to learn it or have to get new jobs. ACORN, you know what I'm talking about!

We have to have a government that cares, that is accountable, and that protects the common good.

ACORN is on the move and it's good to have all of us come together. We do this every two years: share ideas, mourn our losses, and recommit to our struggles. ACORN is bigger and better than we were 2 years ago, and we will be even bigger and better in another 2 years, and 2 years after that, and 2 years after that, and so on and on and on. We won't stop until we win, and victory is not yet in sight!

Mark my words, brothers and sisters. We have big shoulders and we're taking on big fights around the country. We may not win them all, but if they beat us, they will have to whip us first. We are going to fight until we win -- whether its wages or housing or education or urban renewal or stopping predatory lending or bank accountability or immigration rights or voting rights. We will defend our members! We will win for our members!

Come on ACORN, stay with me this weekend, and come ready to fight and win – mark your calendars and commit to work to get every low and moderate income voter to the polls this November. Let's hit the streets and the ballot box.

Our time is now, and now is time for regime change!

The organization grew exponentially during those few years so that both our reach and our grasp had extended, but the basic skeleton of the meeting's management was hard set. ACORN knew where it could both achieve membership success and present strength and power in this framework.

But of course, nothing is perfect and there's always room for improvement, which is part of the fundamental nuts and bolts of all organizing methodology. Following every convention there were lessons learned, both large and small. After the St. Louis Convention in 1996 when several people, including myself, were "picked off" and arrested by the police around the Marriott, and there was difficulty mopping up the actions with busses moving out to home on a rigid schedule while ACORN attorney's and volunteer local lawyers, like St. Louis-based labor lawyer, Art Martin, tried to get people out of jail. We realized that we needed what I referred to as a "cleaner," after the character played by Harvey Kietel in the movie, *Point of No Return*. Someone who at the end of every convention would be assigned to "clean everything down to the nap." It might be things infinitesimally small, like a lost-and-found or more important like making sure someone was sprung from jail and had transport home, but having someone assigned was a lesson learned and from then on important for the overall flow and ease of the convention.

Experience teaches that the best time to make these lists and start remembering for the next time is immediately after the event. Thinking about big meetings and conventions, we'll end with the real-time "rough notes" at the end of the Los Angeles Convention in 2004.

Exhibit 48: Post-Convention Follow-up

MEMORANDUM

July 1, 2004

To: Steve, Carolyn, Helene, and Kevin

Fr: Wade

Re: Random Convention Thoughts for Next Time

Well, we survived another convention – let's hope everyone else will!

Before senility catches up, I wanted to share some random thoughts so that we have these notes for next time, as we continue to try to perfect these efforts around the convention.

1. I think Pittsburgh or someplace in Ohio (Cincinnati or Cleveland or Columbus) are the best prospects for the 2006 convention.
2. I think putting the staff up in the balcony was not a win, and, if we are going to do a banquet in the future, which I'm betting we will do forever now, we need to figure out a way to get everyone on the floor. Additionally, from the balcony one could see the number of empty seats, and they were plentiful, so it's unclear how we served our interest.

3. My god these introductions are too, too long. First, we need to take control of all of them – even if they are written outside, we need an editor to cut them down to 5 sentences or so.
4. The banquet program was way, way too long – 7:40 to 9:20 – kill me next time!!! I think 45-60 minutes is the way outside!!!
5. We have to make sure that ANY of the actions or marches are led by an ACORN Banner. It's ridiculous that we would put more than more than 1000 folks behind a NY banner or any state banner. An assignment for an action is not an opportunity to be off message.
6. We have to remind everyone repeatedly that the ACORN colors are red, black, and white – we need to start doing this 90-120 days out from the convention so that we don't have this number of mess-ups. Particular attention to CA, OR, and MN. Not sure if there were others off program or not.
7. Any staff with a direct role for a major action has to be on program.
8. We have to get control of line organizing staff on large actions. I had a young organizer from Chicago that I finally had to remove to the crowd, because the fool kept trying to move the march line over to the sidewalk on Monday, and thought he had some implicit approval to do so, because he was allowed up front for no apparent reason.
9. We need to make it a priority to update the web and sent out email bulletins to our e-list on every day of the convention. We really dropped the ball on pushing the excitement out on this. And, to the degree we try to make it all "press friendly" – they could not move on this either.
10. We need to figure out a way to copy out the press for the delegates like we used to do – the pics in the latimes were great, but we had no way to take advantage of them.
11. Water problem – still don't know how we missed signal there on water placement for the march – dropped piece on my part.
12. There was some random conversation, and I had a more specific conversation with Jon, that with other shared cost going down, and the costs of the convention continuing to soar, we need to offer states the option of putting aside 1% of gross or something along these lines to a convention account for 2006 and beyond. I think that makes good sense. People just can't get on top of all of this!
13. Lost opportunity – it killed me to read the latimes in the airport and realize that Clinton was in la the first day of our convention doing a book signing. We could have had him @ ulca!
14. UCLA sets a new standard in cost, but also in organization and support – the rooms were good, now if they can just flatten everything next time….
15. Carolyn, I actually want to set up a staff side convention planning team a year out of the next convention, so that we have more involvement at every level on all of this. Let's remember!

As soon as I send this, I'll think of more, but I wanted to get some quick items out there as grist for our mill in planning for next time.

Great job!

Chapter XII: **Where do Issues Go? Campaigns!**

From the first time an organizer meets a prospective member and begins to listen and talk, the trickle begins and quickly turns into a raging torrent of issues. Some of them are petty annoyances while others are longstanding and deep seated grievances that can date back decades. Some speak of grave injustices of equity, race, gender, and income involving discrimination, indifference, and systemic fault and failure. Others lack voice and only speak in the language of shared frustration and some level of pain. Some issues are as immediate as the pothole in the street, the water lapping from the sewer, the dogs barking in the night, and the weeded lot down the street, while others are the stuff of visions and dreams of wholesale renovation and rebuilding.

Organizing is often a translation into language of issues that seek focus and form. Issues frequently find definition in organizational campaigns and action, as organizers and leaders transform anger into action. I have defined this process of an organizer listening for issues for almost 50 years as learning to walk with one eye fixed on the ground in front of you, and the other eye constantly searching the clouds ahead of you. Saul Alinsky memorably defined issues as needing to be "specific, immediate, and realizable," so I had better be a little clearer about this "clouds" thing before confusion sets in to deeply.

Alinsky's dicta here is instructive, though like much of his work, he was trying as much to make a point as create a definition, and he was providing literally a community service by taking issues out of the "pie in the sky" realm where too many of them were soaring aimlessly. Some of the people, at least people who we organize, think in concrete, specific, "scratch where it itches" terms. They are, for the most part, not prone to sweeping prognostications about what might be fine in the future, because they are trying in the main to make it today as best they can. Alinsky was rhetorically jabbing at the left, while worrying about the left-out. At the local level when one begins the organizing process, his prescription still stands the test of time, and even if it is neither totally accurate nor absolutely complete, it still works as a rule of thumb. None of that is to say that these were the only issues or that issues that were not immediately winnable were ignored or discarded, but in the pile of issues confronting the membership, they were sifted and curated in a process that balanced short term gains with longer and more difficult campaigns.

We would find this tellingly in 1977-78 in ACORN as we tried to put together a membership process to develop our "ACORN Peoples' Platform,"[88] as I cannot seem to tire of retelling because of the power of the lesson it taught. When we first began having the conversations at the local group level of what the members believed should be the successful outcome of their vision on issues, the most common response was either

---

[88] Described at length in Gary Delgado's book, *Organizing the Movement: The Roots and Growth of ACORN* (1986)

profound silence or the continuation of more endless conversations about immediate concerns. It was very difficult for people to imagine how things would be, *if they had the power to create the changes,* because the experience of either power or change was largely unknown. It took a lot of meetings over many months and a process of pushing them from the local level to the regional, state, and national for members to begin to learn how to think differently, as if they had the power, and start to really imagine how change would work, and envision what it would look like in program and policy. When they got there it was exhilarating, but the journey from the specific to the general was not easy nor from the immediate to the visionary, partially because we had to suspend the notion of the "realizable," and having suspended disbelief as well, allow people to embrace dreams.

When not involved in a mammoth internal exercise such as the platform process, issues move from the simple to the more complex through campaigns designed to resolve the issues. Issues rise and fall on many grounds, but central to their effectiveness are two overwhelming characteristics: (1) do people care enough about the issue to "vote with their feet" and take the necessary actions to resolve the issue, and (2) does the issue build the organization? Superficially, the casual observer or rookie practitioner might think that the second concern is automatically resolved by the first priority, and frequently, but not always, that is the case. There are some issues where a small number of people might in fact be willing to move forward, but the concern is so tangential that in fact the organization could be marginalized and disempowered, particularly in the initial stages of growth and development where multiple judgments abound at every level and the testing is intense.

The best examples of issues that may not be fatal, but still do not build the organization commonly fall in the "truth to power" category. I have sat through a number of top leadership meetings in ACORN and in Local 100 where controversial issues of the day were extensively debated from giving away the Panama Canal to opposing the war in Iraq to public positions for or against abortion, as discussed earlier. In each case the leadership has argued that personal points of view were secondary to organizational interest, particularly if they felt the issue was both divisive throughout the entire membership or inconsequential in terms of core organizational positions on which the membership had frequently expressed itself. Within our leadership there was a tremendous distrust around what are perceived as "externally" driven issues and agendas, and a suspicion about organizations that lacked an independent base but sought to pull our organizations into a position of serving as their constituency.

There are also issues that may be important and are essential in requiring organizational action, but often are organizationally difficult because of the huge challenges they pose in stabilizing constituency and in sustainability. Some years ago, I was involved in an advanced organizer training outside of Los Angeles and in an "open mic" section the head organizer from Broward County, Florida raised the question of how to service and stabilize a group of migrant farm workers, who a predecessor organizer had assisted in organizing. Answering more questions from the group it turned out that of the original members less than 15 were still in camp, that the camp was 50 miles away on the other side of the county, and that the office was inadequately staffed to be able to provide real support at that distance. It was always next to impossible for us to say "no," but in this situation there was also no plan for building real power in this local group that was transient by definition. Did migrant farm workers need an organization? Absolutely! Could ACORN do the job on this basis? No! I suspect someone's liberalism or perhaps adventurism had gotten us caught in this situation which could only disappoint the constituency and siphon off resources and capacity from the core base of the organization. The problem was more complex than the organizer might have hoped, because we could not answer the threshold question of whether or not this group and the set of issues that concern them would in fact build organization and therefore power, and if that test cannot be passed, then it is not a job we can manage.

Tenant issues and groups can be another example of an important constituency with critical issues, but nonetheless a group that provides huge organizational challenges to service, stabilize, and make sustainable. The critique about building movement through mobilization versus building stable, permanent organization is especially relevant in this context, unless the organization has an exceptionally good servicing program. To some degree we were able to make this leap because of our bank draft system, which moved with the member as they moved, and a better reliance on cell phone technology and email for communication. In Toronto, where the ACORN Canada organizational base was disproportionately located in the many massive tenant based housing complexes that sprawl throughout the city, we have developed a way to move with the member-tenants to organize the new buildings as they moved from one to another, and tenancy is more common and semi-permanent as a residential choice for families. We have also found tenant-based issues dominating in Rome, Edinburgh, Paris, Grenoble, and Bristol so we are not dogmatic on this point, simply stating the experience in many cities that lower income housing is dominated by transient living arrangement provides an organizing challenge, and we embrace that challenge and its opportunity. As public or social housing also declines in many countries and home ownership is an improbable quest, the need and demand for strong tenants organizations will be paramount for ACORN and our constituency in the future growth of the organization.

There are a million issues our constituency feels strongly and deeply about, but no organization can be equally proficient in handling every issue, no organization can engage them simultaneously, and not all of these issues will build the organization or be able to be successfully engaged. Therefore there is a constant dialectic between organizational planning and implementation and membership desires and democracy which has to filter the issues and place them in the queue for action and work. None of this is easy, but all of it is important.

There are a couple of things we need to explore.

First, given how complex the process is, how is it possible that the members are able to drive the program?

Secondly, how do we get past the Alinsky premise and engage issues more deeply and at the level of more fundamental change.

Thirdly, how can we represent and advocate from the base as well as engage and activate the base.

Members at the Wheel of Issues

Voting with your feet is a powerful democratic manifestation, particularly within a mass organization. We believe in the old-fashioned raising of hands and marking of ballots as well, but in some ways internally this is less powerful than the way we count heads at an action or count bottoms in chairs at a meeting about the issues.

We do vote. We vote on a menu of issues in order to prioritize them at the very first meeting of a newly organized local group and at subsequent meetings as well. We vote on issues at the city board level, when the issue rises to that level, and make sure that all of the affiliated organizations in the city have had their say, bartered back and forth, and are ready to move. We do the same thing at a state or provincial level and national level, though less frequently given when those bodies convene. Every two even-numbered years in the United States, we tested the major national campaigns at a national convention with thousands of ACORN delegates from around the country. Every odd-numbered year in ACORN Canada. ACORN United Kingdom now envisions an annual convention, and ACORN India with huge distances and more limited resources has yet to resolve this issue.

Every month, we count the members who are active in meetings and actions around issues. There is a shared report. There is also a campaign report prepared by the research department that catalogued all of the issues and campaigns underway from month to month, quarter to quarter, so that we could monitor the more than 100 offices in the USA and elsewhere and see the trends of major campaigns and their developments and correlate it back to the real activity. In this way we were able to count how many "feet" are voting, and make assessments and adjustments accordingly.

We have made strides to get a better picture of activity that comes with scale. ACORN Canada has a database that allows us to track issues raised by members on the doors, enter them in the database, and respond accordingly. Using these tools we are able to communicate more effectively and target our campaign messages with our members more accurately, but also using the database analytics literally "count the votes" on how various groups of our members line up in their ranking of the many issues in their neighborhood. The age old "seat of the pants" guesswork by the organizers is in effect being substituted by more accurate assessments of actual membership and community input. We also do this with autodialers in many offices. Using robodialers, the newer issues with will become more apparent as they dominate more and the demand to reach even large constituencies is more challenging.

Put it all together and we can be pretty sure we know, democratically, where the majority of our members stand, and what they are willing to do. Putting together the plans and the campaigns is another matter of course.

Self-interest versus Expectations

One problem in the articulation of issues as simply driven by self-interest of individuals is that it too narrowly defines how people really think and what really motivates their activity in organizations and around issues. Forty years ago I used to express this difference as the way that immediate self-interest was offset for many members and leaders by their expectations. By expectations I meant their aspirations and hopes for the future which for many were as powerful, if not more so, than their more individual motivations. None of these words were really adequate to describe the phenomena an organizer sees so frequently that it cannot be ignored, that often some of our people, particularly leaders, who are most active on an issue, in fact have the least self-interest in the resolution. Many are motivated by feelings of solidarity, common experience in the past, a view of what they think is best or most moral or most important to others, and any number of other social, political, class, and even religious motivations that are broader than narrow self-interest can express, but are equally valid, and perhaps even more sustainable for their long term participation. There is probably a better word. Let's hope we find it! In the meantime let's just try to understand how people think and then move.

This notion came early to me because though I began as an organizer believing absolutely and parroting self-interest as the primal motivating force, it did not explain why some people did the things that they did. Simone St. Jacque, a white Springfield WRO leader who lived on the largely African-American "Hill," claimed she had virtually nothing to gain from participation in welfare rights and in some ways it clearly was unnatural for her, but she did so because she simply could not get around the fact she felt she had been dealt a bad hand by a bad man and that divorce should not come with the punishment of poverty. Other leaders were fearless and tireless advocates on different issues even though they had no stake in the issue personally. Were they simply trying to win a place in the community, reconcile their own self-respect, be good neighbors, or what? Perhaps one could argue that these things were self-directed and therefore self-interested, but I swear to god some things just have to be the way they seem, and many of these leaders wanted what was best for everyone and not simply something for themselves. Whatever the concept, it needs to be broad enough to cover the entire range of motivations that make up the complex people that we all are and therefore make up our organizations.

Don't Stop – Go!

Hopefully, this detour helps explain how we are able to deepen the campaigns around particular issues and get past the classic stop signs in the neighborhood or the most immediate, specific, and realizable grievance that presents itself at a community meeting. Alinsky's point was really more than anything else that one cannot build organization by losing, and therefore picking issues in the beginning that are uber-realistic allows the organization to potentially begin its life with a winning record and translate the success into the first building block of power. My point in equally simplistic terms is that one constructs engagement not from self-interest or the simple delivery of goods and services of organizational exchange but by offering members *the right to fight* through an organization. Social scientists might speak of this as "agency" or the organizational provision of "voice." In fact listening to organizer's "raps" at a training session I heard a young organizer in Mesa, Arizona, talk about how he had amended the basic rap in middle-income suburban turf (Mesa after all!) by taking out the word "fight" and substituting the concept of joining to have "a voice in the way the city is run." Whatever. Same, same!

We can prove categorically that people will join on the sole basis of seeking the right to fight or the ability to have a voice and frequently they will attach their own meaning and issues to this architecture later, once they are inside the organization and already defining themselves as part of the membership and paying dues. Perhaps the modern sense of isolation and anomie is moving people to join simply based on the direct invitation. Perhaps the act of joining itself satisfies the search for social ties and networks where none exist in many contemporary settings?

Either way, these deepening commitments have pushed the boundaries of organizing and issues past simple frameworks to allow organizations to engage issues in more and more extensive, enduring, and complex campaigns and subsequently win victories that were incalculable in earlier expressions of community organization. Such work has also continued to lead direct action organizations like ACORN past normal boundaries and limits into larger and larger campaigns and into a broader range of projects from the provision of services to programs increasing long-term sustainability in addition to the standard repertoire of our work.

An excellent example in ACORN's history can be found with the experience with lending (our members want loans) and the financial institutions that provide the money (and are not *giving* the money to our members.) These issues began in the simple discovery in the 1970's of the long term disinvestment in our communities. Members – and often their children – could not get loans to repair houses or to buy houses in the neighborhoods. Disinvestment and racial discrimination led to block-busting as real estate interests flipped neighborhoods for their own profit. Deteriorating communities were cash starved for investment in improvements dividing families that did not have the means to flee from families that did not have the means to flee versus families that tried to outrun the rising tide.

A good example might be the evolution of ACORN's work on housing from the first simple campaigns in Little Rock, when we would put signs up in front of houses saying "This house is NOT FOR SALE" in some neighborhoods and in other areas where hundreds of members would tie red ribbons and streamers around bank branches demanding an end to "redlining" (refusing to loan in certain neighborhoods), to decades of work in more sophisticated direct housing development and partnerships with banks to assure best practice lending standards to campaigns that have targeted newly emerging predatory practices from sub-prime lenders, cash outlets, pay-day lenders, and other targets, many of whom are among the largest companies in the world. Issue campaigns are building blocks that begin at the bottom and stack their way steadily to the top.

We Like it Here House is Not for Sale.

Representing

An evolution worth noting has been the changing organizational role around certain issues involving long-term campaigns where members, leaders, and the organization itself developed deepening capacity and expertise in specific areas. Certainly the financial area was one such example, but I could also cite other issues like living wages, neighborhood policy questions, and a slew of others where ACORN became a voice for its constituency of low and moderate income families virtually independent of individual membership activity. Indeed this was a collective voice legitimized by decades of actions, but advocacy is still inherently different than direct action and membership activism.

Advocacy troubles organizers and organizations. It is the first resort and easy lure of the lazy, whether the wannabe "advocate" or the complicit (and equally lazy!) reporter. In a hotel some years ago I remember picking up a *USA Today* left in the way of these papers in front of the door and seeing an article that caught my eye about the evils of RAL's – refund anticipation loans – which had been a multi-year focus of huge ACORN campaigns against the largest tax preparers in the US and the banks that are behind them and pushing these drugs to the financially desperate. Some fellow, unknown to me, had simply shown up with a smile at the annual meeting of one of the preparers and said that RAL's were evil – end of work and weaponry – and managed to garner a headline for his casual labor. The grant proposal no doubt followed right behind and was already in the mail!

Was I touchy simply because that might have been press ACORN more rightly deserved? Actually, no! Press comes and goes, and if an organization lives by it, the organization will also die from it. More disturbing to me is that the freelance advocate was accountable to no one in any way, shape, or form, and therefore was the most susceptible (and as experience serves) and most easily bought and co-opted, making our campaigns that much harder and the companies that much more resistant to serious settlements and reform.

We have created an entire cottage industry for "middle-man" and brokering operations to sell hygienic, sanitary services to dirty companies trying to whitewash bad practices. Some operate by providing cover for fair housing and racial discrimination. Others come in on lucrative contracts to "claim" that practices are something opposite of what they are. Even when these folks are well intentioned, their lack of accountability alone means that they can cut deals willy-nilly without a second thought to how people are really affected in any final analysis. Many of the large scale environmental organizations could serve as case studies for the disasters that come with such unaccountability.

The irony of the work becomes that we are forced to "represent" and "advocate" in many areas for our broad constituency in addition to our specific membership in order to protect and advance their interests, so it rankles to find that there is often such a small degree of difference accorded to mass organization and real people as opposed to the Lone Rangers.[89]

---

[89] Not to be confused with the ACORN members in the Twin Cities of Minneapolis-St. Paul who were victims of predatory loans and build a very strong ACORN group which they famously called the ACORN Loan Rangers!

Chapter XII: Where do Issues Go? Campaigns!

Chapter XIII: **Strategy and Tactics**

There is no way to reduce the work to a simple formula, but a good way to contemplate strategy and tactics is that strategy is the way we *think* about making the plan for victory in organization building and issue campaigns, and tactics are the way we *act* on those plans.

Gene Sharp, one of the most prominent contemporary advocates and philosophers of nonviolent tactics produced a well-known list of almost two hundred possible nonviolent tactics,[90] and there is little doubt that the list could have been even longer. The overall point that Sharp was really making through this exhausting exercise was that organizers and activists almost always have a wide selection of potential tactics before they are forced to resort to violence, but obviously some forms of violence are also tactical inserts in some organizing and political strategies, so once again as I have argued previously, "there's no substitute for good judgment." The other point that Sharp's list or any other serious thinking about tactics immediately brings to mind is that there are endless variations of potential tactics that might be appropriate depending on the strategy involved and the overall objectives of the organization or the specific campaign.

Some of the more notorious community organizing tactics are those highlighted by Saul Alinsky in his books, Rules for Radicals and Reville for Radicals, when he talks about loading buses to the opera full of folks having eaten beans or crowding into all of the bathrooms at Chicago O'Hare Airport.[91] Virtually everyone can recall the tactic, while few can remember the issue or strategy that the tactic was supposed to advance, which is good evidence of the fact that Alinsky was probably more invested in the story than the factual history involved in any of those events. The best tactics are those that most effectively fit the strategy of the campaign or the organization. Neither of those were good examples of either and both would have been difficult to get real people to actually do them, and of course in the 21st century the airport idea would be impossible to contemplate.

Add to all of these organizing challenges the fact that times "they are a changing." Petitioning and the right to petition governments for change has been a tactical option for several hundred, if not thousand, years which is partially why it is memorialized in the English charter and the fundamental rights won in the American Revolution. Organizers in the late 20th century would scoff at the notion that a petition could be much more than a tactical placeholder in any campaign, yet suddenly, and somewhat dramatically, in the early 21st century fascination with the potential, even if still unproven, of social networking, internet-based petitions are more common than weeds along the rows of our political fields. Even more surprisingly, some turn out to even be effective, and under any reckoning the whole exercise and practice of internet petitioning has altered the landscape that defines petitions in the same way that civil disobedience altered the landscape of

[90] Gene Sharp, http://www.aeinstein.org/nonviolentaction/198-methods-of-nonviolent-action/
[91] "Playboy Interview: Saul Alinsky". Playboy Magazine. March 1972.

race when utilized aggressively by the civil rights movement. Tactics evolve over time and some, the best of them, can adapt to changing situations.

Similarly, tactics like encampments have had a role in the United States and some other countries for more than one-hundred years. In the organizing of the Farmers' Alliance in Texas and other states that drove the populist movement, encampments brought thousands together from farms and country towns to talk, visit, strategize, socialize, hear speeches, and commit to the kinds of actions and work that built the movement. In ACORN we used the tactic in 1982 at our 35-city "Reagan Ranches," as we called them, and again in Dallas in 1984 along the river a short hike from the Republican National Convention, to protest President Ronald Reagan's rending of the social safety net. Dug in encampments by members of the Muslim Brotherhood in city squares in Cairo in protest of the army's removal of President Morsi, a former Brotherhood leader, were so extensive that the public squares were bricked and sandbagged as if they were small urban communities. Of course encampments became the tactic that defined the "Occupy" movement from Wall Street to cities around the country and the world so thoroughly that the power of the tactic devoured any other strategy that might have been intended by the movement.

The challenge of all strategies and tactics is the need for flexibility to continually adapt to the changing circumstances and politics in the give-and-take of campaigns and the ups-and-downs of organization building. In this sense nothing is so dialectical as the constant ebb and flow of strategic and tactical selection and development.

Yet, perhaps not surprisingly, since simple tactics are easier to learn and duplicate than the constantly shifting sands of sophisticated strategy, it is not uncommon that the very repetition that can make such tactics effective and universal, also often overwhelm movements and organizations themselves. Unfortunately, even the best tactics have a half-life of effectiveness that saps their strength given constant repetition. Eventually, the

Gene Sharp.

impact on the public is blunted. Invariably, the target also learns to adapt to the tactic and absorb its strength, rendering what was powerful, impotent. At one point sit-ins were dramatic and game changing in the 1960s, but by the end of the 1970's a sit-in on jobs at a mayor's office in New Orleans or HUD in Dallas would lead to cokes, cookies, and an unexpected overnight stay, rather than a change in position.

Not only does a strategy normally need a diverse set of tactics to be effective, and, yes, they can be wonderfully creative and imaginative and not simply scatological in the Alinsky examples, but the tactics need to be appropriate to the target. In training sessions I used to talk about not using an elephant gun to kill a squirrel despite the realization that few organizers in the room had seen or done either, including myself, but they got the message. The point was all about the need to tailor the tactic to the target. Some targets are more accessible than others and the organizations resources are mismatched to the size, scale, and power of the target. In Montana working with groups of farmers and ranchers taking on a strip mining and giant power companies, I advised for example that they hit the meter readers who were accessible to them since they could not get to the CEO's that were out of range and often in other states. That is a strategic point, but it blends into tactical selection when one considers "how" to hit the meter reader. Where a hundred or a thousand people sitting in at the office of an energy company CEO might be a tactical

Reagan Ranch.

consideration, such a sit-in or demonstration on a working stiff, meter reader would seem way out of proportion, no matter how important the issue or campaign. In a campaign to try to stop construction of the world's largest coal-fired plant in the early 1970's in Arkansas, we took 25 farmers from the eastern side of the River into an Entergy (then Arkansas Power & Light) office in Stuttgart, Arkansas to demand an explanation of how their families and farms were going to be protected from coal dust effluent downwind, and the company was outflanked because they had just *assumed* the farmers would believe any story they spun about the beefits of sulfur as free fertilizer, and of course the press went wild with glee at the juxtaposition of these so-called red-necked farmers demonstrating and demanding.

The other tactical consideration for an organizer looking at appropriateness is whether or not the members will feel comfortable actually implementing the tactic. People "vote with their feet" when it comes to joining an action. Organizing can make a difference on turnout when it comes to visits, calls, and reminder calls, and a dedicated group of "regulars" (members who will come to anything and everything, god love them) or "day-timers" (members who, based on work schedules or lack of work schedules, are available during the day, which is a precious commodity) is essential in building an organization, but when the tactic and its objectives are not clear or it seems embarrassing to some people or too militant or strident for the situation or at the "wrong" stage of the campaign or just not important or worthwhile to justify their time and trouble, no amount of organizing can put people on the bus or in the street. Or, worse, make them happier or stronger when they get back on the bus after it is all said and done.

As a young organizer at MWRO, I ended up having to organize two actions in the early spring of 1970, one on Massachusetts Governor Francis Sargent's "flat grant" for welfare recipients and another targeting U.S. House Speaker John McCormick over issues around the expansion of the Viet Nam War. On the flat grant because it was hurting our members and in many ways pushing it back was life or death for the organization, and on the war because it was important to the national organization's relationships and alliance building in Washington, D.C. in advancing the adequate income campaign, and my instructions from George Wiley and the national leadership were to hit them as hard as we could.

We sussed out that Sargent was speaking to a group one winter evening at the stately Shoreham Hotel in downtown Boston. We purchased a table inside the event scheduled in a banquet hall on the mezzanine level of this grand, old, fancy Boston hotel. We planted several organizers and leaders inside and their job was to make sure the doors were open if we were able to get our people into the hotel, and of course that was the hardest part of the action. At least the action was at night, so we were able to get somewhere between one-hundred fifty and two-hundred of our members on the buses. The strategy was to chant and picket on the outside of the hotel and have our folks inside disrupt at some point, and if we got lucky, had the will, and found the way, we would get everyone into the hotel and make as much mayhem and mess as we could put together to support them. From the unloading point, signs in hand, chanting to the night sky, we made it round the building. As we came up to a bank of revolving entry doors, I pulled ahead of the column of marchers by a couple of strides and rolled from door to door as if I were back on my high school football team, rolling off of one block after another, testing and turning the knobs, until to my shock and surprise, the third or fourth door turned and opened, and I crashed through, signaling the column to follow at which point the lead marchers broke and ran for the door, and before the hotel could react within no time we had virtually everyone in the hotel chanting in the lobby and looking for the stairs to the mezzanine. Memory dims, but I think we got no more than fifty folks up the stairway before we were effectively rebuffed. The table inside had moved a bit too quickly and were as quickly ushered out of the banquet after a brief confusion, and from the lobby and the hallway in front of the banquet we rallied and let out a mighty roar of protest against the flat grant proposal. When the police arrived *en masse* with threats of arrest, we eventually left pumped with adrenaline from the experience.

The McCormick action was roughly the same, though not at night, and instead occurred at a federal office building with about one-hundred fifty folks, though in that instance disproportionately Puerto Rican with many monolingual. We were fortunate to get into the lobby with some few moving up the elevators to the locked door of the Speaker's Congressional field office. Though it was during a recess, he was certainly not there, nor had we expected him to be there. A small press item in the *Herald* and the *Globe* was about all the leverage it bought for NWRO in Washington. On the other hand it was clear to me that many, if not most, of the members at the anti-war action had no clue what we were doing there or what we might have hoped to accomplish, if anything. They were there because of organizational loyalty. It was fun and exciting to a certain degree to some perhaps, but otherwise made little sense to them or to me. I vowed to myself I would never be part of another action where the members were simply "troops," and fodder for maneuvers far afield.

Though there were no arrests or attendant problems, the old guard welfare rights leadership used both of these actions, though they were not there, as prime examples of what they called "Rackley's suicide actions" in the words of South End welfare rights leader Ruth Barkley in order to paint me and the organizing staff as "other," adventuresome, reckless, and perhaps dangerous to the membership. Lessons abound, and whether I agreed with the assessment or not, and certainly I did not, at twenty-one years old, I learned lifetime, career altering lessons about how to present and test the appropriateness of tactics within overall organizational strategy.

It is axiomatic that members want to enjoy the actions and have fun at them. It is equally clear that they do not want to be arrested without some advance notice or warning that it might be coming. Sometimes organizers cannot predict these things, or perhaps we can, but don't. As I write this I am thinking of three examples from ACORN national conventions where there were arrests in Philadelphia 1982, Chicago in 1990, and St. Louis in 1996, all of which are informative in understanding both the organizing tactics and the police tactics which often are the other part of the equation. Though I've mentioned some of these events earlier, let me go into them in more detail to pound the lesson home.

In Philadelphia as we tried to push the Democratic Party to concede to our demands around low income representation, in two different circumstances we targeted state delegations where we knew their hotel arrangements and where our members from particular states present at the ACORN convention could also burst in and confront

members of their own state delegations to agree to our demands. In New York City in 1980 the strategy and the tactic had worked reasonably well with some state delegations pledging to support the demand for low income representation and even in the wildly fancy – and accessible -- hotels of Manhattan, we found no problem getting into the hotels or out of them in terms of police or arrests, once the action had run its course. Philadelphia was an entirely different situation. In Philadelphia the strategy was much the same as in New York, map and mark the state delegations, detach action groups of various numbers depending on the size of the delegation, and seek to engage as many of the party convention delegations as possible with ACORN members from their states. Once again the hotels had been scouted, groups were properly staffed, including with voluntary lawyers, and the tactic was a soft, "meet-and-greet" style action. Furthermore in Philadelphia we had typically had constructive working relationships with the Civil Disobedience Squad, so it was a surprise when varying, random reports began to come in of arrests of organizers and leaders at some of the hotels. The total of arrests was less than a dozen, but since arrests had not been part of the tactical planning, there were delays in some ACORN delegations returning home and all manner of last minute logistical and even financial issues in arranging bail, waiting out the arraignment, and closing out the basic convention staffing.

Why did Philadelphia, where we had a deep base and long experience, turn out so much differently in 1982 than New York City in 1980 where at least at the time, we had not yet begun to organize significantly? In retrospect the action was perhaps too dispersed in Philly, whereas in New York City we were steadily focused on hitting big Manhattan, largely luxury hotels, and the array of locations and the range of sophistication of the hotels in Philly was much more diverse. The arrests tended not to be at the larger, fancier hotels, but at the smaller more remote properties. The local management was perhaps less sophisticated and pulled the trigger on calling the police much more quickly than the more battle hardened New Yorkers. In a majority of the arrests the police actions were immediate and without warning. The police were from different districts and outside of the Civil Disobedience unit which normally only handled the Center City hotel actions, which went off calmly for the most part. This was one of those exceptional situations in which we overestimated the police! In some of the cases where we had people arrested the ratio of our members to the size of the delegation was not as robust as New York either, which may have also hastened the arrests. Finally, I cannot discount the fact that in repeating the 1980 tactic in 1982, that may have allowed more preparation by Democratic state delegations who may have made prior decisions, that if there were the least hints of an action or disruption, "arrest first, ask later."

Civil disobedience squads are a factor in some larger cities worth reckoning with in different ways. In the summer of 1978 in a jobs march and action that terminated around City Hall with the statue of William Penn looking down on us, more than a thousand largely African-American teenagers had marched from the Quaker headquarters to demand summer jobs from then Mayor Frank Rizzo. In that instance I was picked off along with another organizer nearby on a police strategy akin to trying to cut the head off the snake, but other than holding me against a wall for 30 minutes or so, there was clearly no real interest by the unit in keeping me and a volunteer lawyer yelling in the captain's ear was more than enough to spring me and my buddy[92] away in no time.

---

[92]   Bert DeLeeuw

In Chicago 1990 we had one organizer[93] picked off during the march through the financial district solely as a police maneuver as they treied to establish the dominance of their horses and keep us from taking the street, rather than the sidewalk, as we were determined to do, and eventually did do. Later they picked off former ACORN President Elena Hanggi while she was speaking from the middle median to the crowd waiting in front of the office building we had targeted. Another Chicago police effort to send a message about control to the crowd by taking a leader. Though a bit of a nuisance for Craig Robbins and Hanggi, these were tactically appropriate signals between the organization and the police in the silent communications of social change, which did not alter any tactical consideration by either party, but probed the organization and the resistance of the state, kept both parties at the asphalt of the action in a funny balance of forces with complete understanding of each other.

St. Louis was the best and worst of both kinds of tactical probes in actions. We were marching the entire convention delegation through downtown St. Louis along one lane of the street in 1996. The demand was for "first source" hiring for jobs from Marriott Hotel, which we had been pressing in several cities before the convention. The march was loud and orderly, but was clearly focused on Marriott without any sleight of hand that masked our intention to go there. The police were tightly positioned along the march and trying to steer the column away from the Marriott. As we got close enough to the hotel and I moved to veer the march towards the hotel doors, the police swooped in and grabbed me immediately in an effort to turn the column. We had already broken towards the doors, and as always had street blockers and door openers positioned inside and around the hotel to allow the members in. Snatching me, just accelerated the drive to the doors, and the police ended up dragging me into the lobby with them. There was something of a melee as members pushed and pulled to get in and in the back-and-forth, several other members and organizers were pinched, about eight in all.[94] Eventually, all of the members were out again, the impact on the Marriott was nil, our local lawyer, the great Art Martin, managed to get us all out later than night, the charges were never processed surprisingly, and though we made our point, we accomplished little, and never won the campaign, underlining our desperation perhaps more than the ineffectiveness of the tactic in this instance.

Large, mass action tactics present, as you can see, a different set of "nuts and bolts" concerns than many other classic tactics and strategies. They have their own dynamics and a tendency, when most effective, to be right at the razor edge of reckless and out of control.

That razor edge cuts both ways. A too tightly controlled action with no possibility of spontaneity or legitimate ability to serve as the sharp point of popular anger also loses its power to pressure, its capacity to disturb and disrupt, to scare and unsettle. Such an action is like a race car that starts with a roar and runs out of gas before the finish line. It is the difference between a march and a parade, a public hearing or a mass protest, a delegation arriving for a meeting versus a group prepared to sit-in. Each of these tactical

---

[93]   Craig Robbins

[94]   Bryan Kettenring was in this group.

Exhibit 49: Map for action at Philly Convention

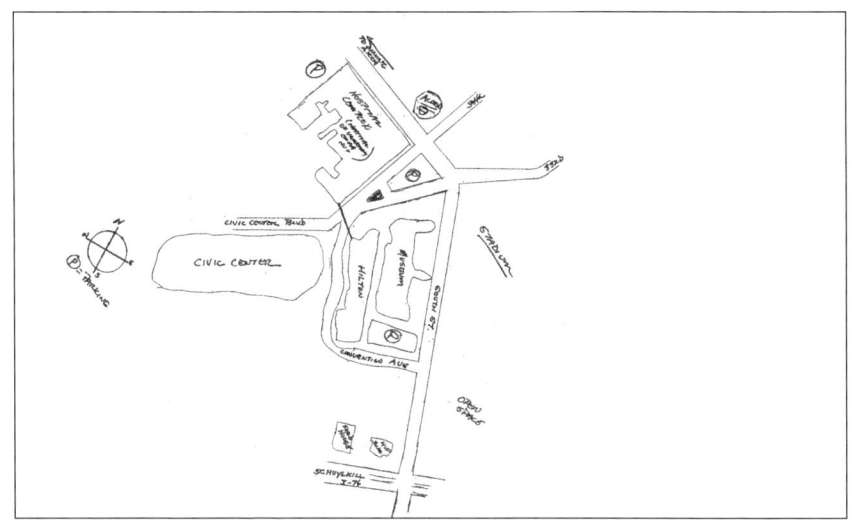

Map for Action at Philly Convention.

options has a purpose and has to be chosen appropriately, but for organizers there are always questions on how loosely or tightly to cinch the rope. It is not our job to dilute peoples' anger and rage about their issues, but at the same time anger itself is a tactic, so if completely unleashed, it can help or hurt the organization, and if out of control is by definition a bad tactic.

Inexperienced organizers also can be easily nicked in these actions, lacking practice or comfort in recognizing the natural flows of popular anger as opposed to the militant fabrication that pushes through the doors to move the march into the street or blocking the intersections. The push to get into some Wall Street banks on Park Avenue may be one thing at the heart of the beast, but a toe-to-toe with Liberty Tax Service workers in a Virginia office park *cul de sac*, where they are the big dog running, is a different thing entirely, especially when *their* base turns out to be angrier and more out of control than ours! Less experienced organizers in those kinds of circumstances can too easily confuse their own militancy and aggression with whether or not the members are all in or turned off. The element of danger can be an essential power of a tactic but the sense of danger can also be a narcotic temptation to adventurism without care, planning, and judgment.

The same thing can be as true of small actions as large demonstrations of thousands. Too many actions too quickly are allowed to evolve into listless charades complete with props without any critical content. Others seem not attuned to the target, but only to the press. Given the decline of the press and the likelihood of any coverage, which has been steadily decreasing over the last fifty years, such actions are likelier to be used more to motivate members and other adherents than to exert any particular pressure on the target. Increasingly, some actions seem expressly designed to communicate and only reflectively to administer any heat. In these actions costumes, props, and sometimes imaginative or outlandish creativity hope to carry the message forward. Some targets are, particularly consumer corporations with known brands in the marketplace, more vulnerable to this kind action than are public officials, big banks, or other industry giants.

It is self-evident that the reason such actions, soft or hard, are in fact called "demonstrations" is by definition based on the fact that they are trying to show or demonstrate to multiple audiences and targets the clarity of the point of the action and the urgent need to resolve the grievance or issue. Sometimes the demonstration is meant to educate, sometimes to pressure, sometimes to measure the levels of anger and outrage, sometimes they are more about the members, and sometimes they are more about the target.

The tactical utility of sound is obviously to disrupt. The tactical purpose of silence is usually to communicate moral righteousness to some audience, either the direct public or the public as connected through print or visual media. These more "symbolic" actions, as opposed to direct actions, are useful tactics in the early stages of a campaign where the purposes often are more educational than meant to pressure. Essentially the basic requirement of symbolic actions is that they vividly and creatively communicate the message.

Sometimes the props can communicate effectively even in more direct and hard hitting actions. In the days when we were moving aggressively after utility companies, a sign in the shape of an electric light bulb was always a crowd pleaser. It is harder to make that point with a new CFL or LED of course, but the well-known silhouette of the classic bulb was always much in evidence. Signs in the shape of dollar signs never caught on as well, though the issues about money were begging for an organizational protest artist. These are fundamental classics in community organizing of course. Few have done the work who have not been involved in actions where uncollected garbage has been delivered to city hall or roaches, rats, and whatever have been dumped on recalcitrant and contemptuous landlords. Likewise there are classic actions involving street corner disruptions and street blockings that are a common staple in protesting speeding cars, danger to children or traffic actions that have harmed children or whatever in the name of the need for traffic signs, signal lights, warnings, slower speeds, speed bumps, or the like.

Where protest is more a part of the culture, actions might include struggle vests, which are common in Korea, or head bans with protest messages worn by all and visible to many that are common in Japan and Korea, or a wide variety of vests in all shapes, sizes, and colors, that are popular in Argentina and some other Latin American countries. Burning targets in effigy is still a staple of protests in India. Flags in Brazil and many European countries are a call to act and preparation for the barricades.

All of these "props" speak to what is now called branding, but are elements that have been part and parcel of actions and organizational building for many, many years. ACORN members had buttons, t-shirts, polo shirts, dress shirts, and after my visits to Brazil, there were always ACORN flags, that were impossible to ignore, and after we began organizing in Latin America more and more there were red ACORN vests that were the equivalent of life size buttons or posters. Are these kinds of props effective? Hell, yes! Adopting red and black as the ACORN colors gave ACORN and its actions an edge. These were not random assemblages, but actions from ACORN, and the fact that they were coming from ACORN spoke to the fact that they would be aggressive and that they would continue persistently until victory.

One of ACORN's classic "tricks of the trade" was always to make sure any signs or posters displayed the name ACORN and the logo on the sign, regardless of what message the members might have written on the rest of the work. In fact over the last years of ACORN and on an ongoing basis in Canada, we even went to the extent of printing standard sign "posters" for actions that already included the colors, ACORN, and the symbol, so that all that had to be added was the message in the middle. None of this is hard, but it is vital to the nuts and bolts details, since a random photo for a newspaper or a camera pan of an action sends a message, so it makes sense to make sure that the organization is linked to the issue, so people are prepared for this in the future.

And, yes, this works. I hate to count the number of times that in mass actions on this issue or that, sometimes where there are thousands of people in the swelling crowd, the camera would almost magnetically go to the waving ACORN flags or the clear and distinctive signs or the red in our members' t-shirts or vests. I can remember a huge immigration reform rally in Denver with a picture in the *New York Times* with ACORN's flags waving in full view. Over the years it was amazing to see the number of other pictures of actions and events where editors or reporters might have left us on the cutting room floor so to speak, where the picture shouted silently ACORN's presence as the camera caught members with their signs or chanting with their t-shirts. Details, details, and, then, more details! Sometimes our coalition partners might be upset about this, but all we could really do is good organizing, what happened after that was beyond our control.

Neither was it unique to ACORN, so this is not some special, private truth. The United Farmworkers raised millions of dollars and won their boycotts based partially on the quick and easy identification of their eagle and their flag. In more recent years labor unions have been easily identified by the purple of SEIU, the green of AFSCME, and the

ACORN Flag at Toronto Occupy.

Chapter XIII: Strategy and Tactics 325

ACORN on poster and signs Louisiana ACORN stop predatory lending.

blue of AFT for example. The AFL-CIO's two hands shaking, though outdated, are difficult to change because it so clearly triggers an immediate identification. I still use ACORN's flags and design in ACORN International work for all of the same reasons. The symbol is easy to draw and hard to forget. In working with other networks of organizations in the United States, the most frequent complement, even if begrudging was praise for how successfully we had branded ACORN. Perhaps that also why it was easier to attack the organization, and the reason it continues to provoke controversy. The ACORN brand stood for something. It spoke of actions, aggressive pursuit, and success in voter registration, housing, and community improvements, which attracted members and their fervent loyalty, and opponents and their continuing antipathy.

The very power of the brand is also the conundrum for the ACORN successor organizations in the United States and why I would maintain that ACORN must and will (should and might?) rise again. Even years after ACORN pulled the plug in the states, the former ACORN organizations are still on any list of groups on the Congressional defunding amendments. Other funders, regardless of how shortsighted their advice might have been at the time, need to come to grips with the reality and not continue to be cowed by the right wing "optics," as many spoke of the problem. The rest is legal quibbling. The left and right are in perfect agreement that these state organizations are simply ACORN with another name, and that either brings joy or hate to the heart depending on your perspective. It is equally clear that simply operating on the state level or past that as national networks by any name, such federations, even PICO and Gamaliel, as good as they are, along with others that have developed, cannot hope to build the kind of brand and discipline that ACORN was able to create as one unitary organization.

More importantly, friends and foes, as well as ACORN's own work for forty years in some cities and communities around the country, created an evergreen legacy with our constituency that is more powerful than any opponents or a federal or state funding ban. Whether me or someone and something else, it is just a matter of time, before ACORN is revived to build again from that base and brand, the devil take the hindmost. Actions and tactics have to communicate, and as long as ACORN continues to communicate in such a dramatic, hardwired, visceral way to the heart and soul of America, it is just a matter of time before its banner is picked up again to rally the troops. It's never about the money; it's all about the masses!

ACORN Tent City to support squatters winning homestead rights in behind the White House in Washington.

Among the most famous ACORN tactics were squatting and street blocking. In the case of squatting or physically occupying abandoned homes in order to link houses that needed families with families that needed homes, the tactic was expressly tailored to fit the needs of the housing campaign which it did spectacularly. The squatting tactic also had a range of subsidiary options. The squatting could be symbolic with an "opening" of the house, a taking of possession, posting a sign, and demanding title, or depending on the campaign, family, and circumstance, we could physically break in, forcibly turn on water and electric, and physically occupy the home with the full neighborhood part of the defense of the property and the squatter. At this level the tactic ratcheted up the pressure many levels especially when the property was controlled by the city or its housing authority and we were trying to win a broader program of homesteading or a $1 purchase program. At that end of the tactical scale it might also involve being willing and able to take arrests for trespassing, which were sometimes provoked by long extended occupation or in the case of federal Housing Urban Development (HUD) owned houses, squatting insured virtually immediate arrest at the point we entered the home. In one day of action HUD arrested around twenty-five people from Columbus, Ohio to Fort Worth, Texas for our demanding that they should move the houses back to people.

Physically squatting was very effective in the cities where we were able to build sympathy for the squatters and their families against the grisly backdrop of an abandoned house. Even though we were breaking the cardinal principle of the United States, the protection of private property, it was so clear that an abandoned and decaying house was in no one's public or private interest so the support was often very strong for the morality of our position as opposed to the technicality of the law, which is an excellent tactical position. Infrequently there was a backfire; the most notorious for us was the case of the charismatic Lisa Redd in Detroit, where after several days of escalating support and sympathy for her, putting incredible pressure on then mayor, Coleman Young, the papers broke the fact that Redd was guilty of so-called welfare fraud. We ended up winning a program in Detroit, but it took us years to do so after that setback. We learned a hard lesson about vetting the public faces and leaders of our campaigns.

Street blocking worked well in winning neighborhood issues particularly when the tactic followed an immediate traffic accident involving any kind of injury, real or perceived, to a child, such as speeding or no signs in a school zone. There the rage and the rationale fit the tactic to the strategy like a hand to a glove.

Street blocking also works well as a general purpose tactical alternative in an escalating strategic situation where we needed to force a governmental target to have to respond on an issue by triangulating an issue for our constituency with critical disruption to a constituency that the city or other governmental entity valued more highly. Not infrequently, in city after city, when push came to shove, ACORN would block traffic at central arteries and times for business commuters to the central business districts in major cities, and it would be hell to pay. Interestingly, there were few tactics that got more attention and less press than street blocking. The tactic was the equivalent of a citizen strike and could be exercised in hit-and-run fashion by relatively few people in certain situations. Twenty folks could create virtual gridlock at a four-way interchange, if they were willing to endure the horn blaring and cursing of the commuters until the police show up, make their point, then dissipate, and turn up again with the same folks or another group at a similar intersection then blocks or ten miles away. Over the years we took relatively few arrests on this tactic, but the message almost invariable got delivered forcibly.

Blocking interstates or flyways was a more dangerous escalation and one that I do not believe we ever tried anywhere more than a handful of times. The speed of the cars and the logistics on expressways were daunting. Dropping a sign or acting on interchanges for entry or exit were easier, and more likely to still engage local police rather than state police, so were more practicable.

Bridges were choke points that were easier to access and more dramatic of course and very frustrating to city forces. The overreaction of the police in New York City to the bridge march by Occupy Wall Street was a turning point in that movement given the initial indifference to the encampment, and their ability to not only take the police rage, but skillfully get the videos out on YouTube and pictures out on other social media, introduced a flagging movement to a larger audience that resonated powerfully. Washington, DC is another city where bridges are a huge choke point. It was fascinating to hear the parry and thrust of internal debate at the AFL-CIO convention during its historic election between John Sweeney and Tom Donahue over the issue of whether or not it was tactically appropriate for labor to block bridges. This debate and Sweeney's initial embrace of more effective and militant tactics seemed to speak to a new strategy for labor and a new tactical period of innovation at the time, though it turned out hope was not a plan.

Unfortunately more imaginative and aggressive tactics have not evolved independently by labor, although many of the tactics of community organizations have been adopted by labor campaigns increasingly. Additionally some of the more effective corporate campaign tactics for labor continue to be under legal and political attack. On the eve of Obama's first election the successful plant closing sit-in at the Chicago door and frame company seemed to herald the prospects of tactical workplace seizures reminiscent of the activity of many workers during the Argentine financial crisis, but this proved to be more flicker than flame.[95]

Strikes which were the tactical nuclear weapon for unions have been falling in number and size almost annually for several decades. More recently a *faux* strike by a few Walmart and fast food workers has proven a widely effective tactic for bringing attention and publicity to the plight of these lower waged workers and their demands for significant pay increases and living wages, though these are not strikes in the classic sense of actions designed to inflict economic loss to a firm's bottom line. These are what we might call in light of the previous conversation "branding strikes" or "publicity" strikes or perhaps symbolic strikes,[96] designed to harm the corporate image more than the real balance sheet of McDonalds or certainly Walmart. Whether these tactics are strategic in the sense of achieving unionization or simply advancing the longstanding campaign for living wages will be closely watched.

The United Farm Workers boycott of grapes and lettuce during the late 1960s and 1970's accompanying the spate of successful organization in California and Arizona seemed to herald a tactical breakthrough there, as did the *de facto* embargo internationally of South Africa around the persistence of apartheid and the Nestle boycott, but boycotts though frequently threatened have not had as impressive a record in recent decades or as ready a weapon in the 21st century arsenal, despite the media effectiveness of the *Color of Change* and *Sleeping Giants*. Partially the law has not evolved to favor the tactic. The penalties for damages can be organizational death sentences. Injunctions have rained like summer showers on unions and others. Even in the best of situations they involve a huge burden of moral rectitude, vast organizational marketplace reach, especially for national and international firms or targets, and significant staffing and financial resources able to be expended over an indeterminate period of time. The checklist before engaging in such boycotts is daunting.

Organizers reading *Trampling out the Vintage*[97] might raise questions about even the effectiveness of many of the UFW boycotts other than the initial ones and whether even in that case we also find a situation where the tactic overwhelmed the strategy, at least if the strategy was to build a union. Although indisputably Chavez and his colleagues built something that has lasted even if what they have is an amalgamation of nonprofits rather than a collective bargaining, dues paying membership-based institution. Reading *Trampling* also makes it impossible to ignore the fact that the success of some tactics also rests on the thin line between the pressure and protest of direct action and gloves-off, no holds barred violence.

---

[95] See *Revolt on Goose Island* by Kari Lydersen (2009).

[96] An interesting discussion of the symbolic strength of some labor organizing work can be found in Jennifer Jihye Chun's *Organizing at the Margins: The Symbolic Politics of Labor in South Korea and the United States*, ILR Press: Ithaca, NY, 2009

[97] Frank Barnacke, *Trampling Out the Vintage: Cesar Chavez and the Two Souls of the United Farm Workers*, 2012.

It is common knowledge and well documented whether in cinematic form in John Sayles's, *Matawan,* Barbara Koppel's *Harlan County* documentary, or numerous other accounts that in mineworker strikes bullets were often blazing. Entering the Service Employees from the United Labor Unions, we often listened with mouths gaping wide to stories of the janitors' strikes in big cities that featured bombs blowing up toilets, as well as receiving fascinating advice in our orientation about where in Manhattan we could buy skunk oil, but it was still something of a surprise to read behind the public persona of Cesar Chavez, the hard fisted, violent "wet works" and pitched, dangerous battles and destruction in the fields. For example I know Chava Bustamente well, and always found him a sweet and gentle man, who would kid me about the time I got him to visit an avian museum with me in Saltillo, Mexico during an Enlace meeting in order to see the bird habitat dioramas, but to read about he and a team of folks chopping down 80 acres of lettuce one night and then getting caught trying to break a scab herder's car window to incinerate his vehicle, says to me that such activity must have been epidemic in the constant strikes in the California fields.

Violence is not only as "American as apple pie" as Baton Rouge born civil rights organizer Rap Brown claimed, but is also *lingua franca* around the world. There are now generations of Palestinians who have been arrested and served time for rock throwing, no matter how ineffective, simply because it was a tactic that defined resistance, even if futile. Say what one may about the failure of the Muslim Brotherhood in governance in Egypt, their willingness to fight military power in the name of whatever definition they hold for democracy and suffer 2000 injuries and 700 deaths is either a profile in courage or something unnameable that few other organizations can even imagine. The willingness of many, whether in China or Prague or Hungary, to face tanks with their own bodies is also past most of our understanding of political action. The self-immolation of Tibetans

Hyatt Boycott Press Conference: Bill Becker, John Sweeney, Mildred Edmond, Gene Upshaw.

in protest of the Chinese occupation or Buddhist priests in protests in Vietnam are tactics that also defy easy categorization.

Hunger strikes are another interesting tactical dilemma. Gandhi and Chavez both used such tactics to increase the moral weight of their demands, as did the suffragettes in England who took such tactics to the point where the brutality of forced feeding itself became part of the state crimes against women in their case, though more recently Irish political prisoners fared less well with the tactic, and prisoners on long term detention in Guantanamo Bay against the US military have certainly failed to get traction, though in both cases such direct actions have underscored the untenable positions of their captors. Hunger strikes by SEIU janitors at the University of Miami while organizing there were interesting, though somehow a mismatch within the strategy.

As direct, and even personal, as some of these tactics might be, there are others, even boycotts that are as personal and indirect, like "greenlining" where individuals and organizations threaten to move their money from one place to another to make various points. Given the size of many financial institutions, it probably goes without saying that such tactics are largely symbolic on the national scene, though their close tactical cousin, the "do not patronize" campaigns run by the NAACP and other civil rights groups in smaller southern towns, where African-Americans were a majority, had devastating impact. Some of these tactics are viable, because they are immeasurable. I remember ACORN's "Turn Off Arkla Day," where we tried to organize people in the early 1970's to protest the rate hikes from the gas company by organizing people to not turn on their gas for a day. Hmmmm….Almost equally difficult was our Boycott Hyatt effort to force the hotel company to negotiate with us in New Orleans, which though instrumental in keeping the pressure on during a seven year legal battle, almost sucked the life out of Local 100 in the process in an excruciating learning process.

Either tactic was less of a shot in the dark than ACORN's Anti-Inflation Campaign several years later. It was a Hail Mary that counted more on a miracle mobilization than actually nuts and bolts organizing. Once again, like the fast food strikes, these are more tactics than real campaigns. Much like physical comedy that depends on the visual impact of the action for the laughs it inspires, these tactics are more like physical communications, somewhat like sheep in wolves' clothing. Similarly when a tactic catches the public and the target unexpectedly, there is also some impact in catching them off guard, for example the way Femen, the Ukrainian feminist group, turns around cultural expectations of sexuality and women, through bare breasted protests of their targets in several countries. More famously Indian women of all generations protested in exactly that way around military and police action around martial law and the rape of women in their community.[98]

Luckily the list is endless and exhaustive. Powerless people and those seeking a voice to win power, create change, and pressure institutions, corporations, and governments pretty much have to try anything and everything, and the closer they can get to the nerve, the great their chance of impact.

---

[98] Nandini Deo and Duncan McDuie-Ra, *The Politics of Collective Advocacy in India: Tools and Traps*, (2011).

The problem at the nuts and bolts level is often less tactical where imaginations seem to run wild, than strategic, requiring more discipline, planning, and consistent organizational activity over extended periods of time, counted in weeks, months, and often years. As importantly, strategy has to be continually adapted to evolving circumstances in any campaign or organizational building endeavor based on the action and reaction of the target. Strategy has to be uniquely designed to local and other situations and circumstances and assemble the timing and sequencing of tactics appropriately.

In sports it is interesting to hear discussions, particularly in American football (not soccer) about "packages." Sports analogies have been passé for decades, but in some ways coaches are the professional "organizers' of these teams, so there are lessons they sometimes offer, and this might be one worth noting. The coaches prepare packages or schemes to prepare tactically to meet the opposing team's effort, whether defensively or offensively. The best coaches are able to constantly adapt to the changing situations on the field, and the same is true for the best organizers. There may be a rough plan for a similar "package" of tactics for a campaign based on research and evaluation of the target (or the other team as we beat this analogy to death!) based on what the members are ready and able to do, and where the organization stands in the overall campaign timing and sequencing, much like the fact that what a team might try on a two-minute drill or when the other side is playing shorthanded is different than what might be effective or necessary early in the game. My point here, if it is not already too painfully obvious, is that good organizers are exhaustively prepared, but they are also flexible and adaptable enough to seize small nuances in the available space to create opportunities for increased leverage and advantage to move the campaign forward.

The difficult organizing problem for those of us organizing the powerless will continue to be that we have to be able to move others in situations where we are trying to unsettle entrenched opponents. Too often it will not be enough, nor will be able to find an accessible choke point or area of leverage sufficient to force concessions, so we will have to move the public and various allies to align with our issues and interests to give us enough heft to carry the fight to victory.

I have always believed in *escalating* and *stair stepping* tactics to create momentum and force campaigns into the center stage of public attention where targets were forced to declare their intentions and the public was forced to take a stand. The strategy is simple. Starting small allows outsiders to try to understand the campaign before the organization gets into full-on conflict and the acceleration careens ahead of both the observers (reporters, insiders, etc.) and the targets themselves. It is a way to set the stage and platform the message that is more manageable for the organization and perhaps in its own way forces the target out of step. In beginning the first ACORN campaign in Arkansas, the first action demanding a furniture benefit was undertaken not by African-American welfare mothers from the iconic and therefore stereotypical East End of Little Rock where many would have expected it to arise, and therefore easily pigeonholed the demand, but from the largely, white women – and men – of Silver City Courts, an almost lily white housing project near the Levy area of North Little Rock. As the first volley of the campaign that action captured huge attention, but then we kept hitting day after day throughout the week on the same target, the head of the state welfare system on the

Capitol grounds with larger groups and more buses on each successive day of the week as the campaign escalated and the voices became more strident and angry since there was no immediate concession.

Such stair stepping leads the public and the target to believe, if the organization can sustain the effort successfully, that momentum is building to a crescendo that is dangerous and uncertain and must be met. Strategically for the organization, the week of demonstrations ends with a chance to recoil and then to strike again at the fixed date the organization has given the target for a positive response, putting pressure on the target to concede to the demand. I had used a similar set of tactics in Springfield, mostly successfully, until it wasn't, on winter coats. In Little Rock the strategy led to a meeting first with the head of the state OEO program and a key aide to the governor, as preparation for a meeting with Governor Winthrop Rockefeller directly, which led to victory through the creation of a free furniture warehouse funded by the state and by Rockefeller personally.

I have used strategic variations on this tactical package dozens of times, but as with the Springfield Winter Coat Riot, not always successfully. In organizing a half-dozen surface parking contractors in New Orleans with 700 workers through the NLRB, we filed one petition after another in a compressed period of time to basically situate the elections like a row of dominos falling on the companies with the same sense of momentum on the union's and workers' part and hopefully creating a sense of resignation and inevitability on behalf of the employers. In that situation in the late-1980's, I got out foxed by the company's various lawyers at the NLRB when they stipulated to a quick election in one of our smaller, weaker units, and took us to election delaying NLRB hearings on some of our larger, stronger bargaining units, so that when the elections were all scheduled the dominos were more stacked to fall against us than for us, so that when we lost the first small unit, it set the momentum so firmly against the unit that after losing three units narrowly, I pulled the rest of the petitions knowing we had been hoisted by our own petard.

More recently in ACORN's Home Savers Campaign around rent-to-own predatory purchasing schemes in Philadelphia, Detroit, Pittsburgh, and elsewhere we have used demand-letters to renegotiate such contracts directed at the target companies in addition to seeking to block them access to foreclosed and tax delinquent properties. This is another good example of a small beginning city to city, which can blow up bigger as it goes national. Surprisingly, it has some impact when companies see there's no end in sight, and negotiating might be a better alternative.

Similarly, when targeting companies on campaigns I am a big believer in strategically going after all of those that control an industry and set the market. I also believe in hitting the biggest first and then working our way down the list to try and force what the UAW in its heroic, Reuther days created as "pattern bargaining." My belief, backed up by enough experience to make it not whimsical, is that the smaller companies are then more easily pushed into falling in line once their larger competitors have already bent to the wheel, where beating the smaller competitors first too often forces the bigger targets to dig in against the organization to prove points within their markets that are fundamentally irrelevant to the organizations' interests and demands.

There are scores of "packages" like those that are my defaults in setting up campaigns and orchestrating various tactical combinations into strategies that with work and luck might be successful. What overrides though is the constant requirement that we have to adapt to changing times to win, if for no other reason that the almost universal law holds that the more we repeat a strategy or tactic, the more likely it is to fail, because the target, whether public or private, will be waiting for you, and, if not waiting, will catch up quickly in their response. After beating HSBC in a huge campaign, as one cycle of our fight against predatory lending practices, I was certainly not surprised when the executive vice president who was the lead negotiator for H&R Block, told me that he had talked to people at his level at HSBC to learn the lessons that they had garnered from their campaign, including on the critical issue of whether or not, if one negotiated with ACORN, could we in fact be expected to honor the agreements we made. In an odd way an ironic clue to our victory with H&R Block had been the "endorsement" of HSBC.

My point is that we work in a real world of serious organizations and determined corporations and governments. There are no easy victories, and to the degree that in representing the powerless our unpredictability is in fact one of the sources of our strength, we have to constantly reshape strategies and tactics, if we want to win, and we have to do so deliberately. As a student of organizing, it is sometime surprising to me how often organizations fall into a tactical and strategic rut of easy predictability and then decline because their constituency is alienated by the inability of the organization to win. This is certainly not just true for community organizations, but true in spades for unions as well.

But, unfortunately we lose even more than we win so we need a fallback or exit strategy for almost every effort as well.

Sometimes we only need a way to retreat and let the campaign season and rebuild or in the alternative to lick our wounds, regroup, and try to probe for another way to mount

Home Savers Detroit 1st Meeting.

a new stage in the effort or as often maintain a heartbeat for the campaign on a form of life support and look for an opening to reignite the campaign. Studies, third-party reports or surveys documenting the need or urgency of the demands or grievances, hearings by experts or legislative bodies, or whatever are decent ways to keep a light burning so that one can still spot the issue across the plains.

The classic exit strategy is legal. Finding a handle that is not trivial, meaning that it would not be bounced out of court and incur potential censure of your organizational lawyer or pro bono legal recruit, but decent enough that it encourages long delays and perhaps even the off chance at real victory if lightning strikes, but at the least allows the leadership and membership to answer proudly in the long interim stages of a campaign, the common question of "What happened to that campaign?" with "We're still fighting, but it's in court now." Usually, that is accompanied by a knowing shrug of the shoulders as well, since everyone understands that it could take forever.

As I have argued, I actually believe in these "holding" strategies, because I really believe over the span of my career that persistence and simply a commitment to never abandoning the fight, but continuing to keep marching, actually wins most of these campaigns over the long haul for the simple reason that our causes are right and victory is only just. As a more inexperienced organizer, I was more desperate to win, and I more adamantly believed that one had to orchestrate the strategy and tactics so that at the highest level of pressure that the organization could produce, we would then break the target and win. It did not take long to realize that the power of "No" was often irrationally and deeply rooted and virtually impossible to dislodge on an ideal campaign timeline of building up to victory over two or three months at the crescendo of the effort, and that it was more likely that we would win as often through persistence (not patience!), if we could prove that we could sustain the campaign as we had on the initial rising of the campaign. I still believe in and advise others about the importance of the three-month

Lisa Donner, Maude Hurd, Alton Bennett, Johnny Clark, H&R Block Negotiating Committee.

time frame, but now believe that we have to be prepared to start and stop repeatedly in order to win some campaigns.

Part of this recognition also flowed from our increasing ability to translate our organizational campaigns effectively into political issues and take advantage of the election cycles in our fallback and exit strategies. If we could politicize an issue and a campaign and convert it into an electoral issue, we could often force response and concessions where candidates and incumbents were most vulnerable. Or, as I describe elsewhere we could move an issue into the electoral arena directly in many venues through the referendum and initiative process. We made this campaign transition on jobs with first preference campaigns, living wages, sales taxes, generic drugs, property tax equalization, banking, and a host of other campaigns.

Increasingly the heart of some labor union strategies, especially where there continues to be union density and frequently where there are public sector employees, the whole point seems to be to get the issue or campaign into the political arena where there might be enough leverage to win. This has certainly been the major direction of the SEIU in the US and was at the heart of the organizing drives we ran for CWA in New Jersey and the AFT in New York City around home-based workers as well. If we organized the workers, and they could leverage the politicians, then we were almost there. The skillful cultivation by our sister local, SEIU 880 of political support for their home care workers over decades, coupled with more than a million dollars in political contributions, finally sealed the deal on adding tens of thousands of members. Looking at a 30-year period where SEIU grew to be the largest union in the United States, one could make a credible case that the strategy was a mixture of various parts of affiliations, symbolic protest, and political leverage.

Always essential to strategic development and planning has also been research in both community organizing, and perhaps even more so in labor organizing in recent decades in the search for leverage and vulnerabilities of targets for campaigns. Unions like UNITE HERE have gone through a long period of privileging researchers even more than organizers as invaluable to their organizing and campaigns. As data and information have become more accessible, research has become a more focused and powerful tool for all organizing though, but the greater resources of institutional labor have made it more effective in those venues. The same could sometimes be said of communications as another powerful strategic weapon.

The fight is never equal, but the more we can bring to the field, the better our prospects.

It is also worth always keeping in mind that whatever tactics we fold into our organizational strategies that are designed to pressure and win are going to be controversial. If any of us had a dollar for every time we were told by someone, putative friend or committed foe, that they "agreed with our strategy, but they disagreed with our tactics," we could fund our organizations forever.

Of course there is nothing unique to ACORN's experience about this. Rev. Martin Luther King expressed this well in his famous, "Letter from a Birmingham Jail" in 1963:

> "I must confess that over the past few years I have been gravely disappointed with the white moderate. I have almost reached the regrettable conclusion that the Negro's great stumbling block in his stride toward freedom is not the White Citizen's Councilor or the Ku Klux Klanner, but the white moderate, who is more devoted to 'order' than to justice; who prefers a negative peace which is the absence of tension to a positive peace which is the presence of justice; who constantly says: 'I agree with you in the goal you seek, but I cannot agree with your methods of direct action'; who paternalistically believes he can set the timetable for another man's freedom; who lives by a mythical concept of time and who constantly advises the Negro to wait for a 'more convenient season.' Shallow understanding from people of good will is more frustrating than absolute misunderstanding from people of ill will. Lukewarm acceptance is much more bewildering than outright rejection."

Chapter XIV: Architecture and Engineering of Actions and Campaigns

God knows some actions *must* be spontaneous, no matter how rare that is. Someone just gets a head of steam, loses their temper, reaches a boiling point, whatever you might call it, and just pops. They shut down the line. They walk off the job. They jump up on a table and "Norma Rae." They step in the street in front of the garbage truck or stand in front of a bulldozer shouting to their neighbors and friends to join them now. Sure, it happens. But, it's rare! Very rare! It may be spontaneous when the first couple of friends jumped into the street in Cairo and said that they had "had enough and weren't going to take it no more," but when they looked behind and saw hundreds and then thousands and turned towards Tahir Square, it was no longer spontaneous, but involved detailed and exact existential calculations at the confluence of risk, anger, and reward.

Almost all of us can recount times when we have acted without thinking, instinctively. Organizations though are not spontaneous, and no campaigns are ever spontaneous. Actions may *look* spontaneous, but most often that reflects excellent organizing and leadership, almost organic and seamless in its synchronization, but ground fine through planning and experience into implementation. Actions and campaigns require a lot of architecture and engineering in order to work and win.

Scaling and Momentum

Not all issues rise to the level of full-scale campaigns, but for the many that do, once an issue is assessed as significantly important to the majority of members, it is time for organizers and others to begin to build a campaign architecture that can hold enough credibility to win. Often this involves options that express choices for review and approval, once fashioned and receiving input and screening by members and leaders that also measures something approaching a degree of difficulty, depending on organizational capacity and commitment.

Invariably some research and legwork is involved in order to find the organizing handles, primary and secondary targets, points of leverage or pressure points as we used to call them, potential allies, and action opportunities. Organizing "handles," as we have described them, are often found in rules and regulations governing the particular issue, or in unexpected appropriations that might be applied, or a sentence in the law that allows more favorable interpretation, or simply in the clarity of a practice so obviously wrong and unjust that it offends everyone generally, and our members or constituency particularly. More simply put: good information is necessary to make a good campaign plan.

Most campaigns embed some notion of "scaling" between the first actions and the hoped for victory where you start small and build to larger actions. The opening salvo of many campaigns begin with something as simple as a letter asking for a meeting or underlining an issue in the community or the delivery of a petition from workers to the boss or a supervisor or from neighborhood residents or tenants or welfare recipients to a representative of the target. However a campaign is built to begin, it has to scale larger and/or more dramatic and/or militant with every action in the sequence of the campaign phase. The pressure has to build on the target. The timing and sequencing has to make the target feel that the campaign and the actions will never stop or go away. Being able to plant that feeling of persistence, pressure and inevitability in the target is designed to force the target to either capitulate or negotiate. That's the architecture the organization is trying to construct.

Momentum is a much more subjective concept in a campaign, and neither architecture nor engineering really describes it well, but it is important nonetheless. As we have discussed, there is nothing static about a campaign. We can plan what we can control and scale it within the time frame, but we also have to react to the responses – or lack of them – from the target. As long as the target engages, or we can force engagement, we are in the thick of the fight. The more difficult situation is when a target goes silent. Regardless, we need to keep on the offensive. We need not respond to every move from the target, but we have to maintain the momentum so that the target gets the message that there will be no end to these troubles without concessions or meaningful negotiations. We can fuel the momentum with other tactics besides direct action as we have suggested. We can release research papers. We can hold walking, bus, or caravan tours on the issue. We call press conferences or plant stories with local weeklies or radio shows where we can guarantee coverage to specific constituencies we are trying to pull into the campaign. We can put videos on YouTube and go wild on social media. We can hold rallies on "our turf" without targets allowing us to demonstrate our strength and show off the support of our allies. We have lots of options that allow us to keep the heat on, even while doing the work for larger direct actions within our plan or seizing opportunities. The key is keeping the target on the defensive.

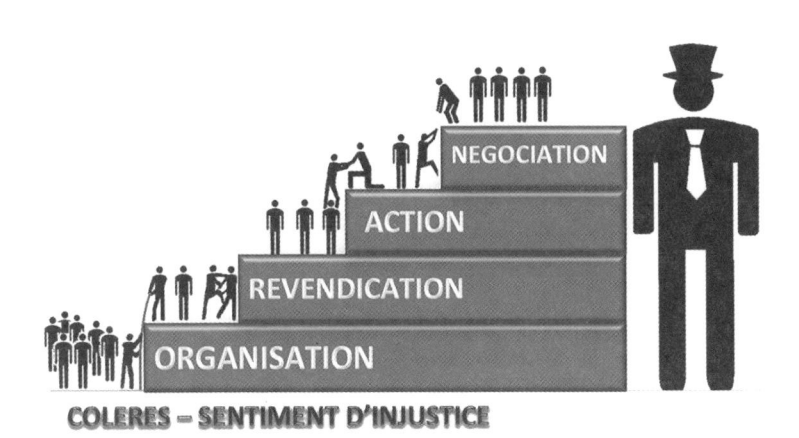

Alliance Citoyene ACORN's action scaling diagram in France.

Chapter XIV: Architecture and Engineering of Actions and Campaigns

Timing

Media interest and the public's attention span are fickle friends of a campaign, so timing is important. For the campaign and its actions to exert pressure they must feel immediate, which compresses the time frame of the campaign. A campaign planning timetable can be assembled in phases that like waves, crest, and then break, and reestablish on another front or perhaps secondary target, while each phase is best compressed in a matter of weeks and at most a few months. Being able to sequence a campaign in this way depends hugely on the organization's capacity and the weight of the issue itself and its ability to fully engage both the constituency and the larger public arena.

Because ratcheting the pressure into a time period can be so vital in determining a campaign's success, it helps to be able to frame the campaign around external events to take some pressure off the organization's ability to carry the campaign and to increase the pressure on the target. This is why external elections are so important for many ACORN organizational campaigns, especially in Mexico, Peru, Honduras, and Argentina where it is often difficult for the collective voice of the poor to be heard. It is also why ACORN targeted tax preparers in the several months before April 15th and hit hardest during the periods when they did most of their returns to impact them the most or when we targeted bank mergers with announced closing dates exploiting the necessity for community reinvestment reviews whose outcomes could create costly delays worth millions if we struck in a timely fashion. The examples are endless. Effective organizational campaigns by the relatively powerless often wield their most strength as negative forces, rather than positive ones. It is always easier for an organization to try to stop something, than it is to start something. Our pressure is always more intense and effective when we disrupt, rather than when we try to initiate and construct.

A million years ago when I began doing this work, I thought we had to be in and out of a campaign in 4 to 6 weeks or we couldn't hold the attention of troops or targets and unless there was some other fabrication or event to keep us going, we needed an exit strategy, as I described in the last chapter. Unquestionably, our odds are better, if we are

Toronto Landlord Licensing Victory.

able to break the target and force them to the table or to capitulation in a shorter time frame when our efforts are at their apex. On the other hand we have found that we can also run campaigns on particularly large issues in cycles, phases, waves or whatever best describes a series of campaign advances over years until we win. In Toronto we have been engaged in a tenant-landlord licensing campaigns with the City for a decade. We have won a truckload of victories and hundreds of millions of worth of repairs along with restrictions and fines for landlords, but we only recently won a version of the landlord licensing we demanded. We're climbing a huge mountain and have established base camps higher and higher, but still haven't reached the peak. We rest. We resupply. We regroup. We leverage the politics. We endure and we persist, and this is one of the advantages a deep-based membership organization has, we can sustain a campaign for years and our leaders and members own the history are enabled by sufficient victories along the way until we make it.

Adequate income, living wages, community development, equitable banking and credit practices, full achievement of rights and entitlements, and a host of other issues are engaged permanently. They never really end, so we have to have the same permanent capacity to continue to fight. This also explains why building power is so vital.

Numbers: Meat and the Motion

Start small and go large is a pretty basic rule of thumb. So is start soft and go hard. The best campaigns are able to engineer these tracks so that they are moving parallel at the target. It's all tricky though. We are working with people, not troops. No matter what we label them, they don't have to suit up for battle unless they want to do so, once again requiring great leadership and good organizing.

Starting small and soft is part of good campaign architecture because it allows the organization to introduce the campaign in the best possible light and a framework providing maximum appeal. Introducing the campaign has two audiences, but the primary audience is most likely the general public, while the secondary objective is beginning to position the target. Or, targets, since in large campaigns with lots of moving pieces, there may be multiple targets requiring a series of organizational actions or initiatives to put the various targets in play. As we have discussed elsewhere, the introductory actions are also meant to build the confidence and resolve of the membership and may therefore not only start small in terms of numbers but even start small in terms of the targets (i.e. the meter reader versus the CEO of the utility).

Organizers and leaders need to have a firm grasp on their capacity to produce turnout at each stage of the campaign. At the beginning five, fifteen, or twenty people is more than adequate, but the numbers have to grow to prove to the public – and the target – that our support for the campaign is growing and that our base is expanding. When the campaign – and its organizers – are not able to align forces and forum so that the numbers seem to have escalated with boots on the ground or bottoms in the chairs or whatever counts as an optimal crowd, pressure relaxes, like air going out of a tire, and the campaign is imperiled. Needlessly, because it was an organizer's primary responsibility to prevent that from happening, it is also a huge failure of campaign engineering.

It is axiomatic in dealing with actions and campaigns that "the threat is more powerful than the action." If the action fails to deliver the numbers or, in the absence of numbers, the anger or rage or reality of the threat, we lose and are only left the option of withdrawing with sufficient grace to be able to rise and fight again.

These can become tactical box canyons, offering no escape or exit with heightening organizational risks that, handled poorly, might either win the campaign or alienate the target and any goodwill and support from the public and allies sufficiently to doom the endeavor and even threaten the organization itself. Invariably, when we cannot muster the numbers, too often we are forced to deliver the heat, and the soft actions are forced to become harder.

This is not inevitable. There are a menu of options available, but it is at this juncture that campaigns find themselves debating civil disobedience, sit-ins, street blocking or whatever lies at the extreme of their tactical range. The postscript for example to ACORN's Marriott Hotel jobs campaign and the arrests and action in St. Louis during our convention in 1996, is that we did not win that campaign. The postscript to the ambush at Liberty Tax Services in Virginia Beach was that we were lucky to negotiate a face saving agreement out of that morass. My point is simply that going hard may not move the target in every case, and may make it difficult, both internally and externally, to revive the campaign.

There is a reason why so much civil disobedience involves almost ritual, symbolic arrests in our conservative political climate. The ability to leverage public support on the morality and rightness of our causes, especially if the issues are complex, is immeasurably difficult tactically. This is not a new problem. There are reasons that civil rights veterans might have prayed for a Bull Connor or even a Pettus Bridge or that labor unions might have exploited their bandaged wounds in the Battle of River Rouge. When the reaction is so fierce, out of proportion, violent, and unjust, it makes our own victories almost inevitable. There are also lessons to be learned from the adverse reactions to welfare rights sit-ins in Secretary Robert Finch's office at HEW in 1970 or even more acutely to shop-ins at Sears demanding credit for welfare recipients.

Real anger cannot be managed or contained. Where I have argued earlier that "anger is a tactic," we are trying to bottle up enough of it to administer a fundamental fear in the target, but this is a highly combustible tactic, and it can as easily deliver victories as administer defeats. At the end game of campaigns we are handling dynamite. Be careful.

One more note on numbers though. Sometimes there is a tension between campaigns that build the organization and campaigns that build the membership. Good examples are foreclosure, predatory, and payday lending campaigns. These are important issues for our constituency. The impacts on our communities are huge. The power that can be built is significant. The need for reform and change is immense. ACORN won amazing things in all of these campaigns. None of them significantly built the membership though, particularly at the community, local group level. There was no density. Victims were everywhere, but they were diffuse. There were few concentrations. Our members rallied around the victims and carried the organization's banners with them arm in arm, but we never could build a critical mass, because the dispersion across the geography was so great and in many cases, like foreclosures, a long way from our traditional base. In an Advocates and Action project in Phoenix in 2009-2010 we would sometimes find entire blocks where 80% of the homes were in the process of foreclosure or going through a forced, quit claim sale, but when we found these clusters they were often miles away from our traditional ACORN groups in the city and located in quickly built, speculative, cheap land developments out, literally, in the desert. They were ready to organize but the numbers were thin. Nonetheless, these campaigns, and others like them, were great for ACORN, loved by the leadership, made change and built power, but they were piddling when it came to growing the organization's membership, creating an internal tension that was significant in ACORN, as it would be in any membership-based organization. Seize these opportunities and campaigns, but make sure as you crawl out on the limb that the trunk of the tree is sturdy and always close at hand.

Negotiations

The end point objective for many campaigns is to force a direct meeting with the target that can lend itself to negotiations, enhancing the opportunity for winning some or all of the organization's demands.

The critical issues surrounding any agreed meeting is whether or not the organization has won a session with a decision maker or simply a public relations person also often called a flak catcher. If the latter situation, then the meeting is meant to defuse the anger and edge of the campaign and assess how small a concession may be adequate to satisfy the organization. With either party the question of good faith bargaining and the authority to conclude an agreement are always appropriate.

Negotiations require extensive preparation and trust within the team, so role plays are as valuable here as they are in door knocking. But the most extensive preparation is wasted unless there are two certainties on the organization's side: first, an assessment of realistic bottom lines where we are willing to settle, and, secondly, an accurate reading of whether or not that bottom line can be sold as adequate to the constituency by the leadership.

I am a big believer in there being a chief negotiator or spokesman for the organization, no matter how many people make take part in the presentations. This prevents the target and/or their team being able to divide our negotiating committee or lead them astray into personal issues, time consuming tangents, or head nodding as if in agreement on positions that are diametrically opposed to the organization. Everyone probes for vulnerabilities on the committee, but having a chief spokesman who will signal whether there is any agreement or not is useful. Caucuses of the committee and the ability for anyone, including staff, to be able to call them are also vital not only in keeping the unity of the committee in place or repositioning in the back-and-forth, but also in order to keep the sessions on track when they are at an impasse or a breaking point, and people may need to calm down or move to another issue or even walk away from the session.

In labor negotiations it is common to articulate the ground rules first, when we invariably make clear that we do not engage in high-low bargaining, because we believe it is a waste of time, but will give you a position very, very close to exactly the limits of where a settlement might be reached. There are also the other formalities of information exchange, frequent separation of discussions between language and economics, and so forth. We believe in "complete proposals" which include economics, because so much of the bargaining bleeds into money, but different unions have different approaches.

Such negotiations do inform community bargaining practices. It is still useful to try to resolve some of the relatively "easy" and inexpensive demands first in order to probe the potential of an overall agreement more realistically than the organization was able to do in its preparation. It allows for a clearing of air to some degree, where both sides are able to let off some steam, but then be moved back to the specific issues.

Negotiations during actions are also very different than negotiations or meetings that are won during an action and scheduled later. Invariably, when a committee of leaders is meeting with the representatives of the target and the members are still on the street, rallying, picketing, chanting, or whenever there is limited time to achieve the demands even if this is the point where the pressure is most intense. It is also very hard to make a deal with a gun at someone's head or at your own. It helps to have some "side" issues that can be resolved in such a situation like not pressing charges if there were arrests, or setting more than one date for the promise of a meeting so it seems more substantial, or agreeing to meet with the CEO and the top leader of the organization, or agreeing that the meeting will be conducted in good faith with dignity and respect for the organization, or whatever puts some flesh on the bones of whatever tentative agreement allows the action to end with people feeling positive and like it was worth what they won.

Whole books could – and should – be written about negotiations, but this is not that book. Nonetheless, I cannot overstate how important tightening down these nuts and bolts can be.

Concession, Claiming the Win, and Converting Wins to Power

Negotiations or a meeting with the target may be what you want, but often what you get is just more talk, even if you have succeeded in engaging the target or if the target cannot avoid you, especially public officials who really have no way to hide, no matter how far they run, or of course silence. Our campaigns provoke people. Often the last thing they want to do in life is meet with us. They are angry. They are hurt. They think they the poor and powerless are undeserving and should be eternally grateful for any crumbs on the table, and certainly not demanding more or better. We are chasing them, and they don't like being caught.

Frequently we have them where we want them, because we have disturbed the peace, we have done our homework, are solid on the issue, and are just plain right. Organizations should never expect a target to have grace. It happens but is exceedingly rare. Targets that confess that they did something wrong and will fix it are even rarer. Saving face always seems more important than saving a community or giving workers justice. Sometimes they will do what we have demanded or some portion of our demands, and do so wordlessly or pontificate that they were "planning to do this anyway," or that "steps were already in motion" on such and such, or basically say anything other than that they had capitulated to a demand, no matter how clear the concession. They are simply trying to serve their own constituency whether it be citizens or consumers or whomever.

Accept that. Take it any way you can get it. We are also only primarily interested in our constituency, so the key is claiming the concession as a victory, no matter how it comes and communicating that victory aggressively and enthusiastically to the membership and "our community." For that matter take the high road and thank the target for the win with some grace and make their pitiful response an additional humiliation. Odds are you will meet that target again so no need to scorch the earth.

Most organizations are very good at claiming the win. Sometimes too good. Be careful not to over claim and try not to ever get caught exaggerating the organization's role or victory. Always accept credit when offered, and give credit to others whether deserved or not. It's a cheap thrill, but worth the price for organizations, like ACORN, that understand that they are always going to be coming back for more.

This is where it helps to have allies, contacts, friends, a network, or whatever you want to call it. All of these folks can convert your work and victories into power. They talk to each other and they often work in different weight classes than the organization, but by systematically managing your "claiming" through these channels you become part of the currency of information and power that they exchange as well and that can leverage your work to other levels and spheres of influence. You want the organization, its mission, and struggles to be part of the "political equation." It is your job to burn up the wires and communicate the wins in these ways.

A political network is not built or maintained like a social network. In the early years of ACORN I would go visit Bill Becker, the president of the Arkansas AFL-CIO, every three or four months, whether I had something pressing for him or not. The AFL-CIO became our best ally in Arkansas, and over the years I used to joke with Bill about how he

California ACORN leaders and ACORN's Bruce Dorpalen (standing) and Mike Shea (far right).

Chapter XIV: Architecture and Engineering of Actions and Campaigns   345 must have wondered what the heck I was doing working a regular route through his office. It was a way for me to learn what was happening in the legislature that might impact our campaigns and to get information that was useful, but more importantly it was a way for him to understand what this strange, new thing ACORN was, how we worked, who we were, and how we fit into the biggest picture of change in the state. It is not enough to win. Winning in and of itself is not power. Victories have to be converted into power in the same way raw materials are converted into fuel.

Exit

And, sometimes — lots of times — we lose. Part of campaign architecture has to include a trapdoor or some kind of exit strategy, so that the organization can pull back and return to fight another day. Lawsuits used to be great for this, but less so increasingly. Reports sometimes work as bridges. Events organized by others where leaders can attend and restate the demands might work. Withdrawn or awarded endorsements have value in politics. It hardly matters, but have something in mind.

Managing the Media

Once upon a time there were daily newspapers that had reporters that occasionally covered local news, including, though this was rarer, in our communities. This was true for television news as well sometimes. Depending on the issue, the campaign, and the actions, organizations could cajole or cower media coverage. It is still possible in some communities and even in some huge cities, like those in India, though there is the additional problem there and in some other countries where reporters expect to

Bank of Montreal Action at ACORN Canada Convention 2015.

be paid or fed or both. The architecture of many campaigns, especially for advocacy organizations even if not community or labor organizations, often depended on the ability to move media into a fight in order to put pressure on the target. Those days have not totally disappeared, but they are different. Whether we have sufficiently adapted our organizational and campaign structure to recognize these changing circumstances is another question. The media business model is in flux, and our ability to mobilize the general public behind our issues is similarly challenged.

Social media is a developing phenomenon. There are intriguing examples of reaction and response from some corporations, particularly consumer-based or public-facing operations and even politicians, who are highly sensitive to activity on Twitter and Facebook. On the whole social media speaks effectively to one's own community and leaps less well to the general public or the target. Every once in a while some organization or advocate bottles lightning, but this kind of viral response is difficult, if not impossible, to predict or direct. Too often we are talking to ourselves which is the opposite of what we need in a campaign.

Classically, looking at a campaign model along the lines sketched by political scientist, Michael Lipsky,[99] media, among other factors, was a critical vector directed at the target and triggering change for the powerless. When numbers make less impact, most often the substitution has trended to bread and circuses. The fabrication of "props" of various kinds has flourished with outlandish costumes, sharks for predatory lending, giant rats for rogue nonunion contractors, and whatever pops up at the limits of the imagination and peoples' willingness to do what is needed to lure or force the press into covering an event or campaign. The problem with props and similar drama is not their uniqueness, but the artificiality of it that detracts from the critical content of the campaign, blunting its impact and effectiveness. It is also no surprise that as media staffing has fallen, the utility of published reports, research papers, and similar tools that can be handled cheaply by an editor just passing something over to the desk, rather than having to put increasingly scarce personnel into the field has become more and more common.

New strategies and tactics are high on the "To Do" list but this is a growing challenge lacking any current semblance of a solution.

Indigenous, Off-the Shelf Campaigns, and "State" Desks

Building large mass-based organizations creates other challenges for campaign architecture and engineering as well. Most of the situations we have been discussing involve campaigns around indigenous issues that emerge from the membership in the dialectical process that noted 20th century American sociologist, C. Wright Mills, referred to as the way a "personal problem" could become a "public issue."[100] These campaigns are natural and organic and often unique to particular communities, cities, or countries and resonate deeply and attract broad support for exactly those reasons. These kinds of campaigns are the meat and potatoes of community organizations, but they are only part

---

[99]   Michael Lipsky, *Protest in City Politics*, (1970).
[100] C. Wright Mills, *The Power Elite*, (1956)

of the array of issues and campaigns that support mass-based organizational activity or national and international organizing.

The nature of organizing is that if a good issue emerges in one community, develops a campaign, and, importantly, builds the organization, it will be copied in as many communities as possible where the issue is also applicable and finds traction. The immense value of citywide, statewide, national, and even international organizations is their ability to duplicate victories widely so that they are spread throughout the constituency. This is part of the way that we truly change the world. In some cases this kind of campaign evangelism started from an indigenous campaign. In other instances it reflects a campaign architecture adapted from generally, almost universal, issues affecting the constituency like the need for higher wages, decent and affordable housing, acquisition and implementation of "rights," elimination of discrimination, and so forth. Organizations, like ACORN, that believe in direct action and a highly participatory and engaged membership, need a constant diet of campaigns to maintain this thrust and deliver to our membership. These larger-than-local campaigns could be packaged and pulled off-the-shelf whenever leadership and staff were ready to move forward with such efforts. A basic research design and support would exist, a general legal perspective on the handles would be available, a network of other organizers would be accessible for advice and experience, and though victory is never guaranteed, the odds would be greatly improved for winning. Such efforts would also build power at the various levels of the organization. Such campaigns were neither crutches nor filler, since they delivered substantial community, membership, and organizational benefits, but neither were they indigenous.

In building an organization and winning campaigns we need tools at the nuts and bolts level that do not depend on genius, brilliant organizing innovators who are rare and far between, but on competent practitioners able to listen well, read and follow directions, implement plans, and achieve consistent success. We need tens of thousands of people willing and able to perform at this level, and the job description cannot be sink-or-swim, good luck and call-me-when-it's-over, if we are going to build mass organizations and the change our members demand. Having campaign designs that work when applying time and energy make a huge difference.

Some campaigns, including these efforts attract interest wider than the organization's discipline and reach, and that is a good thing because it extends the organization's range without generally taxing as many resources. In my brief time with the National Welfare Rights Organization, I admired the "state desk" operation run by Joyce Burson in the national, Washington, DC headquarters. Joyce had been a former welfare recipient and leader of the Brooklyn NWRO affiliate. Her job had been to stay in touch with the scattered welfare recipient organizations around the country that were not staffed by organizers like our team in Massachusetts. In some cases they were self-organized, but in many they benefited from local support from VISTA volunteers or community action program staff or fellow travelers of all sorts and varieties. When there was a national campaign, it was Joyce's job to get the word out, distribute the packet of information that might range from flyers to posters, and talk them through the organizing, actions, and follow-up on the phone until it was done. Carolyn Carr in Little Rock was drafted to a similar task to support our offices in Arkansas in the early ACORN days. When we organized "Reagan Ranches" in 1984 to protest the administration cutbacks, we flogged it to the level that there were almost 100 around the country, more than double our number of offices. Similarly, ACORN's Living Wage Resource Center in our DC-office staffed by Jen Kern helped promote and move the campaign in scores of cities where we did not work.

It all adds up.

Minimum Standards Campaigns

Perhaps the classic benchmark for an organizational building off-the-shelf campaign were the great minimum standard benefit campaigns that some[101] credit to Fred Ross, Cesar Chavez, and Delores Huerta of the United Farmworkers, but were for many years a staple in building the National Welfare Rights Organization into the largest membership organization of poor people in the United States during its brief history. The legal handle for welfare rights was the "equal protection" argument embedded in the US Constitution that essentially holds that where there is access to an entitlement that might have been discretionary in administration, everyone in the same circumstances should be able to receive the same benefit without discrimination. Simply put, if a social worker gave a welfare mother a check for school clothing in Brooklyn for her children in a state run and largely federally funded program, then a mother in Albany or Queens or Troy, New York was similarly entitled. Same for furniture or household supplies or winter clothing or Easter clothing in Massachusetts if the welfare policies there allowed for such "special needs" payments. What was good for any goose, was equally good for the gander.

After Citywide Welfare Rights in New York City won a number of these benefit campaigns on different issues such victories established the minimum standards for what a mother on welfare should be able to receive for her family. Organizers codified the victories into forms that members could fill out and check off the items that they needed and should have received, but had not gotten. These minimum standards campaigns were invaluable in no small part because state and local welfare offices resisted applying the benefits widely therefore giving welfare rights organizations hugely successful and highly winnable campaigns. Bill Pastreich, the founding organizer of Massachusetts Welfare Rights Organization, who preceded my brief stint as head organizer there, always argued that it was an organizer's job to "steal any good campaign whenever they could," and he absolutely grabbed the New York City effort and took it across Massachusetts to great success. Which is not to say it was not a huge and difficult fight to win initially in Boston, because it was, nor that we always won, since the winter coats campaign was a significant defeat, painfully felt in Springfield in the fall of 1969 when I was organizing there, but once won, it could eventually be won everywhere once the campaign was engaged and pursued. It costs state welfare departments millions and triggered flat grant programs that eliminated special needs, and therefore the organizing tool in the welfare rights situation.

---

[101] Felicia Kornbluh, *The Battle for Welfare Rights: Politics and Poverty in Modern America*, University of Pennsylvania Press, 2009.

ACORN ran a similar minimum standards campaign in Rome, Italy to win rent reductions for tenants, though landlords and courts have tried to rollback our victory in much the same way that welfare rights experienced almost 50 years ago. ACORN also attempted to develop other tenant based minimum standard campaigns more recently in Scotland to more moderate success. Mental health consumers with ACORN's MCAN affiliate pursued the same strategy in 2017 with the Alaska Mental Health Trust. Scholars seem curiously divided on the value of minimum standard campaigns in building organization,[102] but not for any good reason that I can determine other than the need to put their noses in the air and substitute their biases for the enthusiasm of members for the benefits that could – and did – win. Regardless understanding the nuts and bolts of minimum standard campaigns, how to build and engineer them, should be part of every organizer and organization's arsenal.

There is never a need to apologize or a reason to shy away from winning in undertaking campaigns to build organization and benefit membership.

Fun and Magic

One caveat that needs to be clearly expressed midst all of this discussion of construction, architecture, engineering and the like: there is still more art and little science to any of this, and that's important to keep constantly in mind. It is also critical to remember that all of this is wildly exciting, nerve wracking to the extreme, scary as hell, and perhaps the most fun for all involved that the combination of life and work ever offers us.

In our New Orleans coffeehouse everyday one or more groups of the Alcohol Anonymous variety meet in the community space on the second floor. They go their way and the rest of the coffeehouse goes its way, normally. When we first took over some years ago it was at first unsettling in some ways to run into one the participants downstairs on my rare visits or when I would join my son to staff the coffee bar on Christmas and Mardi Gras morning, when they would come up to me, grasp my hand, and solemnly express their thanks, and say, "you're saving lives here!"

I don't know anything about that, but I do know that in great campaigns and well executed actions that help cobble together the victories that build the organization, we ennoble life and give it solemn and exhilarating meaning. The work, the fight, and the organization itself enlivens all of us who are part of it, giving our time a larger meaning and purpose than we might have ever imagined, and translating into making a difference for millions, and, yes, in some small but not insignificant ways changing the world, even if only for a moment and in a fleeting way.

The hundred thousandth door knocked, the thousandth campaign and the ten thousandth action is as valued as the first, as raw experience is replaced with finely honed instincts. Soldiers sometimes speak of what others see as courage as simply an eruption of instinctual response that bursts from years of training and repetition. We see the same inexplicable response in the miracle of an athlete's reactions or accomplishments that some speak of as muscle memory, but also spring from training, repetition, and skill.

---

[102] Premilla Nadasen, *Welfare Warriors: The Welfare Rights Movement in the United States*, Routledge, 2005.

Words fail me, but in similar moments in actions I can never cease to recall the same pure magic, whether in Springfield or Boston or Philadelphia or New York or St. Louis or a hundred other times in other places and situations, whether with a hundred or a thousand people, where suddenly I have felt as one with the crowd, able to feel its pulsing heart and anger, and ride that wave of adrenaline and anger to the point of its power and feel that we were unstoppable, unbeatable, and that victory was as certain as the setting of the sun.[103]

Good architecture and engineering increase our ability to share that magic collectively and prevail until victory.

Carolyn Carr Little Rock Office 1976-77.

---

[103] Eugene V. Debs quote speaking of the labor movement was, *"...its historic mission is as certain of ultimate realization as is the setting of the sun."*

Chapter XIV: Architecture and Engineering of Actions and Campaigns   351

Chapter XV: **Big Actions**

If the detail of planning and execution is essential in the experience of conventions and other large meetings, certainly the same can be said of large scale actions. ACORN's philosophy has always been that if you are going to spend the time, money, and energy to pull a thousand or a couple of thousand people together, then it is essential for them and for the organization to put them into action and let them align the beat of the their feet on the streets with the pounding of their hearts and the roar of their voices.

Actions are at the life force of all of ACORN, so frequently what many members – and organizers – remember best about their ACORN experience, including their experience at large scale meetings or conventions, was the actions and marches that marked the high points of their experience. We believed the more actions the better, but largely that depended on the targets and opportunities given in the location, especially if we could advance multiple organizational campaign objectives with the same events, essentially multiplying the impact of the same amount of work and membership involvement.

There are a lot of moving pieces to any action. When we are talking about large marches and big actions, we are really talking about the logistical and tactical problems of scale, rather than something fundamentally different. We had an interesting moment working with ACORN International's affiliate in Grenoble, France, Alliance Citoyenne, when after days of exciting and intense discussions with a great team of organizers, it developed that they distinguished big actions from standard actions by calling them "power actions" signifying their importance in building the organization and its reputation. Though perhaps they were limiting their scope by requiring as much perfection as power through these larger actions, they had a point that often organizations are defined, one way or another, by their large actions, or by their lack of them.

ACORN perhaps does some of that as well by distinguishing between what we called "maintenance" actions, those smaller, sometimes "quick hits" or *rapides accions* as our Latin American organizers constantly refer to them, that kept the local organizations moving and advancing their issues with deep participation of their members and these larger actions that might involve a whole lot more at conventions or as signature events in larger campaigns, perhaps involving members from various cities, states within a region, or whatever might be appropriate to the target. An early ACORN training document from the 1970's insisted that "successful" or "strong" actions include three elements: "surprise, disruption, and timing." By timing the document tried to clarify that ACORN meant that our tactics needed to be unpredictable. Certainly, no matter the size or scale of an action the ability to disrupt in unexpected ways is crucial to success.

Here's another "training" guide on ACORN actions (Exhibit 50)

Exhibit 50: Planning an Action

Planning an Action

1. **Organize Membership Committee to Plan Action**
   - At Committee Meetings: set goals, names of who people will bring are taped to the wall, at each meeting a report is given by each member on their turnout success and plans. Organizers work the lists nightly to ask how members are doing with their lists.

2. **Targets & Demands**
   - Who are the targets?
   - Turning them out: calling them back to reconfirm they will be there even calling them the day of the event --get their home number, beeper number, cell phone number.
   - What are the demands -- what do we want to win in this action?

3. **Scenario**
   - What should this action "look like"?
      Sequence of events
      Staging tactics
      Speakers   Who will speak?
                  How should they be "prepped"?
                  What needs to be said?
                  When should it be said?

4. **Turnout**
   - What is the goal?
   - What is the plan to meet that goal?
   - Membership turnout plan

5. **Materials**
   - Banner/Flags
   - Membership Cards
   - Attendance List
   - Chant Sheets
   - Copies of Press Release
   - Bullhorn
   - Signs
   - "Yes List"
   - Flyers
   - Props
   - Demand Sheet
   - Buttons
   - What else?

6. **Media**
   - What kind of media coverage do we want?
   - Turning them out:
   - call them and tell them about the action
   - fax press release
   - call them back as necessary
   - Have a leader ready to meet & greet them

7. **Ending the Action**
   - Very Important! Defining how Important the member's turn-out and work on this, what we won-- Plan for worst case scenario, so leaders can be prepped to actually find the "win" in the event, point to the next steps & how to win more.
   - Plan B. If you don't win everything--next outreach efforts to build numbers, next meeting date to plan the next action.

Chapter XV: Big Actions

Another thing that might help distinguish between actions large and small is transportation. A local action where neighbors can just meet at a church or a street corner is likely a smaller, maintenance action on a local campaign. An action where people can meet at City Hall on public transportation, buses, trams, or subways, or be dropped off by carpools of leaders, members and organizers, is also likely to be larger, but still relatively speaking not seen as a "big" action depending on the context and the relative comparables. An organizer from an allied organization in the Bronx once famously stood up during an argument that ACORN organizers were having with other organizers and activists in a meeting in Black Mountain, North Carolina years ago and argued that organizers who have never put people on yellow school buses to head off to an action, essentially were not *really* community organizers, and thereby hardly knew action and power from peanut butter and jelly. Often a litmus test for the size of the action is whether or not the organization believes it is in fact time to charter school buses to pull all of their people together.

Buses, trains, and planes can move an action from an individual organizational affair to a mass mobilization. Mobilization of mass actions is an important organizing skill. The naysaying of movements and mass mobilizations by some organizers, should not be allowed to dilute their importance or to belittle the significant skills and organizational talent necessary for putting together such protests, marches, and rallies.

They are what they are, and they aren't what they aren't, but what they are is sometimes powerful and important and having the ability to handle the nuts and bolts well is worthy of respect and teaches huge lessons.

Admittedly it's a specialized literature but even a cursory look at the Taylor Branch series on Martin Luther King[104] gives reasonable perspective on some of the logistical issues and innumerable details involved in putting together the classic civil rights marches. Even the fictionalized movie, Selma[105], offers a vivid look at the many moving pieces involved in such work and is an important window to some of the tactical decisions involved in mass marches confronting persistent opposition.[106] There is a less vivid history in the mass mobilizations against the Vietnam War like the Spring Mobilization that ended in a rally where Rev. Martin Luther King and many others spoke in 1967, and Norman Mailer's Armies of the Night looking at the March on the Pentagon in 1968 is more than vivid, though the nuts and bolts are drowned in his own atmospherics.[107] Another perspective provides a look at the NWRO march and mobilization in Las Vegas to oppose welfare cutbacks gets good treatment in Storming Cesar's Palace: How Black Mothers Fought Their Own War on Poverty by Annelise Orleck. To say that there are not lessons to be learned from such work and that the work is not important or not even organizing is churlish at best. The work teaches and is invaluable while instructing all actions in other contexts as well.

---

[104] Taylor Branch trilogy is: *Parting the Waters: America in the King Years, 1954-63* (1988), *Pillar of Fire: America in the King Years,* 1963-65 (1998), and *At Canaan's Edge: America in the King Years, 1965-1968* (2006)

[105] *Selma*, directed by Ava DuVernay (2014)

[106] Rathke, Wade, *Chief Organizer Report: "Selma for Organizers,"* February 8, 2015, www.chieforganizer.org.

[107] Mailer, Norman, *Armies of the Night*,(1968).

ACORN Union sackcloth action in Bengaluru, India.

    The weight and scale of an action is not simply a matter of numbers and transportation, but also a matter of context. In a smaller city that has hardly ever seen even 50 or 100 people gather together to demand anything or protest against anything at that scale, that is a big action relative to the history and expectations within the culture and community in that situation. A hundred people in that space might be equivalent to a thousand or more in a larger city and even a thousand can be swallowed up in the global megacities now. In Bengaluru we organized a mass protest against closing one of the large marketplaces where our hawkers worked that had been operating steadily for hundreds of years and marched five thousand to the municipal corporation headquarters demanding the development be stopped with our members wearing jute bags as sackcloth to symbolize the fact that the city was threatening to take the "shirts off their backs" and eliminate their livelihoods. Such an action was appropriate in scale. When a year later we tried to symbolize our growing strength and only pulled out a little more than one-thousand, ACORN India organizers were disappointed and saw the action as a failure.

    Sometimes we just do not know the context well enough to predict what a big action might look like. We loaned an organizer to our partner in Indonesia, UPC, the Urban Poor Consortium, for some weeks to put together their first candidate interview rally in Jakarta as elections were returning to people. Talking regularly by Skype with our organizer, we were convinced from what we could count on through our outreach and organizing efforts that we might at most be able to pull out 1000 for the rally and accountability session with the gubernatorial candidates. Our local partner was nonplussed when 7000 turned out, but we were euphoric, while humbly chalking that up as a big lesson learned, as well as a big action!

    Even putting together the actions for between 1500 and 2000 or more people for ACORN Conventions involved significant details. A shorthand list for ACORN's Philadelphia Convention in 2000 gives a hint at what's involved:

Exhibit 51: Action Planning for Philadelphia Convention 2000

Monday Action...June 26th

Staging Area: Broad Street @ Vine
on both sides of the street facing from north To south.

Route

- Broad going south to City Hall
- Cross to City Hall Plaza
- Walk along Plaza to junction of Penn Square and Market
- Cross to Market Street on right hand side of street
- Go from 15th to 16th

Targets

- Lehman Brothers – 1600 Market – 17th floor – Room #1725   [100]
  - Early 30 in 2-3's to floor... [one early bus, early withdrawal from TU]
  - Lobby problems...may have to split out rest of MA to Salomon
- Norwest – 1601 Market – 5th floor – Room #545   [500]
  - Early 40 – 5 from each state on separate bus to split out ahead
  - No problems in lobby...large and should hold everyone...
    one desk/no security
- Salomon Smith Barney – 1650 Market – 44th&45th floor [900]
  - One early bus on non-lobby entrances to upper floor staging
  - Rest through the lobby

Lehman Brothers: Boston – Springfield - Brockton

Norwest: Twins, DC, Albuquerque, Baltimore, Chicago, Texas, Arkansas, Jersey City, Detroit, Colorado, Ohio

Salomon Smith Barney: New York, California, Louisiana, Kansas, Miami, Montana, Philly, Portland, Seattle, Missouri

Lead Inside Action Staff:

Lehman: Lisa Clauson
Norwest: Madeline Talbott
Salomon: Jon Kest

Lead Market Street Management

Mike Shea

Exhibit 51: Action Planning for Philadelphia Convention 2000

Staffing Roles
    Staff on lead buses
    Inside Delegation Staff
    Elevator Staff
    Door Staff (street level)
    Door Staff (target level)
    Police Spotters
    Street blockers
    Radio Crews…

March Staging
- Leadership & Guests Line: Lisa Donner & Carolyn Carr
- West Side column staging – Mike Shea
- East Side column staging – Zack Polett
- Merged line managers (as 2 lines come together crossing to City Hall Plaza
  - Helene O'Brien
  - Beth Butler

March Order[108]

Section I	Craig Robbins
New York	
California	
Louisiana	
Kansas	
Miami	
Montana	
Philly	
Portland	
Seattle	
Missouri	

---

[108] This is the march order from City Hall Plaza to the targets. This order is less critical from the actions to the Federal Reserve, though these folks should group off in rough thirds to move and go.

Exhibit 51: Action Planning for Philadelphia Convention 2000

Section II	Carolyn Siegel
Chicago	Arkansas
Twins	Jersey City
DC	Detroit
Texas	Albuquerque
Baltimore	Ohio
	Colorado

Section III	Bruce Dorpalen
Boston	
Brockton	
Springfield	

Sunday-Suburban Tour - June 25, 2000

Bus Captains (8)

Yard Management – Jeff Ordower

Sunday – N'hood Canvass – June 25, 2000

Bus Captains (25) (Must be here @meeting tonight and should know how to read a map and have some minimal map reading skills…

Other? Talk to Pat and Fred…

Wells Fargo Senior VP confronted by ACORN leaders in Los Angeles Action.

Here's another one four years later in Los Angeles in 2004 on much the same layout:

Exhibit 52: Planning List for Los Angeles Actions 2004

Monday Action...Well, Wells!

Staging Area: City Hall Plaza

We will be dropped off by the busses from UCLA around City Hall. The approximate March order will be moved from that point.

The leading edge of the March will assemble from on Temple from Spring.

Route

- Move out along Temple Street to Grand.
- We will take a left on Grand
- We will proceed past the new Disney-Frank Gehrey Building
- We will turn right into the plaza to the entrance side of the Wells Fargo Bldg (39)
- After the action we will go down hill to Olive and 5th to Pershing Square (79) for lunch and bus pickup.

Targets and Delegations

- Wells Fargo is the primary target
- There will also be a "rally" at Pershing Square with President Marie Elena Durazo, HERE Local #11 about their coming contract problems.

Delegation Wranglers and Guides

Brynne Seibert, Alicia Weber, Janice Mowry, Marta Delgadillo

Staffing Roles

Inside Delegation Staff – Lisa Donner, Becky Gomer, Steve Bradbury

Forward Observation Spotters: Donna Bradford, Julie Roberts from N.J., Zach Polett, Maggie Laslo, Steve Dooley, Myra Glassman, Mildred Simpson, Jose Manuel Escobedo, Odalis Donate, Darlene Anderson – (Wells Team)

Pershing Drones – Carolyn, Sharon Trotter, Glenda Kizzee,

Pershing Lunch – Janet Reasoner + Lez Trujillo, Bruce Dorpalen, Josh Myles, Mike Slater, John Cain, Trevor Fought, Dave Chaos,

Street blockers – Main March

Street blockers – Midwest assign

Street blockers – East assign

Banner Brigade: Paul Richards,

Chapter XV: Big Actions

Exhibit 52: Planning List for Los Angeles Actions 2004

Radio Crews – KNON, KABF
Digital camera folks: Brennan Griffin, Kristy Lefall, Marnie Goodfriend,
Wade Runners   -- Kevin Whelan, Brendan Dugan, Matthew Luskin
Pershing Square Debriefing Stage: Matt Meyers, Marc Seiden
Press – Allison Conyers, Sarah Miller, Jen Kern

March Staging

Leadership & Guests Line: Lisa Donner & Amy Schur
Column staging – Both sites: Helene O'Brien

Action Directors

Overall   Jon Kest

March Order

Midwest	Section I	Madeline Talbott
South	Section II	Beth Butler
West	Section III	Clare Crawford
East	Section IV	Keith Kelleher

The march order for the big action at the national convention in Columbus in 2006 breaks down the groupings more clearly.

Exhibit 53: March Order for Final Action of Columbus Convention

March Order – Monday, July 10th 2006 – Columbus, Ohio

FRONT LINE
NATIONAL OFFICERS AND DIGNITARIES
NATIONAL BOARD

NORTH ATLANTIC

TEXAS	DC
PENN	MARYLAND
CONN	RHODE ISLAND
MASS	DELAWARE
NEW JERSEY	NEW YORK

SOUTH

FLORIDA	KENTUCKY
LOUISIANA	NORTH CAROLINA
ARKANSAS	ALABAMA
SOUTH CAROLINA	TENNESSEE
GEORGIA	MISSISSIPPI

INTERNATIONAL

CANADA	PERU/MX/ARGENTINA

MIDWEST

MISSOURI	WISCONSIN
MICHIGAN	OHIO
MINNESOTA	INDIANA
ILLINOIS	KANSAS
NEBRASKA	

WEST

CALIFORNIA	OREGON
COLORADO	HAWAII
ARIZONA	NEVADA
NEW MEXICO	OKLAHOMA
WASHINGTON	

Assemble in the park once let off the busses by state within your regional grouping for the march.

Jesse Rafert and Dine' Butler, ACORN International Bechaks in Columbus, March 2006.

The basic structure of the actions was always memorable and intricately planned, but "airy" enough to allow tactical flexibility. As a rule, we would always want to get into a building, rather than being caught on the street. At the least we would always want to get some delegation of leaders, appropriately staffed, to the highest seat of power in a location: the office of the CEO, the HUD Secretary's office, the president of the utility company, or whomever the decision maker might be, and where authority and negotiating power might lie. Sometimes it would be enough to get acknowledgment of the receipt of our demands. Other times it would be an agreement for a meeting right then or a fixed date in the future. We understood that our power lay on the street with our people and its half-life was short and exacting, so we wanted to leverage the maximum advantage from the opportunity.

We also knew in the big convention actions that we were time-limited, especially on the final day. We would have the buses packed at dawn and waiting at a staging area as close to the action as practicable so that they could be drawn up quickly once the action was over. A crew of staff, usually canvassers or interns, would have picked up the lunches and have them counted out and labeled for each bus to return. Vans would be ready to move towards the airport with rigid flight schedules. Running these actions was like a high-wire act or trying to make it across a rickety bridge, Wiley Coyote style, where one false step sent you crashing. The euphoria of the members caught in the adrenaline rush of marching, chanting, and direct action could quickly dissipate into hunger, thirst, and, worse, boredom, if they were kept too long waiting for the results of their action amid reports from leaders and negotiators far removed from the street where it was sometimes unknown if they had reached the target or not. The organizer with final responsibility has to be able to monitor and manage the mood.

The changes over time around basic security and access also made mass actions challenging.

In New York in 1992 perhaps the classic ACORN convention action targeted Citibank on Park Avenue. The march route itself was dramatic and exhilarating. Coming out of the tunnels across from Grand Central, we broke the march in two columns in order to confound and maintain the element of surprise with half moving on one side of Park and half the march on the other, designed to remerge in front of Citibank as one side crossed over at the Colgate-Palmolive building. The "door" team had done a brilliant job and of course no matter how disciplined, and this has always been amazing and invigorating to me, whenever the front lines of the march, no matter how struggling, get within 20 or 30 yards of the door, the steady pace and movement, breaks into full-throated roars and whatever sprint people can muster because they all want to be *inside* the building, not outside. Essentially its 1500 to 2000 people all playing capture the flag!

At Citibank, in a world that no longer exists, between the door team and the front lines, we quickly overwhelmed security, seized the doors, and managed to get *everyone* in the building! We also had a group of several hundred in a separate movement coming through the backdoor as well, and we all penetrated the building eventually, marching round and round chanting, in and out among the elevators, controlling the whole first floor of the building as police amassed outside, and we pressed for our negotiating team to report on their progress since the elevators were of course immediately shutdown. There was an additional distraction as a freelance action of sorts tried to push its way into the Citibank "wealth management" office that was accessible to us on the first floor and engaged in a pushing and pulling contest, gaining and then surrendering access, tactically.

For decades I have listened to the arguments about whether such actions have value compared to the risks and whether changing times made them passé. Whether such actions were comfortable for our members or involved physical danger and likely arrests? Others may agree or disagree, but on that day, we won a commitment for direct negotiations with Citibank after years of fighting them and others on discriminatory lending and housing practices and those negotiations led to hundreds of thousands of families owning their own homes, funding for us to help millions of others do the same, and a relationship, albeit forged in conflict and action, that produced victories and progress for our members for decades.

Even in welfare rights where tactically we regularly sat in at welfare centers and offices planted squarely in the ghettos and barrios, like an alien plant in hostile soil that we dominated, we saw offices consolidated and centralized over subsequent years to make them physically and architecturally remote and moated as unassailable castles distant from the poor. There was a global shift of security after September 11, 2000 that dramatically changed target availability, but some of this fortressing in our communities had been in place for decades. Several years later, during the 2004 ACORN Convention, the aggressive campaign focused on Wells Fargo Bank's predatory lending policies had been limited by the tectonic shift in the magnitude of action available on L.A.'s streets.

In the back of our minds we might have imagined a Citibank-Part 2 action, but the early scouting teams, including my own walk through, counted innumerable security personnel, and, just as Citibank became sophisticated internally, so had Wells Fargo

Citibank Action.

adopted protected levels of restricted card entry that made the notion of getting more than a handful inside seem remote. The action plan involved probing the possibilities from the back and front and any other available points, but it was always clear that Plan B was really Plan A, and there was no way that we were going to gain entry. We ended up surrounding the bank with our people and clogging up the area and using security and the police, which is not uncommon, to deliver a copy of the lawsuit we were simultaneously filing and essentially serving the notice of the suit on a vice-president of something after the requisite chanting and demands. In Toronto's 2013 ACORN Canada convention, hitting Bell Canada demanding internet access for lower income families, we ended up only making it as far as a patio outside of the skyscraper's back doors, held off by numerous burly, humorless security, with our advance entry team repelled, and unable to get the robotron security to even take the demands upstairs. Of course in 2015 a large contingent at ACORN Canada's Convention in Montreal overwhelmed the historic headquarters of the Bank of Montreal (BMO) with no security issues at all. There is no guarantee of success or assurance of failure, but it remains "dare to struggle, dare to win."

No matter the target or the times, it does make a difference to have a large, disciplined, and skilled team of organizers with shared experiences and *lots* of practice with direct and mass actions. The HOTROC march in New Orleans was the largest I ever organized with 8000 counted, but it was also one of the most difficult to pull together and though it had tremendous impact and therefore worked, was much more symbolic and more like a parade than having the razor-edged feeling that so many ACORN actions had where each step might yield opportunity. Part of the problem was just the conflict of an organizing culture, shared by the HOTROC team that I managed, and the bureaucratic culture of the additional support grafted on from the AFL-CIO and other unions, well-meaning, but not that experienced in such activity and definitely undisciplined and inclined to showboat.

ACORN Action at Bell Toronto Headquarters 2013.

Not that it really mattered, since the leadership was also ad hoc and more ceremonial including then Mayor of New Orleans Marc Morial and the President of the AFL-CIO John Sweeney. We were essentially marching from the New Orleans Convention Center to Canal Street and then from Canal over towards Lafayette Square and a staged rally about living wages and workers' rights to organize the hotels. We got the job done and for some of our HOTROC team it was the most exciting event of their organizing careers, they claimed, but if I compared the ACORN organizers meeting on the eve of every convention night and then sometimes piling into cars or subways to go and scope out the next day's action targets to the donuts-and-coffee crowds of peacocks trying to parachute in for their piece of the credit as the expected numbers grew for the HOTROC march and sharp elbows nudged their way to the front of the line, I'd have to admit that like sausage or democracy, those were events where bystanders would not want to examine too closely how all of the pieces were baked together.

The advantages of well-trained and disciplined organizers as a key to successful large actions can also be found in the sophistication and complexity that it is possible to handle with such an organizing staff. Good examples can easily be found lots of places, but perhaps nowhere better than the multiple-entry action we pulled off in hitting the meeting site in Philadelphia at the Democratic mid-term convention in 1982. Despite surveillance of our meeting place, we managed to peel off several large delegations and scouting parties in order to deploy them successfully over sky bridges and through various hotels in order to disrupt various Democratic meetings. The main force was later blocked by the horse patrols and ended up marching and chanting in front of the convention, but our separate ACORN cohorts had managed to deliver our message forcibly.

Streets and Permits

Invariably on any larger action that involves marching from an assembly point to the target location, there is the question of whether or not to get a permit from the police or the city officials to allow such activity. ACORN's policy throughout my years was simple: we did not get permits; we did not ask permission to put our feet on the street and make our demands known. Practically speaking, we wanted to avoid the potential of being refused a permit, and tactically we wanted to have maximum flexibility and versatility in controlling both our routes and destination. Fundamentally, I always believed that with thousands of people, we were the eight-hundred pound gorilla and even with hundreds of people we could often fight way above our weight class.

All of which is not to say we were either stupid or reckless. Within days of convention actions and marches, we would dispatch our national legal team along with any locally experienced and adept attorneys that they had cajoled for help to visit the local police and inform that that we were in town, where we were staying, how long we would be around, where we were meeting, and the fact that we would be involved in various actions and events while here. Undoubtedly, the attorneys probably engaged in a fair amount of shrugging and sighing about their difficult clients (us!), but invariably they were able to assure them that there would be sufficient liaison, we were determined but not crazy and violent, and that we had local roots and buses, planes, and trains to catch when it was over and done. Believe it or not, this kind of interchange usually worked fine.

The other question on all such marches is whether to stay on the sidewalk or take the street, and once in the street, how much of the street to take, one lane, two, or the whole thruway. Places like Chicago were notoriously difficult, just as Philadelphia tended to be easier, and New York was usually a breeze, but whatever the city, even when it seemed to be going well, it would only be doing so "up to a point."

In Chicago in 1990, the police grudgingly surrendered one lane going through the financial district, but when various segments of the march tried to gingerly nudge our lane wider, they met it quickly with arrests by picking off an organizer involved (Craig Robbins), as I mentioned earlier. Horses were part of the problem in Chicago in 1990, just as they were daunting in 1982 in Philadelphia. Similarly, we found an entire mounted cavalry of police and their horses drawing an insurmountable wall in front of Madison Square Garden after what had been a joyous romp down Broadway during the march in 1980 to that point, leaving us to rally for a while and then release the crowd to find their buses parked on Eighth Avenue.

In the later years in places like Los Angeles, Detroit, and Columbus, we had little trouble, though we also had different targets and slimmer opportunities as the world changed and tactical options and opportunities changed as well. Additionally as the organization's general size and the numbers at the biennial conventions grew, our reputation and influence grew correspondingly as well making us less threatening to the police, and producing more of a "I've got my job, you've got your job," kind of climate that allowed more leeway and fewer arrests.

Ironically, my only experience with permits and the streets ended up in New Orleans where our alliance with Mayor Marc Morial, toggling between friend and foe, and the more conservative partnership between our union, ACORN, and other much more conservative unions meant that they wanted permits, and the permits were open ended. Unbelievably, we once easily got a permit to take only a couple of hundred people and a brass band right down Canal Street in the center of the city, just as the major HOTROC march was ceded the entire street for as long as we wanted.

In the ACORN Canada convention action in Montreal in June 2015, police came by as we assembled in Victoria Square, only yards from the statue of her highness. We kept to the sidewalks because our real objective was less the streets than the target of the action, the Bank of Montreal (BMO) and its stately, historic headquarters building that seemed the perfect setting to raise our demands about ending predatory lending and their financing of payday lenders, long a core ACORN campaign. Not only did we forsake the street, but crossed over through a side lane to a street just a block away from the BMO address, and then stopped chanting as we entered the square in front of the cathedral so that we could almost blend in with the groups of tourist milling in the square, observed, we hoped, lazily, by the BOM security team. While the main body proceeded through the square a smaller contingent of 30 to 40 had split behind another bank running parallel to our procession past the main statuary of the park until we came to the street in front of the bank, crossed quickly as both columns sought to enter the two primary front entrances, expecting fully in this modern age of high security, post-9/11, and paranoia extreme that a successful action to end the convention might mean getting fifty ACORN members into the bank to rendezvous with the scout team of organizers and the advance team of leaders and negotiators.

Amazingly, we overwhelmed what security existed and as the squad cars of Montreal police arrived the peculiarity of the revolving doors on both entrances meant that the police had to wait as the members poured through, and I was able to stand behind them and shepherd the rest of the members not yet in the bank to the side entrance while the police continued to try and exert control over the main door. Within minutes we had all 250 folks at the action into the bank, past the ornate, columned entryway and in the long expanse in front of the dark wood and marble teller's counters running the width of the bank under the 50 foot ceilings of the bank. Who knows how a concert might have sounded there, but the acoustics were marvelous for the chants and the sharks, symbolizing the predatory behavior, were waved as high as the banners.

You never know what might happen in an action, but as long as you are prepared for the worst and ready for any opportunity, great things can still happen in the magic of the moment driven by the power and passion of the people.

Chapter XVI: **Organizing Math**

Organizers and math are two peas that don't seem to fit in the same pod. In training or directing organizers on our staff, whenever I would begin to talk about "organizing math," I could almost feel the physical shudder and could absolutely see eyes begin to glaze over. Just at the thought that somehow as hard as many of them had spent a lifetime running from anything that had anything to do with math and were firmly committed to the soft side of the more liberal arts, here was a guy telling them that, whoops, you need as much math as mouth for this work.

We tried to keep it simple, but numbers mattered tremendously to the nuts and bolts of ACORN organizing. There was no way to avoid the systematic counting because it was essential in measuring organizational progress and health. Certainly, as I have repeatedly argued, there is no substitute for good judgment. Absolutely there are hundreds of judgments that are made subjectively. Clearly my brothers and sisters who argue the importance of values and faith in providing some of the binding glue for organizing have deep and important contributions to make to any discussion about organizational formation. Nonetheless, once we sign on as organizers determined to build mass organization, the numbers deeply matter, and trump many other considerations if we are truly trying to build mass organizations.

It all starts with the very first organizing drive that a trainee undertakes following the ACORN organizing model. The trainee would need to first find a community or neighborhood or "piece of turf," that could effectively sustain an ACORN local group organization over time. And, over time we had lots of experience to guide the *size* of the population we needed and knew why that took precedence over the *shape* of the community.

When I first began organizing ACORN I believed a successful organization could be built no matter what the size. If there were communities with natural boundaries set by rivers, railroads, expressways, parks or whatever that defined the turf and created some commonality and neighborhood identification, then I was confident that we were ready to rock and roll. Over the years we found that that was both true and false. Yes, the model was strong enough that we could create a local group, get the officers elected, move to action, and see the organization move forward. We could in fact virtually guarantee that result, but we also found over the years that unless we insisted on a threshold size for the community, the organization was not necessarily sustainable on a self-sufficient basis, particularly for a dues-based organization.

The size of the community we would organize was dictated by the numbers we needed. Ideally, we wanted a minimum of 1500 to 2000 families or households to make the organization sustainable and a vehicle for some real power in the area. Sometimes we were successful with only 1000 households, but routinely we were successful with 2500 or more, and certainly we could resolve issues and win campaigns with even smaller neighborhoods, but they were never sustainable.

At a first meeting expectations are predictably low. Many attending are skeptical that anything can be organized in their community, therefore any crowd larger than they predicted seems huge. Members are not organizers so their sense of the numbers can range widely. The best example I can give of how this perspective can get skewed is actually from union organizing when I asked a Hyatt housekeeper after a vote inside the hotel how many workers had been in the meeting, and without hesitation she replied, "thousands!" even though I knew there were less than 400 in the bargaining unit even if everyone had been there. She was telling me an important truth though about numbers. It is not the actual number, but what you think the number *feels* like that matters most in determining the sustainability of the local organization not in financial terms but as something that seems "strong" to its own members.

For the local organization to have sustainability as a vehicle for power in the eyes of its members the organization has to "feel" big and the regular meetings have to "feel" big, especially big enough to get something done and make things happen. A local group monthly meeting with only ten or twelve people doesn't "feel" strong. It feels weak. If the local group meeting even has twenty or twenty-five in attendance every meeting, it will "feel" stronger and more stable. If the average can move up past thirty-five or forty, then all of the members – and the leaders – will feel that the organization is in fact much more than just them and can be a real vehicle for change. A group with one hundred in attendance month after month is a world shaker! Remember, this is all regardless of what the organizer thinks personally, or the organizing staff expects or plans.

To reach those kinds of numbers, the organizing math is straightforward, and you are hard pressed to get there if there are only 500 or even 1000 households in the defined neighborhood turf. The organizing math aligns with certain performance standards that over time and constant repetition move from expectations or surprises to minimum standards for acceptable work. For example in the ACORN Organizing Model we would want to pull out no less than 5% and preferably10% of the number of households to the first formal organizational meeting that created the group.

For an organizing committee to be broadly representative and effective, there needed ideally to be people from the various geographic and demographic areas of the community, but it also had to be large enough to get the job done, especially when it came to filling out the schedule for doorknocking visits on the drive calendar. Ideally, a 20 to 25 person committee was best for 1000 households, 30 for 1500, 40 for 2000 and so forth with 2% as a rule of thumb. But, of course organizing does not occur as part of a mathematical formula and all of the committee never shows up at each of the weekly committee meetings and many fantastic organizing drives with the numbers more or less than ideal are still successful on the principle of hitting the doors "by any means necessary."

There was never an organizer that wanted less than 100 people at the first, formal meeting of a new ACORN organization. We always wanted 10% of the articulated community at the first meeting, and if we had followed the steps, done the doors, hit the marks, found, the issues, made the reminder visits and calls, we could see people coming through the attendance table a half hour before the meeting was even scheduled. We had made the meeting a "happening" that tilted the entire community in a new direction.

The magic number on the organizing math was to enroll 10% of the target community as dues paying members by the time of the first meeting. Many people unfamiliar with organizing are always surprised that so many families would join as dues paying members *before* they had even gone to a first meeting, voted on the officers, debated and selected the first campaign, and determined the first action. People without organizing experience think that organizing is "talk first, decision later," like so much of life, but rarely is that the case for most people. People join because of their *expectations* for the organization and their *aspirations* for themselves and the meaning of their participation, rather than because of the organization's record of accomplishment or their narrow self-interest calculations, which many wrongly believe describes way more about organizational activity than practice ever proves. This phenomenon of membership enrollment is also true whether the organization had been established for 40 years in Arkansas or was organizing for the first time in a megaslum outside of Lima or Buenos Aires.

Novices often try to argue that people will not join an organization until it is established, but on the doors an organizer always finds that in truth people believe that they know the organization from the first time they hear it is organizing. As mentioned earlier, in new cities in the United States when sometimes I was on the doors setting foot on the turf for the first time ever, and there was no chance that people had ever heard of ACORN, I would start the rap as always saying, "you've heard of ACORN, the community organization working in the neighborhood on housing, jobs, and education or whatever… haven't you?" Invariably, everyone would nod to me, that, yes, they knew ACORN. Talking then about what neighbors were saying the organization might do in this particular neighborhood established an emerging consensus and the decision about membership was a "vote" on the organization's mission. There was no need to reserve judgment for some later time. Mostly that is just "testing," a bit of push back on the doors from people to measure the organization and organizer's intention, commitment to their own rap, and passion about their mission. People voted with their membership, just like they would vote "with their feet" in the future practice of the organization. Why? People want to organize! They want an organization!

In organizing in addition to the attention given to the dialogue and dialectic on the doors, a lot of the success of recruitment and enrollment also lies in how well the entry and exit to the actual meeting is managed, especially when it comes to the selection of the people working the table and their skill in handling the attendance list and then converting the sign-ups to membership recruitment. This is an art that is rapidly being lost for lack of diligent care and nurturing of the skill, but when committee members are well selected and trained, it is something to behold. The work starts at the head of the chute as people come in the door and are met by the greeters, and walked hand in hand, arm in arm, to the attendance and sign-up table. Met with a smile and a pre-started attendance list that primes the list with the information correctly filled out in each column, and enough people working the table that lines do not build up but move swiftly, people follow the drill smoothly from one station to another in order to complete the requirements.

It has always been fascinating to me to observe how much of the success of these kinds of operations are based on modeling appropriate and expected behavior from the committee, and then followed as expected by people coming into the meeting. If someone at the top of an attendance list does not fill in their telephone number, then no one below will fill in their number until the sheet flips on the clipboard to a clean sheet. If someone ahead fills it in, then everyone fills it in. Most of this is simply "follow the leader." People can disturb the pattern by "swallowing the 'ask'" and presuming that people will refuse to sign or refuse to give some specific piece of information.

When we were beginning our field work for ACORN Ecuador in partnership with Ruptura, at the time an emerging political party in that country, the executive board of the party was absolutely convinced that no one would give us their cell numbers. We demurred and said, we would see, but we were comfortable that they would. Not surprisingly, just by asking, virtually everyone we met, even opponents of Ruptura and our organizing, gave their number as quickly as they were asked. Why not? We trained our organizers to ask on the assumption that they would get the number. We expected they would succeed. We trained them to ask with that conviction, and, bam, there were never any difficulties. These kinds of stories are legion in organizing. Too often organizers *project* problems onto people rather than asking and then listening and watching to see how people really respond.

Sign up table in Edinburgh, Scotland.

Whether a newly built local organization reached the 10% or 100 member benchmarks by the time of the first meeting, it was important to get there as quickly as possible during the post-organizing drive "cleanup." In the aftermath of the initial community organizing drive the organizer's task was to channel the energy of the new leadership and the continued vibrancy of the organizing committee members, many of whom would invariably have just been elected to key local group offices in recognition of their work and visibility through the drive, into a mop-up which re-visited all of the "yeses" who committed to come to the meeting, but for whatever reason did not actually make it, and all of the people who actually did come to the meeting, signed the attendance list, but for whatever reason did not actually join the organization.

The skill in this, and in all such situations where a commitment was made to the organization that was not fulfilled, is to refuse to take the inaction as a "no," but to always presume that what the person said was in fact what they meant, but that for reasons or

Chapter XVI: Organizing Math

rationales unknown and best left that way actually, they failed to follow through and attend, join, or whatever it might have been. Our job as organizers was to assume that their failure was not a rejection, and in fact to assume that the individual probably feels ashamed and guilty about having broken their word and will appreciate the fact that we do not dwell on it or make them wallow in it. By reaching out and essentially saying, "Darn, did you miss a great meeting! We wanted to come by and visit with you so that you were up to date with what happened and know that we are counting on you for …." Here the hook is the upcoming action or next meeting or joining or whatever the bottom line question and objective might be for that visit or conversation. On their part the prospective member might offer some excuse or reason for having not come through, but the organizer's job is to shrug that off as no problem, and keep moving forward to "yes," and to moving the person the huge existential distance from their house to the meeting, the action, the life of the organization, and their future.

None of this is easy of course. Organizers and leaders are human as well and many of us battle our own demons, insecurities, and the constant trauma of doors being slammed in our faces, both figuratively and literally. It is frequently hard for people not to take this personally. There are many new organizers who will admit to spending hours driving around the block in circles to build up the courage to hit the doors, all of which is also a primary reason why it is always better for an organizer to have taken the time and scheduled a committee member to do the doorknocking, calling, or whatever the task in tandem with the organizer.

This is ridiculous on its face. Organizational participation or inactivity is not personal, and organizers have to get past that argument. We cannot have it both ways. We cannot argue that we are building a membership organization, but somehow let our own personal involvement and issues be like fingers plopped on the scale to weigh down the chances of the organization's growth and success. It's not about us, it's about them.

Marcos Gomez (center) training militantes (organizers) in Quito.

This was always easy for me not only in community organizing but in union organizing as well, where the promises from workers were often about whether or not they would vote for the union. Other organizers often believed that some of the folks saying "yes," were just lying. I always argued that it is more complex. We had to rate people from our organizing contacts on a 1 to 5 scale, whether or not we thought someone was going to vote with us or not. Even when I rated someone as a maybe or even as a flat no, despite their solemn pledge that they were going to vote yes, I still always believed that what they were telling me and others is what they *wanted* to do or *wished* they would do, but often were just too fearful and intimidated to do. In other words they wanted to be yeses, even when they – and we – often knew they were going to be no's.

Being resilient in organizing and always continuing to push the yeses to really be yeses is part of the beauty and craft of the process. Like so much in organizing, I think that we only fail to achieve this at the point we give up trying. As long as we are pushing forward, I absolutely believe the odds are with us, and think that the organizing math backs me up on such a conclusion.

Cleanups were critical, but that does not mean they were easy for an organizer to manage well. Coming from the first meeting, an organizer, even a new trainee, is juggling a lot of balls in the air with both hands. Second and third visits needed to be held with the new officers and meetings scheduled with the new officers to work out their relationships, to more clearly understand their roles, to get their arms around the finances, and of course to plan for the first action and first campaign and the next meeting. Speaking of the first action, organizers often had trouble making sure the turnout mechanisms were being put in place, while integrating the turnout from people who were now members with the ongoing recruitment of additional people in the harvest from the original drive and first meeting.

The goals for a local group were to hit 20% membership density within the designated community within 6 months of initial organizing drive, computed easily enough by dividing the number of members by the total number of households in the territory or drive area. Within a year we looked at a 30% benchmark for density, but often were not as attentive to that objective since we were also pushing the organizer to begin more organizing drives and maintain more local groups, essentially to become a better juggler, rather than simply "polishing the pearl," as we often said. There were some groups in places as diverse as Mountain Pine, Arkansas, NICO in northern Lake Charles, Louisiana, and some tenant and building-based organizations where in fact the numbers even exceeded 50% concentration, but frankly that was more unusual than it was common. In some ways it was sufficient to know that the model could in fact produce those results, even if ACORN never had the resources to expend on staffing to support the mass of our 800 odd local groups by 2008 to achieve quite those numbers. Both the accomplishment and the failure raise other questions perhaps about our choices, but we were building a mass-based constituency organization not a neighborhood organization, so we were clear on our vision and direction.

One question has to do with the ideal ratio in assigning organizers to maintain local groups and support their development. In the early years of building in Arkansas and the initial expansion of the organization nationally in the United States, it was not uncommon for an individual organizer to be servicing as many as seven or eight local groups. Admittedly, this was a load and it kept an organizer hopping from one planning meeting or local group meeting to another virtually every night of the week. The corollary though was that the organizer was forced to develop and depend on leaders and members more because they physically and mentally could not handle the load otherwise. Fast forward 25 and 30 years later and such a load was unheard of anywhere within the organization. It was more likely by the 21st century to find an organizer straining to handle a load of three or four local groups at the most. Undoubtedly such a level of maintenance responsibility was easier to handle, but it was less clear if the organization actually grew more with such attention. In fact it is likely that with the narrower ratio of groups to organizers, that the groups invariably became more staff-dependent, and it is categorically true that the local organizations became much less sustainable, since a smaller number of groups, and therefore members, were carrying the full weight of the organizer, pay, benefits, travel, and per capita office expense.

It is impossible to measure growth whether in a local group, city, statewide or national organization without counting, so we counted all the time. For 38 years in the United States we kept monthly statistics that recorded much of this for every organizer, every office, every city, and every state and was tabulated, summarized, and distributed back to everyone as well. We still do internationally.

From the first office opened in Sioux Falls through the early 20/80 expansion the opening-a-new-office "kit" would include a couple of meeting tables bought in bulk by Carolyn Carr from the surplus supply of Union National Bank in Little Rock and a chart used to tabulate the daily performance of organizers in the new city. Transparency of performance was critical. Everyone knew how everyone else was doing every day, and the system requireed the numbers to be posted daily. This should have meant that the collection of data for the weekly and monthly reports was smooth and easy, but those were not the days when such reports could simply be loaded online and automatically tabulated as was the case by 2008. For decades this was a burdensome hand to hand job that relied as much on the "trailing" offices as on the ones who managed the math and numbers easily. The numbers were assembled thanks to intricate formulas on Lotus and then Excel spreadsheets and then distributed. The performance of both organizers and offices were ranked across all of these categories in these reports.

The reports were essential in building the organization and the ACORN culture of growth and performance, although that does not mean that as important as these reports were to ACORN's success and operations that the process, reports, or transparency of it all were popular. Those offices that understood the purpose were fine, but obviously those trapped at the bottom of the charts were not enthusiastic proponents of the system or the inevitable competition and hierarchy it produced. Sometimes such criticism was fair, especially after 1984 when the offices had variable resources with which to compete. But, not counting the numbers and doing the math does not build mass organization, it only builds something soft and squishy based on supposition and conjecture, and that doesn't put bottoms in chairs and feet on the street. Like it or not, without the numbers we would not have been equally as able to support the offices that needed to be shored up and to maximize the offices that had the potential to do more.

Keeping up with the numbers was also critical in doing the work to determine turnout for actions, meetings, conventions, and any other kind of organizational activity. Often understanding the organizing math is the difference between just guessing at who and what might turnout, and actually organizing and therefore having an accurate prediction on what to expect based on your experience. Simply put, 50 yeses never mean that 50 people will be there at the rough and ready as expected. In fact 50 yeses, depending on the experience and the skill of the organizer, might be translated into a range of between 15 people and 25 with 15 being the low end based on an over optimistic, more gullible, and usually more inexperienced organizer seriously over-counting the yeses by listening to their own rap more closely than the response from the members, and 25 being a more normal assessment of work done, plans made, and predictable response.

A rule of thumb only works well if it is a reasonably accurate gauge of reality. If you really want and need 25 people or 100 or even a 1000 at an event, then depending on all of the factors, most organizers would believe that you would need at least twice to three times as many yeses to have a reasonable expectation of success and that knowledge then dictates the work plan and the timeline. Organizing is more art than science though, so the real conversion of such a rule of thumb is in the range of not being embarrassed on the low end and getting lucky on the high end, both of which can happen, keeping the reality of life and the work from making this a fool's imperfect science. If the issue or the event catches fire, then lightening can strike and give an organizer more than an even break on the numbers. If disaster strikes, snow falls, and rain pours, the experienced organizer will rarely be looking at nothing but empty seats on the bus or chairs in the church, but will still come in at one-third to forty percent of the yeses. Picking this profession means living with adrenaline at the edge of that work or, if that is not comfortable, following your ulcers out the door.

On events where members had "skin in the game," meaning money down for their share of a seat on the bus or deposit on a dorm room at a convention, the planning and work is on a longer timeline and the numbers exist in different relationships to reality in ACORN's experience, and of course the numbers work out differently for short hauls compared to big trips like biannual conventions. Where members might be putting down $10 or $20 per person to roll from New York or Philadelphia or even Boston for a one-day action or rally on a campaign target or lobbying as part of the annual ACORN lobby day, a small deposit was often an excellent predictor on the numbers, and of course the more a member might have ponied up, the better chance that they would follow through rather than blow off the non-refundable deposit, making ten bucks more like an ante and thirty something closer to a sure bet. None of that would make the ratio 100%, but it might put the range between 50 and 75%.

Conventions were trickier because the costs were steeper and frequently for the "fliers" meant serious money and fundraising efforts to enable attendance. The same rules prevailed on deposits. For fliers, fifty was an ante, and one hundred was a serious bet on attendance. Everything was always nonrefundable in principle, though not necessarily 100% in practice. The problem with conventions where the organization was going to move thousands of people is that the fuse to the dynamite was always lit and burning quickly on the calendar. If the member price was $300, $500, or $800 for the airplane fliers, then the office needed to be in motion early enough to have the range of deposits piled up sufficiently to have the members involved in scrimping, saving, and fundraising to be able to get the committed number on the bus or aboard the plane. For example ACORN conventions were invariably held in the summer months, so the best prepared offices came into the Year End/ Year Begin meetings with a chunk of members and money already on the books and in hand perhaps 10% of the total they had pledged or in big offices like New York City in reasonably short travel or bus range as much as 20% might be already committed. The higher the early payments were, then the greater the likelihood of success.

It is important to remember that ACORN conventions involving thousands of people in attendance were largely self-funded affairs by the membership participants. Take as gospel the fact that no one outside of the ranks of the organization itself ever cares a whit about whether or not the membership really runs the organization nor are they willing to invest a dime in governance, leadership development, or direct participation. Most outsiders would not know membership participation, much less democracy, if it bit them in the butt, so they were sure not going to create a free ride adventure of the experience. That is not to say that unions, allies, and others might not buy an ad in the program or even sponsor a member or more to come from their home city to the convention based on the member or office's own hustle and bustle, but nonetheless, these events worked because they were what the members wanted and were willing to spring for. Knowing that, the first list made, even before the calendar would greet the New Year when a convention would be held, would the list of members who had been on the last convention. There were members who never missed a convention from the first one in 1978 until they literally could not attend again or until the last one in 2008 thirty years later.

Nonetheless the trick was to get 50% of what you were going to need to indicate interest before the calendar turned to the new year and to get at least 50% of that number or 25% of the total to have put down their deposits. Ideally by March 1st the interest list was established, up to 50% were fully paid and the scuffle was to get the rest of the money in by the convention itself. In reality most offices were collecting money as the buses rolled away and often in way too many cases still collecting even a couple of months after the convention was over. Some of this work became a little easier in the last several conventions in the 21st century when ACORN began encouraging members to start "saving" money for their convention costs through bank drafts on their accounts on a monthly basis. Nonetheless it was always a lift, and always worth the climb, but new offices and inexperienced organizers often had a painful learning curve, though richly rewarded by the expression on the members' faces as they slumped in their seats on the bus and slept most of the journey home with their ice chests empty and wearing their new convention t-shirts proudly.

Reminder calls in many ACORN offices were compulsive and incessant. In the most productive offices, the time in the field was followed by several hours on the phone from the office. ACORN never bought into the notion that organizers should go home to make their calls rather than rolling to the office after the field for mutual support, suggestion, and accountability. You had to have many years of seniority to work your way into that special place and perk of home-based calling. There were some simple truths.

Bars were for drinking, not for meeting potential members or contacts. Homes were for eating and sleeping, not for working. ACORN believed in the boiler room atmosphere of the movement and political campaigns. The symphony of multiple voices making calls together and building off the success shared by any member of the team would be loud and infectious, and would keep people going until after 9 PM when we believed enough was enough.

The reminder calls for a meeting or an action might involve three or even four "touches" to the member on the phone in addition to the doors, general meetings, or planning meetings in the community. The first call translated the information, created engagement, and won the commitment. The second call was ostensibly an update of more information and solidified the commitment by tightening down additional details, like whether a ride was needed or the rendezvous place for the action or pickup spot for the buses, the third call was the night before and was a final reminder and a count, and then there was the fourth call which was the "day of" call, and might happen at dawn for an early pickup or within the last two hours before the meeting was scheduled that night. Organizers in the larger offices were pulled into regularly scheduled meetings and required to report on their numbers in detail. There was rigor, there was discipline, there was consistency, and it worked. Office after office would have their own math that articulated the effectiveness of this program, and whether it differed by a point or two here or there, it happened in Philadelphia just like it happened in Miami or Toronto or New Orleans, night after night. And, the fact that as an organizer in the ACORN community of organizers you also knew you could call, text, or email a fellow organizer in another city and find them doing the same thing at the same time, made a difference.

For ACORN the numbers all started with building the list and in the beginning that meant stacks of 3x5 cards in as many shades as I could purchase. Each colored 3x5 card signified a different organizing drive and were used on the doors to record interest, issues, and attendance, becoming the living, very physical database for an organizing drive in the 1970's when the notion of having a database *per se* did not really exist. In those days the first "touch" of an organizing drive was a bulk mailing to the list compiled for the drive from crisscross directories (linking phone numbers and addresses) and Polk's City Directory that would list all addresses in the "turf" selected for the drive. After the trainee or office manager or volunteer or organizer, depending on who drew the short straw, had typed up the list, mailing labels would be created first through punch card machines in the 1970s and then through Avery labels as time went on, and then affixed to the 3x5 cards.

The total list produced in this way defined the universe of the drive. Telephone numbers were corrected on the doors. Notes were made on abandoned houses or wrong names or tenants now in or out. Giant rubber bands kept them all together so that the organizers working the group over the years could continue to consult the information, go back, and pull people out of the stack who had been active, once were members, had come but then been lost, or had special interests, issues, or problems. The transition notes from organizer to organizer that annotated these basic cards and lists could be wonderfully detailed, in fact sometimes too detailed as we once learned from a great organizer's notes (Terry Andrews in Philadelphia) that were later found by an excellent leader (Mary Ellen

Smith from South Philly) and created a hullabaloo because the notes were a little too frank on the strengths and weaknesses of various local group leaders. There is no question that the movement to database computer programs whether Excel or Access or FileMaker Pro (and lord the arguments that organizers could have over the merits of each of those programs were legendary and still are with NationBuilder, Action Network, and others!) was an improvement on the old handcrafted system, especially for building a national organization and aggregating so much information for so many people. On the local level though of servicing a community organization, I have often wondered if having the physical cards in your desk for ready information and consultation did not create a closer connection between the organizer and the group that was lost in the transition. You can never go back, but that does not mean that you do not do the work with sometimes a touch of nostalgia or that every new tool is an even trade on all counts with what preceded it.

The same obsession with numbers and lists transferred over to labor and political organizing from the community organizing experience. In 1980 when we first started running union elections with the United Labor Unions, we used the same 3x5 cards that were once the ACORN stock-in-trade. When we got the *Excelsior* list from the National Labor Relations Board (NLRB), I would make up a new set of 3x5 cards for every worker, regardless of who had signed authorization cards, been to meetings, or anything else. I would post all of the cards on a giant bulletin board covered with reddish orange burlap on the 2nd floor of the union's office at 628 Baronne in the Central Business District of New Orleans. I would tack all of the cards on the "No" side of the board, and then restart the process from the several weeks that we received the list to the day of the election, to see if we could move a majority of the cards over to the clear "Yes" side of the board, rather than "Maybe's" in the middle or stuck in the original "No" column. In union organizing our experience was that "maybe's" always voted when there was hard company opposition in the campaign and "maybe's" almost always voted "no," so you had to count them that way. Yeses had to be hard and tested to get to the far right column. The process was laborious to a small degree, but just one of the endless details involved in the work, and it was brutally effective in creating an accurate count before the election.

A cousin of the "count on me" in community organizing for labor organizing was the "why I'm voting yes!" In reaffirming support before an election, the goal was to get a majority of the workers to give personal quotes offering the reasons "why I'm voting yes" alongside their picture. The statement might be as simple as "better pay" or "dignity or respect" or as detailed and lengthy as a worker might offer. The point of the piece was to circulate it to every worker in the last 24 to 72 hours before the election to drive momentum behind the union's victory. If we achieved our goal of being able to demonstrate that more than half of the bargaining unit was solidly committed to voting yes, then often we would win by a large, sweeping margin because people like to vote on the winning side and would be emboldened by their co-workers. It could be dicey if we came out with the leaflet too early because managers would try to flip some of our yeses or pick off someone to serve as an observer for the company at the balloting or anything that might deflate or obstruct our final push.

Accurate counting is also important for electoral work on GOTV in the community from the point of registration to the point of pulling the lever at the voting booth. There, I always favored a 1 to 5 numbering system with 1's indicating sure votes, 2's leaning to yes, 3's maybe, 4's leaning to no's, and 5's hard no's and committed to voting for the other proposition, candidate or party. There are endless variations on the applications, and as important as the organizing math are the metrics involved in determining the vote in that precinct, ward, district or whatever the jurisdiction, and whether or not our efforts increased the total votes as well as the vote recorded by the candidate or the party compared to past elections. We cared deeply whether or not we could make the case that our work among lower income voters was determinant in the final outcome of the election, because our statistical case also leveraged our claim to power and the conversion of the votes to move commitments to actual victories.

When we first dipped our feet in these waters, the process was such in Arkansas that when the polls closed and the count was completed a copy of the vote total and the actual sign-in sheet for registered voters was posted on the door of the polling station. We would be up in the wee hours after an election going from poll location to location on our turf to pick up copies of those sheets from the election judges. We even made a couple of dollars for the organization in those days by calling in the results to counting companies that were servicing local and national television and trying to race the results in first. No doubt in these modern days of real-time data and high speed internet that sounds unbelievably quaint, but for us it also put in our hands an amazing list of regular or chronic voters, as they are called in Louisiana, and an ability to for us to go back through the list and name by name determine what our own get-out-the-vote work had delivered, and therefore as an organizing training lesson was invaluable. I miss those sheets!

Sometimes this worked very well, and sometimes it was difficult to figure out the math in the political equation. A recent experience for ACORN International and ACORN Ecuador in working in partnership with a young political party in its first electoral contests in 2013 is a prime example. There, President Rafael Correra, the left-leaning president of the country in the process of rewriting the constitution had greatly altered the way votes would be counted, not surprisingly favoring his own party and allies. Rather than allowing an individual candidate to win in the election based on the usual plurality of votes, in the mandatory voting, Ecuadorians would have to vote the entire slate (*plancha*) for a party if they wanted to elect any of the members of that slate to office. Previously, there might have been a blend of delegates from different parties if the leading candidates for each of the parties had run well. Despite running a program largely in Quito Norte that successfully built a list of contacts among more than 21,000 people with a significant percentage committing to vote with our allies, this election was peculiar because there would be no baseline we could use to measure the final outcome of the work this election, since this was the first election by a new party under a new system. How many times does that every happen?

The math involved in hitting a half-million or a million new voter registrations was often a gang rush that was more mass engineering than delicate surgery. To get to the numbers needed involved inputs of money and people over the two-year voting cycle mashing the numbers on a daily prediction and expectation of production to end up with the numbers needed to make a difference. The math was more analogous to what it took to put bottoms on buses to a convention, meaning that what often matters most was timing and sequencing. More specifically, we need the ability to start early enough in enough battleground states with enough money to hire and assemble the crews to get the training so that production goals could be realized within the timeframe between start and the final day allowing registrations.

Probably the real scale of our voter registration accomplishment was only fully realized by the same forces that were so committed in 2008 and afterward to shutting ACORN's voter registration efforts down. As the cycle thickened during the spring and summers before an election, the payroll would swell to 5 to 6000 workers involved in voter registration around the country on a part or full-time basis. Training, supervision, and reporting were gargantuan tasks as were collecting the forms, double checking the signatures for accuracy and completion, databasing, collecting the payroll information, getting the checks out or printed on-site from a centralized source, and just the plain and simple logistics of getting the trains to move on time and make it to their destinations. It would have been a miracle if there had not been some errors, and of course, surely there were, given the mountains of paper and the number of times a registration form moved from the signature in the field to the field office to quality control and back to the home office and registrar's office for filing and then doubling checking to make sure the wannabe new voter would actually get to be a real first time voter and pull the lever when it mattered.

As I said before, counting matters!

Organizing Math Driving Sustainability and Strategy

Sure, we talked the math, but we walked it as well.

The 20/80 Campaign initiated in 1975-76 is well known, but looking back at old memos I had written during that period the headline might have been the commitment to expand the organization but the subtext over and over again was focused on the nuts and bolts of what it took to recruit and retain more organizers and make the organization more self-sufficient financially for the long term. The memoranda detailed the plans – and the numbers and formulas – to get us there.

The 100+ Plan[109] was a look at the number of members, dues collected, and internal financing that would allow us to hire unlimited numbers of organizers. At the Year End/Year Begin staff meeting in Little Rock, of the three states (Arkansas, Texas and South Dakota), where ACORN was organized at that time, and thirty staff members expected to be in attendance, the organization was working on a way to hire a staff of over 100 organizers by the end of 1978. This was less a question of meeting membership needs or hiring ability, but more about "guaranteeing a ratio between salary and income which would allow the unlimited increase of organizers within ACORN." The ratio that ACORN was trying to achieve was for organizers to reach "parity between income and salary in 1975 and in most cases to exceed parity and approach the 2.5 ratio inherent in the 100+

---

[109] Rathke, Wade, *"Status Report on '100+ Plan' and General Staff,"* January 3, 1976.

Plan and the Staff Salary and Income Schedules." The ratio was essentially total internal income to staff salary payment.

There was recognition that field organizers with direct membership contact were more likely to have a shot at income self-sufficiency based on dues and internal fundraising events, but also that support staff would have some level of equity in pay, based on whether or not they generated the higher ratio of income to support themselves as well as contribute to the financial security of the whole. These early ACORN memos of the mid-1970's called these folks 4/2 staff, meaning that not only did their work trigger the 2.5 ratio of income generated to salary expense, but they also were paid $4000 per year once they also made a 2 year commitment to work for the organization.[110]

The Million Plus Plan, originally promoted in "late spring 1975"[111] envisioned an ACORN with gross revenues of more than $1,000,000 per year, unheard of then. At the time it was written, ACORN was a three-state operation with a budget of perhaps $250,000. The initiative was really two-fold. As the status report stated, "We made the plan in anticipation of organizational need, but as the various projections and formulas show, the organizational need is fast catching up to a million a year." The second objective though was more strategic and that was to *force a redefinition of the basic understanding of what a community organization* was and cantilever ACORN forward on a new paradigm. We wanted to break the block club, "small is beautiful" mold, so that insiders (members, leaders, and staff) and outsiders (funders, media, politicos, etc.) would start to understand the real potential of community organizations in the ACORN mold, rather than in the ways people had become accustomed to thinking about it all. In order to both develop the internal resources and compete for the external resources sufficient to reach our ambitions, we needed to change the conversation and the expectations of what was possible.

Another memo entitled "Organizer/Member Ratios"[112] calculated the existing ratio of members serviced by each organizer and speculated on what it would take to reach a ratio that would enable sustainability and scale. The 100+ Plan "argued a ratio of 1:500" in order to achieve the balance between dues and internal expense and the cost of an organizer which was central to ACORN growth and maintenance in ACORN system. In 1976 though, as the plans were made and measured, the ratio in Arkansas was 1:200, in South Dakota 1:60, and in Texas 1:111 in terms of total members and obviously less than those numbers perhaps up to half as many who were completely paid up. The numbers needed for full self-sufficiency, not simply what we called "staff self-sufficient," were more in the range of 1:1000, a goal we hoped to achieve over a 10 year time period.

It is impossible to underestimate the seriousness with which ACORN took these programs linking organizing effectiveness, growth and empowerment with financial stability. The "Ratios" memo recognizes that at the time of writing in early 1976, when

---

[110] Thanks to Dewey Armstrong, a 10 year ACORN veteran of that period, who jogged my memory on exactly how the 4/2 program worked.

[111] Rathke, Wade, *"Status Report on Million Plus Plan,"* January 3, 1976.

[112] Rathke, Wade, *"Organizer/Member Ratios,"* January 3, 1976.

ACORN was largely built around small and medium sized cities and rural areas, there would have to be changes.

> "Confronting the problem of how we come to a point where ACORN maintains a 1:1000 ratio, one is obviously talking about the role of an ACORN organizer being much different in practice in coming years, although not in theory, than it is now. The movement in more urban ACORN operations towards larger and larger neighborhoods as we have discussed previously is more suited to the ACORN model, the dues system, and the directions the organization has been moving than are some of the situations we face in rural ACORN operations. But, that is not to say that ACORN should, or will, move away from organizing in states like Arkansas and South Dakota, or in offices like Huron and Stuttgart. The point is only that an ACORN organizer in a more rural area has to be more efficient than an equivalent organizer in an urban area in order to organize the same number of people in perhaps more groups. In short, we have to better define the constituency in our organizing in all areas. In Eastern Arkansas we have to look at not only the 2000 potential members in Stuttgart, but also the additional 3000 Riceland Coop users. We have to know that we are willing to organize the TRAG's and MPCO's in rural areas, or be willing to take the time to make that happen. One organizer could handle 1000 members within the next 3-4 years potentially. This could be achieved by implementation of the ACORN representation structure; better organizer training and training drive supervision; increasing leadership training; a recruiting system which would allow for two years of seasoning by local group organizers before promotion or termination; larger neighborhoods; higher percentages of ACORN members organized in each community or neighborhood; and potentially an Association field organizer pool and campaign organizer pool."[113]

The "Close the Gap/Hold the Line"[114] memo struggled to determine how to balance the membership enrollment with the PUP (paid up percentage), which was especially critical in those days before we might have even imagined automatic bank draft collection ten and twenty years later. In the spring of 1976, ACORN's multi-state growth goal

---

[113] Ibid, pp. 2-3.

[114] Rathke, Wade, *"Close the Gap / Hold the Line,"* April 16, 1976.

was 10% on a membership of roughly 5000[115] with about 3600 of the members still in Arkansas and the other 1400 distributed between South Dakota (325), Texas (560), New Orleans (265), and St. Louis (30), and these new offices geared up to speed between January 1975 and the 18 months following. The analysis shaping the "Close the Gap/Hold the Line" memo was an effort to both accelerate expansion with the recruitment of new members while simultaneously narrowing the percentages of members who were fully paid up on their dues at the same time. The numbers were running above 50% in all cases with the newest offices only open for a month or two at the time of the memorandum near 100%, and the aggregate number for Arkansas at 50.2% and for the Dallas/Fort Worth offices opened in August 1975 at 50.1%. Pages of charts, forms, and specific office-by-office goals attempted to instill a campaign atmosphere for the offices and organizers to try and discipline the pace of expansion with a deeper attention to performance on maintenance, which was always an abiding tension within ACORN. The "gap" in these exhortations was the difference in paid up percentage, while the "line" was the continued commitment to growth. We never won this campaign in my 38 years at the wheel of ACORN in the U.S., and we never lost it. This model is still evolving as defined by a critical ACORN-centric understanding and commitment to the need to be a mass based organization.

As Chief Organizer of both the Association (meaning the multi-state ACORN) and at that time of Arkansas ACORN, the mother ship, these memos reveal the clarity of how the "organizing math" was embedded in the culture and planning of the organization in the mid-1970's at the time when Arkansas was the training center and development platform for all of the organizers leading the expansion effort and the programs driving the organization. The culture would be formed in Arkansas and spread nationally.

The first head organizers for all of the new projects were hired and trained in Arkansas and then dispatched to the expansion projects: Dewey Armstrong from Pulaski County to South Dakota, Meg Campbell and Steve Holt from North Little Rock to Fort Worth and Dallas, respectively, Barbara Friedman from Little Rock to Houston, Zach Polett from Fort Smith to New Orleans, and Mary Lassen from Fayetteville to St. Louis, and so forth. Here is how we stirred the pot with all of these numbers:

"Based on these tables as well as the last feedback report and other organizational operative goals in Arkansas (i.e. 10% growth rate), some average expectations can be formulated. In order to close the gap we should expect that on the average 41 *old members who are now in arrears will become paid in good standing every month through June. This figure is computed by office, not but by organizer, although after mid-May that would only be relevant in North Little Rock.*

In order to hold the line in the areas of dues and growth, we can arrive at the average expectations in this area. From the feedback report, you are familiar with your office average in terms of new members and dues

---
[115] Rathke, Wade, "*ACORN Status Report – 6/76*," June, 1976

collected for the last quarter. In terms of the goals you list on your forms, as well as the average/organizer/month computed from the organizational goals of a 10% growth rate, we need to increase by 37 new members for every field organizer each month. Obviously some of the organizers are already producing at this standard expectation, while others have some distance to travel in order to achieve.

We expect that organizers who have already reached this goal will hold the line on their current rate of new membership growth, and that means particularly in Pine Bluff and Hot Springs. For them their last quarter's average is a minimum standard. There is no way to estimate what their standard expectation should be.

These are not minimum standards on the whole. Judging from the last quarter the minimum standards for increase in paid up members would only have been 8. The increase per organizer per month in new members would only be a little over 21. The average amount of money per organizer per month was only around $150. These then are not minimum standards but the standard expectations for the Close the Gap / Hold the Line Campaign to maintain our progress and erode our problems in the area of responsibility for each field organizer.

Closing the gap will involve something extra from every organizer. Holding the line in some cases will also involve some extra push for some organizers. But, regardless, these are the standards we need to hold in this campaign."[116]

Math and Accountability

The real story is obviously not simply about math or my joke about "organizing math" being essential for some of the math-haters among the ranks of organizer and leaders. Organizing success is really driven more by the hard facts of reporting and numbers that sort out the bull from the brass by leveling the playing field so that articulate rappers, jailhouse lawyers, and one college course political philosophers are forced onto even ground with organizers that are single mothers or high school dropouts or "new" Americans more comfortable in Spanish or their home languages than others on the staff. The organizing tradition is inordinately oral, rather than written, therefore standing in passive, stubborn opposition to 20th and 21st century trends moving the rest of the world. Organizing, as some say, is often about stories of one type or another. Contrary to what many might hope though, stories do not build mass organizations, even if they are

---

[116] Ibid, *"Close the Gap."*

Exhibit 54: Monthly Numbers Report July 31, 2002

Chapter XVI: Organizing Math

valuable in constructing narratives that explain an organization's methods or mission. Numbers convert the individual stories into the facts that matter in public life and therefore political and social changes.

Rome or Edinburgh or Delhi, Quito, or Grenoble, usually means seeing a handwritten, butcher paper chart or wall painted with blackboard paint or modern whiteboard with lines of columns running down and names of groups and organizers running across. Every day when organizers come in, the numbers for the day are put on the chart, totaled every week, every month, and every year. The culture of reporting is a culture of final responsibility and accountability.

If members joined at a meeting the cards are turned in along with the dues for deposit or the signed authorizations now in a more modern banking world for direct deposit from a new member's account to ACORN's account or through credit card exchange or whatever works for the member. The only days that do not happen, are the days when there is no organizing. The results converted into numbers do not become stories, but become standards of what the organization can expect from the work being done in the field. The numbers are like a powerful solvent dissolving the stories that may be moving and profound, or as far fetched and fantastic where homework has been eaten or Martians have landed or rain, snow, sleet and hail have halted the organizer from her appointed rounds. The numbers are facts. The stories always have a little bit of fiction as part of the tale.

None of the foregoing is not to suggest that there has not been resistance to such reporting from 1970 until today as I hit the keyboard now. Weak performance that resists routine reporting is virtually a universal organizing law. Not uncommonly a bad day in the streets is slow to find its way to the charts, whether this has been done 12,000 times before or not. And, doubtlessly, when a head organizer or office director stops paying attention to whether or not the charts are up, filled in daily, and tabulated, the culture of reporting also collapses in lightning quick fashion. Reporting is not simply math after all, but part of the dialectic of organizing progress, so if the supervisor is not commenting, complimenting, critiquing, or adding constructive advice to the emerging information as it hits the charts, then the feedback loop is broken, and organizers rapidly understand that the numbers really do not "matter" as much as they had been led to believe, and as speedily the numbers that document the work also begin a slide to a new, much lower baseline.

Interestingly for some community organizations the resistance to reporting was able in many cases to survive even in the midst of other organizing methodologies that demanded numbers. The fundraising mechanics that were the lifeblood of numerous organizations beginning in the 1970's and extending into this time in some cases involved rigorous reporting and constant measurement of the various interactions parsing recruitment to fine points to evaluate field managers and canvass directors, as well as street canvassers working the blocks or phone canvassers riding the dialers for dollars. The same statistical rigor and reporting for the most part did not migrate over to the community-based efforts that were housing the canvasses and in fact being almost wholly funded by them. In fact almost the opposite happened. Sometimes campaign organizers would be recruited from the canvass outreach staff and on a 3/2 basis work for the organization to advance the organization's campaign three days a week, often without any clear reporting or standards, and then in two days of canvassing raising the money necessary for the campaign organizer to be paid a living wage.

More recently, largely driven more by increased rigor of funders more knowledgeable about electoral work, I have noticed a growing trend for more exhaustive and accurate reporting by various organizations and community organizing networks, even among faith-based organizations where such reporting has been more unusual. PICO Network, Ohio Community Collaborative, and others all issued detailed reports on the number of doors they had visited, families they had registered, and so forth after the 2012 Presidential election. As I have discussed elsewhere (Chapter XVIII on Politics), one of the reasons that ACORN found that electoral work and political action were so effective in building power is that the winners and losers are so clear because the votes are counted and the results are unambiguous, as opposed to much of community organizing where the clarity is often much more muddled.

Labor organizing, as I mentioned earlier, also shares the rigor of reporting since they are membership organizations, like ACORN, and if the work does not convert into real growth, the organizing drives are short lived. Visits, "test" results, attendance, card counts, and finally knowing the numbers going into representation elections are all critical barometers in predicting success or failure. No small part of this experience was why the ACORN reporting and accountability culture was so useful in training a generation of organizers who also seeded the organizing departments in unions throughout North America. Three became organizing directors of the AFL-CIO. The transition for us from community to labor organizing was difficult. We learned a new regime of laws and regulations and some of the differences of tactics and strategy, but the mechanics were well understood and easily transferable. ACORN's slam dunk victory for home childcare workers in partnership with the American Federation of Teachers (AFT) for more than 35,000 workers was difficult at the point that I was first selling the program along with the New York ACORN head organizer, Jon Kest, to the local and the national union, but once the labor politics were done, and the job was basically engineering the drive to get the workers organized, the cards signed, and the election run. We had no problems winning one of the largest labor elections in the 20th century and certainly the largest ever in New York City even though Jon and his team on the ground had never run a real union election before.[117]

We all knew the drill and how to march to the finish.

---

[117] The New York ACORN team had won a separately administered balloting for Work Employment Program (WEP) workers several years before when we were trying to force the City of New York to recognize the workers, so after a fashion, they had "been to the rodeo."

Chapter XVII: Constituency, Institutions, Networks, Alliances, Advocacy

If there was one common refrain about ACORN that always surprised me (there were many refrains, just not that many which surprised me), it was the constant niggling about whether or not ACORN worked with other organizations. My lord in heaven, we worked with thousands of groups and hundreds of coalitions in all different shapes and sizes and did so routinely. Where in the blue blazes did this question really come from?

First and finally, it's all about the base

Having thought a lot about this question, I think part of the query lies with the phenomenal implosion of membership-based organizational formations over the last quarter of the 20th Century though now decreasing in the 21st Century. Where once participation in organizational life was such a constant, that 40 years ago I could fashion an organizer training exercise about member expectations of an organization by first forcing new organizers to discuss their own experiences as members of some kind of organization in their own lives, these days, more often than not, I am met by blank stares and have to mine deeply for any experiences that resonate.

Robert Putnam famously observed in his essay and later book, *Bowling Alone*[118], that bowling was soaring as a sport, but bowling leagues were capsizing, he zeroed in on television as a key culprit, but now in any revised version he would have to substitute the internet or whatever is the latest thing standing in television's place, even as organizational membership in all kinds of institutions continues to plummet. Once at an ACORN Legislative Conference in Washington attended by hundreds of the top ACORN leaders, I listened to them engage Putnam tenaciously because their experience in ACORN was so contrary to the trends that Putnam was discussing. We were two ships passing in the night, both at the time convinced of our course, and likely both ships had been steered truly, but to different shores.

Membership has now fallen in US labor unions to the lowest ebb in over 100 years to hardly 11% in total, or fewer than 1 out of every 8 workers, and is even lower than that among private sector workers alone. Membership in the Boy Scouts of America is half of what it was. Membership in churches is cratering, and participation is dramatically falling even where congregants still claim some link to a religious institution. Membership should be falling in the National Rifle Association in the wake of gun violence, and it is. Membership has caved in all of the established veterans organizations. Membership in large environmental organizations like the Sierra Club is down. Few large mass organizations other than the AARP, favored by the aging demographics of America, would not report declining membership. It is hard to make the case that people are lining up to join and pay dues to any of the legacy organizations of the 20th century.

---

[118] Putnam, Robert, *Bowling Alone* (2000)

On the other hand there are new formations that aggregate people, even if this is hardly what any organizer would call organizing, and it is certainly not an organization. Facebook now has over a two billion members with significant numbers in the United States and wild, off-the-charts numbers in places like Indonesia where concentration exceeds 80% of the population according to various company claims. Twitter has grown rapidly, though it is beyond me to understand why. LinkedIn has millions involved, and the beat goes on in the business pages as social networking finds a place, space, and definition as a common and ubiquitous utility. Social networking is a tool for communication more than it is a substitute for organization itself. I would also bet in a decade all three of these outfits, except for possibly Facebook, will at the least be different, and more likely passé.

An exception might be moveon.org, which emerged in the United States when the founders sought support to oppose the impeachment of President Bill Clinton with petition drives and donations that have now become part of the progressive political equation with the capacity to move millions of dollars and a "membership" of millions. "Tribute bands" to the moveon.org model have now formed with various successes such as www.leadnow.ca in Canada and Getup! in Australia. A joint effort supported by moveon.org and like-minded groups called Aviz.org now claims more than 40,000,000 members worldwide on the same model with a "theory of change" that moving petitions and growth that has led to huge numbers approaching a million members in Brazil and a similar number in France, though much smaller in North America and varying in other countries around the world of course.

All of this gets confusing at some levels but at other levels meets the limited but critical definition of having a base, which is the key element that puts organizations at the table in making change. Or, does it? And, if it does, when does that work, and when does it slip through our fingers like sand?

These questions and others like them are at the heart of the way ACORN approached coalitions, which created both long lasting alliances when they worked and a constant chorus of criticism when misunderstood. ACORN perspective on coalitions is always an initial understanding that the primary motivation for joining coalitions was "to borrow power" that we lacked in order to achieve objectives that we sought organizationally. Viewed from that perspective, the opposite was also true. We sometimes might not join coalitions if we were being asked to "lend power" that we did not believe we could responsibly do without an unacceptable reputational or representational price being paid by the organization.

No Shortcuts, No End Runs

Sheryl Sandberg, the Google and Facebook mogul and now chief operating officer of Facebook, is a contemporary example of the distorted vision that afflicts so many when they think about social change. She infamously has already said that she "always thought that she would run a social movement," and referred to herself as a "pompom girl for feminism," both of which should probably disqualify her from being more than grist for the mill, but are also startling, not simply for their amazing lack of general awareness,

Chapter XVII: Constituency, Institutions, Networks, Alliances, Advocacy

but also from their wildly skewed misunderstanding of how change works, which is an epidemic seemingly without a cure. When even Maureen Dowd, the *New York Times* columnist has to remind her quite simply, that social movements begin at the bottom, not at the top[119] or she could have said, "not at the checkbook," then there is little argument about whether there is out of control confusion about the fundamental differences between social movements and social networking.

The age old organizing problem that this repetitive phenomenon exposes is the difference between advocacy and organizing. Many have righteous causes, longstanding grievances, brilliant individual insights, total sincerity, tireless energy, and persuasive arguments for change, but none of these attributes are precursors or predictors of effectiveness. Rather these are simply small fingers pressed into the dike of flooding noise and trying to find a forum that can recognize the sound of their own voice. Some succeed in finding a voice or in buying the platform allowing them to stand in the public forum and forge their way to the forefront, whether they are Sandberg or the Koch brothers or even Ralph Nader.

Ralph Nader undoubtedly has been one of the more remarkable individual advocates of our time by focusing on a series of consumer-related issues over the last generation. To his credit after being a hounded whistle blower in the legal department at General Motors over safety concerns around the Corvair economy car model, he won an "invasion of privacy" suit against the company and used the settlement to personally finance his consumer crusades. Nader's Raiders went through a period of believing, as legal advocates, that change could come through litigation and racking up some legal and policy successes in the early 1970's when such tactics could still find a moment of favor in the courts and in Congress.

ACORN in fact, was occasionally allied with Nader and various parts of his operation during that time around issues of tax justice and other consumer matters and found various of his operations extremely useful in answering research needs in those days before the internet when Washington access was limited and more privileged and therefore a very important commodity in creating the borrowing and lending of power. I can vividly recall conversations with several of Nader's branches and with Ralph himself about what ACORN could and would or would not do in Arkansas to advance their claims. They recognized earlier than most, a lesson, often forgotten in these times, is that simply speaking in Washington DC whether at the top of your lungs, in courtroom proceedings, or even in the quieter halls of Congress, does not work without a real base in the home districts of politicians that were critical for them to move.

ACORN's original home in Little Rock was also the home district of Congressman Wilbur Mills, Chairman of the House Ways and Means Committee, which had been so important to George Wiley and the National Welfare Rights Organization, and was also important to Nader and countless others depending on the ebb and flow of various issues and his power. The same can be said countless times in hundreds of situations; particularly where moderate politicians are on the fence on critical issues and movement is impossible without having or triggering a real base of their constituents for change. Arkansas was a

---

[119] *New York Times*, February 24, 2013.

bellwether state for decades in that way. Louisiana when both Senator John Breaux and Senator Mary Landrieu were in office was also a critical lever in close votes on key issues, and the list is endless and examples are legion over the decades of ACORN's work and that of its successor organizations on the state level.

Beginning in the 1970's, I would screen and school the constant callers who wanted and needed help in Arkansas and then elsewhere on some favorite issue or cause that meant the world to them but might or might not be marginal or meaty for ACORN and out members. Inevitably I would have to remind them that they were calling because they did not have a base in the city or state that was essential to them and that since that was why they were calling in the first place, in the second place they were going to have to listen carefully to what would be required were ACORN to be willing to carry water for them locally.

Early in ACORN's history when survival was still most tenuous, I was especially wary of such appeals since the memories of having done actions which made little sense in Massachusetts when I was directing MWRO, were still fresh, gaping wounds. As I mentioned earlier, leaders critical of my job performance in Boston would refer internally to these as Rathke's "suicide" actions, so I had vowed when organizing ACORN to never find myself in such an untenable predicament again, and many callers had to hear the story and make the case why their request was somehow fundamental to low-and-moderate income members of ACORN in Arkansas then and tens of places thereafter over the years.

Many of these kinds of interactions become transactional. We were saying, if you want a base that moves with you, then you have to recognize that and take the time, spend the money, and pay the dues to build an organization where you need the strength. There are no short cuts. There is no end run around the issue. If you are not willing or able to build that base, then there is an exchange of power necessary in many instances to move an organization like ourselves with precious and limited resources and staffing to divert our energy from our own work to a different issue and timetable even if only for a limited time and a measured amount.

 Over time, the evolution of the transactional nature of these relationships led to a recognition that in partnerships of unequal resources, in order for the organization to be able to add more to its agenda that usually entailed an investment of additional resources as the price for participation. This is hardly "pay to play," but instead is a realistic assessment that rather than simply a letterhead endorsement or a head-nod of support, the organization would dedicate additional staffing, create events, and lend full-throated support, and irreplaceable prestige to a partner organization or vital coalition then it meant raising the money to pay the bills to create the change. Furthermore, given our commitment to sustainability, moving outside of our own work plan, which involved internal and membership financing, meant that the core revenue stream that paid the bills had to be replaced by revenue that was equal to or hopefully sufficiently greater to those amounts in order to increase capacity, achieve mutual goals, and justify the time and trouble.

In the 21st century the right wing is quick to discount any mutually beneficial organizational relationship. In 2009 Fox News wanted to ask me whether or not ACORN was ever involved in something they called "rent-a-mob," which categorically we were not. The question is disparaging since it insulted the autonomy and integrity of actions by membership organizations. That is not to say that a union or a church or a donor might not pay for the bus that put ACORN members closer to the battleground, but that was a recognition of unequal resources not some kind of bribe or inducement outside of the organization's own natural and inherent interests.

These kinds of relationships covered all kinds of forms and functions.

We would pull out some of our members with a giant check prop to parade for the press in front of Mills' office in Little Rock on tax filing day in conjunction with Nader's Tax Reform Group because fair taxation, especially around equalizing property taxes for our members in Pulaski County was a huge issue for us locally at the time, so the publicity locally and nationally from such a small action helped us as much as it was critical for the Nader group in making their case about taxes before the all-powerful House Ways and Means Committee and Mills as its chairman at that time.

On the other hand in our coalitions with national women's organizations desperate to show diversity in their base, so anxious both because of our place in various spaces around the country and the different colors of many of our leader's faces, the exchange could be harder. We could be great and steadfast allies on wage equity questions and health issues for lower income women, but silent on abortion issues. Repeated votes of our leadership, often dominated numerically by middle aged African-American women produced debate and subsequent votes that indicated deep divisions between personal views based in more conservative religious practices that resisted abortion for the majority but had them voting to support positions politically that favored women's rights to abortion. The organization would end up lining up on the right side, but silently and more invisibly given the discomfort of so many of our leaders and members and their understanding that they had to be true to their own membership base that elected them as leaders and also stand with their allies who supported the organization nationally on so many other fronts.

Equally powerful and pioneering actions on rapes that happened to member's relatives were counter-cultural for neighborhood associations that tended to zoning and clean-ups. In ACORN, not only were rape campaigns in Memphis, Boston and New Orleans master-minded by women led community groups and organizers, especially Beth Butler, but their bold cutting-edge actions and victories made rape a national ACORN campaign. The Congressional legislation sought by the National Violence Against Women Act was floundering when ACORN's national canvass came to the rescue and was later credited by the women's organizations as having helped save it. The issue of rape was considered to be one of the most successful campaign issues of the national canvass, and many staff shared poignant moments that they heard from survivors as related to them on the doors.

Some groups fall into advocacy more easily than others. The environment can hardly be asked to speak for itself, though Katrina, Sandy, and countless other catastrophes seem impossible to ignore, so the need for individuals and organizations to advocate for the collective good in this regard is critical. At the same time there seems little real debate that a continued belief that it is simply enough to be right to win by speaking truth to power

Fox News Interview.

seems more common here and in other largely middle and upper middle income based organizations than it is elsewhere. When there has been a peace movement, like during the Vietnam War, there has certainly been recognition that moving the base was critical to winning the peace, rather than it simply being a matter of advocacy. The volunteer army's replacement of the much hated draft system in the United States, as well as the modern technology of invisible war and guiltless killing, if there is such a concept, has certainly made the strategy of peace movements more difficult, but the need for an active base has not been eliminated.

At the same time, arguably, consumers can in fact speak powerfully for themselves and do so by voting with their dollars through their purchases, as proven decades ago by the success of Cesar Chavez and the United Farm Workers in not only organizing their own base at that time at least but also mobilizing a base of supporters across the country to support and follow their leadership. Women certainly have also built significant organizations to represent and advocate their interests like the National Organization of Women (NOW) and service-based institutions like Planned Parenthood.

The movement of African-Americans evolved from abolitionists and carpetbaggers to participant led slave revolts and movements for representation and power whether it was led by the students of SNCC, the preachers of SCLC, or the ghetto firebrands of the Black Panther Party. Having created and led their own movements and forced support, they have probably succeeded better than any other constituency in demanding and enforcing the inability of anyone else to speak for them or presume to represent them, having proven fully able to speak for and represent themselves which is the essence of empowerment all the way from the local city hall to the White House. The divisions within the Latino community, even though the fastest growing minority in the United States, have created less unity and coherence of voice, though the culture and language still make it difficult for anyone else to claim the ability to advocate their interest and allow the community to work out its own path and sort out leadership between those proven and those poseurs, anointed by external interests and agendas.

Certainly American history has been rich in self-proclaimed advocates and representatives of the poor. The key and critical dividing line between Jane Addams' Hull House, muckrakers, and the good government reformers in the Progressive Era in the United States and the advent of Saul Alinsky and his influential advocacy of a legitimate voice for organizations of the poor is at the heart of the modern recognition of the important role of community organizations in low and moderate income areas. Though still often ignored and omitted from the equation of power and the ability to articulate their own special interests and voice in policy and programs, the advent of ACORN and other community-based organizations forces such voices to be heard and recognized.

Lower income families speaking for themselves with a unique voice is still widely resisted. The poor remain largely a group that dominant societal and political forces believe should continue in silence, perhaps even in shame, and rather than advance separate pleadings and petitions in their own interest, much less demands, since they should be thankful and subservient for whatever crumbs fall their way from the main plate of these times. For these reasons the whole concept of rights for the poor has been difficult for organizations to maintain. Certainly in the 1960's and 1970's, during the major movements to create entitlements, the notion of there being a right to welfare or a recalibration of rights to place tenants on a more equal footing with landlords, and more recently rights for victims of foreclosures or those abused by payday lenders or other profiteers, is very difficult not only to establish, but virtually impossible to maintain.

Being continually marginalized and imperiled, organizations of the poor, like ACORN, must be cautious of entangling relationships that reduce flexibility to respond to our own interests or aggressively protect against constant threats and attacks which are not seen as part of normal political life by more privileged groups and their organizations. The coordinated, blitzkrieg attack on ACORN after the elections of 2008 based on the selectively edited video footage of committed right wing ideologues trying to establish that the poor, via ACORN's services, had no right to seek or own decent, affordable housing, but instead insinuating that this was little more than scam and subterfuge, followed by the kneejerk reaction of Congressional resolutions and bans that were unproven and overreaching, and then the abandonment of the organization by virtually all of its so-called allies, supporters, friends, and funders, would seem to have proven this case for caution conclusively.

Coalitions, Alliances, Partnerships, and Other Relationships

As the decades of ACORN's history rolled the calendar over and the organization became larger and relatively well established, it became clear that the threshold for entry in many coalitions was getting lower and lower over time. Eventually it was less a matter of borrowing or lending power than simply being willing to have someone else somewhere else simply claim that we were involved, put us on the letter head or website and insinuate our participation, regardless of the reality, as our institutional presence alone became a signifier that we cared and were included. We became a box for progressives to check whether or not we were seen as an active part of many coalitions or not. As politics shifted more and more towards Washington and into the hands of the financiers and media, the understanding of the *a priori* of a real base also became more diluted and, frankly, a rarer reality.

In the hierarchy of organizational relationships, coalitions the most ad hoc with the lowest level of entry requirements or participation expectations. Such formations are at the tip of the grassroots and often accurately "name only," as we would refer to them, requiring no commitment from the organization whatsoever.

An alliance among a variety of allied organizations is something larger and more important in my reckoning. In such a formation organizations were in fact coming to the table as relatively equal partners with much higher expectations of relative contributions from each participant depending on their strengths, whether financial or research or lobbying or, as ours usually were, putting the base in action.

"Relatively equal" is the pivotal point here, because no matter the formation there is either a direct or unspoken calculus that defines equity. The pipers always get paid. Whoever brings money to the table in such formations always determines what constitutes equity in the partnerships. Sometimes the barter system of people or sweat in exchange for dollars works out well enough in practice, but that also should not be confused with equity in the relationships.

In recent years I have tried to argue that for alliances to really work such arrangements require extremely transparent commitment to "rules of engagement." Such rules are critical where the alliance might have been created with certain targets and campaign objectives. In my experience one of the more interesting examples of the challenges of such arrangements occurred putting together the various efforts around the organizing and campaign efforts designed to bring Walmart at that time in 2004, the world's largest corporation and largest private sector employer, into some level of corporate responsibility. In the various organizing meetings that led to Walmart Watch, Wakeup Walmart, and our own pilot projects with unions and others in Florida and India through the Walmart Alliance for Reform Now (WARN), the Walmart Workers' Association (WWA), India FDI Watch, and other organizations, we insisted that there should be rules of engagement because so many large and various organizations from SEIU to the Sierra Club with potentially conflicting interests had beefs with Walmart and were excited about finally taking the full measure of the company.

The conflicts were easy to imagine and turn up frequently in labor-community alliances. What happens to the community issues around traffic, crime, or housing, if by some miracle the company were to offer concessions on organizing rights in workplaces? What happens to labor's demand for worker health care and better labor standards if the environmentalists are offered some improvements in the greening of the company? The list goes on and on with such a major company with footprints in virtually every state in the United States and huge operations in other countries as well as being the largest private employer in Mexico and Canada.

The need for rules of engagement that would hold everyone together in the alliance and prevent preemptive settlements dividing and therefore weakening the whole were obvious in principal, but still difficult to enforce in practice, especially nationally where the politics are strained around the constantly shifting seas of Washington and competing legislative agendas. The process worked well on the local level where there was often more equity and fewer moving pieces on the board, but nationally groups invested more lip service than real work into the rules of engagement to our peril, since it is a mistake to underestimate any organizing or campaign target and Walmart was an inestimable opponent.

Our efforts in fact coincided with the corporation's own efforts at remaking their corporate killer image into something a little kinder and gentler by hiring former Clinton Administration operatives to direct their corporate relations program. Some of their efforts were ham-handed, like hiring former civil rights leader, UN ambassador, and Atlanta Mayor Andrew Young to head a fake citizens' group extolling the support for Walmart from regular citizens around the country. But, Walmart did not become the largest company in the world without being smart and tough, and their efforts to calf off the environmental organizations were not only effective but also totally within their own interests commercially in the long run. Because of the sometimes nebulous relationship to any base, many environmental groups that were more rooted in advocacy than membership, were surprisingly easy for Walmart to woo and con, since their own accountability was not an issue. A simple invitation to Bentonville to an environmental conference and some promises around greener packaging and transportation logistics were pretty much enough to do the trick. Walmart invited some environmentalists to an advisory council and others to consult, some to be on contract and some to meetings, and it was not long before only a more membership based operation like the Sierra Club was the last of the inner circle on the campaign still representing the environmentalist ranks, while the movement vis a vis Walmart was in disarray.

Community-labor partnerships are also notoriously difficult to manage effectively for much of the same reasons. To be clear I am a huge advocate and believer in the potential of such partnerships. I think they are part of our hope for the future!

Despite a lot of discussion about the necessity for such partnerships as vital to reenergizing the labor movement in the 21st Century[120], the evidence of true partnerships continues to weaken even though the conviction that such partnerships are necessary has grown steadily. Many of them are of course "in name only." Unions frequently initiate such "partnerships," when they need community support for a particular project or purpose and seek to appeal for community or political support and believe that having community partners makes them appear less self-interested and more focused on the collective good, rather than checkoff and a dime. These transactional alliances disappear quickly, either at the first concession that labor feels it can seize that fulfills its objective or when a conclusion is reached that the objective is unattainable. In such circumstances there is very rarely a commitment to a long term relationship. It goes without saying that these arrangements are not equitable, but unrealistic analysis of some of these relationships has often left community organizations feeling used and exploited, though naiveté hardly excuses the unrequited nature of some of these affairs.

---

[120] Amy Dean and Wade Rathke, "Beyond the Mutual Backscratch: A New Model for Labor-Community Coalitions," New Labor Forum, V.17, #3 (Fall, 2008), pp. 46-56.

Building and trades unions were almost always sketchy partners, since invariably on development-based campaigns seeking community benefit agreements for example, they would try to bolt as soon as there was the first hint that the developer might build union, regardless of the interests of the other partners. An infamous situation in New Jersey occurred when Walmart of all possible dissemblers promised to build all of its stores statewide in Jersey with union labor. It then took Herculean effort by the AFL-CIO to put Humpty-Dumpty back together again in that state.

Community organizations, including ACORN, are not immune from driving the partnerships hard in our interests either. In the vast majority of living wage coalitions we organized over the years when we were most active, especially in putting these matters on the ballot, we drove the effort because we were running the petition drives on the ground to get the measures qualified to face the electorate, and we were the ones raising the money, often considerable sums from our partners in labor and elsewhere. I would argue these partnerships were still very real and viable and perhaps represent "best practices" for such community-labor alliances because there was some real equity in the bartering of various resources, decision making on wage levels, and a lot of the other work. Certainly this was not true in every case. There were some situations where we were junior partners and many where we were carrying almost all of the weight by ourselves.

The fights to win community benefit agreements were important amalgamations of allied interests particularly when they required public funding and approval and where a combination of forces importantly increased leverage on privately led development projects. Interests were varied and hard to align between neighborhood development, security and amenities, union construction, "first preference" hiring of impacted community residents, tax benefits, displacement, relocation, and the creation of affordable housing, all of which created a complicated stew of interests whose ultimate success favored a recipe with the maximum number of favorable ingredients. Something weighted more towards labor often left bitter tastes in the community for example in the agreements negotiated around the development of the Staples Center in Los Angeles. A program that yielded a community benefits agreement more tilted towards affordable housing and low-and-moderate income families, such as the one negotiated by ACORN in the Atlantic Yards area of Brooklyn became controversial with other community interests less committed to income diversity residential housing in rapidly gentrifying Brooklyn. Nonetheless to win sufficiently to reconcile all of these varying interests requires true community-labor partnerships, no matter how difficult to achieve.

Community labor organizing partnerships are more difficult to realize since invariably labor is paying the bills. Sometimes the community participation is simply an effort to win broader support which was often the case in the "labor peace" deals that UNITE HERE would attempt to leverage for labor neutrality agreements in hotels which were the product of private-public partnerships. In other cases for example with the partnerships between ACORN and SEIU, AFT, CWA and other unions often ACORN organizers or teams led by ACORN organizers were doing the actual organizing of the workers. Only in the partnership with the United Federation of Teachers in New York City did a genuine partnership evolve and solidify when the then president of the UFT agreed to provide an ongoing servicing relationship to New York ACORN for the home childcare

Chapter XVII: Constituency, Institutions, Networks, Alliances, Advocacy   397

workers we brought into the organization, as well as a share of the monthly per capita being paid directly to NY ACORN on a monthly basis to support the maintenance of the organization and campaigns among the membership. For all of the huge numbers of members that ACORN helped bring into organizations like SEIU, the agreements were formal and memorialized, but never developed into a permanent partnership architecture after the initial organizing drives were complete. To envision real community labor partnerships, we have to be able to imagine structural, financial, and future governance that links the duality of interests together on an organic and permanent basis.

Some formations like CLU in Boston, Connecticut Center for a New Economy in New Haven, and the Working Partnerships in various cities have created structural entities, though more in the model of LAANE (now standing for A New Economy for All) and the original partnership program in San Jose with the labor council in that city, operate more as research and advocacy organizations in support of labor goals and objectives than a partnership of equal interests. Most of these organizations are campaign-based which also allows there not to be conflicting issues at the base, although being campaign-based they also bring no independent base into the larger fight from the ranks of non-union low-and-moderate income families.

The real odds of coalitions and alliances working in practice the way they should in theory seems to only happen when all parties involved come to grips with the fact that the objective is immeasurably larger than any of them could hope to achieve separately, This is not to say that the drive to achieve special results that inure to individual entities, special interests, or even personal benefits ever ceases, but sometimes it is suspended or at least submerged against the great challenges even if not always for the greater good. Politics and political parties are certainly examples of this as I have argued in the chapter on Politics at some length.

Politics is a great unifier, particularly as the elections move up the ballot and the geography widens, because no organization ever has quite enough members or enough discipline to win all by themselves. Sometimes in narrow districts or fixed geographies it is possible, but otherwise having allies with a stake in the outcome and being willing to reward their participation are essential ingredients to forging victory. Or at least that is the case except when efforts are premised wholly on media or fueled solely by money. When having a base is privileged in politics, then critical alliances and long term partnerships can be formed. When the base is disregarded or devalued, then it is survival of the fittest, and the devil take the hindmost.

By Any Name, By Any Means

What brought organizations like unions or community organizations like ACORN to the table in any potential formation around an issue, campaign or election always comes down to whether or not there is a palpable gain or resolution of a grievance for our defined constituency be it workers or in ACORN's case, low-and-moderate income families. Closing the circle, the core decision would be whether participation benefited that same constituency. More critically, though in membership-based organizations where leaders are elected, boards require accountability, dues fuel the organizational engines, and people come in and out of their own will and volition, voting with both their hands in the air, and their feet walking fast towards you or away from you, all of which means that the litmus test for participation is not what is good in the public interest or the best public policy, but what is best for the members. Internally, these are political organizations no matter the rocks that might be thrown at their castles about the level of democracy or the power of the leadership; they cannot be operated without participation, support, and a high consensus of their membership.

In all my years as an organizer I have always been amazed at how often this fundamental truth is ignored or misunderstood, and at how many organizations were delicate about stating such obvious facts. And, when it was ignored, allies, both real and illusory, are always quick to take advantage of that fact.

Politicians are the best examples of how quickly an organization's role in the partnership can be exploited. A strong case could be persuasively argued that labor, despite providing huge ground troops and financial resources to candidates for office in the Democratic Party in the United States, by not leveraging its influence into concrete organizing tools needed to increase its membership, was an unwitting partner in its own decline. Despite a controversial legacy involving his leadership of the Service Employees International Union (SEIU), Andy Stern with the help of Kirk Adams, Tom Woodruff, and others deserves real credit for recalibrating the exchange of support for politicians into real organizing gains and membership growth, especially for lower wage service workers at the intersection of formal and informal employment and the private and public sector, like home health and home daycare workers. Authors, Jennifer Klein and Eileen Boris, called this organizing strategy, "political unionism,"[121] but while the moment was available in the last decade of the 20th Century and the first decade of the 21st Century, this strategy undeniably helped create the largest successes of our generation of labor organizers. In comparison look at how little the labor movement in the United Kingdom was able to get from Tony Blair and Gordon Brown's New Labor from 1997 through 2010, thirteen years, or the INTUC and others from the "special" relationship to the Congress Party in India.

I can remember being dispatched during Louisiana Senator Mary Landrieu's campaign for re-election in 2004 to visit with her over a cup of coffee at a restaurant on St. Charles Avenue in New Orleans to deliver her a message. Despite all of her campaign's entreaties to SEIU for financial and political support to the international union, I was acting as an emissary from President Stern to let her know that if SEIU wanted to donate to a candidate that would "vote like a Republican, then in the future we would make our contributions directly to a Republican." I put as much sugar in her coffee as I needed to operate a local union in Louisiana, but there was no denying that no support was going to be forthcoming for her.

What goes around comes around, and these relationships are still about borrowing and loaning power, and no matter how many phrases and flourishes accompany the conversation, there is really no way to parse the decision any other way.

---

[121] Jennifer Klein and Eileen Boris, *Caring for America: Home Health Workers In the Shadow of the Welfare State* (Oxford University Press, 2012)

Chapter XVIII: Politics –Proving the Base, Initiatives, and Alternative Parties

As I mentioned previously, in my early life as an organizer, the glib line about power and politics was fairly simply put. They had the money, but we had the numbers. The rap about our numbers being our asset was easy to learn and rolled swiftly over the tongue. People would even nod hopefully, as if it were true. The problem I learned early in organizing ACORN in Arkansas was that when push came to shove, none of the members really believed it. They did not want to sit on the sidelines of elections, as Alinsky had argued in the shadow of the fierce Chicago political machine. They actually wanted to believe that they could impact politics. They wanted in the game, rather than being in the grandstands.

The more I talked to members and leaders, the more it became clear that for all of our slick talk, the members clearly identified the talk of power with politics and politics had no meaning without talking about elections, and elections were not spectator sports, but full dress contact battles. If we wanted to build a membership organization and really build power, then we had to figure out a way to effectively engage in politics.

Little Rock School Board Victory in 1972

At the same time we did not want to get pulled apart by the undertow of partisan politics, on one hand because we declared ourselves to be nonpartisan, and on the other, because at that time in Arkansas, as opposed to much of the rest of the South, there was the stirring of a two-party system.[122] There had virtually always been a Republican Congressional District in the northwestern part of the state around Fayetteville in the Ozarks dating back to divisions around secession, slaves, and the Civil War, but more recently the tensions of race and reform from the Orval Faubus multi-term regime had given rise to the deep pocketed victory of Winthrop Rockefeller as the first elected Republican governor since Reconstruction.

As a fledgling organization we were hardly in the position to presume that we could impact a statewide election, but if "all politics is local," we could not have been more local, and one campaign after another was pushing us in that direction. One anomaly of Little Rock politics at the time was that all elections on the city and schools level were both nonpartisan and at-large with no single member district elections, because of an ill begotten "reform" that among other things had created a weak mayor /city director form of government with a hired so-called "professional" city manager who ran things. People still spoke of wards though and maps published in the local newspapers told the whole story when three quarters of the elected officials in the city lived not only in the 5th Ward in the same affluent neighborhood, but in most cases literally within blocks of

---

[122] Yes, this seems hard to believe these days but in 1970, the one-party was Democratic rather than Republican as it is now, and though at that time Arkansas had consistently voted Democratic on the Presidential side, it was a tossup in other ways. See V.O. Key, Jr., *Southern Politics in State and Nation* (1949).

each other. It was hard for ACORN members to pretend that their issues in schools and neighborhoods meant much to people living in Pleasant Valley or Pulaski Heights or elsewhere in the 5th Ward, and in fact it had been more than a generation since anyone for any locally based election had been victorious without carrying the western suburbs of the 5th Ward. For ACORN this was a looming challenge to our notion that "The People Shall Rule."

A campaign around extending school lunches and getting textbooks in the Little Rock Schools led us rapidly to recognize that we would be hard pressed to win without being able to exert some political pressure, electorally, on the school board members and the annual spring election cycle that pitted candidates against each other for seats in that body. Additionally, we benefited from winning early support for ACORN's organizing in lower income and largely minority communities from an external network of folks, aggressive, smart, underutilized and unrecognized women who had originally emerged in the fights to reopen the schools in the 1957 face-off between Governor Faubus and President Eisenhower on enforcing desegregation orders in the city. People like Mamie Ruth Williams and Pat House had been young mothers then and were part of the activist core of anti-Faubus progressives in the city around race and education especially. By 1970 when ACORN began, their children were older but their politics were the same, as was their curiosity, so when I stumbled into them they had a seasoned network of friends, particularly in the press and politics, where they had a history of offering similar sustenance and support. I knew we needed help, and didn't know exactly what I was looking for, but when I found it, I knew how to take advantage of it. Liberal candidates would seek out their advice or assistance, and quickly, as we became part of that network, we became part of what their mentor, Max Allison, would call the "political equation," because we had a base in areas where no one else did.

After the ACORN board interviewed various school board candidates, Doug Stephens, a psychologist, and Bill Hamilton, the African-American head of the Pulaski County community action program, who we had known already, emerged as a tandem that we could support. Best for ACORN's inaugural foray into this wild world of politics, school and city elections were all nonpartisan, so we could endorse and campaign aggressively, and, we did! When the votes came in, Hamilton had lost narrowly, but Stephens had won convincingly. Not only had he won, but thanks to ACORN's work and support, his victory was decisive enough in the eastern and central part of the city that he won the election even while losing the 5th Ward, turning geographical, class, and racial politics upside down in the city for the first time in more than a generation.

Stephens was then quoted in the daily newspaper crediting his victory to ACORN, making our day, and setting us off on an organizational path that never wavered politically from that first experience in Little Rock. From that point on in Arkansas there was never an election where ACORN leadership did not interview candidates on our issues and frequently make endorsements, backing up our endorsements not with any money or contributions, but with door-to-door work in our neighborhoods.

Making Endorsements but Protecting the Organization First

None of which means we were stupid or cavalier about this direction.

First, we had to make sure that the decision, any decision, about endorsements supporting any candidate would not divide the organization. To win an endorsement required a "super majority," not a simple majority. Depending on whether the endorsement was at the state or local organizational level, the candidate needed either two-thirds or three-quarters support of the board to receive an endorsement. Sometime several ballots were required to win an endorsement in Arkansas. As I have mentioned, the endorsement by the ACORN Political Action Committee (APAC) of Barack Obama for President in 2008 needed 75% and only came on the third balloting over a six-month period as the board was vetting candidates.

Deviations from board consensus and recommendations in politics also had to be disciplined, which meant that once an endorsement by ACORN was made democratically at the board level it had to mean something and be supported by all of the leadership. As I mentioned earlier, in the early years in Arkansas one board chairman "individually" endorsed a friend who was running for Mayor of North Little Rock without going through the appropriate board process. The local group had to fight out this problem of unaccountability within its own membership as well as the city wide and county wide board. The leader did not survive the process. Sometimes when there was a split in support or in the interesting circumstances where some of our own members, taking our motto to heart, would run themselves, it was easier to make some candidates favorable or co-endorse when no one won a supermajority in order to still be engaged, but to also be united.

Similarly, in the early days of the multi-state and emerging national ACORN organization, more conservative members of the board initiated a vote by the national organization condemning the action of then President Jimmy Carter in ceding control of the Panama Canal to the country of Panama. I have told this story earlier in discussing leadership, but perhaps it bears revisiting. The board had an extensive debate on whether or not it was appropriate for ACORN to consider taking a position on an issue that was not coming from the membership process or direct campaign experience, much less an international issue. By a significant, though narrow, margin the national board voted to take no position. A renegade leader in Reno, Nevada representing Nevada ACORN on the board, tried to disaffiliate in protest, leading to one of the few situations where the national board took "receivership" control of the organization[123], forcing new elections of leadership in that state. There were bitter, difficult disputes sometimes involving the press and leaked documents, but they were crucial for the organization to win, if ACORN were to operate politically. In the late 1970's this conflict prompted a hostile local press in Little Rock to unsuccessfully attempt to gain access and entry to ACORN board meetings, as if we were a public body, rather than a nonprofit with our own governance procedures. A newspaper editorial and cartoon campaign was unsuccessfully waged to try and force

---

[123] Article XIII of the ACORN Bylaws allowed the parent organization to assume control of a state body if there were severe issues of mismanagement of resources, external attacks and subversion, or flagrant disregard of the bylaws. It was used sparingly, only two or three times in my thirty-eight years.

reporters to be able to sit into our meetings and reveal our financial information. We were big fish in a small pond. We did not budge.

The role of the ACORN Political Action Committee (APAC) itself was also critical in this regard. Members of the board along with some other politically active members constituted the APAC, so that they could make recommendations to the board or make endorsements in their own name on partisan contests. It was never possible to clearly communicate the differences publicly, nor did we really have much interest in doing so, but this wall of separation was important to shield the various parts of the organization and to give us the separation we needed between some of our tax exempt training, research and development arms, and the basic nonprofit and more political entities within ACORN. Primarily, APAC operated as an independent committee of the board as a whole. During the first decade of the 21st century, we also created a contribution and dues structure for APAC which allowed some more flexibility and compliance with changing state and national election laws and reporting requirements.

Running Members for Office

For an organization like ACORN part of the test of empowerment and the implementation of our motto was whether or not we could also elevate our own members to elected office, and in perhaps an even harder test, hold them accountable to organizational interests and even direction, if, and when, they were elected. From the earliest days of the organization, we were constantly on the lookout for opportunities for our members to have a chance at not only running, but more importantly, winning.

None of this was easy. Once we had broken the seal so to speak and demonstrated that we were not only open to direct political activity, but aggressively and effectively pursuing that direction, it also signaled to one and all that we were open for business politically. Part of the problem for an embryonic organization, as we were in the early 1970's, is that we would inevitably attract ambitious community activists who would now see ACORN as a main chance for elected office. In the immortal words of Steve McDonald, national ACORN's first President and a leader in Little Rock, we also had to beware of emerging leaders "getting the big head."

The pinnacle of empowerment for a community organization would be the ability to translate our principles about the importance of the majority constituency in a democracy into actually being the majority of elected officials. To achieve that goal in elections dominated by lawyers, professionals, and business people was not a simple task. I was motivated though by some historical bellwethers from previous movements and organizations to believe that if we looked hard enough, then we might find opportunities. Certainly the original Black Panther Party in Lowndes County, Alabama had been an interesting effort. I had read about the success of the Western Federation of Miners "taking over" whole mining towns in the West where they were strong from tax collector to sheriff. Closer to home, I had driven down to Crystal City, Texas, and talked to people like Carlos Guerra and Jose Angel Gutierrez with La Raza Unida about their experience in converting a Hispanic majority there into power and actual governance. We had studied, read about, and visited Sunflower County, Mississippi to look at the work of the Mississippi Freedom Democratic Party. How could ACORN do that?

Pulaski County Quorum Court

Search and you shall find. It turned out that Pulaski County, where Little Rock and North Little Rock were located, had an archaic form of government dating back to its establishment as a territory. There was an elected county judge, but there was also a legislative body of sorts responsible for approving the budget, setting property tax rates, and other duties. Individual quorum court justices of the peace also had the power to perform marriages. Targeting the Quorum Court was natural because we had been in a protracted fight to win an equalization of regressive property tax assessments so that our members in lower income, working communities of the county were not paying disproportionately. We had filed scores of appeals. We had done actions on the Assessor. We had demanded that the State of Arkansas order a full, new equalization assessment. The Quorum Court could be part of the mix in winning this campaign.

On the political side what most attracted us was the huge volume of seats that came up every election for justices of the peace. The formula had capped out, but allowed one seat for each eight hundred or so people in the country so that there were more than 450 seats for the Quorum Court that were up for election each term. With so many seats from so many individual districts, many of them almost went begging or were uncontested at the polls, especially in the areas where we had strength. Additionally, given how controversial ACORN was in Arkansas already in our early years, we could run something of a stealth campaign by getting together our candidates and filing them without fanfare for one opening after another at the last minute, moving a campaign, and getting out our vote through a door-to-door, local group meeting to local group meeting process. A lot of the campaign would be simply engineering: getting enough of our members and allies to file in enough districts that we elect our members to the majority of the Quorum Court. Our only real allies were some of our network of friends and, most importantly, Art Martin, the business manager then for the International Ladies Garment Workers' Union (ILGWU) and their Kellwood plant in Little Rock[124], who joined with us in getting about twenty of his members to run as part of this effort to swell our numbers where we needed extra help.

Come Election Day, votes were counted, and the next morning a front page story and headline in the *Washington Post* trumpeted the fact that the upstart community organization, ACORN, and its biracial membership and a coalition of allies had accomplished a "takeover" of the Pulaski County government by electing a functional majority of justices of the peace, some 267.[125] We referred to the Quorum Court as the "largest legislative body in the world." The reaction in Little Rock, predictably, did not include applause. The press lashed at ACORN in the pre-internet world with offense

---

[124] There no longer is an ILGWU, its remnants are now part of UNITE HERE or SEIU, and there no longer is a Kellwood either.

[125] Story was written by Austin Scott, who had been the first African-American reporter ever hired by the Associated Press.

and some embarrassment at the fact that a local story was broken nationally, especially from the *Arkansas Gazette*, which at the time held itself in quite extravagant esteem. The County Judge B. Frank Mackey tried to dismiss the victory as relatively inconsequential. Others argued that the unwieldy nature of the body argued for the kinds of Constitutional amendments that they favored to shrink the Quorum Court down to nine members, which subsequently came to pass as a constitutional amendment.

To ACORN it hardly mattered. In our calculus within four years of founding the organization and two years of embracing politics, which was heresy within community organizing at that time, through an open election our rank-and-file lower income members had turned the Pulaski County upside down. In the most honorable tradition of the work we had functionally taken over a unit of government, whether for a day, a month, a year, or forever.

ACORN says, "You are in my power."
George Fisher cartoon in Arkansas Democrat

Actually it was humbling. On one hand we thought we had just grabbed our piece of the world by the tail, but on the other hand, the first call I answered the next morning was from a member who wanted to know exactly why we weren't doing more to stop the gas company from raising rates. There's nothing that can pull a 25-year old wannabe hotshot organizer down to hard earth more quickly than being reminded of the organizational axiom that "it's not what you did for me yesterday that matters, it's what you did for me today" that members want to know.

The Quorum Court battle was eventually fought to something of a stalemate. In a fight over the county budget and tax plan submitted by the county judge, when he wouldn't recognize our amendments and motions, ACORN members and allies marched out of the meeting and "broke the quorum," so that no business could be done. We fought each other to a draw until the Quorum Court was reorganized on a smaller scale after the Constitutional amendment prevailed. At the nuts and bolts level we had learned that we could take power.

Single Seats versus Multiple Openings and Communities in Transition

We learned some other political lessons pretty quickly as well.

A local group chair in one of our Pine Bluff chapters unilaterally decided he wanted to run for the city council. Though the Pine Bluff ACORN board did not feel ready for the race or confident that the leader could win, there was no stopping him from stepping forward, and the organization was pulled into the election in his wake. As it turned out, he was in fact elected, but having jumped into the water and drug the organization along, he did not feel the kind of debt that Doug Stephens in Little Rock had felt, nor did he feel the same accountability as the hundreds of ACORN members elected as justices of the peace in the Pulaski County Quorum Court. The relationship became tense and troubled. The local board wanted him to come regularly and explain his position and seek advice, but he saw himself as a force to be reckoned with on his own.

Even in races where an individual member had been recruited to run or a favored and endorsed candidate had won, ACORN quickly found in the early 1970's that it was very, very difficult for "one Indian in the fort," as I called it, to prevail, even when they *wanted* to try and implement the organizational agenda or deliver on campaign promises. We faced the familiar tension as well between the good and the perfect. Even in the case of the Pine Bluff member, he was still better than the rest of the lot, just not as good as we wanted him to be within the organizational political culture we were building. Other members, when elected, were ineffective and sometimes uncomfortable with the lonely conflict of being outside of the norms and wanting to get along with other elected officials.

The conclusion we drew, and that guided us wherever practical in the future. was to look for situations where we could run members in multiples so that they could offer each other support if elected and would be more closely bound to the organization and our political program regardless of the outcome. City council and school board races lent themselves to such efforts because they usually had annual or biannual elections to fill some seats. The revamped Quorum Court had clearly delineated districts which allowed us to elect three members out of the nine in Pulaski County during the next election and over a 40 year period there has always been at least one ACORN member elected as a Justice of the Peace to this day.[126]

Over time we realized that we were especially successful in our multiple and "takeover" strategies when we could recognize that there was a mismatch between elected officials and changing demographics. Pine Bluff was such an example because the city was becoming majority African-American and there were no elected African-Americans at the city council or school board level in various districts at the point we started running – and winning – with our members. The ACORN organizational effort was able to coincide with reducing barriers and elevating candidacies from our membership as emerging representatives of previously disempowered minorities. When we rode this wave of change, we were able to successfully elect majorities in school boards in Pine Bluff and several members to the Council. As we expanded outside of Arkansas we were able to elect a single school board member in Sioux Falls, South Dakota in our first try, and then several years later in Bridgeport, Connecticut find the same mismatch between Anglos and Hispanics in that community that we had found with African-Americans in Arkansas. Our members became the first Puerto Ricans elected to city and school seats, and later to the state legislature from Bridgeport. We even pulled off the Western Federation of Miners maneuver by organizing the Georgia-Pacific company town, Mountain Pine, in Garland

---

[126] Currently in 2014, Donna Massey, long time member and leader, and also member of the KABF board is still a duly elected JP on the Quorum Court.

County, Arkansas near Hot Springs so conclusively that 40% of the residents of the town became ACORN dues paying members, and swept the elections to municipalize a park and other town services.

Initiatives and Referenda: Combining Political Strategy and Tactics

In building political power though there were no tactical tools that advanced our strategy on every level more effectively than the utilization of procedures allowing initiated acts and referenda on issues both locally and on a statewide basis. We honed these skills in Arkansas where every statewide election saw contending sides on the class divide fighting for or against the railroad union's "full crew" measure or featherbedding as the railroads termed it, fighting for or against removing the 10% usury cap, repealing right-to-work to allow fairer dues collection for unions, or maintaining the so-called "intangible" property taxation on stocks and bonds. All of these issues spoke to the populist past of Arkansas, but so did the very existence of such tools. States and communities that allowed voters to make binding decisions by initiating petitions of their fellow citizens to put measures on the ballot tended to be located in the western and southern parts of the United States where populist and progressive forces had held greater sway in instituting such citizen accountability and legislative options. The random Midwestern state like Ohio or northeastern state like Massachusetts might also allow these procedures but they were ubiquitous in the parts of the country where ACORN was founded and first branched out, so the tactics became a common weapon in the organizational repertoire.[127]

Lifeline Utility Rates

The serendipity of initiative procedures not only allowed ACORN to build political power in the electoral process but also enabled us to polarize and win on core organizational campaign issues as well, particularly around economic issues. In the early 1970's inflation was pinching lower income families on critical essentials like heat, light, and telephone, most of which were provided by investor owned utilities who were constantly pressuring state regulators for rate increases to guarantee profit margins regardless of service issues and consumer affordability. Huge battles would be fought in the unfavorable arena of Public Service Commission meetings dominated by lobbyists, lawyers, and of course the companies themselves. In some states, once again largely in the South and West, the members of such commissions were elected, giving citizens some leverage, and historically populist programs from such officials had been sufficient for some politicians like Louisiana's Huey Long and others to advance in the wake of their causes. These campaigns were hugely important organizationally, but deeply frustrating. We were losing, even while we were winning, because we were caught in a company driven "high-low" game. One company after another would ask for a gazillion dollar increase, and through herculean efforts, we would beat them back to only a half-gazillion

---

[127] It seemed like déjà vu all over again in 2015 to read that the head of a 100,000 plus local union in California was arguing that having labor seize the initiative process in all the states where available could lead to the revitalization of labor.

at the PSC. ACORN members were proud of their fight and quick to declare victory, but still watching their utility bills go up.

We thought the way to fix this campaign dilemma was to win "lifeline" rates to protect affordable access for lower and fixed income families to these basic services. A low, fixed rate would be set for 400 kilowatt hours of electricity for example allowing everyone to get the minimum level needed to keep plugged in regardless of income. ACORN would routinely propose lifeline rates to counter every requested utility increase. In places like California some form of lifeline had been won through the PUC, but in Arkansas we got nowhere. Finally in 1975 and 1976, we devised a strategy to initiate petitions to have voters approve lifeline rates for electric utilities on the local level, where we believed we could force the regulations to be implemented. Strategically, I was always an "eggs in as many baskets as possible" guy, so we devised a plan to petition in all of the cities where we felt we might be able to get on the ballot, which meant not only Little Rock, but also Hot Springs, Pine Bluff, Fort Smith, and others. In some of these cities we couldn't directly petition because of their smaller size but had to get the city council to act to put the measure on the ballot.

Whether local or statewide the nuts and bolts of initiative petitions always involve some tricky turns and hoops to jump through for those bringing the matter forward. Initiative petitions are not propositions where the tie goes to the runner, because any disputes are likely going to court for adjudication. Every jurisdiction at every level bases the requirement for the number of signatures needed to access the ballot either on the number of registered voters or more often on achieving a threshold of valid signatures as a percentage of the number of voters for either a governor's or a mayor's race at the last election. Depending on the jurisdiction there have been extensive efforts to restrict access to the ballot by citizens by raising the thresholds higher and higher and the requirements

Lifeline Campaign in Arkansas. Jon Kest on right as leader speaks at Hot Springs Rally 1975.

Lifeline petition signing in 1976 in Arkansas.

for petitioners are often now extremely burdensome, though not impossible.[128] As these efforts became more frequently used to attempt to make change, blocking or restricting the use of paid petitioners was also common in many areas. The additional challenge in various jurisdictions involves whether or not there is a long or short window for the actual petitioning to occur. A long timeline of a year or more favors the petitioner since the effort to get the signatures is burdensome and significant. The key organizational problem on the nuts and bolts level is making sure that one submits sufficient valid signatures, whatever the requirements. The normal formula ACORN used was roughly 2:1, two signatures for every one needed, though sometimes we thought we could make it at 1.5:1 or 150% of the number of signatures required.

The other baseline challenge on initiative petitions is in the language itself. Depending on the jurisdiction, the requirements might indicate that the petition language has to be clear so that a "yes" or "no" vote can be unambiguous. Usually only one issue can be addressed in each petition.[129] Some jurisdictions bar citizen action on economic issues[130] in the wake of ACORN's aggressive work on living wage measures at the end of the 20th century and first decade of the 21st. Almost invariably opponents of progressive initiatives go to court in last ditch efforts to block such measures from going forward to the voters at large, which is a smart tactic from their vantage since a knockout punch in

---

[128] Example of British Columbia regulations.

[129] California statewide petitions are one of the exceptions allowing different questions to be part of the same initiative question if the questions are on the same subject, like health or housing.

[130] Under intensive lobbying in state legislatures, restaurant, hotel, and small business trade associations moved to bar living wage and similar initiative centers in states and cities in many southern and western states either across the board as in Texas and Louisiana or except in specific situations like in Florida.

Chapter XVIII: Politics –Proving the Base, Initiatives, and Alternative Parties

the courts is cheaper, quicker, and, usually, surer than going head to head in an election. Parenthetically, New York City elections are also a different breed as well since contending candidates and parties routinely attempt to disqualify candidate petitions in order to slim down the field before an election. The rules and procedures of the Election Board are so arcane and oblique that any efforts involving petitions in New York City are *sui generis* and require special care and attention.

ACORN's first leap into the initiatives pool exposed all of the hazards lying below the surface. Despite our multi-city lifeline strategy, we were blocked in Pine Bluff quickly and we lost early court challenges in some other cities. In Hot Springs there were technical problems which led to a last minute petition drive against several city council men launched by Hot Springs organizer, Jon Kest, and the local leadership, which attracted attention and exerted significant pressure. Nonetheless, the only measure that made it to the actual ballot was the one in Little Rock. For the first time we used a canvass crew to supplement our local group and membership activity, which I still remember vividly since I got to personally be the "field manager" and direct the effort in southwestern Little Rock where we did not have much organizational strength but where we believed that an effort would yield the additional working class voters that we needed to win.

We learned a thousand lessons in this first initiative campaign. Without the money to spend on anything but our field program, where all of our work was focused, Arkansas Power & Light and its parent Middle South Utilities (all now called Entergy) barraged us with radio and television advertisements in the last two weeks of the campaign, a pattern we saw in election after election over my years as Chief Organizer. Remarkably we emerged victorious with solid support in the precincts in the east, south, and central parts of Little Rock and solid support and majorities in the southwest precincts where we worked, despite being plummeted in western Little Rock in the old 5th Ward. A huge victory with the popular votes to prove it!

Unfortunately, we did not prevail on this measure. If they cannot get the courts to stop you on the front end, count on the fact that the opposition will attempt to get the courts to unravel your victory on the back end. Sure enough, a lawsuit was filed for the Arkansas Electric Cooperative (represented by Webster Hubbell and Hillary Clinton of the Rose Law Firm), claiming that they had been injured, because the lifeline rate structure required a fairer payment from large industrial users, now being forced by the measure to pay equitably rather than enjoying a bulk discount. The rural co-op had 20 odd customers in the city limits of Little Rock, probably due to some annexation or another, and they pleaded that they had no large users that could offset the distribution to low income users provided in our lifeline measure. On that slim margin the court ruled that the lifeline measure was an illegal "taking," or property confiscation, which was also sustained on appeal.

As painful as it was to not deliver a victory on the campaign, that initiative alone and the electoral victory altered the permanent political stature of the organization in Little Rock and throughout Central Arkansas. Within political circles just proving that we could master the engineering to get on the ballot and sustain the challenges to force the vote, then prevail with the electorate, built power and in my terms, "proved the base," which is the critical issue in any election. To have the victory stolen in the courts, rightly or wrongly on whatever technicality, is unfortunate, but establishing in an election that the organization does not merely "claim" the base, but can deliver that base even in the teeth of a full assault, is invaluable for community organizations, and not available in too many other venues so effectively.

ACORN never shied from going to this well from 1975 onward, and did so with statewide measures including contests proposing the repeal of the sales tax on food and medicine in Missouri in 1976 and implementation of a statewide lifeline measure in South Dakota as well. We lost in Missouri, though the consolation prize for almost winning (and polling decisive majorities in the urban counties of Kansas City and St. Louis) was that the legislature immediately repealed the tax on medicine though not on food. A similar result was achieved legislatively in Arkansas with ACORN's initiative ballot there.

Over the decades we advanced living wage proposals on the ballot as citywide measures first in Houston and then Denver in the mid-1990s. We were walloped by multi-million dollar expenditures by the hotel and fast food industries at the last minute in these campaigns with very short timelines. In Houston the anti-campaign was patronizing, claiming that we "meant well," but were misdirected. In Denver it was all muscle and iron-fisted attack ads. In both cases we lost by 2 to 1. In Houston we ruled in the lower income 3rd and 5th wards that were the stronghold demographics of our base of lower income African-American and Hispanic members. Similarly we carried our base in convincing terms in Denver despite the onslaught. In River Oaks, the Houston precinct where former President George H. Bush lived, we only got one vote on for the living wage proposal. I've often joked that to this day the neighbors are still looking for that one ACORN voting traitor! We had misjudged the wage level that would not trigger fear votes based on the claims of job losses. We could learn a tactical lesson easily enough, and as long as our base was with us, we could fight in the future with an even stronger hand.

I hate to beat a dead horse here, but obviously ACORN built power, even while losing at the ballot box on these electoral initiatives. In the minds and strategies of our opponents we went from being dangerous disruptors to being players, and therefore even more dangerous disruptions to the usual political order. I have always been clear that lower income families to do not win by losing. They have spent lifetimes losing, so the last thing they need to do is pay dues to lose. I stand by that one hundred percent. At the same time building power is not the same as pure and simple winning, and though people cannot afford to lose, an organization actually can handle some setbacks, particularly if it has greater and growing capacity to win in the future. Sometimes the greater the risks, the greater the rewards, and being able to push the organization to the center of the political agenda and categorically establish the political strength of the organization in the harsh reality of votes cast and turf controlled, takes the political equation past conjecture and closer to a pure proof.

Nowhere was this strategy more successful than in the early years of the 21st century around statewide initiatives to implement various ACORN proposals to increase the minimum wages. As a matter of campaign strategy despite our experience supporting different types of "living wage" campaigns in over one hundred cities, schools, and county jurisdiction, most of which involved creating "prevailing wage" or minimum standards for wages, moving to area wide wage increases opened up the living wage efforts to wider impact and dramatically increased coverage. Efforts to win an increase for all workers in the City of New Orleans dramatically changed the proposition on a citywide level with a key signature gathering petition effort that shrewdly took advantage of municipal elections, when there was a surety that validly registered voters would be participants, increasing the accuracy of petition signatures. The length of the campaign, beginning in late 1990's and culminating in a dramatic election victory in February 2002 created a citywide minimum wage of one dollar over the federal minimum wage. Similar efforts were successful in Santa Fe, New Mexico, and then later on a citywide basis in an ACORN-HERE-led coalition that created a citywide minimum wage successfully in San Francisco in 2004. Both of the efforts in New Mexico and California sustained court challenges. The New Orleans ordinance fell at the Louisiana Supreme Court level after the industry passed a backdoor measure in the state legislature that made citizen initiatives on wage issues illegal.

Statewide initiatives were huge efforts involving significant organizational resources, timing, and engineering. Over the years we used this tactic to implement campaign objectives in Arkansas, South Dakota, Missouri, Florida, Arizona, Ohio, Colorado, and Michigan, mostly through direct formal balloting, and sometimes as threats powerful enough to force legislatures to act, as happened in Michigan and Arkansas, creating compromises to raise state minimum wages in 2010 to forestall ballot measures. After narrowly losing a statewide effort to raise the minimum wage in Missouri in 1996, we came back a second time to win in 2006. The largest effort in 2004 in Florida involved obtaining a million signatures to qualify to raise the minimum wage by one dollar over the federal level, indexed to inflation as well. The initiative was contested at every level in the courts including challenges to the ballot language and to the validity of the petitioning apparatus as well as the signatures themselves. After surviving the legal shenanigans by opponents, the measure passed decisively despite a horrific media blitz by opponents in the closing weeks equating passage of the measure as a disaster equivalent to the three hurricanes that had hit the state that year. The results were huge in terms of

Food and medicine initiative in Missouri, Mary Lassen and members turning in petitions for initiative in Columbia, MO.

money delivered to low wage workers and more than a million workers received raises directly and indirectly as the measure raised the wage floor.[131] Ironically, Senator John Kerry, running for President on the same ballot passed on endorsing the measure and lost narrowly in Florida, and therefore nationally, even as the margin of victory for the ACORN initiative led the ballot.

At the nuts and bolts level we had begun our work with initiatives by simply buying an old van that ACORN converted to a campaign wagon of sorts and used to tour the state to rally support for approving a tax on intangible properties (stocks, bonds, and so forth) in the early 1970's. The van of course promptly threw a rod near Dumas as Harold Medlock, a leader of the Hanger Hill ACORN group in East Little Rock, and I went from town to town in southern Arkansas. Towing the van to a repair shop off Highway 65, somewhere between nowhere and no how, could have served as a metaphor for that unsuccessful though righteous effort. On the other hand the effort required to shift all of the gears and put all of the pieces together to get matters on the ballot from start to finish was often so grueling and tedious that there was little energy or resources left to actually wage the campaign after the effort to achieve a place on the ballot was finished. Husbanding the resources, energy, and organizational discipline to have something left for the race to Election Day was always a struggle.

In the beginning we managed to put measures on the ballot virtually through force of will with staff, members, and volunteers. Often it was a balancing act between the normal work of organizing and maintaining the local groups and the added tasks of scheduling petitioners, clearing turf, which in Arkansas and Missouri often meant hide-and-seek efforts in the limitless parking lots of shopping malls, rural Walmarts, and similar venues, and the constant tallying against the daily production goals we had to make in order to get on the ballot. The other task to master were the usual arcane and obstructionist requirements. The valid signatures, whether in Missouri or Florida or elsewhere, could not just equal the total valid number of registered voters we needed, but often had to also include a specific threshold of signatures by number or percentage from each Congressional District in the state. In Missouri, for example, it was always straightforward to pull the numbers of signatures needed out of St. Louis County or Cass County, where Kansas City was located, and given the wonders of gerrymandering a number of Missouri Congressional districts would touch these major urban centers, so it was often a matter of simple scheduling of turf to pick them up, but nothing got around the fact that sooner or later you had to send teams out to Springfield or Jefferson City to sew up the needed signatures from those districts. Take it as gospel that even when states continued to maintain initiative and referendum procedures, there was no legislative obligation to make it easy for citizens and their community organizations, especially like ACORN, to use these tools to enhance democracy and create a real citizens' voice.

In the first decade of the 21st century when the efforts became larger and more numerous, it also meant more sophistication by ACORN, under the direction of Zach Polett, ACORN's political director, as well as many more resources including paid canvassers and petitioners. Key allies like the National Education Association and the

---

[131] For more exact totals on the Florida results and benefits, as well as other states, see Wade Rathke, *Citizen Wealth* (2009).

Service Employees International Union understood the importance of our initiatives and the way they dovetailed with general get-out-the-vote (GOTV) efforts that would enhance turnout sufficiently to make the difference in key states that in the polarized Presidential politics from Gore/Bush, Kerry/Bush, and then Obama/McCain made areas like Ohio, Arizona, Pennsylvania, and Florida electoral battlegrounds. Coupling these efforts with voter registration and aligning them with what became ACORN's signature turnout efforts created real power and significant controversy. By 2006, the ACORN political operations were trying to raise $20,000,000 for these projects in 2008.

Voter Registration and Turnout

It is inarguable that ACORN forged a new path in community organizing by embracing politics, but voter registration was always a historical tactical staple. Voter registration efforts in East Los Angeles particularly by Fred Ross and Cesar Chavez's Community Service Organization (CSO) were instrumental in the election of Ed Roybal as the first Mexican-American on the Los Angeles City Council. Nick von Hoffman, Saul Alinsky's lead organizer at Chicago's Woodlawn Organization (TWO) after seeing the organization register more than 10,000 new voters in the south side, famously said, "is this all there is to this," and moved on after ten years to become a reporter and television commentator. In similar fashion ACORN began linking its organizing with voter registration and GOTV efforts starting virtually with the founding of the organization in Arkansas.

ACORN quickly found that our initial, largely housing project and near project neighborhood base was significantly under registered in our mixed, white, and African-American groups. Registering to vote was not a second hand, third party process in those days but required a physical trip to the Pulaski County Courthouse to go through the steps to qualify as a voter in 1970. Within six months of founding the organization we approached Pat House, who was the majordomo of an extensive minister and church based, statewide, largely African-American voter registration effort, allegedly tied closely to the Republican governor Winthrop Rockefeller and financed by him directly. The effort was nonpartisan, but the premise was undoubtedly that part of the key to Rockefeller's surprising gubernatorial victories was his ability to win over black votes in the general election, particularly against Orval Faubus, whose early populism had rebranded into racism during the school desegregation fights around the state. ACORN's pitch was that we would link membership turnout to access Title I money for school books and supplies with voter registration for every member who attended the action at the Little Rock School Board offices with a trip to the registrar of voters in the Pulaski Courthouse in what we called a "one-two punch," if they provided us sufficient money to pay for the buses as part of the action. When I returned to get their answer, House was so oblique and circumspect in her response that I was not sure if the answer was "yes" or "no," but as I rose to leave she said "take this," and pushed over a small, brown paper bag. When I reached the street, I opened the bag and looked inside to find enough to pay for a whole lot of buses and then some. This was my first – and last -- introduction to what is known universally in politics as "street money," but in fact it was the first "outside" money I was

New Orleans ACORN leader Frenzella Johnson getting signatures of minimum wage ordinance petion.

able to raise from anyone to support ACORN's early, embryonic efforts. Nonetheless from that day on, voter registration was always part of our program.

Subsequently in Arkansas our main effort was to move voter registration from the cumbersome courthouse based system to one that was directed by roving registrars who were able to be deputized by the County election commissions. We pushed and pulled for years and used our newfound influence through the Quorum Court campaign and our justices of the peace to try and maintain a deputy registrar in each of our local groups in Pulaski County. This capacity allowed us to regularly register members who attended local group meetings as a matter of course, including that item as a standard part of the agenda similar to the opening prayer. When it worked, it was great. When it didn't, we hardly noticed, because it was largely an "add-on" to general organizing and campaign work. Nonetheless, our commitment to registration was constant over the years.

What upgraded this priority years later was the merger of Project Vote into the ACORN family of organizations. Project Vote had been founded by Sandy Newman and directed by him from a base in Washington, D.C. for a number of years.[132] ACORN partnered with Project Vote on various registration drives in different election cycles in states where he had raised money and where we had capacity. It was a breakeven operation, but one that fit in with other work and carried its own weight. Eventually, Sandy decided he wanted to go in some other directions with his life and work. He believed that Project Vote would best be served by an African-American or minority executive director, but was having trouble implementing his notion of that ideal scenario. Finally, unwilling to face another cycle he began talking to various organizations who had partnered with Project Vote and at one point seemed to be turning the operation over to Arnie Graf, a senior Industrial Areas Foundation (IAF) organizer based in

---

[132] Barack Obama ran the Project Vote operation in Chicago under Sandy's leadership, which often confuses the rightwing about whether or not he was directly employed by ACORN before becoming President of the United States. He was a partner with Chicago ACORN during that voter registration effort certainly, but never on the payroll.

Chapter XVIII: Politics –Proving the Base, Initiatives, and Alternative Parties

Baltimore. Arnie ended up with some back problems or perhaps just thought he and the IAF did not want to take on the national weight and responsibility of Project Vote and voter registration. We had continued talking to Sandy about growing larger nationally, and were delighted to take over and direct Project Vote's operation after he left in 1992 and beginning in the 1994 cycle as part of Zach Polett's political shop and overall responsibilities, and jumped at the opportunity. From that point on the trajectory of our voter registration and GOTV operation expanded exponentially from election cycle to election cycle over the next twenty years.[133]

In the early years we managed Project Vote as a more marginal operation, hoping that the contacts and supporters developed by Newman would sustain the operation and indirectly contribute to ACORN's support. Project Vote had the tax status under the federal IRS code allowing registration efforts to be tax exempt if they involved five or six states. We found that most of the contacts did not transfer as seamlessly over to ACORN as we might have hoped. There were also additional challenges in managing a Washington, DC-based office for Project Vote as well as the real direction and leadership from Little Rock and New Orleans, and finding the right Project Vote manager who could navigate the potential contacts and general support. Managing the relationships within the ACORN family and management was also not a trivial task. Eventually we reconciled to the fact that we were going to have to manage the funding as aggressively as we did other programs within ACORN to be able to get to scale.

The basic Project Vote model was interesting at the nuts and bolts level, because it focused exclusively on production, which was both its strength and weakness. In order to register the most people possible, the budgeting was exacting since there was virtually no margin between the cost to pay for the registration staff, verify the registrations, do the database work, and submit the registration forms. Some ACORN cities and states in later cycles would try to opt out of the registration program, arguing that they would lose money in their areas by running the program and registering the voters. Others were willing to move forward with the program even at a break even basis, though the indirect costs were significant in terms of reallocation of organizer supervisory time and resources as well as increasing backlash from opponents, political parties, and partisan election commissioners and the press as we became more successful and therefore more threatening in this area. A few states would come out ahead, but they were anomalies from cycle to cycle. Our voter registration really only worked as a commitment to greater democracy and empowerment, because otherwise it was often a huge pain in the neck to administer and run.

The funding ratio might be as thin as $3 for every individual, fully completed registration card. As various states moved to suppress the vote, especially within our core constituencies of lower income and often minority families, they also moved even more aggressively to suppress our third-party registration efforts. For example the 2008 legislative restrictions in Florida, targeting ACORN particularly, were so onerous in criminalizing any inadvertent error severely that even the League of Women Voters was unwilling to run registration efforts because of the potential liabilities imposed by the law.

---

[133] The decade from 1998 to 2008 was the golden age of our voter registration program in terms of scale.

Exhibit 54: Project Vote

Project Vote breaks all records and the numbers say it all:

- 1,123,270 low- and moderate-income African-American and Latino voters registered in 26 states and 102 metro areas
- 8,713,553 GOTV voter contacts
- 11,000 lawn signs, 25,000 window signs, 1.6 million flyers, 1.3 million doorhangers distributed
- 500,000 mobilized in 2000, 2,293,579 mobilized in 2004
- 50% higher increase in voter turnout than the national average increase over 2000
- 90% of Project Vote canvassers hired from the communities of color in which they worked

4 face-to-face visits + 3 live reminder calls = 50% higher voter turnout than the national average

Other statutes in places like Nevada where ACORN was caught in expensive and difficult legal predicaments in 2008 leading to criminal prosecutions were based on whether or not registration canvassers could be paid "by the card." Some technical violation was found involving a game of 21 played by the registration team that rewarded a bonus in some situations to recruiters hitting that number. Objective observers concurred that all of the dust was kicked up over what was a *de minimus* violation at most.

ACORN, when I was Chief Organizer, followed the letter of the law, but often the laws themselves were so mean spirited that there was no way they might have been obeyed. The reality of voter registration financing whether through ACORN, Project Vote or Working Assets/Credo was always so thin that whether paying by the card or prohibited from doing so, the ratios of income to production were so tight that the organization had to have a guideline or target number of 20 or more registrations per shift or could not affordably run the operation even on a break even basis. Call it a quota, whether expressed in that way or not, there had to be a hard number on production to deliver the results required. In some ways the operating contradiction may have been that people were not paid by the card, but they were certainly fired by the card.

In election cycle after election cycle in 2000, 2002, 2004, 2006, and 2008 the size of the voter registration program grew larger and larger as the organization became more proficient and the resources became more available because of other, compatible though external national priorities that involved "taking back the Senate" or work with our constituency in battleground states on various measures or key races. Our total numbers of new registrants moved in each cycle from 250,000 to 500,000 to over a 1,000,000. Most of these were new registrations, though of course some also include updating address and other information that could have prevented someone from being allowed to vote and therefore disqualify them. Infrequent voters sometimes re-registered, creating duplicates in some cases inadvertently. ACORN operations like the ones in Louisiana paid someone full time on their own initiative and out of their own resources to telephone back through every registration and reconfirm their accuracy, avoiding problems later. Others did not. The national organization beginning in 2006 and intensifying in 2008 established a Little Rock based team of verifiers for registration forms that was utilized by all of the organizations, cutting down errors dramatically.

Nothing involving more than one-million records collected in hundreds of locations by 5000 to 10,000 people can achieve a 100% accuracy rate though, and ACORN's operation did not pretend that we could. Voter registration in the United States is a very local and state-based operation with different rules, procedures, and laws in each jurisdiction, which is part of what creates the chaos of costs and customs that surround both the art and science of registration. Nonetheless in almost every jurisdiction, a registration organization is **required** to submit to the Election Commission or the Registrar of Voters **every** completed form, even if the organization believes the cards are inaccurate or fraudulent. All of this is common sense obviously. ACORN and others should not be the final arbiters of whether or not a voter is qualified. Yet, this also meant that even in obvious situations (Dallas Cowboys, Mickey Mouse, and so forth) that ACORN was required to submit the forms, regardless of the fact that they were in our "discard" stack. ACORN also in numerous cases notified authorities when the organization had reason to believe that cards were being forged or in any way fraudulently acquired.

The nicety of the factual circumstances does not alter the political and public relations blow back generated by partisan opponents of these efforts. There had been a mounting level of opposition to ACORN's voter registration efforts that aligned almost seamlessly with our effectiveness in the early 21st century cycles. There was an orchestrated strategy, particularly in so-called battleground states like Ohio, Pennsylvania, Missouri, and Florida. During that period the Republican Party in the closing weeks of each campaign, either directly, or through its local officeholders or party election officials, would begin to impugn or object to the ACORN efforts. In some cycles they would move to file charges directly with the Federal Election Commission (FEC) about alleged violations by ACORN. In other places they would file state charges. Everything was elaborately coordinated with publicity throughout the state, designed to both mobilize their own adherents and suppress newly registered voters from voting for fear of challenge. But, usually by the following January or February, a couple of months after the election had become history to everyone else, the charges against ACORN would be dismissed or withdrawn and this difficult duet would be dusted off the floor until another political season began.

Starting in 2004, the opposition debuted another part of its playbook. The opposition would find someone supposedly claiming to have been an insider in the ACORN registration operation who would allege there was mischief and monkey business to every press pencil and television microphone within miles in order to cast doubt on the validity of the ACORN registrations. Miami saw this first so-called "whistle-blower" case, which ended in charges and countercharges, suits and countersuits, until, once again, many months later after all is gone and forgotten, they settled with ACORN and slinked away leaving a pile of messy media and lots of legal bills for us to sort through. One of the more ridiculous "whistle-blowers," now with a multi-year run, was a DC-based employee who was let go after she was found using the organization's credit card fraudulently for personal items, but then claimed she had special knowledge of ACORN's relationship to the Democratic Party and the Obama campaign. Not surprisingly this whistle-blower even showed up as part of a sophisticated Tea Party voter suppression effort in the 2012 election, and like a bad penny has been making a career of it all ever since.

This is all major league politics, so of course it is also hard ball in every inning played. Given the inattention and inadequate resources of the press and the 24-hour news cycle of Fox News and its cohorts and the harpy chorus of conservative bloggers and hard right websites, the drifts are deep and the sledding was never easy for the organization. ACORN was caught in the middle because despite being nonpartisan in these registration efforts, invariably when registering lower income men and women, and ordinarily therefore in disproportionately African-American and Hispanic communities, it would be unsurprising if the party preferences did not skew Democratic. Additionally, there was also no party, certainly not the Democrats, who were ever ready to stand and defend the organization when attacked or caught in these heavily partisan crossfires. Nonetheless this was the business of ACORN and its mission to organize the powerless, so it all just came with the package.

ACORN accepted struggle and embraced it. In 2007 at the national ACORN board meeting, throughout the national staff councils, and finally at the ACORN Executive Board level in January 2008, there was a hardy debate, that I requested as Chief Organizer, on whether there was still deep consensus that we should continue to do voter registration directly and do so in the name of ACORN given the uproar we had faced in 2006. I used to joke then that my obituary in the *New York Times* would mention fraudulent registrations, but the question before the leadership was whether the voter registration efforts were hurting the organization and the question before the staff was how close we could come to assuring the leadership that we could run a nearly error-free operation. At the end of the debate the national board at every level voted to continue with the program, feeling it was our obligation and mission to bring our members and constituency into the electorate, and recognizing that there was no one else who would pick up the flag were we to lay it down. This decision turned out to be prophetic, given the space created when ACORN was unable to run the program in 2010 and absent from the field in 2012 and thereafter. In fact the opposition and partisan polarization has without question been chilling and subsequently prevented others from duplicating the ACORN capacity in voter registration.

The other area where ACORN excelled was straightforward get-out-the-vote work among our members and in our communities. After decades of making the case that the "ground" war was more effective in moving voters than the "air" war, there finally developed independent validation of the correctness of our argument. Professor Don Green then at Yale was invited with his researchers to independently evaluate our field program in Phoenix, Arizona. His study of ACORN's field program there was well presented in his book, *Get out the Vote: How to Increase Voter Turnout*,[134] and concluded that no technique mail, phone, or advertising was more effective at turning out voters to an election than the door-to-door, person-to-person contact that was the heart of the ACORN effort and others like us.

This technique has been effective not only in the United States but also in programs that ACORN International and its affiliates have managed in Canadian provincial elections in British Columbia and Ontario, Indonesia in 2008, Ecuador in 2012, and the Netherlands in 2016. In Makassar, the 1.3 million person provincial capital of South Sulawesi in the Indonesian archipelago, we trained 50 "rappers," as our partner, the Urban Poor Consortium (UPC), called them since we were teaching them the "engagement and persuasion rap" for them to move the votes on the mayor's election there. In Ecuador in a partnership with Raptura25 to build a broad based political party and ACORN Ecuador, we ran a program we called *"puerta a puerta y calle."* In Ecuador, working with ACORN Canada, Argentina-born, organizer, Marcos Alejandro Gomez, we put out up to 50 organizers (*brigadistas*) every day to secure voting commitments working door-to-door as well as engaging neighbors on the streets.

One of the keys whether in Ecuador (*cuenta conmigos*) or New Orleans in late 1990s, where New Orleans ACORN originally developed the "count on me's," is moving the field program to engage potential voters sufficiently to have them make an actual commitment to vote. In Ecuador voting is mandatory, though of course everyone still does not vote, so the commitment is in fact to support the party and the organization. In the United States and Canada the commitment is to actually show up to vote and take the election seriously, and vote for a specific candidate and program as well. This long tested ACORN technique became a key ingredient of electoral field programs for the 2012 Obama effort.

Needing and Building Political Parties

In an era in the United States when political parties have largely been dismissed as historical artifacts, useful for little but attracting the junior varsity that wants to work its way up to the playing team one way or another, ACORN was unabashedly a proponent of building parties and the relevance of parties to the empowerment mission of the organization. The arc of history, like justice, is also long, and I always believed, and still believe, that parties are critical political organizations that can and should play important roles in advancing the interests of our constituency. I take some comfort after almost half-a-century in the work that the usefulness of political parties has continued to emerge as robust and vital in the 21st century as it was in earlier times for some of the same and for some new reasons. This is a longer topic than we can handle in this work, but the dominance of media first and, most recently, the internet have now been eclipsed again, by the importance of the base voters and the hard and painstaking work of building

---

[134] Donald Green and Alan S. Gerber, *Get out the Vote: How to Increase Voter Turnout*, 2nd edition, (2008).

that base. For that task, parties are the defining instrument for the establishment of the political framework over time and for achievement of results. The weakness, in fact, of political parties during the lifespan of ACORN's key work in the United States defined ACORN's own political life and work and enhances our commitment to encouraging and building political formations within existing parties and in alternate parties to empower our constituency.

The Quorum Court campaign in 1974 made ACORN one of the bigger fishes in that small pond, but we were not simply outsiders, we were an opposition force and an ally to others committed to moving a more progressive agenda in central Arkansas. Somehow we were both inside and outside the dominant Democratic Party. We may have elected hundreds of our members as part of a stealth strategy, but once elected, many of the functionaries in the local Democratic Party saw our members *qua* justices of the peace, as fresh meat for the party, not as disciplined soldiers for the organization. There were many tense exchanges around loyalties, programs, and policies in those days. We howled when the party would try to recruit our members, albeit elected officials, to raise funds for the party or go to events that conflicted in time and energy with our first priority of building ACORN. Sometimes with some people we were able to work this out, and sometimes we lost good members to the siren song of something that seemed more established and prestigious. We tried our "multiple candidates" technique in winning seats to county and state conventions to overtly promote our issue and ideological agenda, but quickly found that swimming in that deeper pond was more like drowning, than evenly stroking on the surface. All of these experiences forced us to recalibrate our strategy and tactics around the party.

We adamantly believed that we needed a party, but we wanted a party that saw organization and accountability in a clearer, democratic form that aligned with our politics. Out of this tension emerged the defining organizational initiative and campaign of the early years of ACORN, the 20/80 campaign.

20/80

It was no secret that ACORN was never designed to only organize in Arkansas, where I founded the organization. From the very beginnings I was always clear, as were other organizers and the majority of the leaders that we wanted to craft an organizing model that could reach its maximum potential in organizing low-and-moderate income families. We took our first tentative steps outside of Arkansas in a partnership of sorts with an organization in the boot heel area of Missouri, abutting Arkansas, called MDEM (Missouri Delta Ecumenical Ministry) that worked in the several counties of southeastern Missouri, largely on economic development issues. They wanted to expand to include a community base, we wanted to expand out of Arkansas, so in what developed as an ill-advised and ill-fated operation, we tried to grow ACORN in early 1974, through shortcuts and on the cheap, which sometimes can work if everything comes together, but is no way to launch a multi-state or national organization we quickly found.

Part of this cobbled together expansion strategy was an attempt with existing staff and leadership to develop a consensus for growth, but to do so with the least conflict possible among leaders and organizers who were Arkansas-first-and-always proponents. Training and placing an organizer from outside of Arkansas for this project meant no reallocation of our most contentious, and in the leadership's view, precious resource: staff. Furthermore, partnering with another organization meant lower front end costs for an office, equipment, and so forth. Being only a couple of hours drive from Little Rock, and even less from Jonesboro and our operations in the northeastern part of Arkansas, we claimed also meant easier support and supervision from ACORN. This kind of transactional expansion was hard to virulently oppose from either the staff or leadership ranks, because it seemed low risk.

Of course the dangers are real when such a major strategic adjustment in the course of an organization is sold and operated almost as an afterthought. We hired and trained an organizer. The training was brief but seemed to go well in the Baseline area southwest of the city of Little Rock. After we placed the organizer and raised $5000 or so from the Boston-based Sherwood Forest Fund of Anne and Marty Peretz, who I had known from my time with MWRO, to support the early work, we planted the organizer and supported the project loosely from Arkansas. The first groups of ACORN as the American Community Organizations for Reform Now came together reasonably well in a couple of communities, but as the money played out the MDEM commitments also thinned, and before long we were minding a mess with the groups and the organizer bolting to go native as more part of MDEM, than ACORN. The future looked even more fraught. The best judgments made by John Beam, the organizer working from Arkansas on this project, and myself was finally to cut bait and run.

Stepping back from that first stumble at expansion, it was clear to me that we needed deeper consensus on expansion and the program needed to be part of a transformative overall vision for growth of the organization that aligned membership, campaign, and political interests. The 20/80 plan later emerged from this need.

Fortunately, the next opportunity for ACORN to expand was too good for the board and staff to pass up. Early press and attention focused on ACORN's campaigns in Arkansas were starting to break in national sources and in Washington. I received an inquiry from a top aide to Senator John Abourezk from South Dakota, asking if I would be willing to meet with the Senator who felt there were similarities between the demographics in Arkansas and South Dakota, and there was need for a progressive community organization of low-and-moderate income people there like ACORN. Meeting a US Senator in the Capitol in his offices to talk about building ACORN in his state and listening to him explain how by himself as an elected official he just could not do as much as was needed, which was why ACORN had to be in South Dakota was all something of a surreal experience, but he seemed genuine and sincere. We pulled together a budget. David Hunter of the Stern Fund ponied up the most, partially I always believed because he loved getting invited to Washington and having the Senator making the pitch! What did a New York foundation care about South Dakota of all places, much less Arkansas? It hardly mattered since it gave the organization and our expansion plans some sizzle. Abourezk ended up delivering on his commitments by letting us work out of his Sioux Falls office for free, and we were able to do a much better job of coordinating the program using the fancy federal telefax, which none of us had ever seen before, and the dedicated WATS lines and other machinery to get started. When his staff called to ask if we had any problem taking Arab money from overseas to finance the organizing, I had the presence of mind to understand that was way too crazy, so after the first year we were on our own, especially when Tom Dashiell came back from DC to run the office and prepare for his own political career.

We opened up South Dakota on the 21st of January in 1975 with a young organizer from the Arkansas operation, Dewey Armstrong. Ironically it developed that he was also someone with roots in the area both in Minnesota and South Dakota where there was an Armstrong County, part of the military legacy of his family which included George Armstrong Custer. A second organizer was recruited from San Francisco, Tony Fazio, originally from Providence, Rhode Island, and more recently an organizer with the All Peoples' Coalition (APC), at that time an emerging community organization in the Mission District of San Francisco. This was a tighter operation in every way.

It was an experience to work through that first winter in South Dakota, flying up there from Little Rock to Memphis to Chicago, and then over to Sioux Falls, all of which would take more than 12 hours to navigate, assuming I didn't get stuck by the snow in O'Hare Airport, which happened more than once. Needless to say that was enough to convince me that our expansion would be much easier in a circumference around Little Rock. Within five to seven hours drive we could reach St. Louis, Memphis, Houston, Dallas, Fort Worth, and New Orleans, all of which were big, inviting targets, that though lacking the cache of an invitation from a progressive U.S. Senator, made more sense in every other way. In quick order we opened Dallas and Fort Worth in August 1975 and New Orleans in 1976.

At the time there were the first tentative movements towards public financing of elections in national politics. If a candidate raised a minimum amount of money in twenty different states (about $5000), then they qualified for matching money from the federal government for the presidential campaign. In Arkansas at the time, without fail there was a staff meeting convened at 8PM each Wednesday night as was the practice for all of the years I worked in Arkansas and acted as Chief Organizer of the state operation. These meetings could go on for hours and hours, essentially until consensus was reached, usually ending by 10 or 11pm, but sometimes stretching on into the early morning hours. These

Senator Jim Abourezk.

Chapter XVIII: Politics –Proving the Base, Initiatives, and Alternative Parties were as much discussions, as survival contests. There were also statewide staff meetings every month on a Saturday. I first broached the issue at a general staff meeting in a short memo arguing that we should advance a lower income member, one of our leaders, as a candidate for President to promote our issues and expand the organization in the coming five years by 1980 and trigger the matching money.

Perhaps the proposal was so outrageous that the organizers at first did not know exactly how to respond to this "20/80" proposal that ACORN should be organizing in 20 states by 1980 in order to qualify for matching money. Unquestionably people were excited or perhaps titillated. This was wild and crazy, but you could tell by the conversation then, and even more later, that this was also the most important thing that any of us could have ever imagined being part of it, and it gave vision and purpose to all of the hard, daily work of our organizing and a timeline to see the results, come hell or high water. There were of course some naysayers. I remember particularly Mark Schroder, who ran our Jonesboro office after a fashion, and was young, but smart as a whip, who scoffed at the notion of running a member for president, and it did not take much time before I quickly amended that part of the proposal as premature and impractical, probably to everyone's relief.

Instead what held the 20/80 plan together for our expansion was our belief that we needed this range and depth in the organization to win a quota for lower income participation in the major political parties, similar to what had been emerging for women and minorities. It was clear that in the age of Nixon and the aftermath of Vietnam that we had to be able to act on our issues nationally. Nixon had withdrawn from President Johnson's "War on Poverty" as surely as he had pulled out of Saigon, and despite the fact that the helicopters did not land on the roof of the high rise housing projects to evacuate any of the families left in the cities of the United States, we had to expand to a level where we could operate nationally or have the organization at best simply seen as "precious" for our members and at the worst irrelevant and reduced to neighborhood cleanups. In a last gasp for lower income families, we believed that if we could build enough scale perhaps, just perhaps, we could raise the issues of low-and-moderate income people to the top ranks of policy and concern, if we could enhance the access and volume of their voices. Winning a guaranteed level of participation by the poor in the political process at the level of delegate horse trading at national conventions selecting Presidential contenders seemed to be a forum that we could use to advance our members voice.

Critically, the emerging ACORN leadership on the multi-state board from Arkansas, Texas, South Dakota, Louisiana, Tennessee, and Colorado was excited about the strategy, regardless of whether they thought it was really practical or even possible. In one of the first fights of the national board, which critically shaped the future and in fact the very possibility of a future for ACORN as a national organization, Steve McDonald from Arkansas serving as the first president, insisted that the governance structure equalize the voting strength of the states, regardless of membership. As the organization began to expand and organizers were moved from Arkansas to lead the staffs of the new states, there was a fierce backlash that developed from some of the key, older leaders who were concerned that staff and resources to assist in maintaining their local groups would change before they were ready or be reduced in ways they did not want.

The breaking point of these tensions came too late for this rump caucus in 1978 as the central organizing, financial, and legal operations of the national headquarters had already been moved to New Orleans to facilitate the expansion program of the 20/80 program and to accelerate the job-and-employment program initiative of ACORN from the members' community life to their work lives. They had voted for the move and the relocation of the Chief Organizer to facilitate both of those projects to what became known as the Organizing and Support Center in New Orleans, and now several of the old bulls of the board had buyer's remorse, as they saw their voices diluted by the rapid expansion and reduced access. The numerically critical mass of membership was still in Arkansas, but the point where the membership there could dominate in the way that it could when they represented 80% of the national organization had already passed when some of these leaders raised the issue from a provincial Arkansas organizational perspective that they wanted to maintain the national office in Little Rock and reverse the national board voting system to award governing votes based on a membership ratio rather than equal numbers per state. Fortunately, McDonald had always used his credibility and the respect of the other board members to assure the new states coming into ACORN that their votes and voice were as critical to the future of ACORN as Arkansas had been, so there was steel in the decision and policy that could not be bent. As discussed elsewhere, ACORN did not move to finally incorporate as a nonprofit, and instead remained as an unincorporated association of groups until 1978 at the same time as I moved along with the office to New Orleans. The voting system for the Association, as national ACORN was known to distinguish it from Arkansas ACORN, had to be finally determined in those bylaws, so once that fight was fought and won, there were no structural governance obstacles to growth.

Internally, we needed the 20/80 plan to deliver the maximum potential of the organizing staff as well. The initial novelty of what ACORN was trying to do in Arkansas and our willingness to train and develop organizers who were ready to "work long hours for low pay" as our job notices heralded with little qualifications other than owning their own transportation, had attracted a bright, young and spirited group of men and women from all over the country as well as from Arkansas and the South, who jumped at the opportunity and rose to the task. The original staff had been cobbled from VISTA volunteers like Carolyn Carr, Donna Parcziak, Melva Harmon, Sue Hanna and others in and around Arkansas who I had picked up along the trail including Gary Delgado from welfare rights, Herman Davenport, Jay Lipner, and Steve Herman from Legal Aid and Bobbie Cox and Cheryl McCleary from the Arkansas Council of Human Relations. There was the Harvard crew that began with Steve Kest, who started as a summer intern and brought along Seth Borgos, an old friend of the Kest family as a researcher, and Madeline Talbott, Steve Holt, Meg Campbell, Mary Lassen, Zach Polett, Steve Bachman, our lawyer who came from the Harvard Law School, and Joe Fox from St. Louis who came to us from the Harvard Business School – all of whom had done time there. Fred Dorsey, Gene Gibbons, and Dub Gulley were from southern Arkansas and Little Rock and just walked in the door so to speak. Beth Butler was scooped up from a political science course I visited at UALR. John Beam was from Dallas via Northwestern at Chicago, Dewey Armstrong was from the DC area via the University of North Carolina, Mary Jo

Kitchen followed her brother, Bill, down from Johnstown, New York, Jon Kest followed his brother down from Oberlin on a year off, Barbara Friedman made her way over from Los Angeles, Danny Cantor came from Wesleyan, and Mike Shea pulled in from the University of Michigan in a Volkswagen bus along with his wife, Maureen. To keep such a diverse staff, they had to believe two things, firstly, that we could win, and, secondly, that their ambitions had vast room to grow with few ceilings in sight. Expansion offered the opportunity tailored to both since going after a seemingly impossible national objective was exhilarating, and having the opportunity to run operations in their "own" cities and states within the larger ACORN was fuel for the fire of their ambition.

ACORN was perfectly designed to exploit their skills, strengths, and passion. In the first waves of expansion Dewey Armstrong opened up South Dakota followed by Steve Soifer; Meg Campbell was then in Fort Worth and Steve Holt in Dallas with Barbara Friedman and then Madeline Talbott in Houston; Zach Polett opened New Orleans; John Beam and then Beth Butler did the same in Memphis, first Mary Anne Fiske who had been my office manager in Boston with welfare rights brought in St. Louis and then Mary Lassen moved into the slot; and Mike Shea opened up Denver once again following Mary Anne Fiske who was in Colorado Springs then (quite the organizing catalyst after having been a home economics major from Cornell)[135]; Cate Poe and then Steve Kest followed me in Arkansas; Mark Schroeder opened up Reno; Mark Dunlea shoehorned us into Phoenix; and so it went. After the foray into South Dakota, we concentrated on the expanding circle around New Orleans where a quick drive or a short plane ride could allow movement among all of the cities fairly easily.

As planes became more necessary, New Orleans was a better hub and the expansion was farther afield after 1978. A long process and the hope of "shooting with a bigger gun," as Jay Hessey and I called it while negotiating the rough details on several ferry rides across the Mississippi River in the crescent of New Orleans, led to the affiliation of Carolina Action in North and South Carolina and Georgia Action in Atlanta, adding people who would become longtime, permanent organizers and vital staff, like Jay, Jim Fleischman and Bruce Dorpalen, and with them the integration of their fundraising canvass and Peter Wood, Pat McCoy, Fred Brooks, and others who helped fund and fuel the 20/80 growth. Rather than organize farewell parties, we exploited and seized the opportunities presented by life changes. When Jon Kest went back to school, he ended up in Philadelphia, we worked with him to open up Pennsylvania ACORN there along with Fran Streich who became his lifelong partner as well. When people wanted to go back towards the East or to a bigger city, we had plenty, and that meant being able to open up in Bridgeport, Connecticut or Detroit. We tried to affiliate an organization, the Citizens' Action League (CAL) in California, but could not quite make the deal. We had to be in Iowa to make 20/80 work, and so we were. The same was true of Florida, New Mexico, and then finally with Mark Splain and Barbara Bowen, earlier comrades from MWRO as well, and Peter Rider's help, Massachusetts became the 20th state with an ACORN operation just as 1980 broke the calendar.

---

[135] Mary Ann Fiske was doing her Cornell thesis in home economics at MWRO while I was there with work as the office manager being part of the quid pro quo, but in her own way opened the way for us in Missouri, then Colorado, and, finally, New Mexico.

Making the list is simple, but moving organizers around, filling spots that went empty, moving forward, moving backward, and somehow holding all of the pieces together for a rapidly expanding organization with limited resources in those days was its own kind of challenge. In the same way that the legendary organizer of the Nonpartisan League, Arthur C. Townley, used to say that he built the league across the plains and Midwestern states with a "Motel T Ford and five dollar dues," I often say in the early decades of the twenty-first century that we can organize internationally only because we have email, Skype, and cheaper plane fares, but in the late 1970's we had none of these things really. As I mentioned earlier, fax machines were still big, bulky government-only contraptions in 1975 when we opened in South Dakota and it took forever to fly there from Little Rock. There were no cell phones, and our view of modern technology that moved organizing drives started with a WATS line, a Gestefax stencil maker and mimeograph machine, and a later with a Xerox machine. All with bulk mail permits and cheaper postage fueling the communications program.

Few organizers of that era during 20/80 expansion cannot tell stories about the famous US Air Liberty Fares program, which supported much of our travel. Initially for $299 and later for $399 one could fly throughout the US Air system for 14 straight days.[136] While the program lasted we almost always had a couple of Liberty Fares open and being moved between me and various organizers that were on the road for ACORN. These were the old days, pre-9/11, when identification and security checks were unknown, and tickets could be bought in initials and swapped with a line of blarney between men and women around the country. The key lay in the hubs of Philly and Pittsburgh. Frequently organizers literally met each other in a hub, switched tickets while one flew away and the other left to work in the area. Sometime we flew ridiculous routes like Memphis to Pittsburgh and then over to Phoenix, back to Providence and then down through Pittsburgh again and over to Tampa. We all knew the system by heart, and we loved that airline!

No matter how we got there, we were organizing in 20 states in 1980 and then had to contend with both the Republicans and the Democrats in trying to win our demand for low-and-moderate income participation. Where possible we employed an inside-outside strategy, though by default that meant trying both with the Democrats and being shut outside with the Republicans. Nonetheless, starting in the Iowa caucuses in the freezing, snowdrifts of January 1980, I was part of a team of organizers that trudged up to support the members and staff in our offices in Des Moines and Davenport in a door-to-door program as well as constant entreaties to precinct chairs to convince caucus goers to make lower income participation a litmus test for candidate support. We were all over the state dogging and stalking both Senator Ted Kennedy and the surrogates for President Jimmy Carter who was running for re-election, finally meeting with both in various ways to win weak levels of commitment to our demand though the letters were short of outright endorsements.

So we ran members in Iowa, Oklahoma, Michigan and elsewhere, often successfully and ended up with more than 42 delegates and alternates from more than a dozen different states including Iowa, Arizona, Florida, Oklahoma, Arkansas, Texas, Michigan,

---

[136] Thanks to Mark Splain for jogging my memory on the exact fare.

Arkansas, and Louisiana. The tactics were numerous and the member and organizer tales from place to place were legendary. In Iowa in an especially unruly caucus meeting several of our members and organizers were asked to provide the final tally and made sure the numbers aligned with our interests. In Tulsa a volunteer organizer held two chickens for a couple of guys who were ringing their necks in the neighborhood in order to get their commitment to attend the caucus meeting.[137] Many of the caucus states were high dives of different degrees of difficulty, as our numbers were winnowed from the local to the district to the Congressional to the statewide caucuses which operated as the "money" round where the delegates were finally named.

The largest harvest interestingly came in Michigan where the first level of Congressional caucuses defined the numbers. Michigan was unique at the time because to participate in the caucuses required that you actually had to be a member of the Democratic Party. The dues were minimal, but that requirement alone, which was probably meant to privilege union members once upon a time, gave ACORN with our strength at the base, almost a level field sufficient enough for us to compete successfully.[138] The battle royal focused on one district which was also the stronghold for our frequent nemesis, Mayor Coleman Young. With brilliant work by organizers Dewey Armstrong, our political director then, and Madeline Talbott, the Michigan head organizer, the hundreds of ACORN members who were also newly minted dues paying Democrats found themselves in the cavernous hall with significant enough critical mass to be able to ally with the UAW in a Unity slate, win a handful of delegates, advance our demand, and deny Young himself a delegate seat to the national convention. Given all of our bitter fights with Mayor Young over the GM World Headquarters expansion into our neighborhoods, this was especially sweet.

All of which found us in New York in the summer of 1980 holding our third ACORN Convention in 2 years, starting in Memphis in 1978 with our first and then moving on to St. Louis in 1979 with our second, a platform conference, at the same time as the Democratic National Convention which would nominate Jimmy Carter for re-election.[139] ACORN members pressed the demand with actions targeting the various state delegations at their hotels throughout Manhattan and winning support from a number of state delegations, as well as a march down Broadway culminating in a loud protest while hemmed in by horses outside of the convention at Madison Square Garden. Later in a smaller event we tried to press the same demands on the Republicans by offering a view of the "real" Detroit as an alternative "reality" for their program as our members acted as tour guides to several busloads of wide-eyed Republican delegates during their convention, while we stayed in a seminary not far away.

---

[137] This unlikely and hilarious story involved my brother, Dale, in one of the few instances that he doorknocked, fish out of water, in his 30 years with ACORN.

[138] The Jeremy Corbyn crusade in Great Britain fueled by the change in membership voting roles and lowered dues threshold is reminiscent of our work with the Michigan party then.

[139] Gary Delgado's book, *Organizing the Movement: The Roots of ACORN*, Temple University Press, (1986), is a well-known, fairly contemporary analysis of 20/80 and this campaign. Gary returned to ACORN in 1979, at my request, to help construct the ACORN Peoples' Platform and its process.

The end result of our campaign was a concession to our demands made by the Democratic Party to create a special commission, which came to be known as the Leland Commission, headed by Houston Congressman Mickey Leland, to review and make recommendations on how to broaden participation within the Democratic Party for lower income citizens. In hearings after the election in 1981 in Houston and other cities we continued to press the case as our members testified, but the results were modest reforms that were casually implemented over the years more in the minimal letter of the policy than in an emboldened program we had demanded. State parties for years would provide transportation and expenses in some cases to lower income delegates rather than creating the kind of affirmative action program we desired. All of which ended up leaving us dressed up for a political party with nowhere to go.

The Citizens' Party

The advent of the Citizens' Party in the run-up to the 1980 election caught us by surprise and involved a number of our traditional friends and allies in the funding and organizing world. We were heavily recruited by David Hunter of the Stern Fund, who had been a serious and consistent financier of our organizing and expansion program since the early mid-1970's, and his friend, Arch Gilles, also well known in philanthropic circles. Comrades like Bert DeLeeuw, dated back with us to welfare rights and, more importantly, to that period of the late 1970's with the Movement for Economic Justice, originally begun by George Wiley and DeLeeuw, when ACORN worked jointly with other groups around jobs and unemployment efforts following the 1978 recession during the Carter Administration.

We took the Citizens' Party effort seriously and respectfully, and tried to argue that we needed a party where our members' interests and voices could be heard, but we believed the project required a patient, long term commitment to building a base, infrastructure, and permanent capacity. We were willing to commit to such a strategy, but we were not willing to spoil our 20/80 campaign for a short term tactical opportunity that might be a transitory mirage. There was some support for our position, including from Washington State's Dan Leahy, who eventually became the key Citizen Party campaign organizer, but our argument did not prevail, allowing us to be both supportive of their efforts and to withdraw from any Citizen Party participation with principle.[140] The Party ended up supporting a number of ACORN's platform positions and ran Barry Commoner, the well-known environmentalist as their candidate for President. Congressman John Anderson's independent effort though garnered more than 6% of the electoral vote, holding President Carter to only a little past 41% and less than 50 electoral votes in the huge Ronald Reagan landslide when Carter only carried his own Georgia, West Virginia, and Mondale's Minnesota, and the Citizens' Party became another alternative party footnote.

But, timing is everything in politics and our die was already cast in that cycle with our 20/80 effort. Had that not been the situation, we might have played a different role, though

---

[140] Stanley Weiss in *Being Dead is Bad for Business* (2017) takes a somewhat different and more embittered view.

the results both within ACORN and nationally would have been at best only notionally different.[141]

The New Party

ACORN's next venture into the realm of building an alternative party came after another dozen years of hitting our heads against the existing two party wall with some local success, but diminishing ability at the national level. National two-party conventions over these decades continued to be a target for several of our own ACORN conventions, but we were marginalized. The major parties were also dominated by candidates, money, and media, and they became more and more about the show and less and less about substance.

During the races made by Rev. Jesse Jackson, we had access and opportunity and close connections like former ACORN and United Labor Unions organizer, Dan Cantor, who ran the labor desk for Jackson's first campaign. In 1984 ACORN had not endorsed, but in Jackson's 1988 quest for the nomination, ACORN's APAC endorsed Jackson during the primary campaign making his candidacy our debut in presidential endorsements. We launched a "Caravan for Justice" bus tour with our members doing GOTV work in the hinterlands, cities and towns from Missouri to Arkansas to Louisiana to Alabama to Georgia.

We had known Bill Clinton from the time he returned to Arkansas after Yale Law School. Many a time he dropped by my office in Little Rock to shoot the breeze with his feet propped on my desk. He had wrangled an offer for me to run a multi-state voter registration and turnout operation for the McGovern campaign in 1972 under Anne Lewis, which I had the good sense luckily to pass up in order to stick with building ACORN rather than flirt with the distraction. Bill had gone on to run the Texas operation and would send me frequent notes from there on progress or clippings from *Texas Monthly* or congratulations on favorable ACORN press starting to emerge. As his career advanced in Arkansas and became more overtly about his candidacy, we endorsed him in every race from his first foray in the Republican northwestern Arkansas district when he tried to unseat John Hammerschmidt unsuccessfully and then on to his successful run for Attorney General, then a multi-term Governor, win, lose or draw. Sometimes we were excited to do so, and sometimes not. He could be a great friend and a frustratingly, maddening one. His reneging on his pledge to endorse the "right to work" initiative we had joined labor in heartily supporting was especially painful, and people like Bill Becker, then head of the Arkansas AFL-CIO, were never able to forgive his crawfishing on that issue.

Nonetheless all of us were quiet advocates of his dark horse run for the Presidency in the 1992 campaign. He had given our local union dues checkoff for state employees when we were organizing them while he was governor, which made it easy for me to introduce him to the executive board of SEIU when he was running. There was a picture on the front page of the *Washington Post* the day after he was elected in a bear hug with Zach Polett, ACORN's political director next door to our Little Rock office. I still have a painting on

---

[141] This story is in Dan Lieberman's *A Third Party Can Succeed in America: The Story of the Citizen Party*, published by AltInst Books, 2012.

Zach Polett and Clinton the Day After his Election.

my office wall of a campaign event that he and Maude Hurd, ACORN's national president did in front of houses we had squatted and rehabbed in Philadelphia that dates back to that first election.

We were not naïve though. We knew Clinton. We knew Hillary. We knew he would go his way and that it would disappoint progressives, as we had been both heartened and depressed in the past. We were realistic. And, because we were, I was still shopping and my door was always marked "open" for viable political alternatives. By 1992, we thought we had one in the New Party.

Danny Cantor had been talking to Joel Rogers a law, sociology, and political science professor at the University of Wisconsin-Madison, about an intriguing tactic that Joel was advocating from his research that still might have some sturdy legs. It was "fusion." Having read extensively about the Farmers' Alliance and the populist movement, I was familiar with the concept without understanding the full dimensions of what the post-populist era had done to eviscerate the tactic in order to protect the hegemony of the two dominant parties. Meeting with Danny and Joel in Madison, I was encouraged by the commitment to grassroots development, building real capacity, and welcoming, in fact aggressively soliciting our participation. What I had argued were the weaknesses of the Citizen Party effort were the strengths of the New Party effort since it would be a "local first" base-building party, rather than a top-down national effort. I was always more open to building a party qua party and contending for power directly on the ballot, and Joel and Danny were always more worried about the "spoiler" problem than I was, but aside from a couple of sentences, we were on the same page word for word.

There were seven states, including some unlikely venues like Mississippi and South Carolina, where we believed fusion might be legal or at least was not illegal, along with Vermont, New York, Connecticut, and others where there was no question whatsoever about their legality. ACORN came in from the beginning with full representation at every structural level. New Party local chapters were built in Arkansas but also embraced in places like Illinois. We helped bring allied organizations into the fold in Montana. We were part of the coalitions that moved forward in Minnesota. We were part of the first planning meetings in Colorado and the advancement of the New Party became a regular part of Zach Polett and the political department's responsibility and portfolio.

ACORN liked a political formation that saw itself as holding candidates accountable to the party itself. Twenty years of experience with community and grassroots based politics convinced us that this was essential. We wanted to help build a party that was centered on the supporters and members in its base, not candidate-centric as so many formations are. This may have been controversial to others, but organizationally we saw this as an *a priori* and embraced the effort accordingly.

Similarly, ACORN believed that a party should live every day in the life of the community and not just rise from near death every election cycle. We wanted the party to be fighting alongside us hand-in-glove on living wage fights, initiatives for single member districts, voter registration and GOTV efforts. We wanted there to be local campaigns led by the New Party affiliates that we helped direct in Chicago and Little Rock or through Progressive Minnesota or Progressive Dane in Wisconsin. We wanted the endorsement of the New Party to mean something in elections. There were numerous efforts to see if we could ally or combine with other contemporary efforts, particularly Tony Mazzocchi's Labor Party. Danny, Joel, and I met with Tony and the primary organizers of the Labor Party in New York City, and I attended the inaugural convention in Cleveland in 1996. The relationships were positive and friendly, but Tony's insistence that the party not participate in elections was a contradiction in terms to me, and gave ACORN members no real way to understand how their participation would be substantive.

Some of this was controversial. There were some close votes from time to time. There were some party adherents who chafed at the ability of ACORN and ACORN allied representatives to impact voting and direction, but we were "all in" and had the votes that go with that kind of sweat equity. We were knocking on the right doors. Barack Obama was at a New Party fundraiser. Future Mayor of New York Bill de Blasio was intrigued and with us for a while. Gerry Hudson, later Secretary-Treasurer of SEIU was at early planning meetings too. We were in a conversation about change.

Fusion was a harder lift. A tactic is not a strategy. Joel is a brilliant lawyer and a great friend, and put everything into the legal strategy of winning the right to fuse in an increasing number of states by winning a decision on the merits at the Supreme Court. For ACORN we needed and wanted an alternative party so that we had an exit strategy in dealing with the Democrats as much of our base was isolated from party activity and participation given how extensive our organization was in Republican states across the South and the West. We were all for fusion but did not see winning the Supreme Court case as make or break for the New Party. Unfortunately our position was a minority. In 1997 upon losing on a 6-3 decision at the Supreme Court in *Timmons vs. Twin Cities New Party* where the decision held that it was constitutional for Minnesota to bar fusion and rejected our argument that held that we had a constitutional protection of our freedom of association, many felt a stake went through the heart of the New Party.

Joel Rogers (Rock Creek, MT 2013).

A footnote to the New Party experience was certainly the long and extended courtship of Barack Obama to join and help carry the New Party standard in Chicago. We were organizationally close to Obama from our joint work with Project Vote in registration efforts in the city. He was an associate in the Miner, Barnhill civil rights law firm in Chicago and Sarah Siskind, Joel Rogers' wife[142], was a partner in the firm working from their Madison office. The relationships were there and numerous meetings with Obama elicited favorable support without any direct commitment to join the party despite all of our entreaties and cajoling. The New Party endorsed Obama, as did ACORN, in his races both quixotic and victorious, including his election to the Illinois State Senate. He also acted as an attorney for ACORN around enforcement of the National Voter Registration Act (NVRA) in Illinois. We categorically counted him as a friend, though we were frustrated about his unwillingness to commit, a trait that became part of his signature as President. Despite the hue and cry of the right and the Republicans, that's about that, as we might say. Arguably, we were always much, much closer to Bill Clinton, but those times, though acrimonious, never reached the level of toxicity that came in the 21st century to United States politics.

Working Families Party

We stepped back, licked our wounds, and immediately began advocating that the party needed to go back to the basics and build where fusion was legal and move forward to build independently where fusion was still barred, but the need for an alternative, viable party as a voice for our members still remained critical. In 1998 working with the New Party's Dan Cantor, we moved forward along with the Communication Workers, upstate

---

[142] Sarah Siskind was the primary attorney for ACORN in our major class action victory around HSBC predatory lending practices through their subprime, Household Finance unit.

UAW, and New York Citizen Action to found the Working Families Party of New York to compete to become a ballot line party in New York State that could use fusion in its overall strategy.

The Working Families Party moved Jon Green from the Chicago New Party to Connecticut to build the party there connected to the ACORN Connecticut base in Hartford and Bridgeport not long afterwards. Both the WFP in New York particularly and Connecticut since the mid-2000's have proven popular and successful. The WFP in New York achieved the 50,000 vote threshold to secure a position on a secure position on the ballot in 1998 and by 2002 was left standing as the only progressive ballot line party still on the ballot. The base of electoral support continues to build in New York hitting 155000 votes on our line in 2006 and more than 200,000 in 2012. Local success for the WFP has come in individual elections in areas like Hempstead where in coalition with ACORN a longstanding mayor was deposed finally. WFP endorsements and skilled GOTV work

Dan Cantor in Working Families Party Office in Brooklyn.

in some assembly district and Congressional races have meant the difference between victory and defeat. As importantly to ACORN and ACORN's successor organizations in New York, has been the continued commitment of the WFP to the initial principles we held so important in creating a party including the role of the WFP between elections as a campaigning organization around issues as varied as living wages in New York City and fracking in upstate New York.

The success of the WFP in New York and Connecticut has led to expansion in other states where fusion was legal as well as where there seemed to be strategic opportunities to create such electoral space. ACORN was pivotal in helping expand the party into Delaware and South Carolina at the early stages, as well as in various attempts to get something started in Oregon and Washington. More recently the efforts in Oregon have showed encouraging promise. In 2012 the WFP began working with a canvass in

Pennsylvania. There, I was delighted to run into the crew on a visit to Pittsburgh sharing an office with the ACORN successor organization, Action United.

In 2014 they were targeting the seats in Philadelphia that are allocated to a minority party, seeking to displace the Republicans in that position, a similar strategy was used in Hartford in the earlier years of the Connecticut Working Families Party. In 2014 the pivotal role played by the party in the progressive sweep of the New York City Council, and critical role in Bill de Blasio's surprise election on an aggressively progressive platform, has given them a city and statewide platform that promises great things in the future.

The Working Family Party is not yet a national party, of course no more than ACORN in 1980 was really a national organization even with 20 states, but more so because WFP despite what I hope is a burgeoning interest in expansion to new states, does not have a national strategy or ambition yet. But after 15 years with stable leadership and direction by Cantor and other senior staff and leadership, I have a good feeling about the party's future within its existing framework. Cantor's move to head the national formation is very encouraging. Importantly, there will always be a place for mass-based organizations in such a formation.

Unfortunately without an organized, disciplined lower income constituency like ACORN, the party is ill positioned to serve effectively as the kind of partner in progressive change that might have been possible had USA's ACORN continued to thrive. The WFP felt no small amount of the blow back in New York particularly during the anti-ACORN barrage following the 2008 election cycle and were under steady assault and investigation themselves during that period. New York ACORN's successor organization, New York Communities for Change, is still an important part of the WFP, especially in New York City. Barring the hope of ACORN's own return or something very much like it, ACORN can remain proud of the part of its legacy that WFP still represents.

What's the Bottom Line on Politics and Political Action?

ACORN would not have been ACORN if we had not crossed the line in 1972 into direct political involvement. Nonetheless politics may not be for every organization, and many organizations pledge to the government and funders that politics will never touch their lips. As we discussed in Chapter II on structure, many organizations and organizers begin their lives with a tax exempt or charitable status in addition to their commitment to being a nonprofit, and that's their story and their sticking to it. There is a famous story about the great IAF community organizer, Ernie Cortez, at a joint rally organized by UNO along with the Los Angeles AFL-CIO and a number of other unions, where a number of elected officials had been invited as targets to give commitments. Several of the pols jumped over the imaginary fence and started going into their campaign spiels. Cortez ran onto the stage and tried to grab the microphone from them, yelling "We're a c3! We're a c3! We can't be political!"[143] Eventually the meeting calmed down and went its normal course. Though the tale was told to me by a number of participants, perhaps the story is

---

[143] Remember from our earlier discussion that a 501c3 IRS tax determination restricts a nonprofits political activity in exchange for the tax exemption.

more exaggerated and apocryphal than real, but it underlines the point: tax exemption and eschewing direct political activity is wildly important to some community-based organizations.

Even if not making the ACORN choice of simply being a nonprofit and not asking for special tax treatment, there are other paths to travel that alleviate some of the risk to tax exempt organizational partners or subsidiaries and still allow an organization to dip its feet in both rivers. Establishing separate, independent political action committees or arms' length organizations with different structures and governance as partners or cousins to allow members and leaders to become political active in other names is certainly one. ACORN did all of these things to enable various operating arms in diverse spheres to cushion the organization with layers of structural formations to allow the maximum flexibility and range of action, especially political.

No matter what you do though, if you are mentally calculating the risk and whether or not any combination of these steps might protect an organization from attack from opponents or government, there are no guarantees. The daily papers are full of stories of draconian steps taken by governments in Russia, Egypt, China, Turkey, India, and elsewhere to regulate, "crackdown," and dilute any impact of nonprofits. The targets range from deep-pocketed foundations like Soros' Open Society and Ford Foundation to small advocacy, environmental, and community organizations. Don't make the mistake of believing that such repression is limited to authoritarian governments, because so-called liberal democracies may be singing more sweetly, but they are in the same choir. Recent election laws in both Canada and the United Kingdom in the name of registration and campaign finance attempted to silence any organizational advocacy on issues that might have been subsumed in political party platforms, by broad brushing such basic, everyday organizational actions as "political advertising." In my assessment, you can run, but you can't hide when it comes to politics. When your organization makes the decision to contend for power and embraces political action and activity as part of the equation, you sign up for a fight, and there is no fight where you don't stand perhaps a greater chance of losing than winning, than there is in politics, given the long odds in organizing the powerless.

For ACORN there was no choice and no use dancing around our reality. We are determined to build power and our eyes are wide open. Furthermore, it worked for the thirty-eight years of my service as Chief Organizer in the United States, and it continues to work today internationally. There is a long list of ACORN accomplishments in many of our cities, especially in the mega-slums that would not have been possible, as I have argued elsewhere, if we had not had the ability to leverage elections and politics to produce results.

At the same time a compelling case could be made that ACORN was targeted by the right in the Obama election of 2008 because of our voter registration and GOTV efforts and that bulls-eye lingered on our backs, provoking the video scam attacks that set off a chain reaction eventually scuttling the organization. Certainly, most of the "re-branded" components of ACORN in the United States, except in Louisiana by choice and Pennsylvania where their application was rejected, all to my knowledge embraced tax exempt statuses, whether wholeheartedly or not, seemingly believing that political activity had been part of the organization's undoing.

Many might conclude that ACORN had simply "flown to close to the sun." We in fact did build power, which correspondingly made us both invaluable to the progressive forces and our own membership as well as a juicy target for a militant and activist right wing and their media megaphones. The simplest response that I can offer is that we still had, and have, no choice, because without power we cannot make social change and be the vehicle our members demand to change their lives and circumstances. If that's the price, then so be it. The problem is not the flight plan and its trajectory, but whether or not we have armored the plane sufficiently to weather the sun and the storms.

Chapter XIX: Communications and Media

In political science terms organizations are about creating and building "voice;" the ability to be heard and heeded on issues in our interests and to build the power to determine our future. All of this is especially important when it comes to organizing low-and-moderate income families since the poor and have-nots around the world are the most powerless and have the least voice compared to all others. Organizers have voice through their organizations, as do leaders. The very act of organizing gives voice but obviously there are many other forces including the way we communicate, both internally and externally, that amplify the voice and give it more weight and impact.

Internal Communication

There are some constants still… and leaflets, flyers, pamphlets, whatever you might call them, are one of them. Organizers could, and have, written whole books or at least good sized pamphlets about the "do's" and "don'ts" of effective leaflets. I'm still an old school box-in-the-center of the page, less than 25 words guy personally, but no doubt there's some beautiful work being done out there, especially given the advent of computer assisted design. A lot of the strength of flyers though is not in the "meat, but the motion," not in the art, but in the distribution. Even the worst flyer will touch more people and therefore communicate better or hopefully reinforce other and "superior" forms of communication depending on what gets in the most possible hands – and heads – with the most touches.

In the ACORN system nothing worked better than the face-to-face communication on the doors and on the streets to present the message of the organization, lockdown engagement, and move people to meetings or actions. Nothing was ever more powerful in leadership development than the relatively leisurely "second visit" that went deep into a potential leader's apprehensions to create the ambitions to lead and mold the ability to do so in a way that would build the organization.

There is much written about the technique of "one-on-one's" used extensively in various contemporary organizing methodologies to create the groundwork for "relational" organizing. "One-on-one's" are not the same as door knocking, nor are they seen as communication exactly, since they are more overtly designed to build relationships, than to communicate or provide voice. My discomfort with "one-on-ones" comes from two places. One is that the relationship that tries to be built seems personal, rather than organizational from my observation and discussion with many practitioners. Similarly, my other objection is that the "one-on-one" recommendations to share a personal story or personal weakness or rage creates a false equity in the communication that devalues the position and entitlement of the potential member and their relationship to their organization by conflating the organizer to the same level as the organization. Many also maintain that there are ethical questions of a policy that essentially tricks people into baring their souls around their most difficult personal issues in order to create an artificial bond. There are undoubtedly better and worse practices in this area, but under any reckoning as a communications or even basic organizing tool, it is for specialized retail use, not the wholesale mass base building that was at the heart and intention of the ACORN nuts and bolts of organizing.

The telephone continues to be a powerful tool as well. A part of the daily schedule for ACORN organizers was always hours of calling after returning from the neighborhoods: reminder calls, leadership calls, research calls, all kinds of calls, even membership calls. I have often witnessed organizers so effective at developing conversational rapport with calls that they could bump up a member's dues level on the phone and in fact often sign up members on cold calls from a list of members. For the generation of organizers, particularly women in the United States, that came of age with the kind of hours of teenage phone practice that is now the common currency of the internet, texting, and Facebook, some of the phone practice was amazingly effective, personable, and, dare I add, relational. As an organizing skill, the key to "working the blower" was being able to move from rote recitation of the list of points to being able to learn the dialectical call and response of listening and reacting on the phone that duplicated the experience from the doors.

We were also "print people" when it came to communications. Since the beginnings of ACORN there is almost always a membership newsletter or membership newspaper on a regular basis. The predominantly lower income membership of ACORN is still trying to scratch its way up on hands and knees to get over the digital divide, so there is no way to pretend that we were delivering regular, consistent information about issues, campaigns, events, and victories without something in print that people could put in their hands and read. There was a letter from the President, there were features on the Convention or key initiatives, and several pages and many stories were translated into Spanish. We put it on paper, and we put it on the web. We worked it, and we believed in it.

The *United States of ACORN* was news when it came out on a bi-monthly basis and the printer had the mailing house send a copy to every fully paid up dues member on bank draft, while shipping out bundles to every one of the offices in the country. Some offices understood the value of membership communication and some never could quite get their arms around the distribution, so there were long standing jokes in some locations about desks and tables being propped up by old bundles of the *USA's*. Putting out a membership publication cost money though and the costs were shared by all offices, so those with tighter budgets felt the pain more than others sometimes. Nonetheless, this was part of our communications commitment, and we were consistent about it.

We were not afraid of the written word as a communication tool. We did a leadership bulletin, *Vamanos!* for many years to just the key leaders and elected board members around the country on tips and updates in between issues of the *USA*. In the 1970's and 1980's we used bulk rate mailings in organizing drives and occasional membership updates. Starting in the 1980's and going regularly through my time with ACORN, we did several direct mail pieces to our "friends" list and then to our donors who contributed in this way on an annual basis. Times change and money still matters. In gearing up a campaign on the rights of "multiple occupancy tenants" in Edinburgh in 2014 we managed to score a list of tens of thousands with help from the city. A test mailing at great expense to a couple of thousand generated only a handful of responses. So much for mailing on that campaign!

With the advent of the internet we did e-blasts and text message alerts to members where we had that information and to anyone else who had signed up for the news. Our website was robust, if not phenomenal, and did over 50,000 visitors per month, and then went through the roof when the organization was in the news or under attack. Starting around the turn of the century I started a blog continuing my tradition of *Chief Organizer Reports* that I have also done in other forms. Producing these reports daily on the web, via email, daily radio broadcasts, and now even podcasts, requires some work, but so does servicing any "local group" and supporting any organizing base. At this writing these daily "blogs" number more than 4300 posts, and are closing on three million words. Yes, Virginia, communication and accountability also require a lot of discipline!

Mike Miller, the director of Organize, Inc. in San Francisco, met me in 2003, as I was changing planes in San Francisco flying from Tokyo back to New Orleans, because he had something he wanted to ask if we would do. To my surprise he asked us to take over management of *Social Policy* magazine, a quarterly journal with a storied history among organizers, activists, academics and progressives founded in 1970 in the same year that ACORN began, and in fact was perhaps the first place to publish something that I had ever written about ACORN. Due to family illnesses and other challenges, no issues had been published for a year and the finances were a horror with subscriptions in chaos. As we pulled it back together Mike became more a contributor, and we took over the publishing and editing the journal which continues to be an important voice in the field to this day and an incredible gift of solidarity and support for which we have been perpetually grateful.

Social Policy, now a part of Labor Neighbor Research & Training Center (LNRTC) has also developed a press which has published books edited by Joe Szakos about rural organizing[144] and by myself on international organizing[145] as well as my book on ACORN's organizing to rebuild New Orleans after Hurricane Katrina and the lessons we have learned in organizing in the wake of disasters here and abroad.[146] More recent titles have reviewed the twenty-year history of Virginia Organizing as well as books on gun control and environmental advocacy. After publishing *Citizen Wealth*[147] with the San Francisco-based Berrett-Koehler, I quickly learned what many authors could have taught me that authors not only write the books, but they also have to sell them. That being the case, why not eliminate the middle man in the outside publishing company and write what needed to be written to help build organization, rather than to suit some external publisher's notion of what worked and what did not in the wildly beleaguered world of the

---

[144] Sazkos, Joe and Kristen Sazkos, *Lessons from the Field: Organizing in Rural Communities* (2008)

[145] Rathke, Wade, editor, *Global Grassroots: Perspectives on International Organizing* (2011)

[146] Rathke, Wade, *The Battle for the Ninth Ward: ACORN, Rebuilding New Orleans, and the Lessons of Disaster* (2011)

[147] Rathke, Wade, *Citizen Wealth: Winning the Campaign to Save Working Families* (2009)

contemporary print business. *Nuts and Bolts: The ACORN Fundamentals of Organizing* will follow along this same line of artisanal publishing as some now increasingly call it. By whatever name in these days of e-books, e-devices, desktop publishing and the internet, there is a new world of words fighting to find readers, and we believe in the importance and necessity of putting words together and creating a voice to say them and ears to receive them that we will continue to stretch out in that direction and lean hard into the learning curve.

The other magical thing about these forms of print communication is that they stood straight and tall on their own feet. The membership newspapers were part of the membership package that every full paid member was entitled to receive, as was a button and a membership card. *Social Policy* paid its own way through a business model that had survived over decades through individual subscriptions but more importantly through institutional and university subscriptions that more than adequately covered the cost of printing the magazine, allowed for the development of the press and expanded offerings in the niche where we wanted our voice to be heard, and contributed resources to the whole enterprise thereby increasing the sustainability of the organizational project. *Social Policy* was a social enterprise for organizing before the term became popular.

ACORN Radio Stations

The fight for lifeline electricity rates in Little Rock in 1976 was lost in the courts, but had won handily at the ballot box once all of the precincts were counted. Even before the litigation began unraveling the victory, we were learning invaluable lessons from the election. I thought the election would be a landslide, yet it was much closer than we imagined that it might have been simply because the business community and the utility company dumped money into TV and radio in the last two weeks of the campaign creating confusion and narrowing the gap, though not sufficiently. As hard as we worked on the streets to mobilize and deliver our vote, it was impossible to escape the conclusion that we would simply never have the financial resources to offset the fallout from big corporations and other opponents shaking the money tree until it rained down hard on us. We could never compete straight up, but I was desperate to find a way that we could at least try to offset the opposition by creating some way to create a voice for low-and-moderate income families.

At the time our operation in Dallas was reporting some encouraging meetings with a unique and eccentric character named Lorenzo Milam, who had a community radio station on the air called KCHU, and was offering ACORN time to do a community affairs show on the air once they were completely up and running. Our organizers in Dallas/Fort Worth, Meg Campbell and Steve Holt, were very high on Milam and argued that he and his engineer, Jeremy Landsman, and some of his crew, were the gurus of community radio. Milam had planted the idea that perhaps given all of the chaos with the DJs and others at KCHU, ACORN should just take the station over. Who knew what to make of all of that, but it got me thinking that perhaps community radio might be just the vehicle to amplify ACORN's voice and give our members a platform that was uniquely their own.

On one of my next visits to Dallas a meeting with Lorenzo Milam was high on my list. Famously he invited me to dinner at his house along with others like his acting station manager at KCHU at the time, Walter Brock, who later developed WWOZ, the well-known jazz and heritage station in New Orleans. When he served steamed artichoke as the first course, never having eaten artichoke, I looked around surreptitiously to see how my tablemates where attacking this thing, and finally without a clue, turned the artichoke over on its side, and started trying to cut it up with a knife and fork to the great amusement of Lorenzo and his friends, welcoming me to the world of artichokes! Lorenzo was originally from Jacksonville, Florida, and though dealing with the effects of polio as a young adult and towering over his crutches, had fallen in love with radio and, as it developed, been a pioneer in developing listener supported community radio first in the Bay Area, then Seattle, and St. Louis, where he cashed in KDNA on the commercial dial sufficiently to fund other radio experiments around the country.

Dallas had been what he hoped would be his last, great radio station accomplishment when he had won the frequency and the rights to a 100,000 watt station in one of the last top 10 markets that would ever be available on the airwaves. Nonetheless it was not only an expensive proposition to get it up and running, but also in the craziness of the time, its alternative, free spirited reputation as an all-volunteer DJ program had created a sense of false entitlements that Lorenzo, as an advocate and aficionado of open access and the use of the airwaves for all, was not really suited to handling. The appeal of ACORN to Lorenzo was not so much political as it was an appreciation of our discipline and the fact that we could manage the trains on time, so to speak.

In fact he had virtually lost any semblance of control of KCHU and the license holder, the Agape Foundation, by the time I met him. His efforts to introduce us to the cast of characters assembled around the station and insert us into management turned into a donnybrook. On the other hand though, as one of the "fathers of community radio," he was a fount of information and a ready ear for anyone trying to get something going

KABF Logo. KNON's old console on display.

around the country. He told me that there was a construction permit that had been issued in the Tampa/St. Petersburg area for a station up to 60,000 watts, but the guy who had the permit was coming near to the end of his construction permit and extensions and in danger of having the FCC pull the whole thing from him. Perhaps we could find him and either help get the station on the air or maybe he would even give us the permit and let us take a shot. Checking with his engineers he also thought there might be a frequency that we could carve out in Little Rock so that we could broadcast from the mother ship.

We could not easily find the guy who held the permit in Tampa/St. Petersburg. In the days before the internet and Google, it was all shoe leather. ACORN had an office in Miami at the time. We heard from Lorenzo that he thought the fellow might have a girlfriend working at a Denny's near the beach in St. Petersburg. Dewey Armstrong, then the head organizer of Florida ACORN, and I drove up there from Miami one night in hopes that we could catch him somewhere around the end of her shift. The long and short of it was that we ended up finding the guy and meeting with him on a beach in St. Petersburg. He was at wits end and ready to throw up his hands at his inability to raise the money and get the station on the air. We made a deal to take over the construction permit, retain some of his board members, and do what was necessary to go live in Tampa/St. Petersburg. With several years of herculean effort by Joe Fox, who I hired when he graduated from Harvard Business School, the station WMNF was on the air almost hand built by Joe and financed largely by a door-to-door canvass that raised the money to build the station.[148]

The station in Little Rock was longer in coming to fruition. The FCC approved the license to the Arkansas Broadcasting Foundation for KABF at 88.3 FM on the dial for 100,000 watts of power after a painful dispute with the University of Arkansas at Little Rock (UALR) who tried to poach the frequency at the last minute, but finally we prevailed and went on the air August 31, 1984, eight years after this saga began.

Dallas, if anything, endured an even more tortuous journey. After Lorenzo failed to engineer a transition of the station to ACORN in a riotous meeting of the DJs which included some of his own associates subverting his efforts in pique, the inmates took over the prison so to speak. Unfortunately, those trying to keep the station together either never reckoned with the critical importance of Milam's personal subsidies of the station from his own pocket or underestimated his resolve to discontinue such expenditures, so within a short time the station went dark. The FCC is a bear protecting its cubs when it comes to existing licensees, whether full bore top 40 commercial or hardcore alternative progressive like KCHU, but when the lights go out and the signal is down there is no stopping the hounds of hell from barking to the skies to secure the signal, which in the 1980's until today largely meant the deeper pockets of religious broadcasters. In the Dallas instance that meant Rev. Criswell of the powerful First Baptist Church, who at that time

---

[148] If the basketball expression is "the ball don't lie," the organizing expression is, "What goes around comes around," and it was a treat to find out that my organizing director, Dave Kieffer, on the HOTROC campaign in New Orleans, started out his illustrious labor organizing career as a canvasser for WMNF in those early days. I still see Joe Fox on most every trip through Little Rock when I stop by every morning at his Community Bakery down the street from our offices and enjoy a maple donut or a classic cinnamon roll while reading his free New York Times.

Chapter XIX: Communications and Media

was running what would now be called a mega-church with its own radio signal and who also coveted the more powerful frequency held by the Agape Foundation, the 501c3 holding the KCHU license.

Months rolled past a year and nothing was happening, furthermore there was no action by the board which at that point had become dysfunctional. The Criswell/Baptist threat continued to gain momentum with every passing week and month. Finally working with Dallas head organizer Terry Andrews, we bogarted the board back into business by convening a meeting of the ACORN members, like Arquila Smith, Leon Gowans, and Ernest Brown, who were still on the board and any others who still had a heartbeat and responded. At the meeting we simply moved forward with survivors, appointed people to fill the vacancies, and assumed control of the station, proving that patience sometimes produces results, which is often not the default setting for organizers. More honestly, probably we proved again that chutzpah and the willingness to calculate and take the risks and absorb the conflict that might come from all sides, was part of our DNA.

Taking over the station though solved no problems, it simply allowed us to finally control the license and move forward. Moving meant responding to the FCC issues, Criswell and the Baptists and crafting a least some rationale for having been "dark," most of which was a promise to do better. At the end of the dispute we lost the 100,000 watt frequency and our neighbor's covetousness was rewarded, but we were able to at least end up on a trade with 60,000 watts and a fresh slate allowing us to move forward and eventually go on the air on the frequency under the name KNON.

There was an ACORN Hour every week. Local 100 had a show as well. Even today at KABF in Arkansas the successor to Arkansas ACORN, appropriately named, the Arkansas Community Organizations (ACO), perhaps just waiting to once again be ready for "reform now," has a weekly "community voices" show and though Local 100 has gone on and off, they are once again on the air. KNON built a signature audience among our members and a wider listenership as the most popular community radio station in the metroplex reaching 80,000 listeners a week on Arbitron ratings a decade and more than 100,000 now in the 2nd decade of the 21st century with a combination of Tejano, gospel, and other signature shows, many of which saw their volunteer DJs poached to commercial stations given the chops they had developed and popularity at KNON.

KABF has often had a rockier road though in many ways it is still a signature success in achieving the original mission that ACORN had for its community stations. The Arbitron ratings for KABF in this smaller market are now up to 50,000 listeners a week with 53% African-American and 50% from households making less than $30,000 per year. This is hardly the demographic that commercial stations lust after, but is precisely the audience that ACORN hoped it could attract with KABF and KNON with their slogans, the "voice of the people," over the last 30 years. The assault on ACORN by Congress, prompted by a right wing video scammer, also embroiled both stations in issues with the Corporation of Public Broadcasting (CPB) about grants for equipment and capacity that they had received in the past. KABF's financial situation, always more tenuous than KNON, left it imperiled in the years after the 2008 election and limping through 2012 with board disputes, maintenance needs, and the removal of the institutional lifelines that had buoyed it in the past. More recently the station finally was able to reorganize its board and contracted again with me through AM/FM (the Affiliated Media Foundation Movement) in early 2013, as station manager to reorganize, stabilize, and expand the station's outreach in the Middle South as well as hopefully internationally as the voice for ACORN International's organizing footprint. Within three days of stepping in high winds blew the studio antenna down sending a not so subtle message that this "voice of the people" thing is easier said, than heard!

At various times the United States Federal Communications Commission (FCC) has stepped out of its corporate cocoon and allowed more access to bandwidth and frequencies for low power radio at lesser wattage and more limited geographical range. ACORN with AM/FM organized extensively during the mid-late 1980's when a round of low power frequencies opened up near our organizing areas, filing under a host of names for perhaps as many as 100 stations, though all unsuccessful in the end. Many were rejected because of slight technical problems with the application. In other cases the FCC did not want to really make determinations of winners and losers in these areas and would often delay and try to force settlements among the contending parties on sharing relationships. We won some sharing arrangements for limited hours, but without a good way to make them sustainable, most of these drifted away in implementation. In most cases the settlements were really about seeing who had the deepest pockets to buy out the other applicants, and that was never ACORN, so we could not prevail. Too often our radio project was not core to the work ACORN was doing, but seen as a communications luxury, no matter how critical or permanent the capacity, so the resources and staffing commitment was proportionate to the priority.

In 2000 there was another low power application window, and given our lack of success in the 1980's, this was even a lesser emphasis. We applied in three or four locations, prevailing only in Lake Charles, Louisiana, but by the time we found out that the application had been approved it was late 2008 and early 2009, and ACORN was so under attack and internally strained that the Louisiana successor organization A Community Voice could get no traction to fend off last minute challenges from McNeese State and was caught in the meat grinder of the Congressional bill of attainder which McNeese was also willing to exploit, making practical negotiations for license sharing impossible as well. In October 2013, the FCC once again opened up low power frequencies for applications including for the first time in decades in *major* cities around the country, making this a more interesting prospect once again.

Nonetheless with the digital divide still so huge for lower income families, much as it was almost 40 years when we started our initiative in radio, it is hard not to be attracted to the **potential** of community radio no matter the trail of tears and daunted dreams we have experienced on this long road with the medium. Having a centerpiece station like KABF makes me think that if we could develop the content and match that with licenses that were not general audience with all of its temptations but specifically in the niche segment that is the sweet spot of our community and labor organizing mission among lower income families, then there is a special kind of "network" that could be built offering a powerful voice for our constituency. At one level we could uplink programming from central locations in studios in Arkansas with KABF or in New Orleans in our St. Claude building, so that they could be downloaded for simultaneous listening on internet radio or rebroadcast by the smaller low power outlets and matched with specific local programming as they developed the capacity to offer such programming and the staffing to do so.

On another level using both web streaming of the signals to act as "repeaters" of the same content for www.acornradio.org, ACORN International's internet station, maximizes the number of computers or devices, meaning people or places, that can be listening to the radio at any instance, and perhaps as powerfully on both a domestic and international level could allow for "concurrent" listening through devices that enabled on demand listening to pod casts of content from any part of the network as well. Such a system could link "message" shows from the countries about international campaigns or local initiatives with local talk, unique local music, attractive and unique remote broadcasts of live events of all shapes and sizes, and create a robust radio experience. With a little more ubiquity of "smartphones" which at this point seem more likely to dominate communications more quickly than computers and separate internet access, allowing such downloading and concurrent listening without the problem of internet access and the expensive internet metering that still prevails in Mexico, Africa, and many other countries, something with real power and not just potential could be built. Maybe? We'll keep trying!

Within the United States it would be nice to imagine being able to construct partnerships in various states between local unions or state-based or local-based community organizations and ACORN International, AM/FM, and our other radio communication adherents to create mini-networks that could be robust on various levels.

Alas, once again I've jumped ahead of myself intoxicated by my own vision of more capacity, regardless of whether or not others might see the potential. The reality is that I reached out for people in Ohio, Florida, and Pennsylvania, and the response was deafening silence. In fact few were willing to take the risks, and the opportunity is largely one those "woulda, coulda, shoulda" things, rather than an opportunity shared and realized. AM/FM and our family of ACORN International organizations did in fact apply for a frequency for a 100-watt station that would broadcast throughout New Orleans, and lo and behold in early 2015 we finally received FCC approval to construct the station that now has the call letters, WAMF and went on the air in June 2017. We are also helping revive the hopes of a 1500-watt noncommercial in the delta town of Greenville, Mississippi with the legendary Delta Foundation. Willie Cosme, veteran radio volunteer, who first introduced Spanish programming to Arkansas on KABF "cleans" taped broadcasts from KABF which are rebroadcast internationally, in Louisiana, and in Greenville demonstrating the potential that exists in all of this still.

We've even made some progress in creating the "network" we had envisioned so long ago packaging show and my Chief Organizer Reports and Daily Peoples' News broadcasts to many of the emerging low power stations in places like Flagstaff, Seattle, Fayetteville, Jonesboro, Conway, Greenville, Mississippi, Hot Springs and Louisville, as well as our old buddies in Dallas. You never know, if we keep pushing what might happen….

For many though this is "old school" rather than cutting edge, but as a voice for organizing and social movements it is still both interesting and important. At the lowest level the equipment is simple and still relatively cheap, making radio still a significant opportunity.

Importantly as well, despite the lack of love from donors and others, listener supported radio, is just what it says, supported by listeners, which provides a base of sustainability every bit as important as membership dues did for ACORN and labor unions. Given ACORN's experience after 2008, I have frequently touched on my obsession with sustainability as a prerequisite for building ongoing social change through organizations that are vehicles for the empowerment of low and moderate income families, and the listen-support model originally stumbled onto by Lorenzo Milam in the desperate early days of KRAB/FM in Seattle in 1962[149] has become a staple of community radio funding, allowing listeners to "vote" with their ears and dollars in much the same way that members with dues systems do in mass-based organizations. The additional facility of "underwriting," which is direct program support by institutions, organizations, and businesses operating much like (sometimes too much like!) advertising in the commercial radio space also provides important self-sufficiency for radio access to the airwaves. Like community organizations in concept and as partner in practice and principal, a community radio station, whether large like KABF or KNON or smaller in the more finally targeted low power concept, could be as strong as possible, proportionate to its attachment to its core base of listeners in the community. As organizers we have to celebrate that kind of survival and accountability symbiosis.

The other problem here is the classic tension around the definition of viability of such locally based formations and the stress test between volunteers or amateurs often free or low paid and thinly staffed, and professionalization with more staff, higher wages, and less volunteer dependence. This tension played out in organized labor from the early years of the 20th century until the institutionalization of the collective bargaining stability after the great organizing drives of the CIO and the AFL before their merger. In some ways it has played out in the tension between movements and organizations, between the post-Alinsky Industrial Areas Foundation sense of organizers who were fewer and higher paid "professionals" as opposed to the constantly expanding need for organizers by ACORN who were quickly trained in apprenticeship programs with lower wages from start to finish. The same inherent conflict exists in community radio in terms of what defines sustainability. Is it the $50,000 to $100,000 volunteer-based budgets cobbled together year after year through pledge drives and underwriting programs or is it the outside funded, NPR biased, federally granted stations in universities and elsewhere with their million dollar per year budgets, professional, and decently paid staffs that used to be described in the "healthy station" model of CPB and the National Federation of Community Broadcasters (NFCB)? Is the only sustainable local union one that has 50,000 members as opposed to the couple of hundred in a plant or the thousand or two thousand in some local areas? These are endless organizing debates. Clearly I come down on a more catholic basis and am open to many more forms of organizations and institutions especially if they are sustainable financially, accountable democratically, and deeply engaging their constituency.

Radio is worth it in these calculations.

---

[149] Walker, Jesse, *Rebels on the Air: An Alternative History of Radio* (2001).

Television, Not So Much

We (and this really might have been "me and the rat in my pocket") thought that we should also not lose the last, vanishing opportunities to acquire public television channels during the same period we were organizing community radio stations. Jeremy Lansman, Milam's engineer, was working with a television station he had managed to put together outside of Denver in Wheatridge, Colorado that was doing some interesting programming (and is given credit for inventing music videos that became the mainstay and lucrative business model years later for MTV at least for a while). A guy named John Swartz known to our folks was also making things happen on a public channel in Philadelphia outside of the Public Broadcasting System (PBS). So it seemed possible and seemed worth the climb, if such stations were available still in major markets. Cable channels in the late 1970's and 1980's were small and virtually unwatched. Television channels were a powerful attractor, so why not?

We heard of a public channel coming up for potential applications in Denton, Texas twenty-five miles north of Dallas. We pulled together an application but were found lacking.

On the other hand there was an outfit in California, assembled by some of the same progressive elements that had been so seminal in the breakthroughs with noncommercial radio, called CCTN (the California Community Television Network) that had ambitions of applying for and establishing TV channels throughout the state. Unfortunately, as was so often the case, their eyes had been bigger than their stomachs. They had won a license based in Watsonville, California near the coast, a smaller city well known for growing strawberries and other fruit and vegetables. The channel could be engineered from Watsonville so that the real strength of the signal would not only be there but also in San Jose, one of the largest dozen cities in the country. The only problem was that the board of CCTN was running out of time on its construction permit and had little hopes of getting the station on the air, so we ended up with CCTN and appointed new board members from ACORN's northern California leadership as well as Gary Delgado who was then living again in the Bay Area, and Arlene Kimata, the epitome of ACORN talent, sacrifice, and spirit, who had relocated from New York to the West Coast.

Arlene was the heart and soul of our television efforts and the only reason we were able to somehow endure the trials and tribulations and get on the air. Arlene had an unusual package of skills embedded in a deep sense of morality and social justice. She is from Hilo, Hawaii and had gone to the Yale School of Management for a business degree at the point she originally came into our world when she walked in our door in Brooklyn to see if there was a way to work with New York ACORN. She ended up during her brief stay in New York organizing our bulk paper business which for a number of years was a key part of our internal financing program most successfully in Brooklyn, but also generating revenue and income in a number of other organizing offices throughout the country. At its largest point in New York, ACORN bought a shipping container of paper in bulk cases, and then resold and delivered to other nonprofits and businesses in the city. As long as paper was priced at a premium per ream and by case, we could make enough on the margin, especially with mostly volunteer and membership labor to generate good cash flow to support the organizing. When that changed, we stopped moving paper. Until Arlene came on the scene and puzzled out the business with Jon Kest, the head organizer, I used to joke that I was an organizer, "because I didn't want to do heavy lifting." During the years we resold paper in offices from Denver to New Orleans and most everywhere else, I could not use that line, because invariably when I would visit the offices, I would end up going to make a stop with them or helping move cartons of paper from pillar to post. By whatever means necessary…

Arlene signed onto the CCTN board and through patience and persistence over the years managed to finally get the station on the air in November, 1989. Doing so raised our costs to another dimension compared to our radio experience. Studio cameras were pricey in the pre-digital age and remote cameras were heavy and expensive. The early 1980's were good years for ACORN in some ways because even though we were operating everything out of one bank account up until 1984, the canvass was producing at record levels in the early 1980's and there was sufficient "surplus" income that I was comfortable going to the board for approval in making what I argued to them and the staff were significant capital investments in long term organizing capacity for the organization that would never be available in the future.

Thanks to Arlene's pluck and others associated with AM/FM at the time, we got on the air finally. We saw our niche as Spanish language programming to our constituency, and god knows it was totally underserved throughout the area despite dominating the demographics on the coast and in San Jose among lower income families. Programming though was different than in radio. Volunteers could relatively quickly be trained to competently act as disc jockeys on-the-air in radio but that was neither possible on our television station, nor welcomed. In community radio if there was some small snafu and there was dead air for 10 or 20 seconds, listeners were tolerant and for the most part committed to the block of programming and would hang with us. On television they were crazy with the remote control devices and were surfing channels within seconds if there was silence on the station.

Starting from scratch meant that we did not have preset content that would work in those spaces while we developed local programming and studio capacity. We ended up acquiring what we could. The standing joke became how many hours per week consisted

Arlene Kimata at Year-End / Year-Beginning with Beth Butler, Judy Graves, Orell Fitzsimmons.

of "Chico and the Man" reruns on the station. It was not pretty, and that does not even include problems like natural disasters such as the great San Francisco earthquake of 1989 whose epicenter along the San Andreas fault line ran right next to our tower in the mountains between San Jose and the coast, only miraculously not putting us off the air forever and requiring us to start over.

With deeper pockets and greater time than we had, we might have soldiered on and eventually succeeded, but in the mid-1980's as canvass revenues became more marginal and each of the operations, whether a field office in Reno or Des Moines or a giant operation in Chicago or New York had to increasingly stand on its own, there was no way to continue to justify subsidizing a television station in Watsonville-San Jose, when we did not have the money to keep all of ACORN's organizing operations afloat in some cities, so we had to pull the plug.

With hundreds of thousands of dollars of debt owed back to ACORN, this was no simple matter either. It was almost as hard to get off air as it had been to get on the air. We approached a public PBS channel in San Jose but made no progress, and were finally forced to cash out to a religious broadcaster, emerging not quite held whole, but definitely wiser about the real difficulties of the prospects for community television. We won a license in Atlanta as well, but wiser counsel led us to quickly cash out there as well.

Fast forward 30 years and for a couple of thousand dollars investment in a good camera and editing software and you and your cousin can make broadcast quality video and sound. Where broadcast television had set the standards then, with YouTube anyone and everyone can have their own channels and some folks do, including for that matter ACORN International (https://www.youtube.com/channel/UCMaQ6xnuWcgjedV3Ky5L28w), so if we had been back in San Jose now, rather than then, it might have been an entirely different ballgame, but as my son Chaco frequently tells me, "don't sweat the if."

Chapter XX: Why Work and Workers

In some ways it started simply enough.

ACORN members in Little Rock, New Orleans, Memphis, and elsewhere would come to their monthly neighborhood meetings and, as the organization became more successful at winning on local and citywide issues, some started raising their hands from the back of the room looking for action on issues that jumped over the fence into higher and higher weeds. Many of these questions had to do with work and what was right and wrong about the way they were worked and whether any of that was by the rules. Other questions started to arise with issues that were less about laws, rights, and entitlements, and more about wages, unjust firings, and what it might take to change things on their jobs, just as we were changing things in the community.

With an organic structure that never ruled out any issue, where there was a substantial base when the members were raising it, and an organizing culture that was premised on listening, these were questions that were impossible to ignore. Initially, the default response was, "yes, you need to act collectively at work, just as we are doing in the neighborhood with ACORN, but we don't have any experience there, so it makes sense for you to reach out for a union that might know something about your kind of work, your industry and your employer." In short order the member would be referred to the central labor council, if we were totally clueless, or to a specific union if the member's job seemed to fit something handled by the hotel workers or machinists or some specific trade. Unfortunately, and almost universally, another month or more would go by and the same member would be back at the meeting once again raising their hand from the back of the room saying they had followed up, called and left messages to X, Y, or Z union, but never heard a word, so now what ACORN? And, in the middle to late 1970's, we were damned if we knew, but we were listening.

By the late 1970's the United States was enduring a recession during the Administration of President Jimmy Carter. Where we had been able to successfully mount demonstrations of thousands for example in Philadelphia demanding youth job program money every summer, the cupboard was now bare, and workers were looking everywhere for employment. We joined with the Movement for Economic Justice (MEJ), initially founded by George Wiley after he left as Executive Director of the National Welfare Rights Organization (NWRO) and then directed by Bert DeLeeuw, along with other community organizations like Massachusetts Fair Share to mount actions pushing for jobs. In campaigns for jobs for young people in our communities we were discovering then, though perhaps not realizing it until later, that we were banging at the door of a paradigm shift. Federal revenue sources were decreasing to cities. The 60's era of OEO, Legal Services, Model Cities, was finally over, and we were no longer able to hit hard on local mayors in our cities, shake the tree fiercely, and make money fall down like leaves.

For example in a bitter campaign in New Orleans engaging the city's first African-American mayor, Ernest "Dutch" Morial, when we poured into City Hall with hundreds of young people and ended up getting to the second floor and sitting in his office, Morial simply left the office, ordered cokes and cookies, and left us there indefinitely without anything more than a perfunctory meeting and head shaking, certainly nothing resembling real negotiations, and a tactical stalemate that had us slinking out many hours later as our troops trickled out, tired and exhausted, after hours of sitting without results.

Frustration grew and given the notoriously ruthless police department in New Orleans, the next action found 50 of our folks and some organizers trapped, literally, on the streets not far from City Hall in a box canyon where many were beaten, others arrested, and no jobs forthcoming. It was not that the city did not want to give us the jobs, and I have spoken of this many times to the woman in charge of youth hiring at the time, but they simply could not move the money to make the program significant or real.

We organized workers whose employment was being subsidized by the federal government during the recession through the Comprehensive Employment and Training Act (CETA) into associations or informal unions through the Association of CETA Employees (ACE) in New Orleans, Boston, Detroit, and Philadelphia. We mounted campaigns to make sure these CETA "slots" were for the unemployed rather than simply replacing city workers that could no longer be afforded. We handled terminations, payroll delays, and other grievances. We organized in some of the nonprofits where there were vast hosts of CETA workers like the YWCA and others to push for priorities and "first choice" provisions for future jobs. We were on it like "white on rice," but we were not necessarily building real power, and we were surprised to find that established unions were impressed with our resolve and energy but certainly uninterested in moving into the vacuum and taking over the direct organizing of these workers.

In 1978 I had moved the national headquarters office, which we called the "organizing and support center" to New Orleans[150] in order to more effectively support the ACORN expansion as well as to personally direct some of the experiments in adding work-based organizing to the ACORN portfolio. In the early days of the Carter Administration we had been awarded a training and supervision grant that assigned 100 VISTA volunteers from ACTION to a program ACORN developed called CORAP (Community Organization Research & Action Project), headed by Carolyn Carr, a senior member of our staff then based in Washington, D.C. Working with some of the VISTAs assigned to New Orleans, we wanted to see if we could organize household workers (domestics, maids, cooks, and so forth) into a worker association, as the Household Workers Organizing Committee (HWOC).

The initial organizing campaign sought to win full implementation of the provisions of the Fair Labor Standards Act (FSLA) which were extending coverage to domestic workers for the first time effective in 1978, and would raise wages for that labor to $1.65/hour. We built a list in painstaking fashion using crisscross and Polk's directories that frequently identified someone's occupation. Wherever it stopped close to our household worker constituency, which we estimated at that time was over 6000 workers and possibly more, they made the list. Even more names and addresses were developed by working the bus and streetcar stops on Canal Street, Carrollton, along St. Charles, and out on the

---

[150] The politics of the organization, having been founded and expanded from Little Rock, meant that the Little Rock office would always need to be identified as the "home" office of ACORN.

Lakefront where household workers would travel to and from work. In those days in New Orleans, an African-American woman walking back and forth from a bus stop in many neighborhoods only meant one thing, so our odds were good, if we could engage them, that they were working in domestic service. Pay was minimal and paternalistic with the Department of Labor allowing any pay for transportation and the ability to make one's lunch from the boss's refrigerator as an offset against full cash payment of the new minimum wage. Workers were routinely paid less than $1/hour. At many of the public transit transfer stops the minimum wage was referred to by the workers as "top pay" and few had any serious expectation that they would be paid that amount any more than they were paid social security benefits that were also required by law.

We knew that we were organizing home-based workers with special and sensitive relationships with their employers that were deeply cultural. We were careful to always maintain steadfastly that we were categorically NOT building a union, but an association of household workers trying to win their wages and rights on their jobs to full benefits and basic dignity. This was our mantra, over and over, we are not a union. The first meeting went well with more than 50 household workers forming the organization, and the first action we had determined was to march over from our office on Baronne Street in the New Orleans Central Business District to the Department of Labor's Wage and Hours Division only a couple of blocks away on Lafayette Square at the old post office building, where many federal offices were then housed. Since this was a first action, many of the newly elected leaders were wary and tentative, but as they made their way over to the DOL offices they sang and chanted a bit and tried out their new assertiveness about demanding enforcement of the new minimum wage standards. They walked into the DOL offices, and demanded to see the Wage & Hours inspector. Heedless of hours of preparation and practice as organizers, including myself, had cautioned restraint, when he asked the leaders at the front of the crowd, "Who are you," almost as one, they shockingly replied, "We are a union of household workers!" I learned something about what a union was that day that I have taken with me wherever I've worked over the last almost 50 years!

By the hardest, the HWOC won some things. We organized a demonstration and a march in an upper middle income neighborhood near New Orleans' northern boundary of Lake Ponchartrain, called Lake Terrace, going from the park in the center of the subdivision and marching around the neighborhood in order to demand the minimum wage. We filed a complaint against several employers to the Wage and Hour Division, including most notoriously against the Gambino family well known in New Orleans as owners of the popular Gambino's bakery uptown who were paying their maid peonage wages of less than $1.00 per hour, and with much publicity, we won! We also filed suit against the Internal Revenue Service when we could not force them otherwise to send a notice out to all employers who actually claimed to be paying Social Security withholding, notifying the employers that they were also required to pay the new federal minimum wage providing coverage for domestic workers. When we settled the lawsuit with the IRS they not only did the mailing but we were able to get them to pay for public service advertisements on streetcars, buses, and radio.

When we tried to organize a hiring hall where employers could get workers on referral so that household workers could get more full days of work, we were less successful.

We were chasing our own tails and trying to formalize deeply informal employment. We managed to negotiate one contract with a liberal Episcopal campus minister for his family's maid, but that was less on the merits than on the morality of it all.[151] More importantly perhaps by the time we were trying to take that next giant step, we had lost much of our staffing capacity, because push back at the Congressional level about the ACTION grant to CORAP and our use of the VISTAs had ended up with Director and former antiwar activist, Sam Brown, and VISTA head and former Youth Project director, Margery Tabankin, both folding when a subcommittee launched an investigation, and cutting off the grant. The Congressional committee alleged that we were using VISTA volunteers to organize unions among other prohibited practices. Nothing ever came of any of this, but the grant was a long gone, pecan, cher!

The United Labor Unions

We had certainly found that workers would respond. We certainly had a host of work related and wage related issues in the ACORN membership, but the silence of institutional labor was deafening, so much so that any individual union's support was heartening. I can remember some of the long meetings of our organizers who were doing the work, as our worker-based strategies were debated. Should we forge ahead along the same path as we were moving then on the fringes of the labor movement by organizing the unemployed and underemployed? Should we organize independent unions? I can even vividly remember a late night conversation with organizers in Boston where there was a debate about whether it made sense to burrow into the building service local and over a number of years mount an internal challenge and try to redirect the union more aggressively and progressively.[152]

We were torn. We did not want to end up jeopardizing all of ACORN's relationships with unions, which were many and critical, and we actually wanted institutional labor to see our organizing with workers as positive and perhaps even to impact on their organizing or lack of it. At the same time we were excited at what we were hearing about new organizing techniques by independent unions like the hospital workers at Local 1199 and their use of recognition strikes to win bargaining units without going through endless delays and NLRB elections. Coming from the ACORN tradition and moving forward with ACORN's support, we were used to being fiercely independent, but at the same time wanted to be friendly and get support from established unions, partly because we were pretty clear that we thought we were all great organizers, but knew we were total novices when it came to union organizing. Mark Splain who was ACORN's northeastern regional representative, was going to direct the effort, and we were strongly in favor of an

---

[151] Thirty-five years later in 2013 Reverend William Barnwell and his daughter did a Fair Grinds Dialogue and told the story including when the worker later told him, they could talk to her directly, they didn't have to have the "union man" in on every conversation.

[152] What goes around comes around. Thirty-five years later Michael Gallagher, who was part of that very conversation retired from SEIU Local 615, the successor to the old Sullivan BSEIU local, and Peter Rider, a veteran of ULU and ACORN, had served as Secretary-Treasurer of that same local.

independent course. At that juncture we made the decision to found the United Labor Unions.

    We wanted to build the early locals in the cities where we had the most prior involvement already in the jobs and other work-based efforts of ACORN and that meant Boston, Detroit, Philadelphia, and New Orleans, and later Chicago as ACORN and the union moved to open organizing there after 1980. Fitting with our strategy of both building an independent union of lower waged workers and organizing workers that were not only not organized but were also either abandoned or not targets of other established unions in more institutional labor, we focused on very specific groups of unorganized workers in each city in order to build the United Labor Unions.

    In Boston that meant general service workers, including some service and maintenance units like the hotel connected to Children's Hospital and some unorganized manufacturing facilities. In fact, winning a back pay settlement for unjust firing for union activity at the Sweetheart Paper Company in Chelsea led to the number of the local, since $1475 was the amount of back pay, this became Local 1475 of the United Labor Unions. The real growth of the Boston local though was following up on so many of the ACORN local group members that were working in a relatively new occupation as home health aides or chore housekeepers or whatever they might be called. Those workers were doing some of the same things that household workers had done in New Orleans, and in fact the Boston organizers found these home health workers while looking for similar women doing household work.[153] Election and organizing victories at both the nonprofit and some for profit companies that were employing these workers grew the local and were our most significant success in ushering in an organizing initiative that ended up with hundreds of thousands of workers organized over succeeding decades.

    In Philadelphia we organized small shops. The local number of 862 was named after the vote count in the first election won by organizer, Fran Streich, at a rag plant by the vote of 86 to 2 of course. A nasty strike ensued so there was never a contract, and much of what was developed in Philly ended up in smaller contracts for emergency service workers organized by Keith Rohman along with other, smaller shops.

    In Detroit, several smaller shops were the core dues paying members of Local "triple deuce" as the members and organizer, Keith Kelleher, a former Jesuit Volunteer Corps and ACORN organizer, called Local 222. A small machine shop was under contract in pro-union Detroit. We tried to organize a laundry after workers enthusiastically signed our authorization cards but quickly found out in an oft told story now that other unions knew better than to try to organize an establishment that was totally run by the mob. The real thrust of the local and the work of Keith and Danny Cantor, who directed the Detroit initiative after years as an ACORN organizer in Stuttgart, Arkansas, and St. Louis, Missouri, was to organize workers in the huge but totally unorganized fast food industry. We could organize lots of workers in Burger Kings, McDonald's, and even Crystals, but were all taught lifelong lessons in the complexity of NLRB organizing as we peeled back the layers to find some stores owned by franchisees, others under corporate control, and all mixed up in a combo that was a lawyer and bureaucrat's delight, but an organizing

---

[153] Thanks to Mike Gallagher for reminding me of this story. See *ACORN International YouTube*.

nightmare. Significantly, we did organize the Burger King at the Detroit Bus Terminal that was actually owned by Greyhound at the time and ended up bargaining the first fast food contract in the country with them.

Later Kelleher moved to Chicago and began organizing home health care workers there, which seemed to be the main chance for the ULU to get to some kind of real scale in terms of members, if he could manage it. Cantor came down to New Orleans to work with me in organizing Local 100 which was targeting hotel and hospitality workers, certainly the largest employer of workers, especially lower wage workers, in the city and with only one organized hotel, a workforce that seemed uninteresting to established unions or perhaps they had more wisely abandoned the effort against determined employer opposition, which we quickly found ourselves facing.

In New Orleans we targeted the Hyatt Hotel at the Superdome only blocks away from our office which was in the CBD on Baronne Street at the time, parallel to the Dome in the 600 block. Normally it would seem to have made sense. The hotel was based in Chicago and had a reputation of being reasonably union-friendly in many cities. In fact more than 50% of Hyatt's were organized in this largely unorganized industry. Furthermore, the Pritzker Family had other interests in the Superdome and friendly relationships with Edwin Edwards, Louisiana's governor at the time, so everything being equal, let's go! Under Barbara Bowen's steadfast direction, we were able to make contacts on Rampart when workers cashed their checks only a couple of blocks from the hotel. Fairly quickly an organizing committee was formed and we decided to storm the gates by having the organizing committee members inside the hotel pass cards on the big game weekend when managers were preoccupied and workers could rule the floors. The committee rocked, going room to room, and a huge percentage of cards were signed by the workers.

Working with Jim Youngdahl of Little Rock, perhaps the premier labor lawyer in the middle south at the time, we were looking at this 1000+ room hotel without blinking, but realized quickly that our best opportunity was to carve out an "appropriate" unit that was largely "back of the house" or non-tipped workers, which meant in New Orleans a largely African-American workforce with a smattering of Latinos, and mostly housekeepers, laundry workers, and the like. We filed for a representation election at the NLRB office at that time only a few blocks from the Hyatt in an office tower across from the train station. The company, led by its attorney, Archibald Stokes of Atlanta, who was also at the zenith of his career as a management attorney in the hospitality industry nationally, went pedal to the metal, crazy with objections to the unit, fearful that it would create a precedent and lead to vastly increased organizing at the Hyatt and other chains around the country. Whatever we thought we had researched about the Hyatt was thrown out the window by Stokes and his pique at the unit and at having Hyatt workers organized by a fledgling independent union with more ties to community organizing than to the labor establishment that Hyatt was used to dealing with around the country. The RC-hearing lasted for days and days of testimony largely based on the company's challenge of whether or not Local 100, United Labor Unions, was in fact a labor organization at all, and endless testimony introduced by the company sought to establish that the only appropriate unit was wall-to-wall. We thanked our stars that Youngdahl was an old friend and ally and working with us for free!

Hyatt Boycott Picket - Beth Butler 1985.

Stokes refused to turn over the *Excelsior* list that is *pro forma* in all representation elections, giving the union the full election list of the potential bargaining unit with their names and addresses. He had the Hyatt and its management refuse to post notices of the upcoming election, forcing NLRB agents in an equally unusual move to stand in the parking lots and at the employee doors to pass out notices of the time, date, and place of the election. In an unprecedented step he refused to allow the election itself to be held on the Hyatt's property, which meant that workers were released for the election to walk to the NLRB offices, being directed on the street by Board agents, vote, and then walk back to work. Not surprisingly we won the election by a 2 to 1 margin in a unit of more than 350 workers. As part of the decision concierges, bellmen and doormen, and valets had been added to the bargaining unit, though the company failed to significantly expand the unit we had petitioned to represent.

Our leadership, largely from housekeeping, was ecstatic, but winning the election turned out to simply be a way station where we engaged in battle in something like an endless war. Hyatt challenged the election and the unit determination in every possible legal venue until finally *cert* was denied seven years later by the *en banc* federal appeals court and the Supreme Court refused to review that decision.

Our next election was at the Tulane University cafeteria. ACORN leaders from the 9th ward identified this unit where a member's sister, Verna Ardoin, worked. As members of UTNO, Geraldine Bell and Mable Washington were instrumental on this drive. Our election victory for these subcontracted workers at Tulane moved more quickly, but even as we were winning the election we did not realize how close we were coming in our naiveté to getting all of our workers fired precipitously. Having secured a significant majority, we threw down the gauntlet, and called for a recognition action at high noon in the largest of the Tulane cafeterias in their Student Center. Cantor and I joined the workers there and at the stroke of noon with students milling in line, our workers left their posts and tried to present the manager with proof of our majority and demanded that the company (Professional Food Service Management) recognize us immediately. They did not, but they did agree after mayhem had broken out, and our people stopped chanting and went back to work, that they would agree to a quick election, which we won handily. In bargaining a successful contract we finally learned from our lawyers and theirs that our work stoppage was illegal in labor law terms and could have led to the termination of every one of our workers participating. We had narrowly ducked the bullet!

Having founded the ULU in 1980, by 1984 we could assess the situation and count our battle scars everywhere. In Detroit our fast food campaign had been a war of attrition with high turnover, young minimum wage workers, and we had one contract at the bus terminal with Burger King. In Boston we had almost 1000 members after several strikes of home healthcare workers, but having started the fight, we were perplexed how to expand sufficiently. In Philly we had lost the ragpickers strike after a bitter campaign from street to synagogue where we tried to mousetrap the owner, unsuccessfully, ending up with a collection of bargaining orders and small contracts. In Chicago we had jumped out fast in organizing home health, but were already caught in potentially wrenching and costly legal battles enforcing bargaining orders, while employers challenged whether or not our workers were really employees or in fact independent subcontractors. In New Orleans we had a bargaining order with Hyatt and some small contracts with food service subcontractors and a giant mess with a nursing home chain.

Regardless by the mid-1980's ACORN was no longer as financially able to subsidize the building of these locals. Where once we might have envisioned local unions with the ULU in many of the ACORN cities, we were caught in heavy conflict, time dragging, expensive battles in all of the cities where we had begun to organize the union, so inevitably we were forced to recognize that our labor union initiative was no longer a national program but only replicable in a small number of cities at great cost. Furthermore, for the ULU organizers caught in the daily grind, there seemed no certainty of success. To many it seemed that we had little choice but to join a larger union. Though we had had offers in the past to affiliate with the UAW in Detroit, the Teamsters had offered us a charter in New Orleans, and HERE had offered us their existing local in New Orleans, if we would merge, and so forth, we had never taken any of it seriously, and never felt the offers were serious. In fact some were almost venal, like the one from HERE offering a job and a pay raise, but nothing for our members. We were young and idealistic, so what were they thinking?

I was about the last one left dragging my feet, but that was easier for me because I had my feet in many different places, rather than the quicksand pulling down all of our union efforts. Finally, we all agreed to reach out to Gerry Shea who had worked with Mark and me at Massachusetts Welfare Rights in the 1960's, living down the block from us when we were in Boston. Gerry and Bill Pastreich had merged their independent local Hospital Workers 880 into SEIU and Gerry was now an official in their DC offices, and he too had often reached out for us and suggested that we should affiliate with SEIU. He argued that SEIU gave locals more autonomy than any other union in the AFL-CIO and were willing to guarantee that we would have a free hand in our organizing.

We all had issues. I wanted to make sure that we all got enough money to make a difference in subsidies and that SEIU made our Hyatt campaign a priority including a boycott of the hotel. I liked the fact that SEIU had virtually nothing between Atlanta and the West Coast, and made as an additional demand that they would have to merge the existing SEIU local into Local 100 as a condition of the merger, if we affiliated. Keith wanted to make sure they offered access to the SEIU legal department so that he had a chance to win the unit determination on the employee status changes. Mark led the negotiations with Gerry Shea from SEIU and joined us in wanting to make the best deal to move the locals forward but was also prescient enough to understand that for our organizing model to have the impact we had hoped, he was going to have to embed himself within the SEIU structure, so he angled as part of the affiliation for a position as organizing director for healthcare units to accelerate the work in that area.

We ended up with three chartered SEIU locals in Boston, Chicago, and New Orleans in the final affiliation agreement. Our largest local in Boston was on its way. Chicago came into SEIU with nothing but bargaining orders and potential, all of which it realized one hundred fold, and New Orleans came in with a couple of hundred members and a tiger by the tail in a fight with Hyatt where we had won a court ordered bargaining order. The bargaining units we had in Philadelphia were merged into District 925, which was concentrating on women clerical workers and needed the extra members. In Detroit our fast food contract with Burger King and other smaller units in Local 222 were merged into the larger building services local union in Detroit, Local 79 at that time. All three locals as part of the affiliation agreement were promised waivers on per capita dues payments for a three year period and direct organizing subsidies of $2000 per month, which may seem meager now, but were huge then.

Local 100 in New Orleans was chartered in May 1984. Our deal was the same, but different, as all of the agreements were. SEIU under President John Sweeney committed that they would resource our boycott Hyatt campaign to force the hotel chain to finally negotiate an agreement in good faith with Local 100. Jay Hessey, a longtime community organizer in the southeast especially the Carolinas and part of the ACORN family, was recruited to staff the position in Washington.[154] Because the merger of the smaller preexisting local 275 was scheduled to occur within subsequent months, the only affiliation agreement that did not have a future timeline for a permanent affiliation decision was Local 100's.

Implicit in the agreements was the understanding that if the locals developed more extensive organizing proposals, the international would be open on a case by case basis to increase the levels of the subsidy and support to implement those organizing campaigns, which all of us saw as a huge green light for the future. The door was also left open for expansion of the locals then. Part of the attraction of the merger for me and Local 100 was the fact that SEIU was bulked up at the east and west arms on both coasts and in the chest in the Midwest, but had virtually no locals of any size and only sporadic units from Atlanta to San Diego below the Mason-Dixon line with locals in Nashville and Louisville. If we could expand into Arkansas or Mississippi or Texas, it all looked very possible. SEIU would not guarantee our expansion in the agreement, but was winking and nodding "yes" in every discussion.

---

[154] More than 20 years later Jay retired from SEIU as deputy-director of the building service division.

The other thing that seemed important at the time was that we would be protected from raiding by other unions, were that to become an issue, because of Article XX of the AFL-CIO constitution which proposed sanctions on unions poaching members and bargaining units from other affiliated unions. In those days SEIU was not small compared to other unions in the federation with something close to a half-million members in 1984 putting the union in the top ten in size, but because of its relatively lower income, service based membership and long history as predominantly a building services union, was not taken that seriously and certainly not seen as the powerhouse it would become later both in and outside of the house of labor.

The organizing department was small and somewhat dispirited with a relatively thin headquarters staff nestled into a couple of floors on K Street in Washington, D.C, where staffers would marvel over the fact that of 250 odd staff members less than a half-dozen, not including the officers themselves, John J. Sweeney from New York City and Richard "Dick" Cordtz from Detroit, actually had any experience whatsoever working in local unions. Ironically over the next decades that would come to matter less and less to the SEIU culture as the organization grew and centralized, but then in the bloom of promoting local union autonomy particularly because so much of its growth came through affiliation efforts of which ours was at the time a minor one, and only later would be seen as one of the major coups of that time, given the growth that followed.

A marriage of such unequal partners is based more on hope than anything else, with success resting as heavily on happenstance as any real evidence at the time hands were shaken. Definitely mutual trust is not what moves these agreements. We were insistent that our local constitutions and bylaws should be protected, including the article enshrined in each of them that acknowledged the role and relationship to ACORN and asserted that it would continue permanently.

On SEIU's side the relationship with ACORN was more a question mark, than deal breaker, given ACORN's overall size and stature in the mid-80's as well. In a classic bit of finesse in describing to President Sweeney the fact that I was directing both Local 100 and ACORN as Chief Organizer, Gerry Shea had analogized the relationship as similar to the membership some other local union leaders had with the Knights of Columbus by saying, that I was active in ACORN, just as others were involved with the KC.

There was a palpable lack of comfort. The historical comparison for SEIU and Sweeney's embrace of the United Labor Unions had more similarity to the way that John Lewis had recruited Communist organizers for the Mineworkers and then the CIO's expansion. We were new left, community organizers, with more spirit than experience, but in the same way that Lewis worked in collaboration with the communists because they were more committed and disciplined organizers, Sweeney might not trust us given our backgrounds and the ACORN relationship, but he knew he wanted SEIU to grow, and if we were part of what went with that ambition, then so be it. More than once we were told the parable of an arrangement that they had made with the United Domestic Workers in California which had more radical politics and practices than the largely conservative cultural stance of the old janitors' union. The UDW was also organizing home health workers and I had spoken with Greg Akili, a key member of their staff, regularly while organizing the Household Workers' Organizing Committee in New Orleans to share ideas and experiences. The SEIU's spin claimed that financial irregularities led them to walk away from the UDW agreement at their first opportunity, but it was hard to tell if that was really the case or just the facade they built to explain their lack of comfort with the Black Nationalist past and Kwanzaa notoriety that went came the UDW.[155]

The nuts and bolts of such relationships are extremely difficult to parse and the United Labor Unions and SEIU marriage is a case study of the huge success that can come from such blessed events, as well as the inevitable challenges that are inherent in grafting different cultures, political orientations, and views of power together. If we had ever had a notion of "boring from within," such an argument would be ludicrous, but even a notion that we could positively impact the larger union by creating an organizing culture is a tenuous conclusion. Over time it is critical to assess the degree to which the United Labor Unions and its organizers changed SEIU or, as powerfully, the SEIU culture changed the United Labor Unions and its organizers.

Very few organizations have successfully made this transition and lived to tell about it. In recent years there have been a number of examples of closer and closer alliances with institutional labor and more grassroots organizing efforts at the community-labor intersection. During the Sweeney tenure the AFL-CIO central labor bodies were allowed to accept community organizations as direct affiliates of the body with even some voting rights in some places to accommodate the Jobs with Justice structure, as well as individual local organizations from place to place. There is no evidence that this practice ever caught on or is widespread. The National Day Labor Organizing Network (NDLON) composed of day labor centers around the country became an affiliate of the AFL-CIO as well, though in practice this alliance seems largely tentative and symbolic. Individual worker centers sometimes became chartered locals of the Laborers or other unions, but there has been little success with these new, more experimental formations to date.

Certainly, as the United Labor Union locals went into SEIU, in the early years we learned to bend without having to bow. After our first year of affiliation, our three locals asked for a meeting with President Sweeney to assess the progress and experience of the affiliation. After some time we were granted the audience. The meeting was more formal than substantive with both sides expressing their continued good will and best intentions, though we continued to press for more without being crazy about it. Shortly after the meeting the word came back to us from Sweeney via Gerry Shea, who continued to be our handler at the time, that the meeting was all well and good, but there would be no future meetings with all of our locals as a group, because "we were SEIU locals now," and we would be dealt with as individual locals, just as other locals were: it was every man for himself!

There was never a feeling that we were in a situation where it was "one for all, and all for one," with SEIU. I can remember many times in discussions over the years with Kelleher as he would recount his continuing frustrations getting the agenda and interests

---

[155] Twenty odd years later, SEIU was more than glad to rekindle the old love and embrace the legacy, leadership and practice of the UDW, in order to gain hegemony over home healthcare in California over AFSCME and any other pretenders to that throne, making it seem all the more certain that it was a more complex and transactional situation than anything more fundamental.

Helen Miller, President of Local 880, second from left, between Keith Kelleher, Mildred Edmond and other delegates from Local 100 at SEIU 2008 Convention in San Juan, PR.

of homecare workers taken seriously in Illinois that he would good humoredly start off the conversations with me saying, "I'm not having fun playing union anymore."

We were always the square pegs in the round hole, partially because our motivations and interests were always different than those that were normal within the institution, whether it involved the fact that we continued to have rank-and-file members elected as officers for decades or did not pay our stewards or pay for meeting attendance or activity or any number of similar cultural disconnects with the SEIU way of doing things.

Over the years the case could be made easily that our affiliation was a success:

- Local 100 at its highwater mark had 7000 members. Local 880 in Chicago, now United Healthcare Illinois-Indiana now had more than 80,000 until the Supreme Court decision in *Harris* and continues to be one of the largest locals in the union.

- Local 100 was always the largest union in the right-to-work South while part of SEIU, even as the International began forcing us to cede members to form a Texas public employees union and a separate Louisiana public employees union.

- Kirk Adams, starting out at ULU with Local 100, did a stint as Organizing Director of the AFL-CIO, was Chief of Staff several times for SEIU, and one of the few Executive Vice-Presidents of SEIU. First, Helen Miller, President of Local 880 and then Kelleher have been elected to the International Executive Board and then Vice-President. I was on the IEB for 8 years from 1996-2004 representing Local 100 and was President of the Southern Conference while there was one.

- Local 100 and Local 880 were allowed to expand geographically at different times within SEIU in our case to Arkansas and Texas and in 880's case to Indiana and Missouri. At other times we had trouble holding on to these areas and our members as different reorganizing schemes became fashionable within SEIU, particularly as its focus under President Andy Stern increasingly prioritized consolidation.

- Most importantly the kind of organizing we advocate, certainly for lower wage home health and home daycare workers became the major growth areas of the union, adding more than a half-million members to organized labor and hundreds of thousands to SEIU. Even specific organizing niches like Head Start workers and community homes for mentally challenged workers, organized by Local 100, and had moments when they were central organizing priorities within various divisions.

- Certainly it is undeniable that on the transactional side, SEIU was generous. Political contributions in Illinois enabled 880's hard, pioneering work to be rewarded after 20 years of solid organizing. Similar support in Louisiana was helpful in our leveraging the unionization of city workers in New Orleans to fruition and winning an election to raise the living wages in the city. SEIU's support was critical in allowing me to direct the path breaking organizing of hospitality and hotel workers in New Orleans through HOTROC in 1997 through 2001 and among Walmart workers in Florida from 2004 through 2008.[156]

There is also no question that the ACORN relationship in addition to the United Labor Unions affiliation played an important role in the SEIU growth surge that continued into the first decade of the 21st Century. For example for several years SEIU contracted with the ACORN Community Labor Organizing Center (ACLOC) as a pre-hiring placement and payroll service to assess trainees and new hires before formally placing such recruits on staff in a mutually beneficial relationship for SEIU in trying to enlist temporary help on huge organizing drives without making permanent budgetary commitments that were unaffordable in any other way and at the same time making the arrangement organizationally and financially appropriate for ACORN and thereby supporting ACORN's community organizing capacity and general infrastructure at the same time. For a number of years Andy Stern, before and after his election and elevation from SEIU's Organizing Director to SEIU's International President, paid annual membership dues to Local 100 so that he would be qualified as a member of a local as required to run for office in the International Union, recognizing that the internal political climate of Local 100 was stable and our commitment to organizing and growth absolute, where he might have been more vulnerable politically in his home local, 668 in Pennsylvania. Kirk Adams also paid dues to Local 100 for several years, since originally Local 100 was his home local.

These relationships with ACORN were not merely transactional. There was there was a formal agreement negotiated and executed between ACORN and SEIU many years later at the time that ACORN affiliated our various home childcare provider chapters in Los Angeles, Philadelphia, and other cities in SEIU. At one level the agreement spelled out the

---

[156] In reality much of the credit for the support also goes to Kirk Adams and his willingness to take chances while with the AFL-CIO and with SEIU, along with his skill at working the levers inside the institutions to make it happen. Muchas gracias, brother!

transfer of these chapters of workers we had originally organized, largely because SEIU and no other union had been willing to undertake the work because the workers in the wake of the changing welfare system were as often employers of other home childcare workers as they were workers themselves, making it a complex organizing unit to engage. Local 880 had pioneered this work in Illinois, but despite their steadfastness in advocating for such organizing, it fell on deaf ears, as the International tried to get them to focus on home healthcare aides exclusively, leaving ACORN citywide organizations unable to resist requests for organizational support from workers suddenly no longer of welfare, and often as not mini-entrepreneurs. In Los Angeles the relationship to the state and normal employer-employee structures were also in flux, much as had been the case in ACORN and the United Labor Unions organizing of other informal workers job classifications. The counties in California contracted with middlemen agencies, usually larger nonprofits, some created for just such purposes, to handle payroll, reporting, and certification of home daycare providers. Much of ACORN's Los Angeles' chapters' work was focused on putting pressure on the paymaster agencies to recognize or negotiate on wages and working conditions. In the serendipity of organizing we had "found" these workers after more directly building an association of workfare workers in Los Angeles.[157] Good things come to those who do the work!

As unions began to look for more growth opportunities at the intersection between public and private sector workers, home daycare workers were inevitably going to receive more attention, and despite some early success in enrolling more than 1000 dues paying members in Los Angeles, ACORN did not have the capacity to commit to building the necessary scale to grow these associations given smaller growth elsewhere in these ACORN affiliated chapters, over committed resources in our own organizing programs in communities, and the millions that institutional labor unions like AFSCME and SEIU could eventually invest if they decided to organize this workforce. As part of the ACORN-SEIU agreement besides affiliating all the chapters and members where SEIU had an interest and a commitment, ACORN committed ACLOC as a partner in direct organizing around SEIU expansion in this sector.

Based on the ACORN-SEIU agreement, ACLOC provided both organizing supervisors and fully staffed and trained crews of organizers to undertake large scale organizing drives in Iowa, Washington, Illinois (on the 880 final push and election), Massachusetts, and other states.[158] We negotiated and pitched programs with SEIU locals in Maryland, California, Minnesota, and elsewhere.

One of the unique features of the ACORN-SEIU Agreement was the "first refusal" language. Our motivation in ceding our home childcare chapters and members had been to secure commitments for significant increases in union density for such workers. The basic organizing model depended on unions in each state being willing to use their political and organizing leverage to move either governors or legislators sufficiently to win organizing rights for these workers that could put them on the road to increased income

---

[157] Brooks, Fred. (2001). *Innovative organizing practices: ACORN's campaign in Los Angeles organizing workfare workers.* Journal of Community Practice, 9 (4), 65-85.

[158] Ross Fitzgerald, based in Houston, was the field manager for most of these efforts.

and job security. The "first refusal" language meant that we would analyze and offer the opportunity to organize home day care workers first to SEIU, and if they indicated interest, go forward first with them in a partnership in organizing these workers. But, if after a reasonable amount of time, there was no action, we reserved the right to pitch other unions who might be willing to move these workers higher on their organizational and political "ask" list and go forward to see if we could implement an organizing program with them.

In New Jersey for example SEIU had no capacity to leverage either the Governor or the key members of the legislature so despite the interest of the Newark-based school and Head Start local, there was no real statewide clout to be put behind the organizing. The Communications Workers of America (CWA) on the other hand had a significant local presence and a progressive regional leadership. I approached Bob Master, the political director of District One, and our best partner in the Working Families Party of New York, about their interest, and he arranged an airport meeting over a hamburger in LaGuardia with the elected head of the District[159] as both of us were changing planes in different directions. Importantly, CWA in New Jersey was the largest union in the state, having won an election some years ago to represent state employees there. They were very close at the time with Governor Jon Corzine, who was also involved at some level with a woman heading one of the CWA locals. There was interest and in subsequent months there were other meetings with the best of their New Jersey local leadership structure. The organizing director for CWA, Ed Sabol, would pick me up at Newark Airport, and we would drive to a local union headquarters in Jersey City or Newark, make our case, discuss our proposal, and leave them to debate whether or not they were willing to represent the workers and partner with us in the organizing. The Jersey story had both a happy and unhappy ending. We were able to work with CWA and deliver a unit of more than 5000 workers, somewhat smaller than in other states, but we did succeed in getting the workers unionized. On the other hand budget cutbacks faced by the giant state employees bargaining units meant that the lower waged home daycare workers slipped to the bottom of the priority list when it came to wages, benefits, and contract protections and advances.

In Florida, where the potential bargaining units were huge, we also felt there were huge opportunities perhaps politically and perhaps through the official public employees' election and bargaining regime, unique among all of the Southern states, though well known for extensive procedural and organizing delays. SEIU led us to believe for several years that Florida was a place where they would engage, and under the language of our agreement there were regular updates with their public employees division and other headquarters staff about the depth of their interest. Finally seeing no action we told them we were going to pursue NEA, the National Education Association, which had significant organizational and political clout in the state. We met with them both in Tallahassee and then later with the president, organizing director, and others over lunch at the Palace Cafe on Canal Street in New Orleans. Each time we were tantalizingly close to an agreement and there seemed palpable interest, but for whatever reason we were never able to implement an agreement and move forward.

---

[159] This is Chris Shelton now national president of CWA beginning in 2015.

In New York, SEIU's 1199 was interested, but the International did not want the local to be "distracted," though doubtlessly they had the political weight to get the job done. Before we were finally released fully from the "first refusal" agreement, SEIU had me talk to their giant building services local, 32BJ, and its political director, a former ACORN staffer named Peter Colavito, who was interested but frank in saying that he did not think he could deliver the leadership. Hector Figueroa, the Secretary-Treasurer then and later the president and I also talked, but nothing was moving. In the meantime we continued our regular pursuit of Randi Weingarten at that time the head of the largest American Federation of Teachers (AFT) local, the United Federation of Teachers, and a frequent ally of New York ACORN. Every three or four months when I was in New York City, Jon Kest and I would ask to meet with her for a conversation. The first was at a Starbucks for a quick cup of coffee before she headed for a meeting with Mayor Bloomberg. She was intrigued but noncommittal. Over time I think we wore her down. We would go to Starbucks. We would meet for dinner or after work sometimes across from the UFT headquarters in lower Manhattan near Wall Street. We were relentless.

Gradually, Weingarten became more and more intrigued by the notion of burnishing her reputation by including an organizing accomplishment as part of her portfolio in addition to her past as teacher, lawyer, leader, and negotiator. Jon Kest was steadily moving ACORN in New York closer and closer to the UFT on other issues as well and the hiring of Jon's wife, and former ACORN and ULU organizer, Fran Streich, onto the UFT staff also helped make this drive a reality. The other clincher was the happy serendipity of the AFT assigning a new member of their national staff to evaluate and act as a liaison to the project named Jessica Smith. I had fortunately worked closely with Jessica when she was the national organizing director for the Seafarers' International Union (SIU) and had been in New Orleans, regularly using the HOTROC offices for meetings and to comfortably park a new baby, when she was an integral part of the Gulf Coast Mariners' Project supported by the AFL-CIO in the late 1990's while HOTROC and the Campaign for Justice at Avondale were central parts of the Sweeney southern strategy.

The end result was a deal made on several levels. The NY State AFT regional director who vetted the partnership for that part of the organization had been a Midwestern AFT director years before who had negotiated with me over jurisdictional issues between Local 100 and AFT in Texas, but that had been a decade before, and it had been "business" and not personal, so his respect for our organizing had transcended the turf issues, and in fact the state organization really was not interested in these kinds of workers in the way UFT had come to want them, so the AFT made a deal with AFSCME, giving them jurisdiction statewide in order to secure an open field in the New York City area. The ACORN deal with UFT and AFT led to our running the card signing, the organizing, the election, and playing an ongoing role in servicing creating a lasting partnership. The certification election with more than 35000 in the bargaining unit was trumpeted as the largest election in New York City perhaps in history, and certainly since the glory days of organizing by the AFL and the CIO. The per capita payments from the UFT to New York ACORN and its successor organization, New York Communities for Change, were essential to the stability and permanence of the organization. This was a partnership that worked and was able to weather the storms.

Perhaps it even worked too well. Proving that our interest continued to be building greater power and security for lower waged workers and that ACORN had built the staff, scale, and capacity to organize and move units of tens of thousands of workers was significant in big picture terms, but in the smaller bore bureaucracies of big international unions, like SEIU, there were many, even at the very top of the leadership structure, including at times Andy Stern and his key organizing lieutenant, Tom Woodruff, who were uncomfortable that our loyalties remained more to the work and to ACORN than exclusively to SEIU or any one union, making us, despite our record and all evidence to the contrary, seem somehow disloyal in their eyes. Certainly John Sweeney had always been cautious about the ACORN connection, but Stern having initially endorsed the relationship seemed more uneasy as our relationships with other unions broadened through these projects in the 21st Century.

TEAM

The direct election of John Sweeney from SEIU to become a leader of a caucus of dissident unions and then the president of the AFL-CIO, placed us in a position of being more trustworthy and reliable as the "devil" that was known, as opposed to the devil unknown. Sweeny emerged with a mandate for change and no small part of that mandate was rooted in whether or not union growth could be rekindled and that relied on organizing, making it only natural that he and his aides would look at organizers and programs they knew and understood, opening the door wide for us once again especially in New Orleans, since expanding unionization in the South was a key plank in the Sweeney platform.

In the early 1980's even before our tie-up with SEIU, Local100 had tried to bootstrap its way into a citywide strategy for organizing hotel workers based on reaching them in the neighborhoods where they lived. Having rejected earlier affiliation offers from the Teamsters for a separate charter and absorption into the Hotel Workers, we had collaborated with the Teamsters and the Operating Engineers on a joint representation strategy for organizing hotels wall-to-wall where we would have more bargaining clout and share the bargaining and representation later on any workers won.

To implement the strategy we believed it was important to first organize various neighborhoods in central and downtown New Orleans that were heavily populated with hotel workers. We organized under a framework we called TEAM, the Teamsters, Engineers, and ACORN Movement. Our theory was straightforward "community unionism," as it came to be called by many people. Those days in the early 1980's were still the days of Polks' and crisscross city directories that listed each address with its resident's name and phone number. Through painstaking labor, we actually knew this was not theory, but a verifiable fact, because block to block, sometimes house to house, lived hotel workers. Because the experience of winning at the workplace was so unknown and foreign, we argued that by engaging hotel workers around community issues, fighting and winning, we could give people the feeling that they could organize and win at their worksites as well. The idea was somewhat similar to our own experience of following ACORN members into their worksites that had initially led us to union organizing in the first place. Various TEAM groups worked on local campaigns. One group in Central

City fought a proposed garbage incinerator successfully near Napoleon Avenue. Another in the Bywater area dealt with a chemical company in the neighborhood and the environmental hazard of its storage practices, another fought a rape at a school.

Meanwhile, as the door-to-door work identified and engaged hotel workers, there were also list-building petitions at the hotel employee doors seeking signatures of workers who agreed that there should be an increase in the federal minimum wage. Those signatures were integrated into the general door knocking lists as quickly as possible. There were citywide meetings of hotel workers from various hotels that would draw a smattering of workers from hotels large and small. In some cases organizing drives would then spin off of those meetings where there was good leadership or specific issues, allowing the same organizing team to be running both community and workplace drives.

John Sweeny and Wade Rathke.

We supported the drives in very basic ways, since between the Engineers and the Teamsters they only contributed about $5000 to the costs. No small amount of the support came from weekly "dinners" the members organized and that we delivered. Fish and macaroni were staples, and I will never forget the arguments back and forth, usually led by Verna Ardoin, our chief steward at the cafeterias at Tulane, on the necessity of potato salad as part of the sales package of a $2 dinner. Lordy!

The other amazing, big money maker was "tagging." On Saturday mornings the staff would put out a small army of between 30 and 40 kids with tennis ball cans collected from the back of the City Park clubhouse with a slogan on the front, and we would hit the high volume traffic intersections with the kids shaking the cans for dimes and dollars and giving out "tags" which said thanks, who we were, and a word about what the donation's purpose was. Danny Cantor was a master at handling the wildness and organizers like Cecile Richards could go out on Claiborne Avenue at Louisiana Avenue and fill a can within a couple of hours. The young taggers who either had their parents' permission or had forged their parents' names and the ones that would actually still be at corner when it was time for the pickup and not have taken the can and disappeared into the mall or wherever (I think this is now called "leakage"), we would pay out between one-third to one-half of the can to the tagger. For decades thereafter going into a grocery store or gas station with Beth Butler, some former tagger would come up to say hello. This was great money for them. And, for us! We regularly cleared between $1000 and $2000 a Saturday which was crazy money. Eventually we had a tag manager and for quite a while ran the tags on Saturdays and then during the summer on other days as well. It may not have been pretty, but it paid for the work.

    The hotel organizing side of the work was very difficult. We were able to use the Hyatt victory as an example of what was possible, but the other side of that victory was the fact that we were stalled out on appeals by the company that eventually ended only when the U. S. Supreme Court denied the writ of *certiari* and the company finally agreed to bargain in 1984, but that was still years away. The fights to organize new hotels were ferocious and marked by multiple firings and NLRB filings for unfair practices. We came close to organizing the Hotel Dauphine; we went to election, losing narrowly at the Inn on Bourbon, literally on Bourbon Street and Toulouse in the heart of the French Quarter; and, we had strong committees at different times in the Royal Sonesta, Le Pavillion, and Hilton that never could get enough support to file.

    We came very close with drives in a unit of five hotels in the Quarter owned by Century Hotel chain, a local outfit controlled by Mark Smith, which included the St. Louis and the Marie Antoinette, along with others less well known. This one will always stick in my mind because I let the organizing committee talk me into working with them to pull some strings to get me hired on as the weekend, graveyard 11-7 AM shift as night bellman on Saturday and Sundays. This was not long before our son, Chaco, had been borne, so I was somehow working full days in the office with ACORN and the union, dealing with a new baby just out of the hospital and then somehow working the graveyard shift. In a piece of irony since I actually stayed awake to help the guys in the kitchen convince waiters and others to sign with the union, management was so impressed that offered me more hours and two additional nights, Thursday and Friday's from 11 to 7am at the St. Louis, which had an even larger and fancier restaurant. My longtime friend and co-conspirator, Drummond Pike of Tides Foundation fame, still talks of a meeting we had about various business in the patio of the St. Louis Hotel one Saturday night from midnight to 2AM in the morning. After six weeks or so, management finally called me in to fire me for being a union organizer, I honestly have to say that I had never been happier at being fired in my life – I was exhausted. And, of course, we filed charges for an unjust firing and won a settlement forcing the company to pay a couple of hundred dollars for having fired me. Unfortunately, we never could sequence all five properties well enough to win in that chain.

    The only real victory in that surge of elections was at the Fontainebleau Hotel at Tulane and Carrollton, which was not a prime property but nice enough at the time. This was a drive run by Cecile Richards, which we won completely in the maintenance and engineering unit although by a narrow margin and had clearly won "in the box" for the rest of the workers, but the lawyers for the company managed to block the vote count with an argument that took us by surprise. The company claimed that it was not a valid election because the company had taken two loans from the notorious Central States pension fund of the Teamsters, a surprising fact that the Teamsters president, Mitchell Ledet, had perhaps forgotten, but under any circumstances had not shared with us. We lost on appeal.

The World's Fair held in New Orleans was a financial disaster in 1984. The hotels had added more rooms than the Fair could fill, consequently there was a gasping retraction in the market when the tourists did not come streaming into the city. Many of the properties where TEAM had been organizing, like the Smith's Century hotels, went bankrupt as did the Fontainebleau shortly thereafter, while others flipped to new owners, closed ostensibly for renovations for years before emerging under new ownership, and so forth. The industry had changed, and the City and its hoteliers had not reckoned with their altered circumstances correctly. Local ownership already in decline, plummeted with only the deeper pockets of the national chains in good position to weather the storm and look for the opportunity to expand. In the shuck-and-jive of developers and politicians, the Fair was still counted a success because real estate prospects and property values rose with the new properties in the CBD, boom or bust, setting the stage for all of them to continue to push warehouse, light manufacturing and similar jobs out of the CBD and the city, so that tourism and upscale apartments and condominiums could be built for the next wave of urban pioneers looking for a cityscape and river views.

Either way, 1984 found Local 100 with a bargaining order finally upheld at the Hyatt Regency at the Superdome after the United States Supreme Court denied a final writ, forcing the company to agree that they would come to the bargaining table. Given the post-Fair hotel shakeup, it seemed clear that we needed to attend to the problem of the Hyatt now, whether opportunity or challenge, and see if we could survive in the industry at all. The other factor pushing hotel organizing farther back on our agenda came with the affiliation with the Service Employees International Union (SEIU) in May 1984, offering support in mustering a Hyatt Boycott. We had to integrate new opportunities and wider organizing jurisdictions into the Local 100 work plan immediately.

Local 100 leaders in Dallas 2009.

As a condition of the merger, we swallowed up the couple of hundred members of the smaller SEIU 275, but that meant bargaining contracts for janitors in the CBD, nursing homes in Gonzales and Shreveport, the federal Hansen's Disease Center in Carville, a few random state health care worker units in New Orleans, and a community hospital in Bogalusa, across Lake Pontchartrain. Even before the merger we found ourselves tangled up in organizing drives in nursing homes, including a vicious mess that began while organizing a few New Orleans area homes run at the time by a chain managed by the ARA Services healthcare division (now known as ARAMARK), that swelled into a pending election for 700 workers across all seven of their homes in the New Orleans area and overwhelmed the local even as the affiliation with SEIU was pending.[160] Similarly we had to advance quickly into the public sector to both shore up the newly acquired units and rapidly expand into local schools and state jurisdictions in Louisiana if possible. All of these opportunities would build Local 100, but it would take some time to have an opportunity to organize hotels and hospitality workers again.

HOTROC

For years we built the local in New Orleans in tandem with our sister local in Chicago, Local 880. Both of these old United Labor Unions locals grew through stops and starts. The Boston ULU local ended up after several years merging with another SEIU local with more healthcare workers in the Boston area, so for decades we were in daily communication with our brothers and sisters in Chicago, trying to light the way along the dark stretches for each other. Both locals were driven to expand. Local 880 opened an office in St. Louis and won several homecare units in that area and in southern Illinois, while continuing to grow larger and stronger with great victories with National Homecare and other large private providers and patient base building in the Department of Rehabilitative Services (DORS), which would become its platform eventually for supercharged growth. Local 100 first was able to win check off for state employees in Arkansas in a direct meeting with Governor Bill Clinton, expanding our jurisdiction to that state by the mid-1980. Promises around expanding into Texas were harder to convert, but an affiliation with SEIU Local 767, the former Beverly nursing home local based in Houston and directed by our old comrade, Orell Fitzsimmons, seemed natural after a while, and a servicing agreement shifted the Baptist Hospital to Local 100, as well as the Jackson, Mississippi VA Hospital.

In 1992, when Governor Anne Richards, signed Senate Bill SB190, granting automatic check off to school workers throughout the state driven by the worker's choice rather than the district's approval, we were ready almost immediately to go after large public school support units in districts around Harris County (Houston) and Dallas County, that eventually also found us organizing around Corpus Christi, throughout East Texas, deep into the Rio Grande areas of Brownsville, Harlingen, and McAllen, and San Antonio districts throughout Bexar County once we merged the city, school, and county districts

---

[160] The affiliation upset the drive, since the "continuity of representation" issues of the merger would have allowed the company to drag the matter through the courts for years, forcing us in the end to settle the many ULPs and withdraw.

that NAGE, the National Association of Government Employees, another SEIU affiliate, was having trouble minding so far away from their main headquarters in Boston.

Much of this growth for both locals was within the public sector units where collective bargaining was rare or unknown. The opportunity for Local 100 to once again attempt to crack the private sector units where the local was borne came with the election of John Sweeney from SEIU as President of the AFL-CIO.

Sweeney had won on a platform for change, particularly through organizing. His call was essentially that he would lead the federation of all of the unions to the kind of growth that had been experienced in SEIU under his leadership. This meant a rededication of energy and, more importantly, resources to organizing to stem the tide of declines that the entire federation had been experiencing, particularly among private sector workers. Implicit in turning the tide as well was Sweeney's call to organize the South where sunbelt jobs and economies had exploded in the last 30 years of the 20th century building economic powerhouses of Dallas, Houston, Atlanta, Phoenix and Florida cities, while stripping down the old powerhouses in Detroit, Cleveland, St. Louis, and Pittsburgh.

HOTROC March through French Quarter.

Essentially we were in the right place at the right time.

Mark Splain had migrated from SEIU to work with Richard Bensinger at the AFL-CIO's Organizing Institute which had been the only shining light in the *ancien regime* before Sweeney took over. Mark was tired of commuting between his home north of California to Washington, so he traded for a new job as the AFL-CIO's Western Regional Director. Kirk Adams had managed his mother-in-law's last race for re-election as Texas Governor only to fall short to George W. Bush, so he was ready to move back into the labor ranks and signed on as Southern Regional Director, hiring old Louisiana native and civil rights veteran, Ken Johnson, working out of Atlanta.

We were making a case once again for taking another shot at organizing hotel and hospitality workers in New Orleans to organizers who had literally been there and done that with us before. All of us still had the taste in our mouths.

The new fad for financing and assembling the work was through multi-union organizing drives. This was more of challenge, especially since the formal jurisdiction within the AFL-CIO for many of these workers in New Orleans belonged to the Hotel Employees and Restaurant Employees (H.E.R.E.) International Union.

HERE had no interest in organizing hotels and hospitality workers in New Orleans or really much of anywhere in the country. Their local in New Orleans had yo-yoed back and forth between trusteeships for years. A former HERE official, Vince Sirabella, had offered to give us their local years ago, if we merged the Hyatt and signed on with HERE. Furthermore after years of governmental investigation and supervision, Edward Hanley, the union's international president had stepped aside, and John Wilhelm, the Secretary-Treasurer, long respected for his dogged and persistent efforts to organize Yale clericals and then his dramatic organizing success in building the culinary workers local in Las Vegas, had emerged at the helm of the union. This transition was still recent and Wilhelm and his team were still trying to sort through the tensions between the old guard and their new wave, so they had a lot of issues that they felt immensely more important to their union than a large scale organizing drive in New Orleans.

HERE had two organizing strategies tailored to their resources and the strength of their team. The first was an analysis that their growth and leverage, largely because of their Vegas stronghold, was in organizing casinos, not hotels. The other was in "labor peace" strategies whose success depended more on the strength of their research team than their field organizers and national representatives, many of whom were long time veterans of the previous regime. "Labor peace" organized a hotel from the "top down" by trying to leverage employer neutrality agreements and even "card check," rather than elections, from the developers when they were still most vulnerable while trying to win approval, concessions, and even financing from public authorities and sometimes on properties being developed on publicly owned lands as well. HERE's researchers would try to leverage isolated developments with the help of local labor central bodies and other unions, like the construction trades, in order to plant flags around the country, like a hotels being built along the Riverwalk in San Antonio or as part of the Convention Center in Houston.

As part of the power sharing when Wilhelm took over HERE, he also made a deal to retain Ron Richardson, a recently named Executive Vice-President of the union under Hanley and former leader of the Washington, D.C. local union, who was seen as relatively clean, but harmless, and more comfortable at the Washington Hilton piano bar than the bargaining table or picket line. Because the New Orleans HERE local was under trusteeship, New Orleans was in Richardson's bailiwick, making him a mountain to climb every step of the way in trying to build the hotel organizing drives. Nonetheless, Wilhelm was able to drive a hard bargain without having to put up more than a token amount of money, he would end up with an equal share of any gain in membership along with SEIU, essentially because they "owned" the franchise.

The formation that we proposed to all of the parties, including the AFL-CIO, was what we called HOTROC, the Hotel, Hospitality and Restaurants Organizing Committee. SEIU would be an equal partner with HERE on any unit and membership gains in a joint representation agreement. We also brought in the Operating Engineers again to handle maintenance and to contribute proportionately for the 10% of the unit they might gain. Richardson and IUOE local union leader, Peter Babin, it developed later, had bonded

Chapter XX: **Why Work and Workers**   473

decades ago as young organizers, Pete with AFSCME then and Richardson starting out with HERE, at a George Meany Center training program, so they were both happy with all of the arrangements.

To leaven the arrangement somewhat, Wilhelm detailed Karl Lechow to deal with me since I was directing the work. Lechow was a legendary organizer and shadowy character within HERE. He was at the time some kind of untitled special assistant to Wilhelm, but generally carried the authority, if not the title, of organizing director for the union. Lechow personified persistence, and his guarantee was that if he committed to the project, he would never abandon it. His single-mindedness was phenomenal. William Buckley could not have bested him in an argument that at the center of American power and influence, it was not so much, "God, Man, and Yale," as simply Yale leading with the others following far behind. Karl after 20 years was still trying to organize at Yale with the big hospital now his target. Wilhelm had assigned him to Reno where he had been doggedly expanding the union there for years. He had no phone or email at that time that he answered. To reach him I would have to leave a message either at an apartment where he had an answering machine in Los Angeles or with a secretary in the DC office of the International Union. Karl was frank and honest though and had we been able to better compete for his time, it might have made a difference.

Nonetheless with HERE and SEIU on board, even tenuously, HOTROC had a green light to move forward. Our best partner was really the AFL-CIO. Dave Kieffer, a former ACTWU organizer in the South and the architect of a dramatic organizing success among asbestos workers in the construction industry in New York City for the Laborers, was directing a program for the AFL-CIO to develop "lead" organizers. He became the HOTROC campaign manager and brought with him a talented bunch of lead organizers in training who cycled through the project including Deborah Axt (later co-director of Make the Road by Walking in NYC), Dalinda Fermin, who was the training director for SEIU more recently, Maria Wickstrom, who also has been a career organizer with SEIU, and the field director for the campaign, Louis Jamerson, who until recently was organizing director of the giant home care and nursing home local based in Los Angeles and southern California and now runs the teachers' union in Fresno, Califonria. Mike Gallagher was detailed back to New Orleans to give me a hand in the organizing equivalent of a baseball "bench coach." The community organizing team was all recruited from New Orleans.

The key to labor peace in New Orleans was Mayor Marc Morial. Morial was the son of the first African-American Mayor in New Orleans, Ernest "Dutch" Morial. Kirk Adams managed to network his political connections from Richards to Senator Mary Landrieu to end up with a meeting where we sought the help of Bob Tucker, who had an engineering firm that did major business for the Airport Commission. He was the Chairman of the Regional Transit Authority, had been the first African-American assistant to Mayor Moon Landrieu, and most importantly acted as the consigliore for Mayor Marc Morial.

Importantly, HOTROC had done an extensive study on the changing character of the New Orleans hospitality industry and found that the real driver of tourism was the Convention Center rather than the French Quarter, accounting for more than 70% of the incoming visitors. Some fortunes might not have been lost if there had been a clearer recognition of this reality at the time of the Worlds' Fair 15 years earlier. The study and our argument that unionization in New Orleans could take our workforce from its present poverty to a solid working-middle class living standard similar to Las Vegas were the twin pillars of our political argument. With Tucker's help, we were able to win the Mayor's confidence and support because it developed that our analyses aligned, though coming from different directions.

Morial felt the burden heavily that after 30 years of African-American political rule in New Orleans, there had not been sufficient economic development to raise the living standards of the overwhelmingly black majority of the population. He felt this had to happen and was critical to his legacy. Between HOTROC in the hotels, ACORN, and Local 100 with the Greater New Orleans AFL-CIO leading the fight for a "living wage" increase of a dollar an hour over the federal minimum wage, and the Local 100 organizing drive among city workers, Morial understood that we were on the verge of making New Orleans the Las Vegas of the South, and in principal he was sympathetic.

In practice he was a shrewd politician. Before agreeing categorically, he wanted to meet with John Sweeney, as head of the AFL-CIO, and maybe even Andy Stern as well, though Sweeney was his target. There were some things he was looking for that they could help deliver, he felt. The end result was a meeting between Morial, Sweeney, Stern, Kirk Adams, now the AFL-CIO's organizing director, and me in Los Angeles in a hotel room a couple of blocks from the Staples Center where the AFL-CIO Executive Council was breaking tradition and holding its winter meetings in Los Angeles in 1996. Morial was clear. He wanted to help make this happen. He was complimentary of me, HOTROC, and so forth, but to get this job done, he essentially had to make sure that his majority on the City Council was locked tight, and that meant a commitment from us that we would do everything we could to help elect two new members of the City Council to firm up his majority.

With Kirk's help and SEIU's we ended up setting up an independent expenditure effort that spent $150,000 in direct mail and GOTV in behalf of the successful election of two candidates to the council to secure Morial's flanks and either overtly or tacitly support our various organizing programs. At the same time, working with ACORN, we were able to win the increase in the minimum wage overwhelmingly at the ballot box, and though it was later successfully challenged and lost on a 3-8 in a decision of the Louisiana Supreme Court, we were well on our way.

On the hotel and hospitality front there was continual tension though. We pursed the labor peace strategies on several proposed developments on city property or where city authorities were central players including the World Trade Center building owned by the city where a hotel was proposed, another hotel proposed for the Airport, and a hotel that would be built abutting the Plaza de Italia on property controlled by a city-board appointed authority.

This was a continual slog through heavy resistance. Developers are in the "promise them the moon, give them garbage," school of negotiations, doing and saying anything that it might take to get a variance, raise money, win council approvals, and then get their money out and run as quickly as they can. They sold the city castles in the air that often crumbled as soon as you shook their hands and tried to get agreements that might benefit workers, much less offer neutrality to the union in organizing. The only real leverage we had was the fact that in some of these cases the mythical "castles" had to be built on land owned or controlled by the City of New Orleans. But, leverage is a stronger word for persuasion and a long way from the command-and-control that mayors and other politicians would like for their own agendas, and never what they are willing to share for ours.

Endless meetings with boards and commissions ranged from the aggressively hostile at the Ernest "Dutch" Morial Convention Center with a state appointed board by Republican governors dominated by the hospitality industry to the passively hostile Aviation Board to the friendly members of boards populated by New Orleans council members. The Plaza de Italia Commission was the most supportive thanks to the participation of Oliver Thomas, a determinedly pro-union, pro-community Councilman-at-Large.

As the work continued behind the scenes on the labor peace strategy, the work in hotels and hospitality units continued to be the emphasis of the organizing staff. We felt strongly, though not always with the full agreement of our partners, that there was no way to win labor peace without having labor war as well, so we pursued organizing targets directly and aggressively.

We targeted the Convention Center and Superdome food services and catering vendor specifically, our old nemesis, ARA Services. We opened up with a significant NLRB election victory at the Convention Center after a bitter fight with ARA on a unit of 350 workers, full and part-time. The Superdome was a bloodbath though with more than a dozen unfair labor practice firings, many of which ended up in complaints against the company. Unfortunately, the impact of the firings dampened our prospects at prevailing in the election, so we withdrew and did not contend when the rerun was ordered.

Interest was high in the hotels, but elections before the NLRB continued to be unlikely areas for success. A membership-based area wide organization of dues paying "HOTROC" members that dug in for the long term until victory could be achieved might have moved the industry towards unionization over time but a property-by-property strategy was unlikely to do so. We filed and went to election at the Wyndham across from the Convention Center and we were all surprised when the Dallas-based chain claimed that their entire staff worked for them through a subcontracted entity, and not the Wyndham Hotel. We lost narrowly. We also went to election at the Royal Omni, formerly a showpiece hotel the Royal Orleans, once owned by the Stern Family along with the Royal Sonesta.[161] We failed to win there as well in another close election.

At this point the fragile alliances among the partner unions were irreparably frayed. HERE wanted to grab the Convention Center work without committing to the shared agreement. SEIU's more "global" negotiations between Wilhelm and Woodruff made Local 100's work and interests expendable, and the lack of good faith in any dealings with Richardson and others was palpable, as was SEIU's attention span and commitments. With the AFL-CIO's support the project managed to continue until the planes hit the New York Twin Towers in 2001 and collapsed, temporarily at least, the airline industry and tourism market, and many of the developers' sky-high castles tumbled, like Humpty Dumpty,

---

[161] The Stern Fund when it closed down in New York after years of leadership by the legendary foundation executive, David Hunter, tabulated that the largest cumulative level of grants had gone to ACORN.

to the ground. Proposals for hotels at the airport, World Trade Center, and Convention Center all crashed as their options expired after frequently missed deadlines. We finally managed to harvest the work at the Plaza de Italia when Loews successfully built the hotel and years later honored our original agreement brokered by Morial and Oliver Thomas, but by that time HOTROC was no more and Local 100's share of the workforce another broken promise. After Katrina in 2005, the Loews emerged as the only union operated hotel in the city, as the more things changed, the more they stayed the same.

The "consolation" prize, as Kirk Adams, called it for Local 100 during those years was the fact that we were simultaneously organizing thousands of public employees of the City of New Orleans through a direct "labor peace" understanding that we had negotiated with Mayor Morial. The deal was straightforward. There would be no voluntary recognition or card check, but Morial gave his word to me, despite widespread skepticism from others, that the City would not campaign against the union. Additionally, at the point we had majorities, we would have to go to supervised elections by a third party neutral to certify the results. To "petition" we would have to face elections department-by-department, which was not what we would have chosen, but certainly something that Local 100 was comfortable with since we had organized and won elections for 1200 workers in the City of Baton Rouge under similar conditions with an election supervised by a former NLRB Assistant Regional Director and a weird combination of departments.[162] In the spirit of the times we had offered a couple of hundred workers involved in skilled maintenance to the unions that were part of the Southeast Louisiana Building & Construction Trades, even though they contributed no resources, no staff, and signed up no workers.

The bargaining was difficult but concluded successfully with language that preserved organizing rights for future city units on the same terms. This was particularly relevant because we wanted to still pick up the Sewerage & Water Board bargaining unit of almost another 1000 workers in the future. The building trades sent a lawyer to one meeting[163] who pronounced himself satisfied that our interests were all the same and subsequently approved the agreement before it was ratified.

The additional drama on this organizing victory was making sure that the contract was executed and implemented while Mayor Morial was still in office. He had tried to stretch out for a third term, but it was not going to happen. We had been endlessly negotiating with his City Attorney, but wanted to make sure we had executed the agreement before Morial left office. The Building Trades stirred at the 11th hour to see if they could renegotiate their share of the unit and grab 600 or 700 workers instead of the 200 or so they had been promised. They attempted to go behind us to the Mayor to squirrel the deal, and even after we were able to execute the agreement tried to delay processing the check off of membership dues for months on various workers to see if they could mount a challenge, classification by classification.

Regardless this was a historic accomplishment for workers in New Orleans. In fact the cumulative impact of the city workers victory, the HOTROC accomplishments, and

---

[162] There's a long, shaggy dog story on the Baton Rouge victories as well, since we had petitioned for the election to replace the Teamsters local in Baton Rouge after a negotiation where they first agreed and then reneged but after it was too late and Local 100 had prevailed.

[163] William Lurie, later deputy general counsel of the AFL-CIO.

the contract campaign at Avondale shipyards found New Orleans with the highest labor density (over 20%) of any southern city thorough this period.[164] And, then came the deluge of Katrina, when the nuts and bolts tightened on labor throughout the city, but that's ahead of our story.

Organizing Walmart

At the Executive Board meeting of the international union shortly before the 2004 SEIU Convention, I was summoned to meet with Andy Stern, the International President. In a tradition dating back decades in SEIU and likely in all big labor unions these were the times when leadership shakeups and shuffles were the order of the day, and of course slate making occurred for the largely rubber stamped approval of the upcoming general convention.

I had never been a smooth fit for the Executive Board and my position as head of the Southern Conference had also become something of an outlier within the union as conferences were dismantled. More importantly, I had been asked by Stern along with Stephen Lerner from SEIU's Building Services Division and the director of the AFL-CIO's George Meany Center to present our vision for the future of the labor movement and SEIU and other unions role in that future and did so in a paper called" Majority Unionism: Strategies for Organizing the 21st Century Labor Movement"[165] which I presented at the June 2002 meeting of the IEB in Seattle, Washington.

Stephen Lerner's argument was essentially for a consolidation of unions through mergers along sectoral lines with a concerted effort to move away from the tendency towards "general workers" unions, representing scores of workers under one union, to a greater specialization and amalgamation in order to concentrate resources, organizing and bargaining power. Controversially, he argued for an AFL-CIO with perhaps 20 unions rather than 3 or 4 times that number. His general disdain for the AFL-CIO was also evident in his remarks. Regardless of his prescriptions, it was hard to argue about much of his diagnosis of the disease.

My argument was essentially that we needed to build a different organizing model to rejuvenate the labor movement by seeking to become a "majority" organization of workers again rather than a minority organization only trying to hold on to the less than 15% membership density we had then (and now less than 12%), which has shrunk even more radically in the last decade. An NLRB-based organizing model had proven incapable of achieving scale, particularly the scale needed to regain lost membership density. The organizing fundamentals had become too expensive per member gained, too legalistic and susceptible to delays, and too tailored to smaller, more accessible bargaining units. Regardless of the discussion of direct recognition, the level of power that labor had to force such concessions had diminished so completely, that even situational success

---

[164] Rathke, Wade, "Labor's Failure in the South," in *American Crisis, Southern Solutions: From Where We stand, Promise and Peril*, edited by Anthony Dunbar (2008)

[165] Rathke, Wade, "*Majority Unionism: Strategies for Organizing the 21st Century Labor Movement*," either social policy or www.chieforganizer.org

from such strategies similar to "Justice for Janitors" was likely to yield too few members proportionate to the resources and time expended.

In some ways the appendix to Majority Unionism made the case inarguable. The firms with 20,000 or more employees, many of which had arisen in the decades since the 1960's of declining union membership were all non-union or virtually so. Not only was this true of Walmart, the country's largest private sector employer, and other giant retailers, like Target, K-Mart, and others, but it was also true of the giant software and computer related employers, contracting firms, and other service sector companies. Where the CIO had targeted the "new" industrial model of its time, our generation of labor organizers had not been able to develop the vision, resources, or organizing model to similarly organize these new private sector powerhouses. In fact, I argued that recent successes pointed the way to a "majority union" model give the rise of public sector unionization since the 1960's from associational roots as well as the similar trajectory for public and private home health and home daycare workers which had represented the greatest membership successes of our generation, adding more than a half-million members over several decades of patient organization building.

The heart of my argument was that we needed to turn the tables and reformulate the paradigm. We needed to create organizational formations that allowed workers – and not employers – to decide that they wanted a union or some form of worker association. In fact we needed to take employers out of the equation completely, build the organization on a membership basis, put the members into action, and eschew an election or bargaining regime, until we had the organizational strength sufficiently established for the employers to sue for peace and stability. Some of the examples were controversial, like whether or not we should create an "AARP for workers" out of the federation, but the whole point was about altering the way we organized, rather than continuing under any of the currently popular models which were at best simply duplicating our minority status since none had the hopes or aspirations of achieving majority worker power in any sectors.

SEIU's decision was to lean more towards Lerner's argument and push the AFL-CIO for consolidation and greater sectoral concentration, rather than to follow through on a different organizing model as I had argued. There was no debate, just a decision or a drift in a certain direction towards one pole and away from another. There were no arguments or raised voices, just a sense of moving on, leading to meetings in 2004 making it impossible eventually to miss the message. SEIU operated on a kinder-and-gentler corporate model in many ways.

Tom Woodruff, who acted as the organizing director for the union, regardless of the title, argued that Local 100 needed to focus and directly made the case to me that either I choose to work 100% for the union in which case they would make continuing investments in the local or they would find another way to move forward in Louisiana. I made the case that some of our greatest victories whether winning check off in Arkansas because of our relationship to Governor Clinton at the time or the victories with the huge addition of city workers in New Orleans or school workers in Texas came because we were working through community-labor partnerships and relationships. My arguments did not prevail.

On the Local 100 level we were pushed to disgorge more than 1000 members in San Antonio to help cede a public employees local in the state and then forced to cede another 2500 of our public members in Louisiana in the city units in Baton Rouge and New Orleans we had won in recent years and our state and school units including our largest unit in East Baton Rouge among support workers to create the base for a public employees only local in Louisiana. Promises of offsets in compensation for lost dues to allow the Local to regain the membership in private sector jurisdictions and elsewhere we worked were not fulfilled, especially after Katrina collapsed so many of the public units that we had given over.

Woodruff, and then Stern, in a private meeting during the Spring IEB meeting in Washington, before the 2004 Convention in San Francisco argued essentially that it was time for me to "put up or shut up" on the majority union argument and that perhaps I was correct that Walmart was the place to prove out the proposition one way or another. It was flattering that he was asking me to plan and direct the Walmart organizing campaign and put it together, but it was also impossible to miss the fact that after 20 years inside the structure I was also being asked to walk a narrow plank off the SEIU ship into high seas where I could sink or swim, and would be marginalized within SEIU itself with a diminished local union base having watched 3500 members go out the door to two new locals, and an exit from the board to do the Walmart project. The assurance that Helen Miller, the President of our sister local, 880, would be raised to the board was a nice consolation, but there was no way to miss the messages in the bottle.

Walmart Organizing Project

Unions are political institutions and navigating them successfully is tough hammer-and-tong politics that organizers are not particularly trained or skilled at handling. Accustomed to being at the back of the room, rather than the front of the room, the "nuts-and-bolts" are often perplexing as we push for metrics often forgetting our manners while unaccustomed to playing outside our usual positions. I genuinely liked Tom, and respected, much of Woodruff's work, and I imagine he felt the same, but we disagreed on fundamental organizing questions and although I had some influence and a voice within the larger union, he had real power over resources and final decision making authority, so it may have been a conversation among equals, but that did not mean the decisions would contain equal parts of our views.

Nonetheless, Woodruff was right and his argument irresistible, even if challenging, so how could any organizer not jump at the chance to try and organize Walmart's million workers as opposed to fighting a losing battle to hold on to our couple of thousand and a seat on the board that had less and less meaning? So, I might have been pushed, but once I felt the hands on my back, I jumped.

The Walmart strategy I devised with our teams had three components: organizing workers and creating leverage to protect and advance unionization by blocking Walmart expansion domestically in the United States where possible and internationally where much of their future growth was projected. In some ways the easiest piece of our Walmart campaign strategy was organizing the workers.

Walmart Site Fight Action by WARN in St. Petersburgh, Florida.

Rick Smith, who had been SEIU's southern organizing director when their organizing strategy included a regional program, rather than an industry-only emphasis, was seconded over to me by SEIU at my request as my field director on this project, in no small way because of his enthusiasm for our experiments here and because we quickly determined that Florida, where he was based, particularly the Interstate 4 corridor counties between Tampa-St. Petersburg and Orlando, was a major Walmart expansion zone and currently accounted for 4% of the company's gross sales. The company might have been California dreaming – and that state also played a key role in our program as it developed for that reason – but, Florida was their sunshine for sales.

On the worker side of the pilot our objective was straightforward. Contrary to popular presumption that Walmart workers were to cowed to organize, could we prove that workers would join their own union or association even though we were not going to file for a representation election with the NLRB. Ever. Nor were we going to take any steps to negotiate a collective bargaining agreement. Joining the Walmart Workers' Association, as we called the organization, meant that a Walmart worker understood this was going to be their organization and to win they were going to have to "push and shove" within the company to get the job done. Furthermore, they were going to have to agree from the very beginning when they signed up with the WWA that they would pay dues, starting at $10 per month. Despite forgoing an election and a contract, workers would elect their own stewards, handle grievances aggressively and often *en masse*, and take advantage of the company's personnel manual and widely touted "open door" policy in dealing with personnel issues.

It turned out that signing up the workers was the easiest part of the task. At least that was true once we could find them, and that was the challenge. When we found them in their homes, we signed up almost 60% of the Walmart workers where there was a completed visit, but often the more than fifteen organizers we had in the field burned up

Chapter XX: Why Work and Workers

100 to 200 miles chasing contacts to be able to get two or three visits in, and sometimes they were lucky to get even one done.

Part of the problem was the obvious dilemma: we were dead when making contacts in and around the stores. Not that we didn't try, because, oh mercy, did we ever. We sent folks in on the sly, we had people at check cashing locations nearby, we scooped up people in the parking lots, and anything else we could think to do. All of these tactics produced limited results at great risks to the campaign and to workers personal job security.

Most of the lists we organized were built somewhat ingenuously. We acquired the voter file in Florida from the 2004 election contest between George Bush and John Kerry. We then broke the file down and sorted out all households with $50,000 or less income in our targeted Florida counties. Finally, we fed the numbers into an autodialer with a simple question on the call saying that if they worked at Walmart, there might be rights they had and help available to obtain them. If interested, press the number 1. Then the prompt asked for the name and address. Some of the responses were folks who thought they might win something from Walmart or whatever, but many were past or present workers. After every night's calls, we would put the names in the hands of the organizing team and they would chase down the leads. Once we had people, we would move them to connect us to co-workers, establish store by store organizing committees, and move forward, all of the while working the lists until they played out.

Moving the worker-based team on this program within less than 9 months we had signed up almost 1000 members in the Walmart Workers' Association. We had committees and leadership in 35 stores with strength in some individual stores as high as 25 – 30% of the workforce. Finally, in the organizing drive we brought the leadership out publicly on the issue of whether or not Walmart's wage claims were accurate in Florida and whether or not managers, rather than headquarters in Bentonville, had the discretion to adjust hours, more or less, which was most critical to this workforce.

Through excellent research work we were able to determine that though unemployment records for individuals in Florida were not public information, the state would provide the data for all employers with more than certain numbers of employees. By making a freedom-of-information request for the employment security data for all employers with more than 50,000 workers, since there were only two in the state, the grocery store chain Publix and Walmart, it was easy to pick out Walmart based on the listed job descriptions, we could go job-by-job and determine without a doubt that we were looking at Walmart and compute the real wages they paid across the company in Florida, putting to a complete lie the numbers that the company routinely swore were their average wages. Even allowing for the fact that supervisors and workers were bulked soup and nuts together, we were able to categorically establish that the actual average wages paid in Florida were anywhere from $1.50 to $0.75 less than the company claimed. Not that it mattered, and not that anyone anywhere has ever been able to calculate this or stop the company from self-certifying its preposterous wage claims. These were the days before anyone took "big data" seriously or had much interest or capacity in trying to either prove we were wrong or support our position because we were right. Once again we were lost in organizing math!

The constant fight on the floors over hours was the bane of Walmart workers everywhere. It was part of the company's ideology that each store manager had the ability to run their own store. This had been a first principle for Sam Walton, the chain's founder. The fact that computers in Bentonville regularly sliced-and-diced hours on virtually a weekly basis was the reality for the workforce. Thirty-two hours this week could be sixteen the next and even forty a month after that. Workers or "associates," as the company called them, and a few even called themselves, never knew what to expect, which made their livelihoods with Walmart precarious and meant for the workers that they always needed to keep looking for a second job or another job, thereby contributing to the 200-plus% turnover the company experienced every year. No one believed that the manager set the hours, but the ideology was enough for the WWA to win many fights for more hours so that the fiction of locally-based management could be maintained.

These were the central issues that led the leadership of the stores to go public with the organizing drive and the fact that they were building a new type of union. Decent press followed the leaders coming out party including pieces by Steven Greenhouse, then the labor reporter for the *New York Times,* and the papers and media outlets in Tampa and St. Petersburg. The real message was to the company, and they responded aggressively by dispatching their huge labor relations team, reported to be over one-hundred strong, into central Florida to do captive audience meetings where we had strength and to run an anti-card signing or union avoidance campaign throughout the area. One of our key leaders literally had a one-on-one with a Bentonville labor relations operative every day for months with offers of promotions and anything that might work.

After the first several weeks, the anti-union campaign started to evolve and taper off into something of a stalemate with both sides jabbing across the ring at each other and trying to see where we could win something here or there, and the company trying to see where it could turn someone in this store or that one. They quickly realized that there was no card-signing campaign, talk of an election, or a contract: we were something different. It almost seemed like they decided they could live with that and would wait and see. When Human Rights Watch did a report on Walmart's abuse of human rights, we were boring interviews. There was never a firing or even any instances where we filed charges with the NLRB for anti-union activity by the company. I'm not saying there was respect, though later company insiders in Florida at the regional level reported just that, but there was at the least regard. Playing by the rules, so to speak, and waiting and seeing in fact might have been smart for them as it turned out.

The second piece of the strategy that turned out to be remarkably effective focused on stopping the construction of new Walmart superstores in central Florida. Walmart was attempting to significantly increase its penetration in the Florida market which was already formidable. We were organizing a vehicle, WARN – the Walmart Alliance for Reform Now – that would be a community-by-community campaign strike force to evaluate and oppose any proposed Walmart superstore expansion. WARN, as an alliance, sought to build broad based coalitions of organizations from environmentalists to community organizations and neighborhood associations to unions, churches, civil rights groups, NIMBY groups and any others we could find that were willing to ask the hard questions, participate in public hearings, and mobilize to stop construction of the stores.

Our record over the period of the campaign was amazing because through a combination of strategies and tactics we were able to prevent the construction and permitting of 32 consecutive applications to build new Walmart stores.

We found ourselves in some strange meetings with some unique allies. The police chief of Orange County (Orlando) was a willing witness for WARN in a number of hearings on Walmart site applications, agreeing with us time after time that the traffic and crime attracted by Walmart superstores overwhelmed the police and sucked up the equivalent of one-and-a-half fulltime cops. In another meeting that Rick and I handled in the early part of the project we met in a community meeting room of a gated subdivision of $300 to $400,000 dollar homes that didn't want Walmart and its traffic to lower the values of their property. There were some natural allies that Walmart subverted with promises of contributions, like the local branch of the NAACP disappointingly, but for the most part we were able to put together strong alliances around store siting proposals. In other cases the company was cavalier about building on wetlands, so we were able to throw up roadblocks with the Sierra Club and others at our side or at the head of the pack.

In many cases as we developed skill we were able to nip the applications in the bud by having our research team call systematically through the list of planning staff and commissioners in various counties and cities in our targeted counties on a regular rotation to identify any shell corporations, land transactions or zoning inquiries that might indicate that a superstore parcel was being put together and readied for review. When we could identify Walmart's "footprint" in these transactions, we had huge success in getting the political and governmental bureaucracy up in arms and moving into action. Walmart's land department obviously did its best work in the quiet backrooms years before an actual permit application developed. When we got there early and moved preemptively we were extraordinarily effective.

Part of the reason was that we were able to construct our own version of a rough algorithm of where Walmart was likely to want to locate its stores. We visited with several academic and private experts at the University of Florida in Gainesville and read with our research team their book on geo-marketing principles very, very closely so that we could predict with fair accuracy where Walmart would be trying to "fill its straight" in terms of store locations in order to increase its market density without cutting "same store sales" even if it meant cannibalizing another Walmart location with several miles. Using this algorithm, we could use our limited resources to focus on where they were most likely to go and pepper city and county planning and zoning questions about those locations and often get there as quickly as the company was able to do so. We stopped store constructions in St. Petersburg, Tampa, Orlando, Clearwater, Sarasota, and tens of towns in counties along the corridor.

The most dramatic victory was one of our last before the project was halted and that occurred in Sarasota. In a complicated deal Walmart had offered the City Council an enticing proposition. They were willing to build on a "brownfield" environmental danger zone, make some of the improvements for some considerations, and locate the supercenter right in the middle of the food desert in the African-American community in that city. On the face of it this would be a hard project for WARN to beat, and in truth some of our normal allies were conflicted. We knew from ACORN's experience in trying to win living wage measures that although the Florida legislature had moved with speed to block the organization from being able to raise wages on a citywide basis as we had tried to do in New Orleans, Houston, and Denver and succeeded in doing in San Francisco, that it was possible for Florida cities to enact special wage floors where there were projects involved that included direct city investment. In this case Walmart was asking for city participation in the brownfield cleanup and for certain other subsidies and inducements. We then assembled a coalition seeking to raise the wage for retail workers (i.e. Walmart workers especially) and other workers that would be hired in the project area so that the minimum wage for retail workers there would be over $12.00 per hour. Walmart announced, predictably, that they would not build the store if forced to pay a "living wage." We mounted an initiated petition drive and won the election setting the wage at the higher rate for all retail workers. Walmart did not build the store.

In some cases our victories were a little like using antibiotics, and in this case land control campaign tactics and strategies, to combat malaria. In many of the thirty-two odd consecutive victories we won, there is little doubt that in subsequent years they were undoubtedly able to correct their problems or find seams that they could widen to force their way into alternative building sites and over the years after the project was closed, Walmart probably built stores in some of those locations. Nonetheless the Walmart project was designed to establish that we could create leverage and could effectively use "site fights" to block the company's expansion, and so we did. We even held three site fight conferences in St. Petersburg and San Jose for example to rally other sitefighters around the country into action in their communities to block the company.

The other major Walmart expansion effort we sought to block, and did for a number of years, was a proposed distribution center in Merced, California. The heart of the company, particularly under CEO Lee Scott at that time, was distribution and logistics. The company shrewdly built and located distribution centers within a distance from the 150

Organizing India FDI Retail Campaign at India Social Forum (Dharmendra Kumar, Vinod Shetty, Reena Desai).

odd stores that would be serviced by those trucks within the time it took to drive without an overnight stay for the trucker. In California where they were drooling to expand the company, Walmart had repeatedly claimed that they would build one-hundred stores around the Bay Area for example, but had been lucky to build a dozen and did so only after fierce fights and continual delays. Merced, a relatively small and beleaguered city in the central valley, was the proposed site for the distribution center that would service the Bay Area and enable this expansion. The City of Merced was vulnerable to the company's promises since it had been hit hard hit by foreclosures, unemployment, and a host of woes. The company wanted to have the center built across from the newly constructed University of California at Merced. In their proposal hundreds of trucks would be coming in and out of this million square footage warehouse night and day.

We were enlisted into a collaboration that had been assembled by the giant UFCW local in that area, Big 8 as it was called, and the Teamsters locals in the northern California area. The two unions funded the organizing in Merced, largely through direct contributions by the locals and assessed themselves per capita payments for that purpose to WARN. Our best ally was Phil Tucker and his California Health Care Coalition who were a constant source of suggestions and assistance both on the ground and with our union partners who he had worked with over the years in similar capacities on similar fights with some success. Using the issue of truck traffic pollution and its risks to community and children's health, we won substantial support from an array of organizations, politicians, and community residents for studies and plan improvements, delaying the project for almost four years. Interestingly to us at one point we had a team travel south to the nearest Walmart distribution center and were able to talk to a number of the workers and record video interviews with some of them who sent warnings to their fellow workers in Merced about the real story of the work and their experiences, all of which were very powerful antidotes to the company's propaganda. As the economy crashed in Merced with the Great Recession in 2007 and 2008, we were unable to hold our majority in the local city elections against the desperation for jobs and development of any kind.

The final leg of our "three-legged stool" strategy for the Walmart campaign was international. The company had set a huge priority on expansion into India, so we made an equivalent commitment to work to build a national coalition in India to resist modification of foreign direct investment in multi-brand retail, which was needed by Walmart and any of its competitors like Carrefour, Tesco, or Metro to successfully enter the Indian market. Over the previous decade there had been a gradual opening up of the Indian markets for foreign direct investment in other commercial areas, many of which had been closed for the sixty years since Indian independence from Great Britain in reaction to the colonial oppression of the subcontinent. With over twenty million people employed in domestically based retail ranging from hawkers and street sellers to biryani shops to local companies, the impact of big-box entry into the marketplace was seen as potentially catastrophic unless met with sufficient guarantees and protections for communities, employment, and suppliers throughout the chain.

As we organized the India FDI Watch Campaign with unions, commodity brokers, buyers, hawkers, political parties of the right and the left, NGOs, and many others,

Michael Duke, a top executive from Walmart (and later CEO), was meeting to wide publicity and speculation with Prime Minister Singh and calling from the rooftops that India was the number one priority for the company's future and global expansion. Our strategy simply was to create leverage, bargaining power, and protection for our organizing campaign by throwing roadblocks in their path to create delays, costs, and restrictions for the company's inevitable entry into the Indian market. In one rally after another in Mumbai, Delhi, Kolkata, Bengaluru, Chennai, and other cities, the campaign was able to mobilize widespread concern about Walmart by telling the story of the company's practices in the United States, Canada, Germany, and elsewhere, all of which made the case for detailed rules and regulations before opening the doors for multi-brand retail.

The campaign managed to navigate fairly agilely the ebbs and tides of Indian multi-party parliamentary politics. The conservative, right, communalist party (and now ruling party), which is always one of the primary opposition parties to the often ruling Congress Party has traditionally had a strong, secure base among traders and small retail operators, so was a surprising, if sometimes uncomfortable ally. The left parties, both nationally and in Kerala and West Bengal were excellent allies and at the inception of the campaign were part of the coalition government providing, along with legislators from the Chennai area, the balance of power for the ruling Congress Party. Our ability thanks to excellent work by Dharmendra Kumar, ACORN'S Delhi-based campaign director, to block the company at several junctures with elections in the offing and threats from our partners to withdraw from the UPA and bring down the government was critical in preventing implementation of the Prime Minister's FDI liberalization program several times.

With elections looming the Prime Minister attempted to implement the opening of multi-brand retail[166] to recast the Congress Party as a driver of economic progress because the growth rate in India nudged below 5% annually. His action initiated a firestorm with all business of Parliament completely stalemated for several weeks as marches and rallies dominated the news in Delhi and elsewhere around the country. Finally, Singh blinked and withdrew his measure, even though relaxing FDI did not require Parliamentary approval. Singh deferred the whole mess to a study committee. We testified numerous times before the committee and arranged for our folks to do the same repeatedly, but we were not overly optimistic that the final recommendations of the committee would yield protections in line with our longstanding campaign objectives; nonetheless the referral to a special committee postponed the larger, substantive fights for another day.

Finally, a new implementation plan was rolled out early in 2013. The plan contained significant concessions that India FDI Watch had advocated for years through. No multi-brand stores could be built in any city with less than one-million population, though assuredly this includes hundreds of Indian cities. No stores could be built within the city cores, but needed to be built more in suburbs. Significant sourcing (30%) had to come from Indian farmers and businesses. And, importantly, a huge prior investment in

---

[166] Single-brand had been opened several years before allowing a Nike store to open with 51% foreign direct investment. Multi-brand, as it implies, refers to retail establishments selling a wide range of goods and brands.

permanent infrastructure equal to almost 60% of the total investment had to be made before any company could open stores under the modified FDI rules. Many companies, including even Walmart, balked at the high level of this infrastructure commitment and some companies have indicated they will not open in India now, amazingly also including Walmart. Finally, and the reason why the national Parliament was not the key decision maker, each Indian state is empowered to act to approve the introduction of multi-brand retail and FDI within their boundaries.

Practically speaking, the fight goes on. In implementing the program in 2013 the powerful governor of West Bengal and her state-based party threatened to leave the ruling coalition and joined a number of other huge states indicating that they will not allow FDI and multi-brand retail within their jurisdictions. Some certainly have welcomed the change like Maharashtra, the huge state where Mumbai is located, but other very populated areas have indicated that they will not approve the modifications joining Kerala and West Bengal.

Ironically, in looking at the nuts-and-bolts of this third, international piece of the Walmart campaign, our original allies were non-participants virtually from the beginning, and yet ACORN International has persevered, based on commitments we made and the work of ACORN India, regardless of the divisions in the US-labor movement. The AFL-CIO with Jason Judd from their international department, and also a former Local 100 organizer, was active in the early days as the India FDI Watch Campaign was organized, but the UFCW was always ambivalent, preferring to leave any work in India to the global union federation, UNI. UNI's representative at the beginning of the campaign bizarrely offered to independently go meet with the Prime Minister and "cut a deal," which clearly would not work with the rest of the partners in the campaign. The AFL-CIO could not really do more than cheer us on since their Solidarity Center was not legally able to open an office in India and do business and instead maintained an office and listening post in Sri Lanka. In short, despite the fact that this campaign cost – and is still costing – Walmart billions both out of its own pocket and out of loss revenue from their over optimistic projections, we have created leverage that has only in the end helped achieve Indian campaign objectives and built ACORN India, rather than assisting in organizing Walmart.

By most reckonings we had categorically established that, yes, Walmart workers would join a worker-run and worker-led organization that publicly advocated for improvements in hours, wages, and working conditions and fought those issues with some success on the floor of the stores. We had achieved a *de facto detente* with the company that allowed stewards to represent other workers on grievances and that allowed WWA leaders to deal directly with store management. We had also established overwhelmingly that we could slow or stop the company's expansion plans with aggressive organizing, research, and alliance building on sitefights. Finally, we were a factor in creating leverage with attendant costs in lost opportunity and direct expenditures to the company's global growth ambitions.

The incipient incident that slammed the door on the worker organizing was a disagreement between Joe Hansen, the president of the UFCW, and Andy Stern, the president of SEIU. With a core membership and jurisdiction among healthcare workers, Stern was attempting to assemble a coalition of business leaders who were willing to advocate for a federal solution to healthcare coverage and insurance had reached out in various ways to Lee Scott, CEO of Walmart, about their potential common interest in a national program of some sort. In the dynamics of Washington, DC beltway politics, Stern was organizing a press conference to announce big business support for a healthcare plan and wanted to make Lee Scott the rabbit he pulled out of his hat.

In the SEIU version of the dispute, Stern had alerted Hansen of this development, Hansen had demurred on any interest in dealing with their archenemy Walmart, and Stern's staff moved forward to organize the event, clearing the attendance at the press conference with Walmart and the other companies. Hansen at the last minute, only a day before the event, changed his mind and wanted to be part of the press conference. SEIU claimed it was too late at that point to include him based on the agreements with the business leaders, and excluded Hansen from the event, which of course attracted wide attention and national press coverage.

No one disputes that Hansen was then livid. Hansen and UFCW felt that they were deliberately excluded by SEIU and Stern, and worse, were humiliated in front of their members and other parts of the labor movement, because of Walmart's presence at the event, their absence, and the fact that in the hallowed traditions within the house of labor that this was their jurisdiction. There were reportedly harsh words between the two allies and friends about whether SEIU was trying to poach in UFCW's preserve.

Not long before Stern had initiated a schism within the American labor movement by leading several unions, including importantly the UFCW, out of the AFL-CIO to create a rival federation, Change to Win (C2W), after failing to convince the AFL-CIO and its leader, the former president of SEIU, John Sweeney, to reform or concede to their demands. Although smaller unions like HERE and the United Farm Workers were part of the walkout, the key unions were UFCW and the Teamsters, both with more than a million members.

Hansen was so enraged by Stern's embrace of Lee Scott at the press conference that he threatened to pull the UFCW out of Change to Win and reenter the AFL-CIO. As part of his demands to make the peace between the unions, he asked for – and received – an even clearer promise from SEIU that they had no designs on their jurisdiction, especially organizing Walmart, and as proof of their good faith, he demanded an immediate end to the Walmart organizing project that I was running in Florida. Within forty-eight hours I had to lay off virtually the entire worker-based organizing staff in central Florida, hobbling the project. Because ACORN International was supporting the India FDI Watch campaign, that effort continued, and because we had raised some outside money from various sources including foundations, for years we were able to maintain some parts of the WARN operation and provide some servicing for the WWA for a period of time along with the Merced project since it was supported by local unions rather than international ones, but the heart had been ripped out of the work at Stern's embrace.

Perhaps this was inevitable, and there were certainly foreboding signs before the Walmart press conference. Hansen was relatively new as UFCW president at that time and was still securing his base with many UFCW locals, particularly in retail, since he had come out of the meatpacking side of the union. He was not uninterested in the project and was always friendly and supportive in his dealings with me, but part of the reason he

Chapter XX: Why Work and Workers   489

had greenlighted the project in Florida was that his locals were so weak in retail there that win, lose, or draw there was no political downside for the UFCW from our work. Their "assistance" had largely been to assign a representative to the project whose main job was showing up for two or three days per week in the beginning and then more infrequently over time to write reports on our progress for the international. The situation was so ludicrous that eventually we offered to just send him a regular report to save him the trip. When I had talked with Hansen about the results of the project directly and the fact that we had proven that workers would join, would pay dues, and would take action, it had been one of those "good news and bad news" conversations, where the good news was the fact that workers were joining in significant numbers, and the bad news was that workers were joining and he would have to decide if UFCW was willing to make the long term investment to move the nearly 1000 members we had up to 100,000 or 200,000 to make a difference in moving the entire company. Hansen was clearly not ready to double-down then, even if he had wanted to do so given his still tenuous grip on the presidency and even more unstable financial condition of the union in the wake of losing a bitter California strike in what had been their stronghold in no small part because of the threat of Walmart.

Looking at our on-the-ground project, the fact that the UFCW had organized something called Wake Up Walmart directed by former Howard Dean political director, Paul Blank, on a strategy of press events and list building for support in order to essentially compete with Stern's Walmart Watch initiative run by Andrew Grossman from Washington, was another level of distrust no matter how many protestations to the contrary. SEIU was funding Walmart Watch extensively to the tune of millions per year and also trying to mobilize private foundations and rich individuals to support their efforts. Although we worked with both efforts, and I had played a role for Stern in organizing the first discussion meetings that led to the creation of Walmart Watch, there was no denying, regardless of the protestations to the contrary, that this was a duplication of effort founded in fundamental mistrust.

Perhaps the final proof of our success, even in the UFCW's perspective, was the organization of OUR Walmart by the UFCW several years after our Walmart organizing project had finally shut down in St. Petersburg, Orlando, and Merced, which used some of the same methodology and strategy though with some different tactics, including a faux strike, with a hundred or more workers nationally to gain attention to their campaign. It was hard to not acknowledge the similarities when OUR Walmart organizers and consultants with Change to Win and elsewhere would call Rick Smith or myself to ask, essentially, for advice based on our experience. In the end UFCW under a new president abandoned that effort as well.

It's not a pretty story and it's disappointing for what might have been, but this is part of the nuts and bolts of organizing.

It is also a true-life story of what happens in coalitions and alliances of unequal partners and the huge potential and tremendous challenges to making community-labor partnerships work at the highest levels.

Learning by Doing

We have clearly walked both sides of the street. We have correctly seen labor unions as our closest partners and been seen by labor unions as a vital ally. At the same time we have been both inside and outside of the house of labor, navigated the uneasy relationships between competitive organizations, been seen as a captive of certain unions and disloyal by certain unions, so the question inevitably arises, should we have chosen only one path or the other? Not surprisingly, I continue to steadfastly endorse the path we chose, so perhaps more importantly, what would we recommend to others if faced with the same choices?

At one level our members benefited. As I have mentioned earlier, though the organizations were separate, and had to be given legal requirements, the relationship with ACORN was formally acknowledged in the Constitution and Bylaws of the local unions, and continues to be for Local 100. Members of the union were automatically provisional members of ACORN, called for events, contacted when there was a neighborhood organizing drive, alerted for housing events, invited to conventions where many also attended, shared offices, and sometimes even staff. To be fully entitled members of either organization continued to require full dues payment to each. Neither ACORN nor our union family members could afford to waive dues, nor did we believe that we should. Certainly, we could not create a system which encouraged "dues shopping" to determine the cheapest deal on this basis. At the same time many members were paying dues to both our local unions and to ACORN. Helen Miller from Local 880 in Chicago was not only a member, but regularly elected to the national ACORN Association board where she played a vital role. For that matter, union members covered by contracts in multiple facilities also paid dues from each facility. There were joint leadership trainings, joint board meetings, joint staff meetings, joint fundraisers, and mutual solidarity was woven fully into our organizing culture. These relationships were unmitigated organizational assets.

In advocating and advancing community-labor coalitions, our experience on both sides of the line was also an advantage. We knew the language, challenges, and issues firsthand, so, even in the wary environment produced by struggle, there was a high level of trust in such partnerships founded on mutual experience and exchange. Not every union may have been delighted with the fact that we also included local unions and workers' associations in our family of organizations, but there was respect for the work and for the fact that we had been there and done that, just as they had. There was a legacy from these relationships as well that was sufficiently deep that in many cases after ACORN's troubles in the United States, it was often unions, their partnerships, and their support that sustained the successor organizations in Texas, Illinois, New York, Florida, and other states and continues to do so.

More importantly, the ACORN organizing methodology **and** the labor organizing methodology hugely benefited from the cross fertilization of experiences, experiments, campaigns, and mutual understandings. Sustaining so many of our labor unions for years without collective bargaining laws or labor relations laws benefited hugely from our core experiences as community organizers, familiar with direct membership enrollment and the push-and-shove of issues, actions and campaigns. Our ability to embrace both worlds is dramatic in cases like our hawkers organizing in India, hotel workers organizing in Lyon, France, and domestic workers organizing in Morocco. Our ability to advocate and embrace strategies and methodology to adapt to the changing world of labor and soaring numbers of informal workers globally also hearkens a robust future.

As a constituency-based organization of low-and-moderate income families, we really never had a choice but to truly organize the unorganized wherever we found them in whatever way we could do so. Nor in the dysfunction of union jurisdictions, competition, and decline do we have a choice in the future, if we can adapt to a changing world and embrace its potential.

It is terribly difficult and contentious to organize workers in unions and collective associations. It is not for everybody, so decisions should be made carefully. But, someone has to do it, and too often we are the only ones willing to answer the call and respond to the need.

Chapter XXI: Services

Over the last fifty years of community organizing in the United States one of the most stubborn and frequently debated conundrums is whether or not it is possible for community organizations to successfully walk the line between advocacy and action on one side and service delivery on the other without being forced to move exclusively in one direction or another. Since the 1960's and the heyday of government and foundation support for community development, the overwhelming presumption has been that in many cases community organization was simply a gateway, perhaps an adolescent acting out, as an organization evolved to find its "real" purpose in delivering goods and services to the community.

Robert Fisher in his book, *Let the People Decide*,[167] outlines the case most persuasively, seeming to conclude that inevitably the requirements of a servicing regime, like a cancer, drive out the advocacy and political elements of a community organization, because inexorably the organization becomes "professionalized," focused on "deliverables" rather than issues, actions and campaigns, and "other" directions given the fact that the resources needed to support the servicing mechanisms frequently require significant levels of outside funding from governments at various levels or private sources like foundations and other financial sources external to the community itself. Certainly in the time when Fisher was writing examples for his arguments seemed everywhere and were well known. The Woodlawn Organization (TWO), one of the famous 1960's Alinsky organizations became better known as a community development corporation (CDC) running jobs programs and trying to develop shopping centers. They were certainly not the only ones who made that transition and abandoned their history of confrontations and advocacy, even while claiming it as part of their heritage. There was no more bitter irony than Rev. Arthur Brazier, head of TWO, opening his church and moving his membership for a pro-Walmart rally in opposition to ACORN and the rest of the city when the company first tried to open a store in Chicago.

At different times organizations like the Center for Community Change, when run by Dave Ramage and then Pablo Eisenberg seemed to exist largely for the purposes of aiding in the seduction and transition of community organizations into community development corporations.[168] All of this in spite of the facts. David Rusk, former mayor of Albuquerque, and later urban planning expert, argued in a report to the Ford Foundation as detailed in his book, *Cities Without Suburbs*[169] that the actual record of CDCs in successfully rehabilitating and restoring neighborhoods despite the millions of dollars spent was almost a story of universal failure with one of the only exceptions from

---

[167] Fisher, Robert, *Let the People Decide: Neighborhood Organizing in America*, (1984)

[168] This has not been the case under Deepak Bagavara, a former legislative director for ACORN in our DC office, and his leadership of CCC in the 21st century which has been more campaign oriented.

[169] Rusk, David, *Cities without Suburbs* (1993)

his statistical reckoning being a neighborhood in Cincinnati which showed dramatic improvement, though unfortunately that was due to wholesale gentrification.

Starting ACORN in 1970 in the midst of these debates was a polarizing experience. I can still remember Dave Ramage, after he had left CCC and was then running the New World Foundation, asking me in the mid-1970's when I was going to "get serious and begin community development." So, though we eschewed the world of CDCs, we were more receptive to integrating the creation of "alternative" institutions into the ACORN organizing enterprise even from the very beginnings of the organization in the early 1970's in Arkansas when we organized ACORN food buyers' clubs with Kaye Jaeger and the Arkansas Advocate, a brief effort at a monthly paper with Martin Kirby, a former Arkansas Democrat reporter.

Squatting to Housing Development and Loan Counseling

The paradigm between services and direct organizing began to shift for ACORN with the initiation of our squatting campaigns, first in Philadelphia and then nationally. We did not invent the squatting tactic in Philadelphia, though we certainly embraced it and took it to a new level, proving the timeless law of organizing that if something is working somewhere, take it, and make it bigger and better. We had some success in winning houses through squatting campaigns, as long as we did the research, making sure the houses were tax-delinquent houses or had already gone over to city ownership through bank default or simple abandonment as many working families deserted the city core in great city after great city.

In Philadelphia, Detroit, and some other cities ACORN was successful in winning some versions of "homesteading" ordinances. Some of these programs were one-dollar purchases as long as the house was rehabilitated within a certain period of time. In some cases, squatters were able to gain title to the houses they had taken over in the beginning. Often there were other people within ACORN's membership or in the neighborhood who had prized skills like how to turn on the water meters without the company's permission or how to suck into other electrical sources. Dicey business perhaps, but as we often said, we were uniting "people that needed houses with houses that needed people."

Our original program was based on two twin pillars: sweat equity and a land trust.

Sweat equity was premised on the ability of the squatters to put in the hard work of actually fixing the house with their own labor and that of family, friends, and neighbors. Some squatters made great progress, but others found that sometimes their dreams for the houses were much bigger than their skills and resources. Initially setting up the ACORN Housing Corporation (AHC), the mission was to organize support for squatters in Philadelphia and then other cities in somewhat of an enhanced sweat equity program where there was at least one skilled construction supervisor who could help organize support, teach skills, and move people and materials to the work.

Eventually, it became clear that we were trying to graft apples and oranges together. Too many of our people were losing their houses after years of work or were fashioning lives together in houses that were only marginally habitable, if not in some cases even worse than the terrible housing they were escaping in private landlord situations or public

ACORN confronts mayor

Officials promise decision on 'squatters'

After a weekend confrontation between Mayor Jim Inhofe and ACORN members, city officials today say they will decide whether to evict "squatters" from vacant urban renewal homes.

They also will ask District Attorney David Moss to determine if ACORN broke the law.

City officials Friday charged the community action group deliberately misled Spanish-speaking Cuban refugees into believing that paying $16 ACORN membership dues would entitle them to vacant Tulsa Urban Renewal homes on the Tulsa's north side.

ACORN members Saturday confronted Inhofe at his home and charged that the city was using the refugee issue to divert attention from the group's demands for a homesteading program.

"They are talking as if all the squatters are Cubans. That is simply a lie," said ACORN member Gayle Robbins.

Because of high interest rates, TURA has been unable to sell about 30 houses moved there from land used for the airport expansion. The houses have remained vacant, some for almost two years.

Since early March, members of Sooners for Houses, a division of ACORN, have moved into the houses. About two-thirds are occupied by Cuban refugees, many of whom have moved in since April 19. Some have begun repairing the deteriorating homes.

Friday, Richard Soudriette, the mayor's administrative assistant, and Pepe Mendez, former head of the Cuban refugee relocation task force, circulated letters drafted in Spanish, warning the squatters to leave the homes by today. But the city said it has not decided whether to evict them.

That decision rests with City Development Director Dr. John Piercey, who is in Washington, D.C., today with the mayor, Soudriette said.

About 25 ACORN members who rallied at the mayor's home Saturday accused Inhofe of using the racial issue to discredit their demands for a homesteading program.

A livid Inhofe told the group clustered in front of his house, "You can come down to my office anytime, but you do not harass my family at home."

Speaking in Spanish part of the time, Inhofe invited the "squatters" to make applications at the urban renewal offices Monday to buy the homes.

The mayor said the city will attempt to work out a program whereby those who want to buy homes might be able to rent them until financial arrangments can be made.

ACORN has said that a Spanish-speaking interpreter explained to Cuban members that the city did not want them in the houses, "but that they would pay their $16 dues to be part of a group that was fighting to get the homes," said Sheila Gaines, an ACORN interpreter.

"We didn't tell them what they were doing was illegal, because we don't consider it illegal. This is something we want," Gaines said.

Through interpreters, the Cubans attending the meeting said they knew the $16 was for membership dues.

However, two men said that until late last week they thought that the abandoned houses would be theirs once they fixed them up.

Tulsa Squatters Press April 1982.

housing. Many of these houses were also large, perhaps even too large. Sometimes after the crowbar pried open the door, we found homes that looked like their owners had just left for a bit and might be back any minute, but more often we found mantels stolen, copper tubing gone, furnaces ripped out, and even the plumbing gone. Those houses had problems larger than what sweat and brute labor could remedy, because restoring infrastructure was expensive and squatters had more courage and conviction than they had financing. Our members could not live in their dreams, and despite our principled commitment to sweat equity and volunteer labor, we could not reliably resource it in such a way that we could get to any scale in helping our members successfully rehabilitate their houses.

Though there were success stories certainly, we finally isolated sweat equity more and more only to Philadelphia, and increasingly realized that we needed to more clearly move AHC into development, and that is where the land trusts came into prominence. The design of the land trusts was straightforward. For the organization we wanted housing development for our members to insure that the housing was always a community asset providing affordable housing for low-and-moderate income families, rather than creating the random walk for individual citizen wealth for a particular family from collective organizational action. A family could sell but they could only sell for what they had invested in improvements to the home and they could will or gift the home within their family, but the same conditions would apply.

Chapter XXI: Services

Street sign in Houston ACORN development.

This was sometimes an area where we had a failure of will, training, and supervision in believing sufficiently in the "community" and collective values of the land trust. Where it worked best was actually in New York City through MHANY, the Mutual Housing Association of New York, where under the leadership of Ismene Spiliotis, the program was our largest with over 1000 units. After ACORN began organizing in the city in the early 1980's one of the first campaigns involved squatting and housing. Mayor Edward Koch was bitterly opposed to our squatting efforts and to ACORN specifically. MHANY's creation was one of the compromises in our winning the campaign. Koch was willing to finally agree to our having the houses where we were squatting, but insisted that he did not want to be seen capitulating to ACORN, so the houses would have to deeded over from the city to some entity that did not have ACORN in its name, *voila* MHANY!

Housing is a critical issue for our constituency and quickly under normal circumstances becomes a central component of citizen wealth as I have documented elsewhere,[170] which also meant that this could be a contentious issue in some circumstances. Before the housing was won in New York City and earlier in Philadelphia, members could get points or credits to move higher up on the list to get houses when, and if, we won, through a form of sweat equity for participation in the actual campaign to win. Being a member counted for points, but so did participation in meetings, actions, and other organizational activities. All of that was great for the campaign and for building organization, but it also created more and more a sense of entitlement in a certain smaller group of leaders and members. More controversially, after the fact, New York ACORN discovered that way too much of our growth in New York from house meetings that were accelerating our Dominican membership was organized by one of our stars, a great former labor organizer in the Dominican Republic, through an implicit promise she was making that members would be guaranteed future houses. What did people have to

---

[170] Ibid, *Citizen Wealth*, Chapter 3.

496   Nuts & Bolts – The ACORN Fundamentals of Organizing

lose? Our Spanish definitely got better, as we were schooled by that learning experience! Furthermore that also meant that though the land trust or mutual housing practice continued in the New York City operation and farther as the program spread to New Jersey and Connecticut on a smaller scale, it also meant that increasingly it was a more technical and professional operation which included a unionized full-time, maintenance crew.

In addition to New York the real housing development occurred at various levels in Chicago, New Orleans, Houston, and, most notably, Phoenix. Development never got significant traction in Philadelphia and the New Orleans development was mainly after Katrina and never reached full potential. Phoenix and Houston both focused on new construction, rather than rehabbing older properties. Driving along roads named after Houston ACORN and Dallas ACORN in the Houston development was a memorable experience for me and any others who drove through the houses.

But outside of New York City, we never were able to build a model of housing development to the scale needed by a mass membership organization or as consistent with our principles as we had originally wished. On the other hand in adapting to the challenges in Philadelphia in navigating the city politics to allow housing development, AHC under Bruce Dorpalen, developed an important program of housing counseling that did achieve significant scale and wide adoption in more than one third of all ACORN offices in the country.

Housing Counseling

The chicken and the egg are clear in this story. First there was the members' demand for houses, and that forced us into one campaign after another to try to force banks to be accountable to our members and their communities. The passage of the Community Reinvestment Act (CRA) in 1977 gave us enough leverage with the data mined through the Home Mortgage Disclosure Act (HMDA) to gnaw away with the few teeth in the statutes at the impact of the banks' redlining of our neighborhoods and racial discrimination involving our African-American and Latino membership. One demonstration after another by ACORN at Citibank, the banks that became Bank of America, and others eventually brought most of the major banks to the table.

Our interests theoretically were mutual. The banks needed, especially in the early decade of the Act, to clean up their CRA ratings. They did not want us to block their merger and expansion plans by filing objections and asking for hearings by the Federal Reserve, which we won in landmark cases in St. Louis and New Orleans. Every delay was costly with often higher interest rates and lost opportunity costs, and some were sufficient to scuttle the deals, if we were able to stretch them out through the process. Eventually, we were clear that our interests were better served through negotiations, but once at the bargaining table it was also clear that we needed more than AHC's meager development capacity and the program it could deliver to get to the scale of homeownership demanded by our membership. Housing counseling became the natural middle ground. The banks were more comfortable agreeing to loan dollars committed to qualified buyers in our neighborhoods over the life of the agreements, if we could develop the systems that could deliver them potential buyers from our communities who either qualified or whose credit could be gotten in shape to qualify for loans.

Inevitably the devil is in the details when it comes to our members. Over time and regular negotiations, we sought to expand what qualified as income for lending purposes and the types of records substantiating that income, and of course interest levels were also critical. The better the "product" provided by individual banks, the more families we could qualify, and the more loans they could make, so the better their CRA record, and the better both of our performances were under the agreements we negotiated. Yearly evaluations of the ACORN loan portfolio referred by our loan counselors allowed us to keep hammering on these themes, sometimes successfully, sometimes not. In successive agreements banks would do "actions" on us in their own way to try to get a larger share of our volume and to improve their products so that our counselors would move more loans to them. The competition among banks was hardly surprising as the agreements matured because in some of the evaluations, banks like Citi were clear with us that our portfolio of lower income and minority borrowers outperformed their "regular" lending from their own sources and brokers so that when they evaluated the actual performance of the loans, the ACORN loans were simply better.[171]

The AHC housing counseling program relied on ACORN's actions, advocacy, and reputation in the communities to fuel the intake system with "Need a House" flyers, but as importantly, when everything was humming, they trained and managed counselors that could relate well to potential homeowners, assist them in credit repair, work closely with folks through the meeting regimen to prepare them for homeownership, and generally improve the opportunities for their success when they succeeded in getting a

Henry Cisneros on Tour as HUD Secretary.

---

[171] Needless to say this experience contradicts all of the right wing rhetoric about ACORN blackmailing the banks to lend to our members, since they competed for our loans and our portfolio outperformed their normal channels. So there!

loan for a home they selected. The staff was usually drawn from the ranks of prospective homeowners, ACORN members, and the general constituency and trained as counselors from that point to a level of proficiency.

There were some cultural and professional strains between the housing and the organizing staff since some of the organizing staff saw themselves as the elite core of the organization and denigrated the fixed schedules and forty-hour workweek of the housing counselors. The organizers always wanted the counselors to sign-up people who came in through the housing intake as ACORN members and to give ACORN members a preference for housing, while the counselors often did not want to do anything that might rock the boat in the least, especially when the level of funding for housing counseling began to increase significantly from HUD beginning in Henry Cisneros' term as HUD Secretary under President Bill Clinton.

In the early years of the Clinton Administration, Cisneros agreed to have quarterly meetings at HUD with ACORN about housing policy and problems around the country. Cisneros was familiar with ACORN from his time as Mayor of San Antonio and was comfortable in dealings with community organizations from his tenure there. Clinton from his terms as Attorney-General and then Governor of Arkansas had long worked with ACORN, so this regular meeting schedule was not surprising.

ACORN and ACORN Housing were able to use these meetings, and the more serious attention given to our work at this level, to win a deeper evaluation of the merits of our housing counseling program in increasing home ownership of lower income families. ACORN's leaders' explanation, time after time, about the problems they were having breaking through the HUD bureaucracy was invaluable. Gradually the requests for proposals (RFPs) began to increase for housing counseling and AHC was successful in winning these funds to support the program which then also grew steadily. The politics were crucial but the program performance had to justify the funding, and it always did, ranking the AHC program in the top three year after year, and allowing the program at its high point to move tens of thousands into homeowners annually and to assist hundreds of thousands of families per year in offices throughout the country.

No marriage is perfect and as symbiotic as the relationship between ACORN and AHC as its housing subsidiary was, there were certainly also management and organizational challenges at the juncture of organizing and service. In some ways the most minor tensions were those within individual offices which often arose as much from personality issues as programmatic concerns. The depth of the commitment of AHC to the overall membership and organizing culture is best illustrated in the way AHC weathered the wrath and revenge of House Speaker Newt Gingrich after an ACORN action that disrupted his speech before the national association of county commissioners at a Washington, DC hotel. Several hundred ACORN members burst through the room, chanting at the microphone in protest of the Speaker's proposal at that time to curtail the national school lunch program. Gingrich left the stage fuming and his reaction was not long in coming. He quickly determined that AHC had recently won a grant from the AmeriCorps program providing one-hundred AmeriCorps volunteers to help expand the housing counseling program. He raised the roof at HUD accusing AHC of allowing AmeriCorps volunteers that they were supervising to attend the action on him.

Despite the fact that this had not been the case, extensive discussions with the Inspector General of AmeriCorps and clear messages from Harrison Wofford, the director of AmeriCorps made it clear to us and our attorneys that there was little hope in saving the program. There is no question that from that point forward AHC was more on-guard about the blow back that could come from ACORN's more aggressive advocacy, and they joined me whenever I cited the fact that we were willing to pay "a million dollars to take action on our issues," since that was the value of the lost AmeriCorps grant.

The management of AHC never complained to me about the action. No small reason for this lay in the fact that Mike Shea, AHC's executive director, and Bruce Dorpalen, both came out of the organizing side of the ACORN experience and culture. Mike had been initially an organizer, first in Houston, and then Arkansas before becoming head organizer of Colorado ACORN and one of our New Orleans-based regional directors of the ACORN field and expansion program. Bruce had been an organizer first in North Carolina and then head organizer for Georgia ACORN. Over the years some of the institutional pressures may have moved them more towards a housing-centric position, but their core values were ACORN's and in line with the organizing culture of the organization throughout my long years of association with them and many others within AHC, most notably Ismene Spiliotis, and it made a difference that was incalculable in our ability to keep these pieces together.

In short, do not try this at home, unless you have the shared experience and culture that molded and welded all of the pieces of the ACORN family together!

There were certainly also times where we failed to get the most of the combination of housing services and organization building and perhaps failed to fully achieve the potential on both sides of the equation.

- In Washington, D.C. where we had a very active housing counseling operation for many years, it was with some surprise that the head organizer at the time, Melanie Marcus, realized that our District membership had leaped past the District boundaries and we had almost 1000 members in Prince George and Montgomery. These were counties in Maryland where we had no local groups or organizers assigned. Almost all of that membership had come from the people seeking our housing counseling and loan products without the organization exploiting the growth in these working class suburbs as our members fled gentrification and higher prices in +the District so that they could afford housing. It also meant that we were essentially helping our own members move away from our neighborhoods, and not following them with the organization to their new homes!

- We never succeeded in developing a seamless system to enroll members into ACORN who came through the housing program. When HUD began funding the counseling, a condition of receiving the services could not include membership. Various offices were more or less successful in setting up a section of the intake that allowed ACORN organizers or leaders to talk about the organization and invite people to join. Later once ACORN diversified our membership categories, Shea and I worked out a system which was vetted and approved by all of the lawyers whereby ACORN could give housing intake participants a free trial, nonvoting membership, and then follow-up later to enroll the family as full members. The system never worked as well in practice as in theory, and office to office problems in sharing the database also presented obstacles, but it was an improvement.

- In the organic nature of the work it was difficult to ever get all cylinders synchronizing. A strong organizing office might not have a strong counseling operation, so the advantages were not exploited, or a strong counseling operation might not have an equally adept organizing operation creating the same incongruities. Or, we could have both and less than successful working relationships or power dynamics or we could have great relationships which meant "easy" members being enrolled without great work on either side. And, finally we were never able to get to the scale in our housing program where all of the cities where we were organizing enjoyed the benefits of the program, even when AHC developed a phone-based referral system, all of which was disappointing, even if understandable based on available resources.

ACORN Service Centers

The campaign for tax justice launched by ACORN first targeted H&R Block, then Jackson-Hewitt, and finally Liberty Tax Services, the big three of tax preparers. The biggest issue was their predatory products involving advance payment of tax refund checks faster than the Internal Revenue Service could deliver them through Refund Anticipation Loans (RALs) or RACS or whatever a particular company might call them. One of the outcomes of this campaign was the launching of the ACORN Service Center operations around the country. With significant funding from the Marguerite Casey Foundation we launched a campaign directed at Block, as the largest tax preparation service in the country, believing that if we could beat them and win an agreement that it might serve as a pattern in the industry. After more than 500 actions in a short two month period before the beginning of their tax season and with the April 15th tax deadline still looming on the horizon, the company agreed to negotiate with us first in New Orleans and later in Kansas City. We ended up winning a series of reforms including disclosures, some commitments on the phase out of RALs, some language on joint legislative work, and a commitment that the company would fund ACORN to open free tax sites in specific cities that overlapped ACORN operations and Block priorities to expand tax services to lower income and working families. Within a couple of years with additional campaigning we won similar terms from Jackson-Hewitt and Liberty increasing the number of ACORN cities that could participate in these three year support agreements.

The Marguerite Casey Foundation in Seattle had initially provided us resources to prove that the participation rate for families eligible for the EITC (Earned Income Tax Credit) could be raised significantly through an aggressive outreach program that we then successfully piloted in Miami, New Orleans, and San Antonio. With the additional resources negotiated from the tax preparers we were also able to convince the Citi Foundation to come in significantly to expand the program even further, as we

ACORN Service Center in operation in Phoenix on EITC and Taxes.

broadened the platform of the ACORN Service Centers from not only free taxes but also a computerized search for all other federal, state, and local programs so the family might be able to qualify to receive from food stamps to child credits, section 8 housing subsidies, and so forth. We referred to this as an effort to achieve *maximum eligible participation*. Of course a family that might also have an interest in home ownership would be referred over to the AHC home counseling program, if there was one in their city, and later via an 800 number when AHC made that available more broadly.

By 2008, we were handling almost 50,000 tax returns annually from our centers. The housing program was seeing 80 to 100,000 people per year. When we began to add up all of the "touches" the organization was making to low-and-moderate income families in our cities by that point with almost 100 ACORN offices in the United States, we realized that we needed to better integrate as many of these contacts with our direct outreach organizing model for community organizations to accelerate our membership growth. Furthermore, by expanding the initial tax preparation services to a wider range of support that *privileged our members,* we could extend the range of the organization's impact and have the work integrate and cross fertilize more as we continued to build mass organization.

Using an "intake" model to supplement our "outreach" model of direct organizing made the organization more efficient, especially since the cost of field organizers was so expensive from recruitment to training to support and supervision. If we could push more of our constituency through our offices, this increased membership and provided more participation in our community groups when done well. Utilizing the offices better and increasing the flow of people made our investments in "sticks and bricks" more efficient as well.

Do Service Programs Increase Organizational Vulnerability?

Despite what I have argued were the essential organizational compatibilities of a family of organizations with wide ranging services as well as a primary organizational and political life, the attacks on ACORN during the 2008 election campaign and subsequently due to the video scamming by James O'Keefe, Hannah Giles, and conservative forces largely sought to probe ACORN vulnerabilities, specifically targeting the housing counseling program of AHC. The attacks began originally on alleged fraud in the massive, one-million plus voter registration program which I might also argue was a critical service component of the organizations political program.

Seemingly the organization's leadership and new staff management[172] would have believed that they had largely gotten past the voter registration problems despite the hue and cry of conservative pundits, led by Glen Beck, Breitbart News, and Fox News. Presumably despite the quickness at which Obama threw ACORN under the bus in the debates, the election of the first African-American president and his relationship with an organization with a sizable African-American membership that had both endorsed his candidacy, registered, and turned out significant numbers of low-to-moderate income voters, the vast majority of whom no doubt voted for the new President, would have improved rapidly as time passed between the election drama and the everyday tasks of governing.

To give the devil his due, O'Keefe and company clearly saw ACORN as a major progressive institution and inherently part of the consensus driving a new government after the Bush years. As a membership organization with dues and other revenue and without any special tax status, ACORN *per se* was relatively immune from outside attacks. Regardless of any internal problems and leadership squabbles there might have been, and certainly there were some, as there always are, the organization could not be subverted internally with any ease from the outside. Six hundred local groups, thirty-eight state organizations, a staff of more than 500 organizers, a conservative hit squad would have needed the resources and discipline to spend years to infiltrate and disrupt any of the state or city organizations. Furthermore, what's the beef? What could they allege? There was no special IRS status. We were a voluntary, membership organization; no one was forced to join. Much of the recruitment continued to be based on neighborhood-by-neighborhood organizing drives and door-to-door contact that would have been impossible to duplicate. There were no government grants to ACORN, so it would have been, "take your best shot."

The housing operation was a different matter though, and in retrospect must have looked like easy pickings. There were open intakes, set office locations, regular office hours that encouraged walk-in traffic from anybody and everybody. The ACORN Housing Corporation was structured as a 501c3 with tax exempt treatment from the IRS and available 990's clearly indicating that operations received extensive federal funding, adding to its perceived vulnerability to conservative arguments about the fungability of resources, meaning that government money to one part of the family of organizations freed up resources in other, more controversial or political, components of ACORN. The

---

[172] Just a reminder here, I left ACORN in the USA after 38 years as Founder and Chief Organizer on June 2, 2008.

organizations shared office locations, as they should have in order to maximize impact and most efficiently use resources, but giving videographers the advantage of filming an ACORN sign on the front of the building or the door could totally confuse the audience of potential viewers. The operations were not centralized, but distributed around the country giving any scammers multiple opportunities to catch someone off guard and trick them for the purposes of their attack.

Equally important was the very nature of the counseling staff. They were inordinately African-American or Latino, given the low-to-moderate income constituency being served and though well trained on housing and credit issues and versed in the organizational mission and culture, they were primarily hired for their relational skills, regardless of educational or prior work background. They were trained to be helpful, to be problem solvers, to make people comfortable talking about something as private in the national culture as their money and as common as their dreams of homeownership. They were trained to give people the benefit of the doubt and move them to the next step of the process. Certainly they knew that people might fudge about how good their credit was or how much they could count as income, but since all of that would need to be verified, this was less of an issue than getting them comfortable and moving along. They were absolutely not trained to be skeptical or disbelieving. Often they had been in the chairs on the other side of the desk, so empathized with people trying to find housing solutions. In retrospect all of this made them more prone to comments that might be easily manipulated later in an editing room.

And, then of course there is race. White families were part of the mix, but in many offices they were rarities. The housing counseling programs were originally intended, as we have already detailed, to offset housing discrimination in lending, so the outreach was to neighborhoods where minorities were the majority, not to white communities. Anyone could walk in the door without fear of discrimination by ACORN personnel, but in many offices white families or couples would have been unusual and something of an oddity in the day, thereby gaining more attention than a regular visit and prompting perhaps some extra effort by the counselors to engage and even please, given the complex racial dynamics of our culture.

None of these conditions were recipes for disaster. All of them were in fact hallmarks and preconditions of an excellent program. Nonetheless all of these proclivities could provide sufficient grist for the mill for any unscrupulous film editor with a hidden agenda. Similar to a crime procedural on television, where there was access and motive, there could be mischief galore, and that was made for someone like O'Keefe and his unprincipled, ideological pursuit.

It is somewhat amazing that he and Giles had to hit so many ACORN offices in so many different parts of the country to piece together their attack. Many offices smelled out the rats immediately, and shooed them out of the door. In a painful irony they scored most heavily in Baltimore and Brooklyn, where local offices had resisted some of the national training and coordination of the program, making them perhaps more susceptible. In Los Angeles they were ushered out and the cops were called. Most notoriously in the National City office in San Diego County, the counselor played along with their outrageous propositions about needing housing to locate Guatemalan immigrant women they intended to illegally transport across the border and then called a relative in the police department to report them. When he was fired by AHC once the video surfaced on Fox News, he later filed suit and several years after ACORN threw in the towel in 2013 he collected $50,000 from Giles and $100,000 from O'Keefe in a settlement for the damages they had caused him.

By that time ACORN in the United States was no more at least in its original form. When the videos first surfaced, tactically they dribbled them out one by one for maximum impact, trying, and succeeding, in silencing any support or defense of the organization from the left, intimidated by concern about what shoe might drop next. In excellent orchestration far right, conservative Representatives and Senators rushed to put forward Congressional resolutions condemning the organization and in a more dramatic step, defunding ACORN and what eventually emerged as an extensive list of almost 200 organizations that were part of the conspiratorial web, alleged by the right. Both resolutions passed quickly and overwhelmingly, often with some surprising support even from some moderate and liberal Congressmen and Senators.

The elaborately constructed "corporate veil" that underscored the ACORN family of organizations was not maintained, probably could not be maintained, and hardly mattered in the witch hunt that ruled the day. Despite the fact that the supposed scandalous activities were under the stewardship of ACORN Housing Corporation, when attacked the organizational response appropriately was united with ACORN never stepping back from the onslaught and hiding behind the niceties of corporate organizational structure and separation. Initially, I wondered why the organization might have chosen that strategy, rather than allowing AHC to take the first wave, but realistically it would not have mattered. ACORN was the game in this hunt, and ACORN was in the name, so all was fair in this war.

On the other hand, I still wonder why AHC summarily dismissed people like Juan Carlos Vera, the National City loan counselor, without even a suspension and investigation, both of which were out of character and would not have been usual protocol or have even been our lawyers' normal advice, but by then I suppose it was "all hands on deck, and man the battle stations," so standard operating procedures went by the wayside. Having the new CEO in Brooklyn handle the public response nationally along with staff in many of the other cities where the video emerged, rather than the elected leadership and members of the organization, was also outside of the culture of the organization, and I suspect inflamed the situation. I'm sure some half-baked, so-called conflict management expert offered that kind of advice, but it fed into the Fox/O'Keefe/Brietbart strategy, rather than playing to the membership strength of the organization and its deep indigenous values. Certainly, the leadership might not be as glib in handling hardball questions, but their sincerity and commitment to the organization would have resonated with any audience willing to still give the organization a listen for the other side of the story. Where the roots were deep in a community in cities like New Orleans, where the reputation of the organization after 30 years and especially its role in the city's post-Katrina recovery, saw everyone from the Mayor to newspaper columnists coming out to defend the organization and its leadership, the organization was able to weather the storm. There are lessons here.

I suspect that O'Keefe's initial hope had been to uncover some overtly political comments from the housing counselors from his videos. In the wake of the 2008 voter registration brouhaha assuredly ACORN would have been on his radar as a banner carrier for the progressive political forces, so I suspect he hoped to uncover some blatant politicization in the housing program given its tax-exempt status and significant federal funding. When that well ran dry, they elected to go with the bizarre and take advantage of the willingness of the housing counselors to try and be helpful and in some cases "play along," as some of them have testified, for the sake of shock value, betting that the power of the film would be sufficient to overcome any concern for the facts and context involved. And, of course given the now documented way that O'Keefe edited the tapes for the shock impression he wanted, it was way too late for what the rapper, Drake, would call the "fake friends" of ACORN to finally rally behind, far, far behind, the organization.

The collapse of ACORN's political support and the inadequate defense by longstanding political allies exposed a huge organizational weakness. Many of its friends ran for cover or folded like cheap suits, allowing the attack to have an even greater, chilling effect on political organization of the poor and working people than O'Keefe and his comrades might have dreamed possible. The years of investment by ACORN in a Washington-based legislative operation were worthless in the kind of death match that faced ACORN. The political staff in most cases was not from the same school of hard knocks that typified most of the organizing staff, but under any reckoning they were overwhelmed by the swiftness and completeness of the Congressional assault. Having President Obama once again throw the organization under the bus in answer to a question at a press conference about the videos was also a signal to progressive forces at all levels to "duck and cover."

ACORN's attempt to fight the "defunding" bills arguably had its most success in court, but even when the organization was winning some of the early legal battles at the federal district court level on the constitutional argument that the "bills of attainder" were outlawed, the delays typical of the judicial process were starving the organization of resources, especially in the service-based programs. A "bill of attainder" is expressly forbidden by the Constitution, because it prevents a legislature or Congress to attack an individual or organization or corporation without judicial process, evidence presented, hearing or trial, giving the attacked, in this case ACORN, no defense. There can be little doubt that the attack on ACORN was a bill of attainder, but in the polarized world of contemporary politics and the judiciary, the federal appeals court overturned the district court decision on the most spurious of grounds, giving the organization no relief.

In fairness it is impossible to run a perfect program, and this has now been demonstrated often as the O'Keefe model of attack has been repeated countless times subsequently targeting other progressive institutions and their services. Attacks have now occurred, following the same model against National Public Radio, the National Education Association, and others, most notably the Planned Parenthood Association (PPA). The Planned Parenthood attack has been most instructive because the right both followed the model most closely and Planned Parenthood with Cecile Richards, a former United Labor Unions organizer, as President and Chief Executive Officer, most clearly learned and adapted the lessons from the ACORN experience.

Drummond Pike and Wade Sidney Australia.

Planned Parenthood was vulnerable in exactly the way that ACORN was vulnerable through its service delivery system. The O'Keefe clone who scored against them managed to take advantage of a low-level intake worker at a clinic in New Jersey, who was operating outside of the PPA script and guidelines, trying too hard to be helpful and finding hot water as the reward.[173] PPA was bigger and better politically connected with its constituency of women and more tested allies in Congress than ACORN enjoyed as an organization of poor people. Women have been elected in the United States to Congress and some have personal experience with the issues of choice and abortion, which is not so much case for poor people or elected leaders sharing the experience of the poor and valuing the importance of their organizations. Even Barack Obama as a former community organizer with experience with exactly that constituency was clueless. PPA was familiar with the culture wars in a way that ACORN, an organization of outsiders, was not, and was able to beat back – with Presidential support – the Congressional defunding bills.

The other part of the attack drill at the state legislative level has been more difficult for them in a way that was less the case for ACORN. In the ACORN situation a number of Republican governors and Republican controlled legislatures immediately issued executive orders or passed resolutions defunding ACORN as well. This was largely just a dog pile because ACORN and its affiliates, including AHC, received almost no money from state legislative sources. There was a bit in New York and the organization was able to hold on there. Planned Parenthood though had extensive clinic operations in states throughout the country and many of them were funded by state governments and sought legislative approval for the resources they received, which has forced PPA into a number of on-going fights in conservative states to withhold funds or restrict their clinic licensing operations

---

[173] To their credit Planned Parenthood did suspend and investigate while of course saying that, if true, this was outside of their policy and guidelines.

or impose new, burdensome requirements. One of the largest of these attacks in Texas in 2013 led to a dramatic filibuster before being enacted into legislation. Of course 2013 also saw several Republican and Tea Party Congressman propose on-going defunding amendments for ACORN and its "affiliates" to the federal budget bills, two-and-a-half years after ACORN filed for bankruptcy and dissolution. And, at the end of 2016, the Obama Administration was madly trying to solidify harder rules barring discrimination against Planned Parenthood by states refusing funding for health services to any clinics also providing abortions.

In PPA and Richards there are experienced and savvy leadership with excellent political and communication skills and the departments to back them up. The way that Planned Parenthood used the politicized withdrawal of support from the Susan Komen Foundation for the Cure to polarize its supporters to its defense should also be a classic, case study for how progressive institutions can shore up their weak kneed supporters to their advantage, which victimized ACORN.

ACORN finding itself the first organization out of the chute for this new, more aggressive right wing attack strategy in fairness had none of these advantages. This was also before "fake news" has become recognized as a modern media phenomena and fear. Its friends, allies, and partners, even among big, experienced and battle tested unions like SEIU[174], cut and ran, isolating the organization and sending a message to other organizations that it was better to watch from the sidelines than stick your neck out for a bunch of unruly poor people and their organization. The exceptions proved the rule, when longtime funders and supporters like Drummond Pike and the Tides Foundation stood up for ACORN, they were virtually alone.[175]

Nonetheless, we are still left with our original question about whether services caused the cards to topple over for ACORN. The defunding action by Congress in and of itself should not have been cataclysmic for the organization, since ACORN only benefited marginally from anything connected to federal dollars through shared office cost arrangements, that were calculated by rigidly applied per square footage formulas, so profiting the organization not at all, and with contracts with AHC to do the outreach that was vital to both programs.

The action of the IRS for example in ending its "partnership" with ACORN was a classic nonevent. The IRS had similar arrangements with more than 50,000 organizations and agencies involved in providing the VITA (Volunteer Income Tax Assistance) and other than some tax software that for the most part was available elsewhere, provided absolutely no material assistance and not one dollar of resources to the entire ACORN Service Center operation. In fact the discontinuance of the IRS partnership should have been liberating, since it would have allowed members and other participants to pay some nominal fee-for-service costs and not only continue the tax preparation assistance

---

[174] Testifying before a Congressional hearing in the first blushes of the attack on ACORN, Anna Burger, SEIU's Secretary-Treasurer, denied that SEIU had any relationship to ACORN or worked with ACORN, despite all evidence and facts to the contrary. See earlier disaffiliation of Local 100 from SEIU.

[175] Pike stood out even from his own board, which after 30 years as a founding member of the board asked me to move to a "senior advisor" status to "protect" Tides.

being provided, but generate substantial and needed revenues from the operation. The tax operation as a standalone service had such value that H&R Block had made annual inquiries about whether or not ACORN would be willing to sell the entire operation to them. Instead for some inexplicable reason, ACORN under attack reacted to the end of the IRS partnership not with relief, but a weird resignation, announcing that they would totally discontinue assisting tax preparation in the communities where they had become vital.

Part of the problem seems to have simply been a chain reaction that overwhelmed inexperienced management receiving poor advice in every direction from folks without experience with ACORN, its culture, politics, and mission. No small amount of this lies in the sweeping nature of the Congressional defunding actions, naming so many organizations that were part of the ACORN family – as well as some that were in no way related! Furthermore to some, the defunding "ban" seemed to block any relationship with even contractual partners to ACORN affiliates if they received federal dollars. The most extreme and ridiculous of these situations was the abrogation of agreements that ACORN had with banks like Citi and Bank of America, who used the fact that they were receiving billions of dollars in federal bailouts as part of the Great Recession to claim that their attorneys believed that they could no longer legally make the required contractual payments to ACORN without running afoul of the defunding acts. Balderdash!

My analysis would be that none of these events *per se* would have been sufficient to topple ACORN, had there been cohesiveness internally within the organization. Unfortunately the internal life of the organization was anything but calm at that point. A rump caucus of leaders, originally unwittingly sought as allies by new management, had attempted their own internal coup of the leadership and finances, which though unsuccessful did involve litigation in several venues, especially New Orleans. The fact that this rump group, calling itself the "ACORN Eight," also was unprincipled enough to regularly attack ACORN with wild and specious charges on Fox News and in other outlets in Washington, D.C. and elsewhere contributed to the chaos. Similarly, a self-styled whistleblower who had been fired from the Project Vote operation for making unauthorized, personal credit card charges, was trying to fashion a new career for herself as an anti-ACORN spokesperson with yet more crazed and unfounded accusations of ACORN partisan activity. The elected national leadership was virtually removed from sight, when their role could – and should – have been prominent, further confusing the membership and other leadership and contributing to the internal sense of the organization as being rudderless against the storm.

In such a fertile ground of internal dissent, staffing instability, and inexperienced management, the "defunding" measure clearly produced a "rats leaving the sinking ship" kind of mentality. AHC was facing near lethal cuts. The radio stations had Corporate for Public Broadcasting monies which were endangered. A FEMA grant was canceled to the ACORN Institute. Housing development funds were curtailed. Even where Mayors or others stood up, as happened in New Orleans, in support of AHC continuing to develop new housing in the Ninth Ward, ACORN national staff summarily terminated the longtime head organizer prompting the local staff and leadership to go on separately with her rather than what was left of national ACORN.

Replacing the "all for one, and one for all," "an injury to one is an injury to all," culture with a "save yourself first" impulse was devastating to the core of ACORN. For the housing operation to survive under AHC meant convincing HUD that they in fact were a separate organization from ACORN just as their corporate status entailed. Even finally proving that to HUD and changing their name to the Affordable Housing Centers (AHC) was insufficient to save them. Unable to bring unity within the organizing staff, the plan, if it could be called that, was rather than hunker down and weather the storm and struggle through to the other side, to instead let everyone in the parlance of the time "rebrand," so that there could be a survival of the fittest and those remnants of ACORN that could make it would shapeshift to fight another day.

Years later, many leaders have told me that when they voted to disband on the advice of lawyers and staff, they were told that this was a temporary maneuver until the coast cleared, and they would reassemble within a year or so and rebuild the organization. Others say that the model recommended was based on the experience of Citizen Action, a national coalition of organizations that ran into trouble on a mess involving tampering with the internal election of the International Brotherhood of Teamsters (IBT), and several years later pulled the pieces back together as U.S. Action. Of course in that situation the local state organizations were separate entities and retained the names as Wisconsin Citizen Action, New York Citizen Action, and the like, and simply killed off the national coordinating body. In this "reorganization," Humpty Dumpty was being broken up so thoroughly that it was doubtful the pieces could have ever been put back together, as the binding glue was devolving to state or local power, and any notion of national power being built for low-and-moderate income families was abandoned.

In reality the defunding crisis triggered an existential crisis for ACORN, which then decided it could only survive on a transactional basis and needed to abandon its transformational agenda and ambitions. In my view it was not the service component vulnerabilities and income sources that killed ACORN, so much as it was the perfect storm at the worst possible time. I have often said that I cannot second guess the management and leadership of ACORN for the decisions they made in the years after I left the organization, because the pressure and isolation must have been extreme, but that in a perverse way perhaps I was lucky, because I would have only known one way which would have been to go down fighting, even if I was the last organizer collecting the last members' dues decades later.

I have always subscribed to the "rule of seven" common in so many labor union constitutions that you cannot kill the union as long as there are seven members left willing to stand and say the union still lives. I simply do not know how any organizer can ever be part of killing any membership organization.

A new and different generation of organizers may think that organizations are not organic, vital organisms that fit their members like a second skin, but something that can be a chameleon and move from place to place searching for sun or shade. They may be right, and they may be wrong, but on the question of services, they can always be severed and rebuilt. On the question of successors, their roots to ACORN are deep and no matter how hard, can never be denied. They will always be ACORN with another name, and years later, that's still how so many of them are known.

For me, as long as I'm still breathing, then I'm still organizing, and ACORN lives, perhaps in the United States, and certainly around the world. Like we used to say in bargaining: you can beat us, but you're going to have to whip us first. And, as long as I'm organizing, you can never tell what might happen and where.

Postscript: Drinking My Own Kool-Aid and Being Prepared

Not only do I not think that embracing service delivery was not the Achilles heel of US ACORN, but even in the wake of ACORN's demise in the United States, but in 2013 and 2014 while acting as "navigators" enrolling lower income families in the first years of the Affordable Care Act, Local 100 United Labor Unions also used the opportunity to attempt to build permanent organizational service capacity by organizing what we called "Citizen Wealth Centers." The Centers being organized embryonically in New Orleans, Houston, Dallas, and Little Rock where Local 100 was recruiting and supervising navigators were designed to provide the full range of access to entitlements and government programs often difficult to access for lower income families. Not surprisingly these centers were based on the same basic model and framework as the old ACORN Service Centers before them. The difference being that the Citizen Wealth Centers were committed to more sustainability on a fairly minimal fee-for-service basis, which we hoped would create ongoing capacity independent of the need for external financing if we could move them to a critical mass, and if not, would at least create valuable cash flow to expand basic operations.

Learning another lesson though, as navigators of a hugely unpopular program with conservatives and the Fox News crowd, we *assumed* that O'Keefe or his wannabes and acolytes would target the centers and the operations of the navigators in an attempt to discredit the new Obama healthcare initiative, even though we were not direct federal grantees but subcontractors in the three state area. We mandated that our staff undergo extensive training, conversations, and role plays to prepare for what we assumed inevitability would be an attack of the scamsters.

Sure enough, Orell Fitzsimmons directing the Houston office of Local 100 raised the warning flag when an applicant was trying to lure the conversation into areas plainly inappropriate for navigation. Then Kenneth Stretcher, Local 100's Dallas office director, immediately reported a conversation in the office with one applicant who proposed that we file an income statement that could not be substantiated to qualify the applicant for a higher subsidy. We refused and he disappeared.

Days later two of our navigators thought they recognized the same fellow coming back in with another cock-and-bull story that was equally incredible and out-of-bounds. One noticed a red light of some sort flashing in one of the fellow's pockets, and asked him what his cellphone was doing. He denied having a cellphone on him. The navigators kept pressing him for what he was doing with his pockets? Was he recording or filming something? He turned to run out of the office at which point our two middle aged African-American organizers physically chased the young man down the hall, out of the building and into the parking lot where he jumped into a car already moving and driven

Local 100 navigators in Houston.

by a confederate, as our erstwhile troops copied down his license plate, Batman and Robin having foiled another dastardly criminal.

No one was surprised when the young man's picture was featured on the news across Texas as having been part of an O'Keefe team that had successfully burned a number of navigator programs on similar scams who were less prepared than we had been. We would have thought after the ACORN experience that everyone would have been "once burned, twice learned," but amazingly that does not yet seem to be the lesson.

Whether seen in the terms of *Citizen Wealth* and ACORN as "maximum eligible participation" or in a term I quite like as a "movement without marches," [176] it is our organizational duty and obligation to ensure our constituency accesses income security in every way practicable as guaranteed by rights and regulations. That being the case, we have to secure out fortresses in order to create the bridges for our members to successfully cross while recognizing that of course this is a struggle too, and we can never engage the battle too lightly.

---

[176] Lisa Levenstein, *A Movement without Marches: African-American Women and the Politics of Poverty in Post-War Philadelphia*, University of North Carolina Press, 2009.

Chapter XXII: *What in the World?*

As ACORN's membership – and the United States itself – became more and more diverse not only racially, but also ethnically with growing immigrant populations, especially Latinos, expanding the population not only in major cities but also in rural enclaves in the South and West, the ACORN membership reflected these dramatic changes as well. Not surprisingly as this happened and leaders from these communities rose to prominence in the organization, casual conversations increasingly became more adamant over time that members wanted to see their great experiences with ACORN in the United States brought to their home countries where "it was *really* needed," as they often said.

These expressions were especially common in the states along the border. Most of the organizing staff in San Diego actually lived in Tijuana, Mexico and before 9/11, commuted daily to work there. The same was true for leaders of Local 100 in Brownsville and Harlingen, Texas who lived in and around Matamoras. Other Latino leaders in Arizona, Colorado, New Mexico, and throughout Texas frequently raised the subject. On the East Coast we used to hear the same thing in Washington Heights in Manhattan, Brooklyn, and Providence, Rhode Island about the desperate need for ACORN to organize in the Dominican Republic. Some of the national officers of ACORN were from the DR, either Santiago or Santo Domingo or Samana on the coast, and never hesitated to raise the question, and do so adamantly.

But as it happened the first serious organizing outside of the United States and the oldest international affiliate of ACORN International developed in Lima, Peru. There were significant pockets of ACORN membership from Peru in Los Angeles and New Jersey, including some leadership, housing counselors, and organizers. Norka Maldanado, the wife of one of ACORN's senior staff, Craig Robbins, was also from Lima, and one of many student activists who had sought asylum in the United States during the time of *sendero* and the Fujimora dictatorship. When Fujimora was finally pushed out of office and free elections brought Alejandro Toledo the presidency in April 2001, there was a demand for a rebuilding of civil society, and many ex-patriots in the United States and their relatives in Peru, wanted ACORN to be a part of the reconstruction. Traveling there for a week of meetings with ACORN organizer Jeff Ordower we went through a whirlwind of all kinds of meetings including sessions at the Palacio with the chief of staff for the new First Lady at 11:00 PM at night. In one of our last meetings before our departure back to the States we met the leadership of the largest of the voluntary associations of *comedores*, and we loved the idea of what they were trying to do. They had been running 1500 kitchens (*comedors*) in barrios throughout the city feeding 150,000 meals per day for only a couple of *soles*, all with volunteers and commodities given by the government. Under Toledo they wanted to expand to health and other issues, and before leaving we promised that we would help.

And, so ACORN International began with two partnerships in Peru, one with the comedores and another with the national union of municipal water workers, FENTAP,

First Meeting of ACORN Peru in Lima.

which had been decimated under Fujimora, but were fighting against the privatization of water in city after city around the country. We honored our commitment to the comedores, bringing the president to Los Angeles for a month of training and experience, much of it with our Peruvian housing counselors and organizers under Amy Schur's direction, and loaned them an organizer for several months, Lisa Donner, from our national staff. The closer we got to the ground, the clearer it became that the leadership changed every year, and they had no capacity to expand their issue basis, but at the same time we had met many people clamoring for ACORN-style organization in the giant mega-slum San Juan Lurigancho. FENTAP wanted to expand the partnership but also wanted us to organize directly, so within a year by 2002, we were organizing ACORN Peru.

The ACORN board approved the expansion, largely conditioned on ACORN International not taking resources away from existing work by ACORN or reallocating staff. Since our aim was to develop organizers in the countries or using our own immigrant organizers, when they were forced to return to their home countries, these were easy conditions to meet.

A banking partnership with Citi, who owned Banamex, one of the largest Mexican banks allowed us to begin organizing in Tijuana, and then later expanded the work to Mexico City in La Neza, often counted as the largest mega-slum in the world.[177] Several trips to the Dominican Republic organized by key ACORN leaders in New York and Providence saw us finally begin organizing in Santiago. In 2004, Judy Duncan's Canadian work visa expired. Judy had been our lead organizer in Seattle for Washington ACORN and had been doing an excellent job, and was game to go with me to Toronto to organize ACORN Canada, which under her leadership has grown in the last dozen years to be the mother ship for ACORN International. Ercilia Sahores was recruited in Buenos Aires by

---

[177] Mike Davis, *Planet of Slums* (2006)

First action in Duoala, Cameroon.

Dine' Butler, my daughter, who also ended up organizing there for a year, and after Ercilia trained for six months in Tampa with ACORN Florida, organized La Boca, Barraca, and the La Matanza with ACORN Argentina, while supporting the rest of our Latin American offices while she worked with me.

ACORN India evolved in 2005 from the work with India FDI Watch Campaign under Reena Desai with our first operations in Mumbai and Delhi where we hired veteran activists and organizers Vinod Shetty and Dharmendra Kumar respectively. Work in Chennai did not stabilize until much later, but over time the organizing in Bengaluru (Bangalore) did so under the energetic and indefatigable Suresh Kadashan. Suresh's patient and persistent work has now created a series of informal "ACORN" unions of hawkers, domestics, and security workers with over 35000 members and growing also in Chennai and Hyderabad. ACORN Kenya was planned initially for 2006, but delayed a year until the post-election violence had subsided sufficiently for us to begin organizing in the Korogocho slum, the oldest and second largest in Nairobi where we hired active community organizers, Sammy Ndirangu and David Musungu, who have been with us now since the beginning of the organization.

In 2010 the impact of the *golopista* coup in Honduras stirred many to seek out Suyapa Amador, our head organizer in Mexico and a native Hondureno, to try to forge partnerships with coffee cooperatives in Marcela and then to build ACORN community organizations in both Tegucigalpa and San Pedro Sula.

ACORN International's mission had been to concentrate its limited resources on organizing mega-slums, but when contacted by activists wanting to organize in Europe and willing to make the sacrifices to build organization, there was no way to refuse. In 2011 Michal Ulver began ACORN in the Czech Republic first, and contacted me after he had already begun using the name and beginning his work. He knew ACORN had been attacked in the US and felt it stood for struggle, organization, and cooperatives, so when

First meeting of ACORN Kenya in Korogocho.

he contacted me through Facebook and we worked our way through Google translate, it became clear to me that he was serious and that this was something more than a "tribute" band in Prague. The train had already left the station, and we needed to catch up and try to help if there was an AKORN there, so we affiliated them and began to support the organization.

Later that year David Tozzo from Rome also reached out through Facebook, which seems in our developing world of work to be a low barrier threshold to cross for contacts. Tozzo had helped a Roman Senator translate a book of letters between French clerical philosopher, Jacques Martian, and Saul Alinsky, and in so doing heard of ACORN and reached out to me. After we had Skyped several times it became clear that he was interested in trying community organizing and there was a campaign in the wings that might be perfect for launching ACORN in Italy in an exciting and potentially self-sufficient basis. The Italian Parliament in the midst of Italy's financial crisis wanted to bring landlord-tenant leasing out of the black market and into the taxable economy. The "bounty" system they had outlined for tenants, was perfect for an ACORN campaign. Having earlier been invited to Sicily several times where we were also close to encouraging organization, we seized the opportunity to begin ACORN Italy in Rome as well.

More recently in 2013, several tenant activists in Edinburgh, Scotland with the Edinburgh Private Tenants Action Group (EPTAG) reached out (yes by Facebook!) to David in Rome asking about his work and about ACORN. He connected them to me and after another Skype conference with Jon Black and Kier Lawson, the primary organizers of EPTAG, and many exchanges of emails over months, I visited with them in June 2013 while also trying to help out in Prague where Michal and colleagues were trying to encourage us to organize in Guinea in West Africa. After several sessions with interested activists there and in Glasgow, and the chance to hit the doors with them on an interesting campaign at Scotmid, a cooperative that also owns flats in Edinburgh with

Fair Grinds Coffeehouse.

some offbeat practices, EPTAG affiliated with ACORN International and direct organizing of ACORN Scotland began in Pilton among private tenants and council housing issues. In a different vein work in Quito, Ecuador in the fall and spring of 2013, led to our engaging Marlene Cortez as an organizer there who has been steadily building ACORN Ecuador in that country. In 2014, the work in Scotland led us to work with a talented team to build ACORN Bristol in England, and opened doors to us throughout the United Kingdom, where there are now branches in Bristol, London, Birmingham, Reading, Sheffield, and Newcastle on Tyne.

In much the same way I heard from Adrien Roux working with Alliance Citoyenne in Grenoble and ReAct, an organizing support outfit specializing in Francophone Africa and elsewhere. Several visits with Adrien and his co-founders in Paris and Grenoble have now led to their affiliation and extensive training regimens in Ottawa and New Orleans, to plan massive expansion of the organization elsewhere in France where we are now organizing in the working class Parisian suburbs, as well as efforts to build a domestic workers union in Morocco. Additionally, our partnership with ReAct has also led to affiliations and growing organizations using the ACORN model in Cameroon, Liberia, and the Ivory Coast with additional prospects emerging in Nigeria as well. Working with the French team reminds me so much of the early mid-70's ACORN staff in Arkansas that words fail me when trying to describe how exciting this partnership is for the future.

We even have affiliates now in the United States including A Community Voice in Louisiana (formerly Louisiana ACORN) and ANEW in Pittsburgh (directed by a former ACORN organizer). More recently we have even partnered with a former Louisiana ACORN organizer to launch a unique, rights-based membership organization in Alaska called MCAN, the Mental Health Consumers' Action Network. You never know what might happen? We have also launched the ACORN Home Savers Campaign to force accountability and demand renegotiated contracts from predatory companies tries to

ACORN India's recycling cooperative truck, Mumbai, India 2014.

expand contract-for-deed land installment purchases in Philadelphia, Pittsburgh, Akron, Youngstown, Detroit, Atlanta, Little Rock, and Memphis.

ACORN International counts as affiliates or partners in a different way several established organizations where we combine on campaigns, strategic and tactical issues, and sometimes training. These organizations include Asian Bridge, headquartered in Seoul, Korea and directed by Na Hywaoo and the Urban Poor Association working in Indonesia and led by Wardah Hafiz from Jakarta.

With this organizational patchwork of planning, partnership, and seized opportunity, ACORN International is distinctly different in form, if not in focus, in its early stages from ACORN in the United States. We now have more than 200,000 dues paying members in no small part because ACORN Canada has 110,000 of those members, and the work is the same, though much is different, as we still search for a model that both fits fully the needs of the developing world and creates more sustainability and immunity from attack than developed with ACORN US.

A critical difference of course is the fact that ACORN International is a federation, rather than one corporation, with each country organization registered separately in the individual countries as appropriate and freedom of action within the country. ACORN International itself is a 501c3 support organization for these affiliates, each of which have a seat on the board of the organization, as well as a vehicle for special projects, campaigns, and work within the United States as well. ACORN International has no direct employees outside of the US, since the work I do as Chief Organizer is not supported financially by the organization except in the same minimal way that we provide subsistence support to our offices in Latin America, India, and Africa, amounting to an average of about of four or five-hundred dollars per month.

In the short fifteen year history of the organization there have already been two critical phases having to do with resources. While I was with "big" ACORN, as we called the US branch, ACORN International always had an affiliate strong enough to seed new projects, even Canada which benefited from front end loans during the startup from ACORN of almost $100,000. Other projects like Walmart, water privatization fights, labor contracts on campaigns in India and Peru, and even banking agreements, trying to pilot access to lower income families on both sides of the border, could deliver sufficient outside resources to support the growth of the organization externally, as dues and other systems developed more slowly.

After I left ACORN in 2008, those organizations underway at that point were going to need to transition to the new reality of being "stand alone" organizations, so any confusion around the world about whether we were an "NGO," which is universally understood to be a deep-pocketed, donor funded, "first" world operation, rather than a membership-based organization of poorer families and workers, needed to be eliminated while we embraced more fully our identity as a membership based, self-sufficient operation. This was a harder transition for some offices than others. India embraced the change as did Kenya, Peru, and Tijuana, though Buenos Aires, Mexico City, and Santiago found it difficult, resulting in changes of staffing there that were precipitated by the annual ACORN International meeting which was held in the Dominican Republic in 2009. The organization that emerged was stronger and more resilient, and more deeply committed to sustainability despite the difficult course before us.

Watching the funding crises enveloping ACORN in the United States in the fall 2009 convinced us even more firmly that relying for expansion or sustainability on external funding sources was a potential death sentence, so the organization did not refuse any gifts, grants, or donations offered, but began to count as a source of pride and accomplishment each year completed without writing a grant proposal. In addition to some much appreciated gifts during this time which helped smooth the transition, the resources came from my consulting jobs with other organizations like the National Immigration Forum and Casa de Maryland and from speaking at colleges and universities about my book, *Citizen Wealth*, as well as a contract helping on the ground research in India and Peru for unions involved in trying to win living wages for Sodexho workers around the world. The list goes on and on!

Frankly, I was willing to start, and even stay, small for as long as it took, as I watched opponents – and friends – of ACORN prepare its tombstone by starving it to death. We had always preached self-sufficiency at ACORN, but as the organization grew larger the budget soared way past the 2:1 ratio we had maintained on internal to external recourses through for the first two decades of the organization's work, so that by the time I left in 2008, the ratio was closer to 2:1 external to internal, inevitably transferring the fate of the organization to outsiders and those who might at any time convert the purse strings to power and a voice over the organization's future. If I had ten or twenty years to lay the foundations for ACORN International over the future, I wanted to leave the work more certain about the permanence of the organization than turned out to be the case with the "too big to fail" ACORN, which had now given up the ghost.

Going "all in," I threw the bulk of my savings (thanks to distribution of the funds from the ACORN Beneficial Association) into the down payment and borrowed the rest, to buy the only 100% fair-trade coffeehouse in New Orleans, Fair Grinds Coffeehouse in the Faubourg St. John area of Mid-City right off Esplanade Avenue and only four blocks from City Park and Bayou St. John. The owners, former ACORN members, were bailing and demoralized after ten years in business, two of them shuttered and rebuilding after Katrina flooding. The purchase was more for the dilapidated building than the business itself because they had lost all of their financial records due to a hard drive failure, but besides the political appeal of being fair-trade, the second floor provided meeting space for groups in the neighborhood and throughout the city, operating almost as a nonprofit and community center by providing common space for groups and others. We didn't know coffee yet, but we thought we knew community, so this gave us hope.

With 11-months of cash register tickets, my brother, brilliantly, was able to estimate the cash flow, expenses, and chances of profitability of the coffeehouse with what thankfully turned out to be a level of accuracy that was proven out within dollars over the first years of our operations. The business was organized as perhaps the first L3C in Louisiana or Low Profit Limited Liability Corporation, which means a social enterprise, and from the first day we took over the property, October 15, 2011, we began taking 5% of gross sales and donating the money directly to ACORN International which in turn was able to over time provide all of the external support for all of the Latin American organizing offices from Fair Grinds. Now after almost six years of operation, having replaced much of the critical equipment, repaired and painted the building and opened up the balcony for seating, we are not making money, but we are making our payments, paying our bills and taxes, and have been voted the best or one of the best coffeehouses in the city ever since we took over by readers of both the *New Orleans Times-Picayune* and the weekly *Gambit*. Taking another leap we opened Fair Grinds Coffeehouse on St. Claude on April Fools' Day, 2015, which may say it all, but located in our building at Elysian Fields and St. Claude with our offices and developing radio station and other operations, seemed to make sense.

With Fair Grinds and our customers as a ready market, we just acquired the first part of a one-half acre set of lots in the Lower Ninth Ward of New Orleans for the ACORN Farm, which is providing locally grown, organic, permaculture produce as well. Fingers crossed for the future here as we look for more opportunities to create sustainable businesses that can support ACORN International and its growth in various countries. ACORN International also has a mobile 20,000 per month capacity bio-diesel rig half donated from friends and supporters in 2012 and half purchased, and now located in our building in New Orleans. Now, if we can figure out how to make fuel from coffee grounds, rather than just cooking grease, we're set!

Do I recommend the social enterprise strategy? The jury is still out. There is a learning curve, and these are real dollars and real debts, so there is no way to pretend this is an enterprise that can succeed if run out of your back pocket. As we have found in all of our operations of every kind, good, solid, vision-committed management is essential and in our case in a combination of luck, fate, and looking we found Zee Thornton, a veteran of the back of the house skill sets, who was looking to link those skills to the kind of vision we articulated while making it work with Alabama brilliance and personality. . . OK, maybe it was fate, but my point remains that without finding and developing good managers and staff none of this works. Zee and now, Chaco Rathke as manager, have also built a team that collectively believes in what we are doing. We don't do latte art, but the downside might be that sometimes our own staff's volunteer work makes it difficult for us to schedule their real work. There are worse problems. There are no "get rich quick" schemes so it is still hard work.

Luck also counts. Our most successful social enterprise has been the continued publication and performance of *Social Policy,* the 47 year old quarterly we have managed for fifteen years or so. We do a good job, but the business model was established back in the halcyon days when university libraries routinely subscribed to such intellectual and scholarly publications. We have nurtured that business model assiduously, but cannot claim to have invented it, nor can we predict how long it might last, but we cannot understate how important the surplus revenue produced by the journal has provided a lifeline to our sustainability that would be impossible to reinvent today. And, that does not even count the value that *Social Policy* adds to all of work.

There are many projects in many of our country affiliates. ACORN Canada has continued the ACORN Service Center traditions and been hugely successful in this area. AKORN Czech has a combination art gallery and coffeehouse that they are now running to try and muster more resources for their organizing. ACORN Mexico is selling fair-trade Honduran coffee in Mexico City. ACORN Honduras is trying to set up a coffeehouse operation in both cities so that Hondurans can finally taste some of the great, fair-trade coffee grown there, but usually unavailable on the domestic market. ACORN Peru is even trying to figure out a way to market wine that is grown in Chincha, where a new chapter has organized. Our recycling cooperative in the Dharavi community of Mumbai has added a small pickup truck and is making a difference to some of our members on a small scale. We think there is a future in recycling. Some of this may even work, though all of these projects are embryonic now. There is vision and there is energy, so something will come together.

Building a New Resource Model

The model we are trying to develop with some difficulty starts with the recognition that members understand the necessity of paying dues to support their own organization to then moves to the logical next step, which is that members – in fact our constituency everywhere – expect to pay at least something to support any and all services and projects that they see as beneficial.

In ACORN United States we frequently saw people participating in our tax and benefits program volunteer to pay something for the assistance they were receiving. Working with Action United (formerly Pennsylvania ACORN) on this concept as well as ACORN Canada piloting this program in Ottawa with the support of Revenue Canada (the Canadian IRS), even charging $25 or $50 was no impediment. H&R Block taught us that the sweet sauce of their business was that every year 70% or more of their customers would return from the previous year, because they saw Block as a trusted provider. The ACORN Service Center tax preparation programs were seeing much the same percentages, if not higher, from year to year. In the first trial year in Philadelphia asking people to donate $25 or more to support the service, more than $10,000 was raised according to Craig Robbins, then the ACTION United Executive Director. Ottawa and

BC ACORN doubled that figure in 2016. The simple math would have indicated that if ACORN had done 50,000 returns with a $25 donation, the organization would have raised $1,250,000, quickly exceeding the amount of monies that we were being granted to provide the service for free.

Working with former ACORN organizer Teresa Castro in Phoenix, Arizona in 2009-2010, through the Advocates & Action program we wanted to see if we could develop a foreclosure counseling – and action – program to push back on the home foreclosures in Maricopa County that were among the highest in the country. Private services were charging $1500 - $2000 often for little or nothing in terms of relief assistance. We first tried a fee of $500 and then $750 explaining the program and how it would work. Within a year we were grossing $10,000 per month without a dime of outside support. In some ways the program was both too successful and not successful enough. We had no problem in getting people to work with us and pay the money over several months' time, but we had not anticipated the total failure that the Obama foreclosure modification program would be under the direction of the banks themselves. For us that meant that the counselors, and Teresa, were quickly overwhelmed because the case load grew geometrically faster than modifications were achieved, welding some families to us for years when we had estimated we could resolve the cases in six months. We learned many lessons and confirmed our initial hunches about our folks willingness to pay for needed services while taking direct action at the same time, but as the years went by, we could not sustain the project.

In many ways this was an old lesson relearned, rather than a new lesson first taught. The experience with welfare rights special needs checks, ACORN's early members steadfast monthly dues payments made by hand, union members going deeper to pay for arbitrations or job actions, and neighborhood organizations running dinners, bake sales, and raffles to pay for the costs of lawyers and lawsuits to stop expressway construction, should have made the lessons indelible, but the lessons were not always matched with the discipline necessary to implement a total cultural shift in the way the organization worked and was resourced. It was easy to suddenly remember that initially the housing counseling operation was designed to be self-sufficient and financed by the a piece of the payments of closing costs when a house was sold to a new family as well as developer's fees on new projects, which might have been sufficient to save some parts of the counseling operation if there had still been internal income, just as the tax preparation could have been easily saved with or without access to the e-filing system of the IRS based on member loyalty. If as my old Latin teacher had constantly reminded us, "necessity is the mother of invention," ACORN International had to either have a plan or not survive, and the painful picture of big ACORN on its knees was a constant reminder that another way must be possible.

ACORN Italy has been the most self-sufficient operation on our new model thanks to the uniqueness of the initial campaign waged by the organization. In 2011 the Italian Parliament served notice on the country's landlords that they had until June 1st to register their properties on the tax rolls. If they had not done so, then the penalties were severe, and included a form of incentive system or bounty payment for tenants who assisted the state in putting their landlord's property on the rolls. There were some wrinkles. Tenants living in the landlord's personal home were not eligible for a bounty. Tenants moving from the black market into the formal tenancy also likely owed a small tax as well that they would have been required to pay, too. In fact the mutuality of the scam had been part of what had nurtured the informal system. Landlords and tenants would agree on a "wink and a nod" to help each other game the system with the landlords claiming a small break on the rent for the tenant in exchange for their silence.

The new law changed the odds. If a tenant was able to prove that the landlord's property was unregistered and bring it forward to the assessor's attention, the reward for the tenant was normally a reduction of 85-90% of their rent for the term of an Italian lease. An Italian lease runs for four (4) years with a four (4) year option to renew, so effectively the tenant would see a reduction in their rent for up to eight (8) years. If for example a tenant was paying 1000 Euros in rent and successfully navigated the process, then their rent might only be 100 Euros per month for eight (8) years saving them 86400 Euros over the term of their lease.

ACORN Italy devised several simple forms and a straightforward process so a tenant could first determine if their landlords' property was already registered and, if they were uncertain, then trigger the registration process. Additionally, they arranged for other legal and organizational assistance if the tenant was challenged in court by the landlord protesting the procedure in any way. ACORN then needed to do the organizing and outreach to find families that were in this situation and wanted to pursue the actions necessary to win such a significant reduction in their rent.

Where ACORN Italy's sustainability came into play is that ACORN adjusted the dues system to monetize the victory sufficiently to also provide an income stream to support the campaign work, staff, and other community organizing. For ACORN to join with the tenant in this fight, provide them the assistance, forms, and potentially legal support, the tenant not only agreed to pay the basic membership dues of ten euros per month by

Marshalling Support for ACORN Italy's Tenant Bounty Campaign in the Italian Senate in Rome (David Tozzo) to right of picture.

Chapter XXII: What in the World?

direct bank transfer to the organization's account, but to also commit to pay ACORN ten-percent (10%) of the savings achieved that they won for the life of the lease. In the earlier example that would mean that if the savings were 900 euros per month, the victorious tenant would be paying ACORN 90 Euros per month as supplemental dues. The other alternative ACORN Italy offered is a one-time upfront payment to the organization to settle the campaign obligation which would be the equivalent of one year's payment or in the example given above the one-time payment would be 1080 euros. ACORN Italy began the campaign in the fall of 2011 and by summer of 2012 the organization was already completely self-sufficient based on the cash flow of dues generated by tenants joining together and winning these rent reductions not only in Rome, but hearing and reading notices of our work in the press, contacting ACORN to extend the campaign in cities throughout Italy.[178] The organizing math is straightforward and with focus the organization could use this campaign vehicle to spread throughout the country.

Certainly the Italian situation is unique and not necessarily replicable, though we are not sure exactly how rare this might be. In Korea (ROK) there is a bounty system as an incentive to whistleblowers identifying waste, which might be ideal for a community organization firmly rooted on the ground. The United States has paid over $300 million in 2013 to whistleblowers where trials led to convictions. Ralph Nader financed his early work on such efforts. Just saying, there might be a system, if we could develop it and monetize it, and it aligns and privileges our core work and skills.

ACORN Scotland's private tenants were quickly able to identify two similar, though smaller, programs that could help finance their work through winning. The rental deposits by Scottish law are supposed to be collected and handed over to a third-party for safekeeping to assure that tenants satisfactorily completely their leases actually get the money back and that landlords play fair with the requirements. In point of fact many landlords do not bother and there is little state supervision of the large number of private landlords. The law though does allow a tenant to collect two-and-one-half times the deposit from the landlord if they can prove that the landlord did not transfer the deposit monies to a third party. Landlords are fighting ACORN Scotland more aggressively on this measure because they have gotten away with it for so long, and we are trying to work around the costs of having to go to court to collect, but some are winning, and once again ACORN Scotland is collecting a percentage of the deposit refund to cover the cost of the work. A "minimum standards" type campaign is also being done with tenants renting from Scotmid, a large cooperative active in retail business, and similar companies who have also been violating Scottish law by adding additional charges to payments required of a tenant that are not part of the lease for cleaning, keys, and so forth. Straight refunds are due all tenants facing ancillary charges so that is one of the early campaigns of the organization. Such systems do not exist in most of the countries where ACORN

---

[178] Before any reader thinks, darned that sounds easy, think twice. Landlords had their day in 2013 and won a court decision on a technicality to end the program. ACORN Italy spent months into 2014 getting the Senate to correct the language error, saving the program, but the printed version overlooked the change, once again causing chaos. Finally we have won an agreement to redline all tenants benefiting from the program and are now seeking to make the corrected language permanent. Ongoing court and legislative challenges continue to bedevil the program as I write, so the final outcome of this campaign remains in doubt.

organizes internationally, but the general point and practice is inescapable: where we can monetize services or victories we must do so in order to be sustainable and resource the organization.

ACORN continues to attempt to apply the lessons we learned through decades of organizational campaigns in the United States that winning delivered huge benefits to our members and constituency, but also needed to create additional capacity for ACORN itself to continue to fight and win. It was not enough for us to come to an agreement to end discrimination in home lending for our members, we needed to also see the agreements increase our capacity to put our members in the homes and continue to enforce the agreements. When we prevailed with HSBC or the tax preparers in stopping predatory lending practices, as part of those agreements we needed to be able to guarantee organizational capacity to do our outreach (i.e. organizing) and enforce our agreements. Being able to grow and fight another day is not cooptation in agreements won and enforced in struggle.

Local Issues and International Campaigns

The work of ACORN International country to country is obviously as varied as the countries, communities, and cultures where we work.

In many of mega-slums like La Matanza, San Juan de Lurigancho, Korogocho, Nezahualcóyotl, Dharavi, and even smaller informal settlements like Colonias Ramon Amador in Tegucigalpa or the suburbs around San Pedro Sula the issues are fundamental and basic. Frequently access to potable water tops the list. Roads are unpaved and impassable. Sewage runs in rivulets or small canals along the same byways and footpaths. Often these informal settlements are squatter communities, so land title is a huge issue. Schools are wanted or the ability to attend school. Parks or any green spaces are luxuries.

In La Matanza, which in English means The Massacre, named after a long ago battle in the Buenos Aires province, the fight for many of our groups there is for the land title. Many of our families are squatting on abandoned factory sites since the Crisis in 2001 in Argentina. Though the law says that continuous occupancy for eight (8) years should trigger ownership, starting the clock on that timetable and winning basic services in the meantime from the area government is the subject of constant actions. We have gotten closer to victory in recent years, but have a way to go. Land title and the years involved in achieving such recognition have also quickly emerged as the central issues in the southern barrios of Quito, when we were organizing ACORN Ecuador.

In the city of Buenos Aires we organized *mantillas* and throughout the community of La Boca, known to all tourists from around the world for the couple of blocks of bars, tango displays, and differently colored barge boards salvaged for housing by the nearby port workers, but out of the eyes of the tourists we organized residents who were trying to hold on to their housing rather than become part of the gentrifying obsequiousness designed by city planners. In Barreca, another working community next to La Boca, also near the river, we organized around standard urban community issues and members organized their own children's recreation center on a daily basis in space provided by the Uruguayan Club.

In Lima in addition to organizing against privatization of water in communities around the country, we have organized a number of community groups in San Juan Lurigancho over the last ten years. Visiting in 2011 with ACORN International leadership and organizers from around the globe, it was impressive to walk with Orfa Camacho, our head organizer, and local leaders and see the improvements we have won. Potable water for one, but also a school, park, and community center were built in recent years. Roads are paved in many areas. Perhaps most dramatic were the stairways in bright yellow now built of concrete up to the far reaches of where families are still squatting in makeshift housing all over the dry hills of SJL. Many of these victories were won through the ability of the organization to leverage its membership base in one of the last elections where there had been promises of San Juan Lurigancho becoming a separate province and retaining its tax dollars accordingly, and when that promise was not delivered, actions brought these improvements as concessions to our demands. Other organizing won protections and improvements in giant, sprawling apartment complex originally designed for teachers and civil services, but when privatized threatened basic standards and agreements. More recently we have even begun organizing outside of Lima several hours away in the city of Chincha assisting residents in winning services as part of the long extended recovery from an earthquake there now years ago.

In Korogocho, in Nairobi the issues are endless, but the major campaign that has caught the most fire and gained the most traction was the "bursary" campaign. The Kenyan Parliament has enacted legislation that provides money for school fees for post-primary school attendance for poor communities like Korogocho. Unfortunately whether through incompetence, inattention, or corruption, children were not receiving the bursary fees and in fact they were often being diverted to more middle income or better connected throughout Nairobi. Through direct actions, countless meetings, and mass deliveries of application forms throughout the community, ACORN Kenya has been able

Organizing meeting of squatters in La Matanza, Buenos Aires 2011.

Stairs in SJL won by ACORN Peru.

to win significant transfers of bursary funds to our members and children throughout the community. Not enough certainly, since there are only a couple of facilities approaching "high" schools to service almost a half-million people living there. Nonetheless, hundreds of children are now attending what is available in schools there, thanks to ACORN's victory.

Tijuana and Mexico City have been the homes of the *rapidos acciones* or quick hits, especially in Tijuana to force neighborhood cleanups in the city. In the Neza the issue in this mega-slum of 3.5 million people is still the lack of potable water and adequate sewage treatment and disposal. Members of ACORN Mexico are only too willing to show private water bills that add up to 25 to 30% of their income so that they have clean drinking water. Walking into many of their houses means sidestepping and making a way through a maze of plastic barrels and rubber tubing meant to catch whatever rainwater might come their way or to catch and reuse gray water for other purposes. Any extended visit to Nezahualcóyotl means going by the rivers of pollution and the makeshift drying pools that have eddying up along bridges and massive drainage pipes foaming with raw sewage being dumped into the stream. We have won the extension of lines to provide water to several hundred thousand, partially based once again on leverage during the elections as various parties like the PRI or PRD finally address desperate needs before each 6-year Presidential campaign concludes, but still there are members waving their letters, sometimes more than fifteen years old, promising water that still has not been delivered.

In Honduras the politicization of the communities of lower and working income families both in urban and rural communities due to the *golopista* coup and displacement of an elected president, seen by many as populist and a friend to common people, polarized the country, and, as I mentioned earlier, led to intense interest in our organizing there. Membership has grown rapidly since 2010, particularly around the industrial city of San Pedro Sula and Cholomo, the city of *maquilas* (factories), as they style themselves.

Work in Honduras.

Homes and livelihoods are central issues, along with any community services and potable water.

In 2013, we visited land that many of our members were squatting and were trying to farm for bananas and other crops for sale in the marketplaces of San Pedro Sula. Others were desperate to figure out a way around local marketplaces to wrest better prices through the complex of exported goods, way past the experience or ability of ACORN International. Walking in one of our communities we were shown a piece of paved street on an impossibly steep angle that many of our members and neighbors had built themselves because with such an inactive city administration, the road was frequently impassable making work and school impossible as well.

In Tegucigalpa where we eventually won potable water in Colonias Ramon Amador, walking to the far end of the dirt roads crisscrossing the community alongside a stream of sewage cascading over the hillside, we stood for some minutes watching the airplanes land below at the modern airport of the national capitol with a giant Telefonica cell antenna towering on our flank. Much of our organizing seeks to exploit the contradictions that are ubiquitous in these communities.

More recently as international attention has been focused on the human rights drama of Central American refugees trying to cross the border into the United States fleeing from gang violence, drug trafficking, and economic desperation to reunite with family members, ACORN Honduras organized actions at the US Embassy in Tegucigalpa and the First Lady's office in San Pedro Sula demanding more security. Some of the ACORN members were also mothers who had been forced to raise thousands ($3-5000) to send their children to the border, where they were now held in confinement in the US awaiting hearings and likely deportation. The First Lady agreed to provide the resources to allow ACORN members to send the paperwork to the US to retrieve their children.

In India, along with our ongoing India FDI Watch Campaign around multi-brand retail, our work takes on additional levels of complexity and uniqueness. In Dharavi, which many claim to be one of Asia's largest slums and the scene of the popular movie, *Slumdog Millionaire,* our community base has been part of the coalition fighting to prevent the displacement of the million or so residents of the community. The issue in Mumbai that targets Dharavi directly is the fact that its acreage is near downtown and in the last of the mangrove swamps with expensive high-rise apartment blocks, hotels, and office buildings looming all around it. The best we have been able to win along with many others is a delay in the displacement that now seems inevitable. The current agreement is that over a number of years there will be a gradual transfer of residents to other locations, thought to be more stable than this squatted area where some families have now lived – and worked – for decades. The challenge is that Dharavi is more than a place to live, it is where huge numbers of workers make their living in recycling, small manufacturing, furniture making, textile production, dying, and a host of other occupations. The diversity and sustainability of the community has led some outside observers, even the United Kingdom's Prince Charles, to hold the community up as a model of sustainability. People live where they work, and work where they live. Any relocation to 200 meter housing units will certainly not recreate the workspaces and some businesses, like recycling are already co-locating and acquiring additional sites scores of kilometers away on the outskirts of this huge metropolis.

ACORN International in India is more involved in organizing informal worker unions and associations than in any other country, though elements of each part of our work are in every country where we are active. With our Dharavi Project we have become known nationally in India and internationally to some degree for our wastepickers association which also showcases Dharavi Rocks, a popular and unique band of young recyclers using found items (a garbage, not garage, band!) as percussion instruments in a sort of waste can drum circle, a soccer team for various ages at the Jesuit College field nearby, English and other night classes, and a host of other projects. We have a partnership with the Blue Frog, the premier Mumbai jazz club, which has its visiting musicians come by and do concerts or workshops for our members. We do an Eco-Fair annually where our recyclers train school children and others in waste handling techniques.[179]

The heart of the organizing though is the workers' association and increasing the income of our members. We maintain a sorting center and multi-purpose sheds in Dharavi, and have worked out exclusive agreements with the prestigious American School and many others for their cardboard, plastic, and other saleable waste. Recently we bought a pickup to implement a route system and integrate a new 20-acre college that has agreed to provide us all of their recyclables. We have not reached sufficient scale to guarantee livelihood to more than a certain number of the hundreds of thousands of wastepickers, but through direct organizing and through projects of this kind, we are inching forward, as well as achieving more sustainability for the organization itself. Our primary objective

---

[179] Campana, Joseph, *Dharavi: The City Within,* (2012)

is to win for wasterpickers a labor code similar to what has been achieved by mathadi workers, auto rickshaw drivers, and others.[180]

Similarly in Bengaluru we have successfully registered ACORN as a union under the laws of the state of Karnataka in order to be able to represent hawkers and street sellers and domestic workers, and are in the process of registering a union for food sellers and security workers as well. ACORN International believes that we are a natural organization for informal workers, combining our work in the community with our work in workplaces that draw their support and sustenance from those same communities. Furthermore, both constituencies are the same united not only in poverty, but also the fact that a sizable number are internal immigrants from other Indian states, especially Bihar, or are unregistered immigrants from Bangladesh, and not infrequently are Muslim, rather than Hindu. The slums in Bengaluru are smaller and more diffuse than we have found in Delhi and Mumbai, often no more than a couple of hundred families and ACORN India has organized them around livelihood, sanitation, education, and other issues of basic necessities.

Winning the registrations has seen our union membership soar to more than 35,000 members. The ACORN union has also expanded to other cities in Karnataka seeking the level of density that would allow us to be certified as a statewide union there. We have also begun the process of organizing and registering in Chennai as well.

One common issue in all of our areas is often the problem of registration and establishing identify sufficient to receive a "ration" card from the government for a certain level of foodstuffs and cooking fuel. Despite all of the media's touting of internet breakthroughs in trying to devise a biometric identify card for the more than one-billion Indians, in reality current registrations go back to your home village for both voting in the world's so-called "largest democracy" and for the ration cards, ignoring the huge urban migration that has decimated many villages except for special holidays and annual visits, although this is also the only place they would be allowed to vote. As ACORN's organizers often tell me there is no longer vote stuffing as a rule and the rush to steal ballot boxes that were common 15 to 20 years ago has largely disappeared. Furthermore, there is such a thing in India as a "registered slum," meaning usually that the slum is more formal and old enough that the address works for registration for ration cards, there are schools, and water may be delivered by tanker trucks, but unregistered and more informal is out of luck on all of these counts. Part of the organizing advantage of ACORN membership cards and why they are so eagerly sought is that they provide a form of identity often sufficient enough to vote and obtain a card, and almost invariably enough to get the police to back off from their constant harassment of our waste pickers in the streets. Our union membership cards in Karnataka serve the same purpose.

Similarly in Delhi we have also organized associations of auto rickshaw drivers, domestic workers, and waste pickers, largely in East Delhi and Old Delhi where we have concentrated our organizing. We have more than 2000 members in our workers unions in the capital city. Working with our groups and informal worker associations in the ITO (Indian Tax Office) community we were caught up in a campaign to try and stop

---

[180] Rathke, Wade, "The Maharashtra Model: Organizing Informal Workers by Combining Power, Protection, and Politics," Social Policy, v. 41 #1 (2011).

ACORN Canada Convention Ottawa 2017.

some of the displacements there in the run-up to the 2010 fiasco when India hosted the Commonwealth Games, the old British Empire's answer to the Olympics. Our auto rickshaw drivers were banned from driving during the period of the games, therefore losing income and displacements were extreme for many families. We were too late to the fight to impact the situation more than marginally, and our effort to get any international attention to the issue failed to get traction. The Delhi Municipal Corporation (DMC) did allow us to run a night-shelter for men in the ITO area, initially just for the winter, but subsequently year-round and on a continuing basis. Additionally, for years we managed three or four other centers, all for men and migrant workers in Old Delhi, including one in a multi-story building with full services, and after a short break, we now continue to manage four centers.

ACORN Canada is an example of the biological phenomena common in island biodiversity studies where a plant can no longer grow in its native soil but crops up in a different environment and thrives, and in that sense with ACORN in the United States inactive, Canada is where we see ACORN as it was and might still be. ACORN has had big local victories, like the passage of the first living wage bylaw in the country in New Westminster, and forcing what the City of Toronto verifies as hundreds of millions of improvements throughout Toronto in low-and-moderate income apartment complexes as well as landlord-licensing. The first national campaign won major reforms in a number of provinces on the issues of payday lending both stopping some predatory practices, limiting interest levels and frequency of loans, and increasing disclosures. Now with more than 110,000 members, offices in Ottawa, Toronto, the Vancouver area, Hamilton, and the Maritimes with Montreal on the drawing board, four national conventions under its belt, and a seasoned and stable set of head and lead organizers, ACORN Canada, celebrating its fourteenth anniversary, has made a huge leap forward for low-and-moderate income families throughout the country, and the best is clearly yet to come.

The most rapid growth in ACORN in recent years though has been in Europe, beginning in England and now moving rapidly in France. Our growth in various cities in England was triggered by our ability to repurpose so-called community organizers who were part of former Prime Minister Cameron's "Big Society" program. Extending their service and training them in ACORN model organizing techniques, membership-based community organizations were built in London, Reading, Bristol, Newcastle, and Sheffield. The dominant issues have involved winning tenant rights, especially the emerging majority of private tenants with their landlords with the largest victories being approval of a "letting charter of rights" and blocking a council tax in Bristol.

In France after joint training in New Orleans and Ottawa, more than a half-dozen membership-based community organizations have been built in Grenoble with several more springing up in working class and immigrant suburbs of Paris like Aubervilliers and Gennvilliers and expansion plans now in Lyon and elsewhere in the Alps region. Basic victories have been won in public housing as well as surrounding communities on organizing issues from parking areas to security and repairs.

Obviously, there are common ingredients and themes to all of ACORN International's work in each of the countries: local community and worker membership, associations, strong campaigns at various jurisdictional levels on issues both basic and sophisticated, direct actions, use of organizational and political leverage, and persistence. Language, culture, and laws may be different, but the organization is putting people in motion in ways that are working.

Major Campaigns

In recent years ACORN International has increasingly been trying to knit together some common threads that run throughout all of our countries and doing so through campaigns, particularly around remittances, internet access, and tenants.

The Remittance Justice Campaign began in 2010 with the release of our research reports, *The High Cost of Remittances* and *Past Time for Remittance Justice*.[181] Working with our "volunteer army" many of whom were community worker students at George Brown College in Toronto or attending the University of Ottawa, we were able to determine that the average total cost for immigrant families and migrant workers in Canada to remit or transfer money to families, friends and their communities in their home countries was generally about 22% for an average $100 transfer. The G-8 representing the world's largest industrialized economies and the World Bank were claiming the costs were 10%, not necessarily counting the cost of exchange rates and pickup costs for the receiver of the funds. They had called for total costs to be lowered to 5% by 2014. Despite our disagreements about their research and the current state of affairs, we also adopted the 5% goal for total costs of remittances because it would free up almost $40 billion dollars in additional funds to developing countries, even using their figures.

Unfortunately the G-8 and World Bank in standard operating neo-liberalism procedure are claiming that the 5% cap can be reached solely through competition, and

---

[181] Available at *www.acorninternational.org*

citing the lowered costs of transfers between the United States and Mexico as evidence that this is possible. Certainly there has been progress and the two main money transfer organizations (MTOs),Western Union and MoneyGram have competed aggressively against each other and many other players have joined the fray reducing costs significantly compared to ten or twenty years ago. Unfortunately, Mexico is the exception, and not a very good one according to our members with Mexico ACORN and a study done there in cooperation with students at the Clinton School of Public Service affiliated with the University of Arkansas.

The campaign is caught in the limbo-land of international banking where regulations exist in some ways at the national and state or provincial level, but even the World Bank is careful to stress that they are not empowered to give any instructions to individual national banking regulators or national systems like the Federal Reserve or Bank of Canada.[182] Consequently the Remittance Justice Campaign found some positive feedback initially from the Netherlands and banking committees in the United Kingdom, but few other responses other than simple courteous replies or no response at all. In 2012 and again in 2013, Jagmeet Singh introduced a member's bill in the Ontario provincial parliament which in a rare move forced both Western Union and MoneyGram to jointly hire lobbyists for fear of the bill's passage. Similar bills are being prepared in British Columbia and elsewhere. There is also legislative interest and bills moving forward in Honduras, Mexico, and Italy, though the outcome of any of these measures are at best speculative. Initial direct discussions with Western Union were fruitless. They were willing to suggest a contribution, but not to negotiate a less predatory fee structure since they were making billions. MoneyGram hid in their shadow.

Research and action in 2013 in conjunction with social work students at the Georgia State University in Atlanta produced similar evidence of price spreads in the United States. The newly established Consumer Financial Protection Bureau has begun to mention remittances as an area of interest, which we support, but is largely limiting itself to disclosures, which we have found make only a marginal difference in company behavior, and since families are trapped often with little or no choices in some remittance channels, they pay the piper. The *hawala* system, used more informally in India and the Middle East, is working with rates between 0.5 and 1.5% of transactions though it is illegal in many countries, being an informal system. We are tracking down articles in Minnesota that seem to establish a hawala-style system as legal in that state. Attempts to interest Congressman Keith Ellison from Minnesota were in vain, since his staff indicated that they had never considered the problem of costs, only access, particularly for Somalia immigrants in the Congressman's district.

The campaign is worth the work, given the billions at stake for developing countries and the fact that these direct family to family, family to friends, and family to community contributions could fill and surpass the existing gaps and the widespread disinterest and

---

[182] The World Bank was so worried about this issue that after Avaaz.org in circulating a petition in support our campaign included a link to our report, *"The High Cost of Remittances,"* wrote several letters of protest and clarification that they were simply supporting the G-8 without an independent position.

ACORN Canada action on internet.

reduced payments from developed countries, whether the excuses be the countries own finances or the fact that many immigrant sending countries are, sadly, not "strategic."

Internet Access

In the classic way that an issue sometimes starts from small personal problems and then transforms itself to the largest political forums, we first saw an announcement the fall of 2011 in the *New York Times* by the Chair of the Federal Communications Commission (FCC) of the US, touting the great voluntary program that Comcast had agreed to undertake to extend internet access to the poor as a condition to their purchase of NBC/Universal. Supposedly the program would cost lower income families, whose children were eligible for free school lunches or Head Start, a bit less than $10.00 per month for access and qualify them for a Dell computer for only a $150. Since Comcast was the carrier for a number of cities where Local 100 members lived including Houston, Shreveport, and Little Rock, the program seemed a great opportunity for us to move our members, many of them who even worked at Head Start, so we were anxious to see how to enroll our members so that they could participate. Furthermore, the FCC's chair heralded that two other companies, Cox Cable and Times-Warner, had agreed to implement similar programs – voluntarily – in the spring of 2012.

This sounded great! Our first response was, "Where do we sign people up?" Well, that's when the problems began. Early calls in Houston found more than a dozen Comcast offices there, but only one that would allow enrollment for Internet Essentials as they called the program. Calling the various phone numbers associated with the program produced an array of company offerings at various costs with most Comcast responders having being clueless about the program. Huh? We started finding that much of the program was being run by the governmental relations staff. Public officials and politicians were wined and dined by the company, but clearly there was no real concern for outreach to the actual poor who might benefit. In fact the website claimed a lot of so-called partners, but not much in terms of real detail for accessing the program. They claimed to have printed three million fancy brochures and seemed to be trying to get the school systems to do their enrollment for them. If this had not been so clearly part of the written FCC order, we would have thought we were imaging the entire program.

We enlisted our friends and allies with ACTION United in Philadelphia, where Comcast was headquartered, and Pittsburgh to see if they had better luck, so that we could access the program. If anything the Comcast performance was even worse there! From a simple beginning of trying to sign up members to take advantage of a program that almost sounded too good to be true, we found we were in the midst of a campaign to try and force the company to tell the truth and deliver some good.

Calls and complaints to the FCC led nowhere. Letters to the FCC elicited a reply about whether or not it would be all right for them to turn over the complaints to Comcast, which locked us into a vicious circle. Requests for meetings with Comcast in our Shreveport, Houston, and Little Rock brought down teams of governmental relations people from the company, but no real results and precious little information. Initially the company did not want to supply results in terms of the number of people who had successfully enrolled in the program, though finally we were able to get them to provide the numbers, and then we could see why they were so deeply opposed to any transparency or accountability. In huge markets like Philadelphia they had hardly 700 in the program of the hundreds of thousands who could have applied even by the somewhat narrow company-imposed guidelines for eligibility. In the Houston area where even more could enroll they had perhaps 2000. Everywhere the results were abysmal. Discussions with school districts drew complaints and scratching heads since they had no real responsibility or resources for doing the outreach and follow-up either. A meeting we were able to force in Philadelphia when ACTION United threatened to disrupt a banquet honoring David Cohen, the Executive Vice President of the company, ended in him essentially accusing us of trying to shakedown the company rather than responding to the miserable performance by Comcast.

Finally in reading through the FCC website looking for possible "handles" to give us leverage on the campaign, the best we could find was the ability to file complaints under the "truth in advertising" provision. To move the issue we then began assisting our members in all of our cities to fill out FCC complaint forms that we created that would detail their journey in trying to penetrate Internet Essentials, including the numerous times they were told no such program existed or that the lowest package available was three and four times more expensive than the $10.00 per program that was agreed to by the company and the FCC. We had problems enlisting other organizations, because there were no resources for outreach and so many of them were only operating on a transactional basis on campaigns, rather than being able to resource membership-based campaigns seeking simple justice or transformation.

Nonetheless, Local 100, ACORN, and Action United filed scores of complaints with the FCC as well as generating some letters to them from Congressional representatives and some political officials, and as it developed despite their silence, it made a difference. In the late spring of 2012, the FCC fined Comcast $850,000 for "up selling" on the program and added another year (2015) to the requirement that Comcast continue the program. The fine was hardly a wrist slap for a company the size of Comcast, but at least we had established ourselves in the campaign. Unfortunately retracing our steps in the fall of 2012, we found only marginal differences in the program in our cities and access was still a continual struggle.

The other companies, Cox and Times-Warner that had volunteered to deliver an equivalent program were as disappointing, perhaps worse, since the FCC had gotten them on board solely through moral suasion it seemed. Cox was the dominant provider in south Louisiana in Lafayette, Baton Rouge, and New Orleans, and we enlisted our affiliate, A Community Voice, formerly Louisiana ACORN, to join with us there. Times-Warner was the company in Dallas, where Local 100 had an office, staff and membership, so they were high on our list as well. Unfortunately, no programs developed by the original announcement for spring 2012, and no details on the plans – or interest in discussing them – were forthcoming from either company. Cox in the fall of 2012 mustered a small offering in some New Orleans schools, but looked at it more as a one-day special of sorts, so that by 2013, the program had already shutdown.

Dealing with monopoly enterprises[183] and weak, neoliberal regulatory agencies was proving a huge obstacle for the campaign in the United States, but we were "in it to win it," so undaunted, given the critical equity and opportunity issues for lower income families unable to access the internet regularly. In speaking to our brothers and sisters with ACORN Canada we also found the same monopoly conditions in that country with Rogers, Bell Canada, and Telus being the big-three.

With the ACORN Canada convention scheduled for June 2013, in the Spring, the officers of ACORN Canada began sending letters to the companies, starting with Rogers as the largest, asking for a meeting to discuss their programs, or lack of them, for internet access to the poor. Somewhat to our surprise representatives from Rogers replied almost immediately and agreed to a multiple party phone conference to initiate serious conversations with ACORN. We had two proposals. The first was that the company needed to at least have a $10 program equivalent to the Internet Essentials offering. Secondly we wanted them to also have a "lifeline" telephone plan for lower income families similar to what the FCC had been managing in different ways for years that did not exist yet in Canada.

To our pleasant surprise Rogers responded positively to the $10 program request. They indicated that they had been "thinking" about doing something, and in many ways it seemed almost as if they had been waiting for us to knock on their door or perhaps they had been hiding there waiting for us. They claimed a lack of familiarity with the lifeline phone demand, but committed that they would be back to us shortly with a positive proposal on the low cost access plan. While waiting for their reply we switched primary targets and reached out to Bell Canada and Telus. Telus tried to hide from us, but Bell Canada went out of their way to provoke the organization, suggesting basically that we go play in traffic, or as they said, take our issue to the regulators in Canada to "make" them

---

[183] Susan Crawford, *Captive Audience: The Telecom Industry and Monopoly Power in the New Gilded Age*, Yale University Press, 2013.

do it, which was about the same thing, thereby making them the centerpiece of our largest convention action.

Rogers's proposal was to create a $10 per month program in public housing units throughout Toronto: an interesting first step. They challenged us to provide the details for how people would qualify; we countered that we wanted those on the waiting list to also be eligible. We also wanted the program to be national, rather than only Toronto. Further negotiations would have to determine how this first step would develop.

Bell Canada on the other hand dug in even deeper. Hundreds marched from the ACORN Convention to the Bell headquarters and in the beginning easily got everyone into the front lobby and began marching through the building before security assembled to block us further as we chanted in the back patio of the building. An advance team of leaders and staff in the building seeking to deliver a letter to the Bell CEO were stymied one floor below and finally disappointed. After more picketing and chanting on Yonge Street, the march proceeded across the street to Toronto City Hall to seek assistance and a commitment to equitable internet access as a basic utility for all Canadians.[184]

ACORN International sees this campaign as another step on the long road. The issues of access to internet and other telecommunications facilities are critical tools for empowering lower income families around the world and achieving more equity. In Canada now the regulatory body, had finally held hearings, where ACORN has participated and been a stakeholder, on requiring the telecoms to create an affordable internet access program, so we may finally be close to a victory here nationally.

In Kenya like so many other developing countries the internet is metered and very expensive to access by the minute and hour, which means that our organizers and others can access to send and download email messages. The ability to use the internet as a tool to research issues or gain easy familiarity at a Kenya shilling per minute is out of the reach of possibility, making organizing much more difficult. Many observers trumpet the ubiquitous usage of simple cell phones not only for texting but in some cases for money transfers, purchases, and other utilities without reckoning that part of the reason for the cell dependence is the barriers on the internet. In India cell phones are also common and positioned in a highly competitive market, but some of the same challenges exist in terms of computers and the internet. In Mexico the near monopoly that Carlos Slim and his companies have held on telecommunications has not only made him one of the richest men in the world, but also priced out access for tens of millions of Mexicans. There are starting to be signs of change in Mexico, but those prospects will only be helped by more aggressive organizing on this issue.

And, More

Interestingly in ACORN International's experience, the local can also be the global. We have increasing been linking the tenant issues that surface as dominant in Toronto, Ottawa, Edinburgh, Rome, and Bristol in order to fashion "model" campaigns around habitability standards, which we frequently call landlord licensing campaigns since a key demand is to force landlords to be regulated formally by city officials. Frankly, it was

---

[184] Bell Canada is now (2017) negotiating a similar program with ACORN Canada.

exciting to see organizers from all of these cities sharing notes on strategy and tactics in the ACORN annual board and staff meeting in England in the spring of 2014 and again in Paris in 2016 and 2017.

These are issues that make a difference and speak to common concerns and mutual solutions need around the world. Whether Walmart and multi-brand retail, McDonalds, or telecommunications conglomerates, global corporations need to be met by global response and ACORN International can play a role in winning that fight and maintaining that struggle. Working with our partner, ReAct, we are able to also open up additional fronts with transnational, neo-colonial corporate powers like Bollore-Scofin in Africa with its land grabbing plantations, solar, logistics, and other operations. Furthermore, the very local problems of potable water, access to education, land ownership, sanitation, and decent housing also benefit from mutual experience and campaigns.

Political Intersections

As a federation of membership organizations rather than a donor-based NGO, it also gives ACORN avenues of action for the poor that are still uncommon around the world. Some of these opportunities have to do with building political leverage, particularly useful to the poor during elections, especially in countries where mandatory voting is the norm.

In Indonesia for example, we have frequently offered assistance to Wardah Hafiz and the Urban Poor Consortium working throughout the country. As I mentioned earlier, in the first instance in 2007 we loaned an organizer to UPC in Jakarta when they were trying to force politicians running for governor there to halt slum clearance and heed their issues. UPC assigned a team of organizers to the ACORN adviser to learn how to do door-to-door work, so to speak even if there were no doors in the slums and informal settlements, in order to assemble a rally they were organizing for the first time to invite candidates and attempt to demand their acquiescence in exchange for support. We learned as much as UPC when 7000 people turned out to the rally! Unfortunately the candidates were more noncommittal than UPC had hoped, except for the one previously announced as being pro-poor. In late 2008 I visited Makassar with Wardah for a number of days on the island of Sulawesi at UPC's request to train about thirty "rappers" as they had started calling their organizers in the aftermath of our earlier work. Here the assignment was trying to impact the election of the Mayor of Makassar and win sewerage installations and a moratorium on slum clearance along with other organizational issues.

ACORN Canada through a subsidiary, Community Services, Inc. (CSI), following the earlier model in the United States, has frequently contracted for get-out-the-vote efforts with the NDP particularly in ridings in cities throughout Ontario and of course Toronto itself on council and mayoralty races as well and in British Columbia. The organization has a political action committee that has endorsed candidates as well, mainly NDP but also occasionally Liberals, and has organized candidate forums regularly. The Live Green project during Mayor David Miller's term was a project ACORN Canada directed to bring community gardens and tree planting into the social housing projects, and was a testament to its growing political recognition and strength in the city, as was the rapidity which Mayor Rob Ford eliminated the program when he was elected as the next mayor.

Listening to a Question about Potable Water in Colonias San Ramon Tegucigalpa, Honduras.

Maybe he did not realize what he was doing, because as he has said on other occasions, he "was hammered."

More recently, we developed a voter identification and engagement program in Ecuador in the fall of 2012 and spring of 2013 during the national elections there. We were working in partnership with a left, progressive party that though eight years old had never been a ballot-line party and for many of those years part of the governing coalition with Rafael Correa, the President and his party, *Pais*. They had broken with Correa in 2012 over various domestic policy issues, and one-hundred of them had resigned from the government when they were not able to reconcile their differences. In a major effort they had successfully obtained the more than 145,000 signatures needed to place the party on the ballot. When a former WARN organizer in Tampa who was also an Ecuadorian native, reached out for me they wanted to make sure that an independent organization of lower income families was being built, particularly in Quito, so that their voice could be heard by their party and all other parties. Our mission was training organizers to build the lists of potential supporters for both efforts. With the help of Marcos Gomez, an ACORN Canada organizer in Vancouver, who embedded with the campaign, we developed and ran the program for more than three months through the election, we succeeded in identifying more than 25,000 supporters, ran a staff of up to thirty at different times, and ended up at the end of the campaign with one of the most skilled, Marlene Castro, heading up the effort to build ACORN Ecuador in the barrios of south Quito.

In Kenya ACORN's mission around elections, like so many others, was not before the election, but after the election in working to ensure that there was no post-election violence in Korogocho and no repeat of the circumstances of 2008 when tribal outbreaks had been intense and fatal in the slums and throughout the country. Despite the fact that the election was heatedly and closely contested, because of so many efforts, there was not a recurrence of the violence.

More recently we spent weeks in the Netherlands working with a progressive party there to develop a field and phone program to expand turnout and increase the party's share of the electorate. The simple conclusion is that the kind of deep field engagement that is part of the nuts and bolts of the ACORN toolbox has wide application around the world.

In the United States

Does ACORN International work the United States? Obviously ACORN in the United States founded ACORN International while I was Chief Organizer, and even as I left ACORN in 2008 to build out the international work, Maude Hurd, ACORN's President, continued for a time as the President of ACORN International.

Nonetheless, ACORN International has not attempted to reorganize ACORN in the United States in any concerted manner, despite the huge vacuum that exists in the public forum for a mass-based membership organization of low-and-moderate income organizations. Part of this is intentional, and part of this is situational. Clearly, we want the "re-branded" state organizations to succeed as much as possible, so despite the tragedy of 2010, it was appropriate that time and space be given for their progress without any sense of intrusion or interference. Additionally, many had hoped that within a short time these successor organizations would reassemble as a national organization to further ACORN's mission and legacy even if under some other standard. Seven years after shuttering the doors, there is little evidence of reassembling. There has been some work by some of the former state ACORN's, but there is no indication that this is a current plan on any near horizon. The announced "retirement" of Madeline Talbott in Chicago and the untimely and tragic death of Jon Kest in New York, also eliminated some of the key staff with tremendous legacy history within ACORN whose voices at some point might have been influential in a new United States ACORN-like formation. Many other fine organizers still running the new state organizations, especially in large states like Texas, Pennsylvania, North Carolina, and California, may also be preoccupied with solidifying their organizations locally and on a statewide basis without the current additional time and interest to try to forge a new national organization or attempt to glue the pieces back together. Reading quotes by Talbott in the Springfield, Illinois newspaper[185] saying she no longer "believes" in a national organization may also speak to some of the debate on this issue given how hard the task would be and the continued conservative attack which few have the stomach to handle on an ongoing basis. Certainly, they still have a growing support operation in Washington, D.C. that is increasingly stepping out and has merged with others to enhance its capacity and resources, but such an office speaks to mutual self-interest at a level of funding and joint projects rather than a commitment and willingness to surrender some autonomy to national goals and purposes.

As I described earlier in this chapter, ACORN International has not hesitated over the last several years to begin to engage campaigns on remittances and telecommunications equity and internet access in the United States, as well as elsewhere, and in fact have

---

[185] Bernard Shoenberg, "Action Now Trying to Build Base in the City," State Journal-Register, June 21, 2012.

solicited the participation of many interested former state ACORN operations and have received such cooperation in some states like Louisiana, Arkansas, and Pennsylvania. As a federation of organizations, ACORN International has also been more than willing to embrace an array of individual organizations and projects in the United States, whenever we could be helpful or were invited to participate, including most recently supporting the organization of mental health consumers in Alaska and working to organize a campaign to prevent contract-for-deed sales nationally.

Perhaps with more seriousness than humor, we have been more willing to embrace organizations, issues, and campaigns that resonant within the mission and objectives of the organization even if there is not necessarily a permanent organization likely to emerge from the work. Certainly the pilot in Arizona with Advocates & Actions around foreclosure modifications and resistance was an early example, but a call to help save the last four hundred units of public housing in Memphis was also worth time and effort, and has seen rewarding results. Working with people who want to save the water system from over development and protect the health authority for low-and-moderate income families in Austin, Texas, makes sense and if something comes together who knows what organization might evolve. Helping development mass-membership programs for immigrant rights and worker center organizations in Maryland and Illinois has huge value, so it is worth doing. Training and working with organizers who want to build unions of parents so that they decide the future for their children and the schools rather than letting the schools be the playthings of rich people and their private foundations lacking experience with the public school systems. Even affiliating a network of various community groups and interested young organizers trying to make a difference is of value to ACORN International as a "big tent" federation of like-minded groups trying to build power, even in America. The current ACORN Home Savers Campaign is putting boots on the ground in US cities in the Midwest and South, so has promise as well.

Will it build a "new" ACORN? It took thirty years to build ACORN to the level where it legitimately began to have the kind of scope and reach to consistently drive a national agenda and be the platform for lower income and working families to have power. This time ACORN or whatever fills the space will have to even more rigidly, discipline itself to internal self-sufficiency as a survival mechanism. The basic ACORN Model continues to offer many advantages in building deep, responsive organizations and leadership, but ACORN, despite progress in the 21st century, could never solve completely the issues of integrating the local model with the ability to get to the scale necessary.

ACORN International is even farther away from that goal, but is trying to play heavier than our weight by re-learning pages from the early ACORN history of more fully utilizing members, volunteers, and allies. Work in Canada, England, Scotland, France, and other European countries where there are more easily available resources and more stability among low-and-moderate income families offers promise that they might become the "big" ACORN that can both support work in Latin America, Asia, and Africa more easily, as well as possibly help repatriate some of the ACORN experience back into the United States without the fear and loathing that marked its retreat. Until we can find a model that more effectively allows us to expand and bring some consistency to the variety of organizing on our current agenda, there will continue in coming years to be movement on a zigzag path until we find what works best. This is a critical work in progress on every front today.

So Why, if that is What?

It's a big world out there, and it goes without saying, though I'll say it anyway, it's only getting bigger. Like it or not, as hard as it is to get our arms around our home countries, which in my case is the United States, it also seems inarguable to me that we need to begin to build the capacity to create change on the largest map possible if we truly care about inequality and injustice.

Is that because any of us think we have the all of the answers? Heck, no! In fact some of us have come to face the reality that even in our home countries, and even when our countries are as big, rich, and brassy as the USA, we're still just the smallest of fish in a bigger and bigger pond. In fact how do we avoid snickering at the battle of the shrieking bands on whether the USA is in the state of ascendancy or decline, when it is so clear that whichever you choose, we still are a smaller and smaller part of the world around us, and the only certainty is that things will absolutely change. For better or worse, my simple minded view is that we need to organize now as widely as possible in order to create the formations that can play a role is advancing the interests of lower income families regardless of whatever the future may hold.

This is not a Pollyannaish argument that this is one world, doodah, doodah. It is not. How can it be? We're arguing access to affordable health care for all Americans, and 14 million in Africa cannot get any medicine while suffering – and dying – of AIDS with no access to any healthcare. We're finger pointing about how well websites work and most people don't have access to the internet. Everywhere we go, everything is much, much different. We would be foolish to pretend otherwise.

At the same time as organizers, and through our organizations, we have tools, things that we have found work in many situations and in many parts of the world to redress grievances, make change, and build power. Despite all of the changes in the world around us, we also have experiences that have value from hard lessons, bitter defeats, and soaring victories. How can we not share whatever we know and still maintain our commitment to people and the fundamental principle of our work that "we organize the most people possible?"

Many of these principles know no boundaries. Organizing everyone possible is one. Developing leaders, that's another. Letting everyone participate and speak. Majority rule. Never quitting. Self-sufficiency is best. The list goes on and on, even when the context changes.

Will it be the same? No. Can we do as much? Probably not.

But, if we plant, something will grow.

Just a matter of nuts and bolts and then seeing the organizations, campaigns, and miracles that people are able to accomplish together.

And, if we can, then we must.

Chapter XXIII: **Odds and Ends**

Sitting in the patio of the Fair Grinds Coffeehouse on St. Claude Avenue in New Orleans, Adrien Roux, co-founder of one of ACORN International's newest affiliates, the Alliance Citoyenne in France, and coordinator of ReAct, our international partner, we developed almost a daily routine in the stifling heat of August, 2015, that he spent with me, A Community Voice, and Local 100. We would meet almost every afternoon from 3:30 PM to 6:00 PM under a fan and talk about all manner of organizing problems the Alliance might face as well as our emerging affiliates in North Africa in Morocco, Cameroon, and elsewhere. He would ask how ACORN had faced these issues over the last 45 years of organizing and would cajole and beg to get even the roughest draft of *Nuts and Bolts* so he could wrap his mind around these issues, and eventually I succumbed and sent him an early look as he boarded the plane back to France.

Some subjects kept coming up though in our conversations that called to mind some of the ACORN fundamentals that might have been touched on obliquely or perhaps not at all, yet are as fundamental in their own way as "coordinated autonomy" or direct and political action. As *Nuts and Bolts* draws to a close it only seems appropriate to pile them up somewhere as odds and ends that permeate the ACORN methodology before we close.

List Building

The issue of lists and their importance has come up several times, but it's worth underlining, because it is so important in organizing, and so daunting for many who are uncertain how to begin. Once upon a time Polk's Directory, that identified people based on their street addresses and offered work occupations and sometimes phone numbers, and Criss-Cross directories, that matched phone numbers to addresses, were gold. Given the transience of our organizing constituencies and the ubiquity of mobile phones rather than landlines, neither of these old favorites from 40-odd years ago, are reliable tools, even in the case of Polk's are available on-line.

There are still the old tried-and-true alternatives.

Dumpster diving still yields lists from time to time where smaller employers trash, rather than shred, the payroll printouts. Incidentally, dumpster diving is in fact legal in the USA and many other countries, no matter what your mother might tell you, because courts in these jurisdictions have ruled that once put out as "trash," it's essentially "finders keepers, losers weepers." If there is a private sanitation contract hauling from a secured dumpster locked behind a gate, then that's out of bounds legally, though you can take your chances, and many do.

Petitions about one thing or another are also reliable tools. In beginning to organize hotel workers in the mid-1980s in New Orleans, we used a "raise the minimum wage" petition to great effect, in fact so successful that many hotels tried to ban their workers from signing any petitions. In 2017 before we started the Home Savers Campaign we puzzled for months over a list of 158,000 FNMA foreclosure transactions in Michigan, Illinois, and Ohio, before realizing it was useless to us. This is an evergreen problem.

In the age of "big data," organizers would think putting together lists would be a trivial concern in developed countries, even if a continuing challenge in organizing more informal workers globally. If you've got the money, someone may have the list, other than the National Security Agency. You can get voter files and sort them based on income and sluice out names as we did in the Walmart drives to mine our nuggets, but I knew we were on a deathwatch when I could not convince the UFCW to buy the list of retail workers for central Florida countries, even though, relatively speaking, it was a trivial cost. Legitimate lists of almost every description are for sale, but you need to sweat them down to names of value.

An anonymous, supposedly disgruntled worker at Walmart's Bentonville headquarters offered to sell the list of all the company's distribution center workers, but though tempted I ended up passing because I wasn't willing to take the risk, and I couldn't convince another union like the Teamsters or Longshore and Warehouse Workers Union (ILWU) to take a shot at the units. Of course there are also dark ops using hackers to set up shop near an organizing target and see if they can crack the code to produce a workable list. I've never been down that road, but I've been part of the discussion enough times that I know it happens.

In organizing fixed workplaces every organizing committee meeting would discuss who had access to lists of call-ins or relief workers or who could copy sign-in lists on the wall or timecards slotted by the clock. Was there a maintenance man with keys or anyone else that could wander? Who could put their hands on a list and five-finger it home to the union?[186]

In broad-based community organizing, despite the effectiveness of mail and the huge advantage of being able to ask for Mr. or Mrs. Resident when you knock on the door, most organizations are not willing to spend the time and money to build the lists anymore. It is easier and continues to be very effective to hit every door and organize whatever opens. In housing projects and in very low income communities when I was organizing welfare recipients, the job could also get done by going door to door and working the odds that I would find families on the aid. In projects and apartment towers, once an organizing team or an organizer is "in," you just work from top to bottom, door to door. It was fascinating to read that when Johnnie Tillmon organized her group in Los Angeles before the founding of the National Welfare Rights Organization, she was able to convince the manager of the public housing project to give her a list of 500 recipients who lived there Given the rigid rules on recipient privacy and confidentiality that NWRO won, you would NEVER see that happen again!

Lists are harder to build at supermarkets than they once were, especially in the days of Walmart, but it is still possible. Check cashing locations, payday lending shops, banks on known "check-days," mom-and-pops that handle remittances are still magnets for our constituency. We found ourselves talking about many of these locations in trying to suss

---

[186] Did I mention that lists were fundamental? While I'm writing this I just got an email saying a lawyer has employee lists for a bunch of nursing homes and would just love to see me. See what I mean?

out where to find domestic workers in Morocco as we organize there. Where they only have one day off from work, Sunday, needless to say the organizing teams are going to be working that day hard for months to build the lists and visits on that drive.

In list-building, a version of the Archimedes principle applies. Where he argued that if you could stand at the right place with the right lever, you could move the world, we argue something similar. If you make one good contact, careful listening and questions, can allow you to stand right there and build the list from that person to thousands more.

As important as it is to harvest the names, it is equally important to nurture and protect the lists that are built. From ACORN's first days, I always kept a copy of the lists at my home, as well as the office. We have never had safes, but we always secured the lists well. Sometimes we would buy the lesson all over again, especially in the internet world and not password protect the whole list and have someone try to go rouge in an office and take the list. Be prepared. We were when Katrina hit and took all the hard drives out when we evacuated.

Shared Costs

It seems simple, but in order to get to scale, many internal services have to be centralized. How would it ever make sense for the same organization in each office to pay for a separate bookkeeper, supervise its own financial audit, secure its own attorneys, webmasters, database service, internet providers, banking services, and even communication and development departments? Sure, if money were no object and all supervisory skills in these areas were equal, then go for it, but money is always precious as are organizing skills, so decisions need to me made on how to best marshal the talents to get the jobs done by the best people to do them.

In ACORN we believed in centralized services, no matter how many of them might be cursed from time to time, deservedly. It is an imperfect world after all. But if you have centralized services, then how do you equitably pay for them? We used "shared costs."

It all goes back to "organizing math." Let's keep the numbers simple. If the centralized services expenditures totaled $500,000 annually, then that established the level of what needed to be shared. Good so far. Then if the total of the overall aggregate expenditures of all of the organizations utilizing the centralized services added up to $10 million, the level of the shared costs would be 5%. Simple enough, right? The shared costs were collected on a transactional basis. When a check would be written by Citizens' Consulting, Inc. (CCI) which managed the central services, 5% of the total check would be written and transferred over to pay for the shared costs.

That was the basic system. Of course there were numerous bells and whistles. No shared costs for anything but accounting were paid on per capita payments simply forwarded over to international or other labor bodies, when we were affiliated. If a separate audit was required for ACORN Housing for federal grants, then only the housing operations would share that costs. If Local 880 had to pay lawyers directly for its work and did not use the in-house legal department at CCI, then it would not pay a full portion of the legal shared costs. It was not exactly the same principle of "equity and need" that prevailed in the wage system, but obviously equity was the fundamental proposition. The math also generally worked out in such a way that if the organizational component that you governed on the board or served in direct operations accounted for a million of the overall ten million in expenditures then you were likely paying about $50,000 for all your shared costs, everything being equal.

Operations would get a statement from CCI that detailed the cumulative percentage of shared cost for the year, as approved by the board and a breakout of how much went to audit or legal or bookkeeping or whatever. I was paid out of shared cost for example as part of the national operation, and those funds were transferred into a separate organizational account called the Chief Organizer Fund, but since I performed work for ACORN, media operations, housing, labor and other operations it represented a minuscule percentage of each operations shared cost but also provided direct accountability on performance to the collective whole.

It was an intricate system, but manifestly cheaper than each operation would have shouldered alone, and by sharing costs and operation collectively strengthened the whole while adding capacity and infrastructure to the entire family of organizations simultaneously. ACORN Canada has continued the system to pay for the national head organizer, central database, bookkeeping and other systems. Since ACORN International operates more on an "eat what you kill" basis, costs like travel are shared between offices visited.

Shared costs are worth a look when building unified organizations at scale.

Primary Loyalty

"Primary loyalty," what in the world could that concept mean, especially in the modern world where it is seemingly dog-eat-dog, everyone for themselves, and the devil that the hindmost? In fact, loyalty seems an "old school" concept and a bit anachronistic in the modern world. I honestly don't know how anyone could build an organization of the scale and scope of ACORN over all of these years without there being a fundamental principal like primary loyalty.

By primary loyalty I don't mean a blood oath to take a bullet for the organization, and I certainly don't mean primary loyalty to anything other than ACORN, but I do mean that while working on the staff, at the least, the organization is owed your loyalty. Translated into operational reality that means any organizer is welcome to have a million different opinions but is only allowed to express them within the organization and not on the street or in fact outside of the staff itself, where there was ample space and opportunity for discussion so robust that it might even have been uncomfortable for some. Once consensus was reached, protests ceased, and the work went on, as best we were able.

There was no personal versus professional boundary line on primary loyalty for the staff, because there was not a time when suddenly you presented yourself in a different identity than your role as an ACORN staff member. Recently an organizer in one of our cities decided to promote a particular candidate for legislative office in his area. He made several meetings with unions and allies of the organization, identifying himself as employed by ACORN but acting in his personal capacity in advancing the particular party and candidate's interest. Oh, no, that won't go! The organization's leadership and membership make political decisions and policy for the organization, and once they have acted, their decision is not only respected, but also implemented by the staff where appropriate.

There is no such thing as an organizational position versus a personal preference, a public position versus a personal opinion. I used to joke that 7 to 11, I owed to ACORN, and 11 to 7 was mine, and that sent the message pretty clearly about not only primary loyalty but also about what was my personal time.

So, yes, loyalty is a somewhat archaic principal not held widely by many in organizational and political life anymore and seen as hopelessly old fashioned in popular culture, but it is an organizational necessity if we are to build strong, united, battle ready formations. In modern terminology some refer to "speaking with one voice," which gets at the same thing in the sense that it signals that public messages need to be aligned and that internal and external organizational actors "need to be on message," but "primary loyalty" properly speaks of something honored, atavistic, and essential so there is no reason to dance around the issue. If an organization needs loyalty, it needs to be comfortable demanding loyalty, and we were, and continue to be. We worked on the streets, but we didn't put our business on the streets.

We also always give loyalty in return. As I have said and continue to say, the rest, we take to our graves. For those uncomfortable with primary loyalty, there were other places to work and other people to be.

There's Always a History of Struggle

For all the bells and whistles, tools and tips, even nuts and bolts, one thing that we hold certain is that there is always, and I mean always, a history of struggle in every community and workplace *before* we begin organizing. It is the obligation of a good organizer to question closely and listen carefully to learn that history, and if possible the identity of its leaders and warriors. We build organizations, but we didn't invent organizing. Importantly, we are part of a tradition of struggle, so positioning ourselves within that history is essential.

Identifying the history of struggle is critical in two ways. On the obvious level we want to find out as much as we can about the history in that community or workplace in order to build on the tradition, seat ourselves within the fight to resolve historic grievances, if they exist, and to inspire new – or renewed – action. On the other level we need to know in order define our difference if the prior history of struggle ended up in workers getting fired or the community being defeated in order to have people believe that organizing will work.

When a new community organization or union is organized, we often say that we are organizing the unorganized, and that is true, but that is different than whether or not there is a vital history of struggle, organized or individual, in the past. My experience is that we can always find the lineage so that we represent the legacy, just as we will be part of the legacy for future struggles. This is the nature of our tradition. Often when asked "what can the organization do for me," I would answer, "Nothing. All we can do is give you the ability to fight." The rest depends on how much we all put into it.

There are More Reasons Not to Act, Than to Act

It is an amazing thing about people and the power of inertia. People can come up with more reasons against something, than for something; to not act, rather than to act; to do nothing, rather than something; to talk rather than to walk, which is why "final responsibility" is so important in the internal life of an organization, because right or wrong, decisions have to be made, actions have to be taken, and we have to move forward.

The Organization is More Important than the Issue

No matter how important the issue, the campaign, the action, the leader, or the organizer, everything is secondary and less important that protecting and advancing the organization itself, because it is only by protecting the organization that we have the ability to fight – and win – again.

Never Quitting

We only ever finally lose on any issue or campaign, when we quit fighting. As long as we never quit, we always have a chance of winning in the end.

Money and People

In running an organization the two most critical things to always manage are money and people, because you cannot build an organization without both of those forces aligned.

Twenty Percent

There is no fight worse than a fight about money. The smaller the money, often the worse the fight.

Clarity on the front end of any fundraising is critical, especially when it comes to any equitable division that reflects labor expended to raise revenues. Shared costs handles the question of collective services, but how does a large organization, or for that matter any organization with a central, headquarters or national office and field offices, handle the division of any spoils?

ACORN evolved a twenty percent (20%) system. If the national organization wrote the proposal or developed the relationship to the funder or negotiated the contract with the union or campaign that produced money for a particular office or set of operations, twenty-percent would come off the top to support the national operation. On a small office that might be desperate for that $5000 or $10000, seeing $1 or $2000 gone immediately might have pinched a bit, but you cannot build an organization where the local offices and the national offices are in competition with each other for funds, and, simultaneously, each office has responsibility for meeting its budget, making its payroll, and so forth.

The national office also needs to continue to be able to support offices that need resources but whose work might not be as popular for whatever reason. In the United States there might be campaign resources available in certain states that were seen as "battlegrounds" politically or where there were key legislators that might impact on national issues and there were incentives offered to target and move them to trigger a needed vote. If the national organization was making the connections and moving the money, then the split was clear: 20/80, no questions asked.

Did we discuss these internal resource allocations when negotiating contracts to run organizing drives for unions or manage campaigns? No. This was our internal business. We negotiated a rate for the personnel or the contract that included the percentages, and did the work accordingly. Did we discuss these internal divisions when making proposals or raising external monies? No, way! This was family business, not street traffic.

The point is not twenty-percent, but taking care of everything that has to do with raising money and allocating *before* the money is raised, not afterwards where it leads to mess and mayhem.

Permanently Unresolvable Issues

- **Pioneers versus Settlers:** There are versions of this question in evaluating staff, particularly organizers that never go away. When I first broke into the work, I used to hear these terms frequently, though not much over recent decades, and we never had this discussion within ACORN, largely because I never accepted the dichotomy. Nonetheless, the clarity of the contrast gives the argument a level of continual currency. Simply put, a "pioneer" is an organizer that can open new territory or break new ground in new organizing. A "settler" is an organizer who can manage the organization once established and provide the consistency and stability for the organization to grow and win. The concept likely had more relevancy in the old, Alinskyesque notion of replacing organizers every three years, and since that practice was rejected by ACORN and increasingly discounted by the IAF and others, it began to fade. Regardless there are some different skills and abilities in opening offices and operations compared to managing them. Organizers are different than business agents in unions for example. What is not the case is that the skills cannot be taught, and learned, by motivated people in both situations rather than holding a belief that only certain people can be pioneers and other people, perhaps lesser people, must end up as settlers. This argument may not be resolvable, but that does not mean it is not useful.

- **Expansion versus Maintenance:** Everyone in an organization accepts that an organization is either growing or it is dying, but the unsolvable conundrum will always be whether to grow by expanding the organization to new areas be they neighborhoods, cities, countries or constituencies or by maintaining what we have built and blossoming what we have. I fiercely argue that both were complementary, absolutely necessary, and pursued in perfect harmony with each other, and I totally believe both programs are complementary and conjoined. Yet, there is probably no one who ever toiled alongside me who would not have automatically said that I was a stone cold, one-hundred percent, committed expansionist. Wistfully in the early decade of ACORN, late at night, hanging around with the veterans of our heroic, classic age, someone would speculate about what might have been possible in Arkansas if we pulled all of the stars in our firmament back into the state and tried "to take power." It was nostalgic and spoke to the dedication and solidarity of our team, but it was fantasy. Not only was that not possible, because it was not how power is built, but it is also not how people work. If you build a team based on vision and ambition, there's no going backwards, only forwards, and people need space and new worlds to conquer. There is also a marginal utility in how growth can be achieved, and, on the numbers that can be organized and retained in any fixed space, compared to the growth of membership in strength from nothing to something. Understanding that the organization has to expand does not detract from the value of the perfect pearl you are trying to maintain, but an organization has no choice but to grow.

- **Organizers versus Leaders:** At ACORN during my time there was always a clear distinction, some might argue a rigid boundary line, between organizers and leaders. It was part of our culture, as I have described it, organizers at the back, leaders up front; leaders speaking, organizers silent; leaders as spokespeople, organizers as backroom. Nonetheless there was always an irreconcilable tension in this polarity, because the best leaders are also organizers in many cases, and the best organizers are often also seen as leaders, particularly in the internal life of the organization. To outsiders this is either a constant confusion or a suspicious contradiction. The reasons are simple. Despite the different roles of organizers and leaders, both had significant, even if separate, power in the organization. Furthermore, other organizations regularly conflated these roles. In labor unions, leaders were often elected from staff, so staff were often leaders. In civil rights organizations and social movements, organizers and activists often became staff, if there was staff, and were also leaders. In many other community-based organizations staff-types were also occupied leadership roles. Who wouldn't be confused, and in the confusion who wouldn't want to pick and choose whomever they felt most comfortable dealing with and anoint them as leaders, even if non-members and unelected? None of this changed the ACORN fundamentals or culture, but it did complicate the world. Add race to the equation and sometimes gender, and it is easy to see why in some cases even ACORN-veterans found it easier to allow the roles to drift together and conflate. But, this issue is constant, so no sense in pretending that I can resolve it here. We do what we do in ACORN, while others, even among us, do differently, but we like it best our way. Discuss!

Epilogue: **Going Forward**

Organizing wasn't the sprint I had hoped in 1968. As the years passed by since June 18th, 1970 when I drove into Little Rock, Arkansas to begin ACORN, I realized as time passed that the work was a marathon and more. At almost 50 years and counting through the peaks and valleys of ACORN, organizing, and wherever the work took me, eventually the view stretches past any visible horizon.

There is no end to the road. Not because the poor and powerless will always be with us, but because there is never an end to the struggle for justice or peoples' demand to build enough strength to fight for firmer, fairer ground and hold on to it. As long as I work, I can hear the voices rise and hear mine as one in the roar.

It is important for each of us to do our part. I have been lucky to have been able to be both a general in the peoples' army and a water carrier on the peoples' march. Dreams don't get smaller, even as paths get narrower. The wonderful thing about having been part of big, messy, chaotic social movements as well as a strapping, feisty, world making and shaking organization is that it is impossible not to believe, as firm as anyone else's faith, that if I keep working, stay ready, keep plugging and doing my piece to build organization day after day, then when the tectonic plates of people shift and the rare opportunity of movement arises in that turbulence accelerating the possibility and permanence of change, peoples hopes and dreams can come true for a minute and the flesh and bone organization we helped build and nurture can make a difference in how much can happen and how victories can be sustained. Seems idealistic, perhaps even naïve, and certainly romantic, but, as I said before, an organizer's job is learning to walk with one eye on the ground and the other in the sky, and to do so without stumbling or at least without falling.

People like me also have to believe that the next door I hit might open up to the best leader I have ever seen or imagined. The next staff members I meet around the world might develop into a better organizer than any of us ever imagined that we might be. And, doing my small part, they both might be able to carry the fight farther, build stronger, last longer, and win more.

When you write, whether a brief note or something like this, over more than a dozen years you realize that the writing could go on indefinitely adding yet more and more and more as old lessons are remembered and new ones are learned. Anyone will tell you that you have to keep your audience in mind.

Mine is someone like me, and so many of the members, leaders, and organizers I have known and been privileged to join in this amazing enterprise, who have always been desperate to hear how things were done, how the nuts and bolts were fastened to build something big and win, and who want to grab anything available to read or study that might get us there. Going forward I want this book to somehow find its ways into those hands.

Organize, organize, and organize!
Here's hoping!

Acknowledgements

Having been fortunate to do this work for so many years, the debts incurred are too high to ever repay and the creditors number in the thousands, all of whom were critical in advancing the cause and allowing the organizations to survive and thrive. As an organizer on a daily basis I get to watch miracles every time the phone rings, a message is received, or the door is opened, and I see anger join with hope and resolve to engage in fights for collective and individual justice. There is no adequate thanks that can be given for the pleasure of sharing these experiences with so many. The harder the struggle, the more I count myself lucky to have been even a small part of the process.

I acknowledge a debt to all who have joined with me on this path to build these organizations in whatever capacity. I take full responsibility for this book and everything in it, but give thanks for all of the sweat and toil, laughs and shouts, days, years, and dollars that many gave to make this work happen. This book can never do justice to all of that, can never tell all of the stories, cite every turning point, share every lesson, but hopefully it can serve as a small expression of gratitude for our collective enterprise. My thanks to all!

A special thanks to Mary Rowles and our friends at the British Columbia Government and General Employees' Union for their support for this project and our mission. And to the reader who has made it this far, thanks for your interest and good luck taking all of this from here to there.

Exhibits

Exhibit 1a:	ACORN Organizational Flow Chart	5
Exhibit 1b:	ACORN Organizational Flow Chart	37
Exhibit 1c:	ACORN Organizational Flow Chart	37
Exhibit 2:	COUNCIL Salary Scale 2008	122
Exhibit 3:	ACORN International Salary Scale 2012 (to Scott)	127
Exhibit 4:	Certain Staff Policies – ACORN Canada	152
Exhibit 5:	Overview of the Organizing Model	162
Exhibit 6:	Organizing Letter	168
Exhibit 7:	Quick Hits Checklist	169
Exhibit 8:	Membership Recruitment and Building Your Rap: Video Transcript	171
Exhibit 9:	Agenda for Head Organizer Training (Canada)	185
Exhibit 10:	Agenda for New Head Organizer Training (New Mexico 2008)	186
Exhibit 11:	Sample Agendas and Readings from Dialogues	188
Exhibit 12:	Dialogue on Training, St. Petersburg, February 2006	189
Exhibit 13:	Head Organizers' Meeting Agenda (Gatineau, March 2015)	191
Exhibit 14:	Division Directors' Meeting Agenda	194
Exhibit 15:	Management Council Meeting, Brooklyn & Manhattan, 2001	195
Exhibit 16:	Management Council Meeting, Denver, September 2007	197
Exhibit 17:	Mid-Year Agenda, Abiquiu, New Mexico, May 2004	199
Exhibit 18:	Mid-Year Meeting, Glorieta, New Mexico, June 2005	201
Exhibit 19:	Year End – Year Begin Agenda 2006 New Orleans	204
Exhibit 20:	Year End – Year Begin 2001 New Orleans	214
Exhibit 21:	Small Groups Topic 2001	219
Exhibit 22:	Small Groups Topic YE/YB 2003	220
Exhibit 23:	Agenda for First Organizing Committee Meeting– ACORN Los Angeles	240
Exhibit 24:	Organizing Committee Agenda #2 – ACORN Los Angeles	241
Exhibit 25:	Agenda for Organizing Committee #3 – ACORN Los Angeles	243
Exhibit 26:	Agenda for Organizing Committee #4: ACORN Los Angeles	245
Exhibit 27:	Agenda for a Citywide Board Meeting	248
Exhibit 28:	Pennsylvania Statewide Board Agenda, July 2008	250
Exhibit 29:	Association Board Agenda, Fort Worth, Texas, October, 2003	254

Exhibit 30:	Association Board Agenda, Minneapolis, Minnesota, April, 2008	256
Exhibit 31:	Voting Sheet	260
Exhibit 32a:	2003 Office Development	262
Exhibit 32b:	Board Material on Peru Initiative	264
Exhibit 33:	Sporting Proposition from Local 100 – April 6, 2001	265
Exhibit 34:	October 2005 Chart for 2006 ACORN Convention in Columbus	268
Exhibit 35:	Revised Projections for 2006 ACORN Convention in Columbus	271
Exhibit 36:	March Convention Planning Memo	274
Exhibit 37:	Workshop Grid for the Columbus Convention in 2006	277
Exhibit 38:	Workshop Turnout Numbers Collected on Columbus Convention 2006	279
Exhibit 39:	Going to Ground for a Convention	280
Exhibit 40:	Convention Housing Assignments	282
Exhibit 41:	Order of States	284
Exhibit 42:	Numbers on the Order of States	285
Exhibit 43:	Pre-Convention Board Agenda in 2006 Columbus ACORN Convention	287
Exhibit 44:	Stage Seating at 2006 Columbus ACORN Convention	288
Exhibit 45:	Convention Seating Chart – Columbus, Ohio 2006	289
Exhibit 46:	Annotated Agenda for ACORN 2006 Convention	291
Exhibit 47:	Early Draft of Convention Agenda – ACORN Convention 2002 – Chicago	296
Exhibit 48:	Post Convention Follow-up	306
Exhibit 49:	Map for action at Philly Convention	323
Exhibit 50:	Planning an Action	353
Exhibit 51:	Action Planning for Philadelphia Convention 2000	356
Exhibit 52:	Planning List for Los Angeles Actions 2004	359
Exhibit 53:	March Order for Final Action of Columbus Convention	361
Exhibit 54:	Monthly Numbers Report (7.31.02)	385

Photographs and Illustrations

Fishing Camp. Chaco fishing...xiv
Silver Bullet at Rock Creek, Montana..xvi
ACORN members assembling for Los Angeles ACORN Convention 2004 2
ACORN India members gather in assembly in Delhi 3
Early Little Rock Board Meeting Walter Nunn and Wade 1973-74 22
Burnaby chapter of ACORN Canada preparing to vote..........................29
Mary Gonzalez and Greg Galluzzo at Organziers Forum
   Board Meeting with Barbara Bowen..33
John Bauman PICO..34
Rain follows the plow – Go west!...40
Canvass Team in Arizona on Min Wage..44
Wade in Springfield WRO Action 1969..45
Gary Delgado laughing at Fair Grinds Dialogue 47
Samuel Gompers...60
Ship indentation in Hawaii for measuring sandalwood.........................67
Warren, Arkansas local 100 Labor Day Picnic Setup............................71
Local 100, healthcare rally..72
ACORN Street Vendors Union convenes in marketplace in Bengaluru, India.........74
Union Density 1. Union membership in US 1930-2010 76
Union Density 2. United States union membership and inequality, 1910 to 2010 ...76
Local 100 Houston Cafeteria workers 78
Big Bill Haywood..82
AFL-CIO Organizing Institute Trainees in Action................................87
Wade at Year End / Year Beginning to back. Dewey Armstrong Standing.
   John Beam looking and Others 89
Saul Alinsky..91
ACORN Scotland Doorknocking Crew Gathers 106
Bristol ACORN Easton chapter door knocking role playing 109
Organizing Drive Chart (adapted by Alliance Citoyenne ACORN) 116
George Wiley 116
Bill Pastriech at Local 100 Training...117
Little Rock Staff Meeting 1976. Dewey Armstrong, John Beam, Kaye Jaeger 120

ACORN Board and Staff Meeting in Santa Domingo 2008.	126
Phone bank training in Vancouver	135
ACORN "nut" ad	142
Organizers Forum meets in Moscow with persecuted nonprofit of Soldiers Widows and Mothers	146
No Bulldozing	148
First meeting of Easton chapter of ACORN Bristol	161
Organizing committee meeting in Edinburgh, Scotland	167
ACORN Scotland Doorknocking Team	174
Melian Debate from Organizers Training at Colby Ranch in Los Angeles County	185
ACORN Canada head organizers.	190
ACORN International head organizers meeting Paris 2016	198
Estes Park mid-year meeting in 1990s	202
At ACORN YEYB 2006 John Podesta Answers Questions from Tanya Harris,	211
Peter Wood, Fran Streich, Jeff Elmer at Year End/Year Begin Meeting in 1990s	213
Small group meeting at ACORN International organizers meeting in Paris 2014	219
Gloria Wilson, top row middle, between Wade Rathke and Maxine Nelson, Steve McDonald and Mildred Brown in front, at 20th Anniversary 1990	227
Carmen Rivera, Springfield Welfare Rights leader speaking in 1969	229
ELocal 100 officers at Lake Charles Retreat inc. Rebecca Hart, Vickie Cisneros, Larry Roddy, Linda Lathers	230
Elena Hanggi, Bill Whipple, and Willard Johnson	232
Maude Hurd with Judy Duncan and Wade Rathke Boston 2012	223
ACORN Scotland organizing committee working a street stall	242
First meeting of ACORN Scotland neighborhood chapter	247
Grenoble Citywide Board Meetings Outside in Summer 2016	247
ACORN Canada Board Meeting in Toronto	252
Association Board April 2008	256
Mildred Edmond (100) and Kaye Bisnah (AINT) and others touring with San Juan Laranguancho with ACORN Peru Leaders to see Progress	266
First convention action. Front Line Memphis March 1978.	268
ACORN Canada leaders running a workshop on recruitment at Ottawa Convention 2017	283
Bus load up at convention Ottawa 2017	286
Crew works to prepare the convention packets before the crowd comes 2004	287
Detroit 2008 Convention from back to leadership on stage	295

ACORN President Maude Hurd speaking at Wells Fargo Action in Los Angeles	301
We Like it Here House is Not for Sale	314
Gene Sharp	317
E Reagan Ranch	318
ACORN Flag at Toronto Occupy	325
ACORN on poster and signs Louisiana ACORN stop predatory lending	326
ACORN Tent City to support squatters winning homestead rights	327
Hyatt Boycott Press Conference	330
Home Savers Detroit 1st Meeting	334
H&R Block Negotiating Committee	335
Alliance Citoyene ACORN's action scaling diagram in France	339
Toronto Landlord Licensing Victory	340
Alliance Citoyene ACORN's action scaling diagram in France	339
California ACORN leaders and ACORN's Bruce Dorpalen and Mike Shea	345
Bank of Montreal Action at ACORN Canada Convention 2015	346
Carolyn Carr Little Rock Office 1976-77	351
ACORN Union sackcloth action in Bengaluru, India	355
Wells Fargo Senior VP confronted by ACORN leaders in Los Angeles Action	358
ACORN International Bechaks in Columbus, March 2006	362
Citibank Action	364
ACORN Action at Bell Toronto Headquarters 2013	365
Sign up table in Edinburgh, Scotland	371
Marcos Gomez (center) training militantes (organizers) in Quito	372
Fox News Interview	393
ACORN says, "You are in my power." George Fisher cartoon in Arkansas Democrat	405
Lifeline Campaign in Arkansas. Hot Springs Rally 1975	408
Lifeline petition signing in 1976 in Arkansas	409
Food and medicine initiative in Missouri	412
New Orleans ACORN leader Frenzella Johnson getting signatures of minimum wage ordinance petion	415
Senator Jim Abourezk	423
Zach Polett and Clinton the Day After his Election	431
Joel Rogers (Rock Creek, MT 2013)	433
Dan Cantor in Working Families Party Office in Brooklyn	434
KABF Logo. KNON's old console on display	442

Photographs and Illustrations 557

Arlene Kimata at Year-End / Year-Beginning with Beth Butler,
   Judy Graves, Orell Fitzsimmons 449
Hyatt Boycott Picket - Beth Butler 1985 457
Helen Miller, President of Local 880, between Keith Kelleher, Mildred Edmond and
   other delegates from Local 100 at SEIU 2008 Convention in San Juan, PR . . . 462
John Sweeny and Wade Rathke 468
Local 100 leaders in Dallas 2009 470
HOTROC March through French Quarter 472
Walmart Site Fight Action by WARN in St. Petersburgh, Florida 481
Organizing India FDI Retail Campaign at India Social Forum 485
Tulsa Squatters Press April 1982 495
Street sign in Houston ACORN development. 496
Henry Cisneros on Tour as HUD Secretary 498
ACORN Service Center in operation in Phoenix on EITC and Taxes 502
Drummond Pike and Wade Sidney Australia 507
Local 100 navigators in Houston 512
First Meeting of ACORN Peru in Lima 514
First action in Duoala, Cameroon 515
First meeting of ACORN Kenya in Korogocho 516
Fair Grinds Coffeehouse 517
ACORN India's recycling cooperative truck, Mumbai, India 2014 518
Marshalling Support for ACORN Italy's Tenant Bounty Campaign in the
   Italian Senate in Rome (David Tozzo) to right of picture 523
Organizing meeting of squatters in La Matanza, Buenos Aires 2011 526
Stairs in SJL won by ACORN Peru 527
Work in Honduras 528
ACORN Canada Convention Ottawa 2017 531
ACORN Canada action on internet 534
Listening to a Question about Potable Water in
   Colonias San Ramon Tegucigalpa, Honduras 539

Index

20/80 *285, 374, 380, 421-429, 549*
501c3 *146, 444, 503, 518*
A Community Voice *445, 517, 536, 543*
ACORN Academy *100, 103*
ACORN Community Labor Organizing Centers (ACLOC) *463-464*
ACORN Farm *520*
ACORN Housing Corporation (AHC) *141, 148, 260, 494-510, 545*
ACORN Institute *509*
ACORN International *36, 72, 129-130, 326, 352, 379, 420, 445-446, 450, 488-489, 513-546*
ACORN Peoples' Platform *308*
ACORN Political Action Committee (APAC) *403, 430*
ACORN Service Centers *501-502, 511*
action (s) *2, 16, 26, 46, 113-114, 168-169, 213, 224-225, 227, 232, 234, 246, 251, 261, 281, 283, 286, 289-290, 306, 311, 314, 317, 319-326, 329, 331, 338-355, 362-367, 391-392, 404, 428, 436, 438, 451, 492-498*
Action United *435, 521, 535*
advocacy *1, 8, 12, 91, 314, 347, 390, 392-399, 436, 440, 493, 498, 500*
Advocates & Action *541*
Affordable Care Act *511*
affordable housing *348, 394, 397, 495, 510*
AFL-CIO Organizing Institute *85-86, 472*
Africa *446, 517, 518, 538, 541, 542*
    Morocco *492, 517, 543, 545*
    Cameroon *146, 517, 543*
    Korogocho *515, 525-526, 539*
    Kenya *38, 126, 515, 519, 526, 537, 539*
    Nairobi *129, 515, 526*
    Liberia *517*
    Nigeria *517*
    South Africa *147, 329*
    West Africa *516*
    Ivory Coast *517*

African-American(s) *2, 21, 91, 229, 231, 312, 321, 331, 332, 392-393, 401, 406, 411, 414-415, 419, 444, 451, 453, 456, 474-475, 484, 497, 503-504, 511*
American Federation of Teachers (AFT) *387, 466*
AKORN *516, 521*
Alabama *226, 403, 430, 520*
Birmingham *337*
Selma *354*
Alcohol Anonymous *350*
Alford, Boyce *140*
Alinsky, Saul *45, 90, 238, 308, 316, 394, 414, 516*
alliance (s) *30, 131, 389, 394-395, 461, 476, 484, 490*
Alliance Citoyenne *352, 517, 543*
Alliance for a Just Society *30*
allies *21, 119, 149, 212, 259, 276, 290, 332, 338-339, 342, 345, 376, 379, 392, 394, 398-399, 404-405, 413, 484, 487-489, 506-509, 535, 541, 546*
Allison, Max *401*
Aluli, Emmet *67*
AM/FM *445-446, 449*
Amador, Suyapa *515*
American Federation of Labor (AFL-CIO) *38, 46, 63, 72, 75, 84-87, 129, 259, 328, 345, 364-365, 387, 397, 430, 435, 458, 460-462, 466-467, 472-479, 488-489*
American School *529*
AmeriCorps *141, 499*
Ameriquest *276*
Anderson, Charlie *230*
Andrews, Terry *377, 444*
ANEW *517*
Anti-Inflation Campaign *331*
Ardoin, Verna *457, 468*
Argentina *104, 129, 147, 324, 340, 420, 515, 525*
Buenos Aires *99, 104, 129, 370, 514, 519, 525*
Arizona *190, 313, 329, 412, 414, 420, 427, 513, 522, 541*
Mesa *313*

Phoenix *32, 343, 420, 426, 427, 472, 497, 522*
Arkansas *6, 7, 14, 19-20, 22, 33, 41, 46, 49-50, 71, 81, 119, 140, 190, 225, 231, 249, 251-252, 319, 332, 345, 349, 370, 373, 379-383, 390-391, 400-415, 421-427, 430, 432, 443-449, 462, 471, 479, 494, 499-500, 517, 533, 541, 550*
Little Rock *8, 18-19, 25, 46-47, 51, 99, 119, 125, 140, 203, 231, 259, 267, 313, 332-333, 348, 374, 380, 383, 390, 392, 400-427, 430, 432, 441, 443, 451, 456, 511, 518, 534-535, 551*
Pine Bluff *22, 140, 405-410*
Arkansas Council of Human Relations *46, 425*
Arkansas Democrat *141-142, 494*
Arkansas Electric Cooperative *410*
Arkansas Power & Light *319, 410*
Armstrong, Dewey *383, 423, 425, 426, 428, 443*
Asian Bridge *518*
Association Board *195, 239, 253, 259, 261, 265, 267, 286, 491*
autonomy *18, 31-32, 35, 144, 249, 283, 392, 458, 460, 540, 543*
Axt, Deborah *474*
Bachman, Steve *425*
Bank of America *497, 509*
Bank of Montreal (BMO) *364, 367*
banking *67, 148-149, 260, 276, 336, 341, 386, 514, 519, 533, 545*
Barkley, Ruth *237, 320*
Bauman, John *31*
Beam, John *422, 425-426*
Beck, Glen *503*
Becker, Bill *345, 430*
Bell Canada *364, 536-537*
Bell, Geraldine *457*
BJP Party *146*
Black Panther Party *393, 403*
Black, Jon *516*
Blug Frog *529*

Index   559

Borgos, Seth 425
Bowen, Barbara 426, 456
boycott (s) 6, 184, 326, 329, 331, 459, 470
Brazil 147, 324, 389
Breaux, John 391
Breitbart News 503
Brooks, Fred 283, 426
Brown, Sam 141, 454
Burson, Joyce 348
Bush, George 19, 141, 482
Butler, Beth 392, 425-426, 469
Butler, Dine' 515
bylaws 26, 65, 82, 123, 143, 145, 247, 249, 252, 425, 460, 491
California 30-31, 42-43, 77, 88, 99, 110, 184, 195, 288, 329-330, 407, 412, 426, 448, 460, 464, 472, 474, 481, 485-486, 490, 540
Los Angeles 147, 184, 241-242, 267, 309, 366, 397, 414, 426, 435, 463-464, 474-475, 504, 513-514, 544
Oakland 18, 147
San Diego 31, 148, 187, 459, 504, 513
San Francisco 10, 50, 61, 412, 423, 440, 450, 480, 485
Camacho, Orfa 526
Campbell, Meg 383, 425, 426, 441
Canada 5, 11, 36, 54, 126, 129, 146, 152, 161, 247, 288, 310, 311, 325, 364, 367, 389, 395, 420, 436, 487, 514, 518-519, 521, 531-539, 541, 546
British Columbia 420, 533, 538
Montreal 364, 367, 531
Ontario 420, 533, 538
Ottawa 14, 517, 521, 531-532, 537
Vancouver 11, 531, 539
Toronto 11, 18, 310, 340, 364, 377, 514, 531-532, 537-538
Cantor, Danny 426, 431, 455, 468
canvass 2, 9, 24, 41-43, 50, 53, 89, 100, 111-112, 135, 362, 386, 392, 410, 413, 426, 434, 443, 449-450

capacity 11, 28-29, 36, 43, 51-53, 55, 59, 71, 88-89, 136, 138-139, 149, 244, 253, 310, 314, 322, 338, 340-341, 369, 391, 411, 415, 419, 429, 431, 444-446, 449, 454, 463-467, 511, 525
Carolina Action 30, 426
Carr, Carolyn 273, 281, 286, 348, 374, 425, 452
Carter, Jimmy 20, 402, 427, 428, 451
Castro, Marlene 539
Castro, Teresa 522
Catholic Campaign for Human Development (CCHD) 12
Catholic church 12, 23, 43, 90
CCTN (California Community Television Network) 448-449
Center for Community Change 493
Center for Popular Democracy 30
Chavez, Cesar 110, 187, 330, 349, 393, 414
Chicago Fighting Tenants Union 6
child credits 502
Cholomo 527
churches 12, 41, 145, 242, 244, 388, 483
Cincotta, Gail 30
Cisneros, Henry 499
Citi Foundation 501
Citizen Action 30, 43, 434, 510
Citizen Wealth Centers 511
Citizens Against Poverty 47
Citizens' Action League (CAL) 30, 426
Citizens' Consulting, Inc. (CCI) 545
Citizens' Party 429
civil disobedience 316, 321, 342
class 19, 83-85, 90, 92, 100, 236, 312, 407
Clinton, Bill 14, 212, 259, 389, 396, 430, 431, 433, 471, 479, 499, 533
Clinton, Hillary 410, 431
coalition (s) 19, 61, 388-389, 392, 394-398, 432, 483, 490-491
COLA 121, 125

Comcast 187, 534-536
communication 4, 50, 55, 112, 136-140, 236, 310, 322, 331, 336, 389, 427, 438-449, 465, 471, 508, 545
community development corporation (CDC) 493-494
Community Reinvestment Act (CRA) 497
Community Service Organizations (CSO) 110
Community Services, Inc. (CSI) 538
community-labor partnerships 396-397, 479, 490
conflict (s) 52, 395
Congress 13, 141, 146, 320, 326, 390, 392, 394, 399, 400, 413, 428-429, 434, 444-445, 454, 487, 505-509, 533, 535
Congress of Industrial Organizations (CIO) 61, 83
Connecticut 118, 398, 406, 426, 431, 434, 497
constituency 70, 88, 90, 93, 97-98, 112, 123, 130, 136, 157, 309-310, 314-315, 326, 328, 334, 338, 340, 342-348, 373, 393, 398, 403, 418-420, 435, 445, 447, 449, 452, 492, 496, 499, 502, 504, 521
consultant (s) 33, 89, 490
COPE 77
Correra, Rafael 379, 539
Cortez, Marlene 517
Cosme, Willie 446
count-on-me's 111
Cox 534, 536
Cox, Bobbie 425
crises 30, 50, 67, 136-142, 148, 150, 519
culture 21, 49, 80, 83-84, 94, 100, 112, 130-136, 144, 211, 228, 234, 239, 244, 249, 253, 259, 261, 266, 364, 383, 451, 461, 500
Czech Republic (Prague) 38, 130, 515, 521
Davenport, Herman 425
Delgado, Gary 47, 425, 448
Delta Foundation 446
demonstrations 6, 290, 323-324, 333, 451

560 Nuts & Bolts – The ACORN Fundamentals of Organizing

Denver (Colorado) *32, 195, 325, 411, 426, 448-449, 485*
Desai, Reena *515*
desegregation *47, 401, 414*
Dharavi Project *521, 525, 529*
disaster(s) *147, 315, 440, 450*
Donner, Lisa *274, 514*
doorknocking *108, 170, 369, 372*
Dorpalen, Bruce *426, 497, 500*
Dorsey, Fred *425*
Douglass, Fredrick *22*
Dowd, Maureen *390*
Duncan, Judy *129, 161, 514*
Dunlea, Mark *426*
Ecuador (Quito) *371, 379, 420, 517, 525, 539*
Edinburgh Private Tenants Action Group (EPTAG) *516-517*
Edwards, John *259*
Eisenberg, Pablo *493*
EITC (Earned Income Tax Credit) *42, 501*
election (s) *23, 26-27, 101, 104, 233-234, 237, 246, 259, 261, 333, 340, 355, 378-379, 387, 394, 398, 400-403, 406-407, 423, 432, 434-436, 513, 526-527, 538-539*
Ellison, Keith *259, 533*
Employment Policies Institute *141*
endorsements *19, 249, 349, 401, 403, 427, 430, 434*
Egypt (Cairo) *146, 330, 436*
Executive Board *21, 57, 371, 419, 430, 462, 478*
extermal threats *23, 145-146*
Fair Grinds Coffeehouse *519-520, 543*
Farmers' Alliance *81, 317, 431*
Federal Communications Commission (FCC) *145, 443-446, 534-536*
federations *28, 63, 326*
FEMA *509*
Fermin, Dalinda *474*
Fisher, Robert *493*
Fiske, Mary Anne *426*
Fitzsimmons, Orell *471, 511*
Fleischman, Jim *426*

Florida *73, 129, 309, 395, 412-418, 426-427, 442-443, 446, 463, 465, 472, 481-485, 489, 490-491, 515, 544*
Ford, Rob *538*
foreclosure (s) *342, 394, 486, 522*
foreign direct investment (FDI) *36, 38, 395, 485-489, 515, 529*
Foundation (s) *12, 28, 41, 48-49, 51, 92, 145, 436, 489-490, 493, 519, 541*
Fox News *392, 419, 503, 505, 509, 511*
Fox, Joe *425, 443*
France (Grenoble, Paris), *5, 130, 247, 352, 389, 492, 517, 532, 541, 543*
Friedman, Barbara *383, 426*
fundraising *45, 49, 124, 259, 265, 375, 376, 381, 386, 426, 548*
Gallagher, Mike *474*
Galluzzo, Gregory *31*
Gamaliel Network *31, 212, 326*
Georgia (Atlanta) *30, 73, 232, 426, 429-430, 500, 533*
Georgia State University *533*
get-out-the-vote (GOTV) *379, 414, 416, 430, 432, 434, 436, 475*
Gibbons, Gene *425*
Giles, Hannah *503*
Gingrich, Newt *141, 499*
Glynn, Tom *46*
Gomez, Marcos *539*
Gompers, Sam (Samuel) *28, 59, 60, 68, 81*
Grassley, Senator *141*
Green, Don *420*
Guadino, Robert *88*
Guatemala *129, 504*
Guerra, Carlos *403*
Gulley, Dub *425*
Gutierrez, Jose Angel *403*
H&R Block *334, 501, 509, 521*
Hafiz, Wardah *518, 538*
Hagy, Scott *149*
Hall, Andrea *285*
Hamilton, Bill *401*
Hanggi, Elena *322*
Hanna, Sue *425*
Harmon, Melva *425*
Harris v. Quinn *70*

hawkers *355, 486, 492, 515, 530*
Haywood, Bill Big *81*
Herman, Steve *425*
Hessey, Jay *30, 426, 459*
Hobbie, Rev. Wellford *47*
Holt, Steve *383, 425, 426, 441*
home health workers *455, 460*
Home Mortage Disclosure Act (HMDA) *497*
Home Savers Campaign *333, 517, 541, 543*
homesteading *327, 494*
Honduras (San Pedro Sula, Tegucigalpa *38, 129, 340, 515, 521, 527, 528, 533*
Horowitz, David *141*
Hotel Employees Restaurant Employees (HERE) *84, 473*
HOTROC *364, 367, 379, 463, 466, 471, 473, 474-477*
House, Pat, *47, 401, 414*
Household Finance *25*
Houston Independent School District *72, 75*
HSBC *25, 334, 525*
HUD *212, 318, 327, 362, 499, 500, 510*
Hungary *331*
Hunter, David, *49, 422, 429*
Hurd, Maude *232-234, 286, 431, 540*
Hurricane Katrina *31-32, 136, 138, 142, 147-150, 190, 392, 440, 477-478, 480, 497, 505, 520, 545*
HWOC *452, 453*
Hyatt *331, 369, 456, 457-459, 470, 473*
Hywaoo, Na *518*
Illinois (Chicago) *32, 78, 432-433, 462-464, 471, 491, 540, 541, 544*
Chicago *6, 9, 23, 31, 50, 71, 92, 184, 195, 288, 316, 320, 322, 329, 366, 414, 423, 432-434, 450, 455-459, 462, 471*
India *35, 38, 72, 126, 129, 146, 311, 324, 331, 346, 355, 395, 399, 436, 486-492, 515, 518-519, 529-531, 537*
Bengaluru , *72, 355, 487, 515, 530*

Index   561

Bangalore *515*
Delhi *386, 487, 515, 530-531*
Chennai *72, 487, 515, 530*
Hyderabad *72, 515*
Mumbai *487-488, 515, 521, 529-530*
India FDI Watch *395, 486-489, 515, 529*
Indonesia *147, 355, 389, 420, 518, 538*
Industrial Areas Foundation (IAF) *23, 90-93, 415, 435, 549*
Industrial Workers of the World *64, 146*
Iowa *41, 50, 426-428, 464*
Italy (Rome) *38, 130, 350, 516, 522-524, 533*
Jackson-Hewitt *501*
Jackson, Rev. Jesse *259, 430*
Jamerson, Louis *474*
Japan *15, 324*
Johnson, Ken *472*
KABF *145, 443, 444-447*
Kadashan, Suresh *515*
Kelleher, Keith *71, 455*
Kern, Jen *281, 349*
Kerr, Michael *46*
Kerry, John *413, 482*
Kest, Jon *387, 410, 426, 449, 466, 540*
Kest, Steve *274, 425, 426*
Kieffer, Dave *474*
Kimata, Arlene *448*
King, Rev. Martin Luther *337, 354*
Kirland, Lane *85*
Kitchen, Mary Jo *425-426*
Knights of Labor *25, 81*
KNON *145, 444, 447*
Koppel, Barbara *330*
Korea (Seoul) *324, 518, 524*
Ku Klux Klan (KKK) *23*
Kumar, Dharmendra *487, 515*
Kydd, Andrea *118*
La Matanza *515, 525*
Labor Department *134*
Labor Management Disclosure Act (LMDA) *146*
landlords *324, 341, 350, 394, 522-524, 532, 537*
Landrieu, Mary *391, 399, 474*
Lassen, Mary *383, 425, 426*
Latino(s) *456, 513*

Lawson, Kier *516*
Leland Commission *429*
Leland, Mickey *429*
lending *25, 276, 313, 334, 342, 347, 363, 367, 390, 394, 498, 504, 525, 531, 544*
Lerner, Stephen *478*
Lewis, John *83, 187, 238, 460*
Liberty Tax Services *342, 501*
Linton, Rhoda *118*
Lipner, Jay *425*
living wage *123, 265, 314, 329, 336, 341, 349, 365, 387, 397, 409, 411, 432, 434, 463, 475, 485, 519, 531*
Local 100 ULU *57, 70-78, 123, 141, 229, 265, 309, 331, 444, 456, 459-463, 470-480, 488, 491, 511, 513, 534-536*
Local 222 *455, 459*
Local 880 32, 462, 464, 471, 480, 491, 545
Louisiana *20, 41, 46, 195, 230, 252, 373, 379, 391, 399, 407, 412, 418, 424, 428, 430*
Baton Rouge *148, 229, 330, 477, 480, 536*
Lafayette *536*
Lake Charles *373, 445*
New Orleans *8, 18, 21, 23, 31, 32, 49, 94, 136, 147-150, 190, 203, 211-212, 230, 237, 267, 283, 331, 333, 350, 364, 367, 377-378, 392, 399, 412, 416, 420-426, 440, 442, 450-451*
9th Ward (ninth ward) *509, 520*
Shreveport *71, 471, 534*
Mailer, Norman *354*
Majority Unionism *478*
Make the Road by Walking *30*
Manhattan Institute *141*
Marguerite Casey Foundation *501*
Marriott *306, 322, 342*
Martin, Art *305, 322, 404*
Massachusetts *43, 44, 91, 94, 118, 137, 226, 237, 319, 348-349, 391, 407, 426, 451, 464*
Massachusetts Welfare Rights Organization *137, 349, 458*
MCAN (Mental Health Consumers' Action Network) *350, 517*

McCleary, Cheryl *425*
McCormick, John *319*
McCoy, Pat *184, 203, 426*
McDonald, Steve *231, 403, 424*
McKeever, Mother *226*
Mexico (Mexico City, Tijuana) *38, 48, 126, 129, 138, 190, 330, 340, 395, 446, 513-515, 519, 521, 527, 533, 537*
Michigan *412, 426, 427, 428, 544*
Detroit *302, 328, 333, 366, 426, 428, 452, 455, 458-460, 472, 494, 518*
Michigan Democratic Party *145*
Miller, David *538*
Mills, C. Wright *347*
Mills, Wilbur *46, 390*
Minnesota *78, 423, 429, 432, 464, 533*
Mississippi *6, 187, 404, 431, 446, 459, 471*
Greenville *446*
Mississippi Freedom Democratic Party *404*
Missouri (Kansas City, Jefferson City, St. Louis) *20, 252, 411, 412, 413, 418, 421, 430, 455, 462*
Modi, Prime Minister *146*
Montana *31, 318, 432*
Montana's Peoples' Action (MPA) *31*
Mooney, Josie *30*
Morial, Mayor Marc *365, 367, 474-477*
Morsi, President *317*
Musungu, David *515*
NAACP *6, 331, 484*
Nader, Ralph *390, 524*
National Association of Counties *141*
National Education Association (NEA) *233, 413, 465, 506*
National Organization of Women (NOW) *393*
National Organizers Association *26*
National People's Alliance (NPA) *30*
National Public Radio *506*
National Violence Against Women Act *392*

National Welfare Rights Organization (NWRO) 44, 46, 54, 117-118, 231, 320, 348, 354, 451, 544
Ndirangu, Sammy 515
NDP 538
negotiation (s) 225-227, 259, 339, 343-344, 363, 445, 452, 459, 475-476, 497, 537
neighborhood (s) 9, 43-44, 47, 80, 99, 107, 136, 147, 273, 313, 368, 401, 428, 439, 453, 467, 493, 497, 500, 504, 549
network (s) 30, 35, 54, 115, 234, 313, 326, 387, 446
New Jersey 31, 336, 397, 465, 497, 507
New Mexico (Albuquerque) 190, 412, 426, 513
Albuquerque 37, 493
Santa Fe 412
New Party 430-433
New World Foundation 494
New York City 12, 19, 30, 32, 49, 50, 60, 61, 94, 125, 141, 147, 149, 195, 276, 285, 288, 320-321, 328, 336, 349, 351, 363, 366, 375-376, 387, 397, 410, 422, 426, 428, 431, 432, 434, 435, 448, 450, 460, 465-466, 474, 476, 491, 496, 497, 507, 510, 514, 540,
New York Times 84, 325, 390, 419, 483, 534
New Yorker 142, 321
Newberry, Tom 30
NGO 126, 129-130, 486, 519, 538
NLRB 333, 378, 454-457, 469, 476-478, 481, 483
nonprofits 1, 5, 134, 145-146, 329, 436, 448, 452, 464
nonviolent tactics 316
North Carolina 203, 354, 425, 500, 540
Northwest Federation of Community Organizations 30
NTIC (National Tenant Information Center) 30
O'Brien, Helene 148, 184, 261, 274
O'Keefe, James 503-507, 511-512

Obama, Barack 14, 134, 212, 259, 261, 329, 402, 414, 419-420, 432-433, 436, 503, 506, 507-508, 511, 522
Occupy 116, 317, 328
Ohio 141, 261, 273, 327, 387, 407, 412, 414, 418, 446, 544
  Cleveland 261, 432, 472
  Columbus, 32, 141, 273, 327, 366, 460
Oklahoma 81, 85, 427
Organizing Institute (OI) 85-86, 472
outreach 25, 135, 242, 355, 386, 445, 501-502, 504, 508, 523, 525, 534-535
Parcziak, Donna 425
Parents for Justice 226
Pastreich, Bill 118, 237, 349, 358
Peace Corps 88
Pennsylvania 85, 414, 418, 426, 435, 436, 446, 463, 521, 540, 541
Philadelphia 187, 276, 285, 320, 321, 333, 351, 355, 365, 366, 375, 377, 426, 431, 435, 448, 451, 452, 455, 459, 463, 494, 495, 496, 497, 518, 521, 535
Pittsburgh 333, 427, 435, 472, 517, 518, 535
per capita 52, 56, 60-76, 374, 398, 459, 466, 486, 535, 545
permits 366-367, 427
Peru (Lima) 16, 38, 99, 147, 340, 513, 514, 519, 521
PICO 31, 34, 326, 387
Planned Parenthood 212, 393, 506-508
Poe, Cate 426
Polett, Zach 260, 274, 383, 413, 416, 425, 426, 430, 432
politics 8-9, 11, 17, 19, 70, 76-79, 92, 96-99, 140, 187, 203, 253, 259-260, 317, 341, 346, 387, 395-398, 400
poverty 47, 129, 312, 354, 424, 475, 530
Powderly, Terrence 81
predatory lending 25, 276, 334, 347, 363, 367, 525
Project Vote 42, 415-417, 433, 509

props 324-325, 347
protest (s) 6, 324, 331, 354, 546
Pulaski County Legal Aid 46
Putnam, Robert 388
quick hits 168, 352, 527
Quorum Court 14, 232, 404-406, 415, 421
racism 100, 414
radio 99, 138, 144-145, 195, 339, 410, 440-442, 444-449, 453, 509, 520
Ramage, Dave 493-494
Rathke, Chaco 520
Rathke, Dale 281
ReAct 517, 538, 543
Reagan Ranches 317, 349
Reagan, Ronald 317, 429
recruiting 53, 93, 98-99, 121, 134, 138, 511
Rector, Billy 25
Redd, Lisa 328
redlining 313, 497
refund anticipation loans (RAL) 314, 501
remittance (s) 76, 532, 533, 540, 544
Remittance Justice Campaign 532-533
rent-to-own 333
retention 97, 121, 235
revolution 11, 81, 131, 146, 238, 316
Richards, Cecile 212, 468-469, 506
Richardson, Bill 259
Rider, Peter 426
right-to-work (R-t-W), right to work 56-57, 65-66, 68-69, 73-78, 407, 430, 462
risk (s) 77, 102, 104, 137, 342, 363, 411, 444, 446, 482, 486
Rivera, Barbara 226
Rockefeller, Winthrop 225, 333, 400, 414
Roddy, Larry 229
Rogers 536-537
Rogers, Joel 431, 433
Rogers, Larry 232
Ross Sr., Fred 110, 349, 414
Roux, Adrien 517, 543
Ruptura 371
Rusk, David 493
Russia 146, 436
Sahores, Ercilia 129, 514

Index 563

salaries, salary 50, 123, 265
San Andreas Fault 147-148, 450
Sandberg, Sheryl 389
Sanders, Beulah 46
Sargent, Francis 319
school (s) 242, 400-401, 411, 471, 525, 527, 530, 536, 541
Schroeder, Mark 426
SCLC 393
self-sufficiency 51, 130, 244, 265, 381, 447, 519, 541, 542
seniority 97, 116-117, 120-121, 124-125, 283, 376
Service Employees International Union (SEIU) 32, 35-36, 63, 70, 83, 85-86, 88, 259, 326, 331, 336, 395, 397-399, 430, 432, 458-481, 489-490, 508
service worker (s) 399, 455
services 16, 31, 52, 57-58, 61, 82, 144, 312-315, 394, 407-408, 493-494, 500-511, 521-528
shared costs 545-546, 548
Sharp, Gene 316
Shea, Gerry 458-461
Shea, Mike 148, 260, 274, 426, 500
Shetty, Vinod 515
Shur, Amy 274
Sierra Club 388, 395-396, 484
Sri Lanka 38, 488
Sirabella, Vincent 84
slum , 436, 515, 525, 529-530, 538-539
Smith, Mary Ellen 377-378
Smith, Rick 481, 490
Smith, Vera 226
SNCC 393
social media 89, 136, 328, 339, 347
Social Policy 440-441, 521
Sotomayer, Justice 70
South Carolina 30-31, 187, 426, 431, 434
South Dakota 20, 41, 380-383, 406, 411-412, 422-424, 426-427
Splain, Mark 280, 426, 454, 472
Spring Mobilization 354
Springfield Winter Coat Riot 333

squatting 327, 494, 496, 525-526, 528
St. Jacque, Simone 312
staff 24-27, 30-31, 36, 41-43, 46, 50-51, 53, 61, 67, 69, 80-161, 184, 190, 198, 203, 211-213, 224, 229, 233-237, 244, 247, 249, 252-253, 260, 264-267, 273, 276, 281, 283, 286, 289, 309, 320-321, 329, 343, 347-350, 362, 365, 368-369, 373-375, 390-391, 413, 419, 421-427, 459-468, 476-477, 503-511
stair stepping 332-333
Steelworkers 68, 83
Stephens, Doug 401, 406
Stern Fund 49, 422, 429
Stern, Andy 35, 85, 399, 463, 467, 475, 478, 488
steward (s) 52, 58, 62, 71, 75, 81, 111, 118, 121, 137, 229, 266, 462, 468, 481, 488, 505
strategies, strategy 8, 16, 24-25, 46, 72, 109, 116-118, 187, 316-337, 340, 346, 350, 387, 393, 399, 407-408, 410-411, 418, 421, 424, 427, 429, 432, 434-435, 455, 466-467, 476, 480-481, 483, 486-487, 490, 505, 508, 520, 538
street blocking 324, 327-328, 342
Stretcher, Kenneth 511
strike (s) 7, 57, 62, 66, 74, 328-331, 333, 335, 375, 454-455, 458, 483, 490
sub-prime 276, 313
Sweeney, John 84-85, 328, 365, 459, 467, 472, 475, 489
Szakos, Joe 10, 30, 440
Tabankin, Margery 141, 454
tactic (s) 4-5, 16, 18, 23-24, 92, 109, 116, 118, 145, 226, 246, 316-339, 342, 347, 352, 354, 387, 390, 407, 409, 412, 421, 428, 431-432, 482, 484-485, 490, 494, 538
takeover (s) 14, 137, 141-142, 144-145, 404, 406
Talbott, Madeline 184, 425-426, 428, 540
tax, taxes 4, 7, 13, 56, 63, 69, 139, 252, 336, 392, 502, 520

Teamsters 15, 68, 83, 458, 467-468, 470, 486, 489, 510, 544
teamwork 151
Telus 536
tenants, 2, 6, 310, 339, 350, 377, 394, 440, 516-517, 522-524, 532
Tennessee 20, 424
Memphis 8, 392, 423, 426-428, 451, 518, 541
Texas 20, 50, 72, 81, 113, 190, 317, 327, 380-381, 383, 403, 424, 427, 430, 448, 459, 462, 466, 471-472, 479, 491, 508, 512-513, 540-541
Dallas 8, 72, 99, 317-318, 383, 418, 423, 425-426, 441-444, 446, 448, 471-472, 476, 497, 536
Fort Worth 8, 327, 383, 423, 426, 441
Houston 8, 23, 32, 72, 75, 148, 190, 212, 383, 411, 423, 426, 429, 464, 471-473, 485, 497, 500, 511, 534-535
San Antonio 72, 93, 212, 471, 473, 480, 499, 501
The Woodlawn Organization (TWO) 414, 493
Thornton, Zee 520
Tides Center 10-12
Tides Foundation 10, 469, 508
Tillmon, Johnnie 46, 544
Times-Warner 534, 536
Townley, Arthur C. 81, 427
Tozzo, David 516
TRAG (Tri-Rivers Action Group) 252, 382
training 14, 31, 52, 87-88, 90, 92, 97, 100, 102-105, 108, 110-115, 133, 161, 167, 170, 183-188, 234-235, 352, 388
Trampling Out the Vintage 329
Trapp, Shel 30
Turn Off Arkla Day 331
Ulver, Michal, 515
Union Summer 85, 87-88
United Auto Workers (UAW) 46, 62, 83, 86, 333, 428, 434, 458
United Farm Workers (UFW) 88, 329, 393, 489

564   Nuts & Bolts – The ACORN Fundamentals of Organizing

United Food & Commerical Workers (UFCW) 84, 486, 488-490, 544
United Kingdom 5, 38, 57, 59, 130, 247, 311, 399, 436, 517, 529, 533
England 16, 115, 161, 331, 517, 532, 538, 541
Bristol 115, 161, 310, 517, 532, 537
London 161, 246, 517, 532
Newcastle on Tyne 517
Pilton 517
Reading 161, 517, 532
Sheffield 517, 532
Scotland 16, 350, 516
Edinburgh 161, 310, 386, 440, 516
Glasgow 516
United Labor Unions 330, 378, 430, 454-456, 460-461, 463-464, 471, 506, 511
United Steel Workers 61
University of Wisconsin at Madison 39, 51, 431
Urban Poor Association 518
US Action 30
utilities, utility 252, 407-408, 410, 537
UTNO 457
Vietnam 231, 331, 354, 393, 424
Vietnam Veterans Organizing Committee (VVOC) 231
violence 316, 330, 388, 392, 515, 528, 539
Virginia 7 16, 323, 342, 440
Virigina Organizing 10, 30, 440
vision 20, 30, 39, 51, 133, 144, 150, 152, 276, 308, 373, 389, 422, 446, 478-479
VISTA 46, 100, 141, 348, 425, 452-453
VITA (Volunteer Income Tax Assistance) 508
volunteer (s) 42, 46, 52-53, 62, 75, 80-82, 88, 100, 141, 145, 148-149, 237, 281, 283, 306, 322, 348, 377, 393, 413, 425, 428, 442, 444, 446-447, 449, 452, 454-455, 495, 499, 508, 513, 521, 532, 541

voter registration 5, 13, 47, 146, 326, 379-380, 414-419, 430, 432-433, 436, 503, 506
voting 104, 379, 420, 530
wage (s) 90-91, 97-98, 120-125, 129-130, 265-266, 411-413, 451-458, 463-468
Walmart Alliance for Reform Now (WARN) 483-484, 486, 489, 539
Walmart Workers' Association (WWA) 395, 481-482
Walmart, Wal-Mart, WalMart 35-36, 42, 139, 329, 395-396, 413, 463, 473, 479-490, 493, 519, 538, 544
WAMF 446
Washington (Seattle) 30, 129, 442, 446-447, 478, 501, 514
Washington D.C. 141, 273, 319, 388, 390, 395-396, 404, 415, 452, 473, 500, 509, 540
Washington, Mable 457
water issues 327, 494, 514, 519, 525-528, 530, 538, 541
Watson Chapel 23
Welfare Rights 6, 44, 46, 91, 94, 117-118, 137, 226
Western Federation of Miners 81, 403, 406
West Virginia 429
Whelan, Kevin 149
Whipple, Bill 231
Wickstrom, Maria 474
Wiley, George 46, 117, 231, 319, 390
Wiliams, Mamie Ruth 401
Williams College 88
Wilson, Gloria 225
Wilson, Mamie 237
Wimberly, George 140
Wofford, Harris 141
Wood, Peter 283, 426
Woodruff, Tom 399, 467, 479
workers 32, 42, 57-88, 104-107, 124, 135, 144-146, 220, 230, 309-310, 326, 329, 333-338, 344, 349, 365, 369, 378, 387, 393-399, 404, 412-413, 433, 451-492, 513-519, 525, 529-532, 543-547

Working Families Party (WFP) 13, 433-435, 465
Working Partnerships 398
World Bank 532-533
Wright, Joann 281
Wyoming 94, 149
Young, Andrew 396
Young, Coleman 328, 428

Index: 565

About the Author

Wade Rathke first began organizing almost 50 years ago when he dropped out of college to organize against the Vietnam War. Later he organized welfare recipients in Massachusetts, first in Springfield and then statewide from Boston, before leaving for Arkansas to found ACORN in Little Rock in mid-June 1970. A decade later, Wade added labor organizing to his experiences when he and other organizers responded to issues that ACORN members were having in their workplaces, whether home health workers, hotel workers, or fast food workers, and moved to New Orleans to build independent unions that later merged into the Service Employees International Union in 1984. The common themes of these decades as a welfare rights organizer, community organizer, and labor organizer have been how to unite people at the bottom income levels around their issues to build sufficient power so that they could impact their lives, improve their communities, and change the direction of their country. For a generation Wade has been recognized as perhaps the premier organizer of his generation, making this book something of a milestone in that journey.

Wade leading a workshop at a meeting in Paris
Photo: Michal Ulver, ACORN Czech

Wade left ACORN after thirty-eight years as its chief organizer in mid-2008, when the organization had more than 100 offices and close to 500,000 members. Now he continues as Chief Organizer of ACORN International, working in Canada, Mexico, Peru, Honduras, India, Kenya, Italy, Cameroon, Scotland, France, and England and with partnerships in Indonesia, Korea, and the Philippines. Once again he is working to assist in building membership-based organizations largely in the mega-slums that have arisen in some of the world's largest cities. ACORN International is also organizing unions of hawkers and wastepickers in Delhi, Mumbai and Benglauru while supporting worker organizations in other countries as well. In the United States, Wade continues to serve as chief organizer of Local 100, United Labor Unions, headquartered in New Orleans, with members in Louisiana, Arkansas, and Texas.

In recent years Wade has had the opportunity to learn more about other organizing around America and the rest of the world as chair of the Organizers' Forum, which once a year looks at common problems for community and labor organizers, and once a year travels to other countries to learn about the challenges and experiences of organizations elsewhere. Thus far he has led delegations of organizers to Brazil, India, South Africa, Indonesia, Turkey, Russia, Australia, Vietnam, Thailand, Egypt, Cameroon, Bolivia, and Morocco.

As publisher and editor-in-chief of Social Policy, the quarterly journal that has been able to offer a forum for the many voices from organizing, academia, and elsewhere on issues that matter around social change here and abroad. Social Policy Press has also published books on rural organizing, Virginia Organizing, gun safety, and Wade's book, The Battle for the Ninth Ward: ACORN, Rebuilding New Orleans, and the Lessons of Disaster (2011) along with Global Grassroots: Perspectives on International Organizing (2011) where he served as editor. Wade's first book was Citizen Wealth: Winning the Campaign to Save Working Families (2009) published by Berrett-Koehler.

Wade writes a daily blog www.chieforganizer.org, also available as a podcast and distributed to radio stations, especially KABF at www.kabf.org in Little Rock and WAMF at www.wamf.org in New Orleans as well as ACORN's internet station at www.acornradio.org. As a director of the Affiliated Media Foundation Movement (AM/FM, Inc.), Wade services as station manager for these radio outlets as well as acting to support WDSV in Greenville, Mississippi. The ACORN Farm and its memorial orchard are located in the now iconic post-Katrina Lower 9th Ward. Wade enjoys touting what he believes is the only fair trade coffee-and-chicory in the world at the Fair Grinds Coffeehouses in Faubourg St. John and Faubourg Marigny in New Orleans that are owned and operated by ACORN Global Enterprises as social enterprises supporting ACORN's organizing around the world.

Wade's partner, Beth Butler, is also a longtime community organizer and executive director of A Community Voice (formerly Louisiana ACORN). Their two children, Chaco Butler Rathke and Diné Rathke Butler, were born and raised in New Orleans. Chaco is manager of the coffeehouses. Dine' is working as and organizer and researcher with ACORN's Home Savers Campaign in the United States which is currently trying to reshape the predatory rent-to-own and contract for deed housing markets in Ohio, Michigan, Georgia, Arkansas, and Pennsylvania. Wade is easy to find. Calls are not screened and the door is always open if you are on St. Claude Avenue at Elysian Fields, and he happens to be in town. Always follow the work first, and that can be done through www.acorninternational.org. When looking for Wade, the easiest is to check out his website at www.waderathke.org and see where he is and what he is up to. If you want to organize, he's always available at chieforganizer@acorninternational.org.